I0755286

A

HAND-BOOK OF POLITICS

FOR 1876:

BEING A RECORD OF

IMPORTANT POLITICAL ACTION,

NATIONAL AND STATE,

FROM JULY 15, 1874, TO JULY 15, 1876.

BY
HON. EDWARD McPHERSON, LL. D.,
OF GETTYSBURG, PENNA.,
CLERK OF HOUSE OF REPRESENTATIVES U. S., 38TH TO 43D CONGRESS, INCLUSIVE.

[SIXTH EDITION.]

WASHINGTON:
SOLOMONS & CHAPMAN,
Agents for Foreign Statistical and Government Books,
[SUCCESSORS TO PHILP & SOLOMONS.]
1876.

Stereotyped and Printed by
THE INQUIRER P. & P. CO.,
Lancaster, Pa.

PREFACE.

THIS volume has been prepared on the same general plan as the previous volumes of the Series, and, it is hoped, will be found as worthy of confidence and approval.

In its pages have been gathered a great variety of political facts, which at once attest the activity of our political life during the past two years, and indicate the directions of it. Several of the Chapters have great political importance, and all of them are worthy of attention. The IVth, VIIIth and IXth may be indicated as furnishing special attractions to the student of our system—its principles, its modes, and its growth.

The Chapters devoted to the record of parties on pending questions contain, I hope, all the available facts necessary to judge them, distinctly classified, and carefully stated.

In the votes given, Republicans are printed in Roman, Democrats in *Italic*, and Independents in SMALL CAPS; and gentlemen are indicated according to their party relations at the time of voting.

No effort has been spared to ensure accuracy and completeness, and the volume is submitted to the public in the hope that it will meet the want which it is designed to supply, and be accepted as a useful contribution to political history.

EDWARD McPHERSON.

GETTYSBURG, PENNA., *July 15, 1876.*

TABLE OF CONTENTS.

HAND-BOOK OF POLITICS FOR 1876.

I.

MEMBERS OF FORTY-THIRD CONGRESS.

SECOND SESSION, DECEMBER 7, 1874—MARCH 3, 1875.

The Senate.

HENRY WILSON, of Massachusetts, *Vice President of the United States, and President of the Senate.*
George C. Gorham, of California, *Secretary.*
The term of office of each Senator will expire on the 3d of March of the year set opposite to his name.

State	Senator	Term	Senator	Term
Alabama	George E. Spencer	(1879)	George Goldthwaite	(1877).
Arkansas	Stephen W. Dorsey	(1879)	Powell Clayton	(1877).
California	Aaron A. Sargent	(1879)	John S. Hager	(1875).
Connecticut	Orris S. Ferry	(1879)	Wm. W. Eaton,*	(1875).
Delaware	Eli Saulsbury	(1877)	Thomas F. Bayard	(1875).
Florida	Simon B. Conover	(1879)	Abijah Gilbert	(1875).
Georgia	John B. Gordon	(1879)	Thomas M. Norwood	(1877).
Illinois	Richard J. Oglesby	(1879)	John A. Logan	(1877).
Indiana	Oliver P. Morton	(1879)	Daniel D. Pratt	(1875).
Iowa	William B. Allison	(1879)	George G. Wright	(1877).
Kansas	John J. Ingalls	(1879)	James M. Harvey	(1877).
Kentucky	Thomas C. McCreery	(1879)	John W. Stevenson	(1877).
Louisiana	(Vacancy)	(1879)	J. Rodman West	(1877).
Maine	Lot M. Morrill	(1877)	Hannibal Hamlin	(1875).
Maryland	George R. Dennis	(1879)	William T. Hamilton	(1875).
Massachusetts	George S. Boutwell	(1877)	William B. Washburn	(1875).
Michigan	Thomas W. Ferry	(1877)	Zachariah Chandler	(1875).
Minnesota	William Windom	(1877)	Alexander Ramsey	(1875).
Mississippi	James L. Alcorn	(1877)	Henry R. Pease	(1875).
Missouri	Lewis V. Bogy	(1879)	Carl Schurz	(1875).
Nebraska	Phineas W. Hitchcock	(1877)	Thomas W. Tipton	(1875).
Nevada	John P. Jones	(1879)	William M. Stewart	(1875).
New Hampshire	Bainbridge Wadleigh	(1879)	Aaron A. Cragin	(1877).
New Jersey	Fred. T. Frelinghuysen	(1877)	John P. Stockton	(1875).
New York	Roscoe Conkling	(1879)	Reuben E. Fenton	(1875).
North Carolina	Augustus S. Merrimon	(1879)	Matthew W. Ransom	(1877).
Ohio	John Sherman	(1879)	Allen G. Thurman	(1875).
Oregon	John H. Mitchell	(1879)	James K. Kelly	(1877).
Pennsylvania	Simon Cameron	(1879)	John Scott	(1875).
Rhode Island	Henry B. Anthony	(1877)	William Sprague	(1875).
South Carolina	John J. Patterson	(1879)	Thomas J. Robertson	(1877).
Tennessee	Henry Cooper	(1877)	William G. Brownlow	(1875).
Texas	Morgan C. Hamilton	(1877)	James W. Flanagan	(1875).
Vermont	Justin S. Morrill	(1879)	George F. Edmunds	(1875).
Virginia	John W. Johnston	(1877)	John F. Lewis	(1875).
West Virginia	Henry G. Davis	(1877)	Arthur I. Boreman	(1875).
Wisconsin	Timothy O. Howe	(1879)	Matthew H. Carpenter	(1875).

*Qualified February 13, 1875, *vice* William A. Buckingham, deceased, February 4th, 1875.

The House of Representatives.

JAMES G. BLAINE, of Maine, *Speaker.*
Edward McPherson, of Pennsylvania, *Clerk.*

Alabama—Frederick G. Bromberg, James T. Rapier, Charles Pelham, Charles Hays, John H. Caldwell, Joseph H. Sloss, Alexander White, Christopher C. Sheats—8.

Arkansas—Asa Hodges, Oliver P. Snyder, Thomas M. Gunter, William J. Hynes—4.

California—Charles Clayton, Horace F. Page, John K. Luttrell, Sherman O. Houghton—4.

Connecticut—Joseph R. Hawley, Stephen W. Kellogg, Henry H. Starkweather, William H. Barnum—4.

Delaware—James R. Lofland—1.

Florida—Josiah T. Walls, William J. Purman*—2.

Georgia—Andrew Sloan, Richard H. Whiteley, Philip Cook, Henry R. Harris, James C. Freeman, James H. Blount, Pierce M. B. Young, Alexander H. Stephens, Hiram P. Bell—9.

Illinois—Bernard G. Caulfield,† Jasper D. Ward, Charles B. Farwell, Stephen A. Hurlbut, Horatio C. Burchard, John B. Hawley, Franklin Corwin, Greenbury L. Fort, Granville Barrere, William H. Ray, Robert M. Knapp, James C. Robinson, John McNulta, Joseph G. Cannon, John R. Eden, James S. Martin, William R. Morrison, Isaac Clements, Samuel S. Marshall—19.

Indiana—William E. Niblack, Simeon K. Wolfe, William S. Holman, Jeremiah M. Wilson, John Coburn, Morton C. Hunter, Thomas J. Cason, James N. Tyner, John P. C. Shanks, Henry B. Sayler, Jasper Packard, Godlove S. Orth, William Williams—13.

Iowa—George W. McCrary, Aylett R. Cotton, William G. Donnan, Henry O. Pratt, James Wilson, William Loughridge, John A. Kasson, James W. McDill, Jackson Orr—9.

Kansas—David P. Lowe, Stephen A. Cobb, William A. Phillips—3.

Kentucky—Edward Crossland, John Young Brown, Charles W. Milliken, William B. Read, Elisha D. Standiford, William E. Arthur, James B. Beck, Milton J. Durham, George M. Adams, John D. Young—10.

Louisiana‡—Effingham Lawrence, Lionel A. Sheldon, Chester B. Darrall, George L. Smith, Frank Morey, George A. Sheridan—6.

Maine—John H. Burleigh, William P. Frye, James G. Blaine, Samuel F. Hersey,§ Eugene Hale—5.

Maryland—Ephraim K. Wilson, Stevenson Archer, William J. O'Brien, Thomas Swann, William J. Albert, Lloyd Lowndes, jr—6.

*Resigned January 25, 1875, to accept a seat in the Legislature of Florida.

†Qualified February 1, 1875, to fill the vacancy caused by the death, December 17th, 1874, of Hon. John B. Rice.

‡Mr. Lawrence qualified March 3, 1875, in place of J. Hale Sypher, unseated on that day. The House voted down, 87 to 143, a resolution that neither Lawrence nor Sypher had shown himself entitled to the seat; and then adopted without a division a resolution unseating Mr. Sypher. A motion to table the resolution seating Mr. Lawrence was lost, and he was then declared entitled to the seat, 135 to 86. Mr. Sheridan was declared entitled to the seat, without a division, on same day.

§Died February 3, 1875.

Massachusetts—James Buffinton, Benjamin W. Harris, Henry L. Pierce, Samuel Hooper,* Daniel W. Gooch, Benjamin F. Butler, E. Rockwood Hoar, John M. S. Williams, George F. Hoar, Charles A. Stevens,† Henry L. Dawes—11.

Michigan—Moses W. Field, Henry Waldron, George Willard, Julius C. Burrows, William B. Williams, Josiah W. Begole, Omar D. Conger, Nathan B. Bradley, Jay A. Hubbell—9.

Minnesota—Mark H. Dunnell, Horace B. Strait, John T. Averill—3.

Mississippi—Lucius Q. C. Lamar, Albert R. Howe, Henry W. Barry, Jason Niles, George C. McKee, John R. Lynch—6.

Missouri—Edwin O. Stanard, Erastus Wells, William H. Stone, Robert A. Hatcher, Richard P. Bland, Harrison E. Havens, Thomas T. Crittenden, Abram Comingo, Isaac C. Parker, Ira B. Hyde, John B. Clark, jr., John M. Glover, Aylett H. Buckner—13.

Nebraska—Lorenzo Crounse—1.

Nevada—Charles W. Kendall—1.

New Hampshire—William B. Small, Austin F. Pike, Hosea W. Parker—3

New Jersey—John W. Hazelton, Samuel A. Dobbins, Amos Clark, jr., Robert Hamilton, William Walter Phelps, Marcus L. Ward, Isaac W. Scudder—7.

New York—Henry J. Scudder, John G. Schumaker, Simeon B. Chittenden,‡ Philip S. Crooke, William R. Roberts, Samuel S. Cox, Thomas J. Creamer, John D. Lawson, Richard Schell,§ Fernando Wood, Clarkson N. Potter, Charles St. John, John O. Whitehouse, David M. DeWitt, Eli Perry, James S. Smart, Robert S. Hale, William A. Wheeler, Henry H. Hathorn, David Wilber, Clinton L. Merriam, Ellis H. Roberts, William E. Lansing, R. Holland Duell, Clinton D. MacDougall, William H. Lamport, Thomas C. Platt, H. Boardman Smith, Freeman Clarke, George G. Hoskins, Lyman K. Bass, Walter L. Sessions, Lyman Tremain—33.

North Carolina—Clinton L. Cobb, Charles R. Thomas, Alfred M. Waddell, William A. Smith, James M. Leach, Thomas S. Ashe, William M. Robbins, Robert B. Vance—8.

Ohio—Milton Sayler, Henry B. Banning, John Q. Smith, Lewis B. Gunckel, Charles N. Lamison, Isaac R. Sherwood, Lawrence T. Neal, William Lawrence, James W. Robinson, Charles Foster, Hezekiah S. Bundy, William E. Finck,‖ Milton I. Southard, John Berry, William P. Sprague, Lorenzo Danford, Laurin D. Woodworth, James Monroe, James A. Garfield, Richard C. Parsons—20.

Oregon—James W. Nesmith—1.

*Died February 14, 1875.

†Qualified January 27, 1875, in place of Alvah Crocker, died December 26, 1874.

§Qualified December 7, 1874, to fill the vacancy caused by the death of Hon. David B. Mellish, May 23, 1874.

‡Qualified December 7, 1874, to fill the vacancy caused by the resignation of Hon. Stewart L. Woodford, Sept. 30, 1874.

‖Qualified December 7, 1874, to fill the vacancy caused by the resignation of Hon. Hugh J. Jewett, October 1, 1874.

Pennsylvania—Samuel J. Randall, Charles O'-Neill, Leonard Myers, William D. Kelley, Alfred C. Harmer, James S. Biery, Washington Townsend, Hiester Clymer, A. Herr Smith, John W. Killinger, John B. Storm, Lazarus D. Shoemaker, James D. Strawbridge, John B. Packer, John A. Magee, John Cessna, R. Milton Speer, Sobieski Ross, Carlton B. Curtis, Hiram L. Richmond, Alexander W. Taylor, James S. Negley, John M. Thompson,* William S. Moore, Lemuel Todd, Charles Albright, Glenni W. Scofield—27.

Rhode Island—Benjamin T. Eames, James M. Pendleton—2.

South Carolina—Joseph H. Rainey, Alonzo J. Ransier, L. Cass Carpenter,† Alexander S. Wallace, Richard H. Cain—5.

Tennessee—Roderick R. Butler, Jacob M. Thornburgh, William Crutchfield, John M. Bright, Horace H. Harrison, Washington C. Whitthorne, John D. C. Atkins, David A. Nunn, Barbour Lewis, Horace Maynard—10.

Texas—William S. Herndon, William P. McLean, De Witt C. Giddings, John Hancock, Roger Q. Mills, Asa H. Willie—6.

Vermont—Charles W. Willard, Luke P. Poland, George W. Hendee—3.

Virginia—James B. Sener, James H. Platt, jr., J. Ambler Smith, William H. H. Stowell, Christopher Y. Thomas, Thomas Whitehead, John T. Harris, Eppa Hunton, Rees T. Bowen—9.

West Virginia—John J. Davis, J. Marshall Hagans, Frank Hereford—3.

Wisconsin—Charles G. Williams, Gerry W. Hazelton, J. Allen Barber, Alexander Mitchell, Charles A. Eldredge, Philetus Sawyer, Jeremiah M. Rusk, Alexander S. McDill—8.

DELEGATES FROM TERRITORIES.

Arizona—Richard C. McCormick.
Colorado—Jerome B. Chaffee.
Dakota—Moses K. Armstrong.
District of Columbia—Norton P. Chipman.
Idaho—John Hailey.
Montana—Martin Maginnis.
New Mexico—Stephen B. Elkins.
Utah—George Q. Cannon.
Washington—Obadiah B McFadden.
Wyoming—William R. Steele.

Whole number of Representatives......	292
" " " Delegates.............	10
	302

II.

THE SUPPLEMENTARY CIVIL RIGHTS BILL.

[For previous votes on this subject see McPherson's Hand-Book of Politics for 1874, pp. 205-209.]

SENATE BILL.

Forty-third Congress—Second Session.

IN HOUSE.

1875, January 25—Mr. BENJAMIN F. BUTLER moved that the rules be so suspended that the bill of the Senate known as the civil-rights bill (S. No. 1) be taken from the Speaker's table for consideration at the present time, and so continuously until a final disposition shall be had thereof; and that no dilatory motion, save a single motion to adjourn, be allowed, until such bill and any amendments allowed thereto have been finally disposed of.

Which was decided in the negative—yeas 147, nays 93, not voting 48 (two-thirds not having voted in the affirmative), as follow:

YEAS—Messrs. Albright, Averill, Barber, Barrere, Barry, Bass, Begole, Biery, Bradley, Buffinton, Bundy, H. C. Burchard, Burleigh, Burrows, B. F. Butler, Cain, Cannon, Carpenter, Cason, Cessna, Chittenden, A. Clark, jr., Clayton, Clements, C. L. Cobb, S. A. Cobb, Coburn, Conger, Corwin, Cotton, Crooke, Crounse, Crutchfield, Curtis, Darrall, Dawes, Dobbins, Donnan, Duell, Dunnell, Eames, Farwell, Fort, Foster, Garfield, Gooch, Gunckel, Hagans, E. Hale, R. S. Hale, B. W. Harris, Hathorn, J. B. Hawley, J R. Hawley, Hays, G. W. Hazelton, J. W. Hazelton, E. R. Hoar, Hodges, Hoskins, Houghton, Howe, Hubbell, Hunter, Hurlbut, Hynes, Kasson, Kelley, Kellogg, Lamport, W. Lawrence, Lawson, B. Lewis, Loughridge, Lowe, Lynch, Martin, McCrary, J. W. McDill, McKee, McNulta, Merriam, Monroe, Morey, Myers, Negley, Niles, O'Neill, Orr, Orth, Packard, Page, I. C. Parker, R. C. Parsons, Pelham, Pendleton, W. A. Phillips, Pierce, T. C. Platt, Poland, Pratt, Rainey, Ransier, Rapier, W. H. Ray, Richmond, E. H. Roberts, J. W. Robinson, S. Ross, Rusk, H. B. Sayler, Scofield, I. W. Scudder, Sessions, Shanks, Sherwood, L. D. Shoemaker, W. B. Small, Smart, A. H. Smith, H. B. Smith, J. Q. Smith, Snyder, Sprague, Starkweather, Strawbridge, Taylor, C. R. Thomas, J. M. Thompson, Todd, W. Townsend, Tremain, Tyner, Waldron, A. S. Wallace, J. D. Ward, M. L. Ward, Whiteley, Wilber, C. W. Willard, G. Willard, C. G. Williams, J. S. Williams, W. Williams, W. B. Williams, J. Wilson, J. M. Wilson—147.

NAYS.—Messrs. *G. M. Adams, Archer, Arthur, Ashe, Atkins, Banning, Beck, H. P. Bell, Berry, Bland, Blount, Bowen, Bright, Bromberg, J. Y. Brown, Buckner*, R. R. Butler, *J. H. Caldwell, J. B. Clark, jr., Clymer, Comingo, Cook, Cox, Creamer, Crittenden, Crossland, John J. Davis, De Witt, Durham, Eden, Finck, Giddings, Glover, Gunter, R. Hamilton, Han-*

*Qualified January 5, 1875, to fill the vacancy caused by the resignation of Hon. Ebenezer McJunkin, January 1, 1875.

† Qualified December 7, 1874, to fill the vacancy caused by the resignation of Hon. Robert B. Elliott, resigned November 1, 1874.

cock, *H. R. Harris*, *J. T. Harris*, H. H. Harrison, *Hatcher*, *Hereford*, *Herndon*, *Holman*, *Hunton*, Hyde, *Lamar*, *Lamison*, *Leach*, Lofland, Lowndes, *Luttrell*, *Magee*, Maynard, *McLean*, *Milliken*, *Mills*, *Morrison*, *Neal*, *Niblack*, *O'Brien*, *H. W. Parker*, *Perry*, *C. N. Potter*, *Randall*, *Read*, *W. M. Robbins*, *M. Sayler*, *Schell*, Sener, Sheats, Sloan, *Sloss*, J. A. Smith, *Southard*, *Speer*, Stanard, *Standiford*, *A. H. Stephens*, *Stone*, *Storm*, Strait, *Swann*, Thornburgh, *R. B. Vance*, *Waddell*, *E. Wells*, *Whitehead*, *Whitthorne*, *Willie*, *Wolfe*, *F. Wood*, *J. D. Young*, *P. M. B. Young*—93.

House Bill.

January 27—Mr. Benjamin F. Butler called up the motion to reconsider the vote whereby the bill (H. R. No. 796) reported by him from the Judiciary Committee, Dec. 18, 1873, was on January 7, 1874, recommitted to the Committee on the Judiciary.

Mr. Randall raised the question of consideration, upon which the yeas and nays were ordered—pending which he moved that the House adjourn, and also that when the House adjourns it adjourn to meet on Friday next.

Mr. Eldredge moved to amend by striking out Friday and inserting Saturday.

Motions of this sort were repeated, and the yeas and nays called seventy-seven times in a continuous session of forty-six hours and a half, the House adjourning at ten o'clock and twenty-five minutes, A. M., January 29.

February 1—The rules of the House were, after a struggle, amended so as to cut off "dilatory motions" after a certain point.

February 3—The question recurring on the question of consideration of the motion to reconsider, it was agreed to—yeas 148, nays 91, not voting 51.

The motion to reconsider the vote of recommitment was then agreed to—yeas 151, nays 93, not voting 46.

The text of the bill is as follows:

That all persons within the jurisdiction of the United States shall be entitled to the full and equal enjoyment of the accommodations, advantages, facilities, and privileges of inns, public conveyances on land or water, theaters, and other places of public amusement; and also of common schools and public institutions of learning or benevolence supported, in whole or in part, by general taxation, and also the institutions known as agricultural colleges endowed by the United States; subject only to the conditions and limitations established by law, and applicable alike to citizens of every race and color, regardless of any previous condition of servitude: *Provided*, That if any State, or the proper authorities in any State having the control of common schools or other public institutions of learning aforesaid, shall establish and maintain separate schools and institutions, giving equal educational advantages in all respects, for different classes of persons entitled to attend such schools and institutions, such schools and institutions shall be a sufficient compliance with the provisions of this section, so far as they relate to schools and institutions of learning.

Sec. 2. That any person who shall violate the foregoing section by denying to any citizen, except for reasons by law applicable to citizens of every race and color, and regardless of any previous condition of servitude, the full enjoyment of any of the accommodations, advantages, facilities, or privileges in said section enumerated, or by aiding or inciting such denial, shall, for every such offense, forfeit and pay the sum of five hundred dollars to the person aggrieved thereby, to be recovered in an action of debt, with full costs; and shall also, for every such offense, be deemed guilty of a misdemeanor, and, upon conviction thereof, shall be fined not less than five hundred nor more than one thousand dollars, or shall be imprisoned not less than thirty days nor more than one year: *Provided*, That all persons may elect to sue for the penalty aforesaid or to proceed under their rights at common law and by State statutes; and having so elected to proceed in the one mode or the other, their right to proceed in the other jurisdiction shall be barred. But this proviso shall not apply to criminal proceedings, either under this act or the criminal law of any State: *And provided further*, That a judgment for the penalty in favor of the party aggrieved, or a judgment upon an indictment, shall be a bar to either prosecution respectively.

Sec. 3. That the district and circuit courts of the United States shall have, exclusively of the courts of the several States, cognizance of all crimes and offenses against, and violations of, the provisions of this act; and actions for the penalty given by the preceding section may be prosecuted in the territorial, district, or circuit courts of the United States wherever the defendant may be found, without regard to the other party. And the district attorneys, marshals, and deputy marshals of the United States, and commissioners appointed by the circuit and territorial courts of the United States, with powers of arresting and imprisoning or bailing offenders against the laws of the United States, are hereby specially authorized and required to institute proceedings against every person who shall violate the provisions of this act, and cause him to be arrested and imprisoned or bailed, as the case may be, for trial before such court of the United States or territorial court as by law has cognizance of the offense, except in respect of the right of action accruing to the person aggrieved; and such district attorneys shall cause such proceedings to be prosecuted to their termination as in other cases: *Provided*, That nothing contained in this section shall be construed to deny or defeat any right of civil action accruing to any person, whether by reason of this act or otherwise. And any district attorney who shall willfully fail to institute and prosecute the proceedings herein required shall, for every such offense, forfeit and pay the sum of five hundred dollars to the person aggrieved thereby, to be recovered by an action of debt, with full costs, and shall, on conviction thereof, be deemed guilty of a misdemeanor, and be fined not less than one thousand nor more than five thousand dollars: *And provided further*, That a judgment for the penalty in favor of the party aggrieved against any such district attorney, or a judgment upon an indictment against any such district attorney, shall be a bar to either prosecution respectively.

SEC. 4. That no citizen possessing all other qualifications which are or may be prescribed by law shall be disqualified for service as grand or petit juror in any court of the United States, or of any State, on account of race, color, or previous condition of servitude; and any officer or other person charged with any duty in the selection or summoning of jurors who shall exclude or fail to summon any citizen for the cause aforesaid shall, on conviction thereof, be deemed guilty of a misdemeanor, and be fined not more than five thousand dollars.

SEC. 5. That all cases arising under the provisions of this act in the courts of the United States shall be reviewable by the Supreme Court of the United States without regard to the sum in controversy, under the same provisions and regulations as are now provided by law for the review of other causes in said court.

Mr. BENJAMIN F. BUTLER withdrew the motion to recommit.

February 4—The amendment offered by Mr. KELLOGG, as follows:

Strike from the first section the following:

"And also all common schools and public institutions of learning or benevolence supported in whole or in part by general taxation, and also the institutions known as agricultural colleges endowed by the United States."

Strike out also the following:

"*Provided*, That if any State or the proper authorities in any State, having the control of common schools or other public institutions of learning aforesaid, shall establish and maintain separate schools and institutions, giving equal educational advantages in all respects for different classes of persons entitled to attend such schools and institutions, such schools and institutions shall be a sufficient compliance with the provisions of this section so far as they relate to schools and institutions of learning."

Was agreed to, on a count, yeas 128, nays 48.

Mr. CESSNA offered the following as a substitute for the bill of the Judiciary Committee, it being the text of the Senate bill on the Speaker's table:

That all citizens and other persons within the jurisdiction of the United States shall be entitled to the full and equal enjoyment of the accommodations, advantages, facilities, and privileges of inns, public conveyances on land or water, theaters and other places of public amusement, and also of common schools and public institutions of learning or benevolence supported in whole or in part by general taxation, and of cemeteries so supported; and also the institutions known as agricultural colleges endowed by the United States, subject only to the conditions and limitations established by law, and applicable alike to citizens of every race and color, regardless of any previous condition of servitude.

SEC. 2. That any person who shall violate the foregoing section by denying to any entitled to its benefit, except for reasons by law applicable to citizens of every race and color and regardless of any previous condition of servitude, the full enjoyment of any of the accommodations, advantages, facilities, or privileges in said section enumerated, or by aiding or inciting such denial, shall, for every such offense, forfeit and pay the sum of $500 to the person aggrieved thereby, to be recovered in an action on the case, with full costs; and shall also, for every such offense, be deemed guilty of a misdemeanor, and, upon conviction thereof, shall be fined not more than $1,000, or shall be imprisoned not more than one year: *Provided*, That the party aggrieved shall not recover more than one penalty; and when the offense is a refusal of burial, the penalty may be recovered by the heirs at law of the person whose body has been refused burial: *And provided further*, That all persons may elect to sue for the penalty aforesaid or to proceed under their rights at common law and by State statutes; and having so elected to proceed in the one mode or the other, their right to proceed in the other jurisdiction shall be barred. But this proviso shall not apply to criminal proceedings, either under this act or the criminal law of any State.

SEC. 3. That the district and circuit courts of the United States shall have, exclusively of the courts of the several States, cognizance of all crimes and offenses against, and violations of, the provisions of this act; and actions for the penalty given by the preceding section may be prosecuted in the territorial, district, or circuit courts of the United States wherever the defendant may be found, without regard to the other party. And the district attorneys, marshals and deputy marshals of the United States, and commissioners appointed by the circuit and territorial courts of the United States with powers of arresting and imprisoning or bailing offenders against the laws of the United States, are hereby specially authorized and required to institute proceedings against every person who shall violate the provisions of this act, and cause him to be arrested and imprisoned or bailed, as the case may be, for trial before such court of the United States or territorial court as by law has cognizance of the offense, except in respect of the right of action accruing to the person aggrieved; and such district attorneys shall cause such proceedings to be prosecuted to their termination as in other cases: *Provided*, That nothing contained in this section shall be construed to deny or defeat any right of civil action accruing to any person, whether by reason of this act or otherwise.

SEC. 4. That no citizen possessing all other qualifications which are or may be prescribed by law shall be disqualified for service as grand or petit juror in any court of the United States, or of any State, on account of race, color, or previous condition of servitude; and any officer or other person charged with any duty in the selection or summoning of jurors who shall exclude or fail to summon any citizen for the cause aforesaid shall, on conviction thereof, be deemed guilty of a misdemeanor, and be fined not more than $1,000.

SEC. 5. That all cases arising under the provisions of this act in the courts of the United States shall be reviewable by the Supreme Court of the United States without regard to the sum in controversy, under the same provisions and regulations as are now provided by law for the review of other causes in said court.

Mr. WHITE moved the following as a substitute for the said amendment:

That all persons within the jurisdiction of the United States shall be entitled to the full and equal enjoyment of the accommodations, advantages, facilities and privileges of inns, public conveyances on land or water, theaters and other places of public amusement; and also of common schools and public institutions of learning or benevolence supported in whole or in part by general taxation, subject only to the conditions and limitations established by law, and applicable alike to citizens of every race and color, regardless of any previous condition of servitude: *Provided*, That nothing in this act shall be construed to require mixed accommodations (by sitting together), facilities and privileges at inns, in public conveyances on land or water, theaters or other places of public amusement, for persons of different race or color, nor to prohibit separate accommodations, facilities and privileges at inns, in public conveyances on land or water, theaters or other places of public amusement; such separate accommodations, facilities and privileges being equal in equipment and kind for persons of every race and color, regardless of any previous condition of servitude: *And provided further*, That nothing in this act shall be construed to require mixed common schools and public institutions of learning and benevolence for persons of different race or color, nor to prohibit separate common schools for different races or colors, provided the facilities, duration of term, and equipments of such common schools and public institutions for both races in the town, city, school district, or other topographical division, shall be equal in facilities and equipments for both races for the purposes for which such institutions are established.

SEC. 2. That any person who shall violate the foregoing section by denying to any citizen, except for reasons by law applicable to citizens of every race and color, and regardless of any previous condition of servitude, the full enjoyment of any of the accommodations, advantages, facilities, or privileges in said section enumerated, or by aiding or inciting such denial, shall, for every such offense, forfeit the sum of $500 to the person aggrieved thereby, to be recovered in action of debt, with full costs: *Provided*, That no action shall be maintainable under the provisions of this act when equal but separate accommodations, advantages, facilities, or privileges are provided for and are not denied to the party complaining of the violation of this act: *And provided further*, That all persons may elect to sue for the penalty aforesaid or to proceed under their rights at common law and by State statutes; and having so elected to proceed in the one mode or the other, their right to proceed in the other jurisdiction shall be barred.

SEC. 3. That the district and circuit courts of the United States shall have cognizance of all violations of the provisions of this act, and actions for the penalty given by the preceding section may be prosecuted in the territorial, district, or circuit courts of the United States wherever the defendant may be found, without regard to the other party.

SEC. 4. That no citizen, possessing all other qualifications which are or may be prescribed by law, shall be disqualified for service as grand or petit juror in any court of the United States, or of any State, on account of race, color, or previous condition of servitude; and any person charged with any duty in the selection or summoning of jurors who shall exclude or fail to summon any citizen for the cause aforesaid, shall, on conviction, be fined not more than $1,000.

SEC. 5. That all cases arising under the provisions of this act shall be reviewable by the Supreme Court of the United States, without regard to the amount in controversy, in the same manner as now provided by law for the review of other causes in said court.

Which was disagreed to on a count—yeas 91, nays 114.

The question recurring on Mr. CESSNA'S motion, it was disagreed to—yeas 113, nays 148, not voting 28:

YEAS—Messrs. Albert, Barber, Barrere, Bass, Begole, Buffinton, H. C. Burchard, Burleigh, Burrows, B. F. Butler, Cain, Cannon, Carpenter, Cason, Cessna, Clayton, S. A. Cobb, Coburn, Conger, Cotton, Crooke, Crounse, Curtis, Darrall, Dawes, Dobbins, Donnan, Duell, Eames, Field, Fort, Foster, Garfield, Gooch, Harmer, B. W. Harris, Hathorn, J. B. Hawley, J. R. Hawley, G. W. Hazelton, J. W. Hazelton, Hendee, E. R. Hoar, Hodges, Hooper, Hoskins, Houghton, Howe, Hurlbut, Kasson, Kelley, Lamport, Lansing, W. Lawrence, Lawson, Loughridge, Lowe, Lynch, McCrary, J. W. McDill, McNulta, Monroe, Morey, Myers, Negley, Niles, O'Neill, Orth, Packard, Page, R. C. Parsons, Pendleton, Pierce, Pike, Pratt, Rainey, Rapier, Richmond, J. W. Robinson, S. Ross, Rusk, Sawyer, H. B. Sayler, Sessions, Shanks, Sheldon, W. B. Small, Smart, A. H. Smith, G. L. Smith, H. B. Smith, J. Q. Smith, Sprague, Starkweather, C. A. Stevens, Stowell, Sypher, Taylor, W. Townsend, Tyner, Waldron, A. S. Wallace, J. D. Ward, M. L. Ward, Wilber, G. Willard, C. G. Williams, J. M. S. Williams, W. Williams, W. B. Williams, J. Wilson, J. M. Wilson, Woodworth—113.

NAYS—Messrs. *G. M. Adams*, Albright, *Archer*, *Arthur*, *Ashe*, *Atkins*, Averill, *Banning*, *Beck*, *H. P. Bell*, *Berry*, Biery, *Bland*, *Blount*, *Bowen*, Bradley, *Bright*, *Bromberg*, *J. Y. Brown*, *Buckner*, Bundy, R. R. Butler, *J. H. Caldwell*, *Caulfield*, Chittenden, A. Clark, jr., *J. B. Clark, jr.*, F. Clarke, Clements, *Clymer*, C. L. Cobb, *Comingo*, *Cook*, Corwin, *Cox*, *Crittenden*, *Crossland*, Crutchfield, *John J. Davis*, *De Witt*, Dunnell, *Durham*, *Eden*, *Eldredge*, *Finck*, *Giddings*, *Glover*, Gunckel, *Gunter*, Hagans, E. Hale, R. S. Hale, *R. Hamilton*, *Hancock*, *H. R. Harris*, *J. T. Harris*, H. H. Harrison, *Hatcher*, Havens, Hays, *Hereford*, *Herndon*, *Holman*, Hubbell, Hunter, *Hunton*, Hyde, Hynes, Kellogg, *Knapp*, *Lamar*, *Lamison*, *Leach*, B. Lewis, Lofland, Lowndes, *Luttrell*, *Magee*, Martin, A. S. McDill, *McLean*, Merriam, *Milliken*, *Mills*, Moore, *Morrison*, *Neal*, *Nesmith*, *Niblack*, *O'Brien*, Orr, Packer, *H. W. Parker*, I. C. Parker, Pelham, *Perry*, W. W. Phelps, J. H. Platt, jr., Poland, *Potter*, *Randall*, W. H. Ray, *Read*, *W. M. Robbins*, E. H. Roberts, *W. R. Roberts*, *J. C. Robinson*, *M. Sayler*, *R. Schell*, *J. G. Schumaker*, Scofield, H. J. Scudder, I. W. Scudder, Sener, Sheats, L. D. Shoemaker, Sloan, *Sloss*, J. A. Smith, Snyder, *Speer*, Stanard, *Standiford*, *Stone*, *Storm*, Strait, Strawbridge,

Swann, C. Y. Thomas, J. M. Thompson, Thornburgh, Todd, Tremain, *R. B. Vance*, *Waddell*, *E. Wells*, A. White, *Whitehead*, *Whitehouse*, Whiteley, *Whitthorne*, C. W. Willard, *Willie*, *E. K. Wilson*, *Wolfe*, *F. Wood*, *J. D. Young*, *P. M. B. Young*—148.

Mr. SHANKS moved the following as a preamble to the bill:

Whereas, it is essential to just government that we recognize the equality of all men before the law, and hold it is the duty of government in its dealings with the people to mete out equal and exact justice to all, of whatever nativity, race, color, or persuasion, religious or political; and it being the proper object of legislation to enact fundamental principles into law: Therefore, &c.

Which was agreed to—yeas 218, nays 26, not voting 45:

YEAS—Messrs. Albert, Albright, *Archer*, *Ashe*, *Atkins*, Averill, *Banning*, Barber, Barrere, Bass, *Beck*, Begole, Biery, *Bland*, Bradley, *Buckner*, Buffinton, Bundy, H. C. Burchard, Burleigh, Burrows, B. F. Butler, R. R. Butler, Cain, Cannon, Carpenter, Cason, *Caulfield*, Cessna, A. Clark, jr., *J. B. Clark, jr.*, F. Clarke, Clayton, Clements, *Clymer*, C. L. Cobb, S. A. Cobb, Coburn, *Comingo*, Conger, *Cook*, Corwin, Cotton, *Cox*, *Crittenden*, Crooke, Crounse, Crutchfield, Curtis, Darrall, Dawes, *De Witt*, Dobbins, Donnan, Duell, Dunnell, *Durham*, Eames, *Eden*, Field, Fort, Foster, Garfield, *Giddings*, *Glover*, Gooch, Gunckel, *Gunter*, Hagans, E. Hale, *R. Hamilton*, Harmer, B. W. Harris, H. H. Harrison, *Hatcher*, Hathorn, Havens, J. B. Hawley, J. R. Hawley, Hays, G. W. Hazelton, J. W. Hazelton, Hendee, *Hereford*, *Herndon*, E. R. Hoar, Hodges, *Holman*, Hooper, Hoskins, Houghton, Howe, Hubbell, Hunter, Hurlbut, Hyde, Hynes, Kasson, Kelley, Kellogg, *Lamar*, Lamport, Lansing, W. Lawrence, Lawson, *Leach*, Lofland, Loughridge, Lowe, Lowndes, *Magee*, Martin, McCrary, A. S. McDill, J. W. McDill, MacDougall, McKee, McNulta, Merriam, *Mills*, Monroe, Moore, Morey, *Morrison*, Myers, Negley, Niles, *O'Brien*, O'Neill, Orr, Orth, Packard, Packer, Page, *H. W. Parker*, I. C. Parker, R. C. Parsons, Pelham, Pendleton, *Perry*, W. A. Phillips, Pierce, Pike, J. H. Platt, jr., Poland, *C. N. Potter*, Pratt, Rainey, *Randall*, Rapier, W. H. Ray, Richmond, *W. M. Robbins*, E. H. Roberts, *W. R. Roberts*, *J. C. Robinson*, J. W. Robinson, S. Ross, Sawyer, H. B. Sayler, Scofield, H. J. Scudder, I. W. Scudder, Sener, Sessions, Shanks, Sheats, Sheldon, L. D. Shoemaker, Sloan, W. B. Small, Smart, A. H. Smith, G. L. Smith, H. B. Smith, J. A. Smith, J. Q. Smith, Snyder, *Speer*, Sprague, Stanard, *Standiford*, Starkweather, C. A. Stevens, *Storm*, Stowell, Strait, Strawbridge, *Swann*, Sypher, Taylor, C. R. Thomas, C. Y Thomas, J. M. Thompson, Thornburgh, Todd, W. Townsend, Tremain, Tyner, *R. B. Vance*, *Waddell*, Waldron, A. S. Wallace, J. D. Ward, M. L. Ward, *E. Wells*, A. White, *Whitehead*, *Whitehouse*, Whiteley, Wilber, G. Willard, C. G. Williams, J. M. S. Williams, W. Williams, J. Wilson, J. M. Wilson, Woodworth—218.

NAYS—Messrs. *G. M. Adams*, *Arthur*, *H. P. Bell*, *Berry*, *Blount*, *Bowen*, *Bright*, *Bromberg*, *J. Y. Brown*, *J. H. Caldwell*, Chittenden, *Crossland*, *John J. Davis*, *Eldredge*, *Hancock*, *H. R. Harris*, *Hunton*, *McLean*, *Milliken*, *J. W. Nesmith*, *Read*, *Schell*, *Stone*, W. B. Williams, *E. K. Wilson*, *J. D. Young*—26.

The previous question being seconded and the main question ordered, the question was taken, and the bill reported from the Committee on the Judiciary, as amended on motion of Mr. KELLOGG, was passed—yeas 162, nays 100, not voting 27, as follows:

YEAS—Messrs. Albert, Albright, Averill, Barber, Barrere, Bass, Begole, Biery, Bradley, Buffinton, Bundy, H. C. Burchard, Burleigh, Burrows, B. F. Butler, Cain, Cannon, Carpenter, Cason, Cessna, A. Clark, jr., F. Clarke, Clayton, Clements, S. A. Cobb, Coburn, Conger, Corwin, Cotton, Crooke, Crounse, Curtis, Darrall, Dawes, Dobbins, Donnan, Duell, Dunnell, Eames, Field, Fort, Foster, Garfield, Gooch, Gunckel, Hagans, E. Hale, R. S. Hale, Harmer, B. W. Harris, Hathorn, J. B. Hawley, J. R. Hawley, Hays, G. W. Hazelton, J. W. Hazelton, Hendee, E. R. Hoar, Hodges, Hooper, Hoskins, Houghton, Howe, Hubbell, Hunter, Hurlbut, Hyde, Hynes, Kasson, Kelley, Kellogg, Lamport, Lansing, W. Lawrence, Lawson, B. Lewis, Loughridge, Lowe, Lynch, Martin, McCrary, A. S. McDill, J. W. McDill, MacDougall, McKee, McNulta, Merriam, Monroe, Moore, Morey, Myers, Negley, Niles, O'Neill, Orr, Orth, Packard, Packer, Page, I. C. Parker, R. C. Parsons, Pelham, Pendleton, W. A. Phillips, Pierce, Pike, J. H. Platt, jr., Poland, Pratt, Rainey, Rapier, Richmond, E. H. Roberts, J. W. Robinson, S. Ross, Rusk, Sawyer, H. B. Sayler, Scofield, H. J. Scudder, I. W. Scudder, Sessions, Shanks, Sheats, Sheldon, L. D. Shoemaker, W. B. Small, Smart, A. H. Smith, G. L. Smith, H. B. Smith, J. Q. Smith, Snyder, Sprague, Starkweather, C. A. Stevens, Stowell, Strawbridge, Sypher, Taylor, C. R. Thomas, J. M. Thompson, Todd, W. Townsend, Tremain, Tyner, Waldron, A. S. Wallace, J. D. Ward, M. L. Ward, A. White, Whiteley, Wilber, C. W. Willard, G. Willard, C. G. Williams, J. M. S. Williams, W. Williams, W. B. Williams, J. Wilson, J. M. Wilson, Woodworth—162.

NAYS—Messrs. *G. M. Adams*, *Archer*, *Arthur*, *Ashe*, *Atkins*, *Banning*, *Beck*, *H. P. Bell*, *Berry*, *Bland*, *Blount*, *Bowen*, *Bright*, *Bromberg*, *J. Y. Brown*, *Buckner*, R. R. Butler, *J. H. Caldwell*, *Caulfield*, Chittenden, *J. B. Clark, jr.*, *Clymer*, *Comingo*, *Cook*, *Cox*, *Crittenden*, *Crossland*, Crutchfield, *John J. Davis*, *De Witt*, *Durham*, *Eden*, *Eldredge*, *Finck*, *Giddings*, *Glover*, *Gunter*, *R. Hamilton*, *Hancock*. *H. R. Harris*, *J. T. Harris*, H. H. Harrison, *Hatcher*, *Hereford*, *Herndon*, *Holman*, *Hunton*, *Knapp*, *Lamar*, *Lamison*, *Leach*, Lofland, Lowndes, *Luttrell*, *Magee*, *McLean*, *Milliken*, *Mills*, *Morrison*, *Neal*, *Nesmith*. *Niblack*, *O'Brien*, *H. W. Parker*, *Perry*, W. W. Phelps, *C. N. Potter*. *Randall*, W. H. Ray, *Read*, *W. M. Robbins*, *W. R. Roberts*, *J. C. Robinson*, *M. Sayler*, *Schell*, *J. G. Schumaker*, Sloan, *Sloss*, J. A. Smith, *Speer*, Stanard, *Standiford*, *Al. H. Stephens*, *Stone*, *Storm*, *Swann*, C. Y. Thomas, Thornburgh, *R. B. Vance*, *Waddell*, *E. Wells*, *Whitehead*, *Whitehouse*, *Whitthorne*, *Willie*, *E. K. Wilson*, *Wolfe*, *F. Wood*, *J. D. Young*, *P. M. B. Young*—100.

NOT VOTING—Messrs. *Barnum*, Barry, C. L.

Cobb, *Creamer*, Danford, Farwell, J. C. Freeman, Frye, Havens, G. F. Hoar, *Kendall*, Killinger, *Marshall*, Maynard, *Mitchell*, Nunn, T. C. Platt, Purman, Ransier, Sener, Sherwood, W. A. Smith, *Southard*, St. John, Strait, Walls, Wheeler—27.

IN SENATE.

February 15—Mr. EDMUNDS reported back the bill from the Committee on the Judiciary to which it had been referred February 6.

February 27—Mr. THURMAN'S amendment to strike out in section four, line four, the words "or of any State," was disagreed to, yeas 26, nays 40, absent 7:

YEAS—Messrs. *Bayard*, *Bogy*, Carpenter, *Cooper*, *Davis*, *Dennis*, *Eaton*, Ferry of Connecticut, *Goldthwaite*, *Gordon*, *Hager*, *Hamilton* of Maryland, HAMILTON of Texas, *Kelly*, Lewis, *McCreery*, *Merrimon*, *Norwood*, *Ransom*, *Saulsbury*, SCHURZ, Sprague, *Stevenson*, *Stockton*, *Thurman*, TIPTON—26.

NAYS—Messrs. Alcorn, Allison, Anthony, Boreman, Boutwell, Cameron of Pa., Chandler, Clayton, Conkling, Conover, Cragin, Dorsey, Edmunds, Ferry of Michigan, Flanagan, Frelinghuysen, Hamlin, Harvey, Howe, Ingalls, Jones of Nev., Logan, Mitchell, Morrill of Vermont, Morton, Oglesby, Patterson, Pease, Pratt, Ramsey, Robertson, Sargent, Scott, Sherman, Spencer, Stewart, Washburn, West, Windom, Wright—40.

Mr. BAYARD offered the following amendment, to come in at the end of section four:

That sections 820 and 821 of the Revised Statutes of the United States be, and the same are hereby, repealed.

Which was disagreed to, yeas 25, nays 36, absent 12:

YEAS—Messrs. Alcorn, *Bayard*, *Bogy*, *Cooper*, *Davis*, *Dennis*, *Eaton*, Ferry of Connecticut, *Goldthwaite*, *Gordon*, *Hager*, *Hamilton* of Maryland, HAMILTON of Texas, *Kelly*, *McCreery*, *Merrimon*, *Norwood*, *Ransom*, *Saulsbury*, SCHURZ, Sprague, *Stevenson*, *Stockton*, *Thurman*, TIPTON—25.

NAYS—Messrs. Allison, Anthony, Boutwell, Chandler, Clayton, Conkling, Conover, Cragin, Dorsey, Edmunds, Ferry of Michigan, Flanagan, Frelinghuysen, Hamlin, Harvey, Howe, Ingalls, Jones of Nev., Logan, Mitchell, Morrill of Maine, Morrill of Vermont, Morton, Oglesby, Patterson, Pease, Pratt, Ramsey, Robertson, Scott, Sherman, Spencer, Stewart, Washburn, Windom, Wright—36.

[These sections refer to qualifications of jurors, and to the oath required of jurors.]

Mr. THURMAN moved to insert the words "not more than" after the word "pay" in line seven of section two, which was disagreed to, yeas 22, nays 36, absent 15:

YEAS—Messrs. *Bayard*, *Bogy*, *Cooper*, *Davis*, *Dennis*, *Eaton*, *Goldthwaite*, *Gordon*, *Hager*, *Hamilton* of Maryland, HAMILTON of Texas, *Kelly*, *McCreery*, *Merrimon*, *Norwood*, *Ransom*, *Saulsbury*, SCHURZ, Sprague, *Stevenson*, *Stockton*, *Thurman*—22.

NAYS—Messrs. Alcorn, Allison, Boutwell, Chandler, Clayton, Conkling, Conover, Cragin, Dorsey, Edmunds, Ferry of Michigan, Flanagan, Frelinghuysen, Hamlin, Harvey, Howe, Ingalls, Jones of Nev., Logan, Mitchell, Morrill of Maine, Morrill of Vt., Morton, Oglesby, Patterson, Pease, Pratt, Ramsey, Robertson, Scott, Sherman, Spencer, Stewart, Washburn, West, Windom—36.

The bill was then passed, yeas 38, nays 26, absent 9:

YEAS—Messrs. Alcorn, Allison, Anthony, Boreman, Boutwell, Cameron of Pa., Chandler, Clayton, Conkling, Conover, Cragin, Edmunds, Ferry of Michigan, Flanagan, Frelinghuysen, Harvey, Howe, Ingalls, Jones of Nev., Logan, Mitchell, Morrill of Vt., Morton, Oglesby, Patterson, Pease, Pratt, Ramsey, Robertson, Sargent, Scott, Sherman, Spencer, Stewart, Washburn, West, Windom, Wright—38.

NAYS—Messrs. *Bayard*, *Bogy*, Carpenter, *Cooper*, *Davis*, *Dennis*, *Eaton*, Ferry of Connecticut, *Goldthwaite*, *Gordon*, *Hager*, *Hamilton* of Maryland, HAMILTON of Texas, *Kelly*, Lewis, *McCreery*, *Merrimon*, *Norwood*, *Ransom*, *Saulsbury*, SCHURZ, Sprague, *Stevenson*, *Stockton*, *Thurman*, TIPTON—26.

ABSENT—Messrs. Brownlow, Dorsey, FENTON, Gilbert, Hamlin, Hitchcock, *Johnston*, Morrill of Maine, Wadleigh—9.

The bill was approved by President GRANT, March 1, 1875.

Judicial Action Upon It.

1875, March 21—Judge Halmer H. Emmons, U. S. Judge for the Sixth Circuit (Ohio, Michigan, Kentucky and Tennessee), gave the following instructions to the Grand Jury, at the session of the court held in Memphis, Tennessee:

[Newspaper Copy.]

It is to be regretted that a question of such exceptional importance, and one which is producing so much excitement, should come before the court in this form. At an early day, however, and during the term, we are compelled by law to decide the matter you lay before us.

The severe penalties imposed by this law upon prosecuting attorneys and other officials will, we are advised, be attempted to be enforced should the grand jury fail to indict, in the assumption that their action will be controlled by such officers unless the court acts. Every consideration makes it a duty to answer your questions at once.

You ask whether it is a crime for which you have a right to find an indictment, that a negro has been denied "the full and equal enjoyment of the accommodations, advantages, facilities, and privileges of the theatres and inns" of the State. Such a denial is not an offense over which Congress can give this court jurisdiction. Those are matters which the State governments alone control.

The parties who think themselves aggrieved can bring their civil action in this court at once. Any decision we may then make can be reviewed by the supreme court.

In ordinary circumstances, this brief reply is all which we should make. It is all which, as a very general rule, the proprieties of such occasions authorize. But such are the exceptional conditions which attend these complaints before you, and such the excited condition of those classes whom the law was intended to affect, that after much hesitation we have yielded to an earnest request to state in a simple and untechnical form the reason upon which our advice rests. To do this successfully, in haste and without preparation, is still more difficult for a judge than to treat the matter technically when addressing the judicial and professional mind.

Until the three recent amendments to the national constitution, which abolished slavery and attempted to protect the civil and political rights of the freedmen, all parties conceded that the federal government had no power whatever to restrain such an offense as this. The punishment of murder, arson, assaults and batteries, trespasses, frauds, injuries to reputation, of obstructions to the right of attending church, public schools, theatres, and forcing the right of being accommodated in inns, and by common carriers within the State, were matters not only not granted to the general government, but in the the constitution itself expressly reserved to the States. The vast mass of civil and political rights included in the compendious phrase, the right to "life, liberty, and the pursuit of happiness," rested entirely under State protection. To this familiar and unquestioned truism, there was universal assent then and is now. The only question presented for judicial determination is, have these amendments completely revolutionized the whole character of our government; because it is entirely evident that if Congress has the power of regulating the theaters and "other places of amusement" in Memphis and other cities of the Union, this necessarily involves the power of protecting the more sacred and important rights of the colored citizen.

The thirteenth amendment abolished slavery only: it did no more. It gave the freedman no right of protection from the federal government superior to that of his white fellow-citizens, and no exemption from the power of State control which might be exercised against others. The right of legislation secured to Congress in the amendment was that only of creating penalties for a violation of its provisions, and to provide securities against the re-establishment of slavery, either generally or in particular instances. It accords no more authority to enact that he should have the right to vote, to testify, to make contracts, to hold real estate, exercise trades, attend public schools, or any other matter or thing within the limits of a State, than it does to enact the same thing in reference to white men. The utmost effect of this great provision in our constitution was to make the colored man a citizen, equal before the laws with the race which had enslaved him. For this purpose the fourteenth amendment was by no means necessary. So far as the control of Congress is concerned, the States were still free to legislate in reference to what persons should attend theaters, be accommodated at inns, or be transported by common carriers within the States. As an illustration of unquestioned local State power anterior to this amendment, we suggest a fact in the history of the State of Michigan: By the voice of the people, it three times denied the colored race, though taxed, the right of voting. The Supreme Court of that State sustained as lawful the action of a steamboat master excluding a colored person from the steamer's cabin, compelling him to take passage on the deck. These judges were high-toned gentlemen, of far more than ordinary legal culture and ability, and elected to their places by a then strongly predominant anti-slavery party in the State. They sustained the action of the carrier, as a wholesome police regulation, calculated, in view of our American education and prejudices, to secure peace and harmony in that department of commerce and business under his control. It was deemed injudicious that the law should interfere with his action. The State Legislature, also overwhelmingly anti-slavery in sentiment, might have changed this rule, but refused to do so. Against this action, political and judicial, a large and influential portion of the people earnestly struggled and protested. But all understood, from the numerous rulings of the supreme court, there was no power in Congress to interfere with the decision of the judges and the people of the State. Like conditions, in a greater or less degree, characterized nearly every free State in the Union. A nearly similar judgment, arising upon facts since the amendment, has recently been pronounced by the learned judge of the superior court of Cleveland, O., in which he ruled that the manager of a theater might lawfully exclude from the dress circle a colored person of never so much respectability. It would seem to be clear that the abolition of slavery placed the negro in the former States just where he had before stood in the free States. What Congress could not do in reference to a free negro in a northern State, where slavery never existed, before the abolition of slavery, it could not afterward do in regard to one living in the South. We conclude with confidence that the thirteenth amendment did not authorize Congress to interfere with the private and internal regulations of theater managers, hotel keepers, or common carriers within the State, in reference to colored persons, any more than it did in regard to their white fellow-citizens.

It will simplify the subject, before considering the fourteenth amendment, to say that the clauses forbidding the "States to deprive any person of life, liberty, or property, without due process of law, or deny to any person the equal protection of the laws," have no application to this subject. They are intended solely to prevent the arbitrary transfer of property from citizen to citizen without legal adjudication or process, and to prevent the establishment of tribunals for one class of persons varying from those which determine the rights of all. These inhibitions, too, beyond all controversy, are aimed at the action of the *State* only, and have no reference to individuals.

The only provision of the fourteeenth amendment which affects this question is that which provides that "no State shall make or enforce any law which shall abridge the privileges and immunities of citizens of the United States." It would be as useless as it would be improper, in view of the authoritative judgment of the court of last resort, to do more than to explain just what it announces. In what are known as the Slaughter-house cases (16th Wallace) two points were established. First, that this clause prohibited the action of the State alone, and gave Congress no power to legislate against the wrongs and personal violence of the citizen. Second, that the privileges and immunities which a State could not abridge were only that limited class which depended immediately upon the constitution of the United States. They are few in number and of little importance to the great mass of the colored race in their present condition. The right to pass from State to State and to the national capital, to protection upon the high seas and in foreign countries, and a few others, were stated as illustrations. The great body of our civil and political rights, that of acquiring and enjoying property, real and personal, to exercise trades, attend schools and churches, to be protected against personal violence, and enjoy the freedom of opinion, were declared to rest entirely under State protection, and were not included in this amendment.

In reference to the first proposition, that the power of Congress was not called into action under this clause until the State, through its political power, had violated its provisions by passing, or attempting to enforce, some law, obtained the unanimous consent of every member of the court. We do not understand that this is anywhere questioned. This legislation, therefore, when no such exigency has occurred, is without authority, and it is our duty for this reason to advise you not to find an indictment for violation of its provisions.

The second proposition, affirmed by a majority of the court, just as conclusively establishes the invalidity of this law. The character of the wrong done—that of excluding a citizen from a hotel and a theater—is not such as Congress has any right to punish. They, say the Supreme Court, are violations of such rights as attach to citizens of a State, and do not belong to those which he enjoys as a citizen of the United States. It is this latter limited class of rights only which the fourteenth amendment protects. Within this judgment, therefore, there is no power of federal legislation to provide penalties for the violation of any privilege save the few which are enjoyed peculiarly under the federal constitution. The right to go from State to State, to visit the capitol, and other national privileges, Congress may protect. All others, among which are the rights claimed to have been infringed in the present instance, are beyond its control. For this additional reason the law which attempts to protect them is void for the want of power in the body which passed it.

The Slaughter-house cases were well calculated to have elicited a different judgment, if the court had not felt constrained upon principle to decide as it did. A State law had substantially interfered with the trade and calling of a large class of citizens. Every butcher and dealer in meats over a wide-spread territory was compelled to pay an onerous tribute to a single corporation. But their right to carry on a trade, to acquire and dispose of property, was held not to come within the protection of the fourteenth amendment. There was no middle ground for the court; they must hold either that it completely revolutionized the whole theory of our government, and transferred to federal control all those rights hitherto alone protected by State laws; or hold, upon the other hand, that it referred only to a few privileges secured by the national constitution. That court, in the same volume, applied the same principle where a woman in Illinois was rejected as an applicant for admission to the bar. It again decided that such right was not one of the immunities protected by the amendment. In 18th Wallace a State law having deprived a citizen of the right to sell what he owned and possessed, it held that the selling of property was a privilege and immunity protected by State laws and constitutions only, and was not protected by this clause.

With the fact that this interpretation was equivalent to expunging it from the amendments altogether, we have nothing to do. It is true, unquestionably, that any violation of any privilege or immunity protected by the federal constitution, by the State, could be punished and redressed by congressional law before the adoption of this amendment. As now judicially read by the court of last resort, it leaves the organic law in this regard precisely where it was before. It is one of those constructions often resorted to, to prevent consequences serious and revolutionary, which courts believe were not contemplated by legislatures who pass laws, and by the people who adopt constitutions.

We do not deem it indelicate to express our sympathy with the large and respectable class of our fellow-citizens, including beyond question a majority of the more conservative Christian gentlemen of the south, who regret that there exists nowhere in either government, State or national, the power of punishing those mean and cowardly murders which are so frequently disgracing our civilization before the world. Although we have carried the doctrine of local governments in township and county organizations to a great extreme, we find in all its ordinary administrations most beneficial effects. To its universal application, however, most statesmen now agree that there should be some exceptions. In no country but our own is the discreditable fact true that where murder, cruel and shocking outrages, are perpetrated by a dominant party in a narrow region of country, there is no power of punishment, save through the impracticable instrumentality of those who have either committed or sympathized with the crime. When conspiracies and combinations against the property, well-being and life of classes or persons in the small civil divisions of our country include large portions of the constabulary, the magistracy, and the jurors, grand and traverse, the inevitable consequence must be that the offenses they commit, or with which they sympathize, will be perpetrated with impunity. Unless our statesmen, State or national, create some jurisdiction of wider scope, and which will authorize indictments and trial beyond the narrow limits a majority of whose citizens abet the crime to be punished, the nation must still submit to the disgrace of yearly additions of mean and courage-wanting murders of the most innocent and helpless, without the slightest infliction of any legal penalty upon the offenders. It has been our painful duty in repeated instances to charge juries that the federal court had no cognizance of offenses where crimes so cruel and shocking had been proved that court, jury and audience could scarce refrain from tears of sympathy, and where the elegantly-dressed, socially well-connected, and shameless murderers had, in the communities where they had shed innocent blood, not only confessed, but boasted of such crimes; or who had either not been indicted at all, or when tried, had been acquitted by juries, tbeir coadjutors in crime, amid the acclamations of their co-conspirators. In a very recent case it was proved that a young man of wealth, education, and most estimable moral character was shot to death at midday in his own house by a band of ruffians, for no other reason than that he had acted as chairman of a committee to wait upon the governor of his State to solicit his action for the protection of the negroes of his county, who were being driven from their homes, their houses burned and themselves murdered by the lawless conspirators by whom he was killed. The mock trial by which these infamous offenders were triumphantly acquitted was a still greater stain upon our civilization than the monstrous crime it affected to try. It is believed by many of our best citizens that there should be here, as in every other government on earth, some power to bring such wicked men to justice outside of, and uncontrolled by, the wills and hands which have united in their atrocities. As it does not now exist, and as no attempt at alteration is made by the State powers, it is natural that all those whose hearts are not of flint, and hope to be blessed and prosper as they do unto others as they would that others should do unto them, should strive to the uttermost to find the source of protection in the federal constitution. In the present condition of public opinion the remedy should, perhaps, be sought through the political action of the State only. I have but small sympathy with the right of the negro to see the immodest and vulgar displays in the ballet dance, which in modern times so universally disgrace the best theatrical presentations. I would have selected some more precious and beneficent privilege for protection, if the power had existed. We turn from this almost grotesque exercise of national authority, and express our regret only that it cannot be exerted to protect from pillage and murder the humble homes of those peaceful toilers, who quietly and inoffensively labor to support their wives and little ones, and who do not officiously and distastefully thrust themselves in the face of those lighter and less reflective portions of society so frequently found among theatrical audiences. We believe the actual history of this unhappy question demonstrates that where no legal force or constraint is used, the lady and gentleman of solid position and real cultivation are least annoyed by his presence when he is really worthy and cultivated; and when left unstimulated by foreign and wicked influences, his own good sense, guided by public opinion, keeps him in his proper position as uniformly as all other classes of society.

A recent judgment of one of the learned justices of the supreme court, after he enjoyed the benefits of the elaborate arguments, and participating in the dissenting opinions in the Slaughter-house cases, still affirms that violence upon the negro, simply because he is such, finding its sole animus in his race and color, may be made penal by Congressional enactment. This utterance suggests what otherwise we should have deemed impossible, that the supreme court may still find in the thirteenth amendment, which abolishes slavery, or the first clause in the fifteenth, which creates citizenship, so much incidental power to protect what they create, as will sustain a national law punishing the crime, where life, liberty, and property are violently taken, solely on account of the race and color of the party injured. Our sympathies are in that direction. Could we see a plausible path leading to such ground, after what that court has said, we would gladly stand upon it. But so demonstrative appear to us the arguments, in view of the judgments of the Supreme Court already rendered, that a crime perpetrated by one citizen of Tennessee upon another, when it consists in the violation of some right which is enjoyed solely as the citizen of the State, and depends in no degree upon the national constitution, that we feel at liberty to give no different advice.

1875, June 8—Judge Rensselaer R. Nelson, U. S. District Judge in the district of Minnesota, gave the following instructions to the Grand Jury at the session of the court held at Winona:

To answer your question properly it is necessary to examine the fourteenth amendment to the Constitution of the United States. Previous to the adoption of the recent amendments there was certainly no authority given to Congress by any clause in the Constitution to enact such a law as the one under consideration.

The thirteenth amendment abolished slavery and involuntary servitude, except as a punishment for crime, and the fourteenth amendment defines, if it does not absolutely create, citizenship of the United States, and provides under what circumstances a citizen of the United States may become a citizen of a State. It also proclaimed protection to all citizens of the United States in the enjoyment of their privileges and immunities, and equal protection of the laws to all persons within the jurisdiction of the State. The first section of the fourteenth amendment declares that "all persons born or naturalized in the United States are citizens of the United States, and of the State wherein they reside. No State shall make or enforce any law which shall abridge the privileges or immunities of the United States; nor shall any State deprive any person of life, liberty or property, without due process of law; nor deny to any person within its jurisdic tion the equal protection of the laws."

Section 5 provides that "the Congress shall have power to enforce by appropriate legislation the provisions of this amendment."

You will see that the legislation of Congress has been extended, and that of the States curtailed.

The Supreme Court of the United States in the "Slaughter-house cases," reported in 16th Wallace, decided that there is a citizenship of the United States and a citizenship of a State, each possessing certain privileges and immunities distinct from the other; and that the first clause of section 1 of the fourteenth amendment prohibited State legislation from abridging the privileges and immunities of the citizens of the United States only, and did not deprive the State governments from regulating and controlling the great fundamental rights of man, which belong to every citizen of a State, embracing nearly all the civil and political rights for the protection and enforcement of which State governments are established. It decided, therefore, that the right to slaughter animals within the city of New Orleans was not a privilege or immunity owing its existence to the Federal Government, its Constitution or its laws, and that a charter giving exclusive privileges to a corporation in regard to slaughtering animals was not in violation of the fourteenth amendment. There was no question raised or decided in regard to the power of legislation by Congress under this amendment. It was the constitutionality of an internal police regulation of a State that was before the court, and the law creating the corporation was sustained.

I call your attention to this case for the reason that several distinguished Federal and District judges and one eminent Circuit Court judge, in instructing grand juries upon the presentation of a similar question, have considered that the interpretation by the United States Supreme Court of this first section of the fourteenth amendment is a judgment against the constitutionality of the law under consideration. With great respect for the opinion of these judges, I cannot assent to their conclusions; and while I have no sympathy with this kind of Congressional legislation, and believe that the State government should punish all wrong or outrage of this character committed within its limits, still I think that where race, color, nativity, and religious or political belief, furnishes the only reason for the commission of such wrong or outrage, a proper occasion arises for the exercise of the power of Congress under this amendment. The objection urged against such a law is that it seeks to punish in the Federal Courts a violation of certain privileges which pertain to State citizenship. It is not doubted that the punishment of ordinary offenses against persons of any race belongs to the State Governments. They were created for the purpose of protecting life, liberty and the pursuit of individual happiness, and should legislate for this object. Yet as the fourteenth amendment creates citizenship and guarantees the equality of all persons before the law, I think Congress can provide for the punishment of individuals who deprive any person of the enjoyment of the rights of citizenship and of legal equality solely on account of race or color. These rights and privileges are derived from the Federal Government and are under its protection. It will be conceded, I think, that State legislation making it an offense to refuse the enjoyment of hotel accommodations to white persons and permitting the exclusion of all other persons, would be repugnant to this amendment. If so, cannot Congress interpose until some unfriendly and discriminating State law is passed? Must it confine its action to correct obnoxious legislation and not restrain individuals?

In the case of McCulloch vs. The State of Maryland (4th Wheaton, pp. 400–437), the construction of the grant of legislative power under the Constitution as it stood before the recent amendments was fully discussed, and it was decided that within the grant of power to Congress for purposes of legislation it may select any proper means of effecting the object in view, and may adopt any which might be appropriate and which were conducive to the end. Applying the reasoning of the Court to this case, where the express power to enforce the provisions of the amendment is given in the fifth section, it seems to me that Congress can legislate, even though a State had passed no obnoxious law; and may also in advance, by such enactments as it may deem suitable and necessary, remedy the evil against which this amendment proposes to guard.

If the opinion in that case correctly represents the extent of Congressional legislation, the power of Congress can be exerted directly to put down all outrage or discrimination on the part of individuals when the motive originates only in race or color.

I do not deem it necessary at this time to more fully discuss this question. The law, in my opinion, is constitutional.

A Conviction Under the Act.

In Philadelphia, in February, 1876, Rev. Fields Cook, pastor of the Third Baptist colored church of Alexandria, Virginia, was refused sleeping and eating accommodations at the Bingham House, by Upton S. Newcomer, one of its clerks; and upon the trial of the cause, in the U. S. District Court, JOHN CADWALADER, Judge, instructed the jury as follows:

The fourteenth amendment of the Constitution of the United States makes all persons born or naturalized in the United States, and subject to the jurisdiction thereof, citizens of the United States, and provides that no State shall make or enforce any law which shall abridge the privileges or immunities of citizens of the United States; nor shall any State * * * deny to any person within its jurisdiction the equal protection of the laws. This amendment expressly gives to Congress the power to enforce it by appropriate legislation. An act of Congress of March 1, 1875, enacts that all persons within the jurisdiction of the United States shall be entitled to the full and equal enjoyment of the accommodations, advantages, facilities and privileges of inns, public conveyances on land or water, theaters and other places of public amusement, subject only to the conditions and limitations established by law, and applicable alike to citizens of every race and color, and makes it a criminal offense to violate these enactments by denying to any citizen, except for reasons by law applicable to citizens of every race and color, * * * the full enjoyment of any of the accommodations, advantages, facilities or privileges enumerated. As the law of Pennsylvania had stood until the 22d of March, 1867, it was not wrongful for innkeepers or carriers by land or water to discriminate against travelers of the colored race to such an extent as to exclude them from any part of the inns or public conveyances which was set apart for the exclusive accommodation of white travelers. The Legislature of Pennsylania, by an act of 22d of March, 1867, altered the law in this respect as to passengers on railroads. But the law of the State was not changed as to inns by any act of the State Legislature. Therefore, independently of the amendment of the Constitution of the United States and of the act of Congress now in question, the conduct of the defendant on the occasion in question might, perhaps, have been lawful. It is not necessary to express an opinion upon this point, because the decision of the case depends upon the effect of this act of Congress. I am of opinion that under the Fourteenth Amendment of the Constitution the enactment of this law was within the legislative power of Congress, and that we are bound to give effect to the act of Congress according to its fair meaning. According to this meaning of the act I am of opinion that if this defendant, being in charge of the business of receiving travelers in this inn, and of providing necessary and proper accommodations for them in it, refused such accommodations to the witness Cook, then a traveler, by reason of his color, the defendant is guilty in manner and form as he stands indicted. If the case depended upon the unsupported testimony of this witness alone, there might be some reason to doubt whether this defendant was the person in charge of this part of the business. But under this head the additional testimony of Mr. Annan seems to be sufficient to remove all reasonable doubt. If the jury are convinced of the defendant's identity, they will consider whether any reasonable doubt of his conduct or motives in refusing the accommodations to Fields Cook can exist. The case appears to the court to be proved; but this question is for the jury, not for the court. If the jury have any reasonable doubt, they should find the defendant not guilty; otherwise they will find him guilty.

The jury brought in a verdict of guilty, March 1, 1876, and the Court imposed a fine of $500.

III.

BILL TO PROTECT ELECTORS.

Forty-third Congress—Second Session.

IN HOUSE.

1875, February 18—Mr. COBURN, from the Select Committee on Affairs in Alabama, reported the following bill (H. R. 4745), which was read twice and recommitted:

That if two or more persons, within the jurisdiction of the United States, shall invade any of the States of this Union for the purpose of forcibly overthrowing the existing government of said State, or any constituted authority of the same, or for the purpose of interfering in any forcible or unlawful manner with the due execution of the laws of said State or of the United States; or if two or more persons, within the jurisdiction of the United States, shall conspire with any other person or persons for any of the unlawful purposes hereinbefore recited, with intent to commit the same, each person so offending shall be deemed guilty of felony, and, on conviction thereof, shall be punished by fine not exceeding ten thousand dollars and by imprisonment and confinement at hard labor for a term not exceeding ten years, at the discretion of the court trying the same.

SEC. 2. That if two or more persons shall conspire together to overthrow by force or to usurp by violence the State government of any of the States of this Union, or any department thereof; or if any two or more persons shall, in fact, by force and violence attempt to subvert or usurp such State government, or any department thereof; or if any two or more persons shall, by like force and violence, actually overthrow the existing government of any State, or any department thereof; each person so offending shall be deemed guilty of a crime, and, on conviction thereof, shall be fined not less than five hundred dollars nor more than five thousand dollars, and shall be imprisoned not less than one year and not more than twenty years, at the discretion of the court trying the same.

SEC. 3. That any person or persons using or proposing to use fire-arms or other deadly weapons against any peaceable individual or individuals, or assemblages of the same, at or near the place and on the day or days of registration or holding an election for Representatives or Delegates to Congress, for the purpose of intimidating or injuring such individual or individuals while such an election is in progress, and before the same shall have been completed, or before such election has commenced to be held, for the purpose of intimidating such individuals from coming to the same, shall be guilty of a crime, and, on conviction thereof, shall be fined not less than five hundred dollars nor more than two thousand dollars, and imprisoned not less than one year and not more than three years, at the discretion of the court trying the same: *Provided*, That in all prosecutions under this act, the open or concealed carrying of fire-arms or other deadly weapons at such elections or place of registration shall be taken as presumptive evidence of the intent to intimidate under this act.

SEC. 4. That in case the registration-officers appointed under the laws of any State or Territory, where, by the laws of said State or Territory, registration is required as a condition of voting at any election for Representatives in Congress, shall willfully or corruptly refuse or neglect to give any persons entitled to vote, at any precinct or voting-place established under the provisions of the laws of Congress, or of any State or Territory, full and sufficient opportunities to register in the manner prescribed by law, and within the time fixed by law, or shall, by any device or subterfuge, impose conditions or enforce discriminations upon voters or classes of voters not declared in such registration-laws, or shall refuse or neglect, on request made by the voter or his agent, to furnish such voter with a certificate of registration, or such other form of evidence of the same as may by law be required in such State or Territory, such officer shall be deemed guilty of a crime, and, on conviction thereof, shall be fined not less than five hundred dollars nor more than one thousand dollars, or imprisoned not less than six months nor more than two years, or both, at the discretion of the court trying the same.

SEC. 5. That any person or persons who, at any election for a Representative to Congress, shall, by cunning or device, fraud or force, take, or cause to be taken, from the legal custodian or custodians of the same, or from any place where kept in deposit by any such custodian or custodians, the box or boxes of ballots, or the poll-lists, or either of them, or shall carry away, conceal, scatter, deface, mutilate, or destroy said ballots or poll-lists, or any or either of them, before the final count and comparison of the same has been completed, and the result of the election ascertained and publicly announced, or before the time has expired for which such ballots and poll-lists, or either of them, have to be preserved under the laws of the United States, or of such State and Territory, every such person shall be deemed guilty of a crime, and, on conviction thereof, shall be fined not less than five hundred dollars nor more than three thousand dollars, and imprisoned not less than two years nor more than five years, at the discretion of the court trying the same.

SEC. 6. That if in the prosecution of any of the undertakings hereinbefore declared unlawful, or in the commission of any of the offenses hereinbefore set forth, any person not participant in said offenses or unlawful undertakings shall be killed by any persons engaged in the same, or any of them, such killing shall constitute the crime of murder: and any person committing the same, or accessory before the fact to such commission, shall, on conviction thereof, suffer the penalty of death.

SEC. 7. That the district courts of the United States, within their several districts, shall have, exclusively of the courts of the several States, jurisdiction of all crimes and offenses against the provisions of this act, and also, concurrently with the circuit courts of the United States, of all causes, civil or criminal, arising under this act, except as herein otherwise provided; and the jurisdiction hereby conferred shall be exercised in conformity with the laws and practice governing United States courts; and all crimes and offenses committed against the provisions of this act may be prosecuted by the indictment of a grand jury, or, in cases of crimes and offenses not infamous, may be, either by indictment or information, filed by the district attorney in a court having jurisdiction.

SEC. 8. That the supervisors of elections hereafter appointed for any county, parish, or voting-precinct in any Congressional district, at the instance of ten citizens, as provided in existing laws, shall exercise the same powers and perform the same duties as are now given to and required from supervisors in towns and cities of twenty thousand inhabitants or upward. All supervisors of elections within any congressional district may hereafter be appointed from the congressional district; and the judge of the circuit court of the United States within whose circuit such district may be situate shall appoint such supervisors on petition as now provided by law at least thirty days prior to the registration or election in which they are to act; and one of said supervisors, so appointed by said judge, shall be by him denominated as chief supervisor of said congressional district, and shall possess the powers and perform the duties now required by law of a chief supervisor.

SEC. 9. That the provisions of existing laws as to the appointment, powers, and duties of special deputy marshals for cities and towns of twenty thousand inhabitants or upward, in elections for Representatives to Congress, are hereby extended to the several counties, parishes, and voting-precincts in each congressional district, and such special deputies may be selected from any portion of such congressional district.

SEC. 10. That at all elections for representatives in Congress hereafter held, the managers of such elections or board of officers charged with the conduct of the said election, by whatever title denominated, at the several polling-places, shall immediately after the closing of the polls, and before separating or adjourning to any other time or place, count and declare, in the presence of the supervisor and deputy marshal, if any shall have been appointed and shall be present at said polling-place, the result of the vote polled at said place of election, and shall thereupon immediately certify the same so far as relates to Representatives in Congress or presidential electors, if voted for in said election, under the laws of the State, and shall deliver such certificate to said supervisor or deputy marshal, whichever may be present; and such supervisor or deputy marshal, as the case may be, shall at once transmit such certificate to the chief supervisor of the Congressional district, who shall, as soon as practicable, forward the same to the Clerk of the House of Representatives. And the officer or officers charged with the canvassing or consolidation of the vote of any county, city, or parish shall, in like manner, perform such duty in the presence of such supervisor, if present, who shall, if appointed, attend in each county, city, or parish, at the time and place provided by law for such canvass and consolidation.

SEC. 11. That no officer whose office is created by this act shall receive any compensation whatever from the United States for his services, nor shall the compensation heretofore allowed by law to any officer already existing be in any manner increased by reason of anything in this act contained.

SEC. 12. That the ballots, poll-lists, tally-sheets, or other papers which by the law of any State are evidence of an election, and which have been used in elections for Representatives to Congress, shall hereafter be preserved and safely kept by the custodian provided by the laws of the several States until the close of the first session of the Congress to be affected by such election; that either party to an election-contest in the House of Representatives of the United States, in which contest an allegation of fraudulent count or change of ballots is made, may have a subpœna directed to said custodian, who shall, if so required by said subpœna, produce such original ballots, lists, and other papers connected with said election, and the same, after the usual notice to the contestant or contestee, may be examined and compared before any person in the county or parish authorized to take depositions in contested elections, and such person shall certify under his hand and seal, and forward in the manner provided by law, said examination and comparison, to be used as evidence in the case. After said examination and comparison shall be completed, said ballots, lists of voters, and other papers shall be returned to their lawful custodian in the same condition as when by him produced before said examining officer.

SEC. 13. That whenever in any State, or part of a State, the unlawful combinations named in section five thousand two hundred and ninety-nine of the Revised Statutes, and in the first and second sections of this act, shall be organized and armed, and so numerous and powerful as to be able, by violence, to either overthrow or set at defiance the constituted authorities of said State, and of the United States within said State, or when the constituted authorities are in complicity with, or shall connive at, the unlawful purposes of such powerful and armed combinations; and whenever, by reason of either or all of the causes aforesaid, the conviction of such offenders and the preservation of the public safety shall become in such district impracticable, in every such case such combinations shall be deemed a rebellion against the Government of the United States, and, during the continuance of such rebellion, and within the limits of the district which shall be so under the sway thereof, such limits to be prescribed by proclamation, it shall be lawful for the President of the United States, when, in his judgment, the public safety shall require it, to suspend the privilege of the writ of habeas corpus, to the end that such rebellion may be overthrown: *Provided*, That all the provisions of the second section of the act entitled "An act relating to habeas corpus, and regulating judicial proceedings in certain cases," approved March third, eighteen hundred and sixty-three, which relate to the discharge of prisoners other than prisoners of war, and to the penalty for refusing to obey the order of the court, shall be in full force so far as the same are applicable to the provisions of this section: *And provided further*, That the President shall first have made proclamation, as provided by law, commanding such insurgents to disperse.

February 24—Mr. COBURN reported back the bill, when Mr. ELDREDGE raised the question of consideration, which was decided in the affirmative—yeas 170, nays 89, not voting 28:

YEAS—Messrs. Albert, Albright, Averill, Barber, Barrere, Barry, Bass, Begole, Biery, Bradley, Buffinton, Bundy, H. C. Burchard, Burleigh, Burrows, B. F. Butler, R. R. Butler, Cain, Cannon, Carpenter, Cason, Cessna, A. Clark, jr., Clayton, Clements, S. A. Cobb, Coburn, Conger, Corwin, Cotton, Crooke, Crounse, Crutchfield, Curtis, Danford, Darrall, Dawes, Dobbins, Donnan, Duell, Dunnell, Eames, Eldredge, Field, Fort, Frye, Garfield, Gooch, Gunckel, Hagans, E. Hale, Harmer, B. W. Harris, H. H. Harrison, Hathorn, Havens, J B. Hawley, J. R. Hawley, Hays, G. W. Hazelton, J. W. Hazelton, E. R. Hoar, G. F. Hoar, Hodges, Hoskins, Houghton, Howe, Hubbell, Hunter, Hurlbut, Hyde, Hynes, Kasson, Kelley, Kellogg, Lamport, Lansing, W. Lawrence, Lawson, B. Lewis, Lofland, Loughridge, Lowe, Lowndes, Lynch, Martin, Maynard, McCrary, A. S. McDill, J. W. McDill, MacDougall, McKee, McNulta, Merriam, Monroe, Moore, Morey, Myers, Negley, Niles, Nunn, O'Neill, Orr, Orth, Packard, Packer, I. C. Parker, R. C. Parsons, Pelham, Pendleton, W. A. Phillips, Pierce, Pike, J. H. Platt, jr., T. C. Platt, Poland, Pratt, Rapier, W. H. Ray, Richmond, J. W. Robinson, S. Ross, Rusk, H. B. Sayler, Scofield, I. W. Scudder, Shanks, Sheats, Sheldon, Sherwood, L. D. Shoemaker, Sloan, W. B. Small, Smart, A. H. Smith, G. L. Smith, H. B. Smith, J. Q. Smith, Snyder, Sprague, Starkweather, C. A. Stevens, St. John, Stowell, Strait, Strawbridge, Sypher, Taylor, C. Y. Thomas, J. M. Thompson, Thornburgh, Todd, W. Townsend, Tremain, Tyner, A. S. Wallace, Walls, M. L. Ward, Wheeler, A. White, Whiteley, Wilber, G. Willard, C. G. Williams, J. M. S. Williams, W. Williams, W. B. Williams, J. Wilson, J. M. Wilson, Woodworth—170.

NAYS—Messrs. *G. M. Adams, Archer, Arthur, Ashe, Atkins, Banning, Barnum, Beck, H. P. Bell, Berry, Bland, Blount, Bowen, Bright, Bromberg, J. Y. Brown, Buckner, J. H. Caldwell, Caulfield, J. B. Clark, jr., Clymer, Comingo, Cook, Cox, Creamer, Crittenden, Crossland, John J. Davis, De Witt, Durham, Finck, Giddings, Glover, Gunter, R. Hamilton, Hancock, H. R. Harris, J. T. Harris, Hatcher, Hereford, Herndon, Holman, Hunton, Knapp, Lamar, Lamison, Leach, Luttrell, Magee, Marshall, McLean, Milliken, Mills, Morrison, Neal, Nesmith, Niblack, O'Brien, H. W. Parker, Perry, C. N. Potter, Randall, Read, W. M. Robbins, W. R. Roberts, J. C. Robinson, M. Sayler, Schell,* Sener, *Sloss,* J. A. Smith, W. A. Smith, *Southard, Speer, Standiford, Stone, Storm, Swann, R. B. Vance, Waddell, E. Wells, Whitehead, Whitehouse, Whitthorne, Willie, Wolfe, F. Wood, J. D. Young, P. M. B. Young*—89.

February 27—Amendments were submitted by Messrs. B. F. BUTLER, CANNON, and E. R. HOAR.

Mr. B. F. BUTLER's amendment is as follows:

In section 13, line 20, of the bill as printed on the files, after the words "*habeas corpus*," insert "in such insurrectionary district or districts wherein the President deems such powerful and armed combinations to exist, within the limits of either of the following-named States: Louisiana, Arkansas, Mississippi, or Alabama."

Also a new section, add the following:

SEC. 14. The provisions of section 13 of this act shall continue to be in force for and during the term of two years, and from thence until the end of the next session of Congress thereafter, and no longer.

Mr. COBURN moved the previous question on the bill and amendments, which was seconded—yeas 160, nays 107, not voting 20:

YEAS—Messrs. Albert, Albright, Averill, Barber, Barry, Bass, Begole, Bradley, Buffinton, Bundy, Burleigh, Burrows, B. F. Butler, R. R.

Butler, Cain, Cannon, Carpenter, Cason, Cessna, A. Clark, jr., Clayton, Clements, S. A. Cobb, Coburn, Conger, Corwin, Cotton, Crooke, Crounse, Crutchfield, Curtis, Danford, Darrall, Donnan, Duell, Dunnell, Eames, Field, Fort, Foster, Frye, Gooch, Gunckel, Hagans, Harmer, B. W. Harris, H. H. Harrison, Hathorn, Havens, J B. Hawley, Hays, G. W. Hazelton, J. W. Hazelton, E. R. Hoar, G. F. Hoar, Hodges, Hoskins, Houghton, Howe, Hubbell, Hunter, Hurlbut, Hyde, Hynes, Kasson, Kelley, Killinger, Lamport, Lansing, W. Lawrence, Lawson, B. Lewis, Lofland, Loughridge, Lowe, Lowndes, Lynch, Martin, Maynard, McCrary, A. S. McDill, J. W. McDill, MacDougall, McKee, McNulta, Monroe, Moore, Morey, Myers, Negley, Niles, Nunn, O'Neill, Orr, Orth, Packard, Packer, Page, I. C. Parker, R. C. Parsons, Pelham, Pendleton, W. A. Phillips, J. H. Platt, jr., T. C. Platt, Pratt, Rainey, Ransier, Rapier, W. H. Ray, Richmond, J. W. Robinson, S. Ross, Rusk, Sawyer, H. B. Sayler, Scofield, H. J. Scudder, I. W. Scudder, Sessions, Shanks, Sheats, Sheldon, Sherwood, L. D. Shoemaker, Sloan, Smart, A. H. Smith, G. L. Smith, J. Q. Smith, Snyder, Sprague, Starkweather, C. A. Stevens, St. John, Stowell, Strait, Sypher, Taylor, C. Y. Thomas, Thornburgh, Todd, Townsend, Tremain, Tyner, Waldron, A. S. Wallace, Walls, J. D. Ward, M. L. Ward, A. White, Whiteley, Wilber, C. G Williams, J. M S. Williams, W. Williams, W. B. Williams, J. Wilson, J. M. Wilson, Woodworth—160.

NAYS—Messrs. *G. M. Adams, Archer, Arthur, Ashe, Atkins, Banning, Barnum, Beck, H. P. Bell, Berry, Bland, Blount, Bowen, Bright, Bromberg, J. Y. Brown, Buckner,* H. C. Burchard, *J. H. Caldwell, Caulfield,* Chittenden, *J. B. Clark, jr.,* F. Clarke, *Clymer, Comingo, Cook, Cox, Creamer, Crittenden, Crossland, John J. Davis,* Dawes, *De Witt, Durham, Eldredge, Finck, Giddings, Glover, Gunter,* E. Hale, *R. Hamilton, Hancock, H. R. Harris, J. T. Harris, Hatcher,* J. R. Hawley, *Hereford, Herndon, Holman, Hunton,* Kellogg, *Knapp, Lamar, Lamison, Leach, Luttrell, Magee, Marshall, McLean,* Merriam, *Milliken, Mills, Morrison, Neal, Nesmith, Niblack, O'Brien, Perry,* W. W. Phelps, Pierce, Poland, *C. N. Potter, Randall, Read, Robbins,* E. H. Roberts, *W. R. Roberts, J. C. Robinson, M. Sayler, Schell, J. G. Schumaker,* Sener, J. A. Smith, W. A. Smith, *Southard, Speer,* Stanard, *Standiford, A. H. Stephens, Stone, Storm, Swann,* J. M. Thompson, *R. B. Vance, Waddell, E. Wells,* Wheeler, *Whitehead, Whitehouse, Whitthorne,* C. W. Willard, G. Willard, *Willie, E. K. Wilson, Wolfe, F. Wood, P. M. B. Young*—107.

Mr. BUTLER's motion was agreed to—Yeas 164, nays 99, not voting 24:

YEAS—Messrs. Albert, Albright, Averill, Barry, Bass, Begole, Bradley, Buffinton, Bundy, H. C. Burchard, Burleigh, Burrows, B. F. Butler, R. R. Butler, Cain, Cannon, Carpenter, Cessna, Chittenden, A. Clark, jr., F. Clarke, Clayton, S. A. Cobb, Coburn, Conger, Corwin, Cotton, Crooke, Crounse, Crutchfield, Curtis, Danford, Dawes, Donnan, Duell, Dunnell, Eames, Farwell, Field, Fort, Foster, Frye, Garfield, Gooch, Gunckel, Hagans, E. Hale, Harmer, B. W. Harris, H. H. Harrison, Hathorn, Havens, J. B. Hawley, J. R. Hawley, Hays, G. W. Hazelton, J. W. Hazelton, E. R. Hoar, G. F. Hoar, Hodges, Hoskins, Houghton, Hubbell, Hunter, Hurlbut, Hyde, Kasson, Kelley, Kellogg, Killinger, Lamport, Lansing, W. Lawrence, Lawson, B. Lewis, Loughridge, Lowe, Lowndes, Martin, Maynard, McCrary, A. S. McDill, J. W. McDill, MacDougall, McNulta, Merriam, Monroe, Moore, Myers, Negley, O'Neill, Orr, Orth, Packard, Packer, Page, I. C. Parker, R. C. Parsons, Pelham, Pendleton, W. W. Phelps, W. A. Phillips, Pierce, J. H. Platt, jr., T. C. Platt, Poland, Rainey, Ransier, Rapier, W. H. Ray, Richmond, E. H. Roberts, J. W. Robinson, S. Ross, Rusk, Sawyer, H. B. Sayler, Scofield, H. J. Scudder, I. W. Scudder, Sessions, Shanks, Sheats, Sherwood, L. D. Shoemaker, Sloan, Smart, A. H. Smith, G. L. Smith, H. B. Smith, J. Q. Smith, Snyder, Sprague, Stanard, Starkweather, C. A. Stevens, Stowell, Strait, Taylor, C. Y. Thomas, J. M. Thompson, Thornburgh, Todd, W. Townsend, Tremain, Tyner, Waldron, A. S. Wallace, Walls, J. D. Ward, M. L. Ward, Wheeler, A. White, Whiteley, Wilber, C. W. Willard, G. Willard, C. G. Williams, J. M. S. Williams, W. Williams, W. B. Williams, J. Wilson, J. M. Wilson, Woodworth—164.

NAYS—Messrs. *G. M. Adams, Archer, Arthur, Ashe, Atkins, Banning, Barnum, Beck, H. P. Bell, Berry, Bland, Blount, Bowen, Bright, Bromberg, Brown, Buckner, J. H. Caldwell,* Cason, *Caulfield, J. B. Clark, jr., Clymer, Comingo, Cook, Cox, Creamer, Crittenden, Crossland,* Darrall, *John J. Davis, De Witt, Durham, Eldredge, Finck, Giddings, Glover, Gunter, R. Hamilton, Hancock, H. R. Harris, J. T. Harris, Hatcher, Hereford, Herndon, Holman,* Howe, *Hunton,* Hynes, *Knapp, Lamar, Leach,* Lofland, *Luttrell,* Lynch, *Magee, Marshall, McKee, McLean, Milliken, Mills,* Morey, *Morrison, Neal,* Niles, Nunn, *O'Brien, Perry, Randall, Read, W. M. Robbins, W. R. Roberts, J. C. Robinson, M. Sayler, Schell, J. G. Schumaker,* Sener, Sheldon, J. A. Smith, W. A. Smith, *Southard, Speer, Standiford,* St. John, *Stone, Storm, Swann,* Sypher, *R. B. Vance, Waddell, E. Wells, Whitehead, Whitehouse, Whitthorne, Willie, E. K. Wilson, Wolfe, F. Wood, J. D. Young, P. M. B. Young.*—99.

Mr. CANNON'S amendment to strike out the thirteenth section was disagreed to—yeas 121, nays 130, not voting 36:

YEAS—Messrs. *G. M. Adams,* Albert, *Archer, Arthur, Ashe, Atkins, Banning, Barnum, Beck, H. P. Bell, Berry, Bland, Blount, Bowen, Bright, Bromberg, J. Y. Brown, Buckner,* Buffinton, Bundy, H. C. Burchard, Burleigh, *J. H. Caldwell, Caulfield, J. B. Clark, jr., Clymer, Comingo, Cook,* Cotton, *Cox, Creamer, Crittenden, Crossland,* Crounse, Crutchfield, Danford, *John J. Davis,* Dawes, *De Witt, Durham, Eldredge,* Farwell, *Finck,* Foster, Garfield, *Giddings, Glover, Gunter,* E. Hale, *R. Hamilton, Hancock, H. R. Harris, J. T. Harris,* H. H. Harrison, *Hatcher,* J. R. Hawley, *Hereford, Herndon, Holman, Hunton,* Kasson, Kellogg, *Knapp, Lamar, Leach, Luttrell, Magee, Marshall,* McCrary, J. W. McDill, *McLean,* Merriam, *Milliken, Mills, Morrison, Neal, Nesmith, O'Brien. Perry,* W. W. Phelps, *W. A. Phillips,* Pierce.

Poland, *C. N. Potter*, *Read*, *W. M. Robbins*, E. H. Roberts, *W. R. Roberts*, *M. Sayler*, *Schell*, *J. G. Schumaker*, H. J. Scudder, Sener, L. D. Shoemaker, J. A. Smith, J. Q. Smith, W. A. Smith, *Southard*, *Speer*, *Standiford*, *A. H. Stephens*, *Stone*, *Storm*, Strait, *Swann*, Thornburgh, *R. B. Vance*, *Waddell*, *E. Wells*, Wheeler, *Whitehead*, *Whitehouse*, *Whitthorne*, C. W. Willard, G. Willard, W. B. Williams, *Willie*, *E. K. Wilson*, *F. Wood*, *J. D. Young*, *P. M. B. Young*—121.

NAYS—Messrs. Albright, Averill, Barber, Barry, Bass, Begole, Bradley, Burrows, B. F. Butler, R. R. Butler, Cain, Cannon, Carpenter, Cason, Cessna, A. Clark, jr., Clayton, Clements, S. A. Cobb, Coburn, Conger, Corwin, Crooke, Curtis, Darrall, Donnan, Duell, Dunnell, Eames, Field, Frye, Gooch, Hagans, Harmer, B. W. Harris, Hathorn, J. B. Hawley, Hays, G. W. Hazelton, J. W. Hazelton, E. R. Hoar, G. F. Hoar, Hodges, Hoskins, Houghton, Howe, Hubbell, Hunter, Hurlbut, Hyde, Hynes, Kelley, Lansing, W. Lawrence, Lawson, B. Lewis, Lofland, Lowe, Lowndes, Lynch, Martin, Maynard, A. S. McDill, MacDougall, McKee, McNulta, Monroe, Moore, Myers, Negley, Niles, Nunn, O'Neill, Orr, Orth, Packard, Packer, Page, I. C. Parker, R. C. Parsons, Pelham, Pendleton, J. H. Platt, jr., T. C. Platt, Pratt, *Randall*, Ransier, Rapier, W. H. Ray, Richmond, J. W. Robinson, S. Ross, Rusk, Sawyer, H. B. Sayler, Scofield, I. W. Scudder, Sessions, Shanks, Sheats, Sherwood, Sloan, Smart, A. H. Smith, G. L. Smith, H. B. Smith, C. A. Stevens, St John, Stowell, Sypher, Taylor, C. Y. Thomas, J. M. Thompson, Todd, W. Townsend, Tremain, Tyner, Waldron, A. S. Wallace, Walls, J. D. Ward, M. L. Ward, A. White, Whiteley, Wilber, C. G. Williams, J. M. S. Williams, J. Wilson, J. M. Wilson, Woodworth—130.

Mr. E. R. HOAR'S amendment to strike out the first, second, and fourth sections, was disagreed to—yeas 119, nays 126, not voting 42:

YEAS—Messrs. *G. M. Adams*, Albert, *Archer*, *Arthur*, *Ashe*, *Atkins*, *Banning*, *Barnum*, *Beck*, *H. P. Bell*, *Bland*, *Blount*, *Bowen*, *Bright*, *Bromberg*, *J. Y. Brown*, *Buckner*, Bundy, H. C. Burchard, Burleigh, *J. H. Caldwell*, *Caulfield*, Chittenden, *J. B. Clark, jr.*, F. Clarke, *Clymer*, *Comingo*, *Cook*, *Cox*, *Creamer*, *Crittenden*, *Crossland*, Crounse, Danford, *John J. Davis*, Dawes, *De Witt*, *Durham*, Eames, *Finck*, Foster, *Giddings*, *Glover*, Gooch, *Gunter*, E. Hale, *R. Hamilton*, *Hancock*, B. W. Harris, *H. R. Harris*, *J. T. Harris*, H. H. Harrison, *Hatcher*, J R. Hawley, *Hereford*, *Herndon*, E. R. Hoar, G. F. Hoar, *Hunton*, Kasson, Kellogg, *Knapp*, *Leach*, Lowndes, *Luttrell*, *Magee*, *Marshall*, J. W. McDill, *McLean*, Merriam, *Milliken*, *Mills*, *Morrison*, *Neal*, *Nesmith*, *O'Brien*, Pendleton, *Perry*, W. W. Phelps, Pierce, Poland, *C. N. Potter*, *Read*, *W. M. Robbins*, E. H. Roberts, *W. R. Roberts*, *J. C. Robinson*, *M. Sayler*, *J. G. Schumaker*, H. J. Scudder, I. W. Scudder, Sener, *Sloss*, J. A. Smith, J. Q. Smith, W. A. Smith, *Southard*, *Speer*, Stanard, *Standiford*, C. A. Stevens, *Storm*, Strait, *Swann*, *R. B. Vance*, *Waddell*, *E. Wells*, Wheeler, *Whitehead*, *Whitehouse*, *Whitthorne*, C. W. Willard, G. Willard, W. B. Williams, *Willie*, *E. K. Wilson*, *Wolfe*, *F. Wood*, *J. D. Young*—119.

NAYS—Messrs. Albright, Averill, Barber, Barry, Bass, Begole, Bradley, Burrows, R. R. Butler, Cain, Cannon, Carpenter, Cason, Cessna, A. Clark, jr., Clayton, Clements, S. A. Cobb, Coburn, Conger, Crooke, Darrall, Dobbins, Donnan, Duell, Dunnell, Field, Fort, Frye, Gunckel, Hagans, Harmer, Hathorn, Havens, J. B. Hawley, Hays, G. W. Hazelton, J. W. Hazelton, Hodges, Hoskins, Houghton, Howe, Hubbell, Hunter, Hurlbut, Hyde, Hynes, Kelley, Killinger, Lansing, W. Lawrence, Lawson, B. Lewis, Loughridge, Lowe, Lynch, Martin, Maynard, A. S. McDill, MacDougall, McKee, McNulta, Monroe, Moore, Morey, Myers, Negley, Niles, Nunn, O'Neill, Orr, Orth, Packard, Packer, Page, I. C. Parker, R. C. Parsons, Pelham, J. H. Platt, jr., T. C. Platt, Pratt, Rainey, *Randall*, Rapier, W. H. Ray, Richmond, J. W. Robinson, S. Ross, Rusk, Sawyer, H. B. Sayler, Sessions, Shanks, Sheats, Sheldon, Sherwood, L. D. Shoemaker, Sloan, Smart, A. H. Smith, H. B. Smith, Snyder, Sprague, Stowell, Sypher, Taylor, C. Y. Thomas, J. M. Thompson, Thornburgh, Todd, W. Townsend, Tremain, Tyner, Waldron, A. S. Wallace, Walls, J. D. Ward, M. L. Ward, A. White, Whiteley, Wilber, C. G. Williams, J. M. S. Williams, W. Williams, J. Wilson, J. M. Wilson—126.

On ordering the bill, as amended, to be engrossed and read a third time, the yeas were 136, nays 109, not voting 42:

YEAS—Messrs. Albert, Albright, Averill, Barber, Barry, Bass, Begole, Bradley, Bundy, Burrows, R. R. Butler, Cain, Cannon, Carpenter, Cason, Cessna, A. Clark, jr., Clayton, Clements, S. A. Cobb, Coburn, Conger, Corwin, Crooke, Danford, Darrall, Donnan, Duell, Eames, Field, Fort, Frye, Gooch, Gunckel, Hagans, Harmer, B. W. Harris, Hathorn, J. B. Hawley, Hays, G. W. Hazelton, J. W. Hazelton, Hodges, Hoskins, Houghton, Howe, Hubbell, Hunter, Hurlbut, Hyde, Hynes, Killinger, Lansing, W. Lawrence, Lawson, B. Lewis, Lofland, Loughridge, Lowe, Lynch, Martin, Maynard, A. S. McDill, J. W. McDill, MacDougall, McKee, McNulta, Monroe, Moore, Morey, Myers, Negley, Niles, Nunn, O'Neil, Orr, Orth, Packard, Packer, Page, I. C. Parker, R. C. Parsons, Pelham, Pendleton, J. H. Platt, jr., T. C. Platt, Pratt, Rainey, *Randall*, Ransier, Rapier, W. H. Ray, Richmond, J. W. Robinson, S. Ross, Sawyer, H. B. Sayler, Scofield, Sessions, Shanks, Sheats, Sheldon, Sherwood, Sloan, Smart, A. H. Smith, G. L. Smith, J. Q. Smith, Snyder, Sprague, Stevens, St. John, Stowell, Sypher, Taylor, C. Y. Thomas, J. M. Thompson, Thornburgh, Todd, W. Townsend, Tremain, Tyner, Waldron, A. S. Wallace, Walls, J. D. Ward, M. L. Ward, A. White, Whiteley, Wilber, C. G. Williams, J. M. S. Williams, W. Williams, J. Wilson, J. M. Wilson, Woolworth.—136.

NAYS—Messrs. *G. M. Adams*, *Archer*, *Arthur*, *Ashe*, *Atkins*, *Banning*, *Barnum*, *Beck*, *H.P.Bell*, *Berry*, *Bland*, *Blount*, *Bowen*, *Bright*, *Bromberg*, *J. Y. Brown*, *Buckner*, H. C. Burchard, Burleigh, *J. H. Caldwell*, *Caulfield*, *J. B. Clark, jr.*, *Clymer*, *Comingo*, *Cook*, *Cox*, *Creamer*, *Crittenden*, *Crossland*, Crounse, *John J. Davis*, Dawes, *De Witt*, *Durham*, *Eldredge*,

Finck, Foster, Garfield, *Giddings*, *Glover*, *Gunter*, E. Hale, *R. Hamilton*, *Hancock*, *H. R. Harris*, *J. T. Harris*, H. H. Harrison, *Hatcher*, J. R. Hawley, *Hereford*, *Herndon*, E. R. Hoar, G. F. Hoar, *Hunton*, Kasson, Kellogg, *Knapp*, *Lamar*, *Leach*, Lowndes, *Luttrell*, *Magee*, *Marshall*, *McLean*, Merriam, *Milliken*, *Mills*, *Morrison*, *Neal*, *Nesmith*, *O'Brien*, *Perry*, W. W. Phelps, Pierce, Poland, *C. N. Potter*, *Read*, *W. M. Robbins*, E. H. Roberts, *W. R. Roberts*, *J. C. Robinson*, *M. Sayler*, *Schell*, *J. G. Schumaker*, H. J. Scudder, Sener, H. B. Smith, W. A. Smith, *Southard*, *Speer*, Stanard, *Standiford*, Starkweather, *Stone*, *R. B. Vance*, *Waddell*, *E. Wells*, *Whitehead*, *Whitehouse*, *Whitthorne*, C. W. Willard, G. Willard, W. B. Williams, *Willie*, *E. K. Wilson*, *Wolfe*, Willie, *F. Wood*, *J. D. Young*, *P. M. B. Young*—109.

On the passage of the bill the yeas were 135, nays 114, not voting 38, as follow:

YEAS—Messrs. Albright, Averill, Barber, Barry, Bass, Begole, Bradley, Bundy, Burrows, R. R. Butler, Cain, Cannon, Carpenter, Cason, Cessna, A. Clark, jr., Clayton, Clements, S. A. Cobb, Coburn, Conger, Corwin, Crooke, Curtis, Danford, Darrall, Dobbins, Donnan, Duell, Dunnell, Eames, Field, Fort, Frye, Gooch, Gunckel, Hagans, Harmer, B. W. Harris, Hathorn, Havens, J. B. Hawley, Hays, G. W. Hazelton, J. W. Hazelton, Hodges, Hoskins, Houghton, Howe, Hubbell, Hunter, Hurlbut, Hyde, Hynes, Lansing, W. Lawrence, Lawson, B. Lewis, Lofland, Loughridge, Lowe, Lynch, Martin, Maynard, A S. McDill, J. W. McDill, McDougall, McKee, McNulta, Monroe, Moore, Morey, Myers, Negley, Niles, Nunn, O'Neill, Orr, Orth, Packard, Packer, Page, I. C. Parker, R. C. Parsons, Pelham, Pendleton, J. H. Platt, jr., T. C. Platt, Pratt, Rainey, Ransier, Rapier, W. H. Ray, J. W. Robinson, S. Ross, Sawyer, H. B. Sayler, Scofield, Sessions, Shanks, Sheats, Sherwood, Sloan, Smart, A. H. Smith, G. L. Smith, J. Q. Smith, Snyder, Sprague, C. A. Stevens, St. John, Stowell, Sypher, Taylor, C. Y. Thomas, J. M. Thompson, Thornburgh, Todd, W. Townsend, Tremain, Tyner, Waldron, A. S. Wallace, Walls, J. D. Ward, M. L. Ward, A. White, Whiteley, Wilber, C. G. Williams, J. M. S. Williams, W. Williams, J. Wilson, J. M. Wilson, Woodworth—135.

NAYS—Messrs. *Archer*, *Arthur*, *Ashe*, *Atkins*, *Banning*, *Barnum*, *Beck*, *H. P. Bell*, *Berry*, *Bland*, *Blount*, *Bowen*, *Bright*, *Bromberg*, *J. Y. Brown*, *Buckner*, H. C. Burchard, Burleigh, *J. H. Caldwell*, *Caulfield*, *J. B. Clark, jr.*, *Clymer*, *Comingo*, *Cook*, *Cox*, *Cream-er*, *Crittenden*, *Crossland*, Crounse, Crutchfield, *John J. Davis*, Dawes, *De Witt*, *Durham*, *Eldredge*, *Finck*, Foster, Garfield, *Giddings*, *Glover*, *Gunter*, E. Hale, *Hancock*, *H. R. Harris*, *J. T. Harris*, H. H. Harrison, *Hatcher*, J. R. Hawley, *Hereford*, *Herndon*, E. R. Hoar, G. F. Hoar, *Hunton*, Kasson, Kellogg, *Knapp*, *Lamar*, *Leach*, Lowndes, *Luttrell*, *Magee*, *Marshall*, McCrary, *McLean*, Merriam, *Milliken*, *Mills*, *Morrison*, *Neal*, *Nesmith*, *O'Brien*, *Perry*, W. W. Phelps, Pierce, Poland, *C. N. Potter*, *Randall*, *Read*, *W. M. Robbins*, E. H. Roberts, *W. R. Roberts*, *J. C. Robinson*, *M. Sayler*, *Schell*, *J. G. Schumaker*, H. J. Scudder, Sener, L. D. Shoemaker, *Sloss*, H. B. Smith, J. A. Smith, W. A. Smith, *Southard*, *Speer*, Stanard, *Standiford*, Starkweather, *Stone*, *Storm*, *R. B. Vance*, *Waddell*, *E. Wells*, *Whitehead*, *Whitehouse*, *Whitthorne*, C. W. Willard, G. Willard, W. B. Williams, *Willie*, *E. K Wilson*, *Wolfe*, *F. Wood*, *J. D. Young*, *P. M. B. Young*—109.

NOT VOTING—Messrs. *G. M. Adams*, Albert, Barrere, Biery, Buffinton, B. F. Butler, Chittenden, F. Clarke, C. L. Cobb, Cotton, *Eden*, Farwell, J. C. Freeman, R. S. Hale, *R. Hamilton*, Hendee, *Holman*, Kelley, *Kendall*, Killinger, *Lamison*, Lamport, *Mitchell*, *Niblack*, *H. W. Parker*, W. A. Phillips, Pike, Richmond, Rusk, I. W. Scudder, Sheldon, W. B. Small, *A. H. Stephens*, Strait, Strawbridge, *Swann*, C. R. Thomas, Wheeler—38.

[During the consideration of this bill, numerous dilatory motions were made by Democratic members, and a final vote was not reached till midnight on Saturday, February 27th.]

IN SENATE.

March 1—Read and passed to second reading.
March 2—Read second time.
No further action upon it was taken. See p. 183.

IV.

EXECUTIVE AND LEGISLATIVE ACTION ON AFFAIRS IN THE STATES OF ARKANSAS, LOUISIANA, MISSISSIPPI, SOUTH CAROLINA AND TENNESSEE, AND ON THE ADMISSION OF COLORADO AND NEW MEXICO.

Affairs in Arkansas.

[For other facts respecting Arkansas, see McPherson's Hand-Book of Politics for 1874, pp. 87–100.]

At the close of the record, May, 1874, in Hand-Book of Politics, p. 100, Elisha Baxter was recognized as Governor of Arkansas, and in possession of the office. May 18th of that year, the Legislature passed an Act providing for a Convention to frame a new Constitution, to meet July 14, the election to be held June 30, 1874. The Convention met, and framed a Constitution, which was submitted to the people at an election held on 13th of October. At same time, State officers, provided for in the Constitution, were voted for. The vote on Constitution, as declared by the board of supervisors created by the Convention, was "For" 78,697, "Against" 24,807; A. H. Garland was also declared to have received 76,453 votes for Governor, with 50 votes scattering. November 12, 1874, A. H. Garland qualified, and took possession of the Governor's office.

Same day—The newspapers state that Volney V. Smith, elected Lieut. Gov. in 1872 with Elisha Baxter as Governor, claimed from Prest. GRANT recognition as the rightful Governor, Elisha Baxter having "abdicated and abandoned" the office. The claim was not recognized.

President Grant's Message Relating to Affairs in the State of Arkansas, February 8, 1875.

To the Senate of the United States:

Herewith I have the honor to send, in accordance with the resolution of the Senate of the 3d instant, all the information in my possession not heretofore furnished, relating to affairs in the State of Arkansas.

I will venture to express the opinion that all the testimony shows that in the election of 1872 Joseph Brooks was lawfully elected Governor of the State; that he has been unlawfully deprived of the possession of his office since that time; that in 1874 the Constitution of the State was by violence, intimidation, and revolutionary proceedings overthrown, and a new Constitution adopted and a new State government established.

These proceedings, if permitted to stand, practically ignore all rights of minorities in all the States. Also, what is there to prevent each of the States recently re-admitted to Federal relations on certain conditions, changing their constitutions and violating their pledges, if this action in Arkansas is acquiesced in?

I respectfully submit whether a precedent so dangerous to the stability of State government, if not of the National Government also, should be recognized by Congress. I earnestly ask that Congress will take definite action in this matter, to relieve the Executive from acting upon questions which should be decided by the legislative branch of the Government. U. S. GRANT.

EXECUTIVE MANSION, *February* 8, 1875.

Forty-Third Congress—Second Session.

ACTION IN THE HOUSE.

1875, March 2—Mr. POLAND, from the Select Committee on Affairs in Arkansas, reported the following resolution:

Resolved, That the report of the Select Committee on the condition of Affairs in the State of Arkansas be accepted; and in the judgment of this House no interference with the existing government in that State by any department of the Government of the United States is advisable.

Mr. J. D. WARD moved the following as a substitute:

Resolved, That Joseph Brooks, having been by the people of Arkansas elected to the office of Governor of said State under the constitution of 1868, for the period of four years, ending in January, 1877, and said constitution never having been legally overturned or abrogated, and being still in force, he is the lawful Governor of said State of Arkansas.

The question being taken on the substitute, it was disagreed to—yeas 80, nays 152, not voting 55:

YEAS—Messrs. Barry, Bass, Begole, Biery, B. F. Butler, R. R. Butler, Cain, Carpenter, Cason, Cessna, Conger, Crooke, Curtis, Darrall, Donnan, Dunnell, Field, Fort, Harmer, Hathorn, Hays, G. W. Hazelton, J. W. Hazelton, Hodges, Houghton, Howe, Hurlbut, Hyde, Hynes, Kelley, Lawson, B. Lewis, Lofland, Lowe, Lynch, Martin, Maynard, A. S. McDill, MacDougall, McNulta, Moore, Myers, Negley, O'Neill, Orth, Packard, I. C. Parker, Pelham, W. A. Phillips, T. C. Platt, Pratt, Rapier, W. H. Ray, Rusk, Sawyer, Scofield, Sessions, Shanks, Sheats, Sheldon, Sherwood, Sloan, Smart, A. H. Smith, Snyder, Sprague, Stowell, Sypher, Taylor, Todd, W. Townsend, Tremain, Tyner, A. S. Wallace, Walls, J. D. Ward, A. White, Wilber, W. Williams, J. Wilson—80.

NAYS—Messrs. *G. M. Adams*, *Archer*, *Arthur*, *Ashe*, *Atkins*, *Averill*, *Banning*, *Barnum*, Barrere, *Beck*, *H. P. Bell*, *Berry*, *Bland*, *Blount*,

Bowen, Bradley, *Bright*, *Bromberg*, *J. Y. Brown*, *Buckner*, H. C. Burchard, Burleigh, *J. H. Caldwell*, Cannon, *Caulfield*, Chittenden, A. Clark, jr., *J. B. Clark, jr.*, F. Clarke, Clayton, Clements, *Clymer*, S. A. Cobb, *Comingo*, *Cook*, Cotton, *Cox*, *Crittenden*, *Crossland*, Crounse, Danford, *John J. Davis*, Dawes, *De Witt*, *Durham*, Eames, *Eden*, *Eldredge*, *Finck*, Garfield, *Giddings*, *Glover*, Gunckel, *Gunter*, E. Hale, *R. Hamilton*, *Hancock*, B. W. Harris, *H. R. Harris*, *J. T. Harris*, H. H. Harrison, *Hatcher*, Havens, J. R. Hawley, *Hereford*, E. R. Hoar, G. F. Hoar, *Holman*, Hoskins, Hubbell, *Hunton*, Kasson, Kellogg, Killinger, *Knapp*, W. Lawrence, Loughridge, Lowndes, *Luttrell*, *Magee*, *Marshall*, McCrary, J. W. McDill, *McLean*, Merriam, *Milliken*, *Mills*, Monroe, *Morrison*, *Neal*, *Nesmith*, *Niblack*, *O'Brien*, Orr, Packer, *H. W. Parker*, *Perry*, Pierce, Poland, *C. N. Potter*, *Randall*, Ransier, *Read*, Richmond, *W. M. Robbins*, E. H. Roberts, *W. R. Roberts*, *J. C. Robinson*, J. W. Robinson, S. Ross, H. B. Sayler, *M. Sayler*, *Schell*, H. J. Scudder, Sener, L. D. Shoemaker, *Sloss*, H. B. Smith, J. Q. Smith, W. A. Smith, *Southard*, *Speer*, Stanard, *Standiford*, Starkweather, *A. H. Stephens*, C. A. Stevens, *Stone*, *Storm*, Strait, C. R. Thomas, C. Y. Thomas, J. M. Thompson, *R. B. Vance*, M. L. Ward, *E. Wells*, Wheeler, *Whitehead*, *Whitehouse*, Whiteley, *Whitthorne*, C. W. Willard, G. Willard, C. G. Williams, W. B. Williams, *Willie*, *E. K. Wilson*, *Wolfe*, *F. Wood*, Woodworth, *J. D. Young*, *P. M. B. Young*—152.

The question recurring on the resolution reported by the committee, Mr. MAYNARD moved to lay it on the table, which was disagreed to—yeas 94, nays 147, not voting 46:

YEAS—Messrs. Albright, Barber, Barry, Bass, Begole, Biery, B. F. Butler, R. R. Butler, Cain, Carpenter, Cason, Cessna, Clayton, Clements, Coburn, Conger, Crutchfield, Curtis, Darrall, Donnan, Dunnell, Field, Fort, Hagans, Harmer, Hathorn, Havens, Hays, G. W. Hazelton, J. W. Hazelton, Hodges, Hoskins, Houghton, Howe, Hunter, Hurlbut, Hyde, Hynes, Kelley, Lawson, B. Lewis, Lofland, Lowe, Lynch, Martin, Maynard, MacDougall, McKee, McNulta, Moore, Myers, Negley, O'Neill, Orth, Packard, Packer, Page, I. C. Parker, Pelham, W. A. Phillips, J. H. Platt, jr., T. C. Platt, Pratt, Rapier, W. H. Ray, Rusk, Sawyer, Scofield, Sessions, Shanks, Sheats, Sheldon, Sherwood, Sloan, W. B. Small, Smart, A. H. Smith, Snyder, Sprague, Stowell, Sypher, Taylor, Todd, W. Townsend, Tremain, Tyner, A. S. Wallace, Walls, J. D. Ward, A. White, Wilber, C. G. Williams, W. Williams, J. Wilson—94.

NAYS—Messrs. *G. M. Adams*, Albert, *Archer*, *Arthur*, *Ashe*, *Atkins*, Averill, *Banning*, *Barnum*, Barrere, *Beck*, *H. P. Bell*, *Berry*, *Bland*, *Blount*, *Bowen*, Bradley, *Bright*, *Bromberg*, *J. Y. Brown*, *Buckner*, H. C. Burchard, Burleigh, *J. H. Caldwell*, Cannon, *Caulfield*, Chittenden, A. Clark, jr., *J. B. Clark, jr.*, F. Clarke, *Clymer*, S. A. Cobb, *Comingo*, *Cook*, Cotton, *Cox*, *Crittenden*, Crooke, *Crossland*, Crounse, Danford, *John J. Davis*, Dawes, *De Witt*, Dobbins, *Durham*, Eames, *Eden*, *Eldredge*, *Finck*, Garfield, *Giddings*, *Glover*, *Gunter*, E. Hale, *R. Hamilton*, *Hancock*, B. W. Harris, *H. R. Harris*, *J. T. Harris*, H. H. Harrison, *Hatcher*, J. R. Hawley, *Hereford*, E. R. Hoar, G. F. Hoar, *Holman*, Hubbell, *Hunton*, Kasson, Kellogg, Killinger, *Knapp*, *Lamar*, W. Lawrence, Lowndes, *Luttrell*, *Magee*, *Marshall*, McCrary, J. W. McDill, *McLean*, Merriam, *Milliken*, *Mills*, Monroe, *Morrison*, *Neal*, *Nesmith*, *Niblack*, *O'Brien*, Orr, *H. W. Parker*, Pendleton, *Perry*, W. W. Phelps, Pierce, Poland, *C. N. Potter*, *Randall*, *Read*, *W. M. Robbins*, E. H. Roberts, *W. R. Roberts*, *J. C. Robinson*, J. W. Robinson, S. Ross, H. B. Sayler, *M. Sayler*, *Schell*, H. J. Scudder, Sener, L. D. Shoemaker, *Sloss*, H. B. Smith, J. Q. Smith, W. A. Smith, *Southard*, *Speer*, Stanard, *Standiford*, Starkweather, *A. H. Stephens*, C. A. Stevens, *Stone*, *Storm*, Strait, C. R. Thomas, J. M. Thompson, *R. B. Vance*, M. L. Ward, *E. Wells*, Wheeler, *Whitehead*, *Whitehouse*, Whiteley, *Whitthorne*, C. W. Willard, G. Willard, W. B. Williams, *Willie*, *E. K. Wilson*, J. M. Wilson, *Wolfe*, *F. Wood*, *J. D. Young*, *P. M. B. Young*—147.

The resolution was then agreed to—yeas 150, nays 81, not voting 56:

YEAS—Messrs. *G. M. Adams*, Albert, *Archer*, *Arthur*, *Ashe*, *Atkins*, Averill, *Banning*, *Barnum*, Barrere, *Beck*, *H. P. Bell*, *Berry*, *Bland*, *Blount*, *Bowen*, Bradley, *Bright*, *Bromberg*, *J. Y. Brown*, *Buckner*, H. C. Burchard, Burleigh, *J. H. Caldwell*, *Caulfield*, Chittenden, A. Clark, jr., *J. B. Clark, jr.*, F. Clarke, *Clymer*, S. A. Cobb, *Comingo*, *Cook*, Cotton, *Cox*, *Creamer*, *Crittenden*, Crooke, *Crossland*, Crounse, Danford, *John J. Davis*, Dawes, *De Witt*, Dobbins, *Durham*, Eames, *Eden*, *Eldredge*, *Finck*, J. C. Freeman, Garfield, *Giddings*, *Glover*, Gunckel, *Gunter*, E. Hale, *R. Hamilton*, Hancock, B. W. Harris, *H. R. Harris*, *J. T. Harris*, H. H. Harrison, *Hatcher*, J. R. Hawley, *Hereford*, *Herndon*, E. R. Hoar, G. F. Hoar, *Holman*, Hubbell, *Hunton*, Kasson, Kellogg, Killinger, *Knapp*, *Lamar*, W. Lawrence, Lofland, Lowndes, *Luttrell*, *Magee*, *Marshall*, McCrary, A. S. McDill, J. W. McDill, *McLean*, Merriam, *Milliken*, *Mills*, Monroe, *Morrison*, *Neal*, *Nesmith*, *Niblack*, *O'Brien*, Orr, *H. W. Parker*, Pendleton, *Perry*, W. W. Phelps, Pierce, Poland, *C. N. Potter*, *Randall*, *Read*, *W. M. Robbins*, E. H. Roberts, *W. R. Roberts*, *J. C. Robinson*, J. W. Robinson, S. Ross, H. B. Sayler, *M. Sayler*, *Schell*, H. J. Scudder, Sener, L. D. Shoemaker, *Sloss*, H. B. Smith, W. A. Smith, *Southard*, *Speer*, Stanard, *Standiford*, *A. H. Stephens*, C. A. Stevens, *Stone*, *Storm*, Strait, C. R. Thomas, J. M. Thompson, *R. B. Vance*, M. L. Ward, *E. Wells*, Wheeler, *Whitehead*, *Whitehouse*, Whiteley, *Whitthorne*, C. W. Willard, G. Willard, W. B. Williams, *Willie*, *E. K. Wilson*, J. M. Wilson, *Wolfe*, *F. Wood*, *J. D. Young*, *P. M. B. Young*—150.

NAYS—Messrs. Albright, Barry, Bass, Begole, Biery, R. R. Butler, Cason, Cessna, Coburn, Conger, Crutchfield, Curtis, Darrall, Donnan, Dunnell, Field, Fort, Harmer, Hathorn, Havens, Hays, G. W. Hazelton, J. W. Hazelton, Hodges, Hoskins, Houghton, Howe, Hunter, Hurlbut, Hyde, Hynes, Kelley, Lawson, B. Lewis, Lowe, Lynch, Martin, Maynard, MacDougall, McKee, McNulta, Moore, Myers, Nunn, O'Neill, Orth, Packard, Packer, Page, I. C. Parker, Pelham, W. A. Phillips, J. H. Platt, jr., T. C. Platt, Rusk, Sawyer, Scofield, Sessions, Shanks, Sheats,

Sheldon, Sherwood, Sloan, W. B. Small, Smart, A. H. Smith, Sprague, Stowell, Sypher, Taylor, Todd, W. Townsend, Tremain, Tyner, A. S. Wallace, Walls, J. D. Ward, A. White, Wilber, W. Williams, J. Wilson—81.

Louisiana.

[For additional papers respecting affairs in Louisiana, see McPherson's Hand-Book of Politics for 1874, pp. 100–108.]

The papers referring to Louisiana are very voluminous. Only the most important are selected, and they from Senate Ex. Docs. 13 and 17, 2d Sess., 43d Cong., and from newspapers where there are not official copies of the Orders or Proclamations.

1874, August 19—Gov. W. P. Kellogg wrote a letter to President GRANT, in which, after stating his views of the situation of affairs, he respectfully and earnestly suggests that "If the United States troops were returned to their posts in this State, such a course would have a most salutary effect, and would prevent much bloodshed, and probably a formal call upon the President and a renewed agitation of the Louisiana question, which otherwise a quiet, fair election next November would forever set at rest, and fully vindicate your just policy toward us."

U. S. Marshal to the Attorney-General.

[OFFICIAL.]

NEW ORLEANS, *August* 30, 1874.

Attorney-General WILLIAMS:

The registration of voters throughout the State for election of Congressmen commences to-morrow in several parishes. Large bodies of armed and mounted white men have appeared. Through fear of them, the blacks will be unable to register or vote in case of a conflict, which I regard as imminent. I shall be unable to enforce the laws of Congress without a posse of troops. It is believed the mere presence of United States troops in this district will prevent interference with the blacks in their registration. I therefore request, through the Attorney-General, that the Secretary of War order a sufficient force to this district immediately to aid in the discharge of my duty as required by law.

S. B. PACKARD, *U. S. Marshal.*

Governor Kellogg to the Attorney-General.

NEW ORLEANS, *August* 30, 1874.

Hon. GEO. H. WILLIAMS, *Attorney-General:*

A gross outrage has just been perpetrated at Coushatta, Red River Parish, in the northwestern portion of the State. A large number of White-Leaguers from that and other parishes near the Texas and Arkansas line invaded the parish, in order to force the parish officers to resign. They refused; but after a short conflict, in which several persons were killed, to avoid further bloodshed, these officers and other leading republicans surrendered. Red River Parish, a new parish formed some four years since, is strongly republican, there being three colored to one white. It was returned as largely republican by the fusionists at last election. Coushatta, though small, is the most thriving landing on Upper Red River, and is owned mainly by northern men. It is known, however, as one of the strongholds of republicanism in that portion of the State; the people pay taxes, are industrious and law-abiding. A more wanton outrage was never committed in any civilized community, as an investigation will fully show. The White-Leaguers, in order to carry out more effectually their avowed plan of carrying the State by terrifying republicans, and preventing their registering and voting, as was done in 1868, have inaugurated violence in several of the northern parishes. There are no troops in that portion of the State, and, indeed, none in the State, except a company at Colfax. As the evident intention of the White-League is to inaugurate domestic violence and interference with the rights of the colored citizens, especially in the remote parishes where our State militia cannot be sent, and as the registration of voters throughout the State commences to-morrow, I respectfully suggest that the troops now in Mississippi, designed, I believe, to take the place of the Nineteenth Infantry, ordered away in July, be directed to resume the posts vacated by said regiment. A systematic effort has been and is being made by the opposition to create the impression that no troops will, under any circumstances, be sent into the State. The presence of troops, it is believed, will go far to prevent violence and bloodshed. No danger need be apprehended on sanitary grounds, as both city and State are perfectly healthy, not the slightest sign of epidemic disease existing, or likely to occur this season.

WM. P. KELLOGG.

Governor Kellogg to the Attorney-General.

NEW ORLEANS, *August* 31,
via Long Branch, September 1.

Hon. GEO. H. WILLIAMS, *Attorney-General:*

The statement telegraphed you last night regarding the outrage at Red River Parish, has been fully confirmed. * * * Predatory bands of armed men are scouring several of the republican parishes in that portion of the State, driving out republicans and intimidating colored men. Registration commenced to-day, and an openly avowed policy of exterminating republicans.

WM. P. KELLOGG.

The President to the Secretary of War.

LONG BRANCH, N. J., *September* 2, 1874.

General W. W. BELKNAP, *Secretary of War:*

The recent atrocities in the South, particularly in Louisiana, Alabama, and South Carolina, show a disregard for law, civil rights and personal protection that ought not to be tolerated in any civilized government. It looks as if—unless speedily checked—matters must become worse, until life and property there will receive no protection from the local authorities—until such authority becomes powerless. Under such circumstances it is the duty of Government to give all the aid for the protection of life and civil rights legally authorized. To this end I wish you would consult with the Attorney General, who is well informed as to the outrages already committed and the localities where the greatest danger lies, and so order troops as to be available in case of necessity. All proceedings for the protection of the South will be under the Law Department of the Government, and will be directed by the Attorney General in accordance with the provisions of the enforcement acts. No instructions need, therefore, be given the troops ordered into the Southern States, except as they may be transmitted from time to time on advice from the Attorney General, or as circumstances may determine hereafter.

Yours truly, U. S. GRANT.

CIRCULAR OF THE ATTORNEY–GENERAL.

*Instructions to United States Marshals and Attorneys.**

DEPARTMENT OF JUSTICE,
WASHINGTON, *September* 3, 1874.

SIR: Outrages of various descriptions, and in some cases atrocious murders, have been committed in your district by bodies of armed men, sometimes in disguise, and with the view, it is believed, of overawing and intimidating peaceable and law-abiding citizens, and depriving them of the rights guaranteed to them by the Constitution and laws of the United States.

Your attention is directed to an act of Congress passed April 9, 1866, entitled "An act to protect all persons in the United States in their civil rights and to furnish means for their vindication;" and to another passed April 20, 1871, entitled "An act to enforce the provisions of the fourteenth amendment to the Constitution of the United States, and for other purposes;" also, to one passed May 30 [1], 1870, entitled "An act to enforce the right of citizens of the United States to vote in the several States of this Union, and for other purposes," which, with their amendments, make these deeds of violence and blood offenses within the jurisdiction of the General Government.

I consider it my duty, in view of these circumstances, to instruct you to proceed with all possible energy and dispatch to detect, expose, arrest, and punish the perpetrators of these crimes; and, to that end, you are to spare no effort or necessary expense.

Troops of the United States will be stationed at different and convenient points in your district, for the purpose of giving you all needful aid in the discharge of your official duties.

You understand, of course, that no interference whatever is hereby intended with any political or party action not in violation of law; but protection to all classes of citizens, white and colored, in the free exercise of the elective franchise, and the enjoyment of the other rights and privileges to which they are entitled under the Constitution and laws, as citizens of the United States.

These instructions are issued by the authority of the President, and with the concurrence of the Secretary of War.

Very respectfully,
GEO. H. WILLIAMS, *Attorney-General.*

U. S. Marshal Packard to the Attorney-General.

NEW ORLEANS, *September* 13, 1874.

Attorney-General WILLIAMS:

Some morning papers and incendiary notices posted, call upon citizens to close stores and meet at Clay Statue at 11 a. m., to-morrow. Danger of conflict imminent. No troops here at present, but General Emory telegraphs me that he will send detatchment from Jackson to-night. If so, they will arrive to-morrow.

S. B. PACKARD, *U. S. Marshal.*

J. R. Beckwith to the Attorney-General.

NEW YORK, *September* 13, 1874.

Hon. GEO. H. WILLIAMS, *Attorney-General:*

The troops are ordered away from Colfax. If not countermanded, I fear all of the witnesses in late Mapoce trial will be killed.

J. R. BECKWITH.

U. S. Marshal to Attorney-General.

NEW ORLEANS, *September* 14, 1875.

Attorney-General WILLIAMS:

The White League, armed, have occupied the city hall, and have cut the wires of the fire-alarm and police telegraph.

S. B. PACKARD, *U. S. Marshal.*

Gov. Kellogg to the President.

NEW ORLEANS, *September* 14, 1874.

To President GRANT, *Washington:*

Under article four, section 4, of the Constitution of the United States, I have the honor to inform you that the State is now subject to domestic violence of a character that the State forces, under existing circumstances, are unable to suppress, and the legislature not being in session and not being able to be convened within the requisite time to take action in this matter, I respectfully make requisition upon you to take measures to put down the domestic violence and insurrection now prevailing.

WM. P. KELLOGG, *Governor of Louisiana.*

U. S. Marshal to the Attorney-General.

NEW ORLEANS, *September* 14, 1874.

Attorney-General WILLIAMS:

A meeting of about two thousand has been held, and a committee sent, demanding the governor's immediate resignation. The committee was received by assistant attorney-general, also a member of the governor's staff, and by direction of the governor, informed the committee that the

---

* NOTE.—The following telegram from the Associated Press Agent at Washington gives an additional circular to U. S. Marshals issued at a later date:

DEPARTMENT OF JUSTICE,
WASHINGTON, *September* 30, 1874.

SIR: I would suggest that at those points where United States troops are, or may be stationed in your district, some prudent and fearless person in whose judgment you have confidence, and whom the people respect, may be appointed as deputy marshal, to act at once in the arrest of parties committing outrages in the vicinity, so that it may not be necessary in such cases to send for you before the troops can be used for the purpose of arresting those who are guilty of violating the laws of the United States. This of course will not be necessary where you are easily accessible, but where the troops are placed at remote points, before the necessary communication as to the crimes committed can be made, the offenders as a general rule have an opportunity to escape. You will give the deputies the necessary instructions as to procuring warrants, and I need not repeat that it is important that you should delegate this power to none but careful and responsible persons. Very respectfully,

GEORGE H. WILLIAMS, *Attorney-General.*

governor refused to receive any communication from a body of armed men accompanied with a menace. The people assembled at the meeting were generally unarmed, but large bodies of White Leaguers are under arms in the vicinity, awaiting orders. The meeting dismissed, and the people notified to come to Canal street to-night at four o'clock with their arms and blankets, and camp there. Mr. Marr, chairman democratic committee, was chairman of the committee to demand the governor's resignation. There is little doubt of a conflict to-night. I have a company of United States troops guarding the custom house building, that arrived, on my requisition, from Jackson, Miss., this morning. Four companies are *en route* from Holly Springs, expected at four o'clock, if not intercepted as threatened. The armed gathering to-night is avowedly to attempt the overthrow of the State government; if successful, the murder of leading republicans. The local authorities have several hundred men under arms at State-house and arsenals. The State authorities are exercising the utmost discretion, in order that if blood be shed, it will be precipitated by the White League.

S. B. PACKARD, *U. S. Marshal.*

U. S. Marshal to the Attorney-General.

NEW ORLEANS, *September* 14, 1874.

Attorney-General WILLIAMS:

The detachment from Holly Springs arrived at 5 p. m. There was a short fight between the police and White League, between four and five o'clock, before the arrival of the troops. Estimated loss of police fifteen killed and thirty wounded. General Badger, commanding police, was mortally wounded. General Longstreet retired to the State-house, which he holds, no attack having been made. The purpose of the riot is overthrow of the State government. Several United States soldiers are reported arrested by the League while on the street unarmed. The military force is inadequate to protect the public property and keep the peace of the city besides.

S. B. PACKARD, *United States Marshal.*

[From the Newspapers.]

NEW ORLEANS, *September* 14—In pursuance of notice in the words following, posted through the city September 13:

"Citizens of New Orleans: For nearly two years you have been the silent but indignant sufferers of outrage after outrage, heaped upon you by a usurping government. One by one your dearest rights have been trampled upon, until at last, in the supreme height of its insolence, this mockery of a republican government has dared even to deny you that right so solemnly guaranteed by the very Constitution of the United States, which in article two of the amendments, declares that 'The right of the people to keep and bear arms shall not be infringed.'

"In that same sacred instrument, to whose inviolate perpetuity our fathers pledged their lives, their fortunes and their sacred honor, it was also declared that even Congress shall make no law abridging the right of the people peaceably to assemble and to petition the Government for a redress of grievances. It now remains for us to ascertain whether this right any longer remains to us. We therefore call upon you, on Monday morning, the 14th day of September, 1874, to close your places of business, without a single exception, and at 11 o'clock, a. m. to assemble at the Clay statue, on Canal street, and in tones loud enough to be heard throughout the length and breadth of the land declare that you are, of right ought to be, and mean to be free."

A meeting was held and adopted these resolutions:

Resolved, That we reaffirm solemnly the resolutions adopted by the white people of Louisiana in convention, have no desire to deprive colored people of any right to which they are entitled: that W. P. Kellogg is a mere usurper, and we denounce him as such; that his government is arbitrary, unjust and oppressive, and can only maintain itself through Federal interference; that the elections and registration laws under which this election is being conducted were intended to perpetuate usurpation by depriving people, and especially our naturalized citizens, of an opportunity to register and vote, and therefore, in the name of the citizens of New Orleans now in mass meeting, and of the people of the State of Louisiana, whose franchise has been wrested from them by fraud and violence, and all of whose rights and liberties have been outraged and trampled upon, we demand of W. P. Kellogg his immediate abdication.

Resolved, That a committee of five be immediately appointed by the chairman, who shall be a member of the committee, to wait upon W. P. Kellogg, to present him these resolutions, and demand of him immediate answer, and report the result of such interview to this meeting.

R. H. Marr, Jules Tuyes, Samuel Chapin, Samuel Bell and J. M. Saixas, committee, called at the Executive Rooms about noon.

Mr. Marr, as spokesman, said they had called as a committee to interview the Governor. General Dibble said he would convey the intelligence to the Governor. After a brief absence he returned and made a reply which, at the request of Mr. Marr, was reduced to writing, as follows:

"I have communicated with the Governor, and he directs me to say to you he must decline to receive any communication from the committee appointed by the mass-meeting assembled on Canal street. He does so, I am instructed to say, because he has definite and accurate information that there are now assembled several large bodies of armed men in different parts of the city who met at the call which convened the mass-meeting which you represent. He regards this as a menace, and he will receive no communication under such circumstances. He furthermore directs me to say that should the people assemble peaceably, without menace, he would deem it one of his highest duties to receive any communication from them, or entertain any petition addressed to the government.

"I have received and answered you, gentlemen, as a member of his staff.

"HENRY C. DIBBLE,

"Brigadier and Judge Advocate General, Louisiana State Militia."

To which Mr. Marr orally replied as follows:

"We repeat, there are no armed rioters; there are no armed men on Canal street, so far as we know. We came on a mission of peace, and believe that if the Governor had acceded to the proposition we brought to-day, which was to abdicate, it would have pacified the people of Louisiana, and might or would have prevented violence or bloodshed. So far as we are concerned, we are prepared to pledge him no violence in person or property, and we feel in a position, on the contrary, to assure him that there should be perfect immunity to both."

The substance of the foregoing reply was subsequently, by Mr. Marr's request, reduced to writing by the Governor's private secretary and handed to him to read at the mass meeting.

Gen. Dibble, on the part of the Governor, replied: "I have to repeat what I said before, that while there may not be armed men on Canal street, there are armed bodies within a short distance, assembled on the same call as your mass meeting."

NEW ORLEANS, *September* 14—An extra edition of the *Bulletin*, issued at 4 p. m., contains the following proclamation:

To the People of Louisiana: For two years you have borne with patience and fortitude great wrongs. Through fraud and violence the government of your choice has been overthrown and its power usurped. Protest after protest, appeal after appeal to the President of the United States and to Congress, have failed to give you the relief you had the right under the Constitution to demand. The wrong has not been repaired. On the contrary, through the instrumentality of partisan judges, you are debarred from all legal remedy. Day by day taxation has been increasing, with costs and penalties amounting to the confiscation of your property. Your substance squandered, your credit ruined, resulting in failure and bankruptcy of your valued institutions. The right of suffrage is virtually taken from you by the enactment of skillfully-devised registration and election laws. The judicial branch of your government has been stricken down by the conversion of the legal *posse comitatus* of the sheriff to the use of the usurper for the purpose of defeating the decrees of the courts. His defiance of law leading him to use the very force for the arrest of the sheriff while engaged in the execution of the process of the court.

To these may be added a corrupt and vicious legislature, making laws in violation of the Constitution for the purpose of guarding and perpetuating their usurped authority, and a Metropolitan police force, paid by the city, under control of the usurper, quartered upon you to overawe and keep you in subjection. Every public right has been denied, and, as if to goad you to desperation, private arms are seized and individuals arrested. To such extremities are you driven that manhood revolts at any further submission.

Constrained from a sense of duty as legally elected Lieutenant-Governor of the State and acting Governor in the absence of Gov. McEnery, I do hereby issue this my proclamation, calling upon the militia of the State, embracing all males between the ages of eighteen and forty-five years, without regard to color or previous condition, to arms, and assemble under their respective officers for the purpose of driving the usurpers from power.

Given under my hand and seal this 14th day of September, 1874.

D. B. PENN, *Lieutenant Governor.*

GENERAL MILITARY ORDERS.

EXECUTIVE DEPARTMENT.
STATE OF LOUISIANA,
NEW ORLEANS, *Sept.* 14, 1874.

General Order No. 1.

Gen. Frederick N. Ogden is hereby appointed provisional general of the Louisiana State militia. He will at once assume command and organize into companies, regiments and battalions.

General Order No. 2.

Gen. Ogden will report the names of staff, regimental and company officers to this department forthwith to be commissioned.

By command of D. B. PENN,
Lieutenant-Governor and Acting Commander-in-chief of Louisiana State Militia.

NEW ORLEANS, LA., *Sept.* 14.

To the colored people of the State of Louisiana:

In the grand movement now on foot against the enormities of the rule of the Kellogg usurpation, rest assured that no harm is meant towards you, your property, or your rights. Pursue your usual avocations, and you will not be molested. We war against thieves, plunderers and spoilers of the State, who are involving your race and ours in common ruin. The rights of the colored as well as of the white race we are determined to uphold and defend. D. B. PENN,
Lieutenant-Governor and Acting Governor and Commander-in-chief of the Louisiana State Militia.

NEW ORLEANS, *Sept.* 14.—The people seem to have responded with alacrity to the advice given them by Dr. Beard, one of the speakers at the Canal street meeting. By 3 o'clock this afternoon armed men were stationed at the intersection, of all the streets on the south side of Canal street from the river to Clairborne street. About 4 o'clock a body of Metropolitans, numbering about 500, with cavalry and artillery, appeared at the head of Canal street and took position. General Longstreet, who was commanding, accompanied by an orderly, then rode up and down Canal street, ordering the armed citizens to disperse. Some desultory firing soon after occurred along Canal street, and some few casualties are reported on both sides. The Metropolitans are reported to have broken at the first fire, the citizens capturing one piece of artillery. Citizens are now building barricades along Poydras street, having already captured the city hall and taken possession of the fire-alarm telegraph. The police telegraph is worked by a battery at the city hall, and this has been detached therefrom, rendering the police wires useless. There is one company of United States troops here, but they remain at the custom-house, spectators of the lively scenes being enacted in front of them.

The State authorities seem to have great confidence in their ability to deal with what they term an armed mob, and say that unless the people disperse there will be bloody work to-night.

Barricades are erected in all the streets leading from Canal, between Poydras and Canal, and the People's party hold all that portion of the city above Canal. The Metropolitans are massed in and around Jackson square and the St. Louis hotel.

There was quite a sharp fight at the river and on Canal street about 4 o'clock. The number killed is estimated by some as high as fifty, and many wounded. Captain J. M. West, a printer and well-known newspaper correspondent, and E. A. Toledano were killed on the citizens' side. A number of Metropolitans are reported killed, and General Badger severely wounded. The colored men, of which the Metropolitan brigade was largely composed, broke and ran upon the first fire, leaving their white comrades, a number of whom were killed and wounded. Casualties will be reported as they are ascertained.

NEW ORLEANS, *Sept.* 14, 8 p. m.—The streets above Canal street are well filled with armed citizens. The impression now prevails that no further attempt will be made by the Metropolitans to disperse their opponents. The city is remarkably quiet throughout, and no further conflict is apprehended before morning. Most of the barricades are made with street railroad cars. Six or eight citizens and twenty or thirty Metropolitans were killed in the fight this afternoon, and many wounded on both sides.

NEW ORLEANS, *Sept.* 15.—An extra *Picayune* contains the following: "As might have been expected after the decisive victories of yesterday and consequent demoralization of the Kellogg forces, the finish this morning was a very brief affair. About 8.30 o'clock the State house was occupied by the citizens' force, and by 9 o'clock the third precinct station and the Kellogg armory. The last of the Radical government was after a sharp little assault captured, and so ends the Kellogg regime."

The State-house surrendered at 7 this morning to Lieutenant Governor Penn's militia without firing a gun. Governor Penn's militia are about ten thousand strong. All State and city property, the police stations, arsenals and police and fire-alarm telegraphs, are in the possession of the League. Kellogg is in the custom-house, under protection of United States troops. Jackson square police station, under command of General Longstreet, is reported to have just surrendered.

The Kellogg government has been overthrown, and the entire city is in the hands of his opponents. Lieutenant Governor Penn has taken the reins of the government, and will at once install in office all those who were voted for on the same ticket with McEnery in 1872. The courts will at once be organized, and the entire machinery of the government set in motion, not only in this city, but throughout the whole State.

The following dispatch was sent last evening by Acting Governor Penn to the President of the United States:

NEW ORLEANS, *Sept.* 14, 1874.

U. S. GRANT, *President of the United States:*

Hopeless of all other relief, the people of this State have taken up arms to maintain the legal authority of the persons elected by them to the government of the State, against the usurpers who have heaped upon them innumerable insults and wrongs. In so doing they are supported by the great body of intelligent and honest people of the State. They declare their unswerving loyalty and respect for the United States Government and its officers. They war only against the usurpers, plunderers and enemies of the people. They affirm their entire ability to maintain peace and protect life, liberty and the equal rights of all classes of citizens. The party and officials of the United States it shall be our special aim to defend against all assaults, and to treat with the profoundest respect and loyalty. We only ask of you to withhold any aid or protection from our enemies and the enemies of republican rights and of the peace and liberties of the people.

D. B. PENN, *Lieut. Gov. and Actg. Gov.*

Same day—President GRANT issued his Proclamation, giving the parties referred to above, five days in which to abandon their position. For full text of the Proclamation, see chapter of Orders and Proclamations.

Same day—Orders were issued for a concentration of land and naval forces, at New Orleans.

Sept. 17—John McEnery issued an order directing that the State troops now under arms will be at once retired to their homes, and the captured arms be deposited in the Central Station, or at the Third precinct. He also surrendered the capitol and the remainder of the property in New Orleans belonging to the State to Gen. J. R. Brooke, who took possession of the arms and other State property, and was appointed by Gen. Emory to command the city of New Orleans until such time as the State and city governments can be organized. McEnery and Penn presented a written protest against the view that there was then in Louisiana "any assembly or aggregation of insurgents to disperse," and insisting that at that time there was "no trace or vestige remaining of the late usurpation of which William Pitt Kellogg was the head."

Sept. 18—Gen. Emory informed Gov. Kellogg that "the insurgents lately in arms against the State government" have surrendered, and offered him the "necessary military support to re-establish the State government."

Gen. Emory to Adjutant-General.

NEW ORLEANS, *September* 24, 1874.

ADJUTANT-GENERAL *U. S. A.:*

Yesterday was asked by Governor Kellogg to meet him and consult upon making arrests and searches for arms. After mature reflection, I concluded and stated to him that, as military commander, I did not, under my orders, feel myself at liberty to advise or consult with the State authorities upon any political matter connected with administration of State affairs.

W. H. EMORY, *Colonel and Brevet M. G., Commanding.*

NEW ORLEANS, *September* 30, 1874.

ADJUTANT-GENERAL *U. S. A.*

Contending parties here have entered into an

agreement about the registration and election. It may ease matters for the time, but it looks like a recognition of the legal rights of insurgent parties. Negotiations of the kind were what I referred to in my telegram of the 24th, informing you I had formally declined any conference with governor on State politics.

W. H. EMORY, *Commanding.*

NEW ORLEANS, *October* 1, 1874.

SIR: The arrangement by the leaders of contending parties, referred to in my telegrams of yesterday, will probably not be acceded to by the followers of either party; and even if it is acceded, to I think that the good effect of the arrangement, if any, would only last until the election. The democrats expect to carry enough of the Legislature to be masters of the situation. Should they do so, order may rule; but if they are defeated, conflict and violence will be the inevitable consequences, unless suppressed by the presence of strong military force. Therefore, I strongly recommend that no material reduction of force be made until after the election and the meeting of the Legislature.

The leaders of the insurgents have, I am sure, used all their efforts to have the arms taken from the State returned; yet there are fifteen hundred (1,500) stand of improved small-arms, and two (2) howitzers yet missing, and as they are in the hands of individuals whose names are not enrolled, or not even known, I see no way of coercing the holders to give up these arms except by search and seizure and imprisonment of leaders, for which I have no authority.

Admiral Mullany informs me he will leave two (2) ships here, which will be an essential aid in the preservation of peace, as it will give me command of the river, and will enable me, in case of disturbance, to transport troops to the city from the suburbs of the town, where they must necessarily be encamped.

W. H. EMORY, *Commanding.*

NEW ORLEANS, *October* 5, 1874.

I have reliable information that bodies of armed men, from twenty to sixty in each body, meet in the street at night for the purpose of drill, and that armed bodies whose numbers are not known meet in the league room. This comes with information, not so well established, that the object is to force a collision, and cause a military government in place of the Kellogg government. The State government appears powerless to suppress the meetings.

W. H. EMORY, *Commanding.*

NEW ORLEANS, *October* 7, 1874.

To ADJUTANT-GENERAL, *U. S. A.:*

I am informed by the chief of police in this city, whom I consider thoroughly reliable, that he has certain information that White Leaguers repudiate compromise between State officials and democratic leaders, and that another attempt will be made to get possession of State-house and other public offices of the State, if only for a time, as soon as troops leave the city to go into camp, or can for a moment be caught off their guard. Their design seems to be to demonstrate the weakness of the State government and show their determination not to acknowledge that government or submit to it, except by force of the arms of the United States. I think the Leaguers would like to be assailed by the United States troops. They have at least six thousand well-instructed men, accustomed to arms.

W. H. EMORY, *Commanding.*

The Adjutant-General to General Emory.

WASHINGTON, *October* 27, 1874.

General W. H. EMORY, *New Orleans:*

The President would like to know your views as to stationing troops in New Orleans on day of election. The object is to confirm every individual in his legal right to vote. Cannot points be selected near polls where attempts to overawe voters, likely to result in riots, may be made, and troops stationed there a day or two beforehand? It would not be desirable to have soldiers at or too near the polls, as all appearance of military interference, except to secure voters their right to vote, should be avoided. Reply to me.

E. D. TOWNSEND, *Adjutant-General.*

General Emory to the Adjutant-General.

To ADJUTANT-GENERAL, *U. S. A.:*

The troops are now stationed as follows: Eleven companies on river-bank about midway of the port of the traffic, and command the levee as far as Canal street. Ten companies at barracks on eastern extremity of city, and three companies at State-house, in center of city, and one company of cavalry near headquarters, also near center of city, and the fleet lying in the stream. The whole city and river front completely commanded. The troops in taking exercise move about the city daily. The city occupies a narrow strip extending ten miles along river, is divided into fifteen wards, and usually has polls opened at more than one hundred places. The frauds charged, if true, are already consummated in the registrations, and every man having certificate of registration is entitled to vote. To change position of troops now, and place them near the polls, would be inconvenient, owing to the number of polls, if not impracticable, owing to the difficulty of getting accommodations, either of house or grounds, to encamp troops, and would, I think, be less effective, and open to the same objection as placing the troops directly at the polls on election day. If thought best, in addition to the troops already in the city, those from the barracks could be brought in, and companies stationed at five of the most eligible police-stations. All the commands will then be in position to act under the acts approved February 28 and April 20, 1871; and this, in my view, is all the change necessary, if any. As far as my information goes, the leading men of the city and the leading newspapers are using all their best exertions to insure a peaceable and quiet election.

W. H. EMORY, *Commanding.*

NEW ORLEANS, *October* 31, 1874.

To ADJUTANT-GENERAL, *U. S. A.:*

Governor Kellogg has this moment requested that two officers and twenty men be sent to Lafourche Crossing, fifty miles distant by railroad, to prevent apprehended violence and bloodshed at polls on Monday; unless detachment start before seven to-morrow, it cannot reach there in time. Shall it be sent? Please answer.

W. H. EMORY, *Commanding.*

NEW ORLEANS, *October* 31, 1874.

To ADJUTANT-GENERAL, *U. S. A*:

I do not think there will be a conflict, except it be for the custody of the ballot-boxes, or about the count of votes. But as a precaution, unless otherwise directed, will, as suggested in my telegram of the 28th, bring remaining troops from Jackson Barracks to city to keep the peace and prevent possible conflict between armed bodies.

W. H. EMORY, *Commanding.*

The Adjutant-General to General Emory.

WASHINGTON, *October* 31, 1874.

General W. H. EMORY, *New Orleans*:

Two cipher dispatches received; Secretary says no objections to arrangement of troops at barracks; better comply with the request of governor in other dispatches, unless it will weaken you too much.

E. D. TOWNSEND, *Adjutant-General.*

Gen. Emory to the Adjutant-General.

NEW ORLEANS, *November* 4, 1874.

To ADJUTANT-GENERAL *U. S. A.*:

I request that my letter to you of the first of October be considered in connection with my dispatch to you of last night. The situation foreshadowed in that letter still exists, and the views expressed in regard to the reduction of force are still entertained.

W. H. EMORY, *Commanding.*

NOTE.—The dispatch of November 3, 1874, herein cited, referred to the hire of quarters in New Orleans.

The Adjutant-General to Gen. Emory.

WASHINGTON, *November* 16, 1874.

General W. H. EMORY, *U. S. A., New Orleans*:

If troops in New Orleans still occupy the State-house, it is desired by the President that they be transferred to the quarters they are to occupy for the winter. Are there any in State-house?

E. D. TOWNSEND, *Adjutant-General.*

Gen. Emory to the Adjutant-General.

NEW ORLEANS, *November* 17, 1874.

To ADJUTANT-GENERAL *U. S. A.*:

The troops moved as directed. It will slightly increase estimated expense for quarters; while in State-house strict orders were observed not to interfere with free ingress or egress of citizens, or with State affairs.

W. H. EMORY, *Commanding.*

Gov. Kellogg to the President.

NEW ORLEANS, *December* 9, 1874.

President GRANT, *Washington*:

Information reaches me that the White League purpose making an attack upon the State-house, especially that portion occupied by the treasurer of the State; the organization is very numerous and well armed, and the State forces now available are not sufficient to resist successfully any movement they make. With a view of preventing such an attempt, and the bloodshed which would be likely to result should an insurgent body again take possession of the State-house and in dispersing them, I respectfully request that a detachment of United States troops be stationed in that portion of the Saint Louis Hotel which is not used for any of the State officers, where they will be readily available to prevent any such insurrectionary movement as that contemplated.

WM. P. KELLOGG, *Governor of Louisiana.*

Gen. Emory to the Adjutant-General.

NEW ORLEANS, *December* 15, 1874.

To ADJUTANT-GENERAL *U. S. A.*:

The returning-board and people representing opposing party differ on vital questions. Each avers against the other crime of such enormity that, in the present excited state of the public mind, violence is imminent. On the occasion of the fourteenth of September I was informed, in a dispatch dated fifteenth September,* that the President directed you to say previous orders are not to be observed; in consequence of which, my order to Colonel Brooke to recognize Governor Kellogg was revoked, and an interregnum intervened. To avoid future misunderstanding in the impending disturbance, which may happen at any moment, or may not occur until after the meeting of the Legislature in January, I asked to be informed if the instructions contained in your dispatch of September eighteenth are to be considered in force, or if I am to await the result of another application from Governor Kellogg to the President. W. H. EMORY, *Commanding.*

NEW ORLEANS, *December* 15, 1874.

To ADJUTANT-GENERAL *of the Army*:

I should have added to telegram of this same date that the troops have been kept in readiness to move since Saturday.

W. H. EMORY, *Commanding.*

The Adjutant-General to Gen. Emory.

WASHINGTON, *December* 16, 1874.

Col. W. H. EMORY, *New Orleans, La.*:

The President directs that you make arrangements to be in readiness to suppress violence, and have it understood that you will do it.

Please acknowledge receipt.

By order of the Secretary of War:

E. D. TOWNSEND, *Adjutant-General.*

Gen. Emory to the Adjutant-General.

NEW ORLEANS, *December* 16, 1874.

To the ADJUTANT-GENERAL *U. S. A.*:

Telegram received. It is already understood in this community that I will act as directed in the dispatch. W. H. EMORY, *Commanding.*

NEW ORLEANS, *December* 16, 1874.

ADJUTANT-GENERAL, *Washington, D. C.*:

Since my dispatch of yesterday, information comes which I think justifies conclusion that personal violence and armed conflict will not be used

*This dispatch does not appear among the papers transmitted to the Senate.—EDITOR.

by contending parties to settle the pending political troubles in this city.

W. H. EMORY, *Commanding.*

[CONFIDENTIAL.]

NEW ORLEANS, *December* 13, 1874.

SIR: The department commander directs that you hold your command, including the company of artillery, with its guns, in constant readiness to move to this city.

On the receipt of orders from these headquarters, or on hearing at any hour of day or night three guns fired in quick succession from the ships of war in the harbor, you will march your command, by the shortest and most expeditious route, to the custom-house in this city, and report in person to these headquarters for orders.

Acknowledge receipt.

I am, sir, very respectfully, your obedient servant,

E. R. PLATT,
Assistant Adjutant-General.

COMMANDING OFFICER *United States Troops, Jackson Barracks, Louisiana:*

NEW ORLEANS, *December* 19, 1874.

Official copy respectfully furnished the Adjutant-General of the Army, through headquarters Division of the South. The substance of this confidential letter appeared in the New Orleans *Picayune* within a few days from its date. It will explain my telegram of the 16th instant.

W. H. EMORY, *Commanding.*

Secretary of War to Gen. Sheridan.

WASHINGTON CITY, *December* 24, 1874.

General P. H. SHERIDAN, *Chicago, Ill.*:

GENERAL: The President sent for me this morning, and desires me to say to you that he wishes you to visit the States of Louisiana and Mississippi, and especially New Orleans, in Louisiana, and Vicksburgh and Jackson, in Mississippi, and ascertain for yourself, and for his information, the general condition of matters in those localities. You need not confine your visit to the States of Louisiana and Mississippi, and may extend your trip to other States, Alabama, &c., if you see proper; nor need you confine your visit, in the States of Louisiana and Mississippi, to the places named. What the President desires is to ascertain the true condition of affairs, and to receive such suggestions from you as you may deem advisable and judicious.

Inclosed herewith is an order authorizing you to assume command of the Military Division of the South, or of any portion of that Division, should you see proper to do so. It may be possible that circumstances may arise which would render this a proper course to pursue. You can, if you desire it, see General McDowell in Louisville, and make known to him confidentially the object of your trip; but this is not required of you. Communication with him by you is left entirely to your own judgment.

Of course you can take with you such gentlemen of your staff as you wish, and it is best that the trip should appear to be one as much of pleasure as of business, for the fact of your mere presence in the localities referred to will have, it is presumed, a beneficial effect.

The President thinks, and so do I, that a trip south might be agreeable to you, and that you might be able to obtain a good deal of information on the subject about which we desire to learn. You can make your return by Washington and make a verbal report, and also inform me from time to time of your views and conclusions. Yours truly,

WM. W. BELKNAP, *Secretary of War.*

Adjutant-General to Gen. Sheridan.

WASHINGTON, *December* 24, 1874.

Lieut. Gen. P. H. SHERIDAN, *Chicago, Ill.:*

SIR: If in the course of the inspection and investigation the Secretary of War has directed you to make, in his communication of this date, you should find it necessary to assume command over the Military Division of the South, or any portion thereof, the President of the United States hereby authorizes and instructs you to take the command accordingly, and to establish your headquarters at such point as you may deem best for the interests of the public service.

I am, sir, very respectfully, your obedient servant,

E. D. TOWNSEND, *Adjutant-General.*

Mr. Wiltz to the President.

NEW ORLEANS, *January* 4, 1875.

The PRESIDENT OF THE UNITED STATES, *Washington, D. C.:*

I have the honor to inform you that the House of Representatives of this State was organized to-day by the election of myself as speaker, fifty-eight members, two more than a quorum, voting, with a full house present. More than two hours after the organization I was informed by the officer in command of the United States troops in this city that he had been requested by Governor Kellogg to remove certain members of the house from the State House, and that, under his orders, he was obliged to comply with the request. I protested against any interference of the United States with the organization or proceedings of the house, but notwithstanding this the officer in command marched a company of soldiers upon the floor of the house, and by force removed thirteen members, who had been legally and constitutionally seated as such, and who, at time of such forcible removal, were participating in the proceedings of the house. In addition to this, the military declared their purpose to further interfere with force in the business and organization of this assembly, upon which some fifty-two members and the speaker withdrew, declining to participate any longer in the business of the house under the dictation of the military. As speaker, I respectfully appeal to you to know by what authority and under what law the United States Army interrupted and broke up a session of the House of Representatives of the State of Louisiana, and to urgently request and demand that they be ordered to restore the house to the position it occupied when they so interfered; and, further, that they be instructed that it is no part of their duty to interfere in any manner with the internal workings of the general assembly. The house is the representative of the sovereignty of the State, and I know of no law which warrants either the executive of the State or the United

States Army to interfere with its organization or proceedings.
LOUIS A. WILTZ,
Speaker of the House of Representatives of the State of Louisiana.

Gen. Sheridan to the Secretary of War.

NEW ORLEANS, *January* 4, 1875.

W. W. BELKNAP, *Secretary of War:*

It is with deep regret that I have to announce to you the existence in this State of a spirit of defiance to all lawful authority, and an insecurity of life which is hardly realized by the General Government or the country at large. The lives of citizens have become so jeopardized that unless something is done to give protection to the people, all security usually afforded by law will be overridden. Defiance to the laws and the murder of individuals seems to be looked upon by the community here from a standpoint which gives impunity to all who choose to indulge in either, and the civil government appears powerless to punish or even arrest. I have to-night assumed control over the Department of the Gulf.

P. H. SHERIDAN,
Lieutenant-General U. S. A.

Gen. Sheridan to the Secretary of War.

NEW ORLEANS, *January* 5, 1875.

W. W. BELKNAP, *Secretary of War:*

Please say to the President that he need give himself no uneasiness about the condition of affairs here. I will preserve the peace, which it is not hard to do with the naval and military forces in and about the city, and if Congress will declare the White Leagues and other similar organizations, white or black, banditti, I will relieve it from the necessity of any special legislation for the preservation of peace and equality of rights in the States of Louisiana, Mississippi, Arkansas, and the Executive from much of the trouble heretofore had in this section of the country.

P. H. SHERIDAN,
Lieutenant-General U. S. A.

W. W. BELKNAP, *Secretary of War:*

I think that the terrorism now existing in Louisiana, Mississippi and Arkansas could be entirely removed and confidence and fair-dealing established by the arrest and trial of the ringleaders of the armed White Leagues. If Congress would pass a bill declaring them banditti they could be tried by a military commission. The ringleaders of this banditti, who murdered men here on the 14th of last September, and also more recently at Vicksburgh, Miss., should, in justice to law and order and the peace and prosperity of this southern part of the country, be punished. It is possible that if the President would issue a proclamation declaring them banditti, no further action need be taken, except that which would devolve upon me.

P. H. SHERIDAN,
Lieutenant-General U. S. A.

W. W. BELKNAP, *Secretary of War:*

There is some excitement in the rotunda of the Saint Charles Hotel to-night upon the publication by the newspapers of my dispatch to you calling the secret armed organization banditti. Give yourself no uneasiness. I see my way clear enough, if you will only have confidence.

P. H. SHERIDAN,
Lieutenant-General, U. S. A.

Secretary of War to General Sheridan.

WASHINGTON CITY, *January* 6, 1875.

Gen. P. H. SHERIDAN, *New Orleans:*

Your telegrams all received. The President and all of us have full confidence and thoroughly approve your course.

WM. W. BELKNAP, *Secretary of War.*

WASHINGTON, *January* 6, 1875.

Gen. P. H. SHERIDAN, *New Orleans:*

I telegraphed you hastily to-day, answering your dispatch. You seem to fear that we had been misled by biased or partial statements of your acts. Be assured that the President and Cabinet confide in your wisdom and rest in the belief that all acts of yours have been and will be judicious. This I intended to say in my brief telegram.

WM. W. BELKNAP, *Secretary of War.*

General Sheridan to the Secretary of War.

NEW ORLEANS, *January* 6, 1875.

Gen. W. W. BELKNAP, *Secretary of War:*

The city is very quiet to-day. Some of the banditti made idle threats last night that they would assassinate me because I dared to tell the truth. I am not afraid, and will not be stopped from informing the Government that there are localities in this department where the very air has been impregnated with assassination for several years.

P. H. SHERIDAN,
Lieutenant-General Commanding.

NEW ORLEANS, *January* 7, 1875.

W. W. BELKNAP, *Secretary of War:*

Several prominent people have for the last few days been passing resolutions and manufacturing sensational protests for northern political consumption. They seem to be trying to make martyrs of themselves: it cannot be done at this late day; there have been too many bleeding negroes and ostracised white citizens for their statements to be believed by fair-minded people. Bishop Wilmer protests against my telegram of the 4th instant, forgetting that on Saturday last he testified under oath before the congressional committee that the condition of affairs here was substantially as bad as reported by me. I will soon send you a statement of the number of murders committed in this State during the last three or four years, the perpetrators of which are still unpunished. I think that the number will startle you; it will be up in the thousands. The city is perfectly quiet. No trouble is apprehended.

P. H. SHERIDAN,
Lieutenant-General U. S A.

[From the Newspapers.]

NEW ORLEANS, *Jan.* 8.—The following dispatches published here:

NEW ORLEANS, *January* 8.

To W. W. BELKNAP, *Secretary of War:*

I shall send you this evening a report of affairs as they actually occurred here on the 4th instant.

My telegram to you of that date, and those of the 5th and 6th inst., are so truthful of the condition of affairs in this section, and strike so near the water-line, that the ministers of the Gospel and others are appealed to to keep the ship from sinking. Human life has been held too cheaply in this State for many years.

P. H. SHERIDAN, *Lieutenant-General.*

[OFFICIAL.]

NEW ORLEANS, *January* 8, 1875.

Hon. W. W. BELKNAP, *Secretary of War.*

I have the honor to submit the following brief report of affairs as they occurred here in the organization of the State Legislature on January 4, 1875. I was not in command of this military department until 9 o'clock at night on the 4th instant, but I fully indorse and am willing to be held responsible for the acts of the military as conservators of the public peace upon that day. During the few days in which I was in the city prior to the 4th of January, the general topic of conversation was the scenes of bloodshed that were liable to occur on that day, and I repeatedly heard threats of assassinating the governor, and regrets expressed that he was not killed on the 14th of September last; also threats of the assassination of republican members of the house, in order to secure the election of a democratic speaker. I also knew of the kidnapping by the banditti of Mr. Cousinier, one of the members-elect of the Legislature. In order to preserve the peace and to make the State-house safe for the peaceful assembling of the Legislature, General Emory, upon the requisition of the Governor, stationed troops in the vicinity of the building. Owing to these precautions the Legislature assembled in the State house without any disturbance of the public peace. At 12 o'clock William Vigers, the clerk of the last house of representatives, proceeded to call the roll as according to law he was empowered to do. One hundred and two legally-returned members answered to their names; of this number fifty-two were republicans, and fifty were democrats. Before entering the house, Mr. L. A. Wiltz had been selected in caucus as the democratic nominee for speaker, and Mr. Michael Hahn as the republican nominee. Vigers had not yet finished announcing the result, when one of the members, Mr. Billican of Lafourche, nominated Mr. L. A. Wiltz for temporary speaker. Vigers promptly declared the motion out of order at that time, when some one put the question, and, amid the cheers of the democratic side of the house, Mr. Wiltz dashed on to the rostrum, pushed aside Mr. Vigers, seized the speaker's chair and gavel, and declared himself speaker. A protest against this arbitrary and unlawful proceeding was promptly made by members of the majority, but Wiltz paid no attention to their protests, and, upon a motion from some one on the democratic side of the house, declared one Trezevant nominated and elected clerk of the house. Mr. Trezevant at once sprang forward, and occupied the clerk's chair, amidst the wildest confusion over the whole house. Wiltz then again, on another nomination from the democratic side of the house, declared one Flood elected sergeant-at-arms, and ordered that a certain number of assistants be appointed. Instantly a large number of men throughout the hall, who had been admitted on various pretexts, such as reporters, members' friends, and spectators, turned down the lapels of their coats, upon which were pinned blue ribbon badges, on which were printed, in gold letters, the words "Assistant sergeant-at-arms," and the assembly was in the possession of the minority, and the White League of Louisiana had made good its threats of seizing the house; many of the assistant sergeants-at-arms being well known as captains of White League companies in this city. Notwithstanding the suddenness of this movement, the leading republican members had not failed to protest again and again against this revolutionary action of the minority, but all to no purpose; and many of the republicans rose and left the house in a body, together with the clerk, Mr. Vigers, who carried with him the original roll of the house, as returned by the secretary of state. The excitement was now very great. The acting speaker directed the sergeant-at-arms to prevent the egress or ingress of members or others, and several exciting scuffles, in which knives and pistols were drawn, took place, and for a few moments it seemed that bloodshed would ensue. At this juncture Mr. Dupre, a democratic member for the parish of Orleans, moved that the military power of the General Government be invoked to preserve the peace, and that a committee be appointed to wait upon General De Trobriand, the commanding officer of the United States troops stationed at the State house, and request his assistance in clearing the lobby. The motion was declared adopted, a committee of five, of which Mr. Dupre was made chairman, was sent to wait upon General De Trobriand, and soon returned with that officer, who was accompanied by two of his staff officers. As General De Trobriand walked down to the speaker's desk, loud applause burst from the democratic side of the house. General De Trobriand asked the acting speaker if it was not possible for him to preserve order withot appealing to him as a United States Army officer. Mr. Wiltz said it was not. Whereupon the general proceeded to the lobby, and, addressing a few words to the excited crowd, peace was at once restored. On motion of Mr. Dupre, Mr. Wiltz then, in the name of the general assembly of the State of Louisiana, thanked General De Trobriand for his interference in behalf of law and order, and the general withdrew. The republicans had now generally withdrawn from the hall and united in signing a petition to the Governor, stating their grievances and asking his aid, which petition, signed by fifty-two legally-returned members of the house, is in my possession. Immediately subsequent to the action of Mr. Wiltz in ejecting the clerk of the old house, Mr. Billieu moved that two gentlemen from the parish of De Soto, one from Winn, one from Bienville, and one from Iberia, who had not been returned by the returning-board, be sworn in as members; and they were accordingly sworn in by Mr. Wiltz, and took seats upon the floor as members of the house. A motion was now made that the house proceed with its permanent organization, and accordingly the roll was called by Mr. Trezevant, the acting clerk, and Wiltz declared elected speaker and

Trezevant clerk of the house. Acting on the protest made by the majority of the house, the governor now requested the commanding general of the department to aid him in restoring order, and enable the legally-returned members of the house to proceed with its organization according to law. This request was reasonable and in accordance with law. Remembering vividly the terrible massacre that took place in the city on the assembling of the constitutional convention in 1866, at the Mechanics' Institute, and believing that the lives of the members of the Legislature were or would be endangered in case an organization under the law was attempted, the posse was furnished, with the request that care should be taken that no member of the Legislature returned by the returning-board should be ejected from the floor. This military posse performed its duty, under directions from the Governor of the State, and removed from the floor of the house those persons who had been illegally seated, and who had no legal right to be there, whereupon the democrats rose and left the house, and the remaining members proceeded to effect an organization under the State laws. In all this turmoil, in which bloodshed was imminent, the military posse behaved with great discretion. When Mr. Wiltz, the usurping speaker of the house, called for troops to prevent bloodshed, they were given him. When the Governor of the State called for a posse for the same purpose, and to enforce the law, it was furnished also. Had this not been done, it is my firm belief that scenes of bloodshed would have ensued.

P. H. SHERIDAN, *Lieutenant-General.*

NEW ORLEANS, *January* 10, 1875.

Hon. W. W. BELKNAP, *Secretary of War;*

Since the year 1866, nearly thirty-five hundred persons, a great majority of whom were colored men, have been killed and wounded in this State. In 1868 the official record shows that eighteen hundred and eighty-four were killed and wounded. From 1868 to the present time, no official investigation has been made, and the civil authorities in all but a few cases have been unable to arrest, convict and punish perpetrators. Consequently, there are no correct records to be consulted for information. There is ample evidence, however, to show that more than twelve hundred persons have been killed and wounded during this time, on account of their political sentiments. Frightful massacres have occurred in the parishes of Bossier, Caddo, Catahoula, Saint Bernard, Saint Landry, Grant and Orleans. The general character of the massacres in the above-named parishes is so well known that it is unnecessary to describe them. The isolated cases can best be illustrated by the following instances, which I take from a mass of evidence now lying before me of men killed on account of their political principles. In Natchitoches Parish, the number of isolated cases reported is thirty-three. In the parish of Bienville, the number of men killed is thirty. In Red River Parish the number of isolated cases of men killed is thirty-four. In Winn Parish the number of isolated cases where men were killed is fifteen. In Jackson Parish the number killed is twenty; and in Catahoula Parish the number of isolated cases reported where men were killed is fifty; and most of the country parishes throughout the State will show a corresponding state of affairs. The following statements will illustrate the character and kind of these outrages. On the 29th of August, 1874, in Red River Parish, six State and parish officers, named Twitchell, Divers, Holland, Howell, Edgerton and Willis, were taken, together with four negroes, under guard, to be carried out of the State, and were deliberately murdered on the 30th of August, 1874. The White League tried, sentenced, and hung two negroes on the 28th of August, 1874. Three negroes were shot and killed at Brownsville, just before the arrival of the United States troops in this parish. Two White Leaguers rode up to a negro-cabin and called for a drink of water. When the old colored man turned to draw it, they shot him in the back and killed him. The courts were all broken up in this district, and the district judge driven out. In the parish of Caddo, prior to the arrival of the United States troops, all of the officers at Shreveport were compelled to abdicate by the White League, which took possession of the place. Among those obliged to abdicate were Walsh, the mayor, Rapers, the sheriff, Wheaton, clerk of the court, Durant, the recorder, and Ferguson and Renfro, administrators. Two colored men, who had given evidence in regard to frauds committed in the parish, were compelled to flee for their lives and reached this city last night, having been smuggled through in a cargo of cotton. In the parish of Bossier the White League have attempted to force the abdication of Judge Baker, the United States commissioner and parish judge, together with O'Neal, the sheriff, and Walker, the clerk of the court; and they have compelled the parish and district courts to suspend operations. Judge Baker states that the White Leaguers notified him several times that if he became a candidate on the republican ticket, or if he attempted to organize the republican party, he should not live until election.

They also tried to intimidate him through his family by making the same threats to his wife, and when told by him that he was a United States commissioner, they notified him not to attempt to exercise the functions of his office. In but few of the country parishes can it be truly said that the law is properly enforced, and in some of the parishes the judges have not been able to hold court for the past two years. Human life in this State is held so cheaply, that when men are killed on account of political opinions, the murderers are regarded rather as heroes than as criminals in the localities where they reside, and by the White League and their supporters. An illustration of the ostracism that prevails in the State may be found in a resolution of a White League club in the parish of De Soto, which states, "That they pledge themselves under (no ?) circumstances after the coming election to employ, rent land to, or in any other manner give aid, comfort, or credit, to any man, white or black, who votes against the nominees of the white man's party." Safety for individuals who express their opinion in the isolated portions of this State has existed only when that opinion was in favor of the principles and party supported by the Ku-Klux and White League

organizations. Only yesterday Judge Myers, the parish judge of the parish of Natchitoches, called on me upon his arrival in this city, and stated that in order to reach here alive, he was obliged to leave his home by stealth, and after nightfall, and make his way to Little Rock, Ark., and come to this city by way of Memphis. He further states that while his father was lying at the point of death in the same village, he was unable to visit him for fear of assassination; and yet he is a native of the parish, and proscribed for his political sentiments only. It is more than probable that if bad government has existed in this State it is the result of the armed organizations, which have now crystallized into what is called the White League; instead of bad government developing them, they have by their terrorism prevented to a considerable extent the collection of taxes, the holding of courts, the punishment of criminals, and vitiated public sentiment by familiarizing it with the scenes above described. I am now engaged in compiling evidence for a detailed report upon the above subject, but it will be some time before I can obtain all the requisite data to cover the cases that have occurred throughout the State. I will also report in due time upon the same subject in the States of Arkansas and Mississippi. P. H. SHERIDAN,
Lieutenant-General.

President Grant's Special Message on Affairs in the State of Louisiana, January 13, 1875.

To the Senate of the United States:

I have the honor to make the following answer to a Senate resolution of the 8th instant, asking for information as to any interference, by any military officer or any part of the Army of the United States, with the organization or proceedings of the General Assembly of the State of Louisiana or either branch thereof; and also inquiring in regard to the existence of armed organizations in that State, hostile to the government thereof, and intent on overturning such government by force.

To say that lawlessness, turbulence and bloodshed have characterized the political affairs of that State since its reorganization under the reconstruction acts, is only to repeat what has become well known as a part of its unhappy history; but it may be proper here to refer to the election of 1868, by which the Republican vote of the State, through fraud and violence, was reduced to a few thousands, and the bloody riots of 1866 and 1868, to show that the disorders there are not due to any recent causes, or to any late action of the Federal authorities.

Preparatory to the election of 1872 a shameful and undisguised conspiracy was formed to carry that election against the Republicans without regard to law or right, and to that end the most glaring frauds and forgeries were committed in the returns after many colored citizens had been denied registration, and others deterred by fear from casting their ballots.

When the time came for a final canvass of the votes, in view of the foregoing facts, William P. Kellogg, the Republican candidate for governor, brought suit upon the equity side of the United States Circuit Court for Louisiana, and against Warmoth and others, who had obtained possession of the returns of the election, representing that several thousand voters of the State had been deprived of the elective franchise on account of their color, and praying that steps might be taken to have said votes counted, and for general relief. To enable the court to inquire as to the truth of these allegations, a temporary restraining order was issued against the defendants, which was at once wholly disregarded and treated with contempt by those to whom it was directed. These proceedings have been widely denounced as an unwarrantable interference by the Federal judiciary with the election of State officers; but it is to be remembered that by the fifteenth amendment to the Constitution of the United States the political equality of colored citizens is secured, and under the second section of that amendment, providing that Congress shall have power to enforce its provisions by appropriate legislation, an act was passed on the 31st of May, 1870, and amended in 1871, the object of which was to prevent the denial or abridgment of suffrage to citizens, on account of race, color, or previous condition of servitude; and it has been held by all the Federal judges before whom the question has arisen, including Justice Strong of the Supreme Court, that the protection afforded by this amendment and these acts extends to State as well as other elections. That it is the duty of the Federal courts to enforce the provisions of the Constitution of the United States and the laws passed in pursuance thereof, is too clear for controversy.

Section 15 of said act, after numerous provisions therein to prevent an evasion of the fifteenth amendment, provides that the jurisdiction of the Circuit Court of the United States shall extend to all cases in law or equity arising under the provisions of said act and of the act amendatory thereof. Congress seems to have contemplated equitable as well as legal proceedings to prevent the denial of suffrage to colored citizens; and it may be safely asserted that, if Kellogg's bill in the above-named case did not present a case for the equitable interposition of the court, no such case can arise under the act. That the courts of the United States have the right to interfere in various ways with State elections so as to maintain political equality and rights therein, irrespective of race or color, is comparatively a new, and to some seems to be a startling idea; but it results as clearly from the fifteenth amendment to the Constitution and the acts that have been passed to enforce that amendment, as the abrogation of State laws upholding slavery results from the thirteenth amendment to the Constitution. While the jurisdiction of the court in the case of Kellogg *vs.* Warmoth and others is clear to my mind, it seems that some of the orders made by the judge in that and the kindred case of Antoine were illegal. But while they are so held and considered, it is not to be forgotten that the mandates of his court had been contemptuously defied, and they were made while wild scenes of anarchy were sweeping away all restraint of law and order. Doubtless the judge of this court made grave mistakes; but the law allows the chancellor great latitude not only in punishing those who contemn his orders and injunctions, but in preventing the consummation of the wrong which he has judicially forbidden. Whatever may be said or thought of those matters, it was only made known to me that process of the United States court was resisted; and as said act especially provides for the use of the Army and Navy, when necessary, to enforce judicial process arising thereunder, I considered it my duty to see that such process was executed according to the judgment of the court.

Resulting from these proceedings, through various controversies and complications, a State administration was organized with William P. Kellogg as governor, which in the discharge of my duty under section 4, article 4, of the Constitution, I have recognized as the government of the State.

It has been bitterly and persistently alleged that Kellogg was not elected. Whether he was or not is not altogether certain, nor is it any more certain that his competitor, McEnery, was chosen. The election was a gigantic fraud, and there are no reliable returns of its result. Kellogg obtained possession of the office, and in my opinion has more right to it than his competitor.

On the 20th of February, 1873, the Committee on Privileges and Elections of the Senate made a report, in which they say they were satisfied by testimony that the manipulation of the election machinery by Warmoth and others was equivalent to twenty thousand votes; and they add, to recognize the McEnery government "would be recognizing a government based upon fraud, in defiance of the wishes and intention of the voters of the State." Assuming the correctness of the statements in this report, (and they seem to have been generally accepted by the country,) the great crime in Louisiana, about which so much has been said, is, that one is holding the office of governor who was cheated out of twenty thousand votes, against another whose title to the office is undoubtedly based on fraud, and in defiance of the wishes and intentions of the voters of the State.

Misinformed and misjudging as to the nature and extent of this report, the supporters of McEnery proceeded to displace by force in some counties of the State the appointees of Governor Kellogg; and on the 13th of April, in an effort of that kind, a butchery of citizens was committed at Colfax, which in blood-thirstiness and barbarity is hardly surpassed by any acts of savage warfare.

To put this matter beyond controversy, I quote from the charge of Judge Woods, of the United States circuit court, to the jury in the case of the United States *vs.* Cruikshank and others, in New Orleans, in March, 1874. He said:

"In the case on trial there are many facts not in controversy. I proceed to state some of them in the presence and hearing of counsel on both sides; and if I state as a conceded fact any matter that is disputed, they can correct me."

After stating the origin of the difficulty, which grew out of an attempt of white persons to drive the parish judge and sheriff, appointees of Kellogg, from office, and their attempted protection by colored persons, which led to some fighting in which quite a number of negroes were killed, the judge states:

"Most of those who were not killed were taken prisoners. Fifteen or sixteen of the blacks had lifted the boards and taken refuge under the floor of the court-house. They were all captured. About thirty-seven men were taken prisoners; the number is not definitely fixed. They were kept under guard until dark. They were led out, two by two, and shot. Most of the men were shot to death. A few were wounded, not mortally, and by pretending to be dead were afterward, during the night, able to make their escape. Among them was the Levi Nelson named in the indictment.

"The dead bodies of the negroes killed in this affair were left unburied until Tuesday, April 15, when they were buried by a deputy marshal and an officer of the militia from New Orleans. These persons found fifty-nine dead bodies. They showed pistol-shot wounds, the great majority in the head, and most of them in the back of the head. In addition to the fifty-nine dead bodies found, some charred remains of dead bodies were discovered near the court-house. Six dead bodies were found under a warehouse, all shot in the head but one or two, which were shot in the breast.

"The only white men injured from the beginning of these troubles to their close were Hadnot and Harris. The court-house and its contents were entirely consumed.

"There is no evidence that any one in the crowd of whites bore any lawful warrant for the arrest of any of the blacks. There is no evidence that either Nash or Cazabat, after the affair, ever demanded their offices, to which they had set up claim, but Register continued to act as parish judge, and Shaw as Sheriff.

"These are facts in this case, as I understand them to be admitted."

To hold the people of Louisiana generally responsible for these atrocities would not be just; but it is a lamentable fact that insuperable obstructions were thrown in the way of punishing these murderers, and the so-called conservative papers of the State not only justified the massacre, but denounced as Federal tyranny and despotism the attempt of the United States officers to bring them to justice. Fierce denunciations ring through the country about office-holding and election matters in Lousiana, while every one of the Colfax miscreants goes unwhipped of justice, and no way can be found in this boasted land of civilization and Christianity to punish the perpetrators of this bloody and monstrous crime.

Not unlike this was the massacre in August last. Several northern young men of capital and enterprise had started the little and flourishing town of Coushatta. Some of them were republicans and office-holders under Kellogg. They were therefore doomed to death. Six of them were seized and carried away from their homes and murdered in cold blood. No one has been punished; and the conservative press of the State denounced all efforts to that end, and boldly justified the crime.

Many murders of a like character have been committed in individual cases which cannot here be detailed. For example, T. S. Crawford, judge, and P. H. Harris, district attorney, of the twelfth judicial district of the State, on their way to court, were shot from their horses by men in ambush on the 8th of October, 1873, and the widow of the former, in a communication to the Department of Justice, tells a piteous tale of the persecutions of her husband because he was a Union man, and of the efforts made to screen those who had committed a crime which, to use her own language, "left two widows and nine orphans desolate."

To say that the murder of a negro or a white republican is not considered a crime in Louisiana would probaby be unjust to a great part of the people; but it is true that a great number of such murders have been committed and no one has been punished therefor, and manifestly, as to them, the spirit of hatred and violence is stronger than law.

Representations were made to me that the presence of troops in Louisiana was unnecessary and irritating to the people, and that there was no danger of public disturbance if they were taken away. Consequently, early in last summer the troops were all withdrawn from the State, with the exception of a small garrison at New Orleans Barracks. It was claimed that a comparative state of quiet had supervened. Political excitement as to Louisiana affairs seemed to be dying out. But the November election was approaching, and it was necessary for party purposes that the flame should be rekindled.

Accordingly, on the 14th of September, D. B. Penn, claiming that he was elected lieutenant-governor in 1872, issued an inflammatory proclamation, calling upon the militia of the State to arm, assemble and drive from power the usurpers, as he designated the officers of the State. The White Leagues, armed and ready for the conflict, promptly responded.

On the same day the governor made a formal requisition upon me, pursuant to the act of 1795 and section 4, article 4, of the Constitution, to aid in suppressing domestic violence. On, the next day I issued my proclamation, commanding the insurgents to disperse within five days from the date thereof; but before the proclamation was published in New Orleans the organized and armed forces, recognizing a usurping governor, had taken forcible possession of the State-house and temporarily subverted the government. Twenty or more people were killed, including a number of the police of the city. The streets of the city were stained with blood. All that was desired in the way of excitement had been accomplished, and, in view of the steps taken to repress it, the revolution is apparently, though it is believed not really, abandoned, and the cry of Federal usurpation and tyranny in Louisiana was renewed with redoubled energy. Troops had been sent to the State under this requisition of the governor, and as other disturbances seemed imminent, they were allowed to remain there to render the executive such aid as might become necessary to enforce the laws of the State and repress the continued violence which seemed inevitable the moment Federal support should be withdrawn.

Prior to, and with a view to the late election in Louisiana, white men associated themselves together in armed bodies called "White Leagues," and at the same time threats were made in the democratic journals of the State that the election should be carried against the republicans at all hazards, which very naturally greatly alarmed the colored voters. By section 8 of the act of February 28, 1871, it is made the duty of United States marshals and their deputies, at polls where votes are cast for Representatives in Congress, to keep the peace and prevent any violations of the so-called enforcement acts, and other offenses against the laws of the United States; and upon a requisition of the marshal of Louisiana, and in view of said armed organizations and other portentous circumstances, I caused detachments of troops to be be stationed in various localities in the State to aid him in the performance of his official duties. That there was intimidation of republican voters at the election, notwithstanding these precautions, admits of no doubt. The following are specimens of the means used:

On the 14th of October eighty persons signed and published the following at Shreveport:

"We, the undersigned, merchants of the city of Shreveport, in obedience to a request of the Shreveport campaign club, agree to use every endeavor to get our employés to vote the people's ticket at the ensuing election; and in the event of their refusal so to do, or in case they vote the radical ticket, to refuse to employ them at the expiration of their present contracts."

On the same day another large body of persons published in the same place a paper, in which they used the following language:

"We, the undersigned, merchants of the city of Shreveport, alive to the great importance of securing good and honest government to the State, do agree and pledge ourselves not to advance any supplies or money to any planter the coming year who will give employment or rent lands to laborers who vote the radical ticket in the coming election."

I have no information of the proceedings of the returning board for said election which may not be found in its report, which has been published; but it is a matter of public information that a great part of the time taken to canvass the votes was consumed by the arguments of lawyers, several of whom represented each party before the board. I have no evidence that the proceedings of this board were not in accordance with the law under which they acted. Whether in excluding from their count certain returns they were right or wrong, is a question that depends upon the evidence they had before them; but it is very clear that the law gives them the power, if they choose to exercise it, of deciding that way; and *prima facie* the persons whom they return as elected are entitled to the offices for which they were candidates.

Respecting the alleged interference by the military with the organization of the Legislature of Louisiana on the 4th instant, I have no knowledge or information which has not been received by me since that time and published. My first information was from the papers of the morning of the 5th of January. I did not know that any such thing was anticipated, and no orders nor suggestions were ever given to any military officer in that State upon that subject prior to the occurrence. I am well aware that any military interference by the officers or troops of the United

States with the organization of the State Legislature or any of its proceedings, or with any civil department of the Government, is repugnant to our ideas of government. I can conceive of no case, not involving rebellion or insurrection, where such interference by authority of the General Government ought to be permitted or can be justified. But there are circumstances connected with the late legislative imbroglio in Louisiana which seem to exempt the military from any intentional wrong in that matter. Knowing that they had been placed in Louisiana to prevent domestic violence and aid in the enforcement of the State laws, the officers and troops of the United States may well have supposed that it was their duty to act when called upon by the governor for that purpose.

Each branch of a legislative assembly is the judge of the election and qualifications of its own members. But if a mob or a body of unauthorized persons seize and hold the legislative hall in a tumultuous and riotous manner, and so prevent any organization by those legally returned as elected, it might become the duty of the State executive to interpose, if requested by a majority of the members-elect, to suppress the disturbance and enable the persons elected to organize the house.

Any exercise of this power would only be justifiable under most extraordinary circumstances, and it would then be the duty of the governor to call upon the constabulary or, if necessary, the military force of the State. But with reference to Louisiana, it is to be borne in mind that any attempt by the governor to use the police force of that State at this time would have undoubtedly precipitated a bloody conflict with the White League, as it did on the 14th of September.

There is no doubt but that the presence of the United States troops upon that occasion prevented bloodshed and the loss of life. Both parties appear to have relied upon them as conservators of the public peace.

The first call was made by the democrats to remove persons obnoxious to them from the legislative hall; and the second was from the republicans to remove persons who had usurped seats in the Legislature without legal certificates entitling them to seats, and in sufficient number to change the majority.

Nobody was disturbed by the military who had a legal right at that time to occupy a seat in the Legislature. That the democratic minority of the house undertook to seize its organization by fraud and violence; that in this attempt they trampled under foot law; that they undertook to make persons not returned as elected members, so as to create a majority; that they acted under a preconcerted plan, and under false pretenses introduced into the hall a body of men to support their pretensions by force, if necessary; and that conflict, disorder, and riotous proceedings followed, are facts that seem to be well established; and I am credibly informed that these violent proceedings were a part of a premeditated plan to have the house organized in this way, recognize what has been called the McEnery Senate, then to depose Governor Kellogg, and so revolutionize the State government.

Whether it was wrong for the governor, at the request of the majority of the members returned as elected to the house, to use such means as were in his power to defeat these lawless and revolutionary proceedings, is perhaps a debatable question; but it is quite certain that there would have been no trouble if those who now complain of illegal interference had allowed the house to be organized in a lawful and regular manner. When those who inaugurate disorder and anarchy disavow such proceedings, it will be time enough to condemn those who, by such means as they have, prevent the success of their lawless and desperate schemes.

Lieutenant-General Sheridan was requested by me to go to Louisiana to observe and report the situation there, and, if in his opinion necessary, to assume the command, which he did on the 4th instant, after the legislative disturbances had occurred, at 9 o'clock p. m., a number of hours after the disturbances. No party motives nor prejudices can reasonably be imputed to him; but, honestly convinced by what he has seen and heard there, he has characterized the leaders of the White Leagues in severe terms, and suggested summary modes of procedure against them, which, though they cannot be adopted, would, if legal, soon put an end to the troubles and disorders in that State. General Sheridan was looking at facts, and possibly, not thinking of proceedings which would be the only proper ones to pursue in time of peace, thought more of the utterly lawless condition of society surrounding him at the time of his dispatch, and of what would prove a sure remedy. He never proposed to do an illegal act, nor expressed determination to proceed beyond what the law in the future might authorize for the punishment of the atrocities which have been committed, and the commission of which cannot be successfully denied. It is a deplorable fact that political crimes and murders have been committed in Louisiana, which have gone unpunished and which have been justified or apologized for, which must rest as a reproach upon the State and country long after the present generation has passed away.

I have no desire to have United States troops interfere in the domestic concerns of Louisiana or any other State.

On the 9th of December last Governor Kellogg telegraphed to me his apprehensions that the White League intended to make another attack upon the State-house, to which, on the same day, I made the following answer, since which no communication has been sent to him:

"Your dispatch of this date just received. It is exceedingly unpalatable to use troops in anticipation of danger. Let the State authorities be right, and then proceed with their duties without apprehension of danger. If they are then molested, the question will be determined whether the United States is able to maintain law and order within its limits or not."

I have deplored the necessity which seemed to make it my duty under the Constitution and laws to direct such interference. I have always refused except where it seemed to be my imperative duty to act in such a manner under the Constitution and laws of the United States. I have repeatedly and earnestly entreated the people of the South to live together in peace, and obey the laws; and nothing would give me greater pleasure than to see reconciliation and tranquillity everywhere prevail, and thereby remove all necessity for the presence of troops among them. I regret, however, to say that this state of things does not exist, nor does its existence seem to be desired in some localities; and as to those it may be proper for me to say that, to the extent that Congress has conferred power upon me to prevent it, neither Ku-Klux-Klans, White Leagues, nor any other association using arms and violence to execute their unlawful purposes, can be permitted in that way to govern any part of this country; nor can I see with indifference Union men or republicans ostracised, persecuted, and murdered, on account of their opinions, as they now are in some localities.

I have heretofore urged the case of Louisiana upon the attention of Congress, and I cannot but think that its inaction has produced great evil.

To summarize: In September last an armed, organized body of men, in the support of candidates who had been put in nomination for the offices of governor and lieutenant-governor, at the November election, in 1872, and who had been declared not elected by the board of canvassers, recognized by all the courts to which the question had been submitted, undertook to subvert and overthrow the State government that had been recognized by me, in accordance with previous precedents. The recognized governor was driven from the State-house, and, but for his finding shelter in the United States custom-house, in the capital of the State of which he was governor, it is scarcely to be doubted that he would have been killed.

From the State-house, before he had been driven to the custom-house, a call was made, in accordance with the fourth section, fourth article, of the Constitution of the United States, for the aid of the General Government to suppress domestic violence. Under those circumstances, and in accordance with my sworn duties, my proclamation of the 15th of September, 1874, was issued. This served to reinstate Governor Kellogg to his position nominally; but it cannot be claimed that the insurgents have, to this day, surrendered to the State authorities the arms belonging to the State, or that they have in any sense disarmed. On the contrary, it is known that the same armed organization that existed on the 14th of September, 1874, in opposition to the recognized State government, still retain their organization, equipments, and commanders, and can be called out at any hour to resist the State government. Under these circumstances, the same military force has been continued in Louisiana as was sent there under the first call, and under the same general instructions. I repeat, that the task assumed by the troops is not a pleasant one to them; that the Army is not composed of lawyers capable of judging at a moment's notice of just how far they can go in the maintenance of law and order; and that it was impossible to give specific instructions providing for all possible contingencies that might arise. The troops were bound to act upon the judgment of the commanding officer upon each sudden contingency that arose, or wait instructions which could only reach them after the threatened wrongs had been committed which they were called on to prevent. It should be recollected, too, that upon my recognition of the Kellogg government I reported the fact, with the grounds of recognition, to Congress, and asked that body to take action in the matter; otherwise, I should regard their silence as an acquiescence in my course. No action has been taken by that body, and I have maintained the position then marked out.

If error has been committed by the Army in these matters, it has always been on the side of the preservation of good order, the maintenance of law, and the protection of life. Their bearing reflects credit upon the soldiers; and if wrong has resulted, the blame is with the turbulent element surrounding them.

I now earnestly ask that such action be taken by Congress as to leave my duties perfectly clear in dealing with the affairs of Louisiana, giving assurance at the same time that whatever may be done by that body in the premises will be executed according to the spirit and letter of the law, without fear or favor.

I herewith transmit copies of documents containing more specific information as to the subject-matter of the resolution. U. S. GRANT.

Executive Mansion, January 13, 1875.

VOTES IN CONGRESS.

Forty-third Congress—Second Session.

IN HOUSE.

1875, March 1—Mr. G. F. HOAR moved to suspend the rules and pass the following preamble and resolutions:

Whereas, both branches of the Legislature of Louisiana have requested the special committee of this House to investigate the circumstances attending the election and returns thereof in that State for the year 1874; and whereas said committee have unanimously reported that the returning board of that State, in canvassing and compiling said returns and promulgating the result, wrongfully applied an erroneous rule of law, by reason whereof persons were awarded seats in the House of Representatives of Louisiana to which they were not entitled, and persons entitled to seats were deprived of them:

Resolved, That it is recommended to the House of Representatives of Louisiana to take immediate steps to remedy said injustice, and to place the persons rightfully entitled in their seats.

Resolved, That William Pitt Kellogg be recognized as the Governor of the State of Louisiana until the end of the term of office fixed by the constitution of that State.

Which was disagreed to—yeas 155, nays 86, not voting 46, (two-thirds not having voted in the affirmative):

YEAS—Messrs. Albert, Albright, Averill, Barber, Barrere, Barry, Begole, Bradley, Buffinton, Bundy, Burleigh, Burrows, B. F. Butler, R. R. Butler, Cain, Cannon, Carpenter, Cason, Cessna, A. Clark, jr., Clayton, Clements, S. A. Cobb, Coburn, Conger, Corwin, Cotton, Crooke, Danford, Darrall, Dawes, Dobbins, Donnan, Dunnell, Eames, Farwell, Field, Fort, Foster, Frye, Garfield, Gooch, Gunckel, Hagans, E. Hale, Harmer, Hathorn, Havens, J. R. Hawley, Hays,

G. W. Hazelton, J. W. Hazelton, E. R. Hoar, G. F. Hoar, Hodges, Hoskins, Houghton, Howe, Hubbell, Hunter, Hurlbut, Hyde, Kasson, Kelley, Kellogg, Killinger, Lansing, W. Lawrence, Lawson, Loughridge, Lowe, Lynch, Martin, Maynard, McCrary, A. S. McDill, J. W. McDill, MacDougall, McKee, McNulta, Merriam, Monroe, Moore, Morey, Myers, Negley, Nunn, O'Neill, Orth, Packard, Packer, Page, I. C. Parker, R. C. Parsons, Pendleton, W. A. Phillips, T. C. Platt, Poland, Pratt, Rainey, Rapier, W. H. Ray, Richmond, E. H. Roberts, J. W. Robinson, S. Ross, Rusk, Sawyer, H. B. Sayler, Scofield, H. J. Scudder, Sessions, Shanks, Sheats, Sheldon, Sherwood, L. D. Shoemaker, Sloan, Smart, A. H. Smith, G. L. Smith, H. B. Smith, J. A. Smith, J. Q. Smith, Sprague, Stanard, Starkweather, C. A. Stevens, St. John, Stowell, Strait, Sypher, C. Y. Thomas, J. M. Thompson, Thornburgh, Todd, W. Townsend, Tremain, Tyner, Waldron, A. S. Wallace, Walls, J. D. Ward, M. L. Ward, Wheeler, A. White, Whiteley, Wilber, C. G. Williams, J. M. S. Williams, W. Williams, W. B. Williams, J. Wilson, J. M. Wilson, Woodworth—155.

NAYS—Messrs. *G. M. Adams, Archer, Arthur, Ashe, Atkins, Banning, Barnum, Beck, H. P. Bell, Berry, Bland, Blount, Bowen, Bright, Bromberg, J. Y. Brown, Buckner, J. H. Caldwell, Caulfield, J. B. Clark, jr., Clymer, Comingo, Cook, Cox, Creamer, Crittenden, Crossland, John J. Davis, De Witt, Durham, Eden, Eldredge, Finck, Giddings, Glover, Gunter, R. Hamilton, Hancock, H. R. Harris, J. T. Harris, Hatcher, Hereford, Herndon, Holman, Hunton, Knapp, Lamar, Lamison, Leach, Luttrell, Magee, Marshall, McLean, Milliken, Mills, Morrison, Neal, Nesmith, Niblack, O'Brien,* Pierce, *C. N. Potter, Randall, Read, W. M. Robbins, W. R. Roberts, M. Sayler, Schell, Sloss, Southard, Speer, Standiford, Stone, Storm, Swann, R. B. Vance, Waddell, E. Wells, Whitehead, Whitehouse, Whitthorne, Willie, E. K. Wilson, F. Wood, J. D. Young, P. M. B. Young*—86.

Mr. G. F. HOAR then moved that the rules be so suspended as to bring the two resolutions before the House for a separate vote, which was agreed to—yeas 172, nays 85, not voting 30, (two-thirds having voted in the affirmative):

YEAS—Messrs. Albert, Albright, Averill, Barber, Barrere, Barry, Bass, Begole, Bradley, Buffinton, Bundy, H. C. Burchard, Burleigh, Burrows, B. F. Butler, R. R. Butler, Cain, Cannon, Carpenter, Cason, Cessna, A. Clark, jr., Clayton, Clements, S. A. Cobb, Coburn, Conger, Corwin, Cotton, Crooke, Crounse, Danford, Darrall, Dawes, Dobbins, Donnan, Duell, Dunnell, Eames, Farwell, Field, Fort, Foster, J. C. Freeman, Frye, Garfield, Gooch, Gunckel, Hagans, E. Hale, Harmer, B. W. Harris, H. H. Harrison, Hathorn, Havens, J. R. Hawley, Hays, G. W. Hazelton, J. W. Hazelton, E. R. Hoar, G. F. Hoar, Hodges, Hoskins, Houghton, Howe, Hubbell, Hunter, Hurlbut, Hyde, Hynes, Kasson, Kelley, Kellogg, Killinger, Lansing, W. Lawrence, Lawson, Loughridge, Lowe, Lowndes, Lynch, Martin, Maynard, McCrary, A. S. McDill, J. W. McDill, MacDougall, McKee, McNulta, Merriam, Monroe, Moore, Morey, Myers, Negley, Niles, Nunn, O'Neill, Orr, Orth, Packard, Packer, Page, I. C. Parker, R. C. Parsons, Pendleton, W. A. Phillips, J. H. Platt, jr., T. C. Platt, Poland, Pratt, Rainey, Ransier, Rapier, W. H. Ray, Richmond, E. H. Roberts, J. W. Robinson, S. Ross, Rusk, Sawyer, H. B. Sayler, Scofield, H. J. Scudder, Sener, Sessions, Shanks, Sheats, Sheldon, Sherwood, L. D. Shoemaker, Sloan, Smart, A. H. Smith, G. L. Smith, H. B. Smith, J. Q. Smith, Snyder, Sprague, Stanard, Starkweather, *A. H. Stephens*, C. A. Stevens, St. John, Stowell, Strait, Sypher, Taylor. C. Y. Thomas, J. M. Thompson, Thornburgh, Todd, W. Townsend, Tremain, Tyner, Waldron, A. S Wallace, Walls, J. D. Ward, M. L. Ward, Wheeler, A. White, Whiteley, Wilber, G. Willard, C. G. Williams, J. M. S. Williams, W. Williams, W. B. Williams, J. Wilson, J. M. Wilson, Woodworth—172.

NAYS—Messrs. *G. M. Adams, Archer, Arthur, Ashe, Atkins, Banning, Barnum, H. P. Bell, Berry, Bland, Blount, Bowen, Bright, Bromberg, J. Y. Brown, Buckner, J. H. Caldwell, Caulfield, J. B. Clark, jr., Clymer, Cook, Cox, Creamer, Crittenden, Crossland, John J. Davis, De Witt, Durham, Eden, Eldredge, Finck, Giddings, Glover, Gunter, R. Hamilton, Hancock, H. R. Harris, J. T. Harris, Hatcher, Hereford, Herndon, Holman, Hunton, Knapp, Lamison, Leach, Luttrell, Magee, Marshall, McLean, Milliken, Mills, Morrison, Neal, Nesmith, Niblack, O'Brien, Perry, C. N. Potter, Randall, Read, W. M. Robbins, W. R. Roberts, J. C. Robinson, M. Sayler, Schell, J. G. Schumaker, Sloss, Southard, Speer, Standiford, Stone, Storm, Swann, R. B. Vance, Waddell, E. Wells, Whitehead, Whitehouse, Whitthorne, Willie, E. K. Wilson, F. Wood, J. D. Young, P. M. B. Young*—85.

The question being taken on the first resolution, it was agreed to.

The question recurring on agreeing to the second resolution, it was agreed to—yeas 165, nays 89, not voting 33:

YEAS—Messrs. Albert, Albright, Averill, Barber, Barrere, Barry, Bass, Begole, Bradley, Buffinton, Bundy, H. C. Burchard, Burleigh, Burrows, R. R. Butler, Cain, Cannon, Carpenter, Cason, Cessna, A. Clark, jr., Clayton, Clements, S. A. Cobb, Conger, Corwin, Cotton, Crooke, Curtis, Danford, Darrall, Dawes, Dobbins, Donnan, Duell, Dunnell, Eames, Farwell, Field, Foster, J. C. Freeman, Frye, Garfield, Gooch, Gunckel, Hagans, E. Hale, Harmer, B. W. Harris, H. H. Harrison, Hathorn, Havens, J. R. Hawley, Hays, G. W. Hazelton, J. W. Hazelton, E. R. Hoar, G. F. Hoar, Hodges, Hoskins, Houghton, Howe, Hubbell, Hunter, Hurlbut, Hyde, Hynes, Kasson, Kelley, Kellogg, Killinger, Lansing, W. Lawrence, Lawson, Loughridge, Lowe, Lowndes, Lynch, Martin, Maynard, McCrary, A. S. McDill, J. W. McDill, MacDougall, McKee, McNulta, Merriam, Monroe, Moore, Morey, Myers, Negley, Nunn, O'Neill, Orr, Orth, Packard, Packer, Page, I. C. Parker, R. C. Parsons, Pendleton, W. A. Phillips, J. H. Platt, jr., T. C. Platt, Poland, Pratt, Rainey, Ransier, Rapier, W. H. Ray, Richmond, E. H. Roberts, J. W. Robinson, S. Ross, Rusk, Sawyer, H. B. Sayler, Scofield, H. J. Scudder, Sessions,

Shanks, Sheats, Sheldon, Sherwood, L. D. Shoemaker, Sloan, Smart, A. H. Smith, G. L. Smith, H. B. Smith, J. Q. Smith, W. A. Smith, Snyder, Sprague, Stanard, Starkweather, C. A. Stevens, St. John, Stowell, Strait, Sypher, Taylor, C. Y. Thomas, J. M. Thompson, Thornburgh, Todd, W. Townsend, Tremain, Tyner, Waldron, A. S. Wallace, Walls, J. D. Ward, M. L. Ward, Wheeler, A. White, Whiteley, Wilber, C. G. Williams, J. M. S Williams, W. Williams, J. Wilson, J. M. Wilson, Woodworth—165.

NAYS—Messrs. *G. M. Adams, Archer, Arthur, Ashe, Atkins, Banning, Barnum, Beck H. P. Bell, Berry, Bland, Blount, Bowen, Bright, Bromberg, J. Y. Brown, J. H. Caldwell, Caufield, J. B. Clark, jr., Clymer, Cox, Creamer, Crittenden, Crossland, John J. Davis, De Witt, Durham, Eden, Eldredge, Finck, Giddings, Glover, Gunter, R. Hamilton, Hancock, H. R. Harris, J. T. Harris, Hatcher, Hereford, Herndon, Holman, Hunton, Knapp, Lamar, Lamison, Leach, Luttrell, Magee, Marshall, McLean, Milliken, Mills, Morrison, Neal, Nesmith, Niblack, O'Brien, Perry,* Pierce, *C. N. Potter, Randall, Read, W. M. Robbins, W. R. Roberts, J. C. Robinson, M. Sayler, Schell, J. G. Schumaker,* Sener, *Sloss,* J. A. Smith, *Southard, Speer, Standiford, A. H. Stephens, Stone, Storm, Swann, R. B. Vance, Waddell, E. Wells, Whitehead, Whitehouse, Whitthorne, Willie, E. K. Wilson, F. Wood, J. D. Young, P. M. B. Young*—89.

NOT VOTING—Messrs. Biery, *Buckner,* B. F. Butler, Chittenden, F. Clarke, C. L. Cobb, Coburn, *Comingo, Cook,* Crounse, Crutchfield, Fort, R. S. Hale, J. B. Hawley, Hendee, *Kendall,* Lamport, B. Lewis, Lofland, *Mitchell,* Niles, *H. W. Parker,* Pelham, W. W. Phelps, Pike, I. W. Scudder, W. B. Small, Strawbridge, C. R. Thomas, C. W. Willard, G. Willard, W. B. Williams, *Wolfe*—33.

The preamble was then agreed to.

IN SENATE.

Special Session of Fourty-fourth Congress.

March 5—Mr. MORTON offered the following resolution:

Resolved by the Senate, That the State government now existing in Louisiana, and represented by William P. Kellogg as governor, is the lawful government of said State; that it is republican in form; and that every assistance necessary to sustain its proper and lawful authority in said State should be given by the United States, when properly called upon for that purpose, to the end that the laws may be faithfully and promptly executed, life and property protected and defended, and all violators of law, State or national, brought to speedy punishment for their crimes.

March 16—Mr. FRELINGHUYSEN offered the following resolution:

Resolved, That the Senate approve the action heretofore taken by the President of the United States in protecting Louisiana from domestic violence, and are of opinion that he should continue to recognize in that State the existing State government.

March 20—The above was taken up for consideration—yeas 28, nays 24, not voting 20:

YEAS—Messrs. Alcorn, Anthony, Boutwell, Bruce, Burnside, Cameron of Wisconsin, Conkling, Cragin, Edmunds, Ferry of Michigan, Frelinghuysen, Harvey, Hitchcock, Howe, Ingalls, Jones of Nevada, Logan, McMillan, Mitchell, Morrill of Maine, Morrill of Vermont, Morton, Oglesby, Patterson, Robertson, Sherman, Spencer, West—28.

NAYS—Messrs. *Bayard, Bogy,* BOOTH, *Caperton, Cockrell, Cooper, Davis, Eaton, Gordon,* HAMILTON of Texas, *Johnson* of Tennessee, *Jones* of Florida, *Kelley, Kernan, McCreery, Maxey, Norwood, Randolph, Saulsbury, Stevenson, Thurman, Wallace, Whyte, Withers*—24.

Mr. ANTHONY offered the following as a substitute:

That the action of the President in protecting the government in Louisiana, of which William P. Kellogg is the executive, and the people of that State, against domestic violence, and in enforcing the laws of the United States in that State, is approved.

Mr. WHYTE moved that the substitute be postponed until the second Monday in December next, which was disagreed to—yeas 24, nays 30, not voting 18:

YEAS—Messrs. *Bayard, Bogy,* BOOTH, *Caperton, Cockrell, Cooper, Davis, Eaton, Gordon,* HAMILTON of Texas, *Johnson* of Tennessee, *Jones* of Florida, *Kelley, Kernan, McCreery, Maxey, Norwood, Randolph, Saulsbury, Stevenson, Thurman, Wallace, Whyte, Withers*—24.

NAYS—Messrs. Allison, Anthony, Boutwell, Bruce, Burnside, Cameron of Wisconsin, Christiancy, Conkling, Cragin, Edmunds, Ferry of Michigan, Frelinghuysen, Harvey, Hitchcock, Howe, Ingalls, Jones of Nevada, Logan, McMillan, Mitchell, Morrill of Maine, Morrill of Vermont, Morton, Oglesby, Paddock, Patterson, Robertson, Sherman, Spencer, West—30.

Mr. DAVIS moved to strike out the word "approve" in the resolution of Mr. FRELINGHUYSEN; which was disagreed to—yeas 16, nays 23, not voting 33:

YEAS—Messrs. *Bayard, Bogy, Caperton, Cockrell, Cooper, Davis, Gordon, Johnson* of Tennessee, *Jones* of Florida, *McDonald, Norwood, Randolph, Saulsbury, Wallace, Whyte, Withers*—16.

NAYS—Messrs. Allison, Anthony, Boutwell, Bruce, Cameron of Wisconsin, Christiancy, Conkling, Cragin, Ferry of Michigan, Frelinghuysen, Harvey, Hitchcock, Howe, Ingalls, Logan, McMillan, Morrill of Vermont, Morton, Oglesby, Paddock, Patterson, Robertson, West—23.

March 23—Mr. WHYTE moved to amend the amendment of Mr. Anthony, by substituting the following:

That the use of the Army of the United States to enforce the unwarrantable and void order of Judge Durell, issued on the 5th of December, 1872, and directing the United States marshal to seize the building occupied as a State-house for the assembling of the Legislature of Louisiana, and the employment of the soldiers of the United States on the 4th of January, 1875, to invade the hall of the house of representatives of Louisiana, and to eject therefrom persons claiming to be members thereof, are contrary to the spirit of republican institutions and cannot be approved by the Senate of the United States.

Which was disagreed to—yeas 22, nays 33, not voting 17:

YEAS—Messrs. *Bayard, Bogy, Caperton, Cockrell, Cooper, Davis, Dennis, Eaton, Johnson* of Tennessee, *Jones* of Florida, *Kelly, Kernan, McCreery, Maxey, Norwood, Randolph, Saulsbury, Stevenson, Thurman, Wallace, Whyte, Withers*—22.

NAYS—Messrs. Allison, Anthony, BOOTH, Boutwell, Bruce, Cameron of Wisconsin, Conkling, Cragin, Dorsey, Edmunds, Ferry of Michigan, Frelinghuysen, HAMILTON of Texas, Harvey, Hitchcock, Howe, Ingalls, Jones of Nevada, Logan, McMillan, Mitchell, Morrill of Maine, Morrill of Vermont, Morton, Paddock, Patterson, Robertson, Sargent, Sherman, Spencer, Wadleigh, West, Windom—33.

Mr. THURMAN moved to insert at the end of the amendment of the Senator from Rhode Island this proviso:

Provided, That nothing herein contained is meant to affirm that said Kellogg is *de jure* Governor of Louisiana.

Which was disagreed to—yeas 24, nays 33, not voting 15:

YEAS—Messrs. *Bayard, Bogy, Caperton, Cockrell, Cooper, Davis, Dennis, Eaton, Gordon*, HAMILTON of Texas, *Johnson* of Tennessee, *Jones* of Florida, *Kelly, Kernan, McCreery, Maxey, Norwood, Randolph, Saulsbury, Stevenson, Thurman, Wallace, Whyte, Withers*—24.

NAYS—Messrs. Allison, Anthony, BOOTH, Boutwell, Bruce, Burnside, Cameron of Wisconsin, Christiancy, Conkling, Cragin, Dorsey, Edmunds, Ferry of Michigan, Frelinghuysen, Harvey, Hitchcock, Howe, Ingalls, Jones of Nevada, Logan, McMillan, Mitchell, Morrill of Maine, Morrill of Vermont, Morton, Patterson, Robertson, Sargent, Sherman, Spencer, Wadleigh, West, Windom—33.

Mr. THURMAN offered the following proviso:

Provided, That nothing herein contained is meant to affirm that the body of men who assumed to elect P. B. S. Pinchback a Senator of the United States was the Legislature of the State of Louisiana.

Which was disagreed to—yeas 24, nays 31, not voting 17:

YEAS—Messrs. *Bayard, Bogy, Caperton, Cockrell, Cooper, Davis, Dennis, Eaton, Gordon*, HAMILTON of Texas, *Johnson* of Tennessee, *Jones* of Florida, *Kelly, Kernan, McCreery, Maxey, Norwood, Randolph, Saulsbury, Stevenson, Thurman, Wallace, Whyte, Withers*—24.

NAYS—Messrs. Allison, Anthony, Boutwell, Bruce, Burnside, Cameron of Wisconsin, Conkling, Cragin, Dorsey, Edmunds, Ferry of Michigan, Frelinghuysen, Harvey, Hitchcock, Howe, Ingalls, Jones of Nevada, Logan, McMillan, Mitchell, Morrill of Maine, Morrill of Vermont, Morton, Patterson, Robertson, Sargent, Sherman, Spencer, Wadleigh, West, Windom—31.

Mr. THURMAN offered the following proviso:

Provided, That nothing herein contained is meant to approve the military interference of United States troops in the organization of the Legislature of Louisiana on the 4th of January last.

Which was disagreed to—yeas 24, nays 32, not voting 16:

YEAS—Messrs. *Bayard, Bogy, Caperton, Cockrell, Cooper, Davis, Dennis, Eaton, Gordon*, HAMILTON of Texas, *Johnson* of Tennessee, *Jones* of Florida, *Kelly, Kernan, McCreery, Maxey, Norwood, Randolph, Saulsbury, Stevenson, Thurman, Wallace, Whyte, Withers*—24.

NAYS—Messrs. Allison, Anthony, BOOTH, Boutwell, Bruce, Burnside, Cameron of Wisconsin, Conkling, Cragin, Dorsey, Edmunds, Ferry of Michigan, Frelinghuysen, Harvey, Hitchcock, Howe, Ingalls, Jones of Nevada, Logan, McMillan, Mitchell, Morrill of Maine, Morrill of Vermont, Morton, Patterson, Robertson, Sargent, Sherman, Spencer, Wadleigh, West, Windom—32.

The question being taken on agreeing to Mr. ANTHONY'S amendment, it was agreed to—yeas 33, nays 23, not voting 16:

YEAS—Messrs. Allison, Anthony, Boutwell, Bruce, Burnside, Cameron of Wisconsin, Christiancy, Conkling, Cragin, Dorsey, Edmunds, Ferry of Michigan, Frelinghuysen, Harvey, Hitchcock, Howe, Ingalls, Jones of Nevada, Logan, McMillan, Mitchell, Morrill of Maine, Morrill of Vermont, Morton, Paddock, Patterson, Robertson, Sargent, Sherman, Spencer, Wadleigh, West, Windom—33.

NAYS—Messrs. *Bayard, Bogy*, BOOTH, *Caperton, Cockrell, Cooper, Davis, Dennis, Gordon, Johnson* of Tennessee, *Jones* of Florida, *Kelly, Kernan, McCreery, Maxey, Norwood, Randolph, Saulsbury, Stevenson, Thurman, Wallace, Whyte, Withers*—23.

ABSENT—Messrs. Alcorn, Cameron of Pennsylvania, Clayton, Conover, Dawes, *Eaton*, Ferry of Connecticut, *Goldthwaite*, HAMILTON of Texas, Hamlin, *Johnston* of Virginia, *McDonald, Merrimon*, Oglesby, *Ransom*, Wright—16.

The question recurring on the resolution as amended, it was agreed to—yeas 33, nays 24, not voting 15:

YEAS—Messrs. Allison, Anthony, Boutwell, Bruce, Burnside, Cameron of Wisconsin, Christiancy, Conkling, Cragin, Dorsey, Edmunds, Ferry of Michigan, Frelinghuysen, Harvey, Hitchcock, Howe, Ingalls, Jones of Nevada, Logan, McMillan, Mitchell, Morrill of Maine, Morrill of Vermont, Morton, Paddock, Patterson, Robertson, Sargent, Sherman, Spencer, Wadleigh, West, Windom—33.

NAYS—Messrs. *Bayard, Bogy*, BOOTH, *Caperton, Cockrell, Cooper, Davis, Dennis, Gordon*, HAMILTON of Texas, *Johnson* of Tennessee, *Jones* of Florida, *Kelly, Kernan, McCreery, Maxey, Norwood, Randolph, Saulsbury, Stevenson, Thurman, Wallace, Whyte, Withers*—24.

ABSENT—Messrs. Alcorn, Cameron of Pennsylvania, Clayton, Conover, Dawes, *Eaton*, Ferry of Connecticut, *Goldthwaite*, Hamlin, *Johnston* of Virginia, *McDonald, Merrimon*, Oglesby, *Ransom*, Wright—15.

Under the influence of the resolution unanimously adopted by the House of Representatives of the United States, recommending that the House of Representatives of that State seat the persons rightfully entitled thereto from certain districts, the whole subject was, by consent of parties, referred to the Special Committee of the

House who examined into Louisiana affairs, viz.: Messrs. George F. Hoar, William A. Wheeler, William P. Frye, Charles Foster, William Walter Phelps, Clarkson N. Potter and Samuel S. Marshall, who, after careful examination, made an award, which was adopted by the Legislature in April, 1875, and which has been, more or less, faithfully observed. The facts which have transpired under it do not properly claim a place in this record. It is popularly known as the "Wheeler Compromise."

Mississippi.

[From the Newspapers.]

Gov. Ames to the President.

JACKSON, MISS., *July* 29, 1874.

President U. S. GRANT, *Washington:*

I regret to inform you that I find upon returning here that an alarming condition of affairs exists at Vicksburg. Infantry and calvary organizations exist, and it is reported that a number of pieces of artillery have been sent to that city, and these bodies, organized and armed without authority and in violation of law, assume to be guardians of the peace. This is a political controversy. On one side the democrats, represented by the whites, claim that they fear frauds on the part of their opponents. The republicans, consisting mainly of blacks, claim that they fear frauds and also violence on the part of the democrats. At one time a collision and bloodshed was feared by all—now by the republicans, but by the democrats it is disbelieved, only because they have become masters of the situation. It is they, also, who oppose the presence of troops at this time.

Of the causes of this lamentable state of affairs it is now useless to speak. I only seek peace and protection for all. Can there be any serious objection why troops should not be sent there? No harm can result, for troops are in many of our cities; at this moment in two of the cities of this State. Their presence may do great good; it may save many lives; even one would more than compensate for the harm which, if any, I do not see to result from such presence. Will it not be the least of evils to have troops there for any emergency?

ADELBERT AMES, *Governor of Mississippi.*

The President to Gov. Ames.

WASHINGTON, *July* 31, 1874.

The Hon. A. AMES, *Jackson, Miss.:*

The contents of your dispatch have been submitted to the President. He declines to move the troops, except under a call made strictly in accordance with the terms of the Constitution.

W. W. BELKNAP, *Secretary of War.*

Gov. Ames's Second Call.

The following papers are copies of official documents on file in the office of the Attorney-General, in Washington, and are the only full report of these transactions yet printed:

Report of Attorney-General Pierrepont to the President, covering the telegrams and correspondence connected with the second call of Governor Ames for troops.

DEPARTMENT OF JUSTICE, WASHINGTON, D. C.,
Sunday, Sept. 12*th*, 1875.

To the PRESIDENT:

SIR: I report upon the Mississippi disturbance in the order of events. I received your directions on the 9th; forthwith I advised the Adjutant-General to order General Augur to hold his troops in readiness, and to advise Gov. Ames of the fact. I caused a proclamation to be made in duplicate. I telegraphed to Gov. Fish at his country-place, but received no reply until the next day, by reason of an accident which he has explained. Meanwhile I received the following:

[Telegram.]

Dated EDWARDS, MISS., *Sept.* 10, 1875.

To Attorney-General PIERREPONT, *Washington*

Perfect quiet prevails throughout Hinds county; peace officers are not prevented from executing legal, and the good citizens will assist me in discharge of my duties, if needed.

W. H. HARNEY, *Sheriff.*

And also the following, which Secretary BRISTOW assures me is from a most reliable man:

Dated JACKSON, MISS., *Sept.* 10, 1875.

To Gen. B. H. BRISTOW, *Secretary Treasury:*

All is peace here; the tempest in the tea-pot has subsided. The Mayor of our town has tendered to the Sheriff of the county one hundred men, white and colored, if needed, to give assurance to the citizens in any part of the county.

Very respectfully, E. W. CABANANISS.

Also the following, which Gov. Alcorn assures me is from a truthful man, worthy of belief, an able lawyer, but a strong democratic partisan:

Dated JACKSON, MISS., 9 *Sept.*, 1875.

Hon. EDWARDS PIERREPONT, *Attorney-General:*

There are no disturbances in this State now, and no obstructions to the execution of the laws. There has been an unexpected conflict at a political meeting, and some subsequent disturbances, but everything is quiet now; the Governor's call for U. S. troops does not even pretend there is any insurrection against the State government, as required by the Revision of U. S. Statutes of eighteen seventy-five, page ten thirty-four. Peace prevails throughout the State, and the employment of U. S. troops would but increase the distrust of the people in the good faith of the present State government. J. Z. GEORGE,

Chairman Democratic Ex. State Committee.

Yesterday morning I received the following, but they did not come until after I had read them in the Washington newspapers, in which it was stated that they came from Memphis:

[Telegram,]

Dated JACKSON, MISS., 10 *Sept.*, 1875.

To Attorney-General PIERREPONT:

Did not send dispatch. There is no protection for life to colored men in my county. Telegram sent was presented to me by a Captain of one of the military organizations here. For safety to self and property I could not do otherwise I am free to confess my knowledge and convictions are to the contrary.

W. H. HARNEY, *Sheriff, Hinds County.*

Dated JACKSON, MISS., 10 *Sept.*, 1875.
To Attorney-General PIERREPONT.

For my personal safety I desire the telegram sent by me to be kept private. Respectfully,

W. H. HARNEY, *Sheriff.*

I next received the following:

JACKSON, MISS., *Sept.* 11, 1875.
To Hon. EDWARDS PIERREPONT,
Attorney-General U. S.:

I am prepared to prove to your satisfaction that Sheriff Harney was under no duress whatever when he sent his first dispatch to you, and that the contents of that dispatch are true; offers are freely made to the Governor of assistance to preserve the peace should danger of disturbance occur. The people of Mississippi claim the right of American citizens to be heard before they are condemned. I reassert that perfect peace prevails throughout the State, and that there is no danger of disturbance unless incited by the State authorities, which I hope they will not do.

J. Z. GEORGE,
Chairman Dem. Conserv. State Ex. Com.

And then the dispatch from Senator Pease, which follows:

Dated JACKSON, MISS., *Sept.* 11, 1875.
To Hon. EDWARDS PIERREPONT, *Atty. Genl*:

Excitement arising from recent riots at Yazoo City and Clinton has in a great measure subsided. A civil *posse composed of good citizens of all political parties and of sufficient force to protect life and property can be had in any county in the State.*

No effort has as yet been made by State authorities in this direction. Until all legal means have been exhausted, I am of the opinion that federal intervention is unwise, impolitic, and will only tend to aggravate existing difficulties.

H. R. PEASE, *Ex-U. S. Senator.*

On the same day, I received the following:

Dated JACKSON, MISS., 11 *Sept.*, 1875.
To Hon. EDWARDS PIERREPONT, *Atty. Genl*:

SIR: The following dispatches, which appeared in Vicksburg *Herald* of yesterday, and Hinds county *Gazette* of the ninth inst., both democratic papers, are respectfully forwarded for comparison with the dispatches sent you by Chairman of democratic executive committee of this state:

[Special to the Herald.]

YAZOO CITY, *Sept. ninth.*—The latest heard from the Satarlia neighborhood was from a courier who left there last night late. He reported all quiet, with the capture of one negro. Sheriff went through those places that furnished armed negroes, but not one could be found. Even the women and children have gone to the woods. Did every bush contain a United States soldier, the negroes could not be more secure than they are in this county. The whites bear them no malice. Reports come in each day from the Good Hope and Burras places, on Wolf Lake, to the effect that the negroes are armed and have their nightly parades; they are three hundred strong. The Coroner took possession of the Sheriff's office yesterday, but finding out his mistake refused to act, leaving Morgan deputies in full possession. The officer of the night has just reported to your correspondent that all is quiet; the city is kept heavily guarded, and has been ever since the fight, and these expect to continue to do so, regardless of Ames's orders, until the negroes lay down their arms.

Signed C. KNARF.

[Special to the Herald.]

YAZOO CITY, *September 9th.*

We have just read the proclamation of Gov. Ames, of the seventh inst., in which he says civil government is overthrown in Yazoo county.

This is false. Every civil officer of the county is and has been at his post, and in active discharge of his duty except A. L. Morgan, sheriff. He left voluntarily, but his office is open and his deputy in charge of it unmolested.

A. S. EPPERSON, C. V. GWYN, R. S. HUDSON, J. C. PRUETT, E. DWINING, R. BOWMAN, FRANK CAMPBELL.

RAYMOND GAZETTE, *September 9th.* — Saturday night, Sunday and Sunday night, Raymond was a military camp. All the clubs south sent forward large details, and had it been necessary Raymond could have sent two hundred armed men to any locality. The sheriff of Yazoo county is still a fugitive.

A. WARNER,
Chairman Republican State Ex. Com.

Not willing to advise extreme measures unless strictly within the law, and as the call of the Governor was not in strict conformance with the statute, I sent him the following telegram on the morning of the 10th:

DEPARTMENT OF JUSTICE,
WASHINGTON, *Sept.* 10, 1875.
To Governor AMES, *Jackson, Miss.*:

United States forces have been put in readiness. No orders for their movement yet, and no proclamation issued. Everything is ready. Is there such insurrection against the State Government as cannot be put down by State military forces, aided by all the other powers of the State Government and true citizens?

EDWARDS PIERREPONT, *Attorney-General.*

I received no reply. Yesterday morning (the 11th), I sent the following:

DEPARTMENT OF JUSTICE,
WASHINGTON, *Sept.* 11, 1875.
To Governor AMES, *Jackson, Miss.*:

In my dispatch of yesterday morning, in which I mentioned that the troops were held in readiness, I asked whether the situation of the insurrection was such against the State authorities that the State Government by the aid of loyal citizens could not put it down. I have no reply.

EDWARDS PIERREPONT, *Attorney-General.*

Up to eleven o'clock last night no answer came. Meanwhile the telegram above given from Senator Pease, came to hand. Senator Alcorn, late Governor of Mississippi, was present when I received it; he assured me that there was no doubt about Senator Pease, and that full credit should be given to his dispatch and to his suggestion. Between 11 and 12 o'clock last night I received the following:

[Telegram.]

Dated JACKSON, MISS., *Sept.* 11, 1875.
To Attorney-General PIERREPONT:

The necessity which called forth my dispatch of the eighth instant to the President still exists. Your question of yesterday, repeated to-day, asks for information which I gladly give. The violence is incident to the political contest preceding the pending election. Unfortunately, the question of race, which has been prominent in the South since the war, has assumed magnified importance at this time in certain localities. In fact, the race feeling is so intense that protection for the colored people by white organizations is despaired of. A political contest made on the "White Line" forbids it. The history of the colored people since reconstruction, and its bearing on the situation at this time, and a detailed statement of the troubles here, cannot be condensed in a telegram. The Republican party of this State has been opposed to organizing a militia of colored men; it has been believed by them that it would develop a war of races which would extend beyond the borders of this State. The organization of whites alone, where the issue is one of race, would be equally ineffectual. The most complete protection would be found in the strict non-interference of the whites. Contradictions will be numerous; so they were last December; but the report of Congressional committee proved the correctness of my assertions. I am aware of the reluctance of the people of the country to national interference in State affairs; though if there be no violation of the law there can be no interference.

Permit me to express the hope that the odium of such interference shall not attach to President GRANT or the Republican party. As the Governor of a State, I made a demand which cannot well be refused. Let the odium, in all its magnitude, descend upon me. I cannot escape the conscientious discharge of my duty towards a class of American citizens, whose only crime consists in their color. I am powerless to protect. ADELBERT AMES.

These are all the dispatches received since you referred the matter to me. Before that I learned from the United States Attorney at Jackson, in reply to my dispatch, that there were grave disturbances, but that there was no resistance to any United States authority.

After all the delay, Gov. Ames does not answer my question, which I regret. I made it specific, quoting from the statute, in order to bring his call, if possible, within the letter of the law. It is not strictly so now; but in a great emergency I do not think it well to be too stiff about words. The real substance is what we are to look to, and that is my perplexity. I do not think that the Constitution and the laws now invoked were intended for a case where the State authorities were supported by a very large majority of the people, and where the State Government was not found inadequate to the emergency after some effort to quell the riot. This seems to me a matter of much gravity. The Secretary of State will be here to-morrow, Secretaries Bristow and Delano are now here, and the Postmaster General will be here on Tuesday. I send this by special messenger, and await your further instructions, and am

Very respectfully yours,
(Signed) EDWARDS PIERREPONT,
Attorney-General.

NOTE.—The call of Gov. Ames, a copy of the Article of the Constitution referred to, and of the law, is hereto annexed:

Governor Ames to the President.

JACKSON, MISS., *Sept. 8th*, 1875.
President U. S. GRANT, *Washington D. C.:*

Domestic violence prevails in various parts of this State, beyond the power of the State authorities to suppress. The legislature cannot be convened in time to meet the emergency. I therefore, in accordance with Section four, Article four, of the Constitution of the United States, which provides that the United States shall guarantee to every State in this Union a republican form of government, and shall protect each of them against invasion, and on application of the Legislature, or of the Executive when the Legislature cannot be convened, against domestic violence, make this my application for such aid from the Federal Government as may be necessary to restore peace to the State and protect its citizens.

ADELBERT AMES, *Governor.*

ARTICLE IV. SECTION 4. The United States shall guarantee to every State in this Union a Republican form of government, and shall protect each of them against invasion; and, on application of the Legislature or of the Executive (when the Legislature cannot be convened) against domestic violence.

UNITED STATES REVISED STATUTES, SECTION 5297. In case of an insurrection in any State against the government thereof, it shall be lawful for the President, on application of the Legislature of such State, or of the Executive, when the Legislature cannot be convened, to call forth such number of the militia of any other State or States, which may be applied for, as he deems sufficient to suppress such insurrection; or on like application, to employ, for the same purposes, such part of the land or naval forces of the United States as he deems necessary.

The Attorney-General to Gov. Ames.

DEPARTMENT OF JUSTICE,
WASHINGTON, *Sept.* 14, 1875.
To Governor AMES, *Jackson, Miss.:*

This hour I have had dispatches from the PRESIDENT. I can best convey to you his ideas by extracts from his dispatch.

"The whole public are tired out with these annual autumnal outbreaks in the South, and the great majority are ready now to condemn any interference on the part of the Government. I heartily wish that peace and good order may be restored without issuing the proclamation. But if it *is not*, the proclamation must be issued, and if it *is*, I shall instruct the commander of the forces to have *no child's play*.

"If there is a necessity for military interference, there is justice in such interference as to deter evil doers. * * * * * * * I would suggest the sending of a dispatch (or better by private messenger) to Gov. Ames, urging him to strengthen his own position by exhausting his own resources in restoring order, before he receives government aid. He might accept the assistance offered by the citizens of Jackson and elsewhere. * * * * * Gov. Ames and his advisers can be made perfectly secure.

"As many of the troops now in Mississippi as he deems necessary may be sent to Jackson. If he is betrayed by those who offer assistance, he will be in a position to defeat their ends and punish them."

You see by this the mind of the President, with which I and every member of the Cabinet who has been consulted are in full accord. You see the difficulties; you see the responsibilities which you assume.

We cannot understand why you do not strengthen yourself in the way the President suggests; nor do we see why you do not call the Legislature together, and obtain from them whatever powers and money and arms you need. The Constitution is explicit that the executive of the State can call upon the President for aid in suppressing "*domestic violence*" only "*when the Legislature cannot be convened.*" And the law expressly says: "*In case of an insurrection in any State against the government thereof, it shall be lawful for the President, on application of the Legislature of such State, or of the Executive when the Legislature cannot be convened, to call, etc.*" It is the plain meaning of the constitution and the laws, when taken together, that the executive of the State may call upon the President for military aid to quell "domestic violence" only in case of an insurrection in any State against the government thereof, when the Legislature cannot be called together. You make no suggestion even that there is any insurrection against the government of the State, or that the Legislature would not support you in any measures you might propose to preserve the public order.

I suggest that you take all lawful means and all needed measures to preserve the peace by the forces in your own State, and let the country see that the citizens of Mississippi, who are largely favorable to good order, and who are largely Republican, have the courage and the manhood to *fight* for their rights, and to destroy the bloody ruffians who murder the innocent and unoffending freedmen.

Everything is in readiness. Be careful to bring yourself strictly within the Constitution and the laws; and if there *is such resistance to your State authorities as you cannot by all the means at your command suppress*, the President will swiftly aid you in crushing these lawless traitors to human rights.

Telegraph me on receipt of this, and state *explicitly* what you need.

Yours very respectfully,
EDWARDS PIERREPONT, *Attorney-General.*

Citizens of Mississippi to the Attorney-General.

DEPARTMENT OF JUSTICE,
WASHINGTON, *Sept.* 15, 1875.

ATTORNEY-GENERAL:

It is our judgment that your letter of the 14th inst. to Gov. Ames, with the extracts from the President's letter to you, ought to be published in Mississippi, and that the publication would have immense influence in restoring and preserving the public peace. Respectfully,

GEO. M. BUCHANAN, *Sheriff Marshall Co., Miss.*
B. K. BRUCE, *U. S. S.*
A. R. HOWE, *Ex-Mem. Congress.*
JAMES HILL, *Sec. of State.*
A. WARNER, *Chairman Rep. State Ex. Com.*
JOHN B. RAYMOND, *Editor Mississippi "Pilot."*

The Attorney-General to Gov. Ames.

DEPARTMENT OF JUSTICE,
WASHINGTON, *Sept.* 14, 1875.

To Governor AMES, *Jackson, Miss.*:

A special messenger starts with dispatches to you to-day, under the President's direction. If any new outbreak occurs before the messenger reaches you, telegraph at once, and orders will be sent to the Commandiug General.

EDWARDS PIERREPONT, *Attorney-General.*

The President to the Adjutant-General.

LONG BRANCH, N. J., *Sept.* 8, 1875.

ADJUTANT-GENERAL, *U. S. A.*:

You may instruct commanding officer of troops in Mississippi, that he may assist the Governor in maintaining order and preserving life in case of insurrection too formidable for him to suppress. Before telegraphing your order, submit it, with this dispatch, to the Attorney-General, to see if it is entirely legal. Inform Governor Ames of any instructions you give.

U. S. GRANT.

W. P. Harris to Senator Alcorn.

JACKSON, MISS., *Sept.* 14, 1875.

Hon. J. L. ALCORN, *Washington*:

Pease is right. There has not been any resistance offered to any State officer, and none will be offered. Ask Pierrepont to take the opinion of the Attorney-General of Mississippi.

W. P. HARRIS.

Frank Johnston to Senator Alcorn.

JACKSON, MISS., *Sept.* 14, 1875.

JAS. L. ALCORN, *U. S. Senator, Washington*:

On the 5th inst. sheriff called for a posse with approval of Governor. Citizens responded. A mounted posse, headed by deputy sheriff, went to Clinton immediately; the latter found everything quiet, and so reported to the sheriff on his return to Jackson. FRANK JOHNSTON.

The President to Gen. Augur.

WAR DEPARTMENT,
ADJUTANT-GENERAL'S OFFICE,
WASHINGTON, *Sept.* 9, 1875.

To Brigadier General C. C. AUGUR, *U. S. A., Commanding Department South, New Orleans, La.*:

Should the Governor of Mississippi call upon you for assistance in case of insurrection in his State too formidable for him to suppress, the President of the United States directs that you afford him such aid as may be in your power for the purpose of maintaining order and preserving life.

Acknowledge receipt and report action for the President's information.

During the winter of 1875–'6, the Lieuteanant-Governor was removed by impeachment; and articles were also presented impeaching Governor AMES, when, by an arrangement made by counsel, they were withdrawn, and he resigned his office. The State Government is now in wholly different hands.

South Carolina.

Gov. Moses to the President.

[From the Newspapers.]

COLUMBIA, S. C., *Sept.* 25, 1874.

His Excellency U. S. GRANT.

The state of affairs in Edgefield county, in this State, has been for the last ten days of such a character as to threaten the lives and the destruction of the property of law-abiding and peaceful citizens. I have exhausted my efforts with the peaceful and legal means at my command to restore the usual situation. Armed bands are assembled at various points in the county, and have demanded the surrender to them of the State arms in the hands of the regularly organized militia of the State. From this action a reign of terror exists. I issued my proclamation on the 21st instant, commanding these armed bands to disperse and retire to their homes within three days, and hereafter to refrain from a repetition of such actions. They are still under arms. I am powerless to enforce my orders, except by the use of the inexperienced State militia, the employment of which I fear would hasten a conflict, which I desire to avoid.

Having exhausted all means at my command I call upon you, under the Constitution of the United States, for such assistance as will enable me to restore the peace and quiet of the county, and to this end I ask that you will send immediate orders to Col. H. M. Black, commanding United States forces, to report to me with such of his command as it may be found necessary to employ.

Please answer as speedily as possible.

F. J. MOSES, *Governor of South Carolina.*

The President to Gov. Moses.

WASHINGTON, *Sept.* 26, 1874.

Hon. F. J. MOSES, *Columbia, South Carolina:*

SIR: I have to say, by direction of the President, in answer to your telegram of yesterday to him, asking for troops to aid in suppressing disorders in Edgefield, that a company of United States troops is now stationed there, and it is expected and believed that it will afford adequate protection to the lives and property of citizens.

GEORGE H. WILLIAMS, *Attorney-General.*

ATLANTA, GA., Sept. 26.—The troubles in Edgefield county, South Carolina, are ended.

Tennessee.

[From the Newspapers.]

NASHVILLE, TENN., *Sept.* 18.—Gov. Brown of Tennessee sent the following message this afternoon to President Grant:

EXECUTIVE DEPARTMENT,
NASHVILLE, TENN., *Sept.* 18, 1874.

His Excellency U. S. GRANT, *Prest. of the U. S.:*

There were sixteen negroes committed to the jail of Gibson county, in this State, charged with a conspiracy to take the lives of the white citizens of their neighborhood. On the night of the 25th of August, 1874, a party of disguised men violated the jail and took these prisoners forcibly from the jailor, and killed four and wounded two, the remainder escaping and being now at large. The next day I offered a reward of $500 for each of these unknown offenders. The State Court being then in session, took immediate cognizance of the outrage, and the labors of the regular and special term have resulted in the detection and indictment of 41 of the guilty parties, the majority of whom have been arrested, and the remainder will be if they have not fled the country. They are indicted under the second and third sections of the act of the General Assembly of Tennessee of 1869 and 1870, passed on the 30th of January, 1870, entitled "An act to preserve the public peace," and which is in full force. The sections are as follows:

SECTION 2. *Be it further enacted,* That if any person or persons, disguised or in mask, by day or by night, shall enter upon the premises of another, or demand entrance or admission into the house or enclosure of any citizen of this State, it shall be considered *prima facie* evidence that his or their intention is to commit a felony, and such demand shall be deemed an assault with an intent to commit a felony; and the person or persons so offending shall, upon conviction, be punished by imprisonment in the penitentiary for not less than 10 years nor more than 20 years.

SEC. 3. *Be it further enacted,* That if any person or persons so prowling, traveling, riding or walking through the towns or counties of this State, masked in disguise, should or may assault another with a deadly weapon, he or they shall be deemed guilty of an assault with an intent to commit murder in the first degree, and on conviction thereof, shall suffer death by hanging; provided the jury trying the case may substitute imprisonment in the penitentiary for a period of not less than 10 years, nor more than 20 years.

The State authorities have manifested the most earnest desire to enforce the law against the guilty parties, and have demonstrated by these indictments and arrests, not only their disposition but ability to enforce the law and protect all citizens, without regard to race, color, or previous condition of servitude. These efforts, I can assure you, will in no sense be relaxed until the majesty of the law is fully vindicated. Notwithstanding these efforts, with the result stated, the United States Marshal and Commissioner for the Western Division of Tennessee, with the aid of detachments from the Government garrison at Humboldt, have arrived, and are continuing to arrest citizens, and conveying them under guard to Memphis, nearly 100 miles distant, to answer for the same offense charged against them by the State Courts.

As Governor of Tennessee I do most respectfully but earnestly protest against the exercise of jurisdiction by the United States Commissioner and Marshal, without reference to the question whether the offenses are the proper subject of cognizance by the United States Courts, but alone upon the ground that the peace of society will be more certainly preserved and the rights of citizens as well protected by conceding jurisdiction to the State Courts; and I therefore respectfully ask your Excellency to order that no further arrests be made by the Marshal, and that the parties already in his custody be turned over to the proper local tribunals for trial and punishment. I undertake to assure your Excellency that no effort will be spared to enforce the laws and protect the citizens by the officers of the State Goverment throughout the borders of this State, and believe the local authority is ample to protect the people of every race and condition in life. An early reply is respectfully solicited.

JOHN C. BROWN, *Governor of Tennessee.*

WASHINGTON, September 19.—The President this afternoon sent the following telegram to Governor Brown, of Tennessee:

EXECUTIVE MANSION, *Sept.* 18, 1874.

Hon. JOHN C. BROWN, *Governor, Nashville, Tennessee:*

SIR: Your dispatch of yesterday has been received and referred to the United States District Attorney for the Western District of Tennessee for a report, as there is now no official information of his proceedings here. When his report is received I will give you a more definite answer, or have the Attorney-General do so. I will state, however, that it is very gratifying to know that the State authorities of Tennessee are disposed to suppress and punish a class of lawless acts so dangerous to life and so opposed to every political, financial and moral interest of the State. But the Constitution makes it my duty to enforce the acts of Congress, and Congress has passed laws giving the United States jurisdiction in such cases as are referred to in your dispatch.

No special order has been given to the Federal officials in Tennessee farther than the circular of September 3 of the Attorney-General, which is general in its nature and constitutes instructions to all Marshals and District Attorneys wherever violations of said acts may occur. I will add that the State and General Government, as you are well aware, may have concurrent jurisdiction over the same offence, as, for example, in cases of counterfeiting; and the action of the State authorities in such cases does not prevent the General Government from proceeding against the offenders. U. S. GRANT.

Letter of the Attorney-General to Gov. Brown.

[Official.]

DEPARTMENT OF JUSTICE,
WASHINGTON, *October* 10, 1874.

SIR: Referring to your dispatch to the President of the 18th ultimo, asking him to order, in respect to the Gibson County outrage, that no further arrests be made by the marshal, and that the parties already in his custody be turned over to the proper local tribunals for trial, and to the President's answer thereto, in which he stated that your telegram had been referred to the United States district attorney for the western district of Tennessee for information, and that when such report was received a more definite answer would be made to your request, I now have the honor to inclose herewith a copy of that report, detailing the circumstances under which the action of the Federal authorities was taken in that case.

No reasonable doubts can exist as to the jurisdiction of the courts of the United States upon the facts as stated by the district attorney, nor can there be any doubt that it is as much the duty of the President to enforce the so-called enforcement acts as any of the acts of Congress. To admit that persons charged and arrested for a criminal violation of the law of the United States ought to be turned over for trial to the tribunals of the State in which the crimes are committed, upon a demand of the executive thereof, because such persons may also be chargeable, upon the same state of facts, with a violation of State law, would be, as it seems to me, to surrender a power essential to the existence of the national authority, and introduce a practice that would tend more to retard than to promote the administration of justice.

Touching your statement that the parties may be punished under the laws of the State, and therefore that criminal proceedings in the United States court ought to be discontinued, I beg to cite, as a sufficient comment thereon, what Mr. Justice Grier says, in delivering the opinion of the Supreme Court of the United States in the case of Moore *vs.* The People of the State of Illinois, (14 How., 20,) as follows:

"Every citizen of the United States is also a citizen of a State or Territory. He may be said to owe allegiance to two sovereigns, and may be liable to punishment for an infraction of the laws of either. The same act may be an offense or transgression of the laws of both. Thus, an assault upon the marshal of the United States, and hindering him in the execution of legal process is a high offense against the United States, for which the perpetrator is liable to punishment; and the same act may be also a gross breach of the peace of the State, a riot, assault, or a murder, and subject the same person to a punishment, under the State laws, for a misdemeanor or felony. That either or both may (if they see fit) punish such an offender cannot be doubted."

I know of no reason to suppose that the parties arrested will not be fairly tried in the United States court, and, if innocent, acquitted; but, if found guilty, I am sure no one will object to their proper punishment because they were not convicted in a State court.

While, if consistent with his official duty, the President would be pleased to accede to your wishes, he does not feel at liberty to interfere with the judicial proceedings referred to, and they will, therefore, be allowed to proceed in the usual way to a final determination in the courts of the United States.

Very respectfully,

GEO. H. WILLIAMS, *Attorney-General.*

Hon. JOHN C. BROWN, *Governor, Nashville, Tenn.*

Texas.

The subjoined telegram belonging to the period covered by my last Hand-Book (for 1874,) is inserted to complete the record found upon pages 108–112:

WASHINGTON, *January* 12, 1874.
To Governor DAVIS, *Austin*, *Texas:*

Your dispatches and letters reciting the action of the Supreme Court of Texas in declaring the late election unconstitutional, and asking the use of troops to prevent apprehended violence, are received. The call is not made in accordance with the Constitution of the United States and acts of Congress under it, and cannot therefore be granted. The act of the Legislature of Texas providing for the recent election having received your approval, and both political parties having made nominations, and having conducted a political campaign under its provisions, would it not be prudent, as well as right, to yield to the verdict of the people as expressed by their ballots? U. S. GRANT.

Admission of Colorado.

Forty-Third Congress—Second Session.

[For previous proceedings on the bill (H. R. 435) see McPherson's Hand-Book of Politics for 1874, page 220.]

IN SENATE.

1875, February 24—The bill, having been amended, was passed—yeas 43, nays 13, absent 17:

YEAS—Messrs. Alcorn, Allison, Anthony, *Bogy*, Boutwell, Cameron of Pa., Chandler, Clayton, Conkling, Conover, Cragin, Dorsey, Edmunds, Ferry of Michigan, Flanagan, Frelinghuysen, HAMILTON of Texas, Hamlin, Harvey, Hitchcock, Howe, Ingalls, Jones, *Kelly*, Lewis, Logan, Mitchell, Morrill of Maine, Morrill of Vermont, Morton, Oglesby, Pease, Pratt, Robertson, Sargent, Sherman, Spencer, Stewart, TIPTON, Washburn, West, Windom, Wright—43.

NAYS—Messrs. *Bayard*, *Eaton*, *Goldthwaite*, *Gordon*, *Hager*, *Hamilton* of Maryland, *McCreery*, *Merrimon*, *Ransom*, *Saulsbury*, Sprague, *Stevenson*, *Stockton*—13.

IN HOUSE.

1875, March 3—The Senate amendments were agreed to and the bill passed—yeas 164, nays 76, not voting 48, this vote having been taken under an order of the House to take up business on the Speaker's table, a two-thirds vote being required to pass a bill:

YEAS—Messrs. Albert, Albright, Averill, Barber, Barrere, Barry, Bass, Begole, *Berry*, Biery, Bradley, H. C. Burchard, Burleigh, B. F. Butler, R. R. Butler, Cain, Cannon, Carpenter, Cason, *Caulfield*, Cessna, A. Clark, jr., Clayton, Clements, C. L. Cobb, S. A. Cobb, Coburn, *Comingo*, Conger, Corwin, Cotton, *Crittenden*, Crooke, Crounse, Curtis, Danford, Darrall, Dawes, Dobbins, Donnan, Duell, Dunnell, Eames, Farwell, Field, Fort, Foster, J. C. Freeman, Gooch, Gunckel, Hagans, Harmer, B. W. Harris, H. H. Harrison, Hathorn, Havens, J. R. Hawley, Hays, G. W. Hazelton, J. W. Hazelton, Hendee, Hodges, Hoskins, Howe, Hubbell, Hunter, Hurlbut, Hyde, Hynes, Kasson, Kellogg, *Knapp*, Lansing, *E. Lawrence*, W. Lawrence, B. Lewis, Lofland, Lowe, Lowndes, Lynch, Martin, McCrary, A. S. McDill, J. W. McDill, MacDougall, McKee, McNulta, Merriam, Monroe, Morey, *Morrison*, Myers, Negley, *Nesmith*, O'Neill, Orr, Packard, Packer, Page, I. C. Parker, R. C. Parsons, Pelham, Pendleton, W. A. Phillips, J. H. Platt, jr., T. C. Platt, Poland, Pratt, Rainey, Ransier, Rapier, W. H. Ray, Richmond, J. W. Robinson, Rusk, Sawyer, H. B. Sayler, *Schell*, Sener, Sessions, Shanks, Sheats, Sheldon, Sherwood, L. D. Shoemaker, Sloan, *Sloss*, W. B. Small, Smart, A. H. Smith, G. L. Smith, H. B. Smith, J. A. Smith, Sprague, Stanard, Starkweather, C. A. Stevens, St. John, Stowell, Strait, Taylor, C. Y. Thomas, J. M. Thompson, Todd, W. Townsend, Tremain, Tyner, Waldron, A. S. Wallace, Walls, J. D. Ward, M. L. Ward, *E. Wells*, Wheeler, A. White, Whiteley, G. Willard, C. G. Williams, J. M. S. Williams, W. Williams, W. B. Williams, J. Wilson, J. M. Wilson, Woodworth—164.

NAYS—Messrs. *G. M. Adams*, *Archer*, *Arthur*, *Ashe*, *Atkins*, *Banning*, *Barnum*, *Beck*, *H. P. Bell*, *Bland*, *Blount*, *Bowen*, *Bright*, *Bromberg*, *J. Y. Brown*, *Buckner*, *J. B. Clark, jr.*, *Clymer*, *Cook*, *Cox*, *Crossland*, *Durham*, *Eldredge*, *Finck*, *Giddings*, *Glover*, *Gunter*, *R. Hamilton*, *Hancock*, *H. R. Harris*, *J. T. Harris*, *Hatcher*, *Hereford*, *Herndon*, E. R. Hoar, *Holman*, *Hunton*, *Lamar*, Lawson, *Leach*, *Luttrell*, *Magee*, *Marshall*, *McLean*, *Milliken*, *Mills*, *Neal*, *O'Brien*, *H. W. Parker*, *C. N. Potter*, *Randall*, *Read*, *W. M. Robbins*, E. H. Roberts, *W. R. Roberts*, *M. Sayler*, Scofield, *Sheridan*, J. Q. Smith, Snyder, *Southard*, *Speer*, *Standiford*, *Stone*, *Storm*, *Swann*, *R. B. Vance*, *Waddell*, *Whitehead*, *Whitehouse*, *Whitthorne*, C. W. Willard, *Willie*, *E. K. Wilson*, *F. Wood*, *P. M. B. Young*—76.

Admission of New Mexico.

Forty-Third Congress—Second Session.

[For previous proceedings on the bill (H. R. 2418) see McPherson's Hand-Book of Politics for 1874, page 220.]

IN SENATE.

1875. February 24—The bill having been amended was passed—yeas 31, nays 11, absent 31;

YEAS—Messrs. Alcorn, Allison, Anthony, *Bogy*, Boutwell, Cameron of Pa., Cragin, *Dennis*, Dorsey, Ferry of Michigan, Flanagan, Gilbert, *Gordon*, Hamlin, Harvey, Hitchcock, Ingalls, *Kelly*, Lewis, Logan, Mitchell, Oglesby, Patterson, Ramsey, Sargent, Spencer, Stewart, TIPTON, West, Windom, Wright—31.

NAYS—Messrs. Edmunds, Frelinghuysen, *Hamilton* of Maryland, *McCreery*, *Merrimon*, Morton, Pease, Pratt, *Saulsbury*, *Stevenson*, *Stockton*—11.

IN HOUSE.

1875. March 3—The Senate amendments were disagreed to, yeas, 154, nays, 87, not voting 49 (two-thirds not having voted in the affirmative under the order above alluded to):

YEAS—Messrs. Albert, Albright, Averill, Barber, Barrere, Barry, Bass, Begole, Biery, Bradley,

Buckner, Bundy, H. C. Burchard, Burleigh, B. F. Butler, R. R. Butler, Cain, Cannon, Carpenter, Cason, *Caulfield*, Cessna, A. Clark, jr., Clayton, Clements, C. L. Cobb, S. A. Cobb, Coburn, Conger, Corwin, Cotton, *Creamer*, Crounse, Curtis, Danford, Dawes, Dobbins, Donnan, Duell, Dunnell, Eames, Farwell, Field, Fort, Foster, J. C. Freeman, Gooch, Gunckel, Hagans, Harmer, B. W. Harris, H. H. Harrison, Hathorn, Havens, Hays, G. W. Hazelton, J. W. Hazelton, Hendee, Hodges, Hoskins, Howe, Hubbell, Hunter, Hurlbut, Hyde, Hynes, Kasson, Kellogg, *Knapp*, *Lamison*, Lansing, *E. Lawrence*, B. Lewis, Lofland, Loughridge, Lowe, Lowndes, Lynch, Martin, Maynard, McCrary, A. S. McDill, J. W. McDill, MacDougall, McKee, McNulta, Monroe, Morey, Myers, Negley, O'Neill, Orr, Packard, Packer Page, I. C. Parker, R. C. Parsons, Pelham, Pendleton, W. A. Phillips, Pike, J. H. Platt, jr., Rainey, Ransier, Rapier, W. H. Ray, Richmond, J. W. Robinson, Rusk, Sawyer, H. B. Sayler, I. W. Scudder, Sessions, Shanks, Sheats, Sheldon, Sherwood, L. D. Shoemaker, Sloan, *Sloss*, W. B. Small, Smart, A. H. Smith, G. L. Smith, H. B. Smith, J. A. Smith, Stanard, Starkweather, C. A. Stevens, St. John, Stowell, Strait, Taylor, C. Y. Thomas, J. M. Thompson, Todd, W. Townsend, Tremain, Tyner, *Waddell*, A. S. Wallace, Walls, J. D. Ward, M. L. Ward, A. White, Whiteley, Wilber, G. Willard, C. G. Williams, J. M. S. Williams, W. Williams, W. B. Williams, J. Wilson, J. M. Wilson—154.

NAYS—Messrs. *G. M. Adams*, *Archer*, *Arthur*, *Atkins*, *Barnum*, *Beck*, *H. P. Bell*, *Bland*, *Blount*, *Bowen*, *Bright*, *Bromberg*, *J. Y. Brown*, *J. B. Clark, jr.*, *Clymer*, *Comingo*, *Cook*, *Cox*, *Crittenden*, Crooke, *Crossland*, *Durham*, *Eldredge*, *Giddings*, *Glover*, *Gunter*, *R. Hamilton Hancock*. *H. R. Harris*, *J. T. Harris*, *Hatcher* J. R. Hawley, *Hereford*, *Herndon*, E. R. Hoar, *Holman*, *Hunton*, *Lamar*, Lawson, *Luttrell*, *Magee*, *Marshall*, *McLean*, Merriam, *Milliken*, *Mills*, *Mitchell*, *Neal*, *Niblack*, *O'Brien*, *Perry*, W. W. Phelps, Pierce, *C. N. Potter*, *Randall*, *Read*, *W. M. Robbins*, E. H. Roberts, *W. R. Roberts*, *M. Sayler*, *Schell*, Scofield, H. J. Scudder, Sener, *Sheridan*, J. Q. Smith, Snyder, *Southard*, *Speer*, Sprague, *Standiford*, *Stone*, *Storm*, *Swann*, *R. B. Vance*, Waldron, *E. Wells*, *Whitehead*, *Whitehouse*, *Whitthorne*, C. W. Willard, *Willie*, *E. K. Wilson*, *F. Wood*, *P. M. B. Young*—87.

V.

PROPOSED AMENDMENTS TO THE CONSTITUTION OF THE UNITED STATES, SECOND SESSION OF FORTY-THIRD CONGRESS.

[For other Amendments, see McPherson's Hand-book of Politics for 1874, pp. 53–58, and p. 215.]

IN SENATE.

1874, December 15—Mr. WRIGHT proposed a new article:

The President and Vice-President of the United States shall be elected by direct vote of the people, and by ballot. They shall hold their office for the term of six years; and the President shall be ineligible to a re-election.

Every male citizen of the United States, of the age of twenty-one years and upward, residing in each State, District, and Territory thereof, who shall not have been convicted of felony, shall, after registration, be a competent voter at all elections for President and Vice-President of the United States.

The election for President and Vice-President shall be held at the same time in each State, District, and Territory of the United States; and it shall require a majority of all the votes cast to elect to either office. If no person shall receive such majority, another election shall be held, at which the two persons who shall have received the highest vote for either office at the previous election shall alone be voted for, and all votes cast for any other person shall be null and void.

The returns of all elections for President and Vice-President shall be sealed up and transmitted to the Chief Justice of the Supreme Court of the United States. That court shall open and canvass said returns; they shall hear and determine all questions arising thereon; they shall ascertain and declare the result of the election; and grant a certificate accordingly to the persons elected.

The Congress shall have power to pass all laws necessary and proper to carry into effect the provisions of this article.

IN HOUSE.

December 8—Mr. ELLIS H. ROBERTS proposed a new article:

Congress shall not make anything but gold and silver coin a tender in payment of individual debts.

Congress shall pass no law impairing the obligations of contracts.

December 14—Mr. STORM proposed a new article:

The executive power shall be vested in a President of the United States of America. He shall hold his office during the term of six years. No person elected to the office of President shall thereafter be eligible for re-election.

1875, January 25—Mr. MAGINNIS proposed a new article:

Each duly organized Territory of the United States shall be entitled to one Representative in Congress, and also to choose one elector to cast one vote in the election of President and Vice-President of the United States. These Representatives and electors shall have the same qualifications and be entitled to the same rights and privileges as the Representatives and electors from the several States.

On the Presidential Term.

IN HOUSE.

1875, January 26—Mr. POTTER, from the Committee on the Judiciary, reported the following joint resolution:

From and after the next election for a President of the United States the President shall hold his office during the term of six years, and, together with the Vice-President chosen for the same term, be elected in the manner as now provided or may hereafter be provided: but neither the President nor the Vice-President, when the office of President has devolved upon him, shall be eligible for re-election as President.

Mr. JASPER D. WARD moved to lay the resolution on the table, which was disagreed to—yeas 98, nays 139, not voting 51, as follow:

YEAS—Messrs. Averill, Barber, Barrere, Barry, Biery, Bradley, H. C. Burchard, Burleigh, Burrows, B. F. Butler, R. R. Butler, Cain, Carpenter, Cason, A. Clark, jr., F. Clarke, Clements, C. L. Cobb, S. A. Cobb, Coburn, Cotton, Crutchfield, Dobbins, Donnan, Eames, Farwell, Fort, Hagans, R. S. Hale, Harmer, B. W. Harris, J. B. Hawley, G. W. Hazelton, E. R. Hoar, Hodges, Hooper, Houghton, Howe, Hubbell, Hurlbut, Hyde, Kelley, Lofland, Lowe, Lynch, Martin, Maynard, J. W. McDill, Moore, Myers, Negley, Nunn, O'Neill, Orr, Orth, Packard, Page, I. C. Parker, Pelham, Pendleton, T. C. Platt, Pratt, Rainey, Ransier, Rapier, W. H. Ray, Richmond, Scofield, H. J. Scudder, I. W. Scudder, Sessions, Shanks, Sheats, Sheldon, Sherwood, L. D. Shoemaker, Sloan, W. B. Small, Smart, Sprague, Starkweather, St. John, Strait, Taylor, C. R. Thomas, C. Y. Thomas, J. M. Thompson, Todd, W. Townsend, Tyner, Waldron, A. S. Wallace, J. D. Ward, M. L. Ward, Wilber, C. G. Williams, W. Williams, J. Wilson—98.

NAYS—Messrs. *G. M. Adams*, Albert, Albright, *Archer*, *Arthur*, *Ashe*, *Atkins*, *Banning*, Bass, *Beck*, Begole, *Bell*, *Berry*, *Bland*, *Blount*, *Bowen*, *Bright*, *Bromberg*, *J. Y. Brown*, *Buckner*, Buffinton, Bundy, *J. H. Caldwell*, Cannon, Cessna, Chittenden, *J. B. Clark, jr.*, Clayton, *Clymer*, *Comingo*, Conger, *Cook*, *Cox*, *Creamer*, *Crittenden*, *Crossland*, Crounse, *John J. Davis*, Dawes, Dunnell, *Durham*, *Eldredge*, Field, *Finck*, Foster, Garfield, *Giddings*, *Glover*, Gooch, Gunckel, *Gunter*, *R. Hamilton*, *Hancock*, *H. R. Harris*, *J. T. Harris*, H. H. Harrison, *Hatcher*, Hathorn, Havens, J. R. Hawley, *Hereford*, *Herndon*, *Holman*, Hoskins, Hunter, *Hunton*, Kasson, Kellogg, Killinger, *Knapp*, *Lamar*, W. Lawrence, Lawson, *Leach*, Lowndes, *Luttrell*, *Magee*, McCrary, *McLean*, Merriam, *Milliken*, *Mills*, Monroe, Morey, *Morrison*, *Neal*, *Nesmith*, *Niblack*, Niles, *O'Brien*, *H. W. Parker*, *Perry*, W. A. Phillips, Pierce, Poland, *C. N. Potter*, *Randall*, *Read*, *W. M. Robbins*, E. H. Roberts, J. W. Robinson, S. Ross, *M. Sayler*, *Schell*, *J. G. Schumaker*, *Sloss*, A. H. Smith, H. B. Smith, J. A. Smith, J. Q. Smith, Snyder, *Southard*, *Speer*, Stanard, *Standiford*, *Stone*, *Storm*, Strawbridge, *Swann*, Sypher, Thornburgh, Tremain, *R. B. Vance*, *Waddell*, *E. Wells*, A. White, *Whitehead*, Whiteley, *Whitthorne*, C. W. Willard, G. Willard, J. M. S. Williams, W. B. Williams, *Willie*, J. M. Wilson, *Wolfe*, *F. Wood*, *J. D. Young*, *P. M. B. Young*.—139.

NOT VOTING—Messrs. *Barnum*, Corwin, Crooke, Curtis, Danford, Darrall, *De Witt*, Duell, *Eden*, J. C. Freeman, Frye, E. Hale, Hays, J. W. Hazelton, Hendee, Hersey, G. F. Hoar, Hynes, *Kendall*, *Lamison*, Lamport, Lansing, B. Lewis, Loughridge, *Marshall*, A. S. McDill, MacDougall, McKee, McNulta, *Mitchell*, Packer, R. C. Parsons, W. W. Phelps, Pike, J. H. Platt jr., Purman, *W. R. Roberts*, *J. C. Robinson*, Rusk, Sawyer, H. B. Sayler, Sener, G. L. Smith, W. A. Smith, *A. H. Stephens*, Stowell, Walls, Wheeler, *Whitehouse*, *E. K. Wilson*, Woodworth—51.

Mr. J. D. WARD moved to recommit the resolution to the Committee on the Judiciary; which was disagreed to—yeas 109, nays 123, not voting 56, as follow:

YEAS—Messrs. Averill, Barber, Barrere, Bass, Begole, Biery, Bradley, H. C. Burchard, Burleigh, Burrows, B. F. Butler, R. R. Butler, Carpenter, Cason, A. Clark, jr., F. Clarke, Clayton, Clements, C. L. Cobb, S. A. Cobb, Coburn, Conger, Cotton, Crutchfield, Donnan, Dunnell, Eames, Farwell, Fort, Gooch, Hagans, R. S. Hale, Harmer, B. W. Harris, Hathorn, Havens, J. B. Hawley, G. W. Hazelton, E. R. Hoar, Hodges, Hooper, Hoskins, Houghton, Howe, Hurlbut, Hyde, Kelley, B. Lewis, Lofland, Loughridge, Lowe, Lynch, Martin, Maynard, McCrary, J. W. McDill, McNulta, Moore, Myers, Negley, Nunn, O'Neill, Orr, Orth, Packard, Pendleton, T. C. Platt, Poland, Pratt, Rainey, Ransier, Rapier, W. H. Ray, Richmond, S. Ross, Rusk, Scofield, H. J. Scudder, I. W. Scudder, Sener, Sessions, Shanks, Sheats, Sherwood, Sloan, W. B. Small, Smart, A. H. Smith, St. John, Strait, Taylor, C. R. Thomas, C. Y. Thomas, J. M. Thompson, Thornburgh, Todd, W. Townsend, Tyner, Waldron, A. S. Wallace, J. D. Ward, M. L. Ward, Whiteley, Wilber, C. G. Williams, J. M. S. Williams, W. Williams, W. B. Williams, J. Wilson—109.

NAYS—Messrs. *G. M. Adams*, Albert, Albright, *Archer*, *Arthur*, *Ashe*, *Atkins*, *Banning*, *Beck*, *H. P. Bell*, *Berry*, *Bland*, *Blount*, *Bowen*, *Bright*, *Bromberg*, *J. Y. Brown*, *Buckner*, Buffinton, *J. H. Caldwell*, Cannon, Cessna, Chittenden, *J. B. Clark, jr.*, *Clymer*, *Comingo*, *Cook*, *Cox*, *Creamer*, *Crittenden*, *Crossland*, Crounse, *John J. Davis*, Dawes, *Durham*, *Eldredge*, Field, *Finck*, Foster, J. C. Freeman, *Glover*, Gunckel, *Gunter*, *R. Hamilton*, *Hancock*, *H. R. Harris*, *J. T. Harris*, H. H. Harrison, *Hatcher*, J. R. Hawley, *Hereford*, *Herndon*, *Holman*, Hunter, *Hunton*, Kasson, Kellogg, Killinger, *Knapp*, *Lamison*, W. Lawrence, Lawson, *Leach*, Lowndes, *Luttrell*, *Magee*, McKee, *McLean*, Merriam, *Milliken*,

Mills, Monroe, *Morrison*, *Neal*, *Nesmith*, *Niblack*, Niles, *O'Brien*, *H. W. Parker*, *Perry*, W. W. Phelps, W. A. Phillips, Pierce, *C. N. Potter*, *Randall*, *Read*, *W. M. Robbins*, E. H. Roberts, J. W. Robinson, Sawyer, *M. Sayler*, *Schell*, *J. G. Schumaker*, L. D. Shoemaker, *Sloss*, H. B. Smith, J. A. Smith, J. Q. Smith, *Southard*, *Speer*, Sprague, Stanard, *Standiford*, *A. H. Stephens*, *Stone*, *Storm*, Strawbridge, *Swann*, Tremain, *R. B. Vance*, *Waddell*, *E. Wells*, A. White, *Whitehead*, *Whitthorne*, C. W. Willard, G. Willard, *Willie*, J. M. Wilson, *Wolfe F. Wood*, *J. D. Young*, *P. M. B. Young*—123.

The question being taken on the passage of the resolution, it was disagreed to—yeas 134, nays 104, (not voting 50), two-thirds not having voted in the affirmative as follow:

YEAS—Messrs. Albert, Albright, *Archer*, *Arthur*, *Ashe*, *Atkins*, *Banning*, *Beck*, Begole, *H. P. Bell*, *Bland*, *Blount*, *Bowen*, *Bright*, *Bromberg*, *J. Y. Brown*, *Buckner*, Buffinton, Bundy, *J. H. Caldwell*, Cannon, Cessna, Chittenden, *J. B. Clark, jr.*, Clayton, *Clymer*, *Comingo*, *Cook*, *Cox*, *Creamer*, *Crittenden*, *Crossland*, Crounse, Darrall, *John J. Davis*, Dawes, Dunnell, *Durham*, *Eldredge*, Field, *Finck*, Foster, Garfield, *Giddings*, *Glover*, Gooch, Gunckel, *Gunter*, *R. Hamilton*, *Hancock*, *H. R. Harris*, *J. T. Harris*, H. H. Harrison, *Hatcher*, Havens, J. R. Hawley, J. W. Hazelton, *Hereford*, *Herndon*, *Holman*, Hoskins, Hunter, *Hunton*, Kasson, Kellogg, Killinger, *Knapp*, *Lamison*, W. Lawrence, Lawson, *Leach*, Lowndes, *Luttrell*, *Magee*, McCrary, Merriam, *Milliken*, *Mills*, Monroe, *Morrison*, *Neal*, *Nesmith*, *Niblack*, Niles, *O'Brien*, *H. W. Parker*, *Perry*, W. W. Phelps, W. A. Phillips, Pierce, Poland, *C. N. Potter*, *Randall*, *Read*, *W. M. Robbins*, E. H. Roberts, J. W. Robinson, S. Ross, Sawyer, *M. Sayler*, *Schell*, *J. G. Schumaker*, H. J. Scudder, *Sloss*, A. H. Smith, H. B. Smith, J. A. Smith, J. Q. Smith, *Southard*, *Speer*, Stanard, *Standiford*, *A. H. Stephens*, *Stone*, *Storm*, Strait, Strawbridge, Thornburgh, Tremain, *R. B. Vance*, *Waddell*, *E. Wells*, *Whitehead*, *Whitthorne*, C. W. Willard, G. Willard, J. M. S. Williams, W. B. Williams, *Willie*, J. M. Wilson, *Wolfe*, *F. Wood*, *J. D. Young*, *P. M. B. Young*—134.

NAYS—Messrs. Averill, Barber, Barry, Biery, Bradley, H. C. Burchard, Burleigh, Burrows, B. F. Butler, R. R. Butler, Cain, Carpenter, Cason, A. Clark, jr., F. Clarke, Clements, C. L. Cobb, S. A. Cobb, Coburn, Conger, Cotton, Crutchfield, Dobbins, Donnan, Eames, Farwell, Fort, Hagans, E. Hale, R. S. Hale, Harmer, B. W. Harris, Hathorn, J. B. Hawley, G. W. Hazelton, E. R. Hoar, Hodges, Houghton, Howe, Hubbell, Hurlbut, Hyde, Kelley, B. Lewis, Lofland, Loughridge, Lowe, Lynch, Martin, Maynard, J. W. McDill, McKee, McNulta, Moore, Myers, Negley, Nunn, O'Neill, Orth, Packard, Page, I. C. Parker, Pelham, Pendleton, J. H. Platt, jr., T. C. Platt, Pratt, Rainey, Ransier, Rapier, W. H. Ray, Richmond, Rusk, Scofield, I. W. Scudder, Sener, Sessions, Shanks, Sheats, Sherwood, L. D. Shoemaker, Sloan, W. B. Small, Smart, Snyder, Sprague, Starkweather, St. John, Taylor, C. R. Thomas, C. Y. Thomas, J. M. Thompson, Todd, W. Townsend, Tyner, Waldron, A. S. Wallace, J. D. Ward, M. L. Ward, Whiteley, Wilber, C. G. Williams. W. Williams, J. Wilson—104.

IN HOUSE.

1875, January 26—Mr. HARRISON, from the Committee on Elections, reported the following joint resolution:

SECTION 1. The President and Vice-President shall be elected by the direct vote of the people in the manner following: Each State shall be divided into districts equal in number to the number of Representatives to which the State may be entitled in the Congress, to be composed of contiguous territory, and to be as nearly equal in population as may be; and the person having the highest number of votes in each district for President shall receive the vote of that district, which shall count one presidential vote: but no voter in any State shall vote for candidates for President and Vice-President who are both citizens in the same State with himself.

SEC. 2. The person having the highest number of votes for President in a State shall receive two presidential votes from the State at large.

SEC. 3. The person having the highest number of presidential votes in the United States shall be President.

SEC. 4. If two persons have the same number of votes in any State, it being the highest number, they shall receive each one presidential vote from the State at large; and if more than two persons shall each have the same number of votes in any State, it being the highest number, no presidential vote shall be counted from the State at large. If more persons than one shall have the same number of votes, it being the highest number in any district, no presidential vote shall be counted from that district.

SEC. 5. The foregoing provisions shall apply to the election of Vice-President.

SEC. 6. The Congress shall have power to provide for holding and conducting the elections of President and Vice-President. The returns of such elections shall be made to the Supreme Court of the United States within thirty days after the election. Said court shall, under such rules as may be prescribed by law, or by the court in the absence of law, determine any contest in respect of such returns, canvass the same, and declare, within ninety days after such election, by public proclamation, who is elected President and who is elected Vice-President.

SEC. 7. The States shall be divided into districts by the Legislatures thereof, but the Congress may at any time by law make or alter the same.

SEC. 8. No person who has been a Justice of the Supreme Court shall be eligible to the office of President or Vice-President.

Mr. H. BOARDMAN SMITH reported the following as a substitute:

SECTION 1. The President and Vice-President shall be elected by the direct vote of the people in the manner following, but no voter in any State shall vote for candidates for President and Vice-President who are both citizens in the same State with himself.

SEC. 2. In counting the votes the aggregate popular vote in each State for President and

Vice-President shall be respectively divided by the number of Representatives apportioned to such State in the House of Representatives, and twice the result or quotient shall be added to the candidate having the highest number of the popular vote in such State for President, as and for the State vote for such candidate. The person having the highest number of votes in all the States, including the popular vote and the State vote, shall be President, and the person having the highest number of votes in all the States, including the popular vote and the State vote, for Vice-President, shall be Vice-President.

SEC. 3. The Congress shall have power to provide for holding and conducting the elections of President and Vice-President. The returns of such elections shall be made to the Supreme Court of the United States within thirty days after the election. Said Court shall, under such rules as may be prescribed by law, or by the court in the absence of law, determine any contest in respect to such returns, canvass the same, and declare, within ninety days after such election, by public proclamation, who is elected President and who is elected Vice-President.

SEC. 4. No person who has been a Justice of the Supreme Court shall be eligible to the office of President or Vice-President.

No vote was taken upon either.

VI.

PRESIDENT GRANT'S SIXTH AND SEVENTH ANNUAL MESSAGES.

President Grant's Sixth Annual Message, Dec. 7, 1874.

[For his first Inaugural, and his first Annual, see McPherson's History of Reconstruction, pages 416, 533–540; for his second and third Annual, see McPherson's Hand-Book of Politics for 1872, pages 16–27; for his second Inaugural and his fourth and fifth Annual, see McPherson's Hand-Book of Politics for 1874, pages 112–126.]

To the Senate and House of Representatives:

Since the convening of Congress one year ago, the nation has undergone a prostration in business and industries such as has not been witnessed with us for many years. Speculation as to the causes for this prostration might be indulged in without profit, because as many theories would be advanced as there would be independent writers—those who expressed their own views without borrowing—upon the subject. Without indulging in theories as to the cause of this prostration, therefore, I will call your attention only to the fact, and to some plain questions as to which it would seem there should be no disagreement. During this prostration two essential elements of prosperity have been most abundant: labor and capital. Both have been largely unemployed. Where security has been undoubted, capital has been attainable at very moderate rates. Where labor has been wanted, it has been found in abundance at cheap rates, compared with what—of necessaries and comforts of life—could be purchased with the wages demanded. Two great elements of prosperity, therefore, have not been denied us. A third might be added: our soil and climate are unequaled, within the limits of any contiguous territory under one nationality, for its variety of products to feed and clothe a people, and in the amount of surplus to spare io feed less favored peoples. Therefore, with these facts in view, it seems to me that wise statesmanship, at this session of Congress, would dictate legislation, ignoring the past, directing in proper channels these great elements of prosperity to any people. Debt—debt abroad—is the only element that can, with always a sound currency, enter into our affairs to cause any continued depression in the industries and prosperity of our people. A great conflict for national existence made necassary, for temporary purposes, the raising of large sums of money from whatever source attainable. It made it necessary, in the wisdom of Congress—and I do not doubt their wisdom in the premises, regarding the necessity of the times—to devise a system of national currency which it proved to be impossible to keep on a par with the recognized currency of the civilized world. This begot a spirit of speculation involving an extravagance and luxury not required for the happiness or prosperity of a people, and involving, both directly and indirectly, foreign indebtedness. The currency being of fluctuating value, and therefore unsafe to hold for legitimate transactions requiring money, became a subject of speculation in itself. These two causes, however, have involved us in a foreign indebtedness, contracted in good faith by borrower and lender, which should be paid in coin, and according to the bond agreed upon when the debt was contracted—gold or its equivalent. The good faith of the Government cannot be violated toward creditors without national disgrace.

But our commerce should be encouraged; American ship-building and carrying capacity increased; foreign markets sought for products of the soil and manufactories, to the end that we may be able to pay these debts. Where a new market can be created for the sale of our products, either of the soil, the mine, or the manufactory, a new means is discovered of utilizing our idle capital and labor to the advantage of the whole people. But in my judgment the first step toward accomplishing this object is to secure a currency of fixed, stable value; a currency good wherever civilization reigns; one which, if it becomes superabundant with one people, will find a market with some other; a currency which has as its basis the labor necessary to produce it, which will give to it its value. Gold and silver are now the recognized medium of exchange the civilized world over; and to this we should return with the least practicable delay. In view of the pledges of the American Congress when our present legal-tender system was adopted, and the debt contracted, there should be no delay—certainly no unnecessary delay—in fixing by legislation a method by which we will return to specie. To the accomplishment of this end I invite your special attention. I believe firmly that there can be no prosperous and permanent revival of business and industries until a policy is adopted, with legislation to carry it out, looking to a return to a specie basis. It is easy to conceive that the debtor and speculative classes may think it of value to them to make so-called money abundant until they can throw a portion of their burdens upon others. But even these, I believe, would be disappointed in the result if a course should be pursued which will keep in doubt the value of the legal-tender medium of exchange. A revival of productive industry is needed by all classes—by none more than the holders of property, of whatever sort, with debts to liquidate from realization upon its sale. But admitting that these two classes of citizens are to be benefited by expansion, would it be honest to give it? Would not the general loss be too great to justify such relief? Would it not be just as honest and prudent to authorize each debtor to issue his own legal-tenders to the extent of his liabilities? Than to do this would it not be safer, for fear of over-issues by unscrupulous creditors, to say that all debt-obligations are obliterated in the United States, and now we commence anew, each possessing all he has at the time free from incumbrance? These propositions are too absurd to be entertained for a moment by thinking or honest people. Yet every delay in preparation for final resumption partakes of this dishonesty, and is only less in degree as the hope is held out that a convenient season will at last arrive for the good work of redeeming our pledges to commence. It will never come, in my opinion, except by positive action by Congress, or by national disasters which will destroy, for a time at least, the credit of the individual and the State at large. A sound currency might be reached by total bankruptcy and discredit of the integrity of the nation and of individuals. I believe it is in the power of Congress, at this session, to devise such legislation as will renew confidence, revive all the industries, start us on a career of prosperity to last for many years, and to save the credit of the nation and of the people. Steps toward the return to a specie basis are the great requisites to this devoutly to be sought for end. There are others which I may touch upon hereafter.

A nation dealing in a currency below that of specie in value labors under two great disadvantages. First, having no use for the world's acknowledged medium of exchange, gold and silver, these are driven out of the country, because there is no need for their use; second, the medium of exchange in use being of a fluctuating value—for after all it is only worth just what it will purchase of gold and silver, metals having an intrinsic value just in proportion to the honest labor it takes to produce them—a larger margin must be allowed for profit by the manufacturer and producer. It is months from the date of production to the date of realization. Interest upon capital must be charged, and risk of fluctuation in the value of that which is to be received in payment added. Hence high prices, acting as a protection to the foreign producer, who receives nothing in exchange for the products of his skill and labor except a currency good at a stable value the world over.

It seems to me that nothing is clearer than that the greater part of the burden of existing prostration, for the want of a sound financial system, falls upon the working man, who must, after all, produce the wealth, and the salaried man who superintends and conducts business. The burden falls upon them in two ways: by the deprivation of employment, and by the decreased purchasing power of their salaries. It is the duty of Congress to devise the method of correcting the evils which are acknowledged to exist, and not mine. But I will venture to suggest two or three things which seem to me as absolutely necessary to a return to specie payments, the first great requisite in a return to prosperity. The legal-tender clause to the law authorizing the issue of currency by the National Government should be repealed, to take effect as to all contracts entered into after a day fixed in the repealing act; not to apply, however, to payments of salaries by Government or for other expenditures now provided by law to be paid in currency in the interval pending between repeal and final resumption. Provision should be made by which the Secretary of the Treasury can obtain gold as it may become necessary from time to time from the date when specie redemption commences. To this might and should be added a revenue sufficiently in excess of expenses to insure an accumulation of gold in the Treasury to sustain permanent redemption.

I commend this subject to your careful consideration, believing that a favorable solution is attainable, and, if reached by this Congress, that the present and future generations will ever gratefully remember it as their deliverer from a thraldom of evil and disgrace.

With resumption, free banking may be authorized with safety, giving the same full protection to bill-holders which they have under existing laws. Indeed, I would regard free banking as essential. It would give proper elasticity to the currency. As more currency should be required for the transaction of legitimate business, new banks would be started, and in turn banks would wind up their business when it was found that there was a snperabundance of currency. The experience and judgment of the people can best decide just how much currency is required for the transaction of the business of the country. It is unsafe to leave the settlement of this question to Congress, the Secretary of the Treasury, or the Executive. Congress should make the regulation under which banks may exist, but should not make banking a monopoly by limiting the amount of redeemable paper currency that shall be authorized. Such importance do I attach to this subject, and so earnestly do I commend it to your attention, that I give it prominence by introducing it at the beginning of this message.

* * In connection with this subject I call the attention of Congress to a generally conceded fact that the great proportion of the Chinese immigrants who come to our shores do not come voluntarily, to make their homes with us and their labor productive of general prosperity, but come under contracts with head-men, who own them almost absolutely. In a worse form does this apply to Chinese women. Hardly a perceptible percentage of them perform any honorable labor, but they are brought for shameful purposes, to the disgrace of the communities where settled and to the great demoralization of the youth of those localities. If this evil practice can be legislated against, it will be my pleasure as well as duty to enforce any regulations to secure so desirable an end. * * *

* * The deplorable strife in Cuba continues without any marked change in the relative advantages of the contending forces. The insurrection continues, but Spain has gained no superiority. Six years of strife give to the insurrection a significance which cannot be denied. Its duration and the tenacity of its adherence, together with the absence of manifested power of suppression on the part of Spain, cannot be controverted, and may make some positive steps on the part of other powers a matter of self-necessity. I had confidently hoped at this time to be able to announce the arrangement of some of the important questions between this Government and that of Spain, but the negotiations have been protracted. The unhappy intestine dissensions of Spain command our profound sympathy, and must be accepted as perhaps a cause of some delay. An early settlement, in part at least, of the questions between the governments is hoped. In the meantime, awaiting the results of immediately-pending negotiations, I defer a further and fuller communication on the subject of the relations of this country and Spain.

The report of the Secretary of the Treasury, which by law is made directly to Congress and forms no part of this message, will show the receipts and expenditures of the Government for the last fiscal year, the amount received from each source of revenue, and the amount paid out for each of the departments of Government. It will be observed from this report that the amount of receipts over expenditures has been but $2,344,882.30 for the fiscal year ending June 30, 1874, and that for the current fiscal year the estimated receipts over expenditures will not much exceed nine millions of dollars. In view of the large national debt existing and the obligation to add 1 per cent. per annum to the sinking fund—a sum amounting now to over $34,000,000 per annum—I submit whether revenues should not be increased or expenditures diminished to reach this amount of surplus. Not to provide for the sinking fund is a partial failure to comply with the contracts and obligations of the Government.

At the last session of Congress a very considerable reduction was made in rates of taxation and in the number of articles submitted to taxation. The question may well be asked whether or not, in some instances, unwisely. In connection with this subject, too, I venture the opinion that the means of collecting the revenue, especially from imports, have been so embarrassed by legislation, as to make it questionable whether or not large amounts are not lost by failure to collect, to the direct loss of the Treasury, and to the prejudice of the interests of honest importers and taxpayers.

The Secretary of the Treasury, in his report, favors legislation looking to an early return to specie payments, thus supporting views previously expressed in this message. He also recommends economy in appropriations; calls attention to the loss of revenue from repealing the tax on tea and coffee, without benefit to the consumer; recommends an increase of ten cents a gallon on whisky; and further, that no modification be made in the banking and currency bill passed at the last session of Congress, unless modification should become necessary by reason of the adoption of measures for returning to specie payments. In these recommendations I cordially join. I would suggest to Congress the propriety of readjusting the tariff so as to increase the revenue and at the same time decrease the number of articles upon which duties are levied. Those articles which enter into our manufactures, and are not produced at home, it seems to me should be entered free. Those articles of manufacture which we produce a constituent part of, but do not produce the whole, that part which we do not produce should enter free also. I will instance fine wool, dyes, &c. These articles must be imported to form a part of the manufacture of the higher grades of woolen goods. Chemicals used as dyes, compounded in medicines, and used in various ways in manufactures, come under this class. The introduction free of duty of such wools as we do not produce would stimulate the manufacture of goods requiring the use of those we do produce, and therefore would be a benefit to home production. There are many articles entering into "home manufactures" which we do not produce ourselves, the tariff upon which increases the cost of producing the manufactured article. All corrections in this regard are in the direction of bringing labor and capital in harmony with each other, and of supplying one of the elements of prosperity so much needed.

The report of the Secretary of War, herewith attached, and forming a part of this message, gives all the information concerning the operations, wants, and necessities of the Army, and contains many suggestions and recommendations which I commend to your special attention. *

The efficiency of the Navy has been largely increased during the last year. * * *

The report of the Postmaster-General herewith attached, shows that there was an increase of revenue in his Department in 1873 over the previous year of $1,674,411, and an increase of cost of carrying the mails and paying employés of $3,041,468.91. The report of the Postmaster-General gives interesting statistics of his Department, and compares them with the corresponding statistics of a year ago, showing a growth in every branch of the Department. * * *

Your attention will be drawn to the unsettled

condition of affairs in some of the Southern States.

On the 14th of September last the governor of Louisiana called upon me, as provided by the Constitution and laws of the United States, to aid in suppressing domestic violence in that State. This call was made in view of a proclamation issued on that day by D. B. Penn, claiming that he was elected lieutenant-governor in 1872, and calling upon the militia of the State to arm, assemble, and drive from power the usurpers, as he designated the officers of the State government. On the next day I issued my proclamation, commanding the insurgents to disperse within five days from the date thereof, and subsequently learned that on that day they had taken forcible possession of the State-house. Steps were taken by me to support the existing and recognized State government; but before the expiration of the five days the insurrectionary movement was practically abandoned, and the officers of the State government, with some minor exceptions, resumed their powers and duties. Considering that the present State administration of Louisiana has been the only government in that State for nearly two years, that it has been tacitly acknowledged and acquiesced in as such by Congress, and more than once expressly recognized by me, I regarded it as my clear duty, when legally called upon for that purpose, to prevent its overthrow by an armed mob under pretense of fraud and irregularity in the election of 1872.

I have heretofore called the attention of Congress to this subject, stating that on account of the frauds and forgeries committed at said election, and because it appears that the returns thereof were never legally canvassed, it was impossible to tell thereby who were chosen; but from the best sources of information at my command I have always believed that the present State officers received a majority of the legal votes actually cast at that election. I repeat what I said in my special message of February 23, 1873, that in the event of no action by Congress I must continue to recognize the government heretofore recognized by me.

I regret to say that with preparations for the late election decided indications appeared in some localities in the Southern States of a determination, by acts of violence and intimidation, to deprive citizens of the freedom of the ballot because of their political opinions. Bands of men, masked and armed, made their appearance; White Leagues and other societies were formed; large quantities of arms and ammunition were imported and distributed to these organizations; military drills, with menacing demonstrations, were held; and, with all these, murders enough were committed to spread terror among those whose political action was to be suppressed, if possible, by these intolerant and criminal proceedings. In some places colored laborers were compelled to vote according to the wishes of their employers, under threats of discharge if they acted otherwise; and there are too many instances in which, when these threats were disregarded, they were remorselessly executed by those who made them.

I understand that the fifteenth amendment to the Constitution was made to prevent this and a like state of things, and the act of May 31, 1870, with amendments, was passed to enforce its provisions; the object of both being to guarantee to all citizens the right to vote, and to protect them in the free enjoyment of that right. Enjoined by the Constitution "to take care that the laws be faithfully executed," and convinced by undoubted evidence that violations of said act had been committed, and that a wide-spread and flagrant disregard of it was contemplated, the proper officers were instructed to prosecute the offenders, and troops were stationed at convenient points to aid the officers, if necessary, in the performance of their official duties. Complaints are made of this interference by Federal authority; but if said amendment and act do not provide for such interference under the circumstances as above stated, then they are without meaning, force, or effect, and the whole scheme of colored enfranchisement is worse than mockery and little better than a crime. Possibly Congress may find it due to truth and justice to ascertain by means of a committee whether the alleged wrongs to colored citizens for political purposes are real, or the reports thereof were manufactured for the occasion.

The whole number of troops in the States of Louisiana, Alabama, Georgia, Florida, South Carolina, North Carolina, Kentucky, Tennessee, Arkansas, Mississippi, Maryland, and Virginia, at the time of the election were four thousand and eighty-two. This embraces the garrisons of all the forts from the Delaware to the Gulf of Mexico.

Another trouble has arisen in Arkansas. Article 13 of the Constitution of that State (which was adopted in 1868, and upon the approval of which by Congress the State was restored to representation as one of the States of the Union) provides in effect that before any amendments proposed to this constitution shall become a part thereof, they shall be passed by two successive assemblies, and then submitted to and ratified by a majority of the electors of the State voting thereon. On the 11th of May, 1874, the governor convened an extra session of the General Assembly of the State, which on the 18th of the same month passed an act providing for a convention to frame a new constitution. Pursuant to this act, and at an election held on the 30th of June, 1874, the convention was approved, and delegates were chosen thereto, who assembled on the 14th of last July, and framed a new constitution, the schedule of which provided for the election of an entire new set of State officers, in a manner contrary to the then existing election laws of the State. On the 13th of October, 1874, this constitution, as therein provided, was submitted to the people for their approval or rejection, and according to the election returns was approved by a large majority of those qualified to vote thereon, and at the same election persons were chosen to fill all the State, county, and township offices. The governor elected in 1872 for the term of four years turned over his office to the governor chosen under the new constitution; whereupon the lieutenant-governor, also elected in 1872 for the term of four years, claiming to act as governor and alleging that said proceedings by which the new constitution was made and a new set of officers elected were unconstitutional, illegal, and void, called upon me, as provided in section 4, article 4, of the Constitution, to protect the State against domestic violence. As Congress is now investigating the political affairs of Arkansas, I have declined to interfere.

The whole subject of executive interference with the affairs of a State is repugnant to public opinion, to the feeling of those who from their official capacity must be used in such interposition, and to him or those who must direct. Unless most clearly on the side of law, such interference becomes a crime: with the law to support it, it is condemned without a hearing. I desire, therefore, that all necessity for executive direction in local affairs may become unnecessary and obsolete. I invite the attention, not of Congress, but of the people of the United States, to the causes and effects of these unhappy questions. Is there not a disposition on one side to magnify wrongs and outrages, and on the other side to belittle them or justify them? If public opinion could be directed to a correct survey of what is, and to rebuking wrong and aiding the proper authorities in punishing it, a better state of feeling would be inculcated, and the sooner we would have that peace which would leave the States free indeed to regulate their own domestic affairs. I believe on the part of our citizens of the Southern States—the better part of them—there is a disposition to be law-abiding, and to do no violence either to individuals or to the laws existing. But do they do right in ignoring the existence of violence and bloodshed in resistance to constituted authority? I sympathize with their prostrate condition and would do all in my power to relieve them—acknowledging that in some instances they have had most trying governments to live under, and very oppressive ones in the way of taxation for nominal improvements not giving benefits equal to the hardships imposed—but can they proclaim themselves entirely irresponsible for this condition? They cannot. Violence has been rampant in some localities, and has either been justified or denied by those who could have prevented it. The theory is even raised that there is to be no further interference on the part of the General Government to protect citizens within a State where the State authorities fail to give protection. This is a great mistake. While I remain Executive, all the laws of Congress and the provisions of the Constitution, including the recent amendments added thereto, will be enforced with rigor; but with regret that they should have added one jot or tittle to executive duties or powers. Let there be fairness in the discussion of southern questions, the advocates of both, or all political parties, giving honest, truthful reports of occurrences, condemning the wrong and upholding the right, and soon all will be well. Under existing conditions the negro votes the Republican ticket because he knows his friends are of that party. Many a good citizen votes the opposite, not because he agrees with the great principles of state which separate parties, but because generally, he is opposed to negro rule. This is a most delusive cry. Treat the negro as a citizen and a voter—as he is and must remain—and soon parties will be divided, not on the color line, but on principle. Then we shall have no complaint of sectional interference. * * * The attention of Congress is invited to the report of the Secretary of the Interior, and to the legislation asked for by him. * * *

The policy adopted for the management of Indian affairs, known as the peace policy, has been adhered to with most beneficial results. It is confidently hoped that a few years more will relieve our frontiers from danger of Indian depredations.

I commend the recommendation of the Secretary for the extension of the homestead laws to the Indians, and for some sort of territorial government for the Indian Territory. A great majority of the Indians occupying this Territory are believed yet to be incapable of maintaining their rights against the more civilized and enlightened white man. Any territorial form of government given them, therefore, should protect them in their homes and property for a period of at least twenty years, and before its final adoption should be ratified by a majority of those affected. * *

The act of Congress providing the oath which pensioners must subscribe to before drawing their pensions cuts off from this bounty a few survivors of the war of 1812 residing in the Southern States. I recommend the restoration of this bounty to all such. The number of persons whose names would thus be restored to the list of pensioners is not large. They are all old persons, who could have taken no part in the rebellion, and the services for which they were awarded pensions were in defense of the whole country. * * * * * *

The rules adopted to improve the civil service of the Government have been adhered to as closely as has been practicable with the opposition with which they meet. The effect, I believe, has been beneficial on the whole, and has tended to the elevation of the service. But it is impracticable to maintain them without direct and positive support of Congress. Generally the support which this reform receives is from those who give it their support only to find fault when the rules are apparently departed from. Removals from office without preferring charges against parties removed are frequently cited as departures from the rules adopted, and the retention of those against whom charges are made by irresponsible persons, and without good grounds, is also often condemned as a violation of them. Under these circumstances, therefore, I announce that if Congress adjourns without positive legislation on the subject of "civil service reform" I will regard such action as a disapproval of the system, and will abandon it except so far as to require examinations for certain appointees to determine their fitness. Competitive examinations will be abandoned.

The gentlemen who have given their services, without compensation, as members of the board to devise rules and regulations for the government of the civil service of the country, have shown much zeal and earnestness in their work, and to them as well as to myself it will be a source of mortification if it is to be thrown away. But I repeat that it is impossible to carry this system to a successful issue without general approval and assistance, and positive law to support it.

I have stated that three elements of prosperity to the nation, capital, labor, skilled and unskilled, and products of the soil, still remain with us. To direct the employment of these is a problem deserving the most serious attention of Congress. If employment can be given to all the labor offering itself, prosperity necessarily follows. I have expressed the opinion, and repeat it, that the first requisite to the accomplishment of this end is a substitution of a sound currency in place of one of a fluctuating value. This secured, there are many interests that might be fostered to the great profit of both labor and capital. How to induce capital to employ labor is the question. The subject of cheap transportation has occupied the attention of Congress. Much new light on this question will without doubt be given by the committee appointed by the last Congress to investigate and report upon this subject.

A revival of ship-building, and particularly of iron steamship building, is of vast importance to our national prosperity. The United States is now paying over $100,000,000 per annum for freights and passage on foreign ships—to be carried abroad and expended in the employment and support of other peoples—beyond a fair per centage of what should go to foreign vessels, estimating on the tonnage and travel of each, respectively. It is to be regretted that this disparity in the carrying trade exists, and to correct it I would be willing to see a great departure from the usual course of Government in supporting what might usually be termed private enterprise. I would not suggest as a remedy direct subsidy to American steamship lines, but I would suggest the direct offer of ample compensation for carrying the mails between Atlantic sea-board cities and the Continent on American-owned and American-built steamers, and would extend this liberality to vessels carrying the mails to South American States and to Central America and Mexico; and would pursue the same policy from our Pacific sea-ports to foreign sea-ports on the Pacific. It might be demanded that vessels built for this service should come up to a standard fixed by legislation in tonnage, speed, and all other qualities looking to the possibility of Government requiring them at some time for war purposes. The right also of taking possession of them in such emergency should be guarded.

I offer these suggestions believing them worthy of consideration in all seriousness, affecting all sections and all interests alike. If anything better can be done to direct the country into a course of general prosperity, no one will be more ready than I to second the plan. * * *

* * In accordance with section 3, act approved June 23, 1874, I appointed a board to make a survey of the mouth of the Mississippi River, with a view to determine the best method of obtaining and maintaining a depth of water sufficient for the purposes of commerce, &c.; and in accordance with an act entitled "An act to provide for the appointment of a commission of engineers to investigate and report a permanent plan for the reclamation of the alluvial basin of the Mississippi River, subject to inundation," I appointed a commission of engineers. Neither board has yet completed its labors. When their reports are received, they will be forwarded to Congress without delay. U. S. GRANT.

EXECUTIVE MANSION, *December* 7, 1874.

President Grant's Seventh Annual Message.

To the Senate and House of Representatives:

In submitting my seventh annual message to Congress, in this centennial year of our national existence as a free and independent people, it affords me great pleasure to recur to the advancement that has been made from the time of the colonies, one hundred years ago. We were then a people numbering only three millions. Now we number more than forty millions. Then industries were confined almost exclusively to the tillage of the soil. Now manufactories absorb much of the labor of the country.

Our liberties remain unimpaired; the bondmen have been freed from slavery; we have become possessed of the respect, if not the friendship, of all civilized nations. Our progress has been great in all the arts; in science, agriculture, commerce, navigation, mining, mechanics, law, medicine, &c.; and in general education the progress is likewise encouraging. Our thirteen States have become thirty-eight, including Colorado, (which has taken the initiatory steps to become a State,) and eight Territories, including the Indian Territory and Alaska, and excluding Colorado, making a territory extending from the Atlantic to the Pacific. On the south we have extended to the Gulf of Mexico, and in the west from the Mississippi to the Pacific.

One hundred years ago the cotton-gin, the steamship, the railroad, the telegraph, the reaping, sewing, and modern printing machines, and numerous other inventions of scarcely less value to our business and happiness, were entirely unknown.

In 1776, manufactories scarcely existed even in name in all this vast territory. In 1870, more than two millions of persons were employed in manufactories, producing more than $2,100,000,000 of products in amount annually, nearly equal to our national debt. From nearly the whole of the population of 1776 being engaged in the one occupation of agriculture, in 1870 so numerous and diversified had become the occupation of our people that less than six millions out of more than forty millions were so engaged. The extraordinary effect produced in our country by a resort to diversified occupations has built a market for the products of fertile lands distant from the seaboard and the markets of the world.

The American system of locating various and extensive manufactories next to the plow and the pasture, and adding connecting railroads and steamboats, has produced in our distant interior country a result noticeable by the intelligent portions of all commercial nations. The ingenuity and skill of American mechanics have been demonstrated at home and abroad in a manner most flattering to their pride. But for the extraordinary genius and ability of our mechanics, the achievements of our agriculturists, manufacturers, and transporters throughout the country would have been impossible of attainment.

The progress of the miner has also been great. Of coal our production was small; now many millions of tons are mined annually. So with iron, which formed scarcely an appreciable part of our products half a century ago, we now produce more than the world consumed at the beginning of our national existence. Lead, zinc, and copper, from being articles of import, we may expect to be large exporters of in the near future. The development of gold and silver mines in the United States and Territories has not only been remarkable, but has had a large influence upon the business of all commercial nations. Our merchants in the last hundred years have had a success and have established a reputation for enterprise, sagacity, progress, and integrity unsurpassed by peoples of older nationalities. This "good name" is not confined to their homes, but goes out upon every sea and into every port where commerce enters. With equal pride we can point to our progress in all of the learned professions.

As we are now about to enter upon our second centennial—commencing our manhood as a nation—it is well to look back upon the past and study what will be best to preserve and advance our future greatness. From the fall of Adam for his transgression to the present day, no nation has ever been free from threatened danger to its prosperity and happiness. We should look to the dangers threatening us, and remedy them so far as lies in our power. We are a republic whereof one man is as good as another before the law. Under such a form of government it is of the greatest importance that all should be possessed of education and intelligence enough to cast a vote with a right understanding of its meaning. A large association of ignorant men cannot, for any considerable period, oppose a successful resistance to tyranny and oppression from the educated few, but will inevitably sink into acquiescence to the will of intelligence, whether directed by the demagogue or by priestcraft. Hence the education of the masses becomes of the first necessity for the preservation of our institutions. They are worth preserving, because they have secured the greatest good to the greatest proportion of the population of any form of government yet devised. All other forms of government approach it just in proportion to the general diffusion of education and independence of thought and action. As the primary step, therefore, to our advancement in all that has marked our progress in the past century, I suggest for your earnest consideration, and most earnestly recommend it, that a constitutional amendment be submitted to the legislatures of the several States for ratification, making it the duty of each of the several States to establish and forever maintain free public schools adequate to the education of all the children in the rudimentary branches within their respective limits, irrespective of sex, color, birthplace, or religions; forbidding the teaching in said schools of religious, atheistic, or pagan tenets; and prohibiting the granting of any school-funds, or school-taxes, or any part thereof, either by legislative, municipal, or other authority, for the benefit or in aid, directly or indirectly, of any religious sect or denomination, or in aid or for the benefit of any other object of any nature or kind whatever.

In connection with this important question, I would also call your attention to the importance of correcting an evil that, if permitted to continue, will probably lead to great trouble in our land before the close of the nineteenth century. It is the accumulation of vast amounts of untaxed church-property.

In 1850, I believe, the church-property of the United States which paid no tax, municipal or State, amounted to about $83,000,000. In 1860, the amount had doubled; in 1875, it is about $1,000,000,000. By 1900, without check, it is safe to say this property will reach a sum exceeding $3,000,000,000. So vast a sum, receiving all the protection and benefits of government, without bearing its proportion of the burdens and expenses of the same, will not be looked upon acquiescently by those who have to pay the taxes. In a growing country, where real estate enhances so rapidly with time as in the United States, there is scarcely a limit to the wealth that may be acquired by corporations, religious or otherwise, if allowed to retain real estate without taxation. The contemplation of so vast a property as here alluded to, without taxation, may lead to sequestration without constitutional authority and through blood.

I would suggest the taxation of all property equally, whether church or corporation, exempting only the last resting-place of the dead, and, possibly, with proper restrictions, church-edifices.

Our relations with most of the foreign powers continue on a satisfactory and friendly footing.

* * * * *

I am happy to announce the passage of an act by the General Cortes of Portugal, proclaimed since the adjournment of Congress, for the abolition of servitude in the Portuguese colonies. It is to be hoped that such legislation may be another step toward the great consummation to be reached, when no man shall be permitted, directly or indirectly, under any guise, excuse, or form of law, to hold his fellow-man in bondage. I am of opinion also that it is the duty of the United States, as contributing toward that end, and required by the spirit of the age in which we live, to provide by suitable legislation that no citizen of the United States shall hold slaves as property in any other country, or be interested therein. * * * *

The past year has furnished no evidence of an approaching termination of the ruinous conflict which has been raging for seven years in the neighboring island of Cuba. The same disregard of the laws of civilized warfare and of the just demands of humanity which has heretofore called forth expressions of condemnation from the nations of Christendom has continued to blacken the sad scene. Desolation, ruin and pillage are pervading the rich fields of one of the most fertile and productive regions of the earth, and the incendiaries' torch, firing plantations and valuable factories and buildings, is the agent marking the alternate advance or retreat of contending parties.

The protracted continuance of this strife seriously affects the interests of all commercial nations, but those of the United States more than others, by reason of close proximity, its larger trade and intercourse with Cuba, and the frequent and intimate personal and social relations which have grown up between its citizens and those of the island. Moreover, the property of our citizens in Cuba is large, and is rendered insecure and depreciated in value and in capacity of production by the continuance of the strife and the unnatural mode of its conduct. The same is true, differing only in degree, with respect to the interests and people of other nations; and the absence of any reasonable assurance of a near termination of the conflict must, of necessity, soon compel the states thus suffering to consider what the interests of their own people and their duty toward themselves may demand.

I have hoped that Spain would be enabled to establish peace in her colony, to afford security to the property and the interests of our citizens, and allow legitimate scope to trade and commerce and the natural productions of the island. Because of this hope, and from an extreme reluctance to interfere in the most remote manner in the affairs of another and a friendly nation, especially of one whose sympathy and friendship in the struggling infancy of our own existence must ever be remembered with gratitude, I have patiently and anxiously waited the progress of events. Our own civil conflict is too recent for us not to consider the difficulties which surround a government distracted by a dynastic rebellion at home, at the same time that it has to cope with a separate insurrection in a distant colony. But whatever causes may have produced the situation which so grievously affects our interests, it exists, with all its attendant evils operating directly upon this country and its people. Thus far all the efforts of Spain have proved abortive, and time has marked no improvement in the situation. The armed bands of either side now occupy nearly the same ground as in the past, with the difference, from time to time, of more lives sacrificed, more property destroyed, and wider extents of fertile and productive fields and more and more of valuable property constantly wantonly sacrificed to the incendiaries' torch.

In contests of this nature, where a considerable body of people, who have attempted to free themselves of the control of the superior government, have reached such point in occupation of territory, in power, and in general organization, as to constitute in fact a body politic, having a government in substance as well as in name, possessed of the elements of stability, and equipped with the machinery for the administration of internal policy and the execution of its laws, prepared and able to administer justice at home, as well as in its dealings with other powers, it is within the province of those other powers to recognize its existence as a new and independent nation. In such cases other nations simply deal with an actually existing condition of things, and recognize as one of the powers of the earth that body politic which, possessing the necessary elements, has, in fact, become a new power. In a word, the creation of a new state is a fact.

To establish the condition of things essential to the recognition of this fact, there must be a people occupying a known territory, united under some known and defined form of government, acknowledged by those subject thereto, in which the functions of government are administered by usual methods, competent to mete out justice to citizens and strangers, to afford remedies for public and for private wrongs, and able to assume the correlative international obligations, and capable of performing the corresponding international duties resulting from its acquisition of the rights of sovereignty. A power should exist complete in its organization, ready to take and able to maintain its place among the nations of the earth.

While conscious that the insurrection in Cuba has shown a strength and endurance which make it at least doubtful whether it be in the power of Spain to subdue it, it seems unquestionable that no such civil organization exists which may be recognized as an independent government capable of performing its international obligations, and entitled to be treated as one of the powers of the earth. A recognition under such circumstances would be inconsistent with the facts, and would compel the power granting it soon to support by force the government to which it had really given its only claim of existence. In my judgment, the United States should adhere to the policy and the principles which have heretofore been its sure and safe guides in like contests between revolted colonies and their mother country, and, acting only upon the clearest evidence, should avoid any possibility of suspicion or of imputation.

A recognition of the independence of Cuba being, in my opinion, impracticable and indefensible, the question which next presents itself is that of the recognition of belligerent rights in the parties to the contest.

In a former message to Congress I had occasion to consider this question, and reached the conclusion that the conflict in Cuba, dreadful and devastating as were its incidents, did not rise to the fearful dignity of war. Regarding it now, after this lapse of time, I am unable to see that any notable success, or any marked or real advance on the part of the insurgents, has essentially changed the character of the contest. It has acquired greater age, but not greater or more formidable proportions. It is possible that the acts of foreign powers, and even acts of Spain herself, of this very nature, might be pointed to in defense of such recognition. But now, as in its past history, the United States should carefully avoid the false lights which might lead it into the mazes of doubtful law and of questionable propriety, and adhere rigidly and sternly to the rule, which has been its guide, of doing only that which is right and honest and of good report. The question of according or of withholding rights of belligerency must be judged, in every case, in view of the particular attending facts. Unless justified by necessity, it is always, and justly, regarded as an unfriendly act, and a gratuitous demonstration of moral support to the rebellion. It is necessary, and it is required, when the interests and rights of another government or of its people are so far affected by a pending civil conflict as to require a definition of its relations to the parties thereto. But this conflict must be one which will be recognized in the sense of international law as war. Belligerence, too, is a fact. The mere existence of contending armed bodies, and their occasional conflicts, do not constitute war in the sense referred to. Applying to the existing condition of affairs in Cuba the tests recognized by publicists and writers on international law, and which have been observed by nations of dignity, honesty, and power, when free from sensitive or selfish and unworthy motives, I fail to find in the insurrection the existence of such a substantial political organization, real, palpable, and manifest to the world, having the forms and capable of the ordinary functions of government toward its own people and to other States, with courts for the administration of justice, with a local habitation, possessing such organization of force, such material, such occupation of territory, as to take the contest out of the category of a mere rebellious insurrection, or occasional skirmishes, and place it on the terrible footing of war, to which a recognition of belligerency would aim to elevate it. The contest, moreover, is solely on land; the insurrection has not possessed itself of a single sea-port whence it may send forth its flag, nor has it any means of communication with foreign powers except through the military lines of its adversaries. No apprehension of any of those sudden and difficult complications which a war upon the ocean is apt to precipitate upon the vessels, both commercial and national, and upon the consular officers of other powers, calls for the definition of their relations to the parties to the contest. Considered as a question of expediency, I regard the accordance of belligerent rights still to be as unwise and premature, as I regard it to be, at present, indefensible as a measure of right. Such recognition entails upon the country according the rights which flow from it difficult and complicated duties, and requires the exaction from the contending parties of the strict observance of their rights and obligations. It confers the right of search upon the high seas by vessels of both parties; it would subject the carrying of arms and munitions of war, which now may be transported freely and without interruption in the vessels of the United States, to detention and to possible seizure; it would give rise to countless vexatious questions, would release the parent government from responsibility for acts done by the insurgents, and would invest Spain with the right to exercise the supervision recognized by our treaty of 1795 over our commerce on the high seas, a very large part of which, in its traffic between the Atlantic and the Gulf States, and between all of them and the States on the Pacific, passes through the waters which wash the shores of Cuba. The exercise of this supervision could scarce fail to lead, if not to abuses, certainly to collisions perilous to the peaceful relations of the two States. There can be little doubt to what result such supervision would before long draw this nation. It would be unworthy of the United States to inaugurate the possibilities of such result, by measures of questionable right or expediency, or by any indirection. Apart from any question of theoretical right, I am satisfied that, while the accordance of belligerent rights to the insurgents in Cuba might give them a hope and an inducement to protract the struggle, it would be but a delusive hope, and would not remove the evils which this Government and its people are experiencing, but would draw the United States into complications which it has waited long and already suffered much to avoid. The recognition of independence, or of belligerency, being thus, in my judgment, equally inadmissible, it remains to consider what course shall be adopted should the conflict not soon be brought to an end by acts of the parties themselves, and should the evils which result therefrom, affecting all nations, and particularly the United States, continue.

In such event, I am of opinion that other nations will be compelled to assume the responsibility which devolves upon them, and to seriously consider the only remaining measures possible, mediation and intervention. Owing, perhaps, to the large expanse of water separating the island from the peninsula, the want of harmony and of personal sympathy between the inhabitants of the colony and those sent thither to rule them, and want of adaptation of the ancient colonial system of Europe to the present times and to the ideas which the events of the past century have developed, the contending parties appear to have within themselves no depository of common confidence, to suggest wisdom when passion and excitement have their sway, and to assume the part of peace-maker. In this view, in the earlier days of the contest, the good offices of the United States as a mediator were tendered in good faith, without any selfish purpose, in the interest of humanity and in sincere friendship for both parties, but were at the time declined by Spain, with the declaration, nevertheless, that at a future time they would be indispensable. No intimation has been received that in the opinion of Spain that time has been reached. And yet the strife continues with all its dread horrors and all its injuries to the interests of the United States and of other nations. Each party seems quite capable of working great injury and damage to the other, as well as to all the relations and interests dependent on the existence of peace in the island; but they seem incapable of reaching any adjustment, and both have thus far failed of achieving any success whereby one party shall possess and control the island to the exclusion of the other. Under these circumstances, the agency of others, either by mediation or by intervention, seems to be the only alternative, which must, sooner or later, be invoked for the termination of the strife. At the same time, while thus impressed, I do not at this time recommend the adoption of any measure of intervention. I shall be ready at all times, and as the equal friend of both parties, to respond to a suggestion that the good offices of United States will be acceptable to aid in bringing about a peace honorable to both. It is due to Spain, so far as this Government is concerned, that the agency of a third power, to which I have adverted, shall be adopted only as a last expedient. Had it been the desire of the United States to interfere in the affairs of Cuba, repeated opportunities for so doing have been presented within the last few years; but we have remained passive, and have performed our whole duty and all international obligations to Spain with friendship, fairness and fidelity, and with a spirit of patience and forbearance which negatives every possible suggestion of desire to interfere or to add to the difficulties with which she has been surrounded.

The government of Spain has recently submitted to our minister at Madrid certain proposals which it is hoped may be found to be the basis, if not the actual submission, of terms to meet the requirements of the particular griefs of which this Government has felt itself entitled to complain. These proposals have not yet reached me in their full text. On their arrival they will be taken into careful examination, and may, I hope, lead to a satisfactory adjustment of the questions to which they refer, and remove the possibility of future occurrences, such as have given rise to our just complaints.

It is understood also that renewed efforts are being made to introduce reforms in the internal administration of the island. Persuaded, however, that a proper regard for the interests of the United States and of its citizens entitle it to relief from the strain to which it has been subjected by the difficulties of the questions, and the wrongs and losses which arise from the contest in Cuba, and that the interests of humanity itself demand the cessation of the strife before the whole island shall be laid waste and larger sacrifices of life be made, I shall feel it my duty, should my hopes of a satisfactory adjustment and of the early restoration of peace and the removal of future causes of complaint be, unhappily, disappointed, to make a further communication to Congress at some period not far remote, and during the present session, recommending what may then seem to me to be necessary.

The Free Zone, so called, several years since established by the Mexican government in certain of the States of that republic adjacent to our frontier, remains in full operation. It has always been materially injurious to honest traffic, for it operates as an incentive to traders in Mexico to supply without customs-charges the wants of inhabitants on this side the line, and prevents the same wants from being supplied by merchants of the United States, thereby, to a considerable extent, defrauding our revenue and checking honest commercial enterprise.

Depredations by armed bands from Mexico on the people of Texas near the frontier continue. Though the main object of these incursions is robbery, they frequently result in the murder of unarmed and peaceably-disposed persons; and in some instances even the United States post-offices and mail-communications have been attacked. Renewed remonstrances upon this subject have been addressed to the Mexican government, but without much apparent effect. The military force of this Government disposable for service in that quarter is quite inadequate to effectually guard the line, even at those points where the incursions are usually made. An experiment of an armed vessel on the Rio Grande for that purpose is on trial, and it is hoped that, if not thwarted by the shallowness of the river and other natural obstacles, it may materially contribute to the protection of the herdsmen of Texas. * *

The Court of Commissioners of Alabama Claims has prosecuted its important duties very assiduously and very satisfactorily. * *

Among the pressing and important subjects to which, in my opinion, the attention of Congress should be directed, are those relating to fraudulent naturalization and expatriation.

The United States, with great liberality, offers its citizenship to all who in good faith comply with the requirements of law. These requirements are as simple and upon as favorable terms to the emigrant as the high privilege to which he is admitted can or should permit. I do not propose any additional requirements to those which the law now demands. But the very simplicity and the want of unnecessary formality in our law have made fraudulent naturalization not infrequent, to the discredit and injury of all honest citizens, whether native or naturalized. Cases of this character are continually being brought to the notice of the Government by our representatives abroad, and also those of persons resident in other countries, most frequently those who, if they had remained in this country long enough to entitle them to become naturalized, have generally not much overpassed that period, and have returned to the country of their origin, where they reside, avoiding all duties to the United States by their absence, and claiming to be exempt from all duties to the country of their nativity and of their residence, by reason of their alleged naturalization. It is due to this Government itself and to the great mass of the naturalized citizens who entirely, both in name and in fact, become citizens of the United States, that the high privilege of citizenship of the United States should not be held by fraud or in derogation of the laws and of the good name of every honest citizen. On many occasions it has been brought to the knowledge of the Government that certificates of naturalization are held, and protection or interference claimed, by parties who admit that not only they were not within the United States at the time of the pretended naturalization, but that they have never resided in the United States; in others, the certificate and record of the court show on their face that the person claiming to be naturalized had not resided the required time in the United States; in others, it is admitted upon examination that the requirements of law have not been complied with; in some cases even, such certificates have been matter of purchase. These are not isolated cases, arising at rare intervals, but of common occurrence, and which are reported from all quarters of the globe. Such occurrences cannot, and do not, fail to reflect upon the Government and injure all honest citizens. Such a fraud being discovered, however, there is no practicable means within the control of the Government by which the record of naturalization can be vacated; and should the certificate be taken up, as it usually is, by the diplomatic and consular representatives of the government to whom it may have been presented, there is nothing to prevent the person claiming to have been naturalized from obtaining a new certificate from the court in place of that which has been taken from him.

The evil has become so great and of such frequent occurrence that I cannot too earnestly recommend that some effective measures be adopted to provide a proper remedy, and means for the vacating of any record thus fraudulently made, and of punishing the guilty parties to the transaction.

In this connection I refer also to the question of expatriation and the election of nationality.

The United States was foremost in upholding the right of expatriation, and was principally instrumental in overthrowing the doctrine of perpetual allegiance. Congress has declared the right of expatriation to be a natural and inherent right of all people; but, while many other nations have enacted laws providing what formalities shall be necessary to work a change of allegiance, the United States has enacted no provisions of law, and has in no respect marked out how and when expatriation may be accomplished by its citizens. Instances are brought to the attention of the Government where citizens of the United States, either naturalized or native-born, have formally become citizens or subjects of foreign powers, but who, nevertheless, in the absence of any provisions of legislation on this question, when involved in difficulties, or when it seems to be their interest, claim to be citizens of the United States, and demand the intervention of a government which they have long since abandoned, and to which for years they have rendered no service, nor held themselves in any way amenable.

In other cases naturalized citizens, immediately after naturalization, have returned to their native country; have become engaged in business; have accepted offices or pursuits inconsistent with American citizenship, and evidence no intent to return to the United States until called upon to discharge some duty to the country where they are residing, when at once they assert their citizenship, and call upon the representatives of the Government to aid them in their unjust pretensions. It is but justice to all *bona fide* citizens that no doubt should exist on such questions, and that Congress should determine by enactment of law how expatriation may be accomplished, and change of citizenship be established.

I also invite your attention to the necessity of regulating by law the status of American women who may marry foreigners, and of defining more fully that of children born in a foreign country of American parents who may reside abroad; and also of some further provision regulating or giving legal effect to marriages of American citizens contracted in foreign countries. * *

* * The report of the Secretary of the Treasury shows the receipts from customs for the fiscal year ending June 30, 1874, to have been $163,103,833.69, and for the fiscal year ending June 30, 1875, to have been $157,167,722.35, a decrease for the last fiscal year of $5,936,111.34. Receipts from internal revenue for the year ending the 30th of June, 1874, were $102,409,784.90, and for the year ending June 30, 1875, $110,007,-493.58; increase, $7,597,708.68.

The report also shows a complete history of the workings of the Department for the last year, and contains recommendations for reforms and for legislation which I concur in, but cannot comment on so fully as I should like to do if space would permit, but will confine myself to a few suggestions which I look upon as vital to the best interests of the whole people—coming within the purview of "Treasury"—I mean specie resumption. Too much stress cannot be laid upon this question, and I hope Congress may be induced, at the earliest day practicable, to insure the consummation of the act of the last Congress, at its last session, to bring about specie resumption "on and after the 1st of January, 1879," at furthest. It would be a great blessing if this could be consummated even at an earlier day.

Nothing seems to me more certain than that a full, healthy and permanent reaction cannot take place in favor of the industries and financial welfare of the country until we return to a measure of values recognized throughout the civilized world. While we use a currency not equivalent to this standard, the world's recognized standard, specie, becomes a commodity like the products of the soil, the surplus seeking a market wherever there is a demand for it.

Under our present system we should want none, nor would we have any, were it not that custom-dues must be paid in coin, and because of the pledge to pay interest on the public debt in coin. The yield of precious metals would flow out for the purchase of foreign productions, and leave the United States "hewers of wood and drawers of water" because of wiser legislation on the subject of finance by the nations with whom we have dealings. I am not prepared to say that I can suggest the best legislation to secure the end most heartily recommended. It will be a source of great gratification to me to be able to approve any measure of Congress looking effectively toward securing "resumption."

Unlimited inflation would probably bring about specie payments more speedily than any legislation looking to the redemption of the legal-tenders in coin. But it would be at the expense of honor. The legal tenders would have no value beyond settling present liabilities, or properly speaking, repudiating them. They would buy nothing after debts were all settled.

There are a few measures which seem to me important in this connection, and which I commend to your earnest consideration:

A repeal of so much of the legal-tender act as makes these notes receivable for debts contracted after a date to be fixed in the act itself, say not later than the 1st of January, 1877. We should then have quotations at real values, not fictitious ones. Gold would no longer be at a premium, but currency at a discount. A healthy reaction would set in at once, and with it a desire to make the currency equal to what it purports to be. The merchants, manufacturers, and tradesmen of every calling could do business on a fair margin of profit, the money to be received having an unvarying value. Laborers and all classes who work for stipulated pay or salary would receive more for their income, because extra profits would no longer be charged by the capitalist to compensate for the risk of a downward fluctuation in the value of the currency.

Second, that the Secretary of the Treasury be authorized to redeem say not to exceed two million ($2,000,000) dollars monthly of legal tender notes, by issuing in their stead a long bond, bearing interest at the rate of 3.65 per cent. per annum, of denominations ranging from $50 up to $1,000 each. This would in time reduce the legal-tender notes to a volume that could be kept afloat without demanding redemption in large sums suddenly.

Third, that additional power be given to the Secretary of the Treasury to accumulate gold for final redemption, either by increasing revenue, curtailing expenses, or both—it is preferable to do both; and I recommend that reduction of expenditures be made wherever it can be done without impairing Government obligations or crippling the due execution thereof. One measure for increasing the revenue—and the only one I think of—is the restoration of the duty on tea and coffee. These duties would add probably $18,000,000 to the present amount received from imports, and would in no way increase the prices paid for those articles by the consumers.

These articles are the products of countries collecting revenue from exports, and as we, the largest consumers, reduce the duties, they proportionately increase them. With this addition to the revenue, many duties now collected, and which give but an insignificant return for the cost of collection, might be remitted, and to the direct advantage of consumers at home.

I would mention those articles which enter into manufactures of all sorts. All duty paid upon such articles goes directly to the cost of the article when manufactured here, and must be paid for by the consumers. These duties not only come from the consumers at home, but act as a protection to foreign manufacturers of the same completed articles in our own and distant markets.

I will suggest, or mention, another subject bearing upon the problem of "how to enable the Secretary of the Treasury to accumulate balances." It is to devise some better method of verifying claims against the Government than at present exists through the Court of Claims, especially those claims growing out of the late war. Nothing is more certain than that a very large percentage of the amounts passed and paid are either wholly fraudulent, or are far in excess of the real losses sustained. The large amount of losses proven—on good testimony according to existing laws, by affidavits of fictitious or unscrupulous persons—to have been sustained on small farms and plantations, are not only far beyond the possible yield of those places for any one year, but, as every one knows who has had experience in tilling the soil, and who has visited the scenes of these spoliations, are in many instances more than the individual claimants were ever worth, including their personal and real estate.

The report of the Attorney-General, which will be submitted to Congress at an early day, will contain a detailed history of awards made, and of claims pending, of the class here referred to.

* * The condition of our Navy at this time is a subject of satisfaction. It does not contain, it is true, any of the powerful cruising iron-clads which make so much of the maritime strength of some other nations; but neither our continental situation nor our foreign policy requires that we should have a large number of ships of this character, while this situation and the nature of our ports combine to make those of other nations little dangerous to us under any circumstances.

Our Navy does contain, however, a considerable number of iron-clads of the monitor class, which, though not properly cruisers, are powerful and effective for harbor defense and for operations near our own shores. Of these all the single-turreted ones, fifteen in number, have been substantially rebuilt, their rotten wooden beams replaced with iron, their hulls strengthened, and their engines and machinery thoroughly repaired, so that they are now in the most efficient condition, and ready for sea as soon as they can be manned and put in commission.

The five double-turreted iron-clads belonging to our Navy, by far the most powerful of our ships for fighting purposes, are also in hand undergoing complete repairs, and could be ready for sea in periods varying from four to six months. With these completed according to the present design, and our two iron torpedo-boats now ready, our iron-clad fleet will be, for the purposes of defense at home, equal to any force that can readily be brought against it.

Of our wooden navy also, cruisers of various sizes, to the number of about forty, including those now in commission, are in the Atlantic, and could be ready for duty as fast as men could be enlisted for those not already in commission. Of these, one-third are in effect new ships, and though some of the remainder need considerable repairs to their boilers and machinery, they all are, or can readily be made, effective. * *

This constitutes a fleet of more than fifty war-ships, of which fifteen are iron-clad, now in hand on the Atlantic coast. * * * *

It would, in my opinion, be wise at once to afford sufficient means for the immediate completion of the five double-turreted monitors now undergoing repairs, which must otherwise advance slowly, and only as money can be spared from current expenses. Supplemented by these, our Navy, armed with the destructive weapons of modern warfare, manned by our seamen, and in charge of our instructed officers, will present a force powerful for the home purposes of a responsible though peaceful nation.

The report of the Postmaster-General, herewith transmitted, gives a full history of the workings of the Department for the year just passed. It will be observed that the deficiency to be supplied from the General Treasury increased over the amount required for the preceding year. In a country so vast in area as the United States, with large portions sparsely settled, it must be expected that this important service will be more or less a burden upon the Treasury for many years to come. But there is no branch of the public service which interests the whole people more than that of cheap and rapid transmission of the mails to every inhabited part of our territory. Next to the free school, the post-office is the great educator of the people, and it may well receive the support of the General Government. *

The steady growth and increase of the business of the Patent-Office indicates, in some measure, the progress of the industrial activity of the country. The receipts of the Office are in excess of its expenditures, and the Office generally is in a prosperous and satisfactory condition.

The report of the General Land-Office shows that there were 2,459,601 acres less disposed of during this than during the last year. More than one-half of this decrease was in lands disposed of under the homestead and timber-culture laws. The cause of this decrease is supposed to be found in the grasshopper scourge and the droughts which prevailed so extensively in some of the frontier States and Territories during that time as to discourage and deter entries by actual settlers. The cash receipts were less, by $690,-322.23 than during the preceding year.

The entire surveyed area of the public domain is 680,253,094 acres, of which 26,077,531 acres were surveyed during the past year, leaving 1,154,471,762 acres still unsurveyed. * * *

The number of pensioners still continues to decrease, the highest number having been reached during the year ending June 30, 1873. During the last year, 11,557 names were added to the rolls, and 12,977 were dropped therefrom, showing a net decrease of 1,420. But while the number of pensioners has decreased, the annual amount due on the pension-rolls has increased $44,733.13. This is caused by the greatly increased average rate of pensions, which, by the liberal legislation of Congress, has increased from $90.26 in 1872 to $103.91 in 1875 to each invalid pensioner, an increase in the average rate of fifteen per cent. in the three years. During the year ending June 30, 1875, there was paid on account of pensions, including the expenses of disbursement, $29,683,116, being $910,632 less than was paid the preceding year. This reduction in amount of expenditures was produced by the decrease in the amount of arrearages due on allowed claims, and on pensions, the rate of which was increased by the legislation of the preceding session of Congress. At the close of the last fiscal year there were on the pension-rolls 234,821 persons, of whom 210,363 were Army pensioners, 105,478 being invalids and 104,885 widows and dependent relatives; 3,420 were Navy pensioners, of whom 1,636 were invalids and 1,784 widows and dependent relatives; 21,038 were pensioners of the war of 1812, 15,875 of whom were survivors and 5,163 were widows.

It is estimated that $29.535,000 will be required for the payment of pensions for the next fiscal year, an amount $965,000 less than the estimate for the present year.

The method for the treatment of the Indians, adopted at the beginning of my first term, has been steadily pursued, and with satisfactory and encouraging results. It has been productive of evident improvement in the condition of that race, and will be continued, with only such modifications as further experience may indicate to be necessary. * * * *

In nearly every annual message that I have had the honor of transmitting to Congress, I have called attention to the anomalous, not to say scandalous, condition of affairs existing in the Territory of Utah, and have asked for definite legislation to correct it. That polygamy should exist in a free, enlightened and Christian country, without the power to punish so flagrant a crime against decency and morality, seems preposterous. True, there is no law to sustain this unnatural vice, but what is needed is a law to punish it as a crime, and at the same time to fix the status of the innocent children, the offspring of this system, and of the possibly innocent plural wives. But, as an institution, polygamy should be banished from the land.

While this is being done, I invite the attention of Congress to another, though perhaps no less an evil, the importation of Chinese women, but few of whom are brought to our shores to pursue honorable or useful occupations.

As this will be the last annual message which I shall have the honor of transmitting to Congress before my successor is chosen, I will repeat or recapitulate the questions which I deem of vital importance, which may be legislated upon and settled at this session:

First. That the States shall be required to afford the opportunity of a good common-school education to every child within their limits.

Second. No sectarian tenets shall ever be taught in any school supported in whole or in part by the State, nation, or by the proceeds of any tax levied upon any community. Make education compulsory, so far as to deprive all persons who cannot read and write from becoming voters after the year 1890, disfranchising none, however, on grounds of illiteracy who may be voters at the time this amendment takes effect.

Third. Declare church and state forever separate and distinct, but each free within their proper spheres; and that all church-property shall bear its own proportion of taxation.

Fourth. Drive out licensed immorality, such as polygamy and the importation of women for illegitimate purposes. To recur again to the centennial year, it would seem as though now, as we are about to begin the second century of our national existence, would be a most fitting time for these reforms.

Fifth. Enact such laws as will insure a speedy return to a sound currency, such as will command the respect of the world.

Believing that these views will commend themselves to the great majority of the right-thinking and patriotic citizens of the United States, I submit the rest to Congress.

U. S. GRANT.

EXECUTIVE MANSION, *December* 7, 1875.

VII.

PROCLAMATIONS AND ORDERS OF PRESIDENT GRANT.

Proclamation Requiring Certain Disorderly Persons in Louisiana to Disperse, September 15th, 1874.

By the President of the United States of America.

A PROCLAMATION.

Whereas it has been satisfactorily represented to me that turbulent and disorderly persons have combined together with force and arms to overthrow the State government of Louisiana, and to resist the laws and constituted authorities of said State; and

Whereas it is provided in the Constitution of the United States that the United States shall protect every State in this Union, on application of the Legislature, or of the Executive, when the Legislature cannot be convened, against domestic violence; and

Whereas it is provided in the laws of the United States that, in all cases of insurrection in any State, or of obstruction to the laws thereof, it shall be lawful for the President of the United States, on application of the Legislature of such State, or of the Executive when the Legislature cannot be convened, to call forth the militia of any other State or States, or to employ such part of the land and naval forces as shall be judged necessary for the purpose of suppressing such insurrection or causing the laws to be duly executed; and

Whereas the Legislature of said State is not now in session and cannot be convened in time to meet the present emergency, and the Executive of said State, under section 4 of article IV. of the Constitution of the United States and the laws passed in pursuance thereof, has therefore made application to me for such part of the military force of the United States as may be necessary and adequate to protect said State and the citizens thereof against domestic violence, and to enforce the due execution of the laws; and

Whereas it is required that, whenever it may be necessary, in the judgment of the President, to use the military force for the purpose aforesaid, he shall forthwith by proclamation command such insurgents to disperse and retire peaceably to their respective homes within a limited time:

Now, therefore, I, ULYSSES S. GRANT, President of the United States, do hereby make proclamation, and command said turbulent and disorderly persons to disperse and retire peaceably to their respective abodes within five days from this date, and hereafter to submit themselves to the laws and constituted authorities of said State; and I invoke the aid and co-operation of all good citizens thereof to uphold law and preserve the public peace.

In witness whereof I have hereunto set my hand, and caused the seal of the United States to be affixed.

Done at the city of Washington this fifteenth day of September, in the year of our Lord eighteen hundred and seventy-four, and of the Independence of the United States the ninety-ninth.

[SEAL.]

U. S. GRANT.

By the President:
HAMILTON FISH, *Secretary of State.*

Proclamation relative to Foreigners holding Real Estate in the Ottoman Empire, October 29th, 1874.

Whereas, pursuant to the second section of the act of Congress approved the 23d of March last, entitled "An Act to authorize the President to accept for citizens of the United States the jurisdiction of certain tribunals in the Ottoman dominions and Egypt, established or to be established under the authority of the Sublime Porte and of the government of Egypt," the President is authorized, for the benefit of American citizens residing in the Turkish dominions, to accept the recent law of the Ottoman Porte ceding the right of foreigners possessing immovable property in said dominions:

And whereas, pursuant to the authority thus in me vested, I have authorized GEORGE H. BOKER, accredited as Minister Resident of the United States to the Ottoman Porte, to sign, on behalf of this Government, the Protocol accepting the law aforesaid of the said Ottoman Porte, which Protocol and Law are, word for word, as follows:

[Translation.]

The United States of America and His Majesty the Sultan being desirous to establish by a special act the agreement entered upon between them regarding the admission of American citizens to the right of holding real estate granted to foreigners by the law promulgated on the 7th of Sepher, 1284, (January 18th, 1867,) have authorized:

The President of the United States of America, GEORGE H. BOKER, Minister Resident of the United States of America near the Sublime Porte, and

His Imperial Majesty the Sultan, His Excellency A. AARIFI PASHA, His Minister of Foreign Affairs, to sign the Protocol which follows:

PROTOCOL.

The law granting foreigners the right of holding real estate does not interfere with the immunities specified by the treaties, and which will continue to protect the person and the movable property of foreigners who may become owners of real estate.

As the exercise of this right of possessing real property may induce foreigners to establish themselves in larger numbers in the Ottoman Empire, the Imperial government thinks it proper to anticipate and to prevent the difficulties to which the application of this law may give rise in certain localities. Such is the object of the arrangements which follow.

The domicile of any person residing upon the Ottoman soil being inviolable, and as no one can enter it without the consent of the owner, except by virtue of orders emanating from competent authority, and with the assistance of the magistrate or functionary invested with the necessary powers, the residence of foreigners is inviolable on the same principle, in conformity with the treaties, and the agents of the public force cannot enter it without the assistance of the consul or of the delegate of the consul of the Power on which the foreigner depends.

By residence we understand the house of inhabitation and its dependencies: that is to say, the out-houses, courts, gardens, and neighboring enclosures, to the exclusion of all other parts of the property.

In the localities distant by less than nine hours' journey from the consular residence, the agents of the public force cannot enter the residence of a foreigner without the assistance of a consul, as was before said.

On his part the consul is bound to give his immediate assistance to the local authority, so as not to let six hours elapse between the moment which he may be informed and the moment of his departure, or the departure of his delegate, so that the action of the authorities may never be suspended more than twenty-four hours.

In the localities distant by nine hours or more than nine hours of travel from the residence of the consular agent, the agents of the public force may, on the request of the local authority, and with the assistance of three members of the Council of the Elders of the Commune, enter into the residence of a foreigner, without being assisted by the consular agent, but only in case of urgency, and for the search and the proof of the crime of murder, of attempt at murder, of incendiarism, of armed robbery either with infraction or by night in an inhabited house, of armed rebellion, and of the fabrication of counterfeit money; and this entry may be made whether the crime was committed by a foreigner or by an Ottoman subject, and whether it took place in the residence of a foreigner or not in his residence, or in any other place.

These regulations are not applicable but to the parts of the real estate which constitute the residence, as it has been heretofore defined.

Beyond the residence, the action of the police shall be exercised freely and without reserve; but in case a person charged with crime or offence should be arrested, and the accused shall be a foreigner, the immunities attached to his person shall be observed in respect to him.

The functionary or the officer charged with the accomplishment of a domiciliary visit, in the exceptional circumstances determined before, and the members of the Council of Elders who shall assist him, will be obliged to make out a *procès-verbal* of the domiciliary visit, and to communicate it immediately to the superior authority under whose jurisdiction they are, and the latter shall transmit it to the nearest consular agent, without delay.

A special regulation will be promulgated by the Sublime Porte, to determine the mode of action of the local police in the several cases provided heretofore.

In localities more distant than nine hours' travel from the residence of the consular agent, in which the law of the judicial organization of the Velayet may be in force, foreigners shall be tried without the assistance of the consular delegate by the Council of Elders fulfilling the function of justices of the peace, and by the tribunal of the canton, as well for actions not exceeding one thousand piastres as for offences entailing a fine of five hundred piastres only at the maximum.

Foreigners shall have, in any case, the right of appeal to the tribunal of the arrondissement against the judgments issued as above stated, and the appeal shall be followed and judged with the assistance of the consul, in conformity with the treaties.

The appeal shall always suspend the execution of a sentence.

In all cases the forcible execution of the judgments, issued on the conditions determined heretofore, shall not take place without the coöperation of the consul or of his delegate.

The Imperial government will enact a law which shall determine the rules of procedure to be observed by the parties, in the application of the preceding regulations.

Foreigners, in whatever locality they may be, may freely submit themselves to the jurisdiction of the Council of Elders or of the tribunal of the canton, without the assistance of the consul, in cases which do not exceed the competency of these councils or tribunals, reserving always the right of appeal before the tribunal of the arrondissement, where the case may be brought and tried with the assistance of the consul or his delegate.

The consent of a foreigner to be tried as above stated, without the assistance of his consul, shall always be given in writing, and in advance of all procedure.

It is well understood that all these restrictions do not concern cases which have for their object questions of real estate, which shall be tried and determined under the conditions established by the law.

The right of defense and the publicity of the hearings shall be assured in all cases to foreigners who may appear before the Ottoman tribunals, as well as to Ottoman subjects.

The preceding dispositions shall remain in force until the revision of the ancient treaties, a revision which the Sublime Porte reserves to itself the right to bring about hereafter by an understanding between it and the friendly Powers.

In witness whereof the respective plenipotentiaries have signed the Protocol, and have affixed thereto their seals.

Done at Constantinople the eleventh of August, one thousand eight hundred and seventy four. (Signed:) A. AARIFI. [L. S.]
(Signed:) GEO. H. BOKER. [L. S.]

[Translation.]

Law conceding to foreigners the right of holding real estate in the Ottoman Empire.

Imperial Rescript.—Let it be done in conformity with the contents. 7 Sepher, 1284, (January 18, 1867.)

With the object of developing the prosperity of the country, to put an end to the difficulties, to the abuses, and to the uncertainties which have arisen on the subject of the right of foreigners to hold property in the Ottoman Empire, and to complete, in accordance with a precise regulation, the safeguards which are due to financial interests and to administrative action, the following legislative enactments have been promulgated by the order of His Imperial Majesty, the Sultan:

ART. I. Foreigners are admitted, by the same privilege as Ottoman subjects, and without any other restriction, to enjoy the right of holding real estate, whether in the city or the country, throughout the empire, with the exception of the province of the Hédjaz, by submitting themselves to the laws and the regulations which govern Ottoman subjects, as is hereafter stated.

This arrangement does not concern subjects of Ottoman birth who have changed their nationality, who shall be governed in this matter by a special law.

ART. II. Foreigners, proprietors of real estate, in town or in country, are in consequence placed upon terms of equality with Ottoman subjects in all things that concern their landed property.

The legal effect of this equality is—

1st. To oblige them to conform to all the laws and regulations of the police or of the municipality which govern at present or may govern hereafter the enjoyment, the transmission, the alienation, and the hypothecation of landed property.

2d. To pay all charges and taxes under whatever form or denomination they may be, that are levied, or may be levied hereafter, upon city or country property.

3d. To render them directly amenable to the Ottoman civil tribunals in all questions relating to landed property, and in all real actions, whether as plaintiffs or as defendants, even when either party is a foreigner. In short, they are in all things to hold real estate by the same title, on the same condition, and under the same forms as Ottoman owners, and without being able to avail themselves of their personal nationality, except under the reserve of the immunities attached to their persons and their movable goods, according to the treaties.

ART. III. In case of the bankruptcy of a foreigner possessing real estate, the assignees of the bankrupt may apply to the authorities and to the Ottoman civil tribunals, requiring the sale of the real estate possessed by the bankrupt, and which by its nature and according to law is responsible for the debts of the owner.

The same course shall be followed when a foreigner shall have obtained against another foreigner owning real estate a judgment of condemnation before a foreign tribunal.

For the execution of this judgment against the real estate of his debtor, he shall apply to the competent Ottoman authorities, in order to obtain the sale of that real estate, which is responsible for the debts of the owner; and this judgment shall be executed by the Ottoman authorities and tribunals only after they have decided that the real estate of which the sale is required really belongs to the category of that property which may be sold for the payment of debt.

ART. IV. Foreigners have the privilege to dispose, by donation or by testament, of that real estate of which such disposition is permitted by law.

As to that real estate of which they may not have disposed, or of which the law does not permit them to dispose by gift or testament, its succession shall be governed in accordance with Ottoman law.

ART. V. All foreigners shall enjoy the privileges of the present law, as soon as the Powers on which they depend shall agree to the arrangements proposed by the Sublime Porte for the exercise of the right to hold real estate.

Now, therefore, be it known that I, ULYSSES S. GRANT, President of the United States of America, have caused the said Protocol and Law to be made public for the information and guidance of citizens of the United States.

In witness whereof I have hereunto set my hand, and caused the seal of the United States to be affixed.

Done at the city of Washington this twenty-ninth day of October, in the year of our Lord one thousand eight hundred and seventy-four, and of the Independence of the United States of America the ninety-ninth.

[SEAL.]

By the President: U. S. GRANT.

HAMILTON FISH, *Secretary of State.*

5

Proclamation Commanding the Dispersion of all Disorderly and Turbulent Persons in Warren County, Mississippi, December 21st, 1874.

By the President of the United States of America.

A PROCLAMATION.

Whereas, it is provided in the Constitution of the United States that the United States shall protect every State in the Union, on application of the Legislature, or of the Executive (when the Legislature cannot be convened), against domestic violence; and

Whereas, it is provided by the laws of the United States that, in all cases of insurrection in any State, or of obstruction to the laws thereof, it shall be lawful for the President of the United States, on application of the Legislature of such State, or of the Executive (when the Legislature cannot be convened), to call forth the militia of any other State or States, or to employ such part of the land and naval force as shall be judged necessary for the purpose of suppressing such insurrection, or of causing the laws to be duly executed; and

Whereas, the Leglslature of the State of Mississippi, now in session, have represented to me, in a concurrent resolution of that body, that several of the legally elected officers of Warren county, in said State, are prevented from executing the duties of their respective offices by force and violence; that the public buildings and records of said county have been taken into the possession of, and are now held by, lawless and unauthorized persons; that many peaceable citizens of said county have been killed, and others have been compelled to abandon, and remain away from, their homes and families; that illegal and riotous seizures and imprisonments have been made by such lawless persons; and, further, that a large number of armed men from adjacent States have invaded Mississippi to aid such lawless persons, and are still ready to give them such aid; and

Whereas, it is further represented, as aforesaid, by said Legislature, that the courts of said county cannot be held, and that the Governor of said State has no sufficient force at his command to execute the laws thereof in said county and suppress said violence, without causing a conflict of races and endangering life and property to an alarming extent; and

Whereas, the said Legislature, as aforesaid, have made application to me for such part of the military force of the United States as may be necessary and adequate to protect said State and the citizens thereof against the domestic violence hereinbefore mentioned, and to enforce the due execution of the laws; and

Whereas, the laws of the United States require that, whenever it may be necessary, in the judgment of the President, to use the military force for the purposes aforesaid, he shall forthwith, by proclamation, command such insurgents to disperse and retire peaceably to their respective abodes within a limited time.

Now, therefore, I, Ulysses S. Grant, President of the United States, do hereby command said disorderly and turbulent persons to disperse and retire peaceably to their respective abodes within five days from the date hereof; and that they refrain from forcible resistance to the laws, and submit themselves peaceably to the lawful authorities of said county and State.

In witness whereof, I have hereunto set my hand and caused the seal of the United States to be affixed.

Done at the City of Washington, this twenty-first day of December, in the year of our [L.S] Lord, eighteen hundred and seventy-four, and of the Independence of the United States, the ninety-ninth.

By the President: U. S. GRANT.
HAMILTON FISH, *Secretary of State.*

Civil Service Extended, August 31, 1874. Executive Order, No. 4.

[Official.]

It appearing to me, from their trial at Washington and at the city of New York, that the further extension of the civil-service rules will promote the efficiency of the public service, it is ordered that such rules be, and they are hereby, extended to the several Federal offices at the city and in the customs district of Boston, and that the proper measures be taken for carrying this order into effect.

August 31, 1874. U. S. GRANT.

[See allusion to "Civil Service Reform" in his Sixth Annual Message p. 54.]

Extending the Period for the Adjudication of the Alabama Claims, June 2, 1875.

By the President of the United States of America:

A PROCLAMATION.

WHEREAS: By the eighth section of the act of Congress, entitled "An Act for the creation of a Court for the adjudication and disposition of certain moneys received into the Treasury under an award made by the tribunal of Arbitration, constituted by virtue of the first article of the treaty concluded at Washington, the 8th of May, Anno Domini, eighteen hundred and seventy-one, between the United States of America and the Queen of Great Britain, approved June 23, eighteen hundred and seventy-four, it is provided that the judges of the court created by this act shall convene, in the city of Washington, as soon as convenient after their appointment; and the said court shall exist for one year from the date of its first convening and organizing; and should it be found impracticable to complete the work of the said court before the expiration of the said one year, the President may by proclamation extend the time of the duration thereof to a period of not more than six months beyond the expiration of the said one year; and in such case all the provisions of this act shall be taken and held to be the same as though the continuance of the said court had been originally fixed by this act at the limit to which it may be thus extended;" and

WHEREAS, It has been made satisfactorily to appear to me that the said court convened on the 22d of July, 1874, and that a large portion of the business of said court still remains undisposed of, and that it is found impracticable to complete the work of the said court before the expiration of the said year from its first convening and organizing.

Now, therefore, be it known that I, Ulysses S. Grant, President of the United States of America, by virtue of the authority vested in me by the provisions of the said eighth section of the act of Congress aforesaid, do hereby extend the time of the duration of said court of commissioners of Alabama claims for a period of six months after the 22d day of July, A. D., 1875.

In testimony whereof I have hereunto signed my name, and have caused the seal of the United States to be affixed.

Done at the city of Washington, this 2d day of June, A. D., 1875, and of the Independence of the United States, the ninety-ninth.

By the President: U. S. GRANT.
HAMILTON FISH, *Secretary of State.*

VIII.

JUDICIAL DECISIONS AND OPINIONS—NATIONAL AND STATE.

The Kentucky Case under the Enforcement Act of 1870.

SUPREME COURT OF THE UNITED STATES.

No. 145.—October Term, 1875.

The United States, Plaintiffs, vs. Hiram Reese and Matthew Foushee. } In error to the Circuit Court of the United States for the District of Kentucky,

Mr. Chief Justice WAITE delivered the opinion of the Court.

This case comes here by reason of a division of opinion between the judges of the circuit court in the district of Kentucky. It presents an indictment containing four counts, under sections 3 and 4 of the act of May 31, 1870,* (16 Stat., 140,) against two of the inspectors of a municipal election in the State of Kentucky, for refusing to receive and count at such election the vote of William Garner, a citizen of the United States of African descent. All the questions presented by the certificate of division arose upon general demurrers to the several counts of the indictment.

In this court the United States abandon the first and third counts, and expressly waive the

* For copy of this act, see McPherson's Hand-Book of Politics for 1870, pp. 546–550, or McPherson's History of Reconstruction, same pages.—ED.

consideration of all claims not arising out of the enforcement of the fifteenth amendment of the Constitution.

After this concession, the principal question left for consideration is, whether the act under which the indictment is found can be made effective for the punishment of inspectors of elections who refuse to receive and count the votes of citizens of the United States, having all the qualifications of voters, because of their race, color, or previous condition of servitude.

If Congress has not declared an act done within a State to be a crime against the United States, the courts have no power to treat it as such. (U. S. vs. Hudson, 7 Cranch, 32.) It is not claimed that there is any statute which can reach this case, unless it be the one in question.

Looking, then, to this statute, we find that its first section provides that all citizens of the United States, who are or shall be otherwise qualified by law to vote at any election, etc., shall be entitled and allowed to vote thereat, without distinction of race, color, or previous condition of servitude, any constitution, etc., of the State to the contrary notwithstanding. This simply declares a right without providing a punishment for its violation.

The second section provides for the punishment of any officer charged with the duty of furnishing to citizens an opportunity to perform any act which by the constitution or laws of any State is made a prerequisite or qualification of voting, who shall omit to give all citizens of the United States the same and equal opportunity to perform such prerequisite and become qualified on account of the race, color, or previous condition of servitude of the applicant. This does not apply to or include the inspectors of an election, whose only duty it is to receive and count the votes of citizens designated by law as voters, who have already become qualified to vote at the election.

The third section is to the effect that whenever, by or under the constitution or laws of any State, etc., any act is or shall be required to be done by any citizen as a prerequisite to qualify or entitle him to vote, the offer of such citizen to perform the act required to be done, "as aforesaid," shall, if it fail to be carried into execution by reason of the wrongful act or omission "aforesaid" of the person or officer charged with the duty of receiving or permitting such performance or offer to perform, or acting thereon, be deemed and held as a performance in law of such act; and the person so offering and failing as aforesaid, and being otherwise qualified, shall be entitled to vote in the same manner and to the same extent as if he had in fact performed such act; and any judge, inspector, or other officer of election, whose duty it is to receive, count, etc., or give effect to the vote of any such citizen, who shall wrongfully refuse or omit to receive, count, etc., the vote of such citizen, upon the presentation by him of his affidavit stating such offer, and the time and place thereof, and the name of the person or officer whose duty it was to act thereon, and that he was wrongfully prevented by such person or officer from performing such act, shall for every such offense forfeit and pay, etc.

The fourth section provides for the punishment of any person who shall by force, bribery, threats, intimidation, or other unlawful means, hinder, delay, etc., or shall combine with others to hinder, delay, prevent, or obstruct any citizen from doing any act required to be done to qualify him to vote or from voting at any election.

The second count in the indictment is based upon the fourth section of this act, and the fourth upon the third section.

Rights and immunities created by or dependent upon the Constitution of the United States can be protected by Congress. The form and the manner of the protection may be such as Congress, in the legitimate exercise of its legislative discretion, shall provide. These may be varied to meet the necessities of the particular right to be protected.

The fifteenth amendment does not confer the right of suffrage upon any one. It prevents the States, or the United States, however, from giving preference, in this particular, to one citizen of the United States over another, on account of race, color, or previous condition of servitude. Before its adoption this could be done. It was as much within the power of a State to exclude citizens of the United States from voting on account of race, etc., as it was on account of age, property, or education. Now it is not. If citizens of one race having certain qualifications are permitted by law to vote, those of another having the same qualifications must be. Previous to this amendment there was no constitutional guaranty against this discrimination. Now there is. It follows that the amendment has invested the citizens of the United States with a new constitutional right which is in the protecting power of Congress. That right is exemption from discrimination in the exercise of the elective franchise, on account of race, color, or previous condition of servitude. This, under the express provisions of the second section of the amendment, Congress may enforce by "appropriate legislation."

This leads us to enquire whether the act now under consideration is "appropriate legislation" for that purpose. The power of Congress to legislate at all upon the subject of voting at State elections, rests upon this amendment. The effect of article I., section 4, of the Constitution in respect to elections for senators and representatives is not now under consideration. It has not been contended, nor can it be, that the amendment confers authority to impose penalties for every wrongful refusal to receive the vote of a qualified elector at State elections. It is only when the wrongful refusal at such an election is because of race, color, or previous condition of servitude, that Congress can interfere and provide for its punishment. If, therefore, the third and fourth sections of the act are beyond that limit, they are unauthorized.

The third section does not in express terms limit the offense of an inspector of elections, for which the punishment is provided, to a wrongful discrimination on account of race, etc. This is conceded, but, it is urged, that when this section is construed with those which precede it, and to which, as is claimed, it refers, it is so limited. The argument is that the only wrongful act on the part of the officer whose duty it is to receive or permit the requisite qualification, which can dispense with actual qualification under the State laws, and substitute the prescribed affidavit therefor, is that mentioned and prohibited in section 2, to wit: discrimination on account of race, etc., and that consequently section 3 is confined in its operation to the same wrongful discrimination.

This is a penal statute and must be construed strictly; not so strictly, indeed, as to defeat the clear intention of Congress, but the words employed must be understood in the sense they were obviously used. (U. S. vs. Wiltberger, 5 Wheat., 85.) If, taking the whole statute together, it is apparent that it was not the intention of Congress thus to limit the operation of the act, we cannot give it that effect.

The statute contemplates a most important change in the election laws. Previous to its adoption, the States, as a general rule, regulated in their own way all the details of all elections. They prescribed the qualifications of voters and the manner in which those offering to vote at an election should make known their qualifications to the officers in charge. This act interferes with this practice and prescribes rules not provided by the laws of the States. It substitutes, under certain circumstances, performance wrongfully prevented for performance itself. If the elector makes and presents his affidavit in the form and to the effect prescribed, the inspectors are to treat this as the equivalent of the specified requirement of the State law. This is a radical change in the practice, and the statute which creates it should be explicit in its terms. Nothing should be left to construction if it can be avoided. The law ought not to be in such a condition that the elector may act upon one idea of its meaning and the inspector upon another.

The elector, under the provisions of the statute, is only required to state in his affidavit that he has been wrongfully prevented by the officer from qualifying. There are no words of limitation in this part of the section. In a case like this, if an affidavit is in the language of the statute, it ought to be sufficient both for the voter and the inspector. Laws which prohibit the doing of things and provide a punishment for their violation should have no double meaning. A citizen should not unnecessarily be placed where, by an honest error in the construction of a penal statute, he may be subjected to a prosecution for a false oath, and an inspector of elections should not be put in jeopardy because he, with equal honesty, entertains an opposite opinion. If this statute limits the wrongful act which will justify the affidavit to discrimination on account of race, etc., then a citizen who makes an affidavit that he has been wrongfully prevented by the officer, which is true in the ordinary sense of that term, subjects himself to indictment and trial, if not to conviction, because it is not true that he has been prevented by such a wrongful act as the statute contemplated; and if there is no such limitation, but any wrongful act of exclusion will justify the affidavit and give the right to vote without the actual performance of the prerequisite, then the inspector who rejects the vote because he reads the law in its limited sense and thinks it is confined to a wrongful discrimination on account of race, etc., subjects himself to prosecution, if not to punishment, because he has misconstrued the law. Penal statutes ought not to be expressed in language so uncertain. If the legislature undertakes to define, by statute, a new offense and provide for its punishment, it should express its will in language that need not deceive the common mind. Every man should be able to know with certainty when he is committing a crime.

But when we go beyond the third section and read the fourth we find there no words of limitation, or reference, even, that can be construed as manifesting any intention to confine its provisions to the terms of the fifteenth amendment. That section has for its object the punishment of all persons who, by force, bribery, etc., hinder, delay, etc., any person from qualifying or voting. In view of all these facts we feel compelled to say that in our opinion the language of the third and fourth sections does not confine their operation to unlawful discriminations on account of race, etc. If Congress had the power to provide generally for the punishment of those who unlawfully interfere to prevent the exercise of the elective franchise without regard to such discrimination, the language of these sections would be broad enough for that purpose.

It remains now to consider whether a statute, so general as this in its provisions, can be made available for the punishment of those who may be guilty of unlawful discrimination against citizens of the United States, while exercising the elective franchise, on account of their race, etc.

There is no attempt in the sections now under consideration to provide specifically for such an offense. If the case is provided for at all, it is because it comes under the general prohibition against any wrongful act or unlawful obstruction in this particular. We are, therefore, directly called upon to decide whether a penal statute enacted by Congress, with its limited powers, which provides in general language broad enough to cover wrongful acts without as well as within the constitutional jurisdiction, can be limited by judicial construction so as to make it operate only on that which Congress may rightfully prohibit and punish. For this purpose we must take these sections of the statute as they are. We are not able to reject a part which is unconstitutional and retain the remainder, because it is not possible to separate that which is unconstitutional, if there be any such, from that which is not. The proposed effect is not to be attained by striking out or disregarding words that are in the section, but by inserting those that are not now there. Each of the sections must stand as a whole or fall altogether. The language is plain. There is no room for construction, unless it be as to the effect of the Constitution. The question, then, to be determined is, whether we can introduce words of limitation into a penal statute so as to make it specific, when, as expressed, it is general only.

It would certainly be dangerous if the legislature could set a net large enough to catch all possible offenders, and leave it to the courts to step inside and say who could be rightfully detained and who should be set at large. This would, to some extent, substitute the judicial for the legislative department of the government. The courts enforce the legislative will when ascertained, if within the constitutional grant of power. Within its legitimate sphere, Congress is supreme and beyond the control of the courts, but if it steps outside of its constitutional limitations and attempts that which is beyond its reach, the courts are authorized to, and when called upon in due course of legal proceedings must, annul its encroachments upon the reserved power of the states and the people.

To limit this statute in the manner now asked for, would be to make a new law, not to enforce an old one. This is no part of our duty.

We must, therefore, decide that Congress has not as yet provided by "appropriate legislation" for the punishment of the offense charged in the indictment, and that the circuit court properly sustained the demurrers and gave judgment for the defendants.

This makes it unnecessary to answer any of the other questions certified. Since the law which gives the presiding judge the casting vote in cases of division, and authorizes a judgment in accordance with his opinion, (Rev. Stat., sec. 650,) if we find that the judgment as rendered is correct, we need not do more than affirm. If, however, we reverse, all questions certified, which may be considered in the final determination of the case according to the opinion we express, should be answered.

The judgment of the circuit court is affirmed.

Mr. Justice CLIFFORD concurred that the indictment is bad, but for reasons widely different from those assigned by the court. His opinion covers eight printed pages, but there is no summary of his points which compactly presents them.

Mr. Justice HUNT dissented. The following are the points of his dissenting opinion:

1. The fourth count of the indictment charges in substance that the two defendants, inspectors of election, rejected the vote of Garner at a municipal election of the city of Lexington on account of his race and color, he being a citizen of the United States of African descent and a qualified voter.

2. The argument that the 3d and 4th sections of the statute of May 30, 1870, (16 Statutes, 140,) are invalid because they do not use the terms race or color, is not sound, for the reason that they are to be understood as having incorporated into them by reference by the use of the words "as aforesaid" the words without distinction of race or color. Refusing a qualified vote by the "wrongful act aforesaid," means a wrongful act on account of race, color, or previous condition of servitude.

3. The right of voting secured by the 15th amendment is to a particular class of persons, to wit, citizens of the United States, and not for any particular class of elections. *Wherever* the right to vote exists in such a person, its denial or abridgement on account of race, color, or previous condition, at any election, national, State, or municipal, is forbidden by this amendment.

4. A denial by the inspectors of a municipal election, on account of his race or color, of the right of a citizen of the United States to vote at such election, he being qualified in other respects, is a denial by the State within the 15th amendment; and this, although such denial is illegal and in violation of the statute of the State. The word "State" in this amendment includes the agencies and instrumentalities of the State. The inspectors of elections are the agents of the State, having jurisdiction over the subject of receiving and rejecting votes and certifying the results of elections. Although they act illegally and in excess of authority, their certificates are conclusive and their acts are binding upon all parties until vacated by judicial proceedings. For these purposes they are the State.

5. It is competent to Congress to protect and secure this right, by providing for the punishment by fine and imprisonment of those who violate it. The power of enforcing the amendments is not limited to giving an appeal or writ of error to the United States courts from the erroneous decisions of the State courts made upon the subject.

6. If an indictment contain counts that are good and counts that are bad, a judgment of guilty upon the whole indictment will be sustained.

7. In the present case the judgment has been entered discharging the defendants from the whole indictment. As the indictment contains some good counts this judgment is erroneous. It should be reversed and a trial upon the indictment ordered.

The "Grant Parish" case, under the Enforcement Act of 1870.

SUPREME COURT OF THE UNITED STATES.

No. 339.—October Term, 1875.

The United States, Plaintiffs in Error. vs. William J. Cruikshank, William D. Irwin, and John P. Hadnot.	In error to the Circuit Court of the United States for the District of Louisiana.

Mr. Chief Justice WAITE delivered the opinion of the Court.

This case comes here with a certificate by the judges of the Circuit Court for the District of Louisiana that they were divided in opinion upon a question which occurred at the hearing. It presents for our consideration an indictment containing sixteen counts, divided into two series of eight counts each, based upon section 6 of the enforcement act of May 31, 1870. That section is as follows:

"That if two or more persons shall band or conspire together, or go in disguise upon the public highway, or upon the premises of another, with intent to violate any provision of this act, or to injure, oppress, threaten, or intimidate any citizen, with intent to prevent or hinder his free exercise and enjoyment of any right or privilege granted or secured to him by the Constitution or laws of the United States, or because of his having exercised the same, such person shall be held guilty of felony, and, on conviction thereof, shall be fined or imprisoned, or both, at the discretion of the court—the fine not to exceed five thousand dollars, and the imprisonment not to exceed ten years—and shall, moreover, be thereafter ineligible to, and disabled from holding, any office or place of honor, profit, or trust created by the Constitution or laws of the United States." (16 Stat., 141.)

The question certified arose upon a motion in arrest of judgment after a verdict of guilty generally upon the whole sixteen counts, and is stated to be whether "the said sixteen counts of said indictment are severally good and sufficient in law, and contain charges of criminal matter indictable under the laws of the United States."

The general charge in the first eight counts is that of "banding," and in the second eight that of "conspiring" together to injure, oppress, threaten, and intimidate Levi Nelson and Alexander Tillman, citizens of the United States of African descent and persons of color, with the intent thereby to hinder and prevent them in their free exercise and enjoyment of rights and privileges "granted and secured" to them "in common with all other good citizens of the United States by the Constitution and laws of the United States."

The offences provided for by the statute in question do not consist in the mere "banding" or "conspiring" of two or more persons together, but in their banding or conspiring with the intent or for any of the purposes specified. To bring this case under the operation of the statute, therefore, it must appear that the right, the enjoyment of which the conspirators intended to hinder or prevent, was one granted or secured by the Constitution or laws of the United States. If it does not so appear, the criminal matter charged has not been made indictable by any act of Congress.

We have in our political system a government of the United States and a government of each of the several states. Each one of these governments is distinct from the others, and each has citizens of its own who owe it allegiance, and whose rights, within its jurisdiction, it must protect. The same person may be at the same time a citizen of the United States and a citizen of a state, but his rights of citizenship under one of these governments will be different from those he has under the other. (Slaughter-House Cases, 16 Wall., 74).

Citizens are the members of the political community to which they belong. They are the people who compose the community, and who, in their associated capacity, have established or submitted themselves to the dominion of a government for the promotion of their general welfare and the protection of their individual as well as their collective rights. In the formation of a government the people may confer upon it such powers as they choose. The government when so formed may, and when called upon should, exercise all the powers it has for the protection of the rights of its citizens and the people within its jurisdiction, but it can exercise no other. The duty of a government to afford protection is limited always by the power it possesses for that purpose.

Experience made the fact known to the people of the United States that they required a national government for national purposes. The separate governments of the separate States, bound together by the articles of confederation alone, were not sufficient for the promotion of the general welfare of the people in respect to foreign nations, or for their complete protection as citizens of the confederated States. For this reason the people of the United States, "in order to form a more perfect Union, establish justice, insure domestic tranquillity, provide for the common defence, promote the general welfare, and secure the blessings of liberty" to themselves and their posterity, (Const. Preamble,) ordained and established the government of the United States, and defined its powers by a constitution, which they adopted as its fundamental law and made its rule of action.

The government thus established and defined is to some extent a government of the States in their political capacity. It is also, for certain purposes, a government of the people. Its powers are limited in number, but not in degree. Within the scope of its powers, as enumerated and defined, it is supreme and above the States, but beyond it has no existence. It was erected for special purposes and endowed with all the powers necessary for its own preservation and the accomplishment of the ends its people had in view. It can neither grant nor secure to its citizens any right or privilege not expressly, or by implication, placed under its jurisdiction.

The people of the United States resident within any State are subject to two governments, one State and the other national, but there need be no conflict between the two. The powers which one possesses the other does not. They are established for different purposes, and have separate jurisdictions. Together they make one whole and furnish the people of the United States with a complete government, ample for the protection of all their rights at home and abroad. True, it may sometimes happen that a person is amenable to both jurisdictions for one and the same act. Thus, if a marshal of the United States is unlawfully resisted while executing the process of the courts within a State, and the resistance is accompanied by an assault on the officer, the sovereignty of the United States is violated by the resistance, and that of the State by the breach of peace in the assault. So, too, if one passes the counterfeited coin of the United States within a State, it may be an offense against the United States and the State; the United States, because it discredits the coin, and the State, because of the fraud upon him to whom it is passed. This does not, however, necessarily imply that the two governments possess powers in common, or bring them into conflict with each other. It is the natural consequence of a citizenship which owes allegiance to two sovereignties and claims protection from both. The citizen cannot complain, because he has voluntarily submitted himself to such a form of government. He owes allegiance to the two departments, so to speak, and within their respective spheres must pay the penalties which each exacts for disobedience to its laws. In return he can demand protection from each within its own jurisdiction.

The government of the United States is one of delegated powers alone. Its authority is defined and limited by the Constitution. All powers not granted to it by that instrument are reserved to the States or the people. No rights can be acquired under the Constitution or laws of the United States except such as the government of the United States has the authority to grant or secure. All that cannot be so granted or secured are left under the protection of the States.

We now proceed to an examination of the indictment, to ascertain whether the several rights, which it is alleged the defendants intended to interfere with, are such as had been in law and in fact granted or secured by the Constitution or laws of the United States.

The first and ninth counts state the intent of the defendants to have been to hinder and prevent the citizens named in the free exercise and enjoyment of their "lawful right and privilege to peaceably assemble together with each other and with other citizens of the United States for a peaceful and lawful purpose." The right of the people peaceably to assemble for lawful purposes existed long before the adoption of the Constitution of the United States. In fact, it is, and always has been, one of the attributes of citizenship under a free government. It "derives its source," to use the language of Chief Justice Marshall, in Gibbons vs. Ogden, 9 Wheat., 211, "from those laws whose authority is acknowledged by civilized man throughout the world." It is found wherever civilization exists. It was not, therefore, a right granted to the people by the Constitution. The government of the United States when established found it in existence, with the obligation on the part of the States to afford it protection. As no direct power over it was granted to Congress, it remains, according to the ruling in Gibbons vs. Ogden, 9 Wheat., 203, subject to State jurisdiction. Only such existing rights were committed by the people to the protection of Congress as came within the general scope of the authority granted to the national government.

The first amendment of the Constitution prohibits Congress from abridging "the right of the people to assemble and to petition the government for a redress of grievances." This, like the other amendments proposed and adopted at the same time, was not intended to limit the powers of the State governments in respect to their own citizens, but to operate upon the national government alone. (Barron vs. The City of Baltimore, 7 Pet., 250; Lessee of Livingston vs. Moore, 7 Pet., 551; Fox vs. Ohio, 5 How., 434; Smith vs. Maryland, 18 How., 76; Withers vs. Buckley, 20 How., 90; Pervear vs. the Commonwealth, 5 Wall, 479; Twitchell vs. The Commonwealth, 7 Wall., 321; Edwards vs. Elliott, 21 Wall., 557.) It is now too late to question the correctness of this construction. As was said by the late Chief Justice, in Twitchell vs. The Commonwealth, p. 325,) "the scope and application of these amendments are no longer subjects of discussion here." They left the authority of the States just where they found it, and added nothing to the already existing powers of the United States.

The particular amendment now under consideration assumes the existence of the right of the people to assemble for lawful purposes and protects it against encroachment by Congress. The right was not created by the amendment; neither was its continuance guaranteed, except as against congressional interference. For their protection in its enjoyment, therefore, the people must look to the States. There is where the power for that purpose was originally placed, and it has never been surrendered to the United States.

The right of the people peaceably to assemble for the purpose of petitioning Congress for a redress of grievances, or for anything else connected with the powers or the duties of the national government, is an attribute of national citizenship, and as such, under the protection of, and guaranteed by, the United States. The very idea of a government, republican in form, implies a right on the part of its citizens to meet peaceably for consultation in respect to public affairs, and to petition for a redress of grievances. If it had been alleged in these counts that the object of the defendants was to prevent a meeting for such a purpose, the case would have been within the statute and within the scope of the sovereignty of the United States. Such, however, is not the case. The offence, as stated in the indictment, will be made out if it be shown that the object of the conspiracy was to prevent a meeting for any lawful purpose whatever.

The second and tenth counts are equally defective. The right there specified is that of "bearing arms for a lawful purpose." This is not a right granted by the Constitution. Neither is it in any manner dependent upon that instrument for its existence. The second amendment declares that it shall not be infringed; but this, as has been seen, means no more than that it shall not be infringed by Congress. This is one of the amendments that has no other effect than to restrict the powers of the national government, leaving the people to look for their protection against any violation by their fellow-citizens of the rights it recognizes, to what is called in The City of New York vs. Miln, 11 Pet., 139, the "powers which relate to merely municipal legislation, or what was, perhaps, more properly called internal police," "not surrendered or restrained" by the Constitution of the United States.

The third and eleventh counts are even more objectionable. They charge the intent to have been to deprive the citizens named, they being in Louisiana, "of their respective several lives and liberty of person without due process of law." This is nothing else than alleging a conspiracy to falsely imprison or murder citizens of the United States, being within the territorial jurisdiction of the State of Louisiana. The rights of life and personal liberty are natural rights of man. "To secure these rights," says the Declaration of Independence, "governments are instituted among men, deriving their just powers from the consent of the governed." The very highest duty of the States, when they entered into the Union under the Constitution, was to protect all persons within their boundaries in the enjoyment of these "unalienable rights with which they were endowed by their Creator." Sovereignty, for this purpose, rests alone with the states. It is no more the duty or within the power of the United States to punish for a conspiracy to falsely imprison or murder within a state than it would be to punish for false imprisonment or murder itself.

The fourteenth amendment prohibits a State from depriving any person of life, liberty, or property, without due process of law, but this adds nothing to the rights of one citizen as against another. It simply furnishes an additional guaranty against any encroachment by the States upon the fundamental rights which belong to every citizen as a member of society. As was said by Mr. Justice Johnson, in Bank of Columbia vs. Okely, 4 Wheat., 244, it secures "the individual from the arbitrary exercise of the powers of government, unrestrained by the established principles of private rights and distributive justice." These counts in the indictment do not call for the exercise of any of the powers conferred by this provision in the amendment.

The fourth and twelfth counts charge the intent to have been to prevent and hinder the citizens named, who were of African descent and persons of color, in "the free exercise and enjoyment of their several right and privilege to the full and equal benefit of all laws and proceedings, then and there before that time enacted or ordained by the said State of Louisiana and by the United States; and then and there, at that time, being in force in the said State and District of Louisiana, aforesaid, for the security of their respective persons and property, then and there, at that time enjoyed at and within said State and District of Louisiana by white persons, being citizens of said State of Louisiana and the United States, for the protection of the persons and property of said white citizens." There is no allegation that this was done because of the race or color of the persons conspired against. When stripped of its verbiage the case as presented amounts to nothing more than that the defendants conspired to prevent certain citizens of the United States, being within the State of Louisiana, from enjoying the equal protection of the laws of the State and of the United States.

The fourteenth amendment prohibits a State from denying to any person within its jurisdiction the equal protection of the laws; but this provision does not, any more than the one which precedes it, and which we have just considered, add anything to the rights which one citizen has under the Constitution against another. The equality of the rights of citizens is a principle of republicanism. Every republican government is in duty bound to protect all its citizens in the enjoyment of this principle, if within its power. That duty was originally assumed by the States, and it still remains there. The only obligation resting upon the United States is to see that the States do not deny the right. This the amendment guarantees, but no more. The power of the national government is limited to the enforcement of this guaranty.

No question arises under the civil rights act of April 9, 1866, (14 Stat., 27,) which is intended for the protection of citizens of the United States in the enjoyment of certain rights, without discrimination on account of race, color, or previous condition of servitude, because, as has already been stated, it is no where alleged in these counts that the wrong contemplated against the rights of these citizens was on account of their race or color.

Another objection is made to these counts that they are too vague and uncertain. This will be considered hereafter in connection with the same objection to other counts.

The sixth and fourteenth counts state the intent of the defendants to have been to hinder and prevent the citizens named, being of African descent and colored, "in the free exercise and enjoyment of their several and respective right and privilege to vote at any election to be thereafter by law had and held by the people in and of the said State of Louisiana, or by the people of and in the parish of Grant aforesaid." In Minor vs. Happersett, 21 Wall., 178, we decided that the Constitution of the United States has not conferred the right of suffrage upon any one, and that the United States have no voters of their own creation in the States. In U. S. vs. Reese, just decided, we hold that the fifteenth amendment has invested the citizens of the United States with a new constitutional right, which is, exemption from discrimination in the exercise of the elective franchise on account of race, color, or previous condition of servitude. From this it appears that the right of suffrage is not a necessary attribute of national citizenship, but that exemption from discrimination in the exercise of that right on account of race, etc., is. The right to vote in the States comes from the States, but the right of exemption from the prohibited discrimination comes from the United States. The first has not been granted or secured by the Constitution of the United States, but the last has been.

Inasmuch, therefore, as it does not appear in these counts that the intent of the defendants was to prevent these parties from exercising their right to vote on account of their race, etc., it does not appear that it was their intent to interfere with any right granted or secured by the Constitution or laws of the United States. We may suspect that race was the cause of the hostility, but it is not so averred. This is material to a description of the substance of the offence, and cannot be supplied by implication. Everything essential must be charged positively, and not inferentially. The defect here is not in form but in substance.

The seventh and fifteenth counts are no better than the sixth and fourteenth. The intent here charged is to put the parties named in great fear of bodily harm and to injure and oppress them, because, being and having been in all things qualified, they had voted "at an election before that time, had and held according to law by the people of the said State of Louisiana, in said State, to wit: on the 4th day of November, A. D. 1872, and at divers other elections by the people of the State, also before that time had and held according to law." There is nothing to show that the elections voted at were any other than State elections, or that the conspiracy was formed on account of the race of the parties against whom the conspirators were to act. The charge as made is really of nothing more than a conspiracy to commit a breach of the peace within a State. Certainly it will not be claimed that the United States have the power or are required to do mere police duty in the States. If a State cannot protect itself against domestic violence, the United States may, upon the call of the Executive, when the Legislature cannot be convened, lend their assistance for that purpose. This is a guaranty of the Constitution (Art. IV., section 4), but it applies to no case like this.

We are, therefore, of the opinion that the first, second, third, fourth, sixth, seventh, ninth, tenth, eleventh, twelfth, fourteenth and fifteenth counts do not contain charges of a criminal nature made indictable under the laws of the United States, and that consequently they are not good and sufficient in law. They do not show that it was the intent of the defendants, by their conspiracy, to hinder or prevent the enjoyment of any right granted or secured by the Constitution.

We come now to consider the fifth and thirteenth and the eighth and sixteenth counts, which may be brought together for that purpose. The intent charged in the fifth and thirteenth is "to hinder and prevent the parties in their respective free exercise and enjoyment of the rights, privileges, immunities, and protection granted and secured to them respectively as citizens of the United States and as citizens of said State of Louisiana," "for the reason that they, * * * being then and there citizens of said State and of the United States, were persons of African descent and race, and persons of color, and not white citizens thereof," and in the eighth and sixteenth, to hinder and prevent them "in their several and respective free exercise and enjoyment of every, each, all, and singular the several rights and privileges granted and secured to them by the Constitution and laws of the United States." The same general statement of the rights to be interfered with is found in the fifth and thirteenth counts.

According to the view we take of these counts, the question is not whether it is enough, in general, to describe a statutory offence in the language of the statute, but whether the offence has here been described at all. The statute provides for the punishment of those who conspire "to injure, oppress, threaten, or intimidate any citizen, with intent to prevent or hinder his free exercise and enjoyment of any right or privilege granted or secured to him by the Constitution or laws of the United States." These counts in the indictment charge, in substance, that the intent in this case was to hinder and prevent these citizens in the free exercise and enjoyment of "every, each, all, and singular" the rights granted them by the Constitution, etc. There is no specification of any particular right. The language is broad enough to cover all.

In criminal cases, prosecuted under the laws of the United States, the accused has the constitutional right "to be informed of the nature and cause of the accusation." (Amendment VI.) In U. S. vs. Mills, 7 Pet., 142, this was construed to mean that the indictment must set forth the offence "with clearness and all necessary certainty, to apprise the accused of the crime with which he stands charged;" and in U. S. vs. Cook, 17 Wall., 174, that "every ingredient of which the offence is composed must be accurately and clearly alleged." It is an elementary principle of criminal pleading that where the definition of an offence, whether it be at common law or by statute, "includes generic terms, it is not sufficient that the indictment shall charge the offence in the same generic terms as in the definition, but it must state the species—it must descend to particulars." (1 Arch. Cr. Pr. and Pl., 291.) The object of the indictment is, first, to furnish the accused with such a description of the charge against him as will enable him to make his defence, and avail himself of his conviction or acquittal for protection against a further prosecution for the same cause; and, second, to inform the court of the facts alleged, so that it may decide whether they are sufficient in law to support a conviction, if one should be had. For this, facts are to be stated, not conclusions of law alone. A crime is made up of acts and intent, and these must be set forth in the indictment, with reasonable particularity of time, place, and circumstances.

It is a crime to steal goods and chattels, but an indictment would be bad that did not specify with some degree of certainty the articles stolen. This because the accused must be advised of the essential particulars of the charge against him, and the court must be able to decide whether the property taken was such as was the subject of larceny. So, too, it is in some States a crime for two or more persons to conspire to cheat and defraud another out of his property, but it has been held that an indictment for such an offense must contain allegations setting forth the means proposed to be used to accomplish the purpose. This, because, to make such a purpose criminal, the conspiracy must be to cheat and defraud in a mode made criminal by statute, and as all cheating and defrauding has not been made criminal, it is necessary for the indictment to state the means proposed in order that the court may see that they are in fact illegal. (State vs. Parker, 43 N. H., 83; State vs. Keach, 40 Vt., 118; Alderman vs. The People, 4 Mich., 414; State vs. Roberts, 34 Maine, 32.) In Maine it is an offense for two or more to conspire with the intent unlawfully and wickedly to commit any crime punishable by imprisonment in the State prison, (State vs. Roberts,) but we think it will hardly be claimed that an indictment would be good under this statute, which charges the object of the conspiracy to have been "unlawfully and wickedly to commit each, every, all and singular the crimes punishable by imprisonment in the State prison." All crimes are not so punishable. Whether a particular crime be such an one or not is a question of law. The accused has, therefore, the right to have a specification of the charge against him in this respect, in order that he may decide whether he should present his defense by motion to quash, demurrer, or plea; and the court, that it may determine whether the facts will sustain the indictment. So here, the crime is made to consist in the unlawful combination with an intent to prevent the enjoyment of any right granted or secured by the Constitution, etc. All rights are not so granted or secured. Whether one is so or not is a question of law to be decided by the court, not the prosecutor. Therefore, the indictment should state the particulars, to inform the court as well as the accused. It must be made to appear, that is to say, appear from the indictment without going further, that the acts charged will, if proven, support a conviction for the offense alleged.

But it is needless to pursue the argument further. The conclusion is irresistible that these counts are too vague and general. They lack the certainty and precision required by the established rules of criminal pleading. It follows that they are not good and sufficient in law. They are so defective that no judgment of conviction should be pronounced upon them.

The order of the circuit court arresting the judgment upon the verdict is, therefore, affirmed, and the cause remanded with instructions to discharge the defendants.

Mr. Justice Clifford dissented.

Construing the Civil Rights Act of April 9, 1866.

SUPREME COURT OF THE UNITED STATES.

No. 35.—December Term, 1871.

John Blyew and George Kennard, Plaintiffs in Error, vs. The United States.	In error to the Circuit Court of the United States for the District of Kentucky.

Mr. Justice STRONG delivered the opinion of the Court.

The plaintiffs in error, defendants below, were indicted in the Circuit Court for the District of Kentucky for the murder, within that district, of a colored woman named Lucy Armstrong. The indictment contained three counts, all of them charging the murder in the usual form of indictments for that offence, and with sufficient certainty. But, in order to show jurisdiction in the Circuit Court of the United States, an averment was made in the first count that the said Lucy Armstrong was a citizen of the United States, having been born therein, and not subject to any foreign power; that she was of the African race, and was above the age of seventy-five years; that Blyew and Kennard (the persons indicted) were white persons, each of them at the time of the alleged killing and murder above the age of eighteen years; that the said killing and murder, done and committed, as averred, were seen and witnessed by one Richard Foster and one Laura Foster, citizens of the United States, having been born therein and not subject to any foreign power, both of the African race; and that the said Lucy Armstrong, Richard Foster and Laura Foster were then and there denied the right to testify against the said Blyew and Kennard, or either of them, concerning the said killing and murder, in the courts and judicial tribunals of the State of Kentucky, solely on account of their race and color. The second and third counts contained substantially the same averments.

To this indictment the defendants pleaded specially that before it was found they had been in custody of the authorities of the State, and, after examination, had been held to answer for the killing of Lucy Armstrong, which was the same offence as that charged in the circuit court, but on demurrer the plea was overruled, and the case went to trial upon the issues found by a replication to the plea of not guilty. During the progress of the trial the court sealed several exceptions to the admission of evidence offered by the United States, and, a verdict of guilty having been returned, a motion was made in arrest of judgment, which the court also overruled. The ground alleged for this motion was, that "the facts stated in the indictment did not constitute a public offence within the jurisdiction of the court." There are thus three questions presented by the record. They are, *first*, whether the circuit court had jurisdiction of the offence charged in the indictment; *second*, whether the court erred in sustaining the demurrer to the defendants' special plea; and, *third*, whether the evidence to which the defendants objected should have been received.

Addressing ourselves to the first of these questions, it may be remarked that clearly the circuit court had no jurisdiction of the crime of murder committed within the district of Kentucky, unless it was conferred by the third section of the act of Congress of April 9, 1866, entitled "An act to protect all persons in the United States in their civil rights, and furnish the means of their vindication." The first section of that act declared all persons born in the United States, and not subject to any foreign power, excluding Indians not taxed, to be citizens of the United States, and it is enacted that "such citizens, of every race and color, shall have the same right in every State and territory in the United States to make and enforce contracts, to sue, be parties, and give evidence, to inherit, purchase, lease, sell, hold, and convey real and personal property, and to full and equal benefit of all laws and proceedings for the security of person and property as is enjoyed by white citizens, and shall be subject to like punishment, pains, and penalties, and to none other, any law, statute, ordinance, regulation, or custom to the contrary notwithstanding."

The second section enacted "that any person who, under color of any law, statute, ordinance, regulation, or custom, shall subject, or cause to be subjected, any inhabitant of any state or territory to the deprivation of any right, secured or protected by the act, or to different punishment, pains, or penalties, on account of such person having at any time been held in a condition of slavery, or involuntary servitude, except as a punishment for crime, whereof the party shall have been duly convicted, or by reason of his color, or race, than is prescribed for the punishment of white persons, shall be deemed guilty of a misdemeanor, and shall, on conviction thereof, be punished" as therein prescribed.

Then followed the third section, which contains the enactment "that the district courts of the United States, within their respective districts, shall have, exclusively of the courts of the several States, cognizance of all crimes and offenses committed against the provisions of this act, *and also concurrently with the circuit courts of the United States*, of all causes, civil and criminal, affecting persons who are denied, or cannot enforce in the courts or judicial tribunals of the State, or locality, where they may be, any of the rights secured to them by the first section of the act." The section then provided for removal into the federal courts of any suit or prosecution, civil or criminal, which had been, or might thereafter be, commenced against any *such person* for any cause whatever.

It must be admitted that the crimes and offenses of which the district courts are, by this section, given exclusive jurisdiction, are only those which are against the provisions of the act, or those enumerated in the second and sixth sections, and that the "causes, civil and criminal," over which jurisdiction is, by the second clause of the section, conferred upon the district and circuit courts of the United States concurrently, are other than those of which exclusive jurisdiction is given to the district courts. They are described as causes "affecting persons who are denied, or cannot enforce in the courts or judicial tribunals of the State, or locality, where they may be, any of the rights secured to them by the first section of the act. Was, then, the prosecution, or indictment, against these defendants a cause affecting any such person or persons? If it was, then by the provisions of the act it was within the jurisdiction of the court, and if it was not, that court had no jurisdiction.

It was, as we have seen, an indictment for the murder of Lucy Armstrong, a citizen of the United States of the African race, and it contained an averment that other citizens of the United States of the same race, witnessed the alleged murder. It contained also an averment that those other persons, namely, Richard Foster and Laura Foster, as well as the deceased Lucy Armstrong, were, on account of their race and color, denied the right to testify against the defendants, or either of them, of and concerning the killing and murder, in the courts and judicial tribunals of the State of Kentucky.

We are thus brought to the question whether a criminal prosecution for a public offence is a cause "affecting," within the meaning of the act of Congress, persons who may be called to testify therein. Obviously the only parties to such a cause are the government and the persons indicted. They alone can be reached by any judgment that may be pronounced. No judgment can either enlarge or diminish the personal, relative, or property rights of any others than those who are parties. It is true there are some cases which may affect the rights of property of persons who are not parties to the record. Such cases, however, are all of a civil nature, and none of them even touch rights of person. But an indictment prosecuted by the government against an alleged criminal, is a cause in which none but the parties can have any concern, except what is common to all the members of the community. Those who may possibly be witnesses, either for the prosecution or for the defence, are no more affected by it than is every other person, for any one may be called as a witness. It will not be thought that Congress intended to give to the district and circuit courts jurisdiction over all causes, both civil and criminal. They have expressly confined it to causes affecting certain persons. And yet, if all those who may be called as witnesses in a case, and who may be alleged to be important witnesses, were intended to be described in the class of persons affected by it, and if the jurisdiction of the Federal courts can be invoked by the assertion that there are persons who may be witnessess, but who, because of their race or color, are incompetent to testify in the courts of the State, there is no cause either civil or criminal of which those courts may not at the option of either party take jurisdiction. The statute of Kentucky which was in existence when this indictment was found, and which denied the right of Richard Foster and Laura Foster to testify in the courts of the State, enacted as follows: "that a slave, negro, or Indian shall be a competent witness in the case of the commonwealth for or against a slave, negro, or Indian, or in a civil case to which only negroes or Indians are parties, but in no other case." It will be observed that this statute prohibits the testimony of colored persons either for or against a white person in any civil or criminal cause to which he may be a party. If, therefore, they are persons affected by the cause, whenever they might be witnesses were they competent to testify, it follows that in any suit between white citizens, jurisdiction might be taken by the Federal courts whenever it was alleged that a citizen of the African race was or might be an important witness. And such an allegation might always be made. So in all criminal prosecutions against white persons a similar allegation would call into existence the like jurisdiction. We cannot think that such was the purpose of Congress in the statute of April 9, 1866. It would seem rather to have been to afford protection to persons of the colored race by giving to the Federal courts jurisdiction of cases, the decision of which might injuriously affect them either in their personal, relative, or property rights, whenever they are denied in the State courts any of the rights mentioned and assured to them in the first section of the act.

Nor can it be said that such a construction allows little or no effect to the enactment. On the contrary, it concedes to it a far-reaching purpose. That purpose was to guard all the declared rights of colored persons, in all civil actions to which they may be parties in interest, by giving to the district and circuit courts of the United States jurisdiction of such actions whenever in the state courts any right enjoyed by white citizens is denied them. And in criminal prosecutions against them, it extends a like protection. We cannot be expected to be ignorant of the condition of things which existed when the statute was enacted, or of the evils which it was intended to remedy. It is well known that in many of the states, laws existed which subjected colored men, convicted of criminal offences to punishments different from and often severer than those which were inflicted upon white persons convicted of similar offences. The modes of trial were also different, and the right of trial by jury was sometimes denied them. It is also well known that in many quarters prejudices existed against the colored race, which naturally affected the administration of justice in the state courts, and operated harshly when one of that race was a party accused. These were evils doubtless which the act of Congress had in view, and which it intended to remove. And so far as it reaches, it extends to both races the same rights, and the same means of vindicating them.

In view of these considerations we are of opinion that the case now before us is not within the provisions of the act of April 9, 1866, and that the circuit court had not jurisdiction of the crime of murder committed in the district of Kentucky, merely because two persons who witnessed the murder were citizens of the African race, and for that reason incompetent by the law of Kentucky to testify in the courts of that state. They are not persons affected by the cause.

We need hardly add that the jurisdiction of the circuit court is not sustained by the fact averred in the indictment that Lucy Armstrong, the person murdered, was a citizen of the African race, and for that reason denied the right to testify in the Kentucky courts. In no sense can she be said to be affected by the cause. Manifestly the act refers to persons in existence. She was the victim of the frightful outrage which gave rise to the cause, but she is beyond being affected by the cause itself.

The conclusions to which we have come are sustained, we think, fully by the judgment of this court in United States vs. Ortega, 11 Wheat., 467, in which the opinion was delivered by Mr. Justice Washington. It was the case of an indictment in the circuit court for offering violence to the person of the Spanish minister, contrary to the law of nations and the act of Congress. The second section of the third article of the Constitution ordains that the judicial power of the United States shall extend to all cases affecting ambassadors, other public ministers and consuls, and that in all cases affecting ambassadors, other public ministers and consuls, the Supreme Court shall have original jurisdiction. The defendant was convicted, and on motion in arrest of judgment, the question was presented to this court, (and it was the only one decided,) whether it was a case affecting an ambassador, or other public minister. The court unanimously ruled that it was not. The violence out of which the indictment grew was committed upon a public minister, and he was a competent and material witness. But he was ruled to be not a person affected by the case, because it was a public prosecution instituted and conducted by and in the name of the United States, and for the purpose of vindicating the laws of nations and that of the United States, in the person of a public minister, offended by an assault committed on him by a private individual. It is, said the court, a case then, which affects the United States and the individual whom they seek to punish; but one in which the minister himself, although he was the person injured by the assault, has no concern, either in the event of the prosecution, or in the costs attending it. What was meant by the phrase "a case affecting," was thus early defined, and we are bound to presume that Congress, when they used the same word "affecting" in the act of 1866, intended to have it bear its defined meaning. This is according to a well known rule of construction.

An attempt has, however, been made to discriminate between the words "case affecting," as found in the constitutional provision, and the words "cause affecting," contained in the act of Congress. We are unable to perceive any substantial ground for a distinction. The words "case" and "cause" are constantly used as synonyms in statutes and judicial decisions, each meaning a proceeding in court, a suit, or action. Surely no court can have jurisdiction of either a case or a cause until it is presented in the form of an action. We regard, therefore, The United States vs. Ortega as an authority directly in point to the effect that witnesses in a criminal prosecution are not persons affected by the cause. It necessarily results from this that jurisdiction of the offence for which these defendants were indicted, was not conferred upon the circuit court by the act of Congress.

It is unnecessary, therefore, to consider the other questions presented by the record.

The judgment of the circuit court is reversed.

The Chief Justice was not present at the argument, and he has taken no part in the decision.

The Fourteenth Amendment and Woman Suffrage.

SUPREME COURT OF THE UNITED STATES.

No. 182.—October Term, 1874.

Virginia L. Minor and Francis Minor, her husband, Plaintiffs in Error, vs. Reese Happersett.	In error to the Supreme Court of the State of Missouri.

Mr. Chief Justice WAITE delivered the opinion of the Court.

The question is presented in this case, whether, since the adoption of the fourteenth amendment, a woman, who is a citizen of the United States and of the State of Missouri, is a voter in that State, notwithstanding the provision of the constitution and laws of the State, which confine the right of suffrage to men alone. We might, perhaps, decide the case upon other grounds, but this question is fairly made. From the opinion we find that it was the only one decided in the court below, and it is the only one which has been argued here. The case was undoubtedly brought to this court for the sole purpose of having that question decided by us, and in view of the evident propriety there is of having it settled, so far as it can be by such a decision, we have concluded to waive all other considerations and proceed at once to its determination.

It is contended that the provisions of the constitution and laws of the State of Missouri which confine the right of suffrage and registration therefor to men, are in violation of the Constitution of the United States and therefore void. The argument is, that as a woman, born or naturalized in the United States and subject to the jurisdiction thereof, is a citizen of the United States and of the State in which she resides, she has the right of suffrage as one of the privileges and immunities of her citizenship, which the State cannot by its laws or constitution abridge.

There is no doubt that women may be citizens. They are persons, and by the fourteenth amendment "all persons born or naturalized in the United States and subject to the jurisdiction thereof" are expressly declared to be "citizens of the United States and of the State wherein they reside." But, in our opinion, it did not need this amendment to give them that position. Before its adoption the Constitution of the United States did not in terms prescribe who should be citizens of the United States or of the several States, yet there were necessarily such citizens without such provision. There cannot be a nation without a people. The very idea of a political community, such as a nation is, implies an association of persons for the promotion of their general welfare. Each one of the persons associated becomes a member of the nation formed by the association. He owes it allegiance and is entitled to its protection. Allegiance and protection are, in this connection, reciprocal obligations. The one is a compensation for the other; allegiance for protection and protection for allegiance.

For convenience it has been found necessary to give a name to this membership. The object is to designate by a title the person and the relation he bears to the nation. For this purpose the words "subject," "inhabitant," and "citizen" have been used, and the choice between them is sometimes made to depend upon the form of the government. Citizen is now more commonly employed, however, and as it has been considered better suited to the description of one living under a republican government, it was adopted by nearly all of the States upon their separation from Great Britain, and was afterwards adopted in the Articles of Confederation and in the Constitution of the United States. When used in this sense it is understood as conveying the idea of membership of a nation, and nothing more.

To determine, then, who were citizens of the United States before the adoption of the amendment, it is necessary to ascertain what persons originally associated themselves together to form the nation, and what were afterwards admitted to membership.

Looking at the Constitution itself we find that it was ordained and established by "the people of the United States," (Preamble, 1 Stat., 10,) and then going further back, we find that these were the people of the several States that had before dissolved the political bands which connected them with Great Britain, and assumed a separate and equal station among the powers of the earth (Dec. of Ind., 1 Stat., 1), and that had by articles of confederation and perpetual union, in which they took the name of "The United States of America," entered into a firm league of friendship with each other for their common defence, the security of their liberties and their mutual and general welfare, binding themselves to assist each other against all force offered to or attack made upon them, or any of them, on account of religion, sovereignty, trade, or any other pretence whatever. (Art. Confed., sec. 3, 1 Stat., 4.)

Whoever, then, was one of the people of either of these States when the Constitution of the United States was adopted, became *ipso facto* a citizen—a member of the nation created by its adoption. He was one of the persons associating together to form the nation, and was, consequently, one of its original citizens. As to this there has never been a doubt. Disputes have arisen as to whether or not certain persons or certain classes of persons were part of the people at the time, but never as to their citizenship if they were.

Additions might always be made to the citizenship of the United States in two ways; first, by birth, and second, by naturalization. This is apparent from the Constitution itself, for it provides (art. 2, sec. 1,) that "no person except a natural-born citizen, or a citizen of the United States at the time of the adoption of the Constitution, shall be eligible to the office of President," and (art. 1, sec. 8,) that Congress shall have power "to establish an uniform rule of naturalization." Thus new citizens may be born, or they may be created by naturalization.

The Constitution does not, in words, say who shall be natural-born citizens. Resort must be had elsewhere to ascertain that. At common law, with the nomenclature of which the framers of the Constitution were familiar, it was never doubted that all children born in a country of parents who were its citizens became themselves, upon their birth, citizens also. These were natives, or natural-born citizens, as distinguished from aliens or foreigners. Some authorities go further and include as citizens children born within the jurisdiction, without reference to the citizenship of their parents. As to this class there have been doubts, but never as to the first. For the purposes of this case it is not necessary to solve these doubts. It is sufficient for everything we have now to consider that all children born of citizen parents within the jurisdiction are themselves citizens. The words "all children" are certainly as comprehensive, when used in this connection, as "all persons," and if females are included in the last they must be in the first. That they are included in the last is not denied. In fact, the whole argument of the plaintiffs proceeds upon that idea.

Under the power to adopt an uniform system of naturalization, Congress, as early as 1790, provided "that any alien, being a free white person," might be admitted as a citizen of the United States, and that the children of such persons so naturalized, dwelling within the United States, being under twenty-one years of age at the time of such naturalization, should also be considered citizens of the United States, and that the children of citizens of the United States that might be born beyond the sea, or out of the limits of the United States, should be considered as natural-born citizens. (1 Stat., 103.) These provisions thus enacted have, in substance, been retained in all the naturalization laws adopted since. In 1855, however, the last provision was somewhat extended, and all persons theretofore born or thereafter to be born out of the limits of the jurisdiction of the United States, whose fathers were, or should be at the time of their birth, citizens of the United States, were declared to be citizens also. (10 Stat., 604.)

As early as 1804 it was enacted by Congress that when any alien who had declared his intention to become a citizen in the manner provided by law died before he was actually naturalized, his widow and children should be considered as citizens of the United States, and entitled to all rights and privileges as such upon taking the necessary oath (2 Stat., 293,) and in 1855 it was further provided that any woman who might lawfully be naturalized under the existing laws, married, or who should be married to a citizen of the United States, should be deemed and taken to be a citizen. (10 Stat., 604.)

From this it is apparent that from the commencement of the legislation upon this subject alien women and alien minors could be made citizens by naturalization, and we think it will not be contended that this would have been done if it had not been supposed that native women and native minors were already citizens by birth.

But if more is necessary to show that women have always been considered as citizens the same as men, abundant proof is to be found in the legislative and judicial history of the country. Thus, by the Constitution, the judicial power of the United States is made to extend to controversies between citizens of different States. Under this it has been uniformly held that the citizenship necessary to give the courts of the United States jurisdiction of a cause must be affirmatively shown on the record. Its existence as a fact may be put in issue and tried. If found not to exist, the case must be dismissed. Notwithstanding this the records of the courts are full of cases in which the jurisdiction depends upon the citizenship of women, and not one can be found, we think, in which objection was made on that account. Certainly none can be found in which it has been held that women could not sue or be sued in the courts of the United States. Again, at the time of the adoption of the Constitution, in many of the States (and in some probably now) aliens could not inherit or transmit inheritance. There are a multitude of cases to be found in which the question has been presented whether a woman was or was not an alien, and as such capable or incapable of inheritance, but in no one has it been insisted that she was not a citizen because she was a woman. On the contrary, her right to citizenship has been in all cases assumed. The only question has been whether, in the particular case under consideration, she had availed herself of the right.

In the legislative department of the government similar proof will be found. Thus, in the pre-emption laws, (5 Stat., 455, sec. 10,) a widow, "being a citizen of the United States," is allowed to make settlement on the public lands and purchase upon the terms specified, and women, "being citizens of the United States," are permitted to avail themselves of the benefit of the homestead law. (12 Stat., 392.)

Other proof of like character might be found, but certainly more cannot be necessary to establish the fact that sex has never been made one of the elements of citizenship in the United States. In this respect men have never had an advantage over women. The same laws precisely apply to both. The fourteenth amendment did not affect the citizenship of women any more than it did of men. In this particular, therefore, the rights of Mrs. Minor do not depend upon the amendment. She has always been a citizen from her birth, and entitled to all the privileges and immunities of citizenship. The amendment prohibited the State, of which she is a citizen, from abridging any of her privileges and immunities as a citizen of the United States; but it did not confer citizenship on her. That she had before its adoption.

If the right of suffrage is one of the necessary privileges of a citizen of the United States, then the constitution and laws of Missouri confining it to men are in violation of the Constitution of the United States, as amended, and consequently void. The direct question is, therefore, presented whether all citizens are necessarily voters.

The Constitution does not define the privileges and immunities of citizens. For that definition we must look elsewhere. In this case we need not determine what they are, but only whether suffrage is necessarily one of them.

It certainly is nowhere made so in express terms. The United States has no voters in the States of its own creation. The elective officers of the United States are all elected directly or indirectly by State voters. The members of the House of Representatives are to be chosen by the people of the States, and the electors in each State must have the qualifications requisite for electors of the most numerous branch of the State legislature. (Art. 1, sec. 2, Const.) Senators are to be chosen by the legislature of the States, and necessarily the members of the legislature required to make the choice are elected by the voters of the State. (Art. 1, sec. 3.) Each State must appoint in such manner as the legislature thereof may direct, the electors to elect the President and Vice-President. (Art. 2, sec. 2.) The times, places, and manner of holding elections for Senators and Representatives are to be prescribed in each State by the legislature thereof; but Congress may at any time, by law, make or alter such regulations, except as to the place of choosing Senators. (Art. 1, sec. 4.) It is not necessary to inquire whether this power of supervision thus given to Congress is sufficient to authorize any interference with the State laws prescribing the qualifications of voters, for no such interference has ever been attempted. The power of the State in this particular is certainly supreme until Congress acts.

The amendment did not add to the privileges and immunities of a citizen. It simply furnished an additional guaranty for the protection of such as he already had. No new voters were necessarily made by it. Indirectly it may have had that effect, because it may have increased the number of citizens entitled to suffrage under the Constitution and laws of the States; but it operates for this purpose, if at all, through the States and the State laws, and not directly upon the citizen.

It is clear, therefore, we think, that the Constitution has not added the right of suffrage to the privileges and immunities of citizenship as they existed at the time it was adopted. This makes it proper to enquire whether suffrage was coextensive with the citizenship of the States at the time of its adoption. If it was, then it may with force be argued that suffrage was one of the rights which belonged to citizenship, and in the enjoyment of which every citizen must be protected. But if it was not, the contrary may with propriety be assumed.

When the Constitution of the United States was adopted all the several States, with the exception of Rhode Island, had constitutions of their own. Rhode Island continued to act under its charter from the Crown. Upon an examination of those constitutions we find that in no State were all citizens permitted to vote. Each State determined for itself who should have that power. Thus, in New Hampshire, "every male inhabitant of each town and parish with town privileges, and places unincorporated in the State, of twenty-one years of age and upwards, excepting paupers and persons excused from paying taxes at their own request," were its voters; in Massachusetts "every male inhabitant of twenty-one years of age and upwards, having a freehold estate within the commonwealth of the annual income of three pounds, or any estate of the value of sixty pounds;" in Rhode Island "such as are admitted free of the company and society" of the colony; in Connecticut such persons as had "maturity in years, quiet and peaceable behavior, a civil conversation, and forty shillings freehold or forty pounds personal estate," if so certified by the selectmen; in New York "every male inhabitant of full age who shall have personally resided within one of the counties of the State for six months immediately preceding the day of election, * * * if during the time aforesaid he shall have been a freeholder, possessing a freehold of the value of twenty pounds within the county, or have rented a tenement therein, of the yearly value of forty shillings, and been rated and actually paid taxes to the State;" in New Jersey "all inhabitants * * * of full age who are worth fifty pounds, proclamation money, clear estate in the same, and have resided in the county in which they claim a vote for twelve months immediately preceding the election;" in Pennsylvania "every freeman of the age of twenty-one years, having resided in the State two years next before the election, and within that time paid a State or county tax which shall have been assessed at least six months before the election;" in Delaware and Virginia "as exercised by law at present;" in Maryland "all freemen above twenty-one years of age having a freehold of fifty acres of land in the county in which they offer to vote and residing therein, and all freemen having property in the State above the value of thirty pounds current money, and having resided in the county in which they offer to vote one whole year next preceding the election;" in North Carolina, for Senators, "all freemen of the age of twenty-one years who have been inhabitants of any one county within the State for twelve months immediately preceding the day of election, and possessed of a freehold within the same county of fifty acres of land for six months next before and at the day of election," and for members of the House of Commons "all freemen of the age of twenty-one years who have been inhabitants in any one county within the State twelve months immediately preceding the day of any election, and shall have paid public taxes;" in South Carolina "every free white man of the age of twenty-one years, being a citizen of the State and having resided therein two years previous to the day of election, and who hath a freehold of fifty acres of land, or a town lot of which he hath been legally seized and possessed at least six months before such election, or, (not having such freehold or town lot,) hath been a resident within the election district in which he offers to give his vote six months before said election, and hath paid a tax the preceding year of three shillings sterling towards the support of the government;" and in Georgia such "citizens and inhabitants of the State as shall have attained to the age of twenty-one years, and shall have paid tax for the year next preceding the election, and shall have resided six months within the county."

In this condition of the law in respect to suffrage in the several States it cannot for a moment be doubted that if it had been intended to make all citizens of the United States voters, the framers of the Constitution would not have left it to implication. So important a change in the condition of citizenship as it actually existed, if intended, would have been expressly declared.

But if further proof is necessary to show that no such change was intended, it can easily be found both in and out of the Constitution. By Art. 4, Sec. 2, it is provided that "the citizens of each State shall be entitled to all the privileges and immnuities of citizens in the several States." If suffrage is necessarily a part of citizenship, then the citizens of each State must be entitled to vote in the several States precisely as their citizens are. This is more than asserting that they may change their residence and become citizens of the State and thus be voters. It goes to the extent of insisting that while retaining their original citizenship they may vote in any State. This, we think, has never been claimed. And again, by the very terms of the amendment we have been considering (the fourteenth), "Representatives shall be apportioned among the several States according to their respective numbers, counting the whole number of persons in each State, excluding Indians not taxed. But when the right to vote at any election for the choice of electors for President and Vice-President of the United States, representatives in Congress, the executive and judicial officers of a State, or the members of the legislature thereof, is denied to any of the male inhabitants of such State, being twenty-one years of age and citizens of the United States, or in any way abridged, except for participation in the rebellion, or other crimes, the basis of representation therein shall be reduced in the proportion which the number of such male citizens shall bear to the whole number of male citizens twenty-one years of age in such State." Why this, if it was not in the power of the legislature to deny the right of suffrage to some male inhabitants? And if suffrage was necessarily one of the absolute rights of citizenship, why confine the operation of the limitation to male inhabitants? Women and children are, as we have seen, "persons." They are counted in the enumeration upon which the apportionment is to be made, but if they were necessarily voters because of their citizenship unless clearly excluded, why inflict the penalty for the exclusion of males alone? Clearly, no such form of words would have been selected to express the idea here indicated, if suffrage was the absolute right of all citizens.

And still again, after the adoption of the fourteenth amendment, it was deemed necessary to adopt a fifteenth, as follows: "The right of citizens of the United States to vote shall not be denied or abridged by the United States, or by any State, on account of race, color, or previous condition of servitude." The fourteenth amendment had already provided that no State should make or enforce any law which should abridge the privileges or immunities of citizens of the United States. If suffrage was one of these privileges or immunities, why amend the Constitution to prevent its being denied on account of race, etc.? Nothing is more evident than that the greater must include the less, and if all were already protected why go through with the form of amending the Constitution to protect a part?

It is true that the United States guarantees to every State a republican form of government. (Art. 4, sec. 4.) It is also true that no State can pass a bill of attainder, (Art. 1, sec. 10,) and that no person can be deprived of life, liberty, or property without due process of law. (Amendment 5.) All these several provisions of the Constitution must be construed in connection with the other parts of the instrument, and in the light of the surrounding circumstances.

The guaranty is of a republican form of government. No particular government is designated as republican, neither is the exact form to be guaranteed in any manner especially designated. Here, as in other parts of the instrument, we are compelled to resort elsewhere to ascertain what was intended.

The guaranty necessarily implies a duty on the part of the States themselves to provide such a government. All the States had governments when the Constitution was adopted. In all the people participated to some extent, through their representatives elected in the manner specially provided. These governments the Constitution did not change. They were accepted precisely as they were, and it is, therefore, to be presumed that they were such as it was the duty of the States to provide. Thus we have unmistakable evidence of what was republican in form, within the meaning of that term as employed in the Constitution.

As has been seen, all the citizens of the States were not invested with the right of suffrage. In all, save perhaps New Jersey, this right was only bestowed upon men, and not upon all of them. Under these circumstances it is certainly now too late to contend that a government is not republican, within the meaning of this guaranty in the Constitution, because women are not made voters.

The same may be said of the other provisions just quoted. Women were excluded from suffrage, in nearly all the States, by the express provision of their constitutions and laws. If that had been equivalent to a bill of attainder, certainly its abrogation would not have been left to implication. Nothing less than express language would have been employed to effect so radical a change. So also of the amendment which declares that no person shall be deprived of life, liberty, or property without due process of law, adopted as it was as early as 1791. If suffrage was intended to be included within its obligations, language better adapted to express that intent would most certainly have been employed. The right of suffrage, when granted, will be protected. He who has it can only be deprived of it by due process of law, but in order to claim protection he must first show that he has the right.

But we have already sufficiently considered the proof found upon the inside of the Constitution. That upon the outside is equally effective.

The Constitution was submitted to the States for adoption in 1787, and was ratified by nine States in 1788, and finally by the thirteen original States in 1790. Vermont was the first new State admitted to the Union, and it came in under a Constitution which conferred the right of suffrage only upon men of the full age of twenty-one years, having resided in the State for the space of one whole year next before the election, and who were of quiet and peaceable behavior. This was in 1791. The next year, 1792, Kentucky followed with a constitution confining the right of suffrage to free male citizens of the age of twenty-one years, who had resided in the State two years, or in the county in which they offered to vote one year next before the election. Then followed Tennessee, in 1796, with voters of freemen of the age of twenty-one years and upwards, possessing a freehold in the county wherein they may vote, and being inhabitants of the State, or freemen being inhabitants of any one county in the State six months immediately preceding the day of election. But we need not particularize further. No new State has ever been admitted to the Union which has conferred the right of suffrage upon women, and this has never been considered a valid objection to her admission. On the contrary, as is claimed in the argument, the right of suffrage was withdrawn from woman as early as 1807 in the State of New Jersey, without any attempt to obtain the interference of the United States to prevent it. Since then the governments of the insurgent States have been reorganized under a requirement that before their representatives could be admitted to seats in Congress they must have adopted new constitutions, republican in form. In no one of these constitutions was suffrage conferred upon women, and yet the States have all been restored to their original position as States in the Union.

Besides this, citizenship has not in all cases been made a condition precedent to the enjoyment of the right of suffrage. Thus, in Missouri, persons of foreign birth, who have declared their intention to become citizens of the United States, may under certain circumstances vote. The same provision is to be found in the Constitutions of Alabama, Arkansas, Florida, Georgia, Indiana, Kansas, Minnesota, and Texas.

Certainly, if the courts can consider any question settled, this is one. For near ninety years the people have acted upon the idea that the Constitution when it conferred citizenship did not necessarily confer the right of suffrage. If uniform practice long continued can settle the construction of so important an instrument as the Constitution of the United States confessedly is, most certainly it has been done here. Our province is to decide what the law is, not to declare what it should be.

We have given this case the careful consideration its importance demands. If the law is wrong it ought to be changed; but the power for that is not with us. The arguments addressed to us bearing upon such a view of the subject may perhaps be sufficient to induce those having the power to make the alteration; but they ought not to be permitted to influence our judgment in determining the present rights of the parties now litigating before us. No argument as to woman's need of suffrage can be considered. We can only act upon her rights as they exist. It is not for us to look at the hardship of withholding. Our duty is at an end if we find it is within the power of a State to withhold.

Being unanimously of the opinion that the Constitution of the United States does not confer the right of suffrage upon any one, and that the Constitutions and laws of the several States which commit that important trust to men alone are not necessarily void, we affirm the judgment of the court below.

The Union Pacific Railroad Case.

SUPREME COURT OF THE UNITED STATES.

No. 571.—October Term, 1875.

The United States, Appellant, vs. The Union Pacific Railroad Company. } Appeal from the Court of Claims.

Mr. Justice DAVIS delivered the opinion of the Court.

The Union Pacific Railroad Company, conceding the right of the government to retain *one-half* of the compensation due it for the transportation of the mails, military and Indian supplies, and apply the same to reimburse the government for interest paid by it on bonds issued to the corporation to aid in the construction of its railroad and telegraph lines, seeks to establish by this suit its right to the other moiety. The United States, on the other hand, having paid interest on these bonds in excess of the sums credited to the company for services rendered by it, insists upon its right to withhold payment altogether. One of the grounds on which this right of retention is sought to be maintained is by reason of the general right of set-off. It is true this right, as a general proposition, exists in the government, and is commonly exercised by it when settling with those having claims against it. But, manifestly, the rules applicable to ordinary claimants for services rendered the United States do not apply to this controversy. The bonds in question were issued by the United States, in pursuance of a scheme to aid in the construction of a great national highway; in themselves they do not import any obligation on the part of the corporation to pay; and whether when the United States have paid interest on them an obligation arises on the part of the corporation to refund it, depends wholly on the conditions on which the bonds were delivered to the corporation and received by it. These conditions are embodied in the legislation of Congress on the subject; and if, on a fair interpretation of this legislation, the corporation is found to be now a debtor to the United States, the deduction for interest paid on the bonds can be lawfully made. But if the converse of this proposition is ascertained to be true, the government cannot rightfully withhold from the corporation one-half of its earnings.

In construing an act of Congress we are not at liberty to recur to the views of individual members in debate, nor to consider the motives which influenced them to vote for or against its passage. The act itself speaks the will of Congress, and this is to be ascertained from the language used. But courts may with propriety, in construing a statute, recur to the history of the times when it was passed, and this is frequently necessary, in order to ascertain the reason as well as the meaning of particular provisions in it. (Aldridge vs. Williams, 3 Howard, p. 24; Preston vs. Browder, 1 Wheaton, 120.)

Many of the provisions in the original act of 1862 are outside of the usual course of legislative action concerning grants to railroads, and cannot be properly construed without reference to the circumstances which surrounded Congress when the act was passed. The war of the rebellion was in progress, and the country had become alarmed for the safety of the Pacific States, owing to complications with England. In case these complications resulted in an open rupture, the loss of our Pacific possessions was feared, but, even if this fear were groundless, it was quite apparent that we were unable to furnish that degree of protection to the people occupying them which every government owes its citizens. It is true the threatened danger was happily averted, but wisdom pointed out the necessity of making suitable provision for the future. This could be done in no better way than by the construction of a railroad across the continent. Such a road would bind together the widely-separated parts of our common country, and furnish a cheap and expeditious mode for the transportation of troops and supplies. And if it did nothing more than afford the required protection to the Pacific States, it was felt that the government, in the execution of a plain duty, could not justly withhold the aid necessary to build it. And so strong and pervading was this opinion that it is by no means certain the people would not have sanctioned the action of Congress, if it had departed from the traditional policy of the country regarding works of internal improvements, and charged the government itself with the direct execution of the enterprise.

This enterprise was viewed as a national undertaking for national purposes, and the public mind was directed to the end to be accomplished rather than the particular means employed for the purpose. Although this road was a military necessity, there were other reasons active at the time in producing an opinion for its completion besides the protection of an exposed frontier. There was a vast unpeopled territory lying between the Missouri and Sacramento rivers, which was practically worthless without the facilities afforded by a railroad for the transportation of person and property. With its construction the agricultural and mineral resources of this territory could be developed; settlements made where settlements were possible, and thereby the wealth and power of the United States essentially increased. And there was also the pressing want, in times of peace even, of an improved and cheaper method for the transportation of the mails and supplies for the army and the Indians.

It was in the presence of these facts that Congress undertook to deal with the subject of this railroad. The difficulties in the way of building it were great, and by many intelligent persons considered insurmountable.

Although a free people, when resolved upon a course of action, can accomplish great results, the scheme for building a railroad 2,000 miles in length, over deserts, across mountains, and through a country inhabited by Indians jealous of intrusion upon their rights, was universally esteemed at the time to be a bold and hazardous undertaking. It is nothing to the purpose that the difficulties in the way of the undertaking, after trial, in a great measure disappeared, and that the road was constructed at less cost of time and money than was considered possible. No argument can be drawn from the wisdom that comes after the fact. Congress acted with reference to a state of things supposed to exist at the time, and no aid can be derived, in the interpretation of its legislation, from the consideration that the theory on which it proceeded turned out not to be correct. The project of building the road was not conceived for private ends, and the prevalent opinion was that it could not be worked out by private capital alone. It was a national work, originating in national necessities, and requiring national assistance.

The policy of the country, to say nothing of the supposed want of power, stood in the way of the United States taking the work into its own hands. Even if this were not so, reasons of economy suggested that it were better to enlist private capital and individual enterprise in the project. This Congress undertook to do, and the inducements held out were such as it was believed would procure the requisite capital and enterprise. But the purpose in presenting these inducements was to promote the construction and operation of a work deemed essential to the security of great public interests.

It is true the scheme contemplated profit to individuals, for without reasonable expectation of this capital could not be obtained, nor the requisite skill and enterprise; but this consideration does not in itself change the relation of the parties to this suit. This might have been so if the government had incorporated a company to advance private interests, and agreed to aid it on account of supposed incidental advantages which would accrue to the public from the completion of the enterprise. But the government proceeded on a wholly different theory. It promoted the enterprise to advance its own interests, and endeavored to enlist private capital and individual enterprise as a means to an end—the securing a road which could be used for governmental purposes. Whatever obligations, therefore, rest on the company incorporated to accomplish this purpose, must depend on the true meaning of the enactment itself, viewed in the light of cotemporaneous history.

It has been observed by this court that the title of an act, especially in Congressional legislation, furnishes little aid in the construction of it, because the body of the act, in so many cases, has no reference to the matter specified in the title. (Hadden vs. The Collector, 5 Wallace, page 110.) This is true, and we have no disposition to depart from this rule, but the title, even, of the original act of 1862, incorporating the defendant, (12 Stats., p. 489,) seems to have been the subject of special consideration by Congress, for it truly discloses the general purpose Congress had in view in passing it. It is "An act to aid in the construction of a railroad from the Missouri river to the Pacific ocean, and to secure to the government the use of the same for postal, military, and other purposes." That there should, however, be no doubt of the national character of the work which Congress proposed to aid, the body of the act contains these words: "And the better to accomplish the object of this act, namely, to promote the public interest and welfare by the construction of said railroad and telegraph lines, and keeping the same in working order, and to secure to the government at all times (but particularly in time of war) the use and benefits of the same for postal, military, and other purposes, Congress may at any time, having due regard for the rights of said companies named therein, add to, alter, amend, or repeal this act." (See 18th section of charter, 12 Statutes at Large, p. 497.) Indeed, the whole act contains unmistakable evidence that if Congress was put to the necessity of accomplishing a great public enterprise through the instrumentality of private corporations, it took care that there should be no misunderstanding about the objects to be accomplished or the motives which influenced its course of action.

If it had been equally explicit in the provision regarding the bonds to be issued in aid of the road, there would have been no occasion for this suit. But even in this particular, looking to the motives which led to the act, and the objects intended to be effected by it, we do not think there is any serious difficulty to get at the true meaning of Congress. The act itself was an experiment, and must be considered in the nature of a proposal to enterprising men to engage in the work, for there was no certainty that capital, with the untried obstacles in the way, could be enlisted. If enlisted at all, it could only be on conditions which would insure, in case of success, remuneration proportionate to the risk incurred.

The proffered aid was in lands and interest-bearing bonds of the United States. There is no controversy about the terms on which the lands were granted, and the only point with which we have to deal relates to the nature and extent of the obligation imposed by Congress on the company to pay these bonds. It is not doubted that the government was to be reimbursed both principal and interest, but the precise question for decision is, whether the company was required to pay the interest before the maturity of the principal.

The solution of this question depends upon the meaning of the 5th and 6th sections of the original act of 1862, and the fifth section of the amendatory act of 1864. (12 Statutes at Large, 492; 13 Statutes at Large, 359.) The fifth section of the original act contains the undertaking of the government, and the sixth defines the obligation of the company. By the fifth it is provided that on the completion of the road in sections of forty miles, there shall be issued and delivered to the company a certain number of interest-bearing bonds of the United States, payable thirty years after date, with interest payable semi-annually. And "to secure the repayment to the United States, as '*hereinafter provided*,' of the amount of said bonds, together with all interest thereon which shall have been paid by the United States," it was further provided, that the issue and delivery of the bonds should constitute a first mortgage on the property of the company, with a right reserved to the government to declare a forfeiture and take possession of the road and telegraph line in case "of the refusal or failure of the company to redeem said bonds or any part of them when requested to do so by the Secretary of the Treasury, *in accordance with the provisions of the act*." The manifest purpose of this section is to take a lien on the property of the corporation for the ultimate redemption of the bonds, principal and interest, but the manner of redemption and time of it are left for further provision.

That the government was expected in the first instance to pay the interest is clear enough, for the mortgage was taken to secure the repayment of the bonds, "together with all interest thereon which shall have been paid by the United States." This phrase implies a *prior* payment by the United States, whatever may be the duty of the corporation in regard to reimbursement, as subsequently defined. Besides this, when repayment is spoken of, it is understood that something has been advanced which is to be paid back. Apart from this, had it been the intention that the corporation itself should pay the interest as it fell due, phraseology appropriate to such a purpose would have been used. But when and how the reimbursement was to be made was declared to be "as hereinafter provided," that is, in conformity with the terms prescribed in another portion of the act. And that this is so, is evident enough from the latter part of the section, which directs the Secretary of the Treasury to enforce the forfeiture and take possession of the road on failure of the corporation to redeem said bonds or any part of them, (referring to the different periods of their issue,) according to the plan of redemption thus provided, or in other words, "in accordance with the provisions of this act." The obligations imposed on the corporation, or assumed by them, in relation to the repayment of the bonds, are set forth *entire* in the next or sixth section, which, on account of its importance, is set forth at length.

"SEC. 6. And be it further enacted, That the grants aforesaid are made upon condition *that said company shall pay said bonds at maturity*, and shall keep said railroad and telegraph line in repair and use, and shall at all times transmit dispatches over said telegraph line, and transport mails, troops, and munitions of war, supplies and public stores, upon said railroad for the government, whenever required to do so by any department thereof; and that the government shall at all times have the preference in the use of the same for all the purposes aforesaid (at fair and reasonable rates of compensation, not to exceed the amounts paid by private parties for the same kind of service); and *all compensations for services rendered for the government* shall be applied to the payment of said bonds *and interest*, until the whole amount is fully paid. Said company may also pay the United States, wholly or in part, in the same or other bonds, treasury notes, or other evidences of debt against the United States, to be allowed at par, *and after said road is completed*, until said bonds and interest are paid, at least five per centum of the net earnings of said road shall also be annually applied to the payment thereof."

Leaving out of consideration the parts of this section not pertinent to the present inquiry, there are three things, and three only, which the corporation is required to do concerning the bonds in controversy. 1st. To pay said bonds at maturity. 2d. To allow the government to retain the compensation due the corporation for services rendered, and apply the same to the payment of the bonds and interest, until the whole amount is fully paid. 3. To pay over to the government, after the road shall have been fully completed, five per cent. of the net earnings of the road, to be appropriated to the payment of the bonds and interest.

If we take the language used in its natural and obvious sense, there can be no difficulty in arriving at the meaning of the condition "to pay said bonds at maturity," which was imposed upon this corporation. As commonly understood, the word "maturity," in its application to bonds and other similar instruments, refers to the time fixed for their payment, which is the termination of the period they have to run. The bonds in question were bonds of the United States promising to pay to the holder of them one thousand dollars thirty years after date, and the interest every six months. This obligation the government was required to perform, and as the bonds were issued and delivered to the corporation to be sold for the purpose of raising money to construct its road, it is insisted that Congress must have meant to impose a corresponding obligation on the corporation. In support of this construction it is sought to give to the word "maturity" a double signification, applying it to each payment of interest as it falls due as well as to the principal. But this is extending the operation of words by a forced construction beyond their natural and ordinary meaning, which is contrary to all legal rules. Courts cannot supply omissions in legislation, nor afford relief because they are supposed to exist. "We are bound," said Justice Buller in an early case in the King's Bench, "to take the act of Parliament as they have made it; a casus omissus can in no case be supplied by a court of law, for that would be to make laws; nor can I conceive that it is our province to consider whether such a law that has been passed be tyrannical or not." (Jones vs. Smart, 1 Term Reports, 44–52.)

Lord Chief Baron Eyre, in the case of Gibson vs. Minet (1 H. Bl., 569–614), said: "I venture to lay it down as a general rule respecting the interpretation of deeds, that all latitude of construction must submit to this restriction, namely, that *the words may bear the sense* which by construction is put upon them. If we step beyond this line we no longer construe men's deeds, but make deeds for them." This rule is as applicable to the language of a statute as to the language of a deed. The words "to pay said bonds at maturity" do not *bear the sense* which is sought to be attributed to them. They imply, obviously, an obligation to pay both principal and interest when the time fixed for the payment of the principal has passed; but they do not imply an obligation to pay the interest as it accrues and the principal when due. It is one thing to be required to pay principal and interest when the bonds have reached maturity, and a wholly different thing to be required to pay the interest every six months and the principal at the end of thirty years. The obligations are so different that they cannot both grow out of the direct words employed, and it is necessary to superadd other words in order to extend the condition so as to include the payment of semi-annual interest as it falls due. Neither on principle or authority is such a plain departure from the express letter of the statute warranted. And especially is this so when the construction leads to so great an extension of a condition to defeat a grant.

The failure to perform the condition is cause of forfeiture. If the natural meaning of the words be adopted as the true meaning there can be no forfeiture until the bonds themselves have matured. On the contrary, if the construction contended for be allowed, the grants made to the corporation are subject to forfeiture on each occasion that six months' interest falls due and is not met. It would require a pretty large inference to draw from the language used authority to enlarge in a particular so essential the terms of a condition assumed by the corporation when it assented to the act. Besides this, when Congress imposed this condition it well knew that the undertaking of the government bound it to pay to the holder of any bond interest every six months and the principal at the time the bond matured. With this knowledge, dealing as it did with the relations the company was to bear to the government on the receipt of these bonds, had it intended to exact of the company the payment of interest before the maturity of the bonds, it would have declared its purpose in language about which there could be no misunderstanding. But, if the words "to pay said bonds at maturity" do not give notice that this exaction was intended, neither do the other provisions of the sixth section. They created no obligation to keep down the interest, nor were they so intended. The proposition to retain the amount due the company for services rendered, and apply it towards the general indebtedness of the company to the government, cannot be construed into a requirement that the company shall pay the interest from time to time and the principal when due. It was in the discretion of Congress to make this requirement, and then, as collateral to it, provide a special fund or funds out of which the principal obligation could be discharged. This Congress did not choose to do, but rested satisfied with the entire property of the company as security for the ultimate payment of the principal and interest of the bonds delivered to it, and, in the mean time, with special provisions looking to the reimbursement of the government for interest paid by it, and the application of the surplus, if any remained, to discharge the principal. The company, for obvious reasons, might be very willing to accept the bonds of the government on these terms, and very unwilling to come under an absolute promise to pay the current interest as it accrued. If it were in a condition, either during the progress of the work, or on its completion, to earn anything, there was no hardship in the proposed application of the compensation due it; but it can be readily seen, if the company were required to raise money every six months to pay interest, when all its available means were necessary to the prosecution of the work, the burden might be very heavy. Congress did not see fit to impose this burden, and place the company in a position to risk the forfeiture of all its grants, in case of failure to provide the means to pay current interest. Besides, it is fair to infer that Congress supposed that the services to be rendered by the road to the government would equal the interest to be paid; and that this was not an unreasonable expectation, the published statistics of the vast cost of transporting military and naval stores and the mails to the Pacific coast, by the ancient methods, abundantly show.

The views presented regarding the provision, that the government shall retain the compensation for services rendered by the company, either before or after the road is completed, are equally applicable to the provision, that after the road is completed, five per cent. of the net earnings of the road shall be *annually* applied to the payment of bonds and interest. It is not perceived how, on any principle of construction, an obligation of the corporation to pay the interest on the bonds every six months after they shall have been issued can be predicated on the terms of this provision, any more than on the terms of the other. Both are reserved funds out of which the government was to be reimbursed in the first instance the interest it had paid, leaving the surplus, if any, to be applied to the payment of the principal of the bonds.

In addition to all that has been said, there is enough in the scheme of the act, and the purposes contemplated by it, to show that Congress never intended to impose on the corporation the obligation to pay current interest. The act was passed in the midst of war, as has been stated, when the means for national defense were deemed inadequate to the wants of the country, and the public mind was alive to the necessity of uniting by iron bands the destiny of the Pacific States with those of the Atlantic. Confessedly the undertaking was outside of the ability of private capital to accomplish, and only by the helping hand of Congress could the problem, difficult of solution under the most favorable circumstances, be worked out. Local business, as a source of profit, could not be expected while the road was in course of construction, on account of the character of the country it traversed; and whether when completed, as an investment it would prove valuable, was a question for time to determine. But vast as the work was, limited as were the private resources to build it, the growing wants of the country, as well as the existing and future military necessities of the government, demanded that it be completed. Under the stimulus of these considerations Congress acted. It did not act for the benefit of private persons, nor in their interest, but for an object deemed essential to the security of the country, as well as to the prosperity of the country.

Compelled as it was to incorporate a private company to accomplish its object, it proffered the terms on which it would lend its aid, which, if deemed too liberal now, were then considered, with the lights before it, not more than sufficient to engage the attention of enterprising men, who, if not themselves capitalists, were in a position to command the use of capital. These terms looked to ultimate security, rather than immediate reimbursement, and for the obvious reason that the corporation would require all its available means in construction; and to exact from it, while the work was in progress, the obligation to keep down the interest on the bonds of the United States, would tend to cripple the enterprise at a time when the primary object with Congress was to advance it. There could, however, be no reasonable objection to the application "of all compensations for services rendered for the government" from the outset, and "five per cent. of the net earnings after the completion of the road," to the payment of the bonds and interest, and these exactions were accordingly made.

Of necessity there were risks to be taken in aiding with money or bonds an enterprise unparalleled in the history of any free people, which, if completed at all, would require, as was supposed, twelve years in which to do it. But these risks were common to both parties, and Congress was obliged to assume its share and advance the bonds, or abandon the enterprise; for obviously the grant of lands, however valuable after the road was built, could not be available as a resource with which to build it.

If the road were a success, in addition to the benefit it would be to the United States, the corporation would be in a situation to repay advances for interest, and pay the principal when due. If, on the contrary, the investment proved to be a failure, subjecting the private persons who embarked their capital in it to a total loss, there was left for the government the entire property of the corporation, of which immediate possession could be taken on a declaration of forfeiture.

In view of the circumstances under which the act of 1862 was passed, and the purposes to be accomplished by it, appearing as they do in the title as well as the body of the act, and constituting as they do the public history of this legislation, this brief summary presents, as we think, fairly its scope and effect, which are inconsistent with the position asserted by the appellant.

Notwithstanding the favorable terms proposed by Congress the road languished, and the effect of this was the amendatory act of 1864. By this the grant of lands was doubled; a second in lieu of a first mortgage accepted by the government, and a provision inserted that "only one-half of the compensation for services rendered for the government by said companies (meaning this and the auxiliary companies incorporated at the same time) shall be required to be applied to the payment of the bonds issued by the government in aid of the construction of said road."

This amendment was, without doubt, intended merely to modify the provision in the original act so as to allow the government to retain only one-half of the compensation for services rendered, instead of all. Although the requirement in this provision is that the compensation shall be applied to "the payment of bonds," and in the former "to pay the bonds and interest," yet it cannot be supposed that Congress intended to relinquish the right secured in the former act to make the application in the first place to the interest and then to the principal. The purpose of Congress could have been nothing more than to surrender on behalf of the government the right to retain the whole of the companies' earnings, and to accept in lieu of it the right to retain the half, leaving unaffected by this change any right touching this subject secured in the former act. The change was a very material one, and intended, doubtless, as a substantial favor to the companies; but on the principle contended for it would prove, instead of this, to be of no value. Of what possible advantage could it be to these companies to receive payment for one-half their earnings, if they were subject to a suit to recover it back as soon as it was paid? And this is the effect of the provision on the theory that the companies are debtors to the government on every semi-annual payment of interest. They could not, in the nature of things, have accepted the stipulation with an understanding that any such effect would be given it. If the government consents to the diminution of its security, so that only half of the prices due for services are to be applied to the payment of the interest or principal, what is to become of the other half? Surely there is no implication that the government shall retain it; and, if not, who is to get it? Manifestly the companies who have earned the money.

It is very clear that the Congress of 1864 did not suppose, in making this concession, that it would be barren of results, but as the rights of the parties have been settled by the construction given to the original provision on this subject, it is unnecessary to pursue the subject further.

The practice of the government, for a series of years, was in conformity with the views we have taken of the effect of the charter, until the Secretary of the Treasury arrested the payment of the money earned by the companies for services rendered the government, and directed that it be withheld. This action of the secretary brought the subject to the attention of Congress, and the act of March 3, 1871, (16 Stats. at Large, p. 525, section 9,) was passed, directing that one-half of the money due the Pacific Railroad Companies for services rendered, either "heretofore or hereafter," be paid them, leaving open the question of ultimate right for legal decision.

After this, another act was passed on this subject, by virtue of which this suit was instituted by the appellee in the Court of Claims. (Act of March 3, 1873, section 2, 17 Statutes at Large, p. 508.) It is contended that the purpose of this act is to repeal that portion of the charter of the Union Pacific Company containing the provisions we have discussed. But, manifestly, the purpose was very different. It is true, the act directs the Secretary of the Treasury to withhold all payments to the Pacific Companies on account of freights and transportation, but at the same time it authorizes any company thus affected to bring suit in the Court of Claims for "such freight and transportation," and in such suit "the right of such company to recover the same upon the law and the facts shall be determined, and also the rights of the United States upon the merits of all the points presented by it in answer thereto by them." This means nothing more nor less than the remission to the judicial tribunals of the country of the question whether this company, and others similarly situated, had the right to recover from the government one-half of what it earned by transportation, which question was to be determined upon its merits.

The merits of such a question are determined when the effect of the charter is determined. It is hardly necessary to say that it would have been idle to authorize a suit to be brought if it were the intention to repeal the provision on which the suit could alone be predicated.

We cannot go into an argument on the consequences which follow our decision. Consequences are not an element to be considered in the determination of the question whether an act of incorporation is less beneficial to the government than it supposed. And whether an act of Congress be more or less politic and wise it is not our province to determine. When we have declared the meaning of it, if there be power to pass it, our duty in connection with it is ended.

The judgment of the Court of Claims is affirmed.

The Baltimore and Ohio Railroad case, Justice Bradley delivering the Opinion of the Court.

SUPREME COURT OF THE UNITED STATES.

No. 27.—October Term, 1874.

The Baltimore and Ohio Railroad Company, Plaintiff in Error, vs. The State of Maryland.	In error to the Court of Appeals of the State of Maryland.

A stipulation in the charter of a railroad company, that the company shall pay to the State a bonus, or a portion of its earnings, is not repugnant to the Constitution of the United States.

Such a stipulation is different, in principle, from the imposition of a tax on the movement or transportation of goods or persons from one State to another. The latter is an interference with and a regulation of commerce between the States, and beyond the power of the State to impose; the former is not.

The power of a State to construct railroads and other highways, and to impose tolls, fare, or freight for transportation thereon, is unlimited and uncontrolled. The disposition of the revenues thus derived is subject to its own discretion. But a State cannot impose a tax on the movement of persons or property from one State to another.

The cases of Crandall vs. Nevada, 6 Wall., 42, and Freight Tax Cases, 16 Wall., 232, cited and re-affirmed.

Relief from onerous and burdensome rates of transportation imposed under State authority must be sought in the competition of different lines, and, perhaps, in the power of Congress to establish post roads and facilitate military and commercial intercourse between the different parts of the country.

The charter of the Baltimore and Ohio Railroad Company for constructing and operating the branch railroad between Baltimore and Washington, contained a stipulation that the company at the end of every six months should pay to the State one-fifth of the whole amount received for the transportation of passengers. This charter was accepted and complied with for many years: —*Held*,

1st. That this stipulation was not repugnant to the Constitution of the United States.

2d. That it was a contract to pay, and not a receipt of money belonging to the State; and, if unconstitutional, the objection could be set up as a defense to an action brought by the State to recover the money.

3d. That as the alleged unconstitutionality of the stipulation was set up as a defense, the State court was bound to pass upon it: and having decided against the exemption thus claimed, this court is authorized to review the decision.

MILLER, Justice.—I am of opinion that the statute of Maryland requiring the railroad company to pay into the treasury of the State one-fifth of the amount received by it from passengers on the branch of the road between Baltimore and Washington, confined as it is exclusively to passengers, on that branch of the road, was intended to raise a revenue for the State from all persons coming to Washington by rail, and had that effect for twenty-five years, and that the statute is, therefore, void within the principle laid down by this court in Crandall vs. Nevada, 8 Wallace.

In the cases involving the immigration laws of New York and Louisiana, Justice MILLER delivering the opinion, it was held:

1. The case of the City of New York vs. Miln, 11 Peters, 103, decided no more than that the requirement from the master of a vessel of a catalogue of his passengers landed in the city, rendered to the mayor on oath, with a correct description of their names, ages, occupations, places of birth, and of last legal settlement, was a police regulation within the power of the State to enact, and not inconsistent with the Constitution of the United States.

2. The result of the Passenger Cases, 7 How., 283, was to hold that a tax demanded of the master or owner of the vessel for every such passenger, was a regulation of commerce by the State, in conflict with the Constitution and laws of the United States, and, therefore, void.

3. These cases criticised, and the weight due to them as authority considered.

4. In whatever language a statute may be framed, its purpose and its constitutional validity must be determined by its natural and reasonable effect.

5. Hence, a statute which imposes a burdensome and almost impossible condition on the ship-master as a prerequisite to his landing his passengers, with an alternative payment of a small sum of money for each one of them is, in fact, a tax on the ship-owner for the right to land such passengers, and in effect, on the passenger himself, since the ship-master makes him pay it in advance as part of his fare.

6. Such a statute of a State is a regulation of commerce, and when applied to passengers from foreign countries, is a regulation of commerce with foreign nations.

7. It is no answer to the charge that such regulation of commerce by a State is forbidden by the Constitution to say that it falls within the police power of the States, for to whatever class of legislative powers it may belong, it is prohibited to the States if granted exclusively to Congress by that instrument.

8. Though it be conceded that there is a class of legislation which may affect commerce, both with foreign nations and between the States, in regard to which the laws of the States may be valid in the absence of action under the authority of Congress on the same subjects, this can have no reference to matters which are, in their

nature, national, or which admit of a uniform system or plan of regulation.

9. The statutes of New York and Louisiana, here under consideration, are intended to regulate commercial matters which are not only of national but of international concern, and which are also best regulated by one uniform rule, applicable alike to all the seaports of the United States. These statutes are, therefore, void, because legislation on the subjects which they cover is confided exclusively to Congress by the clause of the Constitution which gives to that body the "right to regulate commerce with foreign nations."

10. The constitutional objection to this tax on the passenger is not removed because the penalty for failure to pay does not accrue until twenty-four hours after he is landed. The penalty is incurred by the act of landing him without payment, and is, in fact, for the act of bringing him into the State.

11. This court does not, in this case, undertake to decide whether or not a State may, in the absence of all legislation by Congress on the same subject, pass a statute strictly limited to defending itself against paupers, convicted criminals, and others of that class, but is of opinion that to Congress rightfully and appropriately belongs the power of legislating on the whole subject.

In the case involving the law of California respecting Chinese immigrants, Justice MILLER delivering the opinion, it was held:

1. The statute of California which is the subject of consideration in this case does not require a bond for every passenger, or commutation in money, as the statutes of New York and Louisiana do, but only for certain enumerated classes, among which are "lewd and debauched women."

2. But the features of the statute are such as to show very clearly that the purpose is to extort money from a large class of passengers, or to prevent their immigration to California altogether.

3. The statute also operates directly on the passenger, for, unless the master or owner of the vessel gives an onerous bond for the future protection of the State against the support of the passenger, or pays such sum as the commissioner of immigration chooses to exact, he is not permitted to land from the vessel.

4. The powers which the commissioner is authorized to exercise under this statute are such as to bring the United States into conflict with foreign nations, and which can only belong to the federal government.

5. If the right of the States to pass statutes to protect themselves in regard to the criminal, the pauper, and the diseased foreigner landing within their borders exists at all, it is limited to such laws as are absolutely necessary for that purpose, and this mere police regulation cannot extend so far as to prevent or obstruct other classes of persons from the right to hold personal and commercial intercourse with the people of the United States.

6. The statute of California in this respect extends far beyond the necessity in which the right is founded, if it exists at all, and invades the right of Congress to regulate commerce with foreign nations, and is, therefore, void.

Decision of the U. S. Court of Claims on the Effect of "Amnesty."

1875, April 7.—In the case of John Knote vs. United States, a citizen of West Virginia, who set forth that specified personal property of his was seized and libeled on the ground of his alleged treason and rebellion, and by the decree of the United States District Court for the district and State of West Virginia was condemned and forfeited to the United States, under the act of July 17, 1862, and sold, and the proceeds, amounting to $11,000, paid into the Treasury, an interesting decision was made. He averred that by virtue of the President's proclamation of December 25, 1868, he was pardoned and relieved of all disabilities and penalties attaching to the offence of treason and rebellion, for which said property was confiscated, and by virtue thereof he has been restored to all his rights, privileges or immunities under the Constitution of the United States and the laws made in pursuance thereof, and that he was entitled to receive from the United States the said proceeds of sale, and he prayed judgment for $11,000. The defendants filed a general demurrer to the petition, and on that issue was joined and the case argued and submitted to the Court of Claims.

Judge LORING delivered the opinion of the court, giving the construction of the word "pardon" in the Constitution on the authority of Chief Justice Marshall, according to its significance in English law at the time the Constitution was adopted, and concluding as follows:

When the Constitution gives to Congress the power to dispose of the public property and provides that "no money shall be drawn from the public Treasury except by an appropriation made by law," it positively excludes the President from any control of the National property, real or personal, and so it has always been held. The forfeiture in this case was by the judgment that confiscated it to the United States as absolutely National property then as this capital is now, and as at the time of the adoption of our Constitution. The King's power to restore forfeitures was merely the legal consequence of his title in them, and was not derived from and made no part of his direct prerogative power to pardon crimes. We think that the second section of the second article of the Constitution, in vesting in the President the power to pardon crimes, did not authorize him to restore forfeitures or to dispose of that part of the national property. By the act of July 17, 1862, Congress authorized the President to grant to those who had participated in the rebellion "pardon and amnesty," and both of these words are used in the proclamation of December 25, 1868. The Legislature can neither extend nor restrict the power of the Executive to pardon crimes. The only question arising here is whether the word "amnesty" in the act of Congress authorized the President to restore forfeitures. What may be the technical meaning or effect of the word "amnesty" in other countries under different forms of government and different systems of law is foreign to our subject. But the word "amnesty" does not belong to the common law and has no technical meaning in it, and can be used in it only in the meaning of its synonym in our language, and that is oblivion, for the derivative and literal meaning of "amnesty" is removed from memory, and in the English law oblivion is the synonym of pardon, and it is so used in it, for the act is entitled an act of free pardon, indemnity and oblivion, and these are also its special words of grant; and the case under that act of Tombes, administrator, versus Etherington, heretofore cited, therefore decrees expressly that a grant of "free pardon, indemnity and oblivion" by an act of parliament does not effect or include the restoration of forfeitures. We know of no decision or authority in English law that decides a grant of amnesty is or can be anything more than a grant of oblivion. The word "amnesty" properly belongs to international law, and is applied to treaties of peace following a state of war, and signifies there the burial in oblivion of the particular cause of the strife, so that it shall not be again a cause of war between the parties, and the signification of "amnesty" is fully and practically expressed in the Indian custom of burying the hatchet, and so "amnesty" is applied to rebellions which by their magnitude are brought within the rules of international law, and in which multitudes of men are the subjects of the clemency of the Government. But in these cases and in all cases it means only oblivion, and never expresses or implies a grant. It is observable that the Executive proclamations of pardon previous to that of December 25, 1868, proffered in terms a restoration of property, while the proclamation of December 25, 1868, relied upon in this case, used the words: "Restoration of rights, privileges and immunities." It might be that these words would be satisfied by a mere removal of disabilities, but we have not sought to found an argument on this difference of phraseology. On the whole case, we are of opinion that the proclamation of December 25, 1868, does not entitle the petitioner to a restoration of the confiscated property claimed in his petition, and the order of the court is that the petition be dismissed.

Chief Justice DRAKE did not sit in the trial of this case, or take part in its decision.

Decisions of State Courts.

In INDIANA, November 25, 1874, the Supreme Court submitted an opinion, affirming the constitutionality of certain State legislation on the subject of Public Schools. A full abstract is given of Chief Justice BUSKIRK'S opinion:

Samuel Cary, John Beaver and Worthington Craig vs. Cary Carter. From the Marion Superior Court. This was a proceeding by mandate, on the part of the appellee against the appellants. The appellee in his petition alleges that he was a citizen of the State of Indiana and resided in School District No. 2, in Lawrence Township, Marion County, in the said State, and was a taxpayer therein. That he was the father of two children, Mary and Edward Carter, and the grandfather of Lena and John Carter, all of whom reside with him; that he was a negro of African descent, and that his said children and grandchildren were all negroes of the full blood, and of the same descent; that his children and grandchildren were respectively of the age that entitled them to the benefits of the common-schools in the said district; that there was a common-school for white children in progress in said district, and that his said children and grandchildren presented themselves at the school-house in said district, and demanded admission, and to be taught therein with the white children, but were refused admission by the appellees, Beaver and Craig, the Director and teacher of said school, for the reason that said school was a school for white children, and not for negro children; that after the refusal aforesaid he caused to be served upon the appellants a written request and demand that his said children and grandchildren should be received and taught in said school with the white children of said district, but they were refused admission solely on the ground that they were negroes; that said appellants, and all other persons have wholly neglected, failed and refused to provide any school in said district, or in any adjoining district, near enough for said children to attend as scholars; and that by reason of the said premises, his said children and grandchildren are denied all opportunity to attend any school in said district as abounding in the neighborhood, as in right and law they are entitled to do.

The aid of the Court was requested to declare the right of admission of said negro children in the school for white children, and to compel the appellants to admit them.

It is very plain and obvious to us that by the supplemental act of May 13, 1869, the Legislature has provided for the education of the white and colored children of the State in separate schools; and the question presented for our decision is, whether such legislation is in conflict with the Constitution of the State or the Constitution of the United States.

It is contended that the act in question is repugnant to Sec. 23 of Art. 1, and Sec. 1 of Art. 8, and they use Question 23. The General Assembly shall not grant to any citizen or class of citizens, privileges or immunities which upon the same terms shall not equally belong to all citizens. 1 G. & H. 33.

Sec. 1, Art. 8 (1 G. & H. 48) declares, that knowledge and learning generally diffused throughout a community, being essential to the preservation of a free government, it shall be the duty of the General Assembly to encourage by all suitable means, moral, intellectual, scientific and agricultural improvements, and to provide by law for a general and uniform system of common schools, wherein tuition shall be, without charge, equally open to all.

It is important that we should settle in advance the rules by which we are to be guided in placing a construction upon the constitutional provisions above quoted. In the State vs. Gilson, 36 Ind., 389, we held that it was settled by very high authority that, in placing a construction upon a written constitution, or any clause or part thereof, a court should look to the history of the times, and examine the state of things existing when the Constitution, or any part thereof, was framed and adopted, to ascertain the old law, the mischief, and the remedy.

The Court should also look to the nature and

object of the particular powers, duties and rights in question, with all the aids and lights of contemporary history, and give to the words of each provision just such operation and force consistent with their legitimate meaning as will fairly secure the end proposed. Kendall vs. The United States, 12 Peters, 524; Priggs vs. The Commonwealth, 16 Peters, 539.

After citing a multitude of authorities upon questions of constitutional construction, the Judge proceeds to remark that it is scarcely conceivable that a case can arise where a Court would be justifiable in declaring any part of a written constitution nugatory because of ambiguity. One part may qualify another, so as to explain its operation, or apply it otherwise than the natural construction would require if it stood by itself; but one part is not to be allowed to defeat another, if, by any reasonable construction, the two can be made to stand together.

In support of the above proposition, reference is made in the notes to the following authorities: People vs. Merrill, 21 Wend. 584; Newell vs. People, 7 New York, 109; Wekerson vs. Davis, 3 Barb, 196; People vs. Blodgett, 13 Michigan, 138; United States vs. Fisher, 2 Cranch, 339, and many other decisions of high authority.

The application, he proceeds, of the rules of construction heretofore laid down to the various provisions of our Constitution will conclusively demonstrate that the provisions of the section under examination have no application to the children and grandchildren of the appellee.

One of the cardinal rules of construction is, that courts shall give effect to the intent of the framers of the instrument and of the people in adopting it. Then, as it is manifest that neither the framers of the Constitution, nor the people in adopting it, intended that the children of the African race should participate in the advantages of a general and uniform system of common schools, we possess no power to adjudge to them what was not designed for them.

Another rule of construction is, that, in placing a construction upon one section or clause, courts are required to examine the whole instrument and to give effect, if possible, to the whole instrument; and if different parts seem to conflict, the courts must harmonize them if possible, and lean in favor of a construction which will render every word operative rather than one which may make some idle and nugatory. There is but one construction which will preserve the unity of harmony and consistency of our State Constitution, and that is to hold that it was made and adopted by, and for the exclusive use and enjoyment of, the white race. Any other construction would convict the members of the Constitutional Convention and the voters of the State of the grossest inconsistency, absurdity, and injustice. It would be monstrous to hold that the framers of the Constitution, in adopting, and the voters of the State in ratifying it, intended that the common schools of the State should be open to the children of the African race, when, by the same instrument, that portion of such race as then resided in the State were denied all political rights, privileges, and immunities, and the further emigration of that race into the State was prohibited by the thirteenth article of the Constitution, which received the almost unanimous approval of the voters of the State.

Another important rule of construction is, that the meaning of a Constitution is fixed when it is adopted, and it is not different at any subsequent time when a Court has occasion to pass upon it. A Constitution is infallible, and cannot bend to convenience as modified by public opinion. It is therefore the duty of the Court to declare the law as it is written, leaving to the people in their sovereign capacity to make such change as new Conventions may require, and in our opinion, using the appropriate language of Judge Cooley, "The Court or Legislature which should allow a change in public sentiment to influence it in giving construction to a written constitution not warranted by the intention of its founders, would be justly chargeable with reckless disregard of official oath and public duty."

In the case of Lewis vs. Henly, 2 Ind., 332, this Court was required to place a construction upon a constitutional provision by which interests similar to these were affected, and it was then held that negro children were not entitled to admission to the schools with the white children, and that the Legislature had the right under the Constitution to exclude negro children from our public schools. It was further held that, although the negro might be entitled to share in the fund derived from the sale of lands donated by Congress, yet they would have to do so in separate schools, and not in schools with white children. Both constructions provide for a general and uniform system of common schools. Both provide that the tuition should be free and the schools equally open to all. Both Constitutions deprived the negro of all political rights. If the Legislature, under the Constitution of 1816, had the right to exclude the negro from the public schools for white children, it is difficult to see why it may not be done under the present Constitution.

Having reached the true construction of the Constitution of this State, as it came from the hands of its framers, and received the sanction of her qualified voters, the next step is to find out the extent of its qualification as changed by the Constitution of the United States. Sec 2, of Art. 4 of the Constitution of the United States declares, "That the citizens of each State shall be entitled to all privileges and immunities of citizens in the several States." This section, at an early date, received a construction in the case of Carfield vs. Caryell, which has ever since been recognized and approved. It relates only to "those privileges and immunities which are fundamental," and which all may be comprehended under the following heads: Protection by the Government, with the rights to acquire and possess property of every kind, and to pursue and obtain happiness and safety, subject, nevertheless, to such restraints as the Government may prescribe for the general good of the whole.

In the State et al. Grimes vs. Weban and others, 21 Ohio State 198, the Supreme Court of that State uses the following language: "It would seem, then, that under the Constitution and laws of this State, the right to classify the youth of the State for school purposes, on the basis of color, and to assign them to separate schools for education, both upon well recognized legal principles and the repeated adjudication of this Court, is too firmly established to be now judicially disturbed."

Unquestionably all doubts, where any existed, as to the citizenship of colored persons, and their right to the equal protection of the laws, are settled. But neither of them were denied to them in this State before the adoption of this amendment. At all events, the statutes classifying the youth of the State for school purposes on the basis of color, and the decisions of this Court in relation thereto, were not at all based upon a denial that colored persons were citizens, or that they are entitled to the equal protection of the laws.

It would seem, then, that these provisions of the amendment to the Constitution contain nothing conflicting with the statute authorizing the classification in question. Any State is forbidden to make or enforce any law which will abridge the privileges or immunities of citizens of the United States. This involves the inquiry as to what privileges or immunities are embraced in the inhibition of this clause. We are not aware that this has as yet been judicially settled. The language of the clause, however, taken in connection with other provisions of the amendment, and of the Constitution of which it forms a part, affords strong reasons for believing that it includes such privileges or immunities as are derived from, or recognized by, the Constitution of the United States.

All the privileges of the school-system of this State are derived solely from the Constitution and laws of the State.

The question under consideration is the same that has been heretofore determined in this State, that a classification of the youth of the State for school purposes upon any basis which does not exclude either class from equal school advantages is no infringement of the equal rights of citizens secured by the Constitution of the State. We have seen that the law in the case before us works no substantial inequality of school privileges between the children of both classes in the localities of the parties.

In our opinion, the Court below erred in affirming the action of the Court in special term, and the judgment is reversed, with costs, and the cause is remanded to the Court below, with directions to that Court to overrule the judgment of the Court in special term, in overruling the demurrer to the petition for a mandate.

THE NEXT STEP.

The Plaintiff's lawyers, Gordon, Brown and Lamb, excepted to the opinion and judgment of the Court, and announced their intention to appeal to the Supreme Court of the United States, first, however, asking the Supreme Court of Indiana to grant them a re-hearing.

The opinion of the Superior Court, in the proceeding (April 16th, at Indianapolis) reviewed above, was given by Judge PERKINS, and is thus stated briefly in the newspapers of the day:

Great ability and research have characterized arguments upon the motion. I shall not follow the counsel over the wide field they traversed in argument. I shall limit myself to the statements of a few propositions, which seem to me to support the conclusion to which I have arrived. The ultimate question in the case to be decided is this: Have the children residing in the various districts in the different townships of the State, in which no separate schools have been organized for colored children, a right to attend the school organized in such townships in common with white children? On the 28th of July, 1866, the Fourteenth Amendment became a part of the Constitution of the United States. That amendment ordered that all persons born or naturalized in the United States and subject to the laws and penalties thereof, are citizens of the United States and of the State wherein they reside. Article 8, Section 1, of the Constitution of the State of Indiana, reads: "Knowledge and learning generally diffused throughout a community, being essential to the preservation of free government, it shall be the duty of the General Assembly to encourage, by all suitable means, moral, intellectual, scientific, and agricultural improvement, and to provide by law for a general and uniform system of common schools, wherein tuition shall be without charge and equally open to all." This expression "equally open to all," includes at least all citizens, and the system of common schools is composed of the various district schools of the State. At the date of the taking effect of the Fourteenth Amendment to the Constitution of the United States, the State of Indiana had in operation a system of common schools, wherein tuition was free to white children under 21 years of age, they being citizens of the State; and on the taking effect of that amendment, the several schools composing that system, by virtue of the section above quoted from our State Constitution, became open and free to colored children, also being under 21 years of age. As that amendment placed them in the class of citizens, they had the right to enter and attend those schools until reasonably convenient separate schools, substantially equal in educational advantages, were provided for them by the State; and whenever in any township such schools are not provided for them by the State, colored children, being citizens and under 21 years of age, still retain the right conferred upon citizens' children to attend the common schools, equally with the white children in such locality.

Women as Justices of the Peace.

In MAINE, February 6, 1874, the Supreme Judicial Court were asked these questions:

First. Under the constitution and laws of this State, can a woman, if duly appointed and qualified as a Justice of the Peace, legally perform all acts pertaining to such office?

Second. Would it be competent for the Legislature to authorize the appointment of a married or unmarried woman to the office of Justice of the Peace; or to administer oaths, take acknowledgements of deeds, or solemnize marriages, so that the same shall be legal and valid?

The opinion of the court, drawn by Chief Justice JOHN APPLETON, and concurred in by Justices JONAS CUTTING, JOHN A. PETERS, CHARLES DANFORTH and WM. WIRT VIRGIN, is as follows:

To the questions proposed we have the honor to answer as follows:

Whether it is expedient that women should

hold the office of Justice of the Peace is not an inquiry proposed for our consideration. It is, whether, under the existing constitution, they can be appointed to such office, and can legally discharge its duties.

By the constitution of Massachusetts, of which we formerly constituted a portion, the entire political power of that commonwealth was vested, under certain conditions, in its male inhabitants of a prescribed age. They alone, and to the exclusion of the other sex, as determined by its highest court of law, could exercise the judicial function as existing and established by that instrument.

By the act relating to the separation of the District of Maine from Massachusetts, the authority to determine upon the question of separation, and to elect delegates to meet and form a constitution was conferred upon the "inhabitants of the several towns, districts and plantations in the District of Maine qualified to vote for Governor and Senators," thus excluding the female sex from all participation in the formation of a constitution, and in the organization of the government under it. Whether the constitution should or should not be adopted, was specially, by the organic law of its existence, submitted to the vote of male inhabitants of the State.

It thus appears that the constitution of the State was the work of its male citizens. It was ordained, established and ratified by them, and by them alone. By it the powers of government were divided into three distinct departments: legislative, executive and judicial. By article 6th, section 4, Justices of the Peace are recognized as judicial officers.

By the constitution, the whole political power of the State is vested in its male citizens. Whenever in any of its provisions, reference is made to sex, it is to duties to be done and performed by male members of the community. Nothing in the language of the constitution or in the debates of the convention by which it was formed, indicates any purpose whatever of any surrender of political power by those who had previously enjoyed it, or a transfer of the same to those who had never possessed it. Had any such design then existed, we cannot doubt that it would have been made manifest in fitting and appropriate language. But such intention is nowhere disclosed. Having regard then, to the rules of the common law as to the rights of women, married and unmarried, as then existing—to the history of the past—to the universal and unbroken practical construction given to the constitution of this State and to that of the commonwealth of Massachusetts, upon which that of this State was modelled—we are led to the inevitable conclusion that it was never in the contemplation or intention of those forming our constitution that the offices thereby created should be filled by those who could take no part in its original formation, and to whom no political power was entrusted for the organization of the government then about to be established under its provisions, or for its continued existence and preservation when established.

The same process of reasoning which would sanction the conferring judicial power on women under the constitution would authorize the giving them executive power by making them Sheriffs and Major-Generals.

But while the offices enacted by the constitution are to be filled exclusively by the male members of the State, we have no doubt that the Legislature may create new ministerial offices not enumerated therein, and, if they deem expedient, may authorize the performance of the duties of the offices so created by persons of either sex.

To the first question proposed, we answer in the negative.

To the second, we answer that it is competent for the Legislature to authorize the appointment of a married or unmarried woman to administer oaths, take acknowledgements of deeds or solemnize marriages, so that the same shall be legal and valid.

Justices CHARLES W. WALTON and WM. G. BARROWS unite in a dissenting opinion, and Justice J. G. DICKERSON gave a separate dissenting opinion.

Decision on the Powers of a Constitutional Convention.

In PENNSYLVANIA, the new Constitution was adopted by a vote of a majority of the Convention who made it, November 3, 1873, and was submitted to a vote of the people, December 16, 1873, by whom it was adopted. Pending this vote of the people application was made to Judge STOWE of the District Court for Allegheny county, for an injunction to restrain the Secretary of the Commonwealth from issuing his proclamation for the election—which was refused; and the case was carried to the Supreme Court, by whom an opinion was given, November 3, 1874, which has historical value for its discussion of the powers of a Constitutional Convention. It was delivered by Chief Justice AGNEW, and, so far as it appears, was concurred in by all the Judges:

Robert Woods et al. vs. M. S. Quay, Secretary of State et al. Appeal from the decree of the Court of Common Pleas of Allegheny county. In equity.

The change made by the people in their political institutions, by the adoption of the proposed Constitution since this decree, forbids an inquiry into the merits of the case. The question is no longer judicial, but in affirming the decree we must not seem to sanction any doctrine in the opinion dangerous to the liberties of the people. The claim for absolute sovereignty in the Convention, apparently sustained in the opinion, is of such magnitude and overwhelming importance to the people themselves, it cannot be passed unnoticed. In defence of their just rights, we are bound to show that it is unsound and dangerous. Their liberties would be suspended by a thread more slender than the hair which held the tyrant's sword over the head of Damocles, if they could not, while yet their existing government remained unchanged, obtain from the Courts protection against the usurpation of power by their servants in the convention. When they become complainants, the convention must defend and show their authority.

It was contended in the case of Francis Wells et al. vs. James Bain et al., involving the legality of an ordinance of the Convention, argued at

Philadelphia in December last, that the Convention had the power to ordain ordinances having the present force of law; and the instant power to proclaim a constitution, binding without ratification, irrespective of the matter adopted by the people, to exercise their right to alter or amend their frame of government. This imputed sovereignty in a convention called and organized under a law, as the very means adopted by the people to exercise their reserved right of amendment, owing to the briefness of the time, was not discussed in that case with the fulness the importance of the question to the people demanded.

There is no subject more momentous or deeply interesting to the people of this State than an assumption of absolute power by their servants. The claim of a body of mere deputies to exercise all their sovereignty, absolutely, instantly, and without ratification, is so full of peril to a free people, living under their own instituted government and a well-matured bill of rights, the bulwark and security of their liberties, that they will pause before they allow the claim and inquire how they delegated this fearful power and how they are thus absolutely bound and can be controlled by persons appointed to a special service. Struck by the danger and prompted by self-interest, they will at once distinguish between their *own rights* and the *powers* they commit to others. These rights it is, the judiciary is called in to maintain. The very rights of the people and freedom itself demand, therefore, that no such absolute power shall be imputed to the mere delegates of the people to perform the special service of amendment, unless it is clearly expressed, or as clearly implied, in the *manner* chosen by the people to communicate their authority.

A Convention has no *inherent* rights; it exercises *powers* only. *Delegated* power defines itself. To be delegated it must come in some adopted manner to convey it by some defined means. This adopted *manner* therefore becomes the measure of the power conferred. The right of the people is absolute in the language of the bill of rights, "to alter, reform, or abolish their Government in such *manner* as *they* may think proper." This right being *theirs*, they may impart so much or so little of it as they shall deem expedient. It is only *when* they exercise this right, *and* not before they determine by the mode they choose to adopt, the extent of the powers they intend to delegate. Hence the argument which imputes sovereignty to a Convention, because of the reservation in the bill of rights, is utterly illogical and unsound. The bill of rights is a reservation of rights out of the general powers of government to *themselves*, but is no delegation of power to a Convention. It defines no manner or mode in which the people shall proceed to exercise their right, but leaves that to their after choice. Until then it is unknown how they will proceed, or what powers they will confer on their delegates. Hence we must look beyond the bill of rights to the mode adopted by the people to find the extent of the power they intend to delegate. These modes were stated and discussed in the opinion in Wells et. al. *vs.* Bain et. al. If, by a mere determination of the people to call a Convention, whether it be by a vote or otherwise, the entire sovereignty of the people passes *ipso facto* into a body of deputies or attorneys, so that these deputies can, without ratification, alter a government and abolish its bill of rights at pleasure, and impose at will a new government upon the people without restraints upon the governing power, no true liberty remains. Then the servants sit above their masters by the merest imputation, and a people's welfare must always rest upon the transient circumstances of the hour, which produce the convention and the accidental character of the majority which controls it. Such a doctrine, however suited to revolutionary times, when new governments must be formed as best the people can, is wholly unfitted when applied to a state of peace and to an existing government, instituted by the people themselves and guarded by a well matured bill of rights.

To impute absolute power to a Convention of mere delegates, from a vote on the simple question of calling it, as for example under the act of 1871, is to assume a grant by the people without terms, without the means of limitation, and without any clearly evinced intent. It is an assumption without a just basis against the security, the interest and the welfare of the people, which no body of men have a right to make, and no judicial reason or rule can justify. It contravenes the rightful and necessary prerogative of the people to determine their own institutions by ratification or rejection, and in this respect contravenes the very language and spirit of the Bill of Rights, by which they reserved to *themselves* the right to change their form of government. It also conflicts with that universal rule, that no agent or subordinate can claim the powers, liberties or franchises of the people, except by their express grant, or by a plain and certain implication. What intent is more doubtful? Nay, what clearer *non sequitur* is it, than to affirm, because a people vote to call a Convention, they therefore strip themselves of their most essential power to ratify or reject the work of their delegates? The inference is the very reverse; for a vote for a Convention, which must be called afterwards by law, from its very nature refers the Constitution and powers of a Convention so to be called, to the law, which the people use to accomplish their purpose. Such was the nature of the act of 1871. It was simply an order assuming its mandatory character to call a Convention. It was not a call itself, and it provided no terms in which the call should be made. The people were silent on this point, and therefore no implication can be made against their essential right to protect themselves. The mandatory character of the call does not alter the inference from the vote, or extend the intent evinced by it. The effect of the vote remains simply, that a Convention shall be called. The elector expressed no power to be conferred. The total vote evinced no common terms, and certainly none that the power to be transferred to the Convention when called and organized should be that of absolute will, without ratification or approval. This is tested by a very simple and practical question: Did the people when they voted to call a convention *intend* to strip themselves of the power to ratify or reject the work of their servants? If so, where is the evidence of this intent? Every elector knows as a fact no such proposition was made to him. On the question of power, the minds of the people met on no common ground of intent. The desire of one was not that of another, and a third may have differed from both. Therefore, to *impute* absolute sovereignty of will to the Convention to be called, from the vague and inexpressive implication of the vote on the question of calling a convention, is to assume a grant where none exists, or can be fairly inferred, compatibly with the rights and liberties of the people. Its effect is to declare the impotency of the people, and the absolute potency of their agents. It is to determine a question of authority against the principal, and in favor of the agent or servant, without any evidence of an intention to transmit the power.

The people have the same right to limit the powers of their delegates, that they have to bound the power of their representatives. Each are representatives, but only in a different sphere. It is simply evasive to affirm that the Legislature cannot limit the right of the *people* to alter or reform the government. Certainly it cannot. The question is not upon the power of the Legislature to restrain the *people*, but upon the right of the people, by the instrumentality of the law, to limit their delegates. Law is the highest form of a people's will in a state of peaceful government. When a people act through a law the act is theirs, and the fact that they use the Legislature as their instrument to confer their powers makes them the superiors, and not the Legislature. The idea which lies at the root of the fallacy, that a convention cannot be controlled by law, is that the convention and the people are identical. But when the question to be determined is between the people and the convention, the fallacy is obvious. Such a metonymy may do for a flourish of rhetoric, but not for grave argument. The parties to the question are the people on the one hand and the convention on the other. The people allege an usurpation of power in this, that the convention seek to bind them without their ratification. The question then is, *what* power was conferred? The judiciary sits to decide between them. The people having challenged their power to set a government over them at will, the agents must show their authority to do this. The latter put in evidence the act of 1871 as their authority. Then the issue is, does the act of 1871, simply ordering a Convention to be called, confer this absolute, extraordinary and dangerous power upon a body of men not yet called into being, and which can have neither being nor power except by the further act of the people through the instrumentality of a law. To make the law odious, it is assumed that the Legislature is or may be corrupt. But this is aside from the true question of power. In a governmental and proper sense, *law* is the highest act of a people's sovereignty, while their government and constitution remain unchanged. It is the supreme will of the people expressed in the forms and by the authority of their constitution. It is their own appointed mode through which they govern themselves, and by which they bind themselves. So long as their frame of government is unchanged in its grant of all legislative power, these laws are supreme over all subjects, unforbidden by the instrument itself. The calling of a convention and regulating its action by law is not forbidden in the Constitution. It is a conceded *manner*, through which the people may exercise the right reserved in the bill of rights. It falls, therefore, within the protection of the bill of rights as a very manner in which the people may proceed to amend their Constitution, and delegate the only powers they intend to confer, and as the means whereby they may, by limitation, defend themselves against those who are called in to exercise their powers. The Legislature may not confer powers by law inconsistent with the rights, safety and liberties of the people, because no consent to do this can be implied, but they may pass limitations in favor of the essential rights of the people. The right of the people to restrain their delegates by *law* cannot be denied, unless the power to call a convention by law and the right of self-protection be also denied. It is, therefore, the right of the people and not of the Legislature to be put by law above the convention, and to require the delegates to submit their work for ratification or disapproval.

To argue a want of authority in the law from the alleged character of those who passed it is bad logic, and an undeserved reproach, in view of the liberality of the subsequent act of 1872, which opened a wide door to men of all parties, and filled the convention with the best men in the State. When it is conceded that a convention can be called and organized by law, the number and qualifications of the delegates prescribed, their districts defined, their mode of selection or appointment determined, their time and place of meeting fixed, and their compensation declared by law, the *binding force* of law must be conceded. The convention was a creation of law, and its members the offspring of law—fitly by the mere force of law, without a popular election. How, then, can the power of law be denied? Without it no delegates had existed, and no power had been transmitted to them. It is a solecism and a fallacy to assert that a law has the power to transmit the authority of the people, and yet is a nullity in the terms of its transmission. If the authority of the people passes to the convention outside of the law, the people are left without the means of self-protection except by revolution. Then the singular spectacle is presented of the absolute sovereignty of the people being vested in a body of agents without any known means of transmission or of limitation. But clearly this cannot be when the fundamental rights of the people are at stake. To estop them from their right to accept or reject the work of the convention, there must be an evident channel pointed out, through which their power passed to the convention to ordain at pleasure a constitution or binding ordinances. The force of the argument cannot be avoided, by a reference to the well-known purity of character of the delegates. The *personnel* of the convention has nothing to do with the question of delegated power. It may help to suppress an inquiry into the power, but however presently popular the doctrine of self-imputed sovereignty may be to those whose integrity forbids intentional wrong, as a question of power the doctrine is unfounded in principle, repugnant to right reason, incompatible with safety, dangerous to liberty, and unsuited to times of agitation and excitement, which sometimes overcome the people.

No argument for the implied power of absolute sovereignty in a convention can be drawn from revolutionary times, when necessity begets a new government. Governments thus accepted and ratified by silent submission afford no precedents for the power of a Convention in a time of profound tranquillity, and for a people living under self-established, safe institutions. While Conventions are well-known historical modes of procedure in the formation of Constitutions, they prove nothing; for history does not define their powers, or estop the people from asserting their own. There can be no estoppel by precedent against the fundamental rights of the people. Limits must be set to power. Liberty demands absolute security. No people can be safe in the presence of a divine right to rule, or of self-imputed sovereignty in their servants to bind them without ratification.

Nor is the improbability of a wrong use, or an abuse of power, a sound argument in the light of our own knowledge. We have seen a public sentiment formed and elections carried in a few months, and yet the subject of excitement was as short-lived as it was sudden. Men have been proscribed for religion's sake, and for a foreign birth. Moving like a whirlwind, such excitements have filled a Legislature with its partisans. In our day, conventions, imputing sovereignty to themselves, have ordained secession, dragged States into rebellion against the well-known wishes of their quiet people and erected in the midst of the nation alien State governments, and a Southern Confederacy. The negro is now a citizen and an elector, and yet the time is not long gone by since the word "white" was voted by a former convention into the article on elections. Who can foretell the next subject of agitation? The times abound in contests. Labor and capital are in strife. Agriculture wars on transportation. Communism, internationalism and other forms of agitation excite the world. Let conventions in such seasons possess, by mere imputation, all the powers of the people, and what security is there for their fundamental rights? Not the bill of rights, nor even the particular sentiment that brings the Convention into existence. Once assembled, a Convention, according to this dogma, is all powerful and may annul any declaration in the bill of rights, and proclaim a constitution without let or hindrance. Who will predict what effects may be produced by combinations foreign to the purpose which actuated the call? The fundamental rights of the people, the true principles of civil liberty, the nature of delegated power, and the liability of the people to temporary commotion, all rise up in earnest protest against such a doctrine of imputed sovereignty in the mere servants of the people.

Then look at the constitution of the body to whtch this power may be imputed. The number may be any designated in the law, 133—thirty-three—or three times three. The delegates may not be chosen by the whole people—but by portions of the people of one party, as under the act of 1872. On what principle of sound reason or logical deduction does such a body possess, by mere imputation, all the powers of the people, not conferred on them by law? They possess them by no act of the people independently of law. And certainly there is no popular *afflatus* outside of the law to breathe into them the spirit of prophecy in the name of the people.

In conclusion, we find nothing in the Bill of Rights, in the vote under the act of 1871, or the authority conferred in the act of 1872, nothing in the nature of delegated power, or in the Constitution of the Convention itself, which can justify an assumption that a convention so called, constituted, organized and limited, can take from the people their sovereign right to ratify or reject a constitution or ordinance framed by it, or can infuse present life and vigor into its work before its adoption by the people.

Decree affirmed.

The case of Wells *et al. vs.* Bain *et al.*, referred to in the opinion above, was decided in Philadelphia, December 2, 1873, at Nisi Prius, before GORDON, J., with AGNEW, C. J., SHARSWOOD, WILLIAMS, and MERCUR, JJ., as assessors.

The Constitutional Convention adopted an Ordinance, in which five Commissioners were appointed to conduct the election on the adoption of the Constitution, in Philadelphia, the sixth section of the act of the Legislature of 1872, having provided that "*the election to decide for or against the adoption of the new constitution or specific amendments, shall be conducted as the general elections of this Commonwealth are now by law conducted.*"

Bills were filed by citizens praying an injunction to restrain the Commissioners of Philadelphia from expending any money in relation to the election, and the Commissioners appointed by the Convention from holding such election.

The Court, after argument, held that the ordinance relating to the election in the city of Philadelphia is flatly opposed to the Act of 1872, and is therefore illegal and void. The Opinion, which is elaborate, concludes with this paragraph:

"The Convention is not a co-ordinate branch of the Government. It exercises no govermental power, but is a body raised by law, in aid of the popular desire to discuss and propose amendments, which have no governing force so long as they remain propositions. While it acts within the scope of its delegated powers, it is not amenable for its acts; but when it assumes to legislate, to repeal and displace existing institutions before they are displaced by the adoption of its propositions, it acts without authority, and the citizens injured thereby are entitled, under the Declaration of Rights, to an *open* Court and to redress at our hands."

The election was held under the general election law, all over the State.

IX.

CONSTITUTIONAL AMENDMENTS, MADE AND PENDING, IN VARIOUS STATES.

Alabama.

At an election held, November 16, 1875, a new Constitution, adopted by a Convention, was ratified by the following vote: For, 95,672; Against, 30,004.

Among the Declaration of Rights are the following:

That all persons resident in this State born in the United States, or naturalized, or who shall have legally declared their intention to become citizens of the United States, are hereby declared citizens of the State of Alabama, possessing equal civil and political rights.

That the privilege of the writ of *habeas corpus* shall not be suspended by the authorities of this State.

That the exercise of the right of eminent domain shall never be abridged nor so construed as to prevent the General Assembly from taking the property and franchises of incorporated companies and subjecting them to public use the same as individuals. But private property shall not be taken for or applied to public use, unless just compensation be first made therefor; nor shall private property be taken for private use, or for the use of corporations, other than municipal, without the consent of the owner; *Provided, however*, that the General Assembly may, by law, secure to persons or corporations the right of way over the lands of other persons or corporations, and by general laws provide for and regulate the exercise by persons and corporations of the rights herein reserved; but just compensation shall, in all cases, be first made to the owner. *And provided*, That the right of eminent domain shall not be so construed as to allow taxation or forced subscription for the benefit of railroads or any other kind of corporations other than municipal, or for the benefit of any individual or association.

That every citizen has a right to bear arms in defense of himself and the State.

That no form of slavery shall exist in this State, and there shall be no involuntary servitude, otherwise than for the punishment of crime, of which the party shall have been duly convicted.

The right of suffrage shall be protected by laws regulating elections, and prohibiting, under adequate penalties, all undue influences from power, bribery, tumult, or other improper conduct.

The people of this State accept as final the established fact that from the Federal Union there can be no secession of any State.

No educational or property qualification for suffrage or office, nor any restraint upon the same on account of race, color or previous condition of servitude, shall be made by law.

Other provisions are:

Election for Senators and Representatives shall be on the first Monday in August, 1876, and biennially—the terms of Senators to be four years, Representatives two, and the Legislature to meet biennially. Their pay to be $4 a day, and 10 cents a mile travel to and from the capital. Not more than thirty-three Senators, and not more than one hundred Representatives.

A member of either house expelled for corruption, shall not thereafter be eligible to either house; and punishment for contempt or disorderly behavior, shall not bar an indictment for the same offense.

No Senator or Representative shall, during the term for which he shall have been elected, be appointed to any civil office of profit, under this State, which shall have been created or the emoluments of which shall have been increased during such term, except such offices as may be filled by election by the people.

No person hereafter convicted of embezzlement of public money, bribery, perjury, or other infamous crime, shall be eligible to the General Assembly, or capable of holding any office of trust or profit in this State.

No special or local law shall be enacted for the benefit of individuals or corporations, in cases which are or can be provided for by a general law, or where the relief sought can be given by any court of this State; nor shall the operation of any general law be suspended by the General Assembly for the benefit of any individual, corporation or association.

No local or special law shall be passed, on a subject which cannot be provided for by a general law, unless notice of the intention to apply therefor shall have been published in the locality where the matter or things to be affected may be situated; which notice shall be at least twenty days prior to the introduction into the General Assembly of such bill; and the evidence of such notice having been given, shall be exhibited to the General Assembly before such bill shall be passed. *Provided*, That the provisions of this Constitution, as to special or local laws, shall not apply to public or educational institutions of or in this State, nor to industrial, mining, immigration, or manufacturing corporations or interests, or corporations for constructing canals, or improving navigable rivers or harbors of this State.

The General Assembly shall pass general laws, under which local and private interests shall be provided for and protected.

No bill shall be passed giving any extra compensation to any public officer, servant or employé, agent or contractor, after the services shall have been rendered or contract made; nor shall any officer of the State bind the State to the payment of any sum of money but by authority of law.

No appropriation shall be made to any charitable or educational institution not under the absolute control of the State, other than Normal schools established by law for the professional training of teachers for the public schools of the State, except by a vote of two-thirds of all the members elected to each house.

No act of the General Assembly shall authorize the investment of any trust funds by executors, administrators, guardians and other trustees, in the bonds or stock of any private corporation; and any such acts now existing are avoided, saving investments heretofore made.

When the General Assembly shall be convened in special session, there shall be no legislation upon subjects other than those designated in the proclamation of the Governor calling such session.

A member of the General Assembly who shall corruptly solicit, demand or receive, or consent to receive, directly or indirectly, for himself or for another, from any company, corporation, or person, any money, office, appointment, employment, reward, thing of value or enjoyment, or of personal advantage or promise thereof, for his vote or official influence, or for withholding the same; or with an understanding, expressed or implied, that his vote or official action shall be in any way influenced thereby; or who shall solicit or demand any such money or other advantage, matter or thing aforesaid, for another, as the consideration of his vote or official influence, or for withholding the same; or shall give or withhold his vote or influence in consideration of the payment or promise of such money, advantage, matter or thing to another, shall be guilty of bribery, within the meaning of this Constitution, and shall incur the disabilities provided thereby for such offence, and such additional punishment as is or shall be provided by law.

Any person who shall, directly or indirectly, offer, give or promise any money or thing of value, testimonial, privilege or personal advantage, to any Executive or Judicial officer, or member of the General Assembly, to influence him in the performance of any of his public or official duties, shall be guilty of bribery, and be punished in such manner as shall be provided by law.

The offense of corrupt solicitation of members of the General Assembly, or of public officers of this State, or of any municipal division thereof, and any occupation or practice of solicitation of such member or officers, to influence their official action, shall be defined by law, and shall be punished by fine and imprisonment.

The General Assembly shall not tax the property, real and personal, of the State, counties or other municipal corporations, or cemeteries; nor lots in incorporated cities or towns, or within one mile of any city or town, to the extent of one acre, nor lots one mile or more distant from such cities or towns, to the extent of five acres, with the buildings thereon, when the same are used exclusively for religious worship, for schools, or for purposes purely charitable; nor such property, real or personal, to an extent not exceeding twenty-five thousand dollars in value, as may be used exclusively for agricultural or horticultural associations of a public character.

The General Assembly shall by law prescribe such rules and regulations as may be necessary to ascertain the value of personal and real property exempted from sale under legal process by this Constitution, and to secure the same to the claimant thereof as selected.

The State shall not engage in works of internal improvement, nor lend money or its credit in aid of such; nor shall the State be interested in any private or corporate enterprise, or lend money or its credit to any individual, association or corporation.

The General Assembly shall pass such penal laws as they may deem expedient to suppress the evil practice of duelling.

It shall be the duty of the General Assembly to regulate by law the cases in which deductions shall be made from the salaries of public officers for neglect of duty in their official capacities, and the amount of such deductions.

The Governor shall have power to remit fines and forfeitures, under such rules and regulations as may be prescribed by law, and after conviction, to grant reprieves, commutation of sentence and pardons (except in cases of treason and impeachment); but pardons, in cases of murder, arson, burglary, rape, assault with intent to commit rape, perjury, forgery, bribery and larceny, shall not relieve from civil and political disability unless specifically expressed in the pardon.

The Governor shall have power to disapprove of any item or items of any bill making appropriations of money, embracing distinct items, and the part or parts of the bill approved shall be the law, and the item or items of appropriations disapproved shall be void, unless repassed accordding to the rules and limitations prescribed for the passage of other bills over the Executive veto; and he shall, in writing, state specifically the item or items he disapproves.

Every male citizen of the United States, and every male person of foreign birth, who may have legally declared his intention to become a citizen of the United States before he offers to vote, who is twenty-one years old or upwards, possessing the following qualifications, shall be an elector, and shall be entitled to vote at any election by the people, except as hereinafter provided:

First. He shall have resided in the State at least one year immediately preceding the election at which he offers to vote.

Second. He shall have resided in the county for three months, and in the precinct, or ward, for thirty days immediately preceding the election at which he offers to vote; provided, that the General Assembly may prescribe a longer or shorter residence in any precinct in any county, or in any ward in any incorporated city or town having a population of more than five thousand inhabitants, but in no case to exceed three months; and provided, that no soldier, sailor or marine in the military or naval service of the United States shall acquire a residence by being stationed in this State.

All elections by the people shall be by ballot, and all elections by persons in a representative capacity shall be *viva voce.*

The following classes shall not be permitted to register, vote or hold office:

First. Those who shall have been convicted of treason, embezzlement of public funds, malfeasance in office, larceny, bribery, or other crime punishable by imprisonment in the penitentiary.

Second. Those who are idiots or insane.

It shall be the duty of the General Assembly to pass adequate laws giving protection against the evils arising from the use of intoxicating liquors at all elections.

The Constitution creates Senatorial and Representative districts, to remain till the apportionment made after the census of 1880.

The personal property of any resident of this State to the value of one thousand dollars, to be selected by such resident, shall be exempted from sale on execution, or other process of any court, issued for the collection of any debt contracted since the thirteenth day of July, eighteen hundred and sixty-eight, or after the ratification of this Constitution.

Every homestead not exceeding eighty acres, and the dwelling and appurtenances thereon, to be selected by the owner thereof, and not in any city, town, or village, or in lieu thereof, at the option of the owner, any lot in the city, town, or village, with the dwelling and appurtenances thereon, owned and occupied by any resident of this State, and not exceeding the value of two thousand dollars, shall be exempted from sale on execution, or any other process from a court, for any debt contracted since the thirteenth day of July, eighteen hundred and sixty-eight, or after the ratification of this Constitution. Such exemption, however, shall not extend to any mortgage lawfully obtained, but such mortgage or other alienation of such homestead, by the owner thereof, if a married man, shall not be valid without the voluntary signature and assent of the wife to the same. But this shall not be so construed as to prevent a laborer's lien for work done and performed for the person claiming such exemption, or a mechanic's lien for work done on the premises.

All taxes levied on property in this State shall be assessed in exact proportion to the value of such property: *Provided, however,* The General Assembly may levy a poll tax, not to exceed one dollar and fifty cents on each poll; which shall be applied exclusively in aid of the public school fund, in the county so paying the same.

No power to levy taxes shall be delegated to individuals or private corporations.

The General Assembly shall not have the power to levy, in any one year, a greater rate of taxation than three-fourths of one per centum on the value of the taxable property within this State.

No county in this State shall be authorized to levy a larger rate of taxation, in any one year, on the value of the taxable property therein, than one-half of one per centum.

The property of private corporations, associations and individuals of this State, shall forever be taxed at the same rate; Provided, This section shall not apply to institutions or enterprises devoted exclusively to religious, educational or charitable purposes.

The General Assembly shall establish, organize, and maintain a system of public schools throughout the State, for the equal benefit of the children thereof, between the ages of seven and twenty-one years; but separate schools shall be provided for the children of citizens of African descent.

The General Assembly shall also provide for the levying and collection of an annual poll tax, not to exceed one dollar and fifty cents on each poll, which shall be applied to the support of the public schools in the counties in which it is levied and collected.

No money raised for the support of the public schools of the State shall be appropriated to or used for the support of any sectarian or denominational school.

No corporation shall issue stock or bonds, except for money, labor done, or money or property actually received; and all fictitious increase of stock or indebtedness shall be void. The stock and bonded indebtedness of corporations shall not be increased, except in pursuance of general laws, nor without the consent of the persons holding the larger amount in value of stock, first obtained at a meeting to be held after thirty days' notice given in pursuance of law.

The General Assembly shall not have the power to establish or incoporate any bank or banking company, or moneyed institution, for the purpose of issuing bills of credit, or bills payable to order or bearer, except under the conditions prescribed in this Constitution.

No banks shall be established otherwise than under a general banking law, nor otherwise than upon a specie basis.

All bills, or notes issued as money, shall be, at all times, redeemable in gold or silver, and no law shall be passed sanctioning, directly or indirectly, the suspension, by any bank or banking company, of specie payment.

Holders of bank notes, and depositors who have not stipulated for interest, shall, for such notes and deposits, be entitled, in case of insolvency, to the preference of payment over all other creditors.

Every bank or banking company shall be required to cease all banking operations within twenty years from the time of its organization, (unless the General Assembly shall extend the time), and promptly thereafter close its business; but shall have corporate capacity to sue, and shall be liable to suit, until its affairs and liabilities are fully closed.

No bank shall receive, directly or indirectly, a greater rate of interest than shall be allowed by law to individuals for lending money.

The State shall not be a stockholder in any bank, nor shall the credit of the State ever be given, or loaned, to any banking company, association, or corporation.

All railroads and canals shall be public highways, and all railroad and canal companies shall be common carriers. Any association or corporation organized for the purpose shall have the right to construct and operate a railroad between any points in this State, and to connect, at the State line, with railroads of other States. Every railroad company shall have the right with its road to intersect, connect with, or cross any other railroad, and shall receive and transport, each, the others' freight, passengers, and cars, loaded or empty, without delay or discrimination.

The General Assembly shall pass laws to correct abuses and prevent unjust discrimination and extortion in the rates of freights and passenger tariffs on railroads, canals and rivers in this State.

No railroad or other transportation company shall grant free passes, or sell tickets or passes at a discount, other than as sold to the public generally, to any member of the General Assembly, or to any person holding office under this State or the United States.

No person holding an office of profit under the United States, except Postmasters whose annual salary does not exceed two hundred dollars, shall, during his continuance in such office, hold any office of profit under this State; nor shall any person hold two offices of profit at one and at the same time under this State, except justices of the peace, constables, notaries public and commissioners of deeds.

No Convention shall hereafter be held for the purpose of altering or amending the Constitution of this State, unless the question of Convention or no Convention shall be first submitted to a vote of all the electors of the State, and approved by a majority of those voting at said election.

Arkansas.

A few of the important provisions only, of the new Constitution, are given:

Every male citizen of the United States, or male person who has declared his intention of becoming a citizen of the same, of the age of twenty-one years, who has resided in the State twelve months, in the county six months, in the voting precinct or ward one month, next preceding the election, shall be entitled to vote. No law shall be enacted whereby the right to vote at any election shall be made to depend upon any previous registration of the elector's name.

All elections by the people shall be by ballot. Every ballot shall be numbered in the order in which it shall be received, and the number recorded by the election officers on the list of voters, opposite the name of the elector who presents the ballot. The election officers shall be sworn or affirmed not to disclose how any elector shall have voted, unless required to do so as witnesses in a judicial proceeding, or proceeding to contest an election.

The Supreme Court shall be composed of three judges; one of whom shall be chief justice, elected as such; two of whom shall constitute a quorum. The term of office shall be eight years.

The State shall ever maintain a general, suitable and efficient system of free schools, whereby all persons in the State, between the ages of six and twenty-one years, may receive gratuitous instruction.

No money belonging to the public school fund, or to the State, for the benefit of schools or universities, shall ever be used for any other than for the respective purposes to which it belongs.

The General Assembly shall provide, by general laws, for the support of common schools by taxes, which shall never exceed in any one year two mills on the dollar in the taxable property of the State; and by an annual per capita tax of one dollar, to be assessed on every male inhabitant of the State over the age of twenty-one years; *Provided*, The General Assembly may, by general law, authorize school-districts to levy, by a vote of the qualified electors of such districts, a tax not to exceed five mills on the dollar in any one year for school purposes; *Provided further*, That no such tax shall be appropriated to any other purpose, nor to any other district than that for which it was levied.

The supervision of public schools, and the execution of the laws regulating the same, shall be vested in and confided to such officers as may be provided for by the General Assembly.

All property subject to taxation shall be taxed according to its value. The General Assembly shall not have power to levy State taxes for any one year to exceed, in the aggregate, one per cent. of the assessed valuation of the property for that year.

Senators and representatives, and all judicial and executive, State and county officers, and all other officers, both civil and military, before entering on the duties of their respective offices, shall take and subscribe to the following oath or affirmation: "I do solemnly swear (or affirm) that I will support the Constitution of the United States, and the Constitution of the State of Arkansas, and that I will faithfully discharge the office upon which I am now about to enter."

California.

The proposed Amendments to the Constitution, proposed by the Legislature of 1873–4, and printed in McPherson's Hand-Book of Politics for 1874, pp. 58–60, were agreed to only in part by the Legislature of the twenty first session (1875–6), and were not submitted to the people for their approval.

Instead, at the election of 1875, the vote was taken on the question of calling a Constitutional Convention; which was disagreed to—"For" a Convention, 34,374; "Against," 25,552—total vote for Governor at same election, 122,939.

At same time, a proposed amendment providing that the laws shall be published in such a manner as the Legislature shall direct, as a substitute for the 21st section of Article eleven of the State Constitution, requiring publication in Spanish—was also lost.

An act was passed April 3, 1876, recommending to the electors of the State, at the first general election for members of the Legislature after the passage of this act, to vote for or against calling a Convention to revise and change the Constitution of the State.

Connecticut.

A vote of the people was taken, October 4, 1875, on two Constitutional Amendments, which were adopted, as follows:

THE FIRST.

SECTION 1. A general election for Governor, Lieutenant Governor, Secretary of State, Treasurer, Comptroller and Members of the General Assembly, shall be held on the Tuesday after the first Monday of November, 1876, and annually thereafter for such officers as are herein, and may be hereafter prescribed.

SEC. 2. The State officers above named, and the senators from those districts having even numbers, elected on the Tuesday after the first Monday of November, 1876, and those elected biennially thereafter on the Tuesday after the first Monday of November, shall respectively hold their offices for two years from and after the Wednesday following the first Monday of the next succeeding January. The senators from those districts having odd numbers, elected on the Tuesday after the first Monday of November, 1876, shall hold their offices for one year from and after the Wednesday following the first Monday of January, 1877; the electors residing in the senatorial districts having odd numbers shall, on the Tuesday after the first Monday of November, 1877, and biennially thereafter, elect senators who shall hold their offices for two years from and after the Wednesday following the first Monday of the next succeeding January. The representatives elected from the several towns on the Tuesday after the first Monday of November, 1876, and those elected annually thereafter, shall hold their offices for one year from and after Wednesday following the first Monday of the next succeeding January.

SEC. 3. There shall be a stated session of the General Assembly in Hartford, on the Wednesday after the first Monday of January, 1877, and annually thereafter on the Wednesday after the first Monday of January.

SEC. 4. The persons who shall be severally elected to the State Offices and General Assembly on the first Monday of April, 1876, shall hold such offices only until the Wednesday after the first Monday of January, 1877.

SEC. 5. The General Assembly elected in April, 1876, shall have power to pass such laws as may be necessary to carry into effect the provisions of this amendment.

THE SECOND.

The General Assembly shall have power, by a vote of two-thirds of the members of both branches, to restore the privileges of an elector to those who may have forfeited the same by a conviction of crime.

The vote on the first was: "For," 41,264; "Against," 2,525. On the second: "For," 31,-619; "Against," 11,363.

Four other amendments were before the Legislature of 1775, having been continued over by a majority vote from the previous year:

That no county, city, town, or other municipality shall ever become a subscriber to the capital stock of, or loan its credit in aid of, any railroad or private corporation.

Judges of Common Pleas and Probate, and all other Judges of inferior courts, shall be appointed in the manner now provided, for such terms, not exceeding six years, as the General Assembly may determine by law.

From and after the expiration of the term of Senators elected in April, 1876, the Senate shall consist of not less than forty-one nor more than forty-nine members. The General Assembly of 1876 shall divide the State into Senatorial districts, and in forming them neither the whole or part of one county shall be joined to the whole or part of another county to form a district, regard to be had to population in such apportionment, and no town shall be divided, unless for the purpose of forming more than one district within such town. The districts, when established, shall continue the same until the session of the General Assembly next after the completion of the next census of the United States, when the districts may be changed, but not again till after the next census.

After the first Wednesday in May, 1877, the Senate shall be composed of members chosen annually. The General Assembly of May, 1876, shall divide the State into Senatorial Districts, not less than thirty-five nor more than forty-five. [The manner of forming districts is the same as provided in the preceding proposed amendment. See Miscellaneous Chapter.]

The following items from the newspapers give the result on the above:

HARTFORD, *June* 9, 1875.—The House to-day defeated the proposed constitutional amendment extending the term of the Judges of the Probate and of the Superior Courts to not exceeding six years. The chief objection was to the Judges of the Probate Court, the present term of one year giving a chance for rotation.

June 23—The Senate to-day passed a constitutional amendment, forbidding the bonding of towns in aid of railroads or other private corporations. The vote stood—Yeas, 15; Nays, 6. The amendment was defeated in the House. In the House, a constitutional amendment redistricting the State and making the number of Senators not less than 41 nor more than 49 was defeated —yeas, 105; nays, 121.

The present number of Senators is 21, whose term has been for one year; of Representatives 246, also for one year.

Florida.

The Constitutional Amendments adopted by the Legislature of 1874—an abstract of which can be found in McPherson's Hand Book of Politics for 1874, pp. 62, 63—were ratified by the succeeding Legislature, and adopted by the people, and are now a part of the organic law of that State.

Georgia.

A bill passed the House of Representatives at the late session—yeas 117, nays 27—to provide for calling a Constitutional Convention, to consist of 194 delegates, to be elected in January, 1877, but it failed to become a law.

Kentucky.

In November, 1874, a call for a Constitutional Convention was defeated, a majority of all the qualified voters being necessary to a call. The affirmative votes were 85,466 out of 288,316.

Louisiana.

In November, 1874, the following Constitutional Amendments were ratified by the people: For first amendment, 69,419; against, 60,070; for second, 70,824; against, 59,634; for third, 70,499; against, 59,995; for fourth, 69,750; against, 59,640; for fifth, 67,234; against, 59,-528.

No. 1. The issue of consolidated bonds authorized by the General Assembly of the State, at its regular session in the year 1874, is hereby declared to create a valid contract between the State and each and every holder of said bonds, which the State shall by no means and in no wise impair. The said bonds shall be a valid obligation of the State in favor of any holder thereof, and no court shall enjoin the payment of the principal thereof, or the levy and collection and payment; the judicial power shall be exercised when necessary. The tax required for the payment of the principal and interest of said bonds shall be assessed and collected each and every year until the bonds shall be paid, principal and interest, and the proceeds shall be paid by the Treasurer of State to holders of said bonds as the principal and interest of the same shall fall due, and no further legislation or appropriation shall be requisite for the said assessment and for such payment from the treasury.

No. 2. Whenever the debt of the State shall have been reduced below twenty-five million dollars, the constitutional limit shall remain at the lowest point reached, beyond which the public debt shall not thereafter be increased, and this rule shall continue in operation until the debt is reduced to $15,000,000, beyond which it shall not be increased. Nor shall taxation for all State purposes, excepting the support of public schools, ever exceed twelve and a half mills on the dollar of the assessed valuation of the real and personal property in the State, except in case of war or invasion.

No. 3. The revenue of each year derived from taxation upon real, personal and mixed property, or from licenses, shall be devoted solely to the expenses of the said year for which it shall be raised, excepting any surplus remain, which shall be directed to sinking the public debt. All appropriations and claims in excess of revenue shall be null and void, and the State shall in no manner provide for their payment.

No. 4. Article —. The city of New Orleans shall not hereafter increase her debt, in any manner or form, or under any pretext. After the first day of January, 1875, no evidence of indebtedness or warrant for payment of money shall be issued by any officer of said city, except against cash actually in the treasury; but this shall not be so construed as to prevent a renewal of matured bonds at par, or the issue of new bonds in exchange for other bonds; provided the city debt be not thereby increased, nor to prevent the issue of drainage warrants to the transferee of contract, under act No. 30 of 1871, payable only from drainage taxes, and not otherwise; any person violating the prohibitions of this article shall, on conviction, be punished by imprisonment for not less than two nor more than ten years, and by fine of not less than three dollars nor more than ten thousand dollars.

No. 5 changes the day for holding the general election from "the first Monday" to the "first Tuesday after the first Monday."

Maine.

At the election in September, 1876, several Amendments to the Constitution of the State were ratified by the people. The principal are these:

In case the full number of Senators to be elected from each district shall not have received a plurality of votes, "the members of the House of Representatives and such Senators as shall have been elected, shall, from the highest numbers of the persons voted for on said lists, equal to twice the number of Senators deficient, in every district, if there be so many voted for, elect by joint ballot the number of Senators required."

The Legislature shall, from time to time, provide, as far as practicable, by general laws, for all matters appertaining to special or private legislation.

Corporations shall be formed under general laws, and shall not be created by special acts of the Legislature, except for municipal purposes and in cases where the object of the corporation cannot otherwise be attained; and, however formed, they shall forever be subject to the general laws of the State.

The Legislature shall, by a two-thirds concurrent vote of both branches, have the power to call Constitutional Conventions for the purpose of amending this Constitution.

The Governor shall nominate, and with the advice and consent of the Council, appoint all other civil and military officers, whose appointment is not, by this Constitution, or shall not by law be otherwise provided for; and every such nomination shall be made seven days, at least, prior to such appointment.

Judges of municipal and police courts shall be appointed by the executive power in the same manner as other judicial officers, and shall hold their offices for the term of four years; *Provided, however*, that the present incumbents shall hold their offices for the term for which they were elected.

All taxes upon real and personal estate assessed by the authority of this State, shall be apportioned and assessed equally, according to the just value thereof.

The Legislature shall never, in any manner, suspend or surrender the power of taxation.

The Legislature may enact laws excluding from the right of suffrage, for a term not exceeding ten years, all persons convicted of bribery at any election, or of voting at any election under the influence of a bribe.

Maryland.

The following amendment to section eight of article four, was submitted to the people November 2, 1875, and adopted by a vote of 53,355 "for" to 21,474 "against" it:

SEC. 8. The parties to any cause may submit the same to the Court for determination without the aid of a jury, and in all suits or actions at law, issues from the Orphans' Court, or from any Court sitting in equity, and in all cases of presentments or indictments for offences, which are or may be punishable by death, pending in any of the Courts of law in this State, having jurisdiction thereof, upon suggestion in writing under oath of either of the parties to said proceedings, that such party cannot have a fair and impartial trial in the Court in which the same may be pending, the said Court shall order and direct the record of proceedings in such suit or action, issue, presentment or indictment, to be transmitted to some other Court having jurisdiction in such case for trial; but in all other cases of presentment or indictment pending in any of the Courts of law in this State, having jurisdiction thereof, in addition to the suggestion in writing of either of the parties to such presentment or indictment, that such party cannot have a fair and impartial trial in the Court in which the same may be pending, it shall be necessary for the party making such suggestion to make it satisfactorily appear to the Court that such suggestion is true, or that there is reasonable ground for the same; and thereupon the said Court shall order and direct the record of proceedings in such presentment or indictment to be transmitted to some other Court, having jurisdiction in such cases, for trial; and such right of removal shall exist upon suggestion in cases when all the judges of said court may be disqualified under the provisions of this Constitution to sit in any such case; and said Court to which the record of proceedings in such suit or action, issue, presentment or indictment may be so transmitted, shall hear and determine the same in like manner as if such suit or action, issue, presentment or indictment had been originally instituted therein; and the General Assembly shall make such modification of existing law as may be necessary to regulate and give force to this provision.

Massachusetts.

IN SENATE.

1876, March 8—The Committee on Woman's Suffrage reported the following

RESOLVE

Providing for an Amendment of the Constitution to secure the Elective Franchise and the Right to hold Office to Women.

Resolved, By both houses, the same being agreed to by a majority of the senators and two-thirds of the members of the house of representatives present and voting thereon, that it is expedient to alter the constitution of this Commonwealth by adopting the subjoined article of amendment, and that the same, as thus agreed to, be entered on the journals of both houses, with the yeas and nays taken thereon, and referred to the general court next to be chosen, and that the same be published, to the end that if agreed to by the general court next to be chosen in the manner provided by the constitution, it may be submitted to the people for their approval and ratification, in order that that it may become a part of the constitution of the Commonwealth.

ARTICLE OF AMENDMENT.

Every female citizen of twenty-one years of age and upwards (excepting paupers and persons under guardianship), who has the educational qualification required by the twentieth article of the amendments to the constitution, who shall have resided within the Commonwealth one year, and within the city, town or district in which she may claim a right to vote, six calendar months next preceding any election of governor, lieutenant-governor, senators, or representatives, or other officers, and who shall have paid by herself, or her parent, master or guardian, any state or county tax, which shall within two years next preceding such election, have been assessed upon her in any city, town or district of this Commonwealth, shall have a right to vote in any such election, and shall be eligible to all offices, upon the same terms, conditions and qualifications, and subject to the same restrictions as male citizens.

This Resolve passed the Senate, March 16—yeas 22, nays 15; and was defeated in the House of Representatives, March 28, by a vote of 77 yeas to 127 nays, two-thirds not voting for it.

Michigan.

The proposed amendments to the Constitution of the State—an abstract of which was given in McPherson's Handbook of Politics for 1874, pp. 63–66—were submitted to popular vote in November, 1874, and were rejected—the vote being "For the amendments," 39,285; "against," 124,034. The section securing "Woman Suffrage," which was separately submitted, was also rejected: "for," 40,077; "against," 135,957.

Minnesota.

At the election in 1875, four proposed amendments to the Constitution of the State were voted upon.

The first amendment, changing Section 4 of Article VI, provides for the formation of judicial districts composed of contiguous territory, and the election of judges for a term of seven years, and also provides that every District Judge shall reside within the district at the time of his election and during his continuance in office.

The second amendment says the Legislature may provide by law that any woman, 21 years of age and upward, may vote at any election for school officers, or upon any measure relating to schools, and may also be eligible to hold any office pertaining solely to the management of schools.

The third amendment directs the Legislature to provide for the safe investment of the principal and interest of all funds arising from the sale of certain lands in United States bonds, or the bonds of Minnesota or other States, issued after the year 1860.

The fourth proposition so amends Section 3 of Article X. as to make stockholders in any corporation (except those for carrying on a manufacturing or mechanical business) liable only for all unpaid installments on stock owned by them or transferred for the purpose of defrauding creditors.

These amendments were adopted.

Under the new law allowing women to vote for school officers, about two hundred and fifty of them recently went to the polls at an election in Minneapolis.

Missouri.

A new Constitution was devised by a Constitutional Convention, which was called by a small majority in a popular vote of over 220,000, in November, 1874. It was submitted to a vote of the people October 30, 1875, and was adopted by the following vote: "For," 90,600; "Against," 14,362.

The instrument is very elaborate in its provisions. The chief points of interest will appear in the annexed abstract.

There are several changes in the "Bill of Rights." The old Constitution contained this clause, which is omitted from the new:

1. That all men are endowed with the inalienable right to life, liberty, the fruits of their own labor, and the pursuit of happiness.

The clause in the old, which provides, at length, against any civil disqualification, except for crime, of any person on account of color, and that such person is not to be debarred from the jury box, the courts, the schools, or otherwise unduly hindered in any way, is also omitted from the new.

Section 5 of the old Constitution reads:

That the people of this State have the inherent, sole and exclusive right to regulate the internal government and police thereof, and of altering and abolishing their Constitution and form of government whenever it may be necessary to their safety and happiness, but every such right shall be exercised in pursuance of law, and consistently with the Constitution of the United States.

Section 2 of the new is substituted for it, as follows:

That the people of this State have the inherent, sole and exclusive right to regulate the internal government and police thereof, and to alter and abolish their Constitution and form of government whenever they may deem it necessary to their safety and happiness: *Provided,* such change be not repugnant to the Constitution of the United States.

Sections 6 and 7 of the old Constitution are:

That this State shall ever remain a member of the American Union; that the people thereof are part of the American Nation; and that all attempts, from whatever source, or upon whatever pretext, to dissolve said Union, or to sever said Nation, ought to be resisted with the whole power of the State.

That every citizen of this State owes paramount allegiance to the Constitution and Government of the United States, and that no law or ordinance of this State, in contravention or subversion thereof, can have any binding force.

Sections 3 and 4 of the new are substituted for them:

That Missouri is a free and independent State, snbject only to the Constitution of the United States; and as the preservation of the States and the maintenance of their Governments are necessary to an indestructible Union, and were intended to co-exist with it, the Legislature is not authorized to adopt, nor will the people of this State ever assent to, any amendment or change of the Constitution of the United States which may in any wise impair the right of local self-government belonging to the people of this State.

That all constitutional government is intended to promote the general welfare of the people; that all persons have a natural right to life, liberty and the enjoyment of the gains of their own industry; that to give security to these things is the principal office of government, and that, when government does not confer this security, it fails of its chief design.

Other sections of the new Bill of Rights are as follows:

That no money shall ever be taken from the public Treasury, directly or indirectly, in aid of any church, sect or denomination of religion, or in aid of any priest, preacher, minister or teacher thereof, as such; and that no preference shall be given to, nor any discrimination made against, any church, sect or creed of religion, or any form of religious faith or worship.

That no religious corporation can be established in this State, except such as may be created under a general law for the purpose only of holding the title to such real estate as may be prescribed by law for church edifices, parsonages and cemeteries.

That the right of no citizen to keep and bear arms in defense of his house, person and property, or in aid of the civil power, when thereto legally summoned, shall be called in question; but nothing herein contained is intended to justify the practice of wearing concealed weapons.

That no person elected or appointed to any office or employment of trust or profit under the laws of this State, or any ordinance of any municipality in this State, shall hold such office without personally devoting his time to the performance of the duties to the same belonging.

That no person who is now, or may hereafter become, a Collector or Receiver of public money, or assistant or deputy of such Collector or Receiver, shall be eligible to any office of trust or profit in the State of Missouri under the laws thereof, or of any municipality therein, until he shall have accounted for and paid over all the public money for which he may be accountable.

That no private property can be taken for public use with or without compensation, unless by the consent of the owner, except for private ways of necessity, and except for drains and ditches across the lands of others for agricultural and sanitary purposes, in such manner as may be prescribed by law; and that whenever an attempt is made to take private property for a use alleged to be public, the question whether the contemplated use be really public shall be a judicial question, and, as such, judicially determined, without regard to any legislative assertion that the use is public.

That private property shall not be taken or damaged for public use without just compensation. Such compensation shall be ascertained by a jury or Board of Commissioners of not less than three freeholders, in such manner as may be prescribed by law; and until the same shall be paid to the owner, or into the court for the owner, the property shall not be disturbed or the proprietary rights of the owner therein divested. The fee of land taken for railroad tracks without consent of the owner thereof, shall remain in such owner, subject to the use for which it is taken.

That the privilege of the writ of habeas corpus shall never be suspended.

The right of trial by jury, as heretofore enjoyed, shall remain inviolate; but a jury for the trial of criminal or civil cases, in courts not of record, may consist of less than twelve men, as may be prescribed by law. Hereafter a grand jury shall consist of twelve men, any nine of whom concurring may find an indictment or a true bill.

That there cannot be in this State either slavery or involuntary servitude, except as a punishment for crime, whereof the party shall have been duly convicted.

The House of Representatives is to be chosen every second year, to consist of two hundred—the Senate of thirty-four members, to be chosen for four years. The Senators are to be chosen in districts to be made by the Legislature.

The ratio of representation for the House of Representatives shall be ascertained at each apportioning session of the General Assembly, by dividing the whole number of inhabitants of the State by the number two hundred. Each county having one ratio or less, shall be entitled to one Representative; each county having two and a-half times said ratio, shall be entitled to two Representatives; each county having four times said ratio, shall be entitled to three Representatives; each county having six times said ratio, shall be entitled to four Representatives; and so on above that number, giving one additional member for every two and a-half additional ratios.

When any county shall be entitled to more than one Representative, the County Court shall cause such county to be subdivided into districts of compact and contiguous territory, corresponding in number to the Representatives to which such county is entitled, and in population as nearly equal as may be, in each of which the qualified voters shall elect one Representative, who shall be a resident of such district: *Provided*, That when any county shall be entitled to more than ten Representatives, the Circuit Court shall cause such county to be subdivided into districts, so as to give each district not less than two nor more than four Representatives, who shall be residents of such district; the population of the districts to be proportioned to the number of Representatives to be elected therefrom.

The General Assembly is forbidden to hold adjourned sessions. When the session is prolonged beyond seventy days, the members shall receive after that time but $1 per day, the pay before that time being $5 per day, mileage allowed as at present. Each member will be allowed $30, from which to furnish himself with stationery. No member is to be allowed mileage for any extra session called in less than a day after the adjournment of a regular session.

A large number of conditions and a very minute particularity are required in the passage of a bill. All local and special legislation is prohibited. No local law shall be passed unless notice to apply for the same be given at least thirty days before, and in the locality to be effected by it.

The word "white" is stricken out of the limitation on the Governorship. A majority of two-thirds of all the members of each house is required to pass a bill over the Governor's veto. When a bill containing several items of appropriation is presented to the Governor, he may at pleasure veto any one or several items, giving his objections therefor, and allowing the remainder of the bill to pass; thus giving him the liberty of discriminating between the proper and improper items, passing the one and rejecting the other.

The Supreme Court is made to consist of five Judges, instead of three, and their term of service is made ten years in place of six.

Every association, except those for benevolent, religious or educational purposes, is required, on filing articles of incorporation, to deposit with the State Treasurer $50 on capital stock of $50,000 or less, and $5 on every additional $10,000 capital stock. No special law creating a corporation can be passed. It is made a criminal offense for bankers or corporations to receive deposits of money when they know they are in failing circumstances, and by law they may be held personally responsible for such misdemeanors, when it has been proven that they have been committed with their assent. Railroads are declared public highways, the companies common carriers, and the General Assembly is given power to legislate for the regulation of their tariffs, fixing the maximum, and guarding against discrimination in freight or passenger rates. Every railroad company shall keep books for public inspection, which shall display the amount of stock subscribed, the names of the owners, amounts paid, and other particulars of stock transactions which are of general interest. The rolling stock is declared personal property, liable to execution and sale as other personal effects, and no railroad or street railroad is allowed to traverse any street or public highway without the consent of the local authorities.

Provision is made for the maintenance of public schools and free education for all persons between the ages of six and twenty years; separate schools for colored children are to be provided and maintained; State and county funds for school purposes are to be established, and where the local funds are insufficient an appropriation, not greater than twenty-five per cent. of the State revenue, exclusive of the interest and sinking fund, is to be applied annually to the support of the public schools. The school tax is limited to forty cents on every $100, except in a city, where $1 is allowed; and in the county sixty-five cents on the $100 may be levied by a majority of those voters who are also tax-payers.

All public money is to be placed to the credit of the State at some banking-house of good standing, which shall be approved by the Governor and Attorney-General; demanding, also, that the banker give sufficient security, and pay a reasonable interest for the use of the State funds.

The Legislature shall not surrender nor suspend the power to tax corporations nor corporate property, and all taxes will be levied and collected by general laws. In place of the former provision requiring one-fourth of one per cent. to be set apart for interest and sinking fund, the General Assembly shall levy a tax only sufficient to pay interest, and raise $250,000 annually for sinking fund.

The State tax on property, except where necessary to pay interest on bonded debt, is limited to twenty cents on the $100 valuation; and whenever the taxable property of the State shall amount to $900,000,000, the rate shall not exceed fifteen cents. Taxation in cities and towns is to be levied by population rates. For county purposes, in counties having $6,000,000 or less, 50 cents on the $100; over $6,000,000 and less than $10,000,000, 40 cents on the $100; in counties having $30,000,000 or more, 35 cents on the $100. In cities having a population of thirty thousand or more, the rate shall not exceed $1 on the $100 valuation; a population less than thirty thousand and over ten thousand, not over 60 cents on the $100; with less than ten thousand and over one thousand, not over 50 cents on the $100; with less than one thousand population, not more than 25 cents on the $100 valuation. For erecting public buildings, these limits may be exceeded by a two-thirds vote of all the tax-payers.

No county, city, town, township, or school district, shall be allowed to become indebted to an amount exceeding the income and revenue provided for any one year, without a two-thirds vote of all the qualified voters; and even then, not to an amount exceeding 5 per cent. of the taxable property therein, except that such per cent. may be exceeded for building court houses and jails.

The power of the Legislature to form new counties is restricted, and charters of cities and towns must be amended only in accordance with general laws.

The city of St. Louis will be allowed to extend its limits so as to include the parks and other convenient and contiguous territory, and frame its own charter, which may be amended at intervals of two years; provided, always, that the amendments are in accordance with the Constitution and laws of the State. There shall be two houses of legislation for the city, instead of one, as at present.

Among the prohibitions of legislative power are these:

No debt to be created except to pay off existing bonds; or to provide for an unforeseen emergency or deficiency, not exceeding $250,000, to be paid in not more than two years; or where the emergency, or deficiency, involves a liability of over $250,000, the Assembly shall submit an act providing for the loan, and containing a tax to pay interest and principal in not more than thirteen years; and on the act being submitted to the qualified voters and ratified by two-thirds majority, the act shall be irrepealable till the liability be extinguished.

The General Assembly shall have no power to give or to lend, or to authorize the giving or lending of the credit of the State in aid of or to any person, association or corporation, whether municipal or other, or to pledge the credit of the State in any manner whatsoever, for the payment of the liabilities, present or prospective, of any individual, association of individuals, municipal or other corporation whatsoever.

The General Assembly shall have no power to make any grant, or to authorize the making of any grant, of public money or thing of value to any individual, association of individuals, municipal or other corporation whatsoever: *Provided*, That this shall not be so construed as to prevent the grant of aid in a case of public calamity.

The General Assembly shall have no power to authorize any county, city, town or township, or other political corporation or subdivision of the State now existing, or that may be hereafter established, to lend its credit, or to grant public money or thing of value, in aid of or to any individual, association or corporation whatsoever, or to become a stockholder in such corporation, association or company.

The General Assembly shall have no power to grant, or to authorize any county or municipal authority to grant, any extra compensation, fee or allowance to a public officer, agent, servant or contractor, after service has been rendered or a contract has been entered into and performed in whole or in part, nor pay nor authorize the payment of any claim hereafter created against the State, or any county or municipality of the State, under any agreement or contract made without express authority of law; and all such unauthorized agreements or contracts shall be null and void.

The General Assembly shall have no power hereafter to subscribe or authorize the subscription of stock on behalf of the State in any corporation or association, except for the purpose of securing loans heretofore extended to certain railroad corporations by the State.

The General Assemby shall have no power to release or alienate the lien held by the State upon any railroad, or in any wise change the tenor or meaning, or pass any act explanatory thereof; but the same shall be enforced in accordance with the original terms upon which it was acquired.

The General Assembly shall have no power to release or extinguish, or authorize the releasing or extinguishing, in whole or in part, the indebtedness, liability or obligation of any corporation or individual to this State, or to any county or other municipal corporation therein.

The General Assembly shall have no power to make any appropriation of money, or to issue any bonds or other evidences of indebtedness, for the payment, or on account, or in recognition of any claims audited, or that may hereafter be audited, by virtue of an act entitled "An act to audit and adjust the war debt of the State," approved March 19, 1874, or any act of a similar nature, until after the claims so audited shall have been presented to and paid by the Government of the United States to the State of Missouri.

Neither the General Assembly, nor any county, city, town, township, school district, or other municipal corporation, shall ever make an appropriation, or pay from any public fund whatever, anything in aid of any religious creed, Church, or sectarian purpose; or to help to support or sustain any private or public school, academy, seminary, college, university, or other institution of learning, controlled by any religious creed, Church, or sectarian denomination whatever; nor shall any grant or donation of personal property or real estate ever be made by the State, or any county, city, town or other municipal corporation, for any religious creed, church or sectarian purpose whatever.

The property, real and personal, of the State, counties and other municipal corporations, and cemeteries, shall be exempt from taxation. Lots in incorporated cities or towns, or within one mile of the limits of any such city or town, to the extent of one acre, and lots one mile or more distant from such cities or towns, to the extent of five acres, with the buildings thereon, may be exempted from taxation when the same are used exclusively for religious worship, for schools, or for purposes purely charitable; also such property, real or personal, as may be used exclusively for Agricultural or Horticultural Societies: *Provided*, That such exemptions shall be only by general law.

All laws exempting property from taxation, other than the property above enumerated, shall be void.

No person shall be prosecuted in any civil action or criminal proceeding for or on account of any act by him done, performed or executed between the first day of January, one thousand eight hundred and sixty-one, and the twentieth day of August, one thousand eight hundred and sixty-six, by virtue of military authority vested in him, or in pursuance of orders from any person vested with such authority by the Government of the United States, or of this State, or of the late Confederate States, or any of them, to do such act. And if any action or proceedings shall have been, or shall hereafter be instituted against any person for the doing of any such act, the defendant may plead this section in bar thereof.

Every male citizen of the United States, and every male person of foreign birth who may have declared his intention to become a citizen of the United States, not less than one year nor more than five years before he offers to vote, who is over 21 years of age, shall be a voter if he shall have resided in Missouri one year, and in the county, city, or town at least sixty days immediately preceding the election.

Nebraska.

In November, 1875, a new Constitution was adopted, of which the following abstract is taken from *The Republic* for September, 1875, p. 155:

It prohibits special legislation; abolishes all fee compensation for State officers; confers the right of suffrage upon all male citizens of the United States, and all foreign-born citizens who have taken out naturalization papers; prohibits sectarian instruction in schools supported in whole or part by the State, and prohibits the acceptance by the State of any grant, conveyance or bequest of money or property to be used for sectarian purposes; prohibits the diversion of State revenue for any local purpose; limits its county taxes to 1½ per cent.; prohibits subscriptions by municipalities to railroads, but allows donations of money when sanctioned by a majority vote; confers on the legislature large powers over railroad management; declares railroads to be public highways and authorizes the Legislature to establish maximum rates of freight and transportation; prohibits municipalities from incurring indebtedness for ordinary purposes exceeding 5 per cent. of the assessed value of property; provides that each Legislator and State officer shall subscribe to an oath not to take or accept a bribe, under penalty; makes drunkenness a cause for impeachment and removal from office.

There are two coupon or separate clauses—one prohibiting the removal of the State Capital, except by a majority vote of the people, the other providing for an expression of the people as to their preference for U. S. Senator, prior to the meeting of the Legislature, which shall elect such official.

The vote on the Constitution was "For," 30,202; "Against," 5,474.

New Jersey.

On Tuesday, September 7, 1875, a vote was taken on the subjoined amendments to the Constitution of that State:

First Amendment.

ARTICLE I.

RIGHTS AND PRIVILEGES.

Insert as paragraph 19, a new paragragh, as follows:

"19. No county, city, borough, town, township or village shall hereafter give any money or property, or loan its money or credit, to or in aid of any individual, association or corporation, or become security for, or be directly or indirectly the owner of, any stock or bonds of any association or corporation."

The vote was: For, 70,441; Against, 26,111.

Second Amendment.

Insert as paragraph 20, a new paragraph, as follows:

"20. No donation of land or appropriation of money shall be made by the State or any municipal corporation to or for the use of any society, association or corporation whatever."

Change the number of present paragraph 19 to number 21.

The vote was: For, 70,390; Against, 26,106.

Third Amendment.

ARTICLE II.

RIGHT OF SUFFRAGE.

Section I.

Strike out the word "white" between the word "every" and the word "male" in the first line.

Add to the paragraph the following:

"And provided further, that in time of war no elector in the actual military service of the State, or of the United States, in the army or navy thereof, shall be deprived of his vote by reason of his absence from such election district; and the Legislature shall have power to provide the manner in which, and the time and place at which, such absent electors may vote, and for the return and canvass of their votes in the election districts in which they respectively reside."

The vote was: For, 68,664; Against, 27,756.

Fourth Amendment.

Section II.

Strike out all of the second section after the word "bribery."

The vote was: For, 69,867; Against, 26,636.

Fifth Ameadment.

ARTICLE IV.

LEGISLATIVE.

Section I.

Paragraph 3—Strike out the words "second Tuesday of October," and insert in lieu thereof the words "first Tuesday after the first Monday in November."

The vote was: For, 70,686; Against, 25,846.

Sixth Amendment.

Section IV.

Paragraph 7—Strike out the following words: "A compensation for their services, to be ascertained by law, and paid out of the treasury of the State; which compensation shall not exceed the sum of three dollars per day for the period of forty days from the commencement of the session, and shall not exceed the sum of one dollar and fifty cents per day for the remainder of the sesson. When convened in extra session by the Governor they shall receive such sum as shall be fixed for the first forty days of the ordinary session. They shall also receive the sum of one dollar for every ten miles they shall travel in going to and returning from their place of meeting on the most usual route,"

And insert in lieu thereof the following:

"Annually the sum of five hundred dollars during the time for which they shall have been elected, and while they shall hold their office, and no other allowance or emolument, directly or indirectly, for any purpose whatever.

Also strike out the word "per diem."

The vote was: For, 69,093; Against, 27,438.

Seventh Amendment.

Section VII.

Paragraph 4—Add to the paragraph the following:

"No law shall be revived or amended by reference to its title only, but the act revived, or the section or sections amended, shall be inserted at length. No general law shall embrace any provision of a private, special or local character. No act shall be passed which shall provide that any existing law, or any part thereof, shall be made or deemed a part of the act, or which shall enact that any existing law, or any part thereof, shall be applicable, except by inserting it in such act."

The vote was: For, 70,358; Against, 26,178.

Eighth Amendment.

Paragraph 6—Insert the word "free" between the word "public" and the word "schools," and add to the paragraph the following:

"The Legislature shall provide for the maintenance and support of a thorough and efficient system of free public schools for the instruction of all the children in this State between the ages of five and eighteen years."

The vote was: For, 69,674; Against, 26,834.

Ninth Amendment.

Strike out paragraph 8, as follows:

"8. The assent of three-fifths of the members elected to each house shall be requisite to the passage of every law for granting, continuing, altering, amending or renewing charters for banks or money corporations; and all such charters shall be limited to a term not exceeding twenty years."

Change the number of present paragraph 9 to 8.

The vote was: For, 70,035; Against, 26,473.

Tenth Amendment.

Insert as paragraph 9, a new paragraph, as follows:

"9. No private, special, or local bill shall be passed, unless public notice of the intention to apply therefor, and of the general object thereof, shall have been previously given. The Legislature, at the next session after the adoption thereof, and from time to time thereafter, shall prescribe the time and mode of giving such notice, the evidence thereof, and how such evidence shall be preserved."

The vote was: For, 70,586; Against, 25,917.

Eleventh Amendment.

Insert as paragraph 11, a new paragraph, as follows:

"11. The Legislature shall not pass private, local or special laws in any of the following enumerated cases, that is to say:

"Laying out, opening, altering and working roads or highways.

"Vacating any road, town plot, street, alley or public grounds.

"Regulating the internal affairs of towns and counties; appointing local officers or commissions to regulate municipal affairs.

"Selecting, drawing, summoning or empaneling grand or petit jurors.

"Creating, increasing or decreasing the per centage or allowance of public officers during the term for which said officers were elected or appointed.

"Changing the law of descent.

"Granting to any corporation, association or individual any exclusive privilege, immunity or franchise whatever.

"Granting to any corporation, association or individual the right to lay down railroad tracks.

"Providing for changes of venue in civil or criminal cases.

"Providing for the management and support of free public schools.

"The Legislature shall pass general laws providing for the cases enumerated in this paragraph, and for all other cases which, in its judgment, may be provided for by general laws. The Legislature shall pass no special act conferring corporate powers, but they shall pass general laws under which corporations may be organized and corporate powers of every nature obtained, subject, nevertheless, to repeal or alteration at the will of the Legislature."

The vote was: For, 69,385; Against, 27,131.

Twelfth Amendment.

Insert as paragraph 12, a new paragraph, as follows:

"12. Property shall be assessed for taxes under general laws, and by uniform rules, according to its true value."

The vote was: For, 51,701; Against, 44,967.

Thirteenth Amendment.

Section VIII.

Insert as paragraph 2, a new paragraph, as follows:

"2. Every officer of the Legislature shall, before he enters upon his duties take and subscrbe the following oath or affirmation: 'I do solemnly promise and swear (or affirm) that I will faithfully, impartially and justly perform all the duties of the office of ———, to the best of my ability and understanding; that I will carefully preserve all records, papers, writings or property intrusted to me for safe keeping by virtue of my office, and make such disposition of the same as may be required by law.' "

The vote was: For, 70,554; Against, 25,955.

Fourteenth Amendment.

ARTICLE V.

EXECUTIVE.

Paragraph 6—After the word "legislature," where it occurs first in said paragraph, insert the words "or the senate alone."

The vote was For, 70,066; Against, 26,451.

Fifteenth Amendment.

Paragraph 7—Add to the paragraph the following:

"If any bill presented to the governor contain several items of appropriations of money, he may object to one or more of such items while approving of the other portions of the bill. In such case he shall append to the bill, at the time of signing it, a statement of the items to which he objects, and the appropriation so objected to shall not take effect. If the Legislature be in session he shall transmit to the house in which the bill originated a copy of such statement, and the items objected to shall be separately reconsidered. If, on reconsideration, one or more of such items be approved by a majority of the members elected to each house, the same shall be a part of the law, notwithstanding the objections of the governor. All the provisions of this section in relation to bills not approved by the governor shall apply to cases in which he shall withhold his approval from any item or items contained in a bill appropriating money."

The vote was: For, 70,949; Against, 25,623.

Sixteenth Amendment.

Paragraph 8—Add to the paragraph the following:

"Nor shall he be elected by the Legislature to any office under the government of this State or of the United States, during the term for which he shall have been elected Governor."

The vote was: For, 70,459; Against, 26,019.

Seventeenth Amendment.

ARTICLE VII.

APPOINTING POWER AND TENURE OF OFFICE.

Section I.

MILITIA OFFICERS.

Paragraph 5—After the words "major generals," insert the words "the adjutant general and quartermaster general."

The vote was: For, 70,026; Against, 26,476.

Eighteenth Amendment.

Paragraph 9—Strike out the words "the adjutant general, quartermaster general and."

Also strike out the word "other."

The vote was: For, 69,989; Against, 26,481.

Nineteenth Amendment.

Section II.

CIVIL OFFICERS.

Paragraph 1—Strike out the word "and" (where it occurs first) in the paragraph, and insert after the word "appeals" the following words: "and judges of the inferior court of common pleas."

The vote was: For, 68,700; Against, 27,806.

Twentieth Amendment.

Change the number of present paragraph 3 to number 2, and strike therefrom the following words: "and the keeper and inspectors of the State prison;" and insert in lieu thereof the words "and comptroller."

The vote was: For, 69,051; Against, 27,447.

Twenty-first Amendment.

Also, strike out the words "one year" in the second clause of paragraph 2 of section 2, and insert in lieu thereof the words "three years."

The vote was: For, 68,569; Against, 27,937.

Twenty-second Amendment.

Change the number of present paragraph 4 to number 3, and strike out the word "and" where it occurs between the word "chancery" and the word "secretary."

Also, insert after the word "State" the words: "and the keeper of the State prison."

The vote was: For, 69,245; Against, 27,249.

Twenty-third Amendment.

Change the number of present paragraph 5 to number 4.

The vote was: For, 69,444; Against, 27,053.

Twenty-fourth Amendment.

Change the number of present paragraph 6 to number 5.

The vote was: For, 68,896; Against, 27,630.

Twenty-fifth Amendment.

Change the number of present paragraph 7 to number 6, and strike therefrom the words "annually," "annual" and "they may be re-elected until they shall serve three years, but no longer." Insert after the word "assembly" the following words: "and they shall hold their offices for three years;" and add to the paragraph the following words: "sheriffs shall annually renew their bonds."

The vote was, For, 69,127; Against, 27,264.

The remaining Amendments, 26th, 27th, and 28th, as follows:

Change the number of present paragraph 8 to number 7.

Change the number of present paragraph 9 to number 8.

Change the number of present paragraph 10 to number 9.

Change the number of present paragraph 11 to number 10.

Were adopted by a like vote.

NOTE.—As the School article stood in the old Constitution of 1844, it provided (Art. IV. sec. 6), that designated moneys of the State "shall be annually appropriated to the support of the public schools for the equal benefit of all the people of the State." One of the amendments above, inserts the word "free" between "public" and "schools," so as to give the State moneys not only to the public schools, but to those which are free also. This is regarded as a blow at the project of giving part of the school moneys to parochial schools. The object of that amendment is further secured by a proposed amendment providing that "no donation of land, or appropriation of money shall be made by the State or any municipal corporation to or for the use of any society, association or corporation whatever,"—which is held to preclude State assistance being extended to any Church for the support of its schools; while still another amendment provides that no special law shall be passed "granting to any corporation, association, or individual, any exclusive privilege, immunity, or franchise whatever."

New York.

The proposed amendments to the Constitution of that State, given in McPherson's Hand-Book of Politics for 1874, pp. 69–72, were submitted to popular vote in November, 1874, with this result.

Amendment Art. II. For, 357,635; Against, 177,033.

Amendment Art. III., pt. 1.* For, 325,904; Against, 206,029.

Amendment Art. III., pt. 2. For, 435,313; Against, 98,050.

Amendment Art. IV. For, 336,197; Against, 196,125.

Amendment Art. VII. For, 428,200; Against, 104,129.

Amendment Art. VIII., pt. 1.† For, 337,891; Against, 194,236.

Amendment Art. VIII., pt. 2. For, 336,237; Against, 195,047.

Amendment Art. X., Sec. 9. For, 335,548; Against, 194,933.

Amendment Art. XII. For, 352,514; Against, 179,365.

Amendment Art. XV. For, 351,693; Against, 177,923.

Amendment Art. XVI. For, 446,883; Against, 85,758.

The following proposed amendment is pending:

Resolved, That Article IX. of the Constitution be amended by the addition of the following sections:

SEC. 2. Free common schools shall be maintained throughout the State forever. The Legislature shall provide for the instruction in the branches of elementary education in such schools of all persons in the State between the ages of 5 and 21 years, for the period of at least 28 weeks in each year.

SEC. 3. Neither the money, property, or credit of the State, nor of any county, city, town, village, or school district, shall be given, loaned, or leased, or be otherwise applied, to the support or in aid of any school or instruction under the control or in charge of any church, sect, denomination, or religious society; nor to, or in aid of any school in which instruction is given peculiar to any church, creed, sect, or denomination; nor to, or in aid of any such instruction; nor to or in aid of any school or instruction not wholly under the control and supervision and in charge of the public school authorities.

This section shall not prohibit the Legislature from making such provision for the education of the blind, the deaf and dumb, and juvenile delinquents, as it may deem proper, except in institutions in which instruction is given peculiar to any church, creed, sect, denomination, or religious society; nor shall it apply to or effect the Cornell University Endowment Fund, hitherto pledged and appropriated.

Resolved, That the foregoing amendment be referred to the Legislature to be chosen at the next general election of Senators, and that in conformity with Section 1 of Article XIII of the Constitution, it be published for three months previous to the time of such election.

It passed the House of Representatives, 119 to 2, and the Senate, and will be referred to the Legislature of 1878; and, if approved by that body, will be submitted to a direct vote of the people in the fall of that year.

North Carolina.

1875, August 5—A Constitutional Convention was chosen, which agreed upon the following Amendments, to be submitted to popular vote at the November election in 1876:

IN DECLARATION OF RIGHTS:

Section 24, insert the words:

Nothing herein contained shall justify the practice of carrying concealed weapons, or prevent the Legislature from enacting penal statutes against said practice.

Section 25, insert the words:

But secret political societies are dangerous to the liberties of a free people, and should not be tolerated.

LEGISLATIVE DEPARTMENT.

Sections 4 and 8 of Article 2 are stricken from the Constitution. The latter divided the State into Representative districts, the former into senatorial.

The Legislature shall meet biennially on the "first Wednesday after the first Monday in January next after their election."

Insert new sections:

SEC. 25. The terms of office for Senators and members of the House of Representatives shall commence at the time of their election.

SEC. 27. The election for members of the General Assembly shall be held for the respective districts and counties, at the places where they are now held, or may be directed hereafter to be held, in such manner as may be prescribed by law, on the first Thursday in August, in the year one thousand eight hundred and seventy, and every two years thereafter. But the General Assembly may change the time of holding the election.

SEC. 28. The members of the General Assembly for the term for which they have been elected, shall receive as a compensation for their services the sum of *four dollars* per day for each day of their session, for a period not exceeding sixty days; and should they remain longer in session, they shall serve without compensation. They shall also be entitled to receive ten cents per mile, both while coming to the seat of government and while returning home, the said distance to be computed by the nearest line or route of public travel. The compensation of the presiding officers of the two Houses shall be six dollars per day and mileage.

* Down to, and including section 8.
† First paragraph of Art. VIII.

EXECUTIVE DEPARTMENT.

Amend tenth section so as to read:

SEC. 10. The Governor shall nominate, and by and with the advice and consent of a majority of the Senators elect, appoint all officers, whose offices are established by this Constitution, and whose appointments are not otherwise provided for.

SEC. 17. The General Assembly shall establish a Department of Agriculture, Immigration and Statistics, under such regulations as may best promote the agricultural interests of the State, and shall enact laws for the adequate protection and encouragement of sheep husbandry.

JUDICIAL DEPARTMENT.

Amend section 2 so as to read as follows:

The judicial power of the State shall be vested in a Court for the trial of Impeachments, a Supreme Court, Superior Courts, Courts of Justices of the Peace, and such other Courts inferior to the Supreme Court as may be established by law.

Make these sections read as follow:

SEC. 6. The Supreme Court shall consist of a Chief Justice and two Associate Justices.

SEC. 7. The terms of the Supreme Court shall be held in the city of Raleigh, as now, until otherwise provided by the General Assembly.

Add to section on Supreme Court, these words:

And the jurisdiction of said Court over "issues of fact" and "questions of fact," shall be the same exercised by it before the adoption of the Constitution of one thousand eight hundred and sixty-eight, and the Court shall have the power to issue any remedial writs necessary to give it a general supervision and control over the proceedings of the inferior Courts.

Section 10 shall read:

The State shall be divided into nine judicial districts, for each of which a judge shall be chosen; and there shall be held a Superior Court in each county at least twice in each year, to continue for such time in each county as may be prescribed by law. But the General Assembly may reduce or increase the number of districts.

SEC. 12. That every Judge of the Superior Court shall reside in the district for which he is elected. The Judges shall preside in the Courts of the different districts successively, but no Judge shall hold the Courts in the same district oftener than once in four years; but in case of the protracted illness of the Judge assigned to preside in any district, or of any other unavoidable accident to him, by reason of which he shall become unable to preside, the Governor may require any Judge to hold one or more specified terms in said district, in lieu of the Judge assigned to hold the Courts of said district.

SEC. 13. The General Assembly shall have no power to deprive the Judicial Department of any power or jurisdiction which rightfully pertains to it, as a coördinate department of the government; but the General Assembly shall allot and distribute that portion of this power and jurisdiction, which does not pertain to the Supreme Court, among the other courts prescribed in this Constitution, or which may be established by law, in such manner as it may deem best; provide also a proper system of appeals, and regulate by law, when necessary, the methods of proceeding in the exercise of their powers, of all the Courts below the Supreme Court, so far as the same may be done without conflict with other provisions of this Constitution.

SEC. 22. The Justices of the Supreme Court shall be elected by the qualified voters of the State, as is provided for the election of members of the General Assembly. They shall hold their offices for eight years. The Judges of the Superior Courts, elected at the first election under this amendment shall be elected in like manner as is provided for Justices of the Supreme Court, and shall hold their offices for eight years. The General Assembly may, from time to time, provide by law that the Judges of the Superior Courts, chosen at succeeding elections, instead of being elected by the voters of the whole State, as is herein provided for, shall be elected by the voters of their respective districts.

SEC. 23. All vacancies occurring in the offices provided for by this article of this Constitution shall be filled by the appointments of the Governor, unless otherwise provided for, and the appointees shall hold their places until the next regular election for members of the General Assembly, when elections shall be held to fill such offices. If any person, elected or appointed to any of said offices, shall neglect and fail to qualify, such office shall be appointed to, held and filled as provided in case of vacancies occurring therein. All incumbents of said offices shall hold until their successors are qualified.

SEC. 25. The several Justices of the Peace shall have jurisdiction, under such regulations as the General Assembly shall prescribe, of civil actions founded on contract, wherein the sum demanded shall not exceed two hundred dollars, and wherein the title to real estate shall not be in controversy; and of all criminal matters arising within their counties where the punishment cannot exceed a fine of fifty dollars, or imprisonment for thirty days. And the General Assembly may give to Justices of the Peace jurisdiction of other civil actions, wherein the value of the property in controversy does not exceed fifty dollars. When an issue of fact shall be joined before a Justice, on demand of either party thereto he shall cause a jury of six men to be summoned, who shall try the same. The party against whom judgment shall be rendered in any civil action may appeal to the Superior Court from the same. In all cases of a criminal nature, the party against whom judgment is given may appeal to the Superior Court, where the matter shall be heard anew. In all cases brought before a Justice he shall make a record of the proceedings, and file the same with the Clerk of the Superior Court for his county.

SEC. 28. In case the General Assembly shall establish other courts inferior to Supreme Court, the presiding officers and clerks thereof shall be elected in such manner as the General Assembly may from time to time prescribe, and they shall hold their offices for a term not exceeding eight years.

SEC. 29. Any Judge of the Supreme Court or of the Superior Courts, and the presiding officers of such Courts inferior to the Supreme Court as may be established by law, may be removed from office for mental or physical inability upon a concurrent resolution of two-thirds of both houses of the General Assembly. The Judge or presiding officer, against whom the General Assembly may be about to proceed, shall receive notice thereof, accompanied by a copy of the causes alleged for his removal, at least twenty days before the day on which either House of the General Assembly shall act thereon.

SEC. 30. Any Clerk of the Supreme Court, or of the Superior Courts, or of such Courts inferior to the Supreme Court as may be established by law, may be removed from office for mental or physical inability; the Clerk of the Supreme Court by the Judges of said Court, the Clerks of the Superior Courts by the Judge riding the district, and the Clerks of such Courts inferior to the Supreme Court as may be established by law, by the presiding officers of said Courts. The Clerk against whom proceedings are instituted shall receive notice thereof, accompanied by a copy of the causes alleged for his removal, at least ten days before the day appointed to act thereon, and the Clerk shall be entitled to an appeal to the next term of the Superior Court, and then to the Supreme Court, as provided in other cases of appeals.

SEC. 31. The amendments made to the Constitution of North Carolina by this Convention shall not have the effect to vacate any office or term of office now existing under the Constitution of the State, and filled, or held, by virtue of any election or appointment under the said Constitution, and the laws of the State made in pursuance thereof.

SUFFRAGE AND ELIGIBILITY TO OFFICE.

Amend Section 1 so as to read as follows:

Every male person born in the United States, and every male person who has been naturalized, twenty-one years old or upward, who shall have resided in the State twelve months next preceding the election, and ninety days in the county in which he offers to vote, shall be deemed an elector. But no person who, upon conviction or confession in open court, shall be adjudged guilty of felony, or of any other crime infamous by the laws of this State, and hereafter committed, shall be deemed an elector, unless such person shall be restored to the rights of citizenship in a mode prescribed by law.

MUNICIPAL CORPORATIONS.

SEC. 14. The General Assembly shall have full power by statute to modify, change or abrogate any and all of the provisions of this Article, and substitute others in their place, except sections seven, nine and thirteen.

EDUCATION.

Add the following words to ninth article:

And the children of the white race and the children of the colored race shall be taught in separate public schools, but there shall be no discrimination made in favor of, or to the prejudice of, either race.

Substitute for section 4 of Article 9 the following new sections:

SEC. 4. The proceeds of all lands that have been or hereafter may be granted by the United States to this State, and not otherwise appropriated by this State or the United States; also, all moneys, stocks, bonds and other property now belonging to any State fund for purposes of education; also the net proceeds of all sales of the swamp lands belonging to the State, and all other grants, gifts or devises that have been or hereafter may be made to this State and not otherwise appropriated by the State or by the term of the grant, gift or devise, shall be paid into the State treasury; and, together with so much of the ordinary revenue of the State as may be by law set apart for that purpose, shall be faithfully appropriated for establishing and maintaining in this State a system of free public schools, and for no other uses or purposes whatsoever.

SEC. 5. All moneys, stocks, bonds and other property belonging to a county school fund; also, the net proceeds from the sale of estrays; also, the clear proceeds of all penalties and forfeitures, and of all fines collected in the several counties for any breach of the penal or military laws of the State; and all moneys which shall be paid by persons as an equivalent for exemption from military duty, shall belong to and remain in the several counties, and shall be faithfully appropriated for establishing and maintaining free public schools in the several counties of this State: *Provided*, That the amount collected in each county shall be annually reported to the Superintendent of Public Instruction.

PUNISHMENTS, PENAL INSTITUTIONS AND PUBLIC CHARITIES.

Add to Section 1 of Article 11, the following:

The foregoing provision for imprisonment with hard labor shall be construed to authorize the employment of such convict labor on public works, or highways, or other labor for public benefit, and the farming out thereof where and in such manner as may be provided by law; but no convict shall be farmed out who has been sentenced on a charge of murder, manslaughter, rape, attempt to commit rape, or arson. *Provided*, That no convict whose labor may be farmed out shall be punished for any failure of duty as a laborer except by a responsible officer of the State; but the convicts so farmed out shall be at all times under the supervision and control, as to their government and discipline, of the Penitentiary Board, or some officer of this State.

ON AMENDMENTS.

Substitute for sections 1 and 2 the following:

SECTION 1. No Convention of the people of this State shall ever be called by the General Assembly, unless by the concurrence of two-thirds of all the members of each House of the General Assembly, and except the proposition, Convention or No Convention, be first submitted to the qualified voters of the whole State, at the next general election, in a manner to be prescribed by law. And should a majority of the votes cast be in favor of said Convention, it shall assemble on such day as may be prescribed by the General Assembly.

SEC. 2. No part of the Constitution of this State shall be altered unless a bill to alter the same shall have been agreed to by three-fifths of each House of the General Assembly. And the amendment or amendments so agreed to shall be submitted at the next general election to the qualified voters of the whole State, in such manner as may be prescribed by law. And in the event of their adoption by a majority of the votes cast, such amendment or amendments shall become a part of the Constitution of this State.

MISCELLANEOUS.

Add this new section:

SEC. 8. All marriages between a white person and a negro, or between a white person and a person of negro descent to the third generation inclusive, are hereby forever prohibited.

By an Ordinance of the Convention, the Amendments are to be voted upon as a whole, and the returns made to the Chief Justice. If ratified, they are to take effect, January 1, 1877.

Ohio.

The proposed new Constitution, a full abstract of which was given in McPherson's Hand-Book of Politics for 1874, pp. 72–77, was submitted to a vote of the people, August 18, 1874, and was rejected. The vote "for" the Constitution, was 102,885; "against," 250,169—majority against, 147,284. The vote on the "Separate Propositions" was as follows: "For" Minority Representation in elections for three or more Supreme and Circuit Court Judges at one time, 73,615; "against," 259,415. "For" the "Railroad Aid" section, 45,416; "against," 296,648. "For" the "License" section, 172,252; "against," 179,538. The total number of votes cast was 360,427.

At the October election in 1875, two amendments, submitted by the General Assembly at its previous session, were voted upon. They are as follow:

AMENDMENT TO ARTICLE IV., RELATING TO THE JUDICIARY.

SECTION 22. A Commission, which shall consist of five members, shall be appointed by the Governor, with the advice and consent of the Senate, the members of which shall hold office for the term of three years from and after the first day of February, 1876, to dispose of such part of the business then on the dockets of the Supreme Court as shall, by arrangement between said Commission and said Court, be transferred to such Commission; and said Commission shall have like jurisdiction and power in respect to such business as are or may be vested in said Court; and the members of said Commission shall receive a like compensation for the time being, with the Judges of said Court. A majority of the members of said Commission shall be necessary to form a quorum or pronounce a decision, and its decision shall be certified, entered and enforced as the judgments of the Supreme Court, and disposed of as if said Commission had never existed. The clerk and reporter of said Court shall be the clerk and reporter of said Commission, and the Commission shall have such other attendants, not exceeding in number those provided by law for said Court, which attendants said Commission may appoint and remove at its pleasure. Any vacancy occurring in said Commission shall be filled by appointment of the Governor, with the advice and consent of the Senate, if the Senate be in session, and if the Senate be not in session, by the Governor, but in such last case, such appointment shall expire at the end of the next session of the General Assembly. The General Assembly may, on application of the Supreme Court, duly entered on the journal of the Court and certified, provide by law, whenever two-thirds of such [each] house shall concur therein, from time to time, for the appointment in like manner of a like Commission with like powers, jurisdiction and duties; provided, that the term of any such Commission shall not exceed two years, nor shall it be created oftener than once in ten years.

This amendment received 339,076 votes, and there were 98,561 votes against it; and having received a majority of the whole number of electors voting at said election, was declared adopted.

AMENDMENT PROVIDING FOR TAXING DOGS.

Notwithstanding the provisions of the second section of this article, the General Assembly shall have power to provide by law for the assessment of a special tax on dogs without regard to value, and to provide for the confiscation and killing of such animals upon failure or refusal of the owner, keeper or harborer thereof, to pay such special tax.

This amendment received 278,005 votes, and there were 73,801 against it, and as it did not receive the votes of a majority of the whole number of electors voting at said election, it was declared *not* adopted.

The total vote on Governor was 590,090.

Pennsylvania.

The Commission alluded to on page 84 of McPherson's Hand-Book of Politics for 1874—consisting of Messrs. Daniel Agnew, Benjamin Harris Brewster, Samuel E. Dimmick, Andrew T. McClintock, W. H. Playford, William A. Wallace and Henry W. Williams—reported to the Legislature, January 29, 1875, the following

PROPOSED AMENDMENTS.

Article II. Section 2. Add to the end of the section the following:

"Nor shall a member of either House be permitted to resign pending a trial by the House, or an inquiry into his conduct, which may lead to his expulsion."

Article III. Section 3. Strike out the word "*general*" in the first line. The section will then read:

"No bill, except appropriation bills, shall be passed, containing more than one subject, which shall be clearly expressed in its title."

Article III. Section 15. Amend, by inserting after the word "schools," in the fourth line, the following:

"All other appropriations for charitable and educational purposes, which may be made by a majority vote, shall be embraced in one bill; and all appropriations for such purposes, requiring a vote of two-thirds of the members elected to each House, shall be embraced in one bill. This section will then read:

"The general appropriation bill shall embrace nothing but appropriations for the ordinary expenses of the Executive, Legislative and Judicial Departments of the Commonwealth, interest on the public debt, and for public schools; all other appropriations for charitable and educational purposes, which may be made by a majority vote, shall be embraced in one bill, and all appropriations for such purposes, requiring a vote of two-thirds of the members elected to each House, shall be embraced in one bill; all other appropriations shall be made by separate bills, embracing but one subject."

Article V. Section 2. Insert after the word "*shall,*" in the second clause, "be commissioned by the Governor," and after the words "twenty-one years," the words "beginning on the first Monday of January next after their election."

Article V. Section 3. Strike out the whole clause relating to the original jurisdiction of the Supreme Court, and substitute the following:

"They shall have original jurisdiction in cases of injunction, where a corporation or a public officer is a party defendant, of *habeas corpus, mandamus,* and *quo warranto,* but shall not exercise any other original jurisdiction."

Article V. Section 5. Strike out the entire section and substitute the following:

"SEC. 5. A single county shall be made a separate judicial district only when the business therein shall render it necessary; but no single county containing a population of less than fifty thousand shall be erected into a separate judicial district.

"In separate districts composed of single counties, the office of associate judge, not learned in the law, shall cease to exist when the commissions of such associates in office, at the time of the creation of the district, shall expire.

"In each separate district composed of a single county, one judge, learned in the law, shall be elected to preside therein, and an additional judge or judges, learned in the law, elected only when the business therein shall render it necessary; but no additional law judge shall be elected therein, unless it contain a population of seventy-five thousand. Sufficient provision by law shall be made for the holding of special courts therein, in case of the necessary absence or sickness of the presiding judge, or of his disability by reason of interest, kinship or otherwise.

"Existing separate districts of single counties shall be abolished in all counties wherein the population is less than fifty thousand, and in counties of greater population wherein the business shall not require their continuance; and for this purpose the General Assembly shall re-district the State for judicial purposes, at the session succeeding the next decennial census, to take effect in the abolished separate districts, when the commissions of the judges elected therein, in the year 1874, shall expire. All commissions issued upon elections to fill vacancies accruing in the meantime in the separate districts thus abolished, shall be subject to the provisions of this section for re-districting the State."

REMARKS.—The purpose of this amendment is to change the basis of the judicial system as founded by the new Constitution on population. Business, not population, must determine the necessity for separate single county districts. A purely agricultural county, having a population of 40,000, rarely requires its Courts to sit more than six, eight or ten weeks in the year. A table accompanying this report, drawn from the actual sittings of the Courts in the years 1872 and 1873, as taken from the minutes by the several prothonotaries, will exhibit the effect of the change to the basis of 40,000, contained in the original section. A judge employed so small a part of his time has too little to do, and will retrograde instead of improving.

There is no county in this Commonwealth having a population of 40,000 or less, which affords enough of legal business to occupy a judge profitably to himself or his district. No judge can afford to preside in such a district. No such district can afford to shut up its judge to business so small in amount and so circumscribed in character.

Instead, therefore, of requiring every county having a population of 40,000 to be made a separate district, without regard to the volume of its legal business, it would be wiser to fix a limit below which the Legislature may not go, and leave the question of the erection of separate districts in counties above that limit, to the exercise of a sound legislative discretion upon consideration of all the circumstances in each particular case. An inspection of the table will show that the office of President Judge in some of the agricultural districts is almost a sinecure, while in some of the mining, manufacturing and other business counties, the Courts are constantly employed. Such was the case in 1872 and 1873, when only thirty judicial districts existed; the effect of the population basis was suddenly to raise the number of districts, in 1874, to forty-four, many of which are positively unnecessary. If the State were justly re-districted according to its business wants, it is fair to say that the districts would be reduced below thirty, and but few of the present associates learned in the law would be required, except in large cities and densely populous counties. In a matter so important, when both business and population are changing, a discretion must be left to the representatives of the people. The subject is one that appeals only to the public good, and to no self-interest.

The disparity in the judicial districts and in the labors of the judges is shown by the following facts taken from the table: In five single county districts, with an average population in each of 41,918, the courts sat less than seven weeks in the year. In three single county districts, average population 39,203, courts sat eight and nine weeks. In four single county districts, average population 60,547, courts sat ten and eleven weeks. In three single county districts, average population 50,167, courts sat thirteen and fifteen weeks. In five single county districts, average population 62,373, courts sat sixteen and seventeen weeks. In three single county districts, average population 114,385, courts sat nineteen and twenty weeks; and in four single county districts, average population 102,075, courts sat twenty-two, twenty-three and twenty-four weeks. The same disparity exists in the compound districts composed of two or more counties each. In district No. 41 courts were held but eight weeks in the year. In five districts, Nos. 16, 22, 26, 43 and 44, the courts sat ten, eleven and twelve weeks. In four districts, Nos. 14, 18, 20 and 39, they sat fourteen, fifteen and sixteen weeks. In three districts, Nos. 4, 25 and 27, they sat eighteen and twenty weeks. In three districts, Nos. 12, 17 and 24, they sat twenty-one and twenty-two weeks. In these compound districts the traveling of the judge from county to county must also be considered, especially in districts composed of three or four counties. Another fact to be noticed is that in some of the districts in which the courts sat the longest, the business was done by a single president judge.

Article V. Section 9. Strike out the words "learned in the law" in the first and second lines, and add at the end of the section the following:

"The president or other law judge of said courts shall, in the absence of his associates, constitute a quorum."

Article V. Section 15. Insert in the middle clause, after the word "shall," the words "be commissioned by the Governor, and shall;" and after the words "ten years," the words "beginning on the first Monday of January next after their election."

Article V. Section 16. Strike out the entire section: "Whenever two Judges of the Supreme Court are to be chosen for the same term of service, each voter shall vote for one only, and when three are to be chosen, he shall vote for no more than two; candidates highest in vote shall be declared elected."

REMARKS.—The purpose of this amendment is to return to a direct election of the people for the Judges of the Supreme Court. The effect of the section, as it stands, is to deprive the people of an invaluable right—that of selecting those who administer their laws—and to invest it in an irresponsible body, unknown to any legitimate form of government, and subject to no correction. It is an anomalous, irregular and anti-democratic expedient, to reach a purpose foreign to the true principles of right government.

When two judges are to be chosen for the court in the last resort, in which the final exposition of the laws should accord with the genius and sentiment of the whole people, no reason of sound principle or of public welfare should exclude the citizens from the choice of both.

Why should they be confined to a ballot for one, leaving the selection of the other to accident or the management of an irresponsible convention; or worse, perhaps, to the cunning manipulation of this uncertain, ungoverned collection of partisans? The novelty means simply that a minority, no matter how it is composed, shall make appointments to office. Great or small, its voice is all-potent, no matter how accidental, or how it misrepresents genuine public sentiment.

From the very nature of public affairs, they are constantly varying, necessarily requiring changes of administration to meet the popular will. When these changes come, why should not the popular voice be heard in the election of Judges in accord with the people themselves? But this invention seeks to repress the popular will by taking from the citizen one of his ballots and striking down his power to oppose any one he may deem bad or unfit. It is his right, necessary to the enjoyment of true liberty, to vote against, as well as *for* candidates. But this device takes away that power. There is no longer a contest before the people, wherein the citizen may strike the unfit man of his own party by voting for his opponent; and no matter how he casts his single ballot, the incompetent or unfit man, by an ingenious stroke of art, is successful ere the election has begun. Nor is the right vain or useless, since four times have the people abandoned party lines in voting for Supreme Judges, after the amendment of 1850 had invested them with the power of choice.

The people have had no opportunity of voting directly upon this anomaly. We think the opportunity should be given to them, and we have therefore reported an amendment to strike out the sixteenth section of the fifth article.

Article V. Section 18. Insert after the words "*paid by the State*," at the end of the first clause, the following: "Such compensation may be increased, but shall not be diminished during their continuance in office."

Article V. Section 21. Strike out the words: "as herein provided," at the end of the section, and substitute the following:

"Of prothonotaries of the Supreme Court, criers, tipstaves, auditors, commissioners to take testimony, examiners, masters in chancery, and such other officers necessary in the administration of justice, in the said court, as shall be provided by law. The prothonotaries of the Supreme Court shall hold their offices for a term of three years, if they shall so long behave themselves well, and until their successors shall be appointed and qualified; but may be removed by the said court for misbehavior in office or upon conviction of any infamous or disgraceful offence."

Article VIII. Section 17. Strike out the words "members of the General Assembly," in the first clause, and insert after the word "thereto," at the end of the second clause, the following:

"At the trial of a contested election of a Senator or a Representative before a committee of either House, a Judge of the Supreme Court to be assigned thereto by the said Court, shall preside, and shall decide questions regarding the admissibility of evidence, and shall, at the request of the committee, pronounce his opinion upon the questions of law involved in the trial."

Article IX. Section 1. Insert after the words "corporate profit" in the last line but one, the following:

"Property owned by colleges, academies, and other institutions of learning not used for private gain;" and add at the end of the section the words "and hospitals."

The section will then read:

"All taxes shall be uniform on the same class of subjects within the territorial limits of the authority levying the tax, and shall be levied and collected under general laws; but the General Assembly may by general laws exempt from taxation public property used for public purposes, actual places of religious worship, places of burial not used or held for private or corporate profit, property owned by colleges, academies, and other institutions of learning not used for private gain, institutions of purely public charity, and hospitals."

REMARKS.—The purpose of this amendment is to enable the Legislature, in the exercise of their sound discretion, to exempt institutions of learning from taxation. Education is a State interest, and its benefits belong to the people. When an institution of learning is used for its proper end, and not for private gain, it subserves the welfare and best interest of the people themselves.

There is no sound reason why such institutions should be taxed. They radiate their benefits in another and better form by diffusing what is more valuable to the community than money returned by taxation into the public treasury at the expense of the ability of those institutions to attain their greatest good. Many of the colleges of the State have been founded or largely endowed through the munificent donations of private citizens. A policy which would permit such institutions to be taxed would be illiberal and an unjust imposition upon private benefactions, tending to their repression and to public injury.

Article IX. Section 8. Strike out the words, "*at any one time*," in the last line of the section.

REMARKS.—The purpose of this amendment is to limit the aggregate indebtedness which a city may contract, to ten per cent. As the section stands, it is open to a doubt whether there is any limit to the amount of the indebtedness which a city may contract, if its debt exceeded seven per centum at the time of the adoption of the Constitution. An inference might be drawn from the words "*at any one time*," that the intent of this part of the section was merely to limit the amount of the addition to be made to the debt *at a given time*, leaving no limit to the *number* of additions to be made, or upon the total amount of indebtedness.

Article XIV. Section 6. Amend by adding at the end of the section the following:

"All fines and penalties shall be paid into the treasury of the proper county."

REMARKS.—The purpose of this amendment is to correct an inequality arising from the present laws disposing of fines and penalties. In some counties these are appropriated to a single school district, or to a law association, or to other purposes. The expenses of the administration of justice are borne by the people of the whole county. It is but equitable that the results of this administration should be distributed equitably to the whole population, and not to individuals, or to particular districts of persons. In one of the counties of the Commonwealth at the fall term of 1874, fines amounting to nearly $1,800, were, by a local law, diverted from the county treasury to that of the school district composed of the county town. A leading thought of the Convention was the introduction of uniformity into the laws of the State, and this is evidenced among other provisions by section twenty-six of the fifth article, declaring that all laws relating to courts shall be general and of uniform operation.

Article XIV. Section 7. Strike out this section:

"Three county commissioners and three county auditors shall be elected in each county where such officers are chosen, in the year one thousand eight hundred and seventy-five, and every third year thereafter; and in the election of said officers each qualified elector shall vote for no more than two persons, and the three persons having the highest number of votes shall be elected; any casual vacancy in the office of county commissioner or county auditor shall be filled by the court of common pleas of the county in which such vacancy shall occur, by the appointment of an elector of the proper county who shall have voted for the commissioner or auditor whose place is to be filled."

REMARKS.—The objections to this section are serious and practical. The system of county management has always been a matter of law, and wisely so as absolutely necessary to accomodate it to the changes in times, places, and circumstances. But this section establishes an unalterable and fundamental rule, which no exigency can modify or dispense with. It also destroys all experience and knowledge acquired in the management of county affairs, by turning out the whole board of commissioners or auditors at one and the same time. Under the old system two commissioners or auditors always remained in office to preserve the skill and knowledge acquired in the service. By the wholesale turning out required by the section, the clerk becomes practically the board of commissioners, and these, when coming in all together, must look to him for guidance in their duties. The auditors have not even this aid, but must endeavor to settle the accounts of the officers with the small knowledge that plain and unlearned men have who in the county generally fill the office of auditors.

The purpose of the section was to adapt the system to the new mode of voting. It seems to us the good proposed to be gained by it, bears no proportion to the evils it will entail.

If the people really desire to elect these officers in the mode proposed by this section, this will leave them at liberty to do so. They can pass laws providing for their election upon the cumulative plan, or the restricted, if they please. If, after trying the experiment, they should conclude that it was not best to continue it, they could abandon it without waiting to change the Constitution. The section was at best but an experiment; and experiments are more easily and safely tried in statutes, than in constitutional provisions.

Article XVI. Section 4. Strike out the whole section: "In all elections for directors or managers of a corporation, each member or shareholder may cast the whole number of his votes for one candidate, or distribute them upon two or more candidates, as he may prefer."

REMARKS.—Article XVI. Section 4. This section is very obscure, and difficult to interpret. In ordinary corporation elections each stockholder casts a certain number of votes for each candidate; the number of votes being governed by the number of shares he holds. No matter how many directors or managers there may be, his right is to cast his whole vote for every one, because he has the same right of selection of every one who is to manage his affairs as a corporation. But by the terms of the section, he can cast the whole number of his votes for only one director, and if there be more than one, he must *distribute* his votes among them. If there be seven directors, (and oftentimes there are twelve or more,) and if he have three shares or three votes, he can, according to the new rule in the section, cast these three votes, at most, for only three directors.

He is thus deprived of voting for all the others; and even when he has as many votes as candidates, he is compelled to distribute them in such manner that he loses the power he had hitherto.

The proceeding is exceedingly anomalous, and restrains rather than enlarges the power of the shareholder.

If the purpose of the draughtsman of this section was to provide that each shareholder might "cumulate" upon *one* candidate the whole number of votes he can cast for *all* the directors, if voting upon all his shares of stock for each director, it would appear that it is not accomplished well. Either the purpose of the section is not clear, or it is imperfectly expressed.

Article XVI. Section 5. Strike out the words "do any" in the first line and insert the words "engage in" in lieu thereof.

The section will then read:

"No foreign corporation shall engage in business in this State without having one or more places of business, and an authorized agent or agents in the same, upon whom process may be served."

REMARKS.—The purpose of this amendment is to obviate an interpretation which would prevent a foreign corporation from doing any *single* act relating to its affairs without complying with the requirements of the section. A corporation not intending to engage in business in the State may find it necessary to do a particular act not within the mischief to be remedied.

Article XVI. Section 10. Strike out the last clause, to wit, the words: "No law hereafter enacted shall create, renew or extend the charter of *more than one corporation.*"

REMARKS.—The purpose of this amendment is to harmonize the section with the provision in the seventh section of the third article, that the General Assembly shall not pass any local or special law "creating corporations, or amending, renewing or extending the charters thereof." According to the seventh section of the third article, the Legislature can pass no special law to create, extend or renew charters. Yet from the terms of the last clause of the tenth section of the sixteenth article, an inference might be drawn that a special act could be passed if it contained a charter of not more than one corporation.

The third section of the third article confines legislation to single subjects. The last clause of this tenth section is useless, and its removal will prevent apparent conflict.

Article XVII. Section 9. Amend by inserting the words, "or extended," between the word "constructed" and the word "within."

The section will then read:

"No street passenger railway shall be constructed or extended, within the limits of any city, borough or township, without the consent of its local authorities."

REMARKS.—The purpose of this amendment is to embrace a case as clearly within the evil to be remedied as that now provided for in the section. An existing passenger railway constructed with the assent of the city over certain streets, may without its assent, be extended to other streets to the great injury of the public. The well known legislation to enable the Union Passenger Railway Company in Philadelphia to extend its railway into Market street, between Front and Ninth streets, affords an illustration of the omission intended to be supplied by the word "*extended.*"

Rhode Island.

The following proposed Amendments to the Constitution are now pending:

ARTICLE ——

All soldiers and sailors of foreign birth, citizens of the United States, who served in the Army or Navy of the United States during the late war, from this State, and who were honorably discharged from such service, shall have the right to vote in the election of all civil officers, and on all questions in all legally organized town, district or ward meetings, upon the same conditions, and under and subject to the same restrictions, as native born citizens.

ARTICLE ——

Every male native citizen of the United States, of the age of twenty-one years, who has had his residence and home in the State two years, and in the town or city in which he may offer to vote, six months next preceding the time of voting, whose name shall have been registered in the town or city where he resides, on or before the last day of December, in the year next preceding the time of his voting, shall have a right to vote in the election of all civil officers, and on all questions in all legally organized town, district or ward meetings; provided, that no person shall, at any time, be allowed to vote in the election of the city council of any city, or upon any proposition to impose a tax, or for the expenditure of money, in any town or city, unless he shall within the year next preceding have paid a tax assessed upon his property, valued at least at one hundred and thirty-four dollars. This amendment shall take, in the Constitution of the State, the place of Sections 2 and 3 of Article 2, which sections are hereby annulled and rescinded.

ARTICLE ——

Section 17, Article IV., of the Constitution of the State is hereby annulled and rescinded.

[This amendment looks to the adoption of a general corporation law.]

[The first Amendment passed the HOUSE OF REPRESENTATIVES March 22, 1876—yeas 49, nays 30; the SENATE—yeas 30, nays 0.

The second passed the HOUSE March 17—yeas 50, nays 2; the SENATE—yeas 32, nays 0.

The third passed the HOUSE March 9—yeas 47, nays 0; the SENATE—yeas 26, nays 0.]

Texas.

On the first Monday in August, 1875, the people, by a majority of nearly two-thirds, voted in favor of having a Constitutional Convention, and elected ninety delegates to form it. The Convention met September 6, and adjourned November 22. On the third Tuesday in February, 1876, the vote on ratification was taken, and resulted in the adoption of the Constitution by a large majority. The Convention passed sundry ordinances—one in relation to railroads, one dividing the State into Senatorial and Representative districts, another dividing it into Judicial districts, another fixing the terms of District Courts; another prohibited the registration of voters, and the election of the Legislature fixed by law for December, 1875—thus exercising a power which is brought under review in the decision of the Supreme Court of Pennsylvania printed herein.

An abstract of the principal provisions of the Constitution is appended.

In the "Bill of Rights" are these articles:

Texas is a free and independent State, subject only to the Constitution of the United States; and the maintenance of our free institutions and the perpetuity of the Union depend upon the preservation of the right of local self-government unimpaired to all the States.

No religious test shall ever be required as a qualification to any office, or public trust, in this State; nor shall any one be excluded from holding office on account of his religious sentiments, provided he acknowledge the existence of a Supreme Being.

No person shall be disqualified to give evidence in any of the courts of this State on account of his religious opinions, or for the want of any religious belief, but all oaths or affirmations shall be administered in the mode most binding upon the conscience, and shall be taken subject to the pains and penalties of perjury.

No money shall be appropriated or drawn from the treasury for the benefit of any sect or religious society, theological or religious seminary; nor shall property belonging to the State be appropriated for any such purposes.

The writ of *habeas corpus* is a writ of right, and shall never be suspended. The Legislature shall enact laws to render the remedy speedy and effectual.

The Senate shall consist of 31 members, never to be increased, to serve for four years. The House of 93 members, and never to exceed 150, to serve for two years. Legislature to meet every two years.

No person who at any time may have been a collector of taxes, or who may have been otherwise entrusted with public money, shall be eligible to the Legislature, or to any office of profit or trust under the State government, until he shall have obtained a discharge for the amount of such collections, or for all public moneys with which he may have been entrusted.

A member who has a personal or private interest in any measure or bill, proposed or pending before the Legislature, shall disclose the fact to the house of which he is a member, and shall not vote thereon.

Bills must be read on three several days in each house. After a bill or resolution has been considered and defeated by either house of the Legislature, no bill containing the same substance shall be passed into a law during the same session. The civil and criminal laws shall be digested every ten years. Lotteries prohibited. Creation of State debt prohibited except to supply casual deficiencies of revenue, repel invasion, or pay existing debt, and shall not exceed $200,000 at any time. Extra compensation to officer or contractors prohibited.

The Legislature shall have no power to give or to lend, or to authorize the giving or lending, of the credit of the State in aid of, or to any person, association or corporation, whether municipal or other; or to pledge the credit of the State in any manner whatsoever, for the payment of the liabilities, present or prospective, of any individual, association of individuals, municipal or other corporation whatsoever.

The Legislature shall have no power to make any grant, or authorize the making of any grant, of public money to any individual, association of individuals, municipal or other corporation whatsoever; *provided*, that this shall not be so construed as to prevent the grant of aid in case of public calamity.

The Legislature shall have no power to authorize any county, city, town, or other political corporation, or sub-division of the State, to lend its credit, or to grant public money or thing of value, in aid of or to any individual, association, or corporation whatsoever; or to become a stockholder in such corporation, association or company.

The Legislature shall have no power to grant, or to authorize any county or municipal authority to grant, any extra compensation, fee or allowance to a public officer, agent, servant or contractor, after service has been rendered, or a contract has been entered into, and performed in whole or in part; nor pay, nor authorize the payment of, any claim created against any county or municipality of the State, under any agreement or contract, made without authority of law.

The Legislature shall have no power to release or alienate any lien held by the State upon any railroad, or in any wise change the tenor or meaning, or pass any act explanatory thereof; but the same shall be enforced in accordance with the original terms upon which it was acquired.

The Legislature shall have no power to release or extinguish, or authorize the releasing or extinguishing, in whole or in part, the indebtedness, liability or obligation of any incorporation or individual to this State, or to any county, or other municipal corporation therein.

If any bill presented to the Governor contains several items of appropriation, he may object to one or more of such items, and approve the other portion of the bill, subject to be overruled by a two-thirds vote of each house.

The Supreme Judges to be elected and hold office for six years, and be paid not over $3,500 a year.

Qualified electors shall be male citizens 21 years of age, citizens of the United States, and residents of Texas one year next preceding the election, and the last six months in the district or county in which he offers to vote, and foreign-born who have declared their intention to become citizens under the laws of the United States, similarly qualified as above, electors to vote in the election precinct of their residence. But the following persons shall not vote: Idiots and lunatics, paupers supported by any county, persons convicted of felony, subject to such exceptions as the Legislature may make, and all soldiers, marines and seamen employed in the service of the army or navy of the United States. In municipal elections, to determine expenditure of money or assumption of debt, only those shall be qualified to vote who pay taxes on property in said city or incorporated town; *provided*, that no poll tax for the payment of debts thus incurred shall be levied upon the persons debarred from voting in relation thereto.

In all elections by the people the vote shall be by ballot, and the Legislature shall provide for the numbering of tickets, and make such other regulations as may be necessary to detect and punish fraud and preserve the purity of the ballot box; but no law shall ever be enacted requiring a registration of the voters of this State.

It shall be the duty of the Legislature of the State to establish and make suitable provision for the support and maintenance of an efficient system of public free schools.

All funds, lands and other property heretofore set apart and appropriated for the support of public schools; all the alternate sections of land reserved by the State out of grants heretofore made or that may hereafter be made to railroads, or other corporations, of any nature whatsoever; one-half of the public domain of the State; and all sums of money that may come to the State from the sale of any portion of the same, shall constitute a perpetual public school fund.

There shall be set apart annually not more than one-fourth of the general revenue of the State, and a poll tax of one dollar on all male inhabitants in this State between the ages of twenty-one and sixty years, for the benefit of the public free schools.

The lands herein set apart to the public free school fund shall be sold under such regulations, at such times and on such terms as may be prescribed by law; and the Legislature shall not have power to grant any relief to the purchasers thereof. The comptroller shall invest the proceeds of such sales, and of those heretofore made, as may be directed by the Board of Education herein provided for, in the bonds of this State, if the same can be obtained, otherwise in United States bonds; and the United States bonds now belonging to said fund shall likewise be invested in State bonds, if the same can be obtained on terms advantageous to the school fund.

The principal of all bonds and other funds, and the principal arising from the sale of the lands heretofore set apart to said school fund, shall be the permanent school fund; and all the interest derivable therefrom, and the taxes herein authorized and levied, shall be the available school fund, which shall be applied annually to the support of the public free schools. And no law shall ever be enacted appropriating any part of the permanent or available school fund to any other purpose whatever; nor shall the same or any part thereof ever be appropriated to or used for the support of any sectarian school; and the available school fund herein provided shall be distributed to the several counties according to their scholastic population, and applied in manner as may be provided by law.

All lands heretofore or hereafter granted to the several counties of this State for education, or schools, are of right the property of said counties respectively to which they were granted, and title thereto is vested in said counties, and no adverse possession or limitation shall ever be available against the title of any county. Each county may sell or dispose of its lands in whole or in part, in manner to be provided by the Commissioners' Court of the county. Actual settlers residing on said lands shall be protected in the prior right of purchasing the same to the extent of their settlement, not to exceed one hundred and sixty acres, at the price fixed by said court, which price shall not include the value of existing improvements made thereon by such settlers. Said lands and the proceeds thereof, when sold, shall be held by said counties alone as a trust for the benefit of public schools therein; said proceeds to be invested in bonds of the State of Texas, or of the United States, and only the interest thereon to be used and expended annually.

Separate schools shall be provided for the white and colored children, and impartial provision shall be made for both.

The Governor, Comptroller and Secretary of State shall be a Board of Education.

Taxation shall be equal and uniform. All property, whether owned by natural persons or corporations, other than municipal, shall be taxed in proportion to its value, which shall be ascertained as may be provided by law. The Legislature may impose a poll tax. It may also impose occupation taxes, both upon natural persons and upon corporations, other than municipal, doing any business in this State. It may also tax incomes of both natural persons and corporations, other than municipal, except that persons engaged in mechanical and agricultural pursuits shall never be required to pay an occupation tax; and two hundred and fifty dollars worth of household and kitchen furniture, belonging to each family in this State, shall be exempt.

Legislature may exempt, by general laws, public property used for public purposes; actual places of religious worship; places of burial not held for private or corporate profit; all buildings used exclusively and owned by persons or associations of persons for school purposes (and the necessary furniture of all schools), and institutions of purely public charity; and all laws exempting property from taxation other than the property above mentioned, shall be void.

The ordinary State tax shall not exceed fifty cents on the $100 valuation, and the ordinary county or municipal tax shall not exceed one-half of the State tax. An Assessor of Taxes, to be elected by the people for two years, is created, the Sheriff to be the collector.

Any railroad corporation or association, organized under the law for the purpose, shall have the right to construct and operate a railroad between any points within this State, and to connect at the State line with railroads of other States. Every railroad company shall have the right, with its road, to intersect, connect with or cross any other railroad; and shall receive and transport each the other's passengers, tonnage and cars, loaded or empty, without delay or discrimination, under such regulations as shall be prescribed by law.

Railroads heretofore constructed, or that may hereafter be constructed in this State, are hereby declared public highways, and railroad companies common carriers. The Legislature shall pass laws to correct abuses and prevent unjust discrimination and extortion in the rates of freight and passenger tariffs on the different railroads in this State; and shall from time to time pass laws establishing reasonable maximum rates of charges for the transportation of passengers and freight on said railroads, and enforce all such laws by adequate penalties.

Railroad consolidation of parallel lines, or by purchase of other lines, is prohibited.

The Legislature is prohibited from issuing "Treasury warrants," "Treasury Notes," or paper of any description intended to circulate as money. The legal rate of interest shall not exceed eight per cent. in the absence of contract, and may be twelve under contract. Excess of this last shall be deemed usury.

Members of the Legislature, and all officers, before they enter upon the duties of their offices, shall take the following oath or affirmation: "I, (.... ......) do solemnly swear (or affirm), that I will faithfully and impartially discharge and perform all the duties incumbent upon me as .... according to the best of my skill and ability, agreeably to the Constitution and laws of the United States and of this State; and I do further solemnly swear (or affirm), that since the adoption of the constitution of this State, I, being a citizen of this State, have not fought a duel with deadly weapons, within this State nor out of it, nor have I sent or accepted a challenge to fight a duel with deadly weapons, nor have I acted as second in carrying a challenge, or aided, advised or assisted any person thus offending. And I furthermore solemnly swear (or affirm), that I have not directly nor indirectly paid, offered or promised to pay, contributed, nor promised to contribute any money, or valuable thing, or promised any public office or employment, as a reward for the giving or withholding a vote at the election at which I was elected (or if the office is one of appointment, to secure my appointment). So help me God."

All property, both real and personal, of the wife, owned or claimed by her before marriage, and that acquired afterward by gift, devise or descent, shall be her separate property; and laws shall be passed more clearly defining the rights of the wife, in relation as well to her separate property as that held in common with her husband. Laws shall also be passed providing for the registration of the wife's separate property.

No corporate body shall hereafter be created, renewed or extended with banking or discounting privileges.

Every person, corporation, or company, that may commit a homicide, through wilful act, or omission, or gross neglect, shall be responsible, in exemplary damages, to the surviving husband, widow, heirs of his or her body, or such of them as there may be, without regard to any criminal proceeding that may or may not be had in relation to the homicide.

The Legislature shall have power, and it shall be its duty, to protect by law from forced sale a certain portion of the personal property of all heads of families, and also of unmarried adults, male and female.

The homestead of a family shall be, and is hereby protected from forced sale, for the payment of all debts except for the purchase money thereof, or a part of such purchase money, the taxes due thereon, or for work and material used in constructing improvements thereon, and in this last case only when the work and material are contracted for in writing, with the consent of the wife given in the same manner as is required in making a sale and conveyance of the homestead; nor shall the owner, if a married man, sell the homestead without the consent of the wife, given in such manner as may be prescribed by law. No mortgage, trust deed or other lien on the homestead shall ever be valid, except for the purchase money therefor, or improvements made thereon, as herein before provided, whether such mortgage or trust deed, or other lien, shall have been created by the husband alone, or together with his wife; and all pretended sales of the homestead involving any condition of defeasance shall be void.

The homestead, not in a town or city, shall consist of not more than two hundred acres of land, which may be in one or more parcels, with the improvements thereon; the homestead in a city, town, or village, shall consist of lot or lots, not to exceed in value five thousand dollars, at the time of their designation as the homestead, without reference to the value of any improvements thereon; *provided*, that the same shall be used for the purposes of a home, or as a place to exercise the calling or business of the head of a family, and that any renting of the homestead shall not change the character of the same when no other homestead has been acquired.

Three millions acres of the public domain are hereby appropriated and set apart for the purpose of erecting a new State capitol and other necessary public buildings at the seat of government, said lands to be sold under the direction of the Legislature.

This instrument became the organic law of the State on the third Tuesday of April last, and the first Legislature under it met on the third Tuesday of April last. The regular election hereafter will be on the Tuesday next after the first Monday in November, every second year.

NOTE.—I notice that on the 13th of March, 1876, Mr. BLAINE presented the petition of a convention of colored people of Texas, January 14th, 1876, representing that the proposed new Constitution deprives the colored people of their school privileges, violates the reconstruction act in this respect, and proposes to devote the agricultural land grant to the education of whites alone; which was referred to the committee on the Judiciary.

Virginia.

The following proposed Amendments were adopted by the Legislatures of 1874–5, and of 1875–6, and are now submitted to the people, to be voted on at the general election, November 7, 1876:

Strike out Section 1, Article III., respecting elective franchise and qualifications for office, as follows:

Article III. Section 1. Every male citizen of the United States, twenty-one years old, who shall have been a resident of this State twelve months, and of the county, city, or town in which he shall offer to vote, three months next preceding any election, shall be entitled to vote upon all questions submitted to the people at such election: Provided, that no officer, soldier, seaman, or marine of the United States army or navy shall be considered a resident of this State by reason of being stationed therein: and provided also, that the following persons shall be excluded from voting: *First.* Idiots and lunatics. *Second.* Persons convicted of bribery in any election, embezzlement of public funds, treason or felony. *Third.* No person who, while a citizen of this State, has, since the adoption of this Constitution, fought a duel with a deadly weapon, sent or accepted a challenge to fight a duel with a deadly weapon, either within or beyond the boundaries of this State, or knowingly conveyed a challenge, or aided or assisted in any manner in fighting a duel, shall be allowed to vote or hold any office of honor, profit, or trust, under this constitution.

And in lieu thereof insert the following:

SECTION 1. Every male citizen of the United States, twenty-one years old, who shall have been a resident of the State twelve months, and of the county, city, or town in which he shall offer to vote three months next preceding any election, and shall have paid to the State, before the day of election, the capitation tax required by law, for the preceding year, shall be entitled to vote for members of the General Assembly and all officers elected by the people: provided, that no officer, soldier, seaman, or marine of the United States army or navy, shall be considered a resident of this State, by reason of being stationed therein: and provided also, that the following persons shall be excluded from voting: *First.* Idiots and lunatics. *Second.* Persons convicted of bribery in any election, embezzlement of public funds, treason, felony or petit larceny. *Third.* No person who, while a citizen of this State, has, since the adoption of this constitution, fought a duel with a deadly weapon, sent or accepted a challenge to fight a duel with a deadly weapon, either within or beyond the boundaries of this State, or knowingly conveyed a challenge, or aided or assisted in any manner in fighting a duel, shall be allowed to vote or hold any office of honor, profit, or trust, under this constitution.

Strike out section 4, article 3, as follows:

Article III. Section 4. The General Assembly shall, at its first session under this Constitution, enact a general registration law; and every person offering or applying to register shall take and subscribe, before the officer charged with making a registration of voters, the following oath: "I, ————————, do solemnly swear (or affirm) that I am not disqualified from exercising the right of suffrage by the Constitution framed by the Convention which assembled in the city of Richmond on the third of December, eighteen hundred and sixty-seven, and that I will support and defend the same to the best of my ability."

SCHEDULE.

2. That all elections held subsequently to the ratification of these amendments by the people, before the adjournment of the next regular session of the Legislature, held after such ratification, shall be had and conducted under and in accordance with the election laws and registration laws which may be in force at the time of such ratification, unless the same shall have been sooner amended or repealed by the General Assembly.

Strike out sections 2, 3, 4, 5, 6, and 8 of Art. 5, concerning the legislative department, as follows:

Article V. Section 2. The house of delegates shall be elected biennially by the voters of the several cities and counties, on the Tuesday succeeding the first Monday in November, and shall be distributed and apportioned as follows:

SEC. 3. The Senators shall be elected for the term of four years, for the election of whom the counties, cities, and towns shall be divided into not more than forty districts. Each county, city and town of the respective districts, at the time of the first election of its delegate or delegates under this Constitution, shall vote for one or more Senators. The Senators first elected under this constitution, in districts bearing odd numbers, shall vacate their offices at the end of two years, and those elected in districts bearing even numbers, at the end of four years; and vacancies occurring by expiration of term shall be filled by the election of Senators for the full term.

SEC. 4. At the first session of the General Assembly after the enumeration of the inhabitants of the State by the United States, a re-apportionment of Senators and members of the house of delegates, and every tenth year thereafter, shall be made.

SEC. 5. Any person may be elected Senator who, at the time of election, is actually a resident within the district, and qualified to vote for members of the General Assembly according to this Constitution; and any person may be elected a member of the house of delegates who, at the time of election, is actually a resident within the county, city, town, or election district, qualified to vote for members of the General Assembly according to this Constitution. The removal of any person elected to either branch of the General Assembly from the city, county, town, or district for which he was elected, shall vacate his office.

POWERS AND DUTIES OF THE GENERAL ASSEMBLY.

SEC. 6. The General Assembly shall meet annually, and not oftener, unless convened by the Governor in the manner prescribed by this Constitution. No session of the General Assembly, after the first under this Constitution, shall continue longer than ninety days, without the concurrence of three-fifths of the members elected to each house; in which case the session may be extended for a further period, not exceeding thirty days. Neither house, during the session of the General Assembly, shall, without the consent of the other, adjourn for more than three days, nor to any other place than that in which the two houses shall be sitting. A majority of the members elected to each house shall constitute a quorum to do business; but a smaller number may adjourn from day to day, and shall have power to compel the attendance of absent members, in such manner and under such penalty as each house may prescribe.

SEC. 8. The members of the General Assembly shall receive for their services a compensation, to be ascertained by law, and paid out of the public treasury; but no act increasing such compensation shall take effect until after the end of the term for which the members of the house of delegates voting thereon were elected; and no Senator or Delegate, during the term for which he shall have been elected, shall be appointed to any civil office of profit under the commonwealth, which has been created, or the emoluments of which have been increased during such term, except offices filled by election by the people.

And insert in lieu thereof the following:

SEC. 2. The house of delegates shall be elected biennially by the voters of the several cities and counties, on the Tuesday succeeding the first Monday in November, and shall, from and after the Tuesday succeeding the first Monday in November, eighteen hundred and seventy-nine, consist of not more than one hundred, and not less than ninety members.

SEC. 3. From and after the same date, the senate shall consist of not less than thirty-three nor more than forty members. They shall be elected for the term of four years—for the election of whom, the counties, cities, and towns shall be divided into districts. Each county, city, and town of the respective districts shall, at the time of the first election of its delegate or delegates under this amendment, vote for one or more senators. The senators first elected under this amendment, in districts bearing odd numbers, shall vacate their offices at the end of two years; and those elected in districts bearing even numbers, at the end of four years: and vacancies occurring by expiration of term shall be filled by the election of senators for the full term.

SEC. 4. An apportionment of Senators and members of the House of Delegates shall be made at the regular session of the General Assembly next preceding the Tuesday after the first Monday in November, eighteen hundred and seventy-nine, or sooner. A reapportionment shall be made in the year eighteen hundred and ninety-one, and every tenth year thereafter.

QUALIFICATIONS OF SENATORS AND DELEGATES.

SEC. 5. Any person may be elected senator who, at the time of election, is actually a resident within the district, and qualified to vote for members of the General Assembly according to this Constitution; and any person may be elected a member of the House of Delegates who, at the time of election, is actually a resident within the county, city, town, or election district, qualified to vote for members of the General Assembly according to this Constitution. But no person holding a salaried office under the State Government shall be capable of being elected a member of either House of the General Assembly. The removal of any person elected to either branch of the General Assembly, from the city, county, town, or district for which he was elected, shall vacate his office.

POWERS AND DUTIES OF THE GENERAL ASSEMBLY.

SEC. 6. The General Assembly shall meet once in two years, and not oftener, unless convened by the Governor in the manner prescribed in this Constitution. No session of the General Assembly, after the first under this amendment, shall continue longer than ninety days, without the concurrence of three-fifths of the members elected to each House; in which case the session may be extended for a further period, not exceeding thirty days. Neither house during the session of the General Assembly, shall, without the consent of the other, adjourn for more than three days, nor to any other place than that in which the two houses shall be sitting. A majority of the members elected to each house shall constitute a quorum to do business; but a smaller number may adjourn from day to day, and shall have power to compel the attendance of absent members in such manner and under such penalty as each house may prescribe.

SEC. 8. The members of the General Assembly shall receive for their services a salary, to be ascertained by law, and paid out of the public treasury; but no act increasing such salary shall take effect until after the end of the term for which the members of the House of Delegates voting thereon were elected; and no senator or delegate, during the term for which he shall have been elected, shall be appointed to any civil office of profit under the commonwealth, which has been created, or the emoluments of which have been increased during such term, except offices filled by election by the people.

Add the following sections at the end of the article:

SEC. 23. The Legislature shall have power to provide for the government of cities and towns, and to establish such courts therein as may be necessary for the administration of justice.

SEC. 24. The General Assembly shall have power, by two-thirds vote, to remove disabilities incurred under clause third, section one, article third of this Constitution, with reference to duelling.

X.

THE "PUBLIC CREDIT ACT" OF 1869, AND THE "RESUMPTION ACT" OF 1875.

The "Public Credit Bill" of the Fortieth Congress.

Fortieth Congress—Third Session.

IN HOUSE.

1869, January 20—Mr. SCHENCK introduced, by unanimous consent, the following bill (H. R. 1744):

An act to strengthen the public credit and relating to contracts for the payment of coin.

Be it enacted, &c., That in order to remove any doubt as to the purpose of the Government to discharge all just obligations to the public creditors, and to settle conflicting questions and interpretations of the law, by virtue of which such obligations have been contracted, it is hereby provided and declared, that the faith of the United States is solemnly pledged to the payment in coin, or its equivalent, of all the interest-bearing obligations of the United States, except in cases where the law authorizing the issue of any such obligation has expressly provided that the same may be paid in lawful money, or other currency than gold or silver; *Provided, however,* That before any of said interest-bearing obligatons not already due shall mature, or be paid before maturity, the obligations not bearing interest, known as United States notes, shall be made convertible into coin at the option of the holder.

SEC. 2. That any contract hereafter made specifically payable in coin, and the consideration of which may be a loan of coin, or a sale of property, or the rendering of labor or service of any kind, the price of which, as carried into the contract, may have been adjusted on the basis of the coin value thereof at the time of such sale, or the rendering of such service or labor, shall be legal and valid, and may be enforced according to its terms; and on the trial of a suit brought for the enforcement of any such contract, proof of the real consideration may be given.

February 23—The previous question demanded and the main question ordered—yeas 101, nays 43, not voting 78.

February 24—Mr. SHANKS moved that the bill be laid on the table, which was disagreed to—yeas 54, nays 133, not voting 35.

Mr. NIBLACK moved to strike out the first section, which was disagreed to—yeas 54, nays 130 (not voting 38), as follow:

YEAS—Messrs. *Archer*, Jehu Baker, *Barnes*, Beatty, *Beck*, C. C. Bowen, *Burr*, R. R. Butler, A. Cobb, Coburn, Deweese, Donnelly, Eggleston, Ela, *Eldredge*, Farnsworth, *Fox*, *Getz*, *J. S. Golladay*, Goss, Gravely, *Grover*, *Haight*, Hawkins, *Holman*, B. F. Hopkins, *Humphrey*, Hunter, Ingersoll, *J. A. Johnson*, *T. L. Jones*, *Kerr*, *Knott*, Loan, *Marshall*, *McCormick*, *Mungen*, *Niblack*, Orth, F. A. Pike, *Pruyn*, *L. W. Ross*, Shanks, A. F. Stevens, Stokes, *F. Stone*, Taffe, *Tift*, *Van Auken*, *Van Trump*, H. D. Washburn, J. T. Wilson, *F. Wood*, *P. M. B. Young*—54.

NAYS—Messrs. Allison, Ames, G. W. Anderson, Arnell, D. R. Ashley, J. M. Ashley, *Axtell*, Baldwin, Banks, *Barnum*, Beaman, Benjamin, Benton, Bingham, W. J. Blackburn, Blaine, A. Blair, Boutwell, Boyden, *Boyer*, Bromwell, *Brooks*, Broomall, Buckley, Cake, *Chanler*, Churchill, R. W. Clarke, S. Clarke, Clift, Corley, Cornell, Covode, Cullom, Delano, Dickey, N. F. Dixon, Dockery, G. M. Dodge, Driggs, Eckley, T. D. Eliot, J. T. Elliott, Ferriss, T. W. Ferry, W. C. Fields, *Glossbrenner*, Gove, J. A. Griswold, Halsey, Harding, Heaton, Higby, J. Hill, Hooper, *J. Hotchkiss*, C. D. Hubbard, *R. D. Hubbard*, Hulburd, Jenckes, A. H. Jones, Judd, Julian, Kelley, Kellogg, Kelsey, J. H. Ketcham, Kitchen, Koontz, Laflin, Lash, G. V. Lawrence, W. Lawrence, Logan, J. Lynch, Mallory, Marvin, Maynard, McKee, Mercur, G. F. Miller, W. Moore, Moorhead, Mullins, Myers, Newsham, Norris, O'Neill, H. E. Paine, Perham, Peters, Pettis, *C. E. Phelps*, C. W. Pierce, Pile, Plants, Poland, Pomeroy, H. Price, Prince, Raum, Robertson, Roots, P. Sawyer, Schenck, Scofield, Shellabarger, W. C. Smith, Spalding, Starkweather, T. E. Stewart, Stover, *Taber*, C. N. Taylor, F. Thomas, J. Trimble, Trowbridge, Twichell, C. Upson, Van Aernam, B. Van Horn, H. Ward, C. C. Washburn, W. B. Washburn, Welker, Whittemore, T. Williams, W. Williams, J. F. Wilson, Windom—130.

Mr. ALLISON moved to strike out the second section, which was lost—yeas 72, nays 100 (not voting 50), as follow:

YEAS—Messrs. Allison, Jehu Baker, Beatty, *Beck*, Benton, C. C. Bowen, Bromwell, B. F. Butler, Cake, Clift, A. Cobb, Coburn, B. C. Cook, Cornell, Cullom, Deweese, Dickey, Donnelly, Eckley, Ela, *Eldredge*, Farnsworth, Ferriss, T.W. Ferry, *Fox*, *J. S. Golladay*, Goss, Gravely, Hawkins, *Holman*, Hooper, B. F. Hopkins, Hunter, Ingersoll, Kelley, Kelsey, *Knott*, Koontz, W. Lawrence, Loan, Loughridge, J. Lynch, Maynard, G. F. Miller, W. Moore, Morrell, Mullins, *Mungen*, Myers, *Niblack*, Nunn, O'Neill, Orth, Peters, Robertson, *L. W. Ross*, P. Sawyer, Shanks, Shellabarger, W. C. Smith, A. F. Stevens, Stokes, Taffe, F. Thomas, *Tift*, C. Upson, *Van Trump*, H. D. Washburn, T. Williams, W. Williams, J. T. Wilson, *P. M. B. Young*—72.

NAYS—Messrs. Ames, G. W. Anderson, *Archer*, Arnell, D. R. Ashley, J. M. Ashley, *Axtell*, Baldwin, Banks, *Barnes*, *Barnum*, Beaman, Benjamin, W. J. Blackburn, A. Blair, Boyden, *Boyer*, *Brooks*, Broomall, Buckley, R. R. Butler, Callis, *Chanler*, Churchill, R. W. Clarke, Corley, Covode, Dawes, Delano, N. F. Dixon, G. M. Dodge, Driggs, Edwards, T. D. Eliot, J. T. Elliott, W. C. Fields, *Getz*, *Glossbrenner*, Gove, J. A. Griswold, *Grover*, *Haight*, Halsey. A. C. Harding, Heaton, *J. Hotchkiss*, C. D. Hubbard, *R. D. Hubbard*, Hulburd, Jenckes, *J. A. Johnson*, A. H. Jones, *T. L. Jones*, Judd, Julian, *Kerr*, Ketcham, Kitchen, Laflin, Lash, G. V. Lawrence, Mallory, Marvin, *J. R. McCormick*, McKee, Mercur, Moorhead, Newsham, Norris, H. E. Paine, Perham, *C. E. Phelps*, C. W. Pierce, F. A. Pike, Plants, Poland, Pomeroy, H. Price, *Pruyn*, Raum, Schenck, Scofield, Spalding, Starkweather, T. E. Stewart, *F. Stone*, Stover, *Taber*, C. N. Taylor, Trowbridge, Twichell, Van Aernam, *Van Auken*, B. Van Horn, H. Ward, W. B. Washburn, Welker, Whittemore, J. F. Wilson, *F. Wood*—100.

The bill was ordered engrossed and read a third time, and passed finally—yeas 121, nays 60 (not voting 41), as follow:

YEAS—Messrs. Allison, Ames, G. W. Anderson, Arnell, D. R. Ashley, J. M. Ashley, *Axtell*, Baldwin, Banks, *Barnum*, Beaman, Benjamin, Benton, W. J. Blackburn, Blaine, A. Blair, Boyden, *Boyer*, *Brooks*, Broomall, Buckley, Callis, *Chanler*, Churchill, R. W. Clarke, S. Clarke, Clift, Corley, Cornell, Cullom, Dawes, Delano, N. F. Dixon, G. M. Dodge, Driggs, Eckley, T. D. Eliot, J. T. Elliott, Ferriss, T. W. Ferry, W. C. Fields, Garfield, *Getz*, *Glossbrenner*, Gove, J. A. Griswold, Halsey, A. C. Harding, Heaton, Higby, J. Hill, Hooper, *J. Hotchkiss*, C. D. Hubbard, *R. D. Hubbard*, Hulburd, Jenckes, A. H. Jones, Judd, Julian, F. W. Kellogg, Kelsey, Ketcham, Kitchen, Koontz, Laflin, Lash, G. V. Lawrence, J. Lynch, Marvin, Maynard, McKee, Mercur, G. F. Miller, W. Moore, Moorhead, Morrell, Mullins, Myers, Newcomb, Newsham, Norris, O'Neill, H. E. Paine, Perham, Peters, Pettis, *C. E. Phelps*, Plants, Poland, Pomeroy, H. Price, Raum, Robertson, *Robinson*, Roots, P. Sawyer, Schenck, Scofield, Shellabarger, W. C. Smith, Spalding, Starkweather, T. E. Stewart, Stover, *Taber*, C. N. Taylor, Trowbridge, Twichell, C. Upson, Van Aernam, B. Van Horn, R. T. Van Horn, H. Ward, C. C. Washburn, W. B. Washburn, Welker, Whittemore, T. Williams, J. F. Wilson, Windom—121.

NAYS—Messrs. *Archer*, Jehu Baker, Beatty, *Beck*, C. C. Bowen, Bromwell, *Burr*, B. F. Butler, R. R. Butler, Cake, A. Cobb, Coburn, B. C. Cook, Covode, Deweese, Donnelly, Eggleston, Ela, *Eldredge*, Farnsworth, *Fox*, French, *J. S. Golladay*, Goss, *Grover*, *Haight*, Hawkins, *Holman*, B. F. Hopkins, *Humphrey*, Hunter, Ingersoll, *J. A. Johnson*, *T. L. Jones*, Kelley, *Kerr*, *Knott*, W. Lawrence, Loughridge, *Marshall*, *McCormick*, *Mungen*, *Niblack*, Nunn, Orth, F. A. Pike, *L. W. Ross*, Shanks, A. F. Stevens, Stokes, *F. Stone*, Taffe, F. Thomas, *Tift*, *Van Trump*, H. D. Washburn, W. Williams, J. T. Wilson, *F. Wood*, *P. M. B. Young*—60.

IN SENATE.

February 26—The bill was reported back from the Committee on Finance, amended so as to read as follows:

AN ACT relating to the public debt.

Be it enacted, &c., That in order to remove any doubt as to the purpose of the Government to discharge all just obligations to the public creditors, and to settle conflicting questions and interpretations of the laws by virtue of which such obligations have been contracted, it is hereby provided and declared, that the faith of the United States is solemnly pledged to the payment in coin, or its equivalent, of all the obligations of the United States, except in cases where the law authorizing the issue of any such obligation has expressly provided that the same may be paid in lawful money or other currency than gold and silver.

SEC. 2. That any contract hereafter made specifically payable in coin, and the consideration of which may be a loan of coin, or a sale of property, or the rendering of labor or service of any kind, the price of which, as carried into the contract, may have been adjusted on the basis of the coin value thereof at the time of such sale or the rendering of such service or labor, shall be legal and valid, and may be enforced according to its terms.

February 27—Mr. HENDERSON moved to amend the first clause of the second section by making it read as follows:

That any contract hereafter made specifically payable in coin shall be legal and valid, and may be enforced according to its terms.

Which was not agreed to—yeas 10, nays 35, as follow:

YEAS—Messrs. Cole, Conkling, Corbett, *Dixon*, Fessenden, Henderson, Pomeroy, Ross, Stewart, Trumbull—10.

NAYS—Messrs. Abbott, Anthony, Cameron, Cattell, Chandler, Conness, Cragin, *Davis*, *Doolittle*, Drake, Edmunds, Ferry, Frelinghuysen, Harlan, Howe, Kellogg, *McCreery*, McDonald, Morgan, Morrill of Vermont, Morton, Nye, Osborn, Patterson of New Hampshire, Ramsey, Rice, Sawyer, Sherman, Sumner, Thayer, Wade, Welch, Willey, Williams, Wilson—35.

Mr. BAYARD moved to strike out the second section, which was not agreed to—yeas 7, nays 36, as follow:

YEAS—Messrs. Chandler, Cole, *Davis*, *Doolittle*, Fowler, Howe, Wade—7.

NAYS—Messrs. Abbott, Anthony, Cameron, Cattell, Conkling, Conness, Corbett, Cragin, *Dixon*, Drake, Edmunds, Ferry, Fessenden, Frelinghuysen, Harlan, Kellogg, *McCreery*, McDonald, Morgan, Morrill of Vermont, Morton, Nye, Osborn, Patterson of New Hampshire, Pomeroy, Ramsey, Ross, Sherman, Stewart, Sumner, Thayer, Trumbull, Welch, Willey, Williams, Wilson—36.

Mr. HENDERSON moved to amend the first section so as to make it read as follows:

That it is hereby provided and declared that the faith of the United States is solemnly pledged to an early resumption of specie payment by the Government, in order that conflicting questions touching the mode of discharging the public indebtedness may be settled and that the same may be paid in gold.

Which was not agreed to—yeas 8, nays 34, as follow:

YEAS—Messrs. Cole, *Davis*, Henderson, Morton, Pomeroy, Robertson, Ross, Spencer—8.

NAYS—Messrs. Anthony, Cattell, Conkling, Conness, Corbett, Cragin, *Dixon*, Edmunds, Ferry, Fessenden, Frelinghuysen, Grimes, Harlan, Harris, Howard, McDonald, Morgan, Morrill of Maine, Morrill of Vt., Nye, Osborn, Patterson of New Hampshire, Sawyer, Sherman, Stewart, Sumner, Thayer, Tipton, Wade, Warner, Welch, Willey, Williams, Wilson—30.

The bill as amended by the report of the Committee on Finance, was then passed—yeas 30, nays 16, as follow:

YEAS—Messrs. Abbott, Cattell, Conkling, Conness, Corbett, Cragin, *Dixon*, Edmunds, Ferry, Fessenden, Frelinghuysen, Grimes, Harlan, Harris, Howard, Morgan, Morrill of Maine, Morrill of Vermont, Nye, Patterson of New Hampshire, Robertson, Sawyer, Sherman, Stewart, Sumner, Thayer, Tipton, Willey, Williams, Wilson—30.

NAYS—Messrs. Cole, *Davis*, *Doolittle*, Fowler, Henderson, *Hendricks*, *McCreery*, McDonald, Morton, Osborn, *Patterson* of Tennessee, Pomeroy, Ross, Spencer, Wade, Welch—16.

The title was amended so as to read "An act in relation to the public debt."

March 2—The House non-concurred in the amendments of the Senate, and a committee of conference (Messrs. SCHENCK, ALLISON, and NIBLACK) appointed.

Same day—The Senate insisted on its amendments, and appointed Messrs. SHERMAN, WILLIAMS, and MORTON a conference committee.

March 3—The committee reported the following bill:

AN ACT to strengthen the public credit, and relating to contracts for the payment of coin.

Be it enacted &c., That in order to remove any doubt as to the purpose of the Government to discharge all just obligations to the public creditors, and to settle conflicting questions and interpretations of the laws by virtue of which such obligations have been contracted, it is hereby provided and declared, that the faith of the United States is solemnly pledged to the payment in coin, or its equivalent, of all the obligations of the United States not bearing interest, known as United States notes, and of all the interest-bearing obligations of the United States, except in cases where the law authorizing the issue of any such obligation has expressly provided that the same may be paid in lawful money or other currency than gold and silver. But none of said interest-bearing obligations not already due shall be redeemed or paid before maturity, unless at such time United States notes shall be convertible into coin at the option of the holder, or unless at such time bonds of the United States bearing a lower rate of interest than the bonds to be redeemed can be sold at par in coin. And the United States also solemnly pledges its faith to make provision at the earliest practicable period for the redemption of the United States notes in coin.

SEC. 2. That any contract hereafter made specifically payable in coin, and the consideration of which may be a loan of coin, or a sale of property, or the rendering of labor or service of any kind, the price of which, as carried into the contract, may have been adjusted on the basis of the coin value thereof at the time of such sale or the rendering of such service or labor, shall be legal and valid, and may be enforced according to its terms; and on the trial of a suit brought for the enforcement of any such contract, proof of the real consideration may be given.

Same day—The Senate agreed to the report—yeas 31, nays 24, as follows:

YEAS—Messrs. Abbott, Anthony, Cameron, Cattell, Chandler, Conkling, Conness, Corbett, Cragin, *Dixon*, Drake, Edmunds, Ferry, Fessenden, Frelinghuysen, Harris, Howard, Morgan, Morrill of Maine, Morrill of Vermont, Nye, Patterson of New Hampshire, Ramsey, Sherman, Stewart, Sumner, Trumbull, Van Winkle, Warner, Willey, Williams—31.

NAYS—Messrs. *Bayard*, *Buckalew*, Cole, *Davis*, *Doolittle*, Fowler, *Hendricks*, Kellogg, *McCreery*, McDonald, Morton, *Norton*, Osborn, *Patterson* of Tennessee, Robertson, Ross, Sawyer, Spencer, Sprague, Thayer, Tipton, *Vickers*, Wade, *Whyte*—24.

Same day—The HOUSE adopted the report—yeas 117, nays 59 (not voting 48), as follow:

YEAS—Messrs. Allison, Ames, Arnell, D. R. Ashley, J. M. Ashley, *Axtell*, A. H. Bailey, *Barnes*, *Barnum*, Beaman, Benjamin, Benton, Bingham, A. Blair, Boutwell, C. C. Bowen, Boyden, *Brooks*, Broomall, Buckley, Cake, Callis, *Chanler*, Churchill, R. W. Clarke, S. Clarke, Clift, Corley, Cornell, Cullom, Dawes, Dickey, N. F. Dixon, G. M. Dodge, Eckley, T. D. Eliot, J. T. Elliott, Ferriss, T. W. Ferry, W. C. Fields, Garfield, Gove, Griswold, Halsey, Haughey, Heaton, Higby, J. Hill, Hooper, *J. Hotchkiss*, *R. D. Hubbard*, Hulburd, Jenckes, A. H. Jones, Judd, Julian, F. W. Kellogg, Kelsey, Ketcham, Laflin, Lash, G. V. Lawrence, Lincoln, Logan, J. Lynch, R. Mallory, Marvin, Maynard, McCarthy, McKee, Mercur, G. F. Miller, W. Moore, Moorhead, Morrell, Mullins, Myers, Newsham, Norris, O'Neill, H. E. Paine, Perham, Peters, *C. E. Phelps*, Pile, Plants, Poland, H. Price, Prince, Raum, Robertson, *Robinson*, Roots, P. Sawyer, Schenck, Scofield, Shellabarger, W. C. Smith, Starkweather, A. F. Stevens, T. E. Stewart, Stover, Sypher, *Taber*, C. N. Taylor, Trowbridge, Twichell, Upson, B. Van Horn, Van Wyck, H. Ward, C. C. Washburn, W. B. Washburn, Welker, Whittemore, J. F. Wilson, Woodbridge—117.

NAYS—Messrs. *G. M. Adams*, *Archer*, Jehu Baker, Beatty, *Beck*, *Boyer*, Bromwell, *Burr*, B. F. Butler, R. R. Butler, *Cary*, Cobb, Coburn, B. C. Cook, Deweese, Dockery, Donnelly, Eggleston, *Eldredge*, Farnsworth, *Getz*, *J. S. Golladay*, Goss, *Haight*, A. C. Harding, Hawkins, *Holman*, B. F. Hopkins, Hunter, Ingersoll, *J. A. Johnson*, *T. L. Jones*, *Kerr*, *Knott*, W. Lawrence, *Marshall*, *McCormick*, *McCullough*, *Mungen*, *Niblack*, Orth, *Pruyn*, *Randall*, *Ross*, Shanks, *Sitgreaves*, *F. Stone*, F. Thomas, *Tift*, *L. S. Trimble*, Van Aernam, *Van Auken*, *Van Trump*, H. D. Washburn, W. Williams, S. F. Wilson, *F. Wood*, *Woodward*, *P. M. B. Young*—59.

The President, ANDREW JOHNSON, "pocketed" the bill, it having been presented to him for his approval March 3, 1869, the day of the adjournment of Congress.

The "Public Credit Act" of the Forty-First Congress.

Forty-First Congress—First Session.

This bill became a law March 18, 1869, being the first act approved by President GRANT:

Be it enacted, &c., That in order to remove any doubt as to the purpose of the Government to discharge all just obligations to the public creditors, and to settle conflicting questions and interpretations of the law by virtue of which such obligations have been contracted, it is hereby provided and declared, that the faith of the United States is solemnly pledged to the payment in coin or its equivalent of all the obligations of the United States not bearing interest, known as United States notes, and of all the interest bearing obligations of the United States, except in cases where the law authorizing the issue of any such obligation has expressly provided that the same may be paid in lawful money or other currency than gold and silver. But none of said interest-bearing obligations not already due shall be redeemed or paid before maturity unless at such time United States notes shall be convertible into coin at the option of the holder, or unless at such time bonds of the United States bearing a lower rate of interest than the bonds to be redeemed can be sold at par in coin. And the United States also solemnly pledges its faith to make provision at the earliest practicable period for the redemption of the United States notes in coin.

IN HOUSE.

1869, March 12—Mr. SCHENCK introduced the bill passed at third session of Fortieth Congress, and "pocketed" by President JOHNSON (for which see proceedings above).

Mr. BURR moved that it be laid on the table; which was disagreed to—yeas 54, nays 85, not voting 54.

Mr. ALLISON moved to strike out the second section as printed before, which was agreed to—yeas 87, nays 56 (not voting 50), as follow:

YEAS—Messrs. Allison, Ames, *Archer*, A. H. Bailey, Beaman, Beatty, *Beck*, *Biggs*, Bingham, *Bird*, C. C. Bowen, *Burr*, B. F. Butler, Cake, Cessna, A. Cobb, Coburn, Cullom, N. Davis, Deweese, *Dickinson*, Dyer, *Eldredge*, Farnsworth, Ferriss, T. W. Ferry, Fitch, *Getz*, *Golladay*, *Haldeman*, E. Hale, *Hamill*, Hawkins, Hay, *Hoag*, *Holman*, Hooper, B. F. Hopkins, Ingersoll, Jenckes, *T. L. Jones*, Kelsey, *Kerr*, Knapp, *Knott*, W. Lawrence, Loughridge, J. Lynch, *Marshall*, *Mayham*, *McCormick*, *McNeely*, *Moffet*, J. H. Moore, S. P. Morrill, *Mungen*, *Niblack*, O'Neill, Orth, *Reading*, P. Sawyer, Scofield, Shanks, W. C. Smith, J. E. Stevenson, *Stiles*, *F. Stone*, Stoughton, *Strader*, *Swann*, *Sweeney*, Taffe, *L. S. Trimble*, Tyner, R. T. Van Horn, W. B. Washburn, Welker, *E. Wells*, Wilkinson, C. W. Willard, W. Williams, *E. M. Wilson*, J. T. Wilson, Winans, *Winchester*, Witcher, *Woodward*—87.

NAYS—Messrs. Armstrong, Asper, *Axtell*, Banks, Benjamin, Bennett, A. Blair, Boles, Boyd, Buffinton, Burdett, R. R. Butler, Churchill, C. L. Cobb, Conger, Cowles, Dawes, Dockery, Donley, Finkelnburg, Fisher, Garfield, Gilfillan, Heaton, G. F. Hoar, *J. A. Johnson*, A. H. Jones, Judd, Julian, Ketcham, Laflin, Lash, Logan, McGrew, Mercur, W. Moore, Packard, H. E. Paine, Palmer, Poland, Pomeroy, Prosser, Roots, Sanford, Sargent, Schenck, P. Sheldon, John A. Smith, Stokes, Strickland, Tanner, Twichell, H. Ward, C. C. Washburn, W. A. Wheeler, Whittemore—56.

The bill was engrossed and read a third time—yeas 93, nays 48, not voting 52; and was passed—yeas 97, nays 47 (not voting 49), as follow:

YEAS—Messrs. Allison, Ambler, Ames, Armstrong, Arnell, Asper, *Axtell*, A. H. Bailey, Banks, Beaman, Benjamin, Bennett, Bingham, A. Blair, Boles, Boyd, Buffinton, Burdett, Cessna, Churchill, C. L. Cobb, B. C. Cook, Conger, Cowles, Cullom, Dawes, Donley, Duval, Dyer, Farnsworth, Ferriss, T. W. Ferry, Finkelnburg, Fisher, Fitch, Gilfillan, E. Hale, J. B. Hawley, Heaton, G. F. Hoar, Hooper, G. W. Hotchkiss, Jenckes, A. H. Jones, Judd, Julian, Kelsey, Ketcham, Knapp, Laflin, Lash, W. Lawrence, J. Lynch, Maynard, McCrary, McGrew, Mercur, J. H. Moore, W. Moore, S. P. Morrill, Negley, O'Neill, Packard, H. E. Paine, Palmer, D. Phelps, Poland, Pomeroy, Prosser, Roots, Sanford, Sargent, P. Sawyer, Schenck, Scofield, P. Sheldon, John A. Smith, W. C. Smith, W. Smyth, Stokes, Stoughton, Strickland, Tanner, Tillman, Twichell, W. H. Upson, R. T. Van Horn, H. Ward, C. C. Washburn, W. B. Washburn, Welker, W. A. Wheeler, Whittemore, Wilkinson, C. W. Willard, W. Williams, Winans—97.

NAYS—Messrs. *Archer*, Beatty, *Beck*, *Biggs*, *Bird*, *Burr*, B. F. Butler, R. R. Butler, A. Cobb, Coburn, *Crebs*, Deweese, *Dickinson*, *Eldredge*, *Getz*, *J. S. Golladay*, Hawkins, *Holman*, B. F. Hopkins, *J. A. Johnson*, *T. L. Jones*, *Kerr*, *Knott*, *Marshall*, *Mayham*, *McCormick*, *McNeely*, *Moffet*, *Mungen*, *Niblack*, Orth, *Reading*, *Reeves*, *Rice*, Shanks, *J. S. Smith*, *Stiles*, *F. Stone*, *Strader*, *Sweeney*, Taffe, *L. S. Trimble*, Tyner, *Van Trump*, J. T. Wilson, *Winchester*, *Woodward*—47.

IN SENATE.

March 9—The following bill was reported from the Committee on Finance (S. 56):

A BILL to strengthen the public credit, and relating to contracts for the payment of coin.

Be it enacted, &c., That in order to remove any doubt as to the purpose of the Government to discharge all just obligations to the public creditors, and to settle conflicting questions and interpretations of the laws by virtue of which such obligations have been contracted, it is hereby provided and declared, that the faith of the United States is solemnly pledged to the payment in coin, or its equivalent, of all the interest-bearing obligations of the United States, except in cases where the law authorizing the issue of any such obligation has expressly provided that the same may be paid in lawful money or other currency than gold and silver: *Provided, however*, That before any of said interest-bearing obligations not already due shall mature or be paid before maturity, the obligations not bearing interest, known as United States notes, shall be made convertible into coin at the option of the holder.

SEC. 2. That any contract hereafter made specifically payable in coin, and the consideration of which may be a loan of coin, or a sale of property, or the rendering of labor or service of any kind, the price of which, as carried into the contract, may have been adjusted on the basis of the coin value thereof at the time of such sale or the rendering of such service or labor, shall be legal and valid, and may be enforced according to its terms.

March 11—Mr. HOWARD moved to insert the word "written" before "contract" in the 2d section where it first occurs; which was agreed to.

Mr. SUMNER moved to strike out the 2d section; which was agreed to—yeas 28, nays 15, as follow:

YEAS—Messrs. *Bayard*, Boreman, Carpenter, *Casserly*, Conkling, Corbett, Cragin, Ferry, Fessenden, Gilbert, Harris, Kellogg, McDonald, *Norton*, Nye, Pratt, Robertson, Sawyer, Schurz, Scott, Sprague, Stewart, *Stockton*, Sumner, *Thurman*, Trumbull, *Vickers*, Wilson—28.

NAYS—Messrs. Abbott, Anthony, Brownlow, Drake, Grimes, Hamlin, Morrill, Morton, Osborn, Patterson, Ramsey, Ross, Sherman, Warner, Williams—15.

Mr. THURMAN moved to add to the 1st section the following proviso:

Provided, That nothing herein contained shall apply to the obligations commonly called five-twenty bonds.

Which was not agreed to—yeas 12, nays 31, as follow:

YEAS—Messrs. *Bayard*, Boreman, *Casserly*, Morton, *Norton*, Osborn, Pratt, Ross, Sprague, *Stockton*, *Thurman*, *Vickers*—12.

NAYS—Messrs. Abbott, Anthony, Brownlow, Carpenter, Conkling, Corbett, Cragin, Drake, Fenton, Ferry, Gilbert, Grimes, Hamlin, Harris, Kellogg, McDonald, Morrill, Nye, Patterson, of N. H., Ramsey, Sawyer, Schurz, Scott, Sherman, Stewart, Sumner, Tipton, Trumbull, Warner, Willliams, Wilson—31.

Mr. MORTON moved to strike from section 1st the words, "authorizing the issue of any such obligation;" which was not agreed to—yeas 14, nays 32, as follow:

YEAS—Messrs. *Bayard*, Brownlow, *Casserly*, Morton, *Norton*, Pomeroy, Pratt, Robertson, Ross, Spencer, Sprague, *Stockton*, *Thurman*, *Vickers*—14.

NAYS—Messrs. Abbott, Anthony, Boreman, Carpenter, Cattell, Corbett, Cragin, Drake, Fenton, Ferry, Fessenden, Gilbert, Grimes, Hamlin, Howard, Howe, Morrill, Patterson, Ramsey, Sawyer, Schurz, Scott, Sherman, Stewart, Sumner, Thayer, Tipton, Warner, Willey, Williams, Wilson, Yates—32.

March 15—This bill was then laid aside and the House bill (H. R. 7) taken up; and it passed the SENATE—yeas 42, nays 13, as follow:

YEAS—Messrs. Abbott, Anthony, Boreman, Brownlow, Cameron, Cattell, Chandler, Conkling, Corbett, Cragin, Drake, Edmunds, Fenton, Ferry, Fessenden, Gilbert, Grimes, Harris, Howard, Kellogg, McDonald, Morrill, Nye, Patterson, of N. H., Pool, Pratt, Ramsey, Robertson, Sawyer, Schurz, Scott, Sherman, Stewart, Sumner, Thayer, Tipton, Trumbull, Warner, Willey, Williams, Wilson, Yates—42.

NAYS—Messrs. *Bayard*, Carpenter, *Casserly*, Cole, *Garrett Davis*, Morton, Osborn, Rice, Ross, Spencer, *Stockton*, *Thurman*, *Vickers*—13.

The Resumption Act of the Forty-Third Congress.

Forty-Third Congress—Second Session.

IN SENATE.

1874, Dec. 21—MR. SHERMAN, from the Committee on Finance, reported the following bill:

An act to provide for the resumption of specie payments.

Be it enacted, &c., That the Secretary of the Treasury is hereby authorized and required, as rapidly as practicable, to cause to be coined at the mints of the United States, silver coins of the denominations of ten, twenty-five, and fifty cents, of standard value, and to issue them in redemption of an equal number and amount of fractional currency of similar denominations, or, at his discretion, he may issue such silver coins through the mints, the sub-treasuries, public depositaries, and post-offices of the United States; and, upon such issue, he is hereby authorized and required to redeem an equal amount of such fractional currency, until the whole amount of such fractional currency outstanding shall be redeemed.

SEC. 2. That so much of section three thousand five hundred and twenty-four of the Revised Statutes of the United States as provides for a charge of one-fifth of one per centum for converting standard gold bullion into coin is hereby repealed, and hereafter no charge shall be made for that service.

SEC. 3. That section five thousand one hundred and seventy-seven of the Revised Statutes of the United States, limiting the aggregate amount of circulating-notes of national banking-associations, be, and is hereby, repealed; and each existing banking-association may increase its circulating-notes in accordance with existing law without respect to said aggregate limit; and new banking-associations may be organized in accordance with existing law without respect to said aggregate limit; and the provisions of law for the withdrawal and redistribution of national bank currency among the several States and Territories are hereby repealed. And whenever and so often, as circulating-notes shall be issued to any such banking-association, so increasing its capital or circulating-notes, or so newly organized as aforesaid, it shall be the duty of the Secretary of the Treasury to redeem the legal-tender United States notes in excess only of three hundred million of dollars, to the amount of eighty per centum of the sum of national-bank notes so issued to any such banking-association as aforesaid, and to continue such redemption as such circulating-notes are issued until there shall be outstanding the sum of three hundred million dollars of such legal-tender United States notes, and no more. And on and after the first day of January, anno Domini eighteen hundred and seventy-nine, the Secretary of the Treasury shall redeem, in coin, the United States legal-tender notes then outstanding on their presentation for redemption, at the office of the assistant treasurer of the United States in the city of New York, in sums of not less than fifty dollars. And to enable the Secretary of the Treasury to prepare and provide for the redemption in this act authorized or required, he is authorized to use any surplus revenues, from time to time, in the Treasury not otherwise appropriated, and to issue, sell, and dispose of, at not less than par, in coin, either of the descriptions of bonds of the United States described in the act of Congress approved July fourteenth, eighteen hundred and seventy, entitled, "An act to authorize the refunding of the national debt," with like qualities, privileges, and exemptions, to the extent necessary to carry this act into full effect, and to use the proceeds thereof for the purposes aforesaid. And all provisions of law inconsistent with the provisions of this act are hereby repealed.

Which was read and passed to a second reading.

Dec. 22—The bill was taken up—yeas 39, nays 18—and read a second time and considered as in Committee of the Whole.

Mr. THURMAN moved to add as a new section:

SEC. 4. That from and after June 30, 1875, one-twentieth part of the customs duties shall be payable in United States legal-tender notes, or in national-bank notes; and after June 30, 1876, one-tenth, and after June 30, 1877, one-fifth part thereof may be so paid.

Mr. BOGY moved to amend the amendment by substituting for it the following: That on and after July 1, 1875, duties on imports may be paid in legal-tender notes or coin, at the option of the importer.

Which was disagreed to.

Mr. THURMAN'S amendment was then disagreed to—yeas 16, nays 33, not voting 24, as follow:

YEAS—Messrs. *Bayard*, *Bogy*, *Cooper*, *Davis*, *Dennis*, *Goldthwaite*, *Hager*, *Hamilton* of Maryland, *Johnston* of Virginia, *McCreery*, *Merrimon*, *Norwood*, *Ransom*, *Saulsbury*, *Stevenson*, *Thurman*—16.

NAYS—Messrs. Allison, Anthony, Boutwell, Cameron of Pennsylvania, Carpenter, Clayton, Cragin, Edmunds, FENTON, Ferry of Michigan, Flanagan, Frelinghuysen, HAMILTON of Texas, Hamlin, Harvey, Howe, Ingalls, Logan, Morrill of Maine, Morrill of Vermont, Morton, Patterson, Pease, Pratt, Sargent, SCHURZ, Scott, Sherman, Spencer, Washburn, West, Windom, Wright —33.

ABSENT—Messrs. Alcorn, Boreman, Brownlow, Buckingham, Chandler, Conkling, Conover, Dorsey, Ferry of Connecticut, Gilbert, *Gordon*, Hitchcock, Jones of Nevada, *Kelly*, Lewis, Mitchell, Oglesby, Ramsey, Robertson, Sprague, Stewart, *Stockton*, TIPTON, Wadleigh—24.

Mr. SCHURZ offered the following amendment, to be inserted in section 3, after the words "and no more:"

Provided, That not less than $2,000,000 of legal-tender notes shall be retired monthly by the Secretary of the Treasury, and that the legal-tender notes so retired shall be canceled and destroyed.

Which was disagreed to—yeas 6, nays 44, not voting 23, as follow:

YEAS—Messrs. *Bayard*, FENTON, *Hager*, *Hamilton* of Maryland, HAMILTON of Texas, SCHURZ—6.

NAYS—Messrs. Allison, Anthony, *Bogy*, Boutwell, Cameron of Pennsylvania, Carpenter, Chandler, Clayton, *Cooper*, Cragin, *Davis*, *Dennis*, Edmunds, Ferry of Michigan, Flanagan, Frelinghuysen, *Goldthwaite*, Hamlin, Harvey, Howe, Ingalls, *Johnston* of Virginia, Logan, *Merrimon*, Morrill of Maine, Morton, Oglesby, Patterson, Pease, Pratt, Ramsey, *Ransom*, Sargent, *Saulsbury*, Scott, Sherman, Spencer, Sprague, *Stevenson*, *Thurman*, TIPTON, Washburn, West, Wright —44.

ABSENT—Messrs. Alcorn, Boreman, Brownlow, Buckingham, Conkling, Conover, Dorsey, Ferry of Connecticut, Gilbert, *Gordon*, Hitchcock, Jones of Nevada, *Kelly*, Lewis, *McCreery*, Mitchell, Morrill of Vermont, *Norwood*, Robertson, Stewart, *Stockton*, Wadleigh, Windom—23.

Mr. HAMILTON, of Texas, offered the following amendment: In section 1, after the word "them" insert "at their current value;" and after the words "redemption of" strike out the words "an equal number and amount of;" so as to read:

And to issue them at their current value in redemption of fractional currency of similar denominations.

Which was disagreed to—yeas 3, nays 40, not voting 30, as follow:

YEAS—Messrs. *Cooper*, HAMILTON of Texas, TIPTON—3.

NAYS—Messrs. Allison, Anthony, *Bogy*, Boutwell, Carpenter, Chandler, Clayton, Cragin, *Dennis*, Edmunds, FENTON, Ferry of Michigan, Flanagan, Frelinghuysen, *Goldthwaite*, *Hager*, Hamlin, Harvey, Howe, Ingalls, *Johnston* of Virginia, Logan, *Merrimon*, Morrill of Maine, Morton, Oglesby, Patterson, Pease, Pratt, Ramsey, Sargent, *Saulsbury*, Scott, Sherman, Spencer, *Stevenson*, *Thurman*, Washburn, West, Wright —40.

ABSENT—Messrs. Alcorn, *Bayard*, Boreman, Brownlow, Buckingham, Cameron of Pennsylvania, Conkling, Conover, *Davis*, Dorsey, Ferry of Connecticut, Gilbert, *Gordon*, *Hamilton* of Maryland, Hitchcock, Jones of Nevada, *Kelly*, Lewis, *McCreery*, Mitchell, Morrill of Vermont, *Norwood*, *Ransom*, Robertson, SCHURZ, Sprague, Stewart, *Stockton*, Wadleigh, Windom—30.

The bill was then passed—yeas 32, nays 14, not voting 27, as follow:

YEAS—Messrs. Allison, Anthony, Boutwell, Carpenter, Chandler, Clayton, Cragin, Edmunds, Fenton, Ferry of Michigan, Flanagan, Frelinghuysen, Hamlin, Harvey, Howe, Ingalls, Logan, Morrill of Maine, Morton, Oglesby, Patterson, Pease, Pratt, Ramsey, Sargent, SCHURZ, Scott, Sherman, Spencer, Washburn, West, Wright —32.

NAYS—Messrs. *Bogy*, *Cooper*, *Davis*, *Dennis*, *Goldthwaite*, *Hager*, HAMILTON of Texas, *Johnston* of Virginia, *Merrimon*, *Ransom*, Sprague, *Stevenson*, *Thurman*, TIPTON—14.

ABSENT—Messrs. Alcorn, *Bayard*, Boreman, Brownlow, Buckingham, Cameron of Pennsylvania, Conkling, Conover, Dorsey, Ferry of Connecticut, Gilbert, *Gordon*, *Hamilton* of Maryland, Hitchcock, Jones of Nevada, *Kelly*, Lewis, *McCreery*, Mitchell, Morrill of Vermont, *Norwood*, Robertson, *Saulsbury*, Stewart, *Stockton*, Wadleigh, Windom—27.

IN HOUSE.

December 23—Mr. MAYNARD moved that the bill be made a special order for January 7, 1875, to the exclusion of all other orders, and from day to day till disposed of; which was agreed to by unanimous consent.

1875, January 7—Mr. MAYNARD called the previous question upon the third reading and passage of the bill, which was seconded—yeas 100, nays 91, and the main question ordered—yeas 124, nays 107, not voting 57, as follow:

YEAS—Messrs. Albert, Averill, Barber, Barrere, Barry, Bass, Begole, Biery, Bradley, H. C. Burchard, Burleigh, Burrows, R. R. Butler, Cain, Carpenter, Cason, Cessna, Clayton, Clements, S. A. Cobb, Corwin, Cotton, Crooke, Crounse, Curtis, Danford, Donnan, Duell, Farwell, Fort, J. C. Freeman, Frye, Garfield, Gunckel, E. Hale, Harmer, H. H. Harrison, Hathorn, J. B. Hawley, Hays, G. W. Hazelton, J. W. Hazelton, Hodges, Hooper, Houghton, Howe, Hunter, Hynes, Kasson, Killinger, Lamport, Loughridge, Lowe, J. R. Lynch, Martin, Maynard, McCrary, A. S. McDill, J. W. McDill, MacDougall, McNulta, Monroe, Negley, O'Neill, Orr, Orth, Packard, Packer, Page, R. C. Parsons, Pelham, Pendleton, Pike, T. C. Platt, Poland, Pratt, Purman, W. H. Ray, Richmond, E. H. Roberts, J. W. Robinson, Rusk, Sawyer, H. B. Sayler, Scofield, I. W. Scudder, Sener, Sessions, Shanks, Sheats, L. D. Shoemaker, W. B. Small, Smart, A. H. Smith, H. B. Smith, J. A. Smith, J. Q. Smith, Snyder, Sprague, Stanard, St. John, Strawbridge, Sypher, Taylor, C. R. Thomas, C. Y. Thomas, J. M. Thompson, Thornburgh, Todd, Tremain, Tyner, Waldron, A. S. Wallace, J. D. Ward, M. L. Ward, Wheeler, A. White, Whiteley, Wilber, G. Willard, J. M. S. Williams, W. Williams, W. B. Williams, J. Wilson—124.

NAYS—Messrs. *Archer*, *Arthur*, *Ashe*, *Atkins*,

Banning, Beck, H. P. Bell, Berry, Blount, Bowen, Bright, Bromberg, J. Y. Brown, Buffinton, *J. H. Caldwell*, Chittenden, *J. B. Clark, jr.*, F. Clarke, *Clymer, Comingo, Cook, Cox, Crittenden, Crossland*, Crutchfield, Dawes, *De Witt*, Eames, *Eldredge*, Field, *Finck, Giddings, Glover*, Gooch, *Gunter*, Hagans, *R. Hamilton, Hancock*, B. W. Harris, *H R. Harris, J. T. Harris, Hatcher*, Havens, J. R. Hawley, Hendee, *Hereford, Herndon*, E. R. Hoar, G. F. Hoar, *Holman*, Hoskins, *Hunton*, Kelley, Kellogg, *Knapp, Lamar, Lamison*, Lansing, W. Lawrence, Lawson, *Leach*, Lowndes, *Magee, Marshall, McLean*, Merriam, *Milliken, Mills, Morrison*, Myers, *Neal, Nesmith, Niblack*, Niles, *H. W. Parker*, I. C. Parker, *Perry*, Pierce, *Randall, Read, W. M. Robbins, M. Sayler, Schell*, H. J. Scudder, Sherwood, *Sloss*, W. A. Smith, *Southard*, Starkweather, *A. H. Stephens, Stone, Storm, Swann*, W. Townsend, *R. B. Vance, E. Wells, Whitehead, Whitehouse, Whitthorne*, C. W. Willard, *Willie, E. K. Wilson, Wolfe, F. Wood*, Woodworth, *J. D. Young, P. M. B. Young*—107.

NOT VOTING—Messrs. *G. M. Adams*, Albright, *Barnum, Bland, Buckner*, Bundy, B. F. Butler, Cannon, A. Clark, jr., C. L. Cobb, Coburn, Conger, *Creamer*, Darrall, *John J. Davis*, Dobbins, Dunnell, *Durham, Eden*, Foster, R. S. Hale, Hersey, Hubbell, Hurlbut, Hyde, *Kendall*, B. Lewis, Lofland, *Luttrell*, McKee, *Mitchell*, Moore, Morey, Nunn, *O'Brien*, W. W. Phelps, W. A. Phillips, J. H. Platt, jr., *C. N. Potter*, Rainey, Ransier, Rapier, *W. R. Roberts, J. C. Robinson*, S. Ross, *J. G. Schumacker*, Sheldon, Sloan, G. L. Smith, *Speer, Standiford*, Stowell, Strait, *Waddell*, Walls, C. G. Williams, J. M. Wilson—57.

The question being taken on the passage of the bill, it was decided in the affirmative—yeas 136, nays 98, not voting 54, as follow:

YEAS—Messrs. Albert, Averill, Barber, Barrere, Barry, Bass, Begole, Biery, Bradley, H. C. Burchard, Burleigh, Burrows, R. R. Butler, Cain, Carpenter, Cason, Cessna, Chittenden, Clayton, Clements, S. A. Cobb, Corwin, Cotton, Crooke, Crounse, Curtis, Danford, Dobbins, Donnan, Duell, Eames, Farwell, J. C. Freeman, Frye, Garfield, Gunckel, E. Hale, Harmer, H. H. Harrison, Hathorn, J. B. Hawley, Hays, G. W. Hazelton, J. W. Hazelton, Hendee, Hodges, Hooper, Hoskins, Houghton, Howe, Hunter, Hynes, Kasson, Kellogg, Killinger, Lamport, Lansing, W. Lawrence, Loughridge, Lowe, Lowndes, J. R. Lynch, Martin, Maynard, McCrary, A. S. McDill, J. W. McDill, MacDougall, McKee, McNulta, Merriam, Monroe, Moore, Myers, Negley, O'Neill, Orr, Orth, Packard, Packer, Page, R. C. Parsons, Pelham, Pendleton, A. F. Pike, T. C. Platt, Poland, Pratt, Purman, W. H. Ray, Richmond, E. H. Roberts, J. W. Robinson, Rusk, Sawyer, H. B. Sayler, Scofield, I. W. Scudder, Sener, Sessions, Shanks, Sheats, L. D. Shoemaker, W. B. Small, Smart, A. H. Smith, H. B. Smith, J. A. Smith, J. Q. Smith, Sprague, Stanard, Starkweather, St. John, Strawbridge, Taylor, C. R. Thomas, C. Y. Thomas, J. M. Thompson, Thornburgh, Todd, Tremain, Tyner, Waldron, A. S. Wallace, J. D. Ward, M. L. Ward, Wheeler, A. White, Whiteley, Wilber, G. Willard, J. M. S. Williams, W. Williams, W. B. Williams, J. Wilson, J. M. Wilson—136.

NAYS—Messrs. *G. M. Adams, Archer, Arthur, Ashe, Atkins, Banning, Beck, H. P. Bell, Berry, Blount, Bowen, Bright, Bromberg, J. Y Brown*, Buffinton, *J. H. Caldwell, J. B. Clark, jr.*, F. Clarke, *Clymer, Comingo, Cook, Cox, Crittenden, Crossland*, Crutchfield, Dawes, *De Witt, Eldredge*, Field, *Finck, Giddings, Glover*, Gooch, *Gunter*, Hagans *R. Hamilton, Hancock*, B. W. Harris, *H. R. Harris, J. T. Harris, Hatcher*, Havens, J. R. Hawley, *Hereford, Herndon*, E. R. Hoar, G. F. Hoar, *Holman, Hunton*, Kelley, *Knapp, Lamar, Lamison*, Lawson, *Leach, Magee, Marshall, McLean, Milliken, Mills, Morrison, Neal, Nesmith, Niblack*, Niles, *H. W. Parker*, I. C. Parker, *Perry*, Pierce, *Randall, Read, W. M. Robbins M. Sayler, Schell*, H. J. Scudder, Sherwood, *Sloss*, W. A. Smith, *Southard, A. H. Stephens Stone, Storm, Swann*, W. Townsend, *R. B. Vance, Waddell, Wells, Whitehead, Whitehouse, Whitthorne*, C. W. Willard, *Willie, E. K. Wilson, Wolfe, F. Wood*, Woodworth, *J. D. Young, P. M. B. Young*—98.

NOT VOTING—Messrs. Albright, *Barnum, Bland, Buckner*, Bundy, B. F. Butler, Cannon, A. Clark, jr., C. L. Cobb, Coburn, Conger, Creamer, Darrall, *John J. Davis*, Dunnell, *Durham, Eden*, Fort, Foster, R. S. Hale, Hersey, Hubbell, Hurlbut, Hyde, *Kendall*, B. Lewis, Lofland, *Luttrell, Mitchell*, Morey, Nunn, *O'Brien*, W. W. Phelps, Phillips, J. H. Platt, jr., *C. N. Potter*, Rainey, Ransier, Rapier, *W. R. Roberts, J. C. Robinson*, S. Ross, *J. G. Schumacker*, Sheldon, Sloan, G. L. Smith, Snyder, *Speer, Standiford*, Stowell, Strait, Sypher, Walls, C. G. Williams—54.

Approved January 14, 1875—[See President GRANT'S Message on the subject, in subsequent chapter].

XI.

PROPOSED AMENDMENTS TO THE CONSTITUTION OF THE UNITED STATES—FORTY-FOURTH CONGRESS.

First Session—Forty-Fourth Congress.

The following propositions of amendment were made:

IN SENATE.

1875, December 8—Mr. MORTON proposed the following:

I. The President and Vice-President shall be elected by the direct vote of the people in the manner following: Each State shall be divided into districts, equal in number to the number of Representatives to which the State may be entitled in the Congress, to be composed of contiguous territory, and to be as nearly equal in population as may be; and the person having the highest number of votes in each district for President shall receive the vote of that district, which shall count one presidential vote.

II. The person having the highest number of votes for President in a State shall receive two presidential votes from the State at large.

III. The person having the highest number of presidential votes in the United States shall be President.

IV. If two persons have the same number of votes in any State, it being the highest number, they shall receive each one presidential vote from the State at large; and if more than two persons shall have each the same number of votes in any State, it being the highest number, no presidential vote shall be counted from the State at large. If more persons than one shall have the same number of votes, it being the highest number in any district, no presidential vote shall be counted from that district.

V. The foregoing provisions shall apply to the election of Vice-President.

VI. The Congress shall have power to provide for holding and conducting the elections of President and Vice-President, and to establish tribunals for the decision of such elections as may be contested.

VII. The States shall be divided into districts by the Legislatures thereof, but the Congress may at any time by law make or alter the same.

1876, January 31—Mr. WRIGHT proposed the following:

After the year eighteen hundred and seventy-six, the President and Vice-President of the United States shall be elected by a direct vote of the people of the several States, and the electors in each State shall have the same qualifications as the electors of the most numerous branch of the State Legislature.

The person receiving the greatest number of votes for President shall be the President, and the person receiving the greatest number of votes for Vice-President shall be the Vice-President; but if two or more persons shall each receive an equal and the greatest number of votes for President, then the House of Representatives shall, from such persons, immediately choose the President; and if two or more persons shall each receive an equal and the greatest number of votes for Vice-President, then the Senate shall, from such persons, immediately choose the Vice-President. In such elections, each House shall vote viva voce, and each member shall have one vote; and the person receiving a majority of the votes cast shall be elected; and, in case of a tie, the presiding officer shall determine it.

The election for President and Vice-President shall be held at the time now provided by law for choosing the electors of such officers, but Congress may prescribe a different time, which shall be the same in all the States; and Congress shall prescribe the manner of holding and conducting such election, and making the returns thereof; and, in case of failure so to do, that duty shall devolve, in the order named, first, on the President of the United States; second on the Legislature of each State within that State; and, third, upon the chief executive of each State within that State.

The returns shall be canvassed at the time and in the manner now provided, or which may be hereafter provided, by the joint rules of the two Houses, or by law, by and in the presence of both Houses of Congress, who shall be the judges (each House voting separately) of the returns and election; but in case the two Houses shall not agree, then the matter of disagreement shall be referred to the Supreme Court of the United States, which shall forthwith decide the same, and such decision shall be final.

January 31—Mr. WRIGHT proposed the following:

The Senate of the United States shall be composed of two members from each State, who shall hereafter be elected by a direct vote of the people thereof for six years; and the electors in each State shall have the same qualifications as the electors of the most numerous branch of the State legislature; but Congress may, by law, provide for conducting and holding the election and canvassing the vote.

March 22—Mr. EDMUNDS proposed the following:

ARTICLE XII.

That the twelfth article of the amendments of the Constitution be, and the same is hereby, abrogated, and in the place thereof the following be, and the same is hereby, ordained and established, namely:

The electors shall meet in their respective States, and vote by ballot for President and Vice-President, one of whom at least shall not be an inhabitant of the same State with themselves; they shall name in their ballots the person voted for as President, and in distinct ballots the person voted for as Vice-President, and they shall make distinct lists of all persons voted for as President, and for all persons voted for as Vice-President, and of the number of votes for each; which lists they shall sign and certify, and transmit sealed to the seat of Government of the United States, directed to the presiding justice of the Supreme Court of the United States. And the Supreme Court, at a time and place to be fixed by law, shall publicly open all the certificates and count the votes, and the person having the greatest number of votes for President, considered by the court to have been lawfully given and certified, shall be President, if such number be a majority of the whole number of electors lawfully appointed; and if no person have such majority, the state of the votes shall be immediately certified to the House of Representatives, and then, from the persons having the highest number, not exceeding three on the list of those voted for as President, the House of Representatives shall choose immediately, by a viva voce vote, the President; but the vote shall be taken by States, the representation from each State having one vote; and if the votes of any State shall not show a majority for any one candidate, the vote of such State shall not be reckoned. A quorum of the House of Representatives for the purpose of such election shall consist of a member or members from two-thirds of the States, and a majority of all the States shall be necessary to a choice; and if, on the first vote, there shall be a failure to elect, further votes shall immediately continue to be taken until a President shall be elected.

And if the House of Representatives shall not choose a President, when the right of choice shall devolve upon them, before the fourth day of March next following, then the Vice-President shall act as President, as in the case of the death or other constitutional disability of the President. The person having the greatest number of votes for Vice-President, to be counted and determined as in case of President as before provided, shall be Vice-President, if such number be a majority of the whole number of electors appointed. And if no person have a majority, then from the two highest numbers on the list, the Senate shall choose a Vice-President; a quorum for the purpose shall consist of two-thirds of the whole number of Senators, and a majority of the whole number shall be necessary to a choice. But no person constitutionally ineligible to the office of President shall be eligible to that of Vice-President of the United States.

SEC. 2. No person holding the office of a Justice of the Supreme Court of the United States shall be eligible to be elected as President or Vice-President until the expiration of two years next after he shall have ceased to be such justice.

PETITION FOR AN AMENDMENT.

1876, January 17—Mr. BOUTWELL presented a memorial of citizens of Massachusetts, praying an amendment of the Constitution of the United States so that every member of Congress shall be directly responsible to the electors of his district, who may at any time recall him if he does not justify their confidence in him; which was referred to the Committee on the Judiciary.

IN HOUSE.

1875, December 14—Mr. BLAINE proposed the following:

ARTICLE XVI.

No State shall make any law respecting an establishment of religion, or prohibiting the free exercise thereof; and no money raised by taxation in any State for the support of public schools, or derived from any public fund therefor, nor any public lands devoted thereto, shall ever be under the control of any religious sect; nor shall any money so raised or lands so devoted be divided between religious sects or denominations.

1875, December 14—Mr. RANDALL proposed the following:

ARTICLE XVI.

1. From and after the next election for a President of the United States, the President shall hold his office during the term of six years, and, together with the Vice-President chosen for the same term, be elected in the manner as now provided, or may hereafter be provided; but neither the President, nor the Vice-President, when the office of President has devolved upon him, shall be eligible for re-election as President.

1875, December 14—Mr. CARTER H. HARRISON proposed the following:

ARTICLE XVI.

From and after the election for President of the United States next following the ratification of this article, the President shall hold his office during the term of six years, and, together with the Vice-President chosen for the same term, be elected in the manner as now provided, or may hereafter be provided. But neither the President nor the Vice-President, when the office of President is devolved upon him, shall be eligible for re-election as President, but shall be, from and after the expiration of his office as President, unless the same be by impeachment, a Senator for life for the United States at large, and as such Senator shall have the same privileges as other Senators, except that he shall not vote as Senator, nor shall he be President pro tempore of the Senate, and the same immunities and compensation; but his attendance upon the sessions shall not be compulsory, nor shall his compensation be abridged by reason of his non-attendance.

1875, December 14—Mr. MORRISON proposed the following:

ARTICLE XVI.

1. From and after the next election for a President of the United States, the President shall hold his office during the term of six years, and, together with the Vice-President chosen for the same term, be elected in the manner as now provided, or may hereafter be provided; but the President shall not be eligible for more than six years in any term of twelve years.

1875, December 14—Mr. MCCRARY proposed the following:

All civil officers of the United States, except judges of the Supreme and inferior courts, the heads of Departments, and those whose duties are temporary in their character, shall hold office for a term of four years, unless a longer term shall be fixed by law. Congress may by law provide for the election by the people of postmasters and other officers whose duties are to be performed within the limits of any State or part of a State; but the President shall have the power of removal of any such officer, whether appointed or elected, for any cause affecting the incumbent's character, habits, or other qualifications, excepting political or religious opinions.

1876, January 6—Mr. REAGAN proposed the following:

First. That the words "and direct taxes," where they occur in the first line of clause three, section two, article one, of the Constitution, be stricken out.

Second. That the following words be added to the end of clause one, section eight, of article one, of the Constitution, namely:

"And direct taxes, when levied by the United States, shall be apportioned between the several States and Territories and the District of Columbia in proportion to the value of the property in each; and each State, Territory and the District of Columbia shall have the right to collect its portion of the same, if it elect to do so, by its own officers, and from subjects of taxation provided by its own laws, and pay the same over to the United States, as may be provided by law. And on the refusal or failure of any State, Territory, or the District of Columbia, to collect and pay over its portion of any such tax, the same shall be collected as may be provided by the laws of the United States."

January 6—Mr. OLIVER proposed the following:

After the year eighteen hundred and seventy-six, the President and Vice-President of the United States shall be elected by a direct vote of the people of the several States, and the electors in each State shall have the same qualifications as the electors of the most numerous branch of the State Legislature.

The person receiving the greatest number of votes for President shall be the President, and the person receiving the greatest number of votes for Vice-President shall be the Vice-President; but if two or more persons shall each receive an equal and the greatest number of votes for President, then the House of Representatives shall, from such persons, immediately choose the President; and if two or more persons shall each receive an equal and the greatest number of votes for Vice-President, then the Senate shall, from such persons immediately choose the Vice-President. In such elections, each House shall vote *viva voce*, and each member shall have one vote; and the person receiving the majority of the votes cast shall be elected; and, in case of a tie, the presiding officer shall determine it.

The election for President and Vice-President shall be held at the time now provided by law for choosing the electors of such officers, but Congress may prescribe a different time, which shall be the same in all the States; and Congress shall prescribe the manner of holding and conducting such election, and making the returns thereof; and, in case of failure so to do, that duty shall devolve, in the order named, first, on the President of the United States; second, on the Legislature of each State within that State; and, third, upon the chief executive of each State within that State.

The returns shall be canvassed at the time and in the manner now provided, or which may be hereafter provided, by the joint rules of the two Houses, or by law, by and in the presence of both Houses of Congress, who shall be the judges (each House voting separately) of the returns and election; but in case the two Houses shall not agree, then the matter of disagreement shall be referred to the Supreme Court of the United States, which shall forthwith decide the same, and such decision shall be final.

January 13—MR. BENNETT, Delegate from the Territory of Idaho, offered the following resolution, which was agreed to:

Whereas several propositions for amendments to the Constitution of the United States in relation to the manner of the election of President and Vice-President have been submitted to the House and referred to the Committee on the Judiciary: Therefore,

Resolved, That, in the consideration of such propositions, the Committee on the Judiciary be, and hereby is, requested to inquire into the expediency of incorporating into such constitutional amendments a provision granting to the citizens of the United States residing in the organized Territories the same privileges of voting for President and Vice-President as may be granted to such citizens residing in the States.

January 17—MR. O'BRIEN proposed the following:

ARTICLE XVI.

SECTION 1. No State shall make any law respecting an establishment of religion, or prohibiting the free exercise thereof; and no minister or preacher of the gospel or of any religious creed or denomination shall hold any office of trust or emolument under the United States or under any State; nor shall any religious test be required as a qualification for any office or public trust in any State or under the United States.

SEC. 2. No money received by taxation in any State for the support of public schools, or derived from any public fund therefor, nor any public lands devoted thereto, shall ever be under the control of any religious sect; nor shall any money so raised nor lands so devoted be divided between religious sects or denominations; nor shall any minister or preacher of the gospel, or of any religious creed or denomination, hold any office in connection with the public schools in any State, nor be eligible to any position of trust or emolument in connection with any institution, public or private, in any State or under the United States, which shall be supported in whole or in part from any public fund.

January 17—Mr. NEW proposed the following:

ARTICLE XVI.

From and after the next election for the President of the United States, the President shall hold his office during the term of four years, and, together with the Vice-President chosen for the same term, be elected in the manner now provided by law, or as may hereafter be provided, but neither the President, the Vice-President, or any other person in the office of President, as devolved upon him by law, shall be eligible to the office of President a third time.

January 18—Mr. CHARLES G. WILLIAMS proposed the following:

ARTICLE XVI.

No State shall make any law respecting an establishment of religion, or prohibiting the free exercise thereof; and no money raised by taxation in any State for the support of public schools, or derived from any public fund therefor, nor any public lands devoted thereto, shall ever be under the control of any religious sect; nor shall any money so raised or lands so devoted be divided between religious sects or denominations; neither shall money raised by taxation in any State be appropriated for the maintenance of any sectarian school or sectarian institution.

1876, January 18—Mr. FAULKNER proposed the following:

The President shall have power to disapprove of any item or items of any bill making appropriations of money embracing distinct items; and the part or parts of the bill approved shall be the law, and the item or items of appropriation disapproved shall be void, unless repassed according to the rules and limitations prescribed for the passage of other bills over the executive veto.

January 19—Mr. SPRINGER proposed the following:

The Congress shall not pass any local or special laws in any of the following enumerated cases; that is to say, for—

Granting pensions, bounties, lands, or prize-money to any person or persons; or for correcting the records of any department of the Government in reference thereto;

Granting relief to any person or persons; or

authorizing the payment of any claim against the United States or any officer thereof, except appropriations in general laws, to pay the judgments of courts or commissions authorized by law;

Remitting fines, penalties, or forfeitures, creating, increasing, or decreasing fees, percentage, or allowances of public officers during the term for which said officers are elected;

Granting to any corporation, association, or individual the right to lay down railroad-tracks, or amending existing charters for such purpose, by conferring any special or exclusive privilege upon such corporation or association which it does not already have;

Granting to any corporation, association, or individual any special or exclusive privilege, subsidy, immunity, or franchise whatever;

Regulating the practice of courts, or conferring special jurisdiction, in a particular case, on any of the courts of the United States, or commissions for the auditing of claims against the same.

In all other cases where a general law can be made applicable, no special law shall be enacted, and in all cases the courts may determine whether any special law could have been embraced in a general enactment.

January 24—Mr. LAPHAM proposed the following:

From and after the adoption of this amendment, the official term of the President shall commence on the first day of May instead of the fourth day of March, except when the first day of May shall fall on Sunday, in which case said term shall commence on the first Tuesday in May; and the President in office, when this amendment shall take effect, shall hold his office until the first day of May, in the year when his office would terminate under the present Constitution, and until his successor shall have been duly elected and qualified, and each successive President shall hold his office until his successor shall have been duly elected and qualified.

January 24—Mr. ALPHEUS S. WILLIAMS proposed the following:

ARTICLE XVI.

SECTION 1. Senators and Representatives in Congress are prohibited from soliciting appointments to, or removals from, office.

SEC. 2. Congress may create a civil-service commission of not less than five or more than nine persons, to be chosen once in every four years, in such manner as may be prescribed by law, and may confer on such commission absolute advisory and confirmatory powers in regard to appointments to and removals from office.

SEC. 3. Congress may provide that civil officers whose duties require them to reside in the several States may be elected by the people of their respective States, districts and localities, subject, however, to removal by the civil-service commission, under such rules and regulations as may be prescribed by law; but no officer so elected shall be removed for religious or political reasons.

SEC. 4. Congress shall have power to enforce this article by appropriate legislation.

January 24—Mr. JAMES WILSON proposed the following:

ARTICLE —.

SECTION 1. After the year eighteen hundred and eighty-two, the annual meeting of the Congress shall be on the first day of January, (or on the next day when the first falls on Sunday,) or on such other day in the month of January as may be prescribed by law.

SEC. 2. The term of office of Representatives elected to the Forty-seventh Congress shall expire on the last day of December, in the year eighteen hundred and eighty-two.

SEC. 3. The term of office of Representatives elected to the Forty-eighth Congress shall begin on the first day of January, in the year eighteen hundred and eighty-three, and that of Representatives to the succeeding Congresses shall begin on the first day of January every second year thereafter.

SEC. 4. The terms of office of Senators which, under the present official tenure, would expire with the third day of March, eighteen hundred and eighty-three, eighteen hundred and eighty-five, and eighteen hundred and eighty-seven, shall expire with the close of the month of December next preceding said years respectively; and thereafter the official term of Senators shall begin on the first day of January.

February 7—Mr. OLIVER proposed the following:

From and after the fourth day of March, in the year eighteen hundred and eighty-one, the term of office of the President and Vice-President of the United States shall be six years; and after said date no person shall be eligible for election to the office of President who has held such office within two years immediately preceding such election, or who has ever held such office longer than four years.

February 21—Mr. COOK proposed the following:

That no money shall be appropriated by any one Congress, or session of the same, over and above the annual estimates sent to Congress by the executive department; but this restriction shall not prevent Congress from diminishing the said estimates if they think proper.

March 6—Mr. CHARLES G. WILLIAMS proposed the following:

ARTICLE XVI.

The House of Representatives shall be composed of members chosen every third year by the people of the several States.

Immediately after they shall have assembled in consequence of the first election following the ratification of this article, they shall be divided as equally as may be into three classes.

The seats of the members of the first class shall be vacated at the expiration of the first year; of the second class, at the expiration of the second year; and of the third class, at the expiration of the third year; so that one-third may be chosen every year.

June 12—Mr. LORD proposed the following:

ARTICLE —.

SECTION 1. All postmasters, marshals, assessors, and collectors, except collectors of customs duties, shall be chosen for a term of four years at a general election by the electors of the district, city, town or village in which the duties of their offices are to be performed.

SEC. 2. The Congress shall enact suitable laws

to execute the foregoing article, and to insure the faithful discharge of the duties of such officers, and for their removal by the President for official misconduct; and in case of a removal, for an appointment until the next general election, and for filling vacancies in such offices.

ARTICLE —.

SECTION 1. The Congress shall enact suitable laws for the prevention and punishment of official misconduct and to insure official accountability.

SEC. 2. No person indicted for bribery or for converting the public money, or called as a witness in relation thereto, shall be excused from testifying on the ground that his testimony will tend to criminate himself; and any person convicted of such bribery or conversion shall not be pardoned, and shall be disqualified from holding any office of honor, trust, or profit under the United States.

Votes on Amendment Proposing Ineligibility of the President.

IN HOUSE.

1876, January 18—Mr. KNOTT, from the Committee on the Judiciary, reported the following:

Be it resolved, etc., (*two-thirds of each House concurring therein*,) That the following be proposed to the legislatures of the several States as an amendment to the Constitution of the United States, which, when ratified by three-fourths of said legislatures, shall be valid as a part of said Constitution:

ARTICLE XVI.

No person who has held, or may hereafter hold, the office of President shall ever again be eligible to said office.

January 26—Mr. FRYE, from the minority of of the Committee, proposed the following substitute for the proposed article given above:

From and after the fourth day of March, in the year one thousand eight hundred and eighty-five, the term of office of President and Vice-President of the United States shall be six years; and any person having been elected to and held the office of President, or who, for two years, has held such office, shall be ineligible to a re-election.

Mr. FRYE's substitute was then disagreed to—yeas 108, nays 144 (not voting 37), as follow:

YEAS—Messrs. C. H. Adams, *Ashe*, G. A. Bagley, *J. H. Bagley, jr.*, J. H. Baker, BANKS, Blaine, Bradley, W. R. Brown, H. C. Burchard, Burleigh, *Cate*, Chittenden, *Clymer*, *Cochrane*, Conger, Crapo, Crounse, Farwell, *Faulkner*, Foster, C. Freeman, Frost, Frye, Garfield, *R. Hamilton*, *Hancock*, Haralson, *Hardenbergh*, B. W. Harris, *C. H. Harrison*, *Hatcher*, Hathorn, Hendee, Henderson, *A. S. Hewitt*, *Hopkins*, Hoskins, *House*, Hubbell, Hurlbut, Joyce, Kasson, *Kehr*, Ketchum, Kimball, King, *F. Landers*, *Lane*, Lapham, W. Lawrence, Leavenworth, *Luttrell*, E. W. M. Mackey, *L. A. Mackey*, MacDougall, McCrary, Miller, Monroe, *Morgan*, Norton, Oliver, O'Neill, Packer, *J. Phelps*, W. A. Phillips, Pierce, Piper, Plaisted, T. C. Platt, A. POTTER, Rainey, *Randall*, *Reagan*, *J. Reilly*, *Riddle*, *J. Robbins*, *C. B. Roberts*, M. S. Robinson, S. Ross, Sampson, *Sheakley*, *Singleton*, Sinnickson, A. H. Smith, Strait, Stowell, *Teese*, Thornburgh, *Throckmorton*, W. Townsend, *Turney*, Van Vorhes, *R. B. Vance*, *Walling*, *Warren*, *Wells*, Wheeler, J. D. White, *Whiting*, G. Willard, A. Williams, *A. S. Williams*, *J. D. Williams*, *Willis*, J. Wilson, Woodworth, *Yeates*—108.

NAYS—Messrs. *Ainsworth*, ANDERSON, *Atkins*, *Bagby*, W. H. Baker, Ballou, *Banning*, *Barnum*, *Beebe*, *S. N. Bell*, *Blackburn*, Blair, *Bland*, *Boone*, *Bradford*, *Bright*, *J. Y. Brown*, *Buckner*, *S. D. Burchard*, *Cabell*, *J. H. Caldwell*, CAMPBELL, *Candler*, Cannon, *Caulfield*, *Chapin*, *J. B. Clarke*, *J. B. Clark, jr.*, *Collins*, *Cook*, *Cowan*, *Culberson*, *Cutler*, *Joseph J. Davis*, Davy, *DeBolt*, Denison, *Dibrell*, *Douglas*, Dunnell, *Durand*, *Durham*, Eames, *Eden*, *Egbert*, *Felton*, *Forney*, Fort, *Franklin*, *Fuller*, *Gause*, *Glover*, *Goodin*, *A. H. Hamilton*, *H. R. Harris*, *J. T. Harris*, *Hartzell*, *Haymond*, *Hereford*, *G. W. Hewitt*, *Hill*, *Holman*, *Hooker*, Hunter, *Hunton*, *Hurd*, Hyman, *T. L. Jones*, *Knott*, *G. M. Landers*, *Levy*, *B. B. Lewis*, *Lord*, Lynch, *Lynde*, Magoon, *Maish*, J. W. McDill, *McMahon*, *Meade*, *Metcalfe*, *Milliken*, *Mills*, *Morrison*, *Mutchler*, Nash, *Neal*, *New*, *Odell*, Page, *E. Y. Parsons*, *Payne*, *J. F. Philips*, *Poppleton*, *Powell*, Pratt, *D. Rea*, *A. V. Rice*, *W. M. Robbins*, *M. Ross*, Rusk, *Savage*, *M. Sayler*, *Scales*, Seelye, *Slemons*, R. Smalls, *W. E. Smith*, *Southard*, *Sparks*, *Springer*, *Stenger*, *Stevenson*, *Stone*, *Swann*, *Tarbox*, *Terry*, *C. P. Thompson*, *P. F. Thomas*, M. I. Townsend, *Tucker*, Tufts, *J. L. Vance*, *Waddell*, Waldron, *C. C. B. Walker*, *G. C. Walker*, A. S. Wallace, Walls, *Walsh*, *Ward*, G. W. Wells, *Whitehouse*, *Wigginton*, *Wike*, C. G. Williams, *J. Williams*, *J. N. Williams*, W. B. Williams, *Wilshire*, *B. Wilson*, *F. Wood*, Woodburn, *C. Young*—144.

February 2—Mr. REAGAN moved the following substitute:

That no person who has held or may hereafter hold the office of President shall ever thereafter be eligible to said office.

That the term of office of President and Vice-President of the United States shall be six years from and after the 4th of March, 1881.

Mr. NEW moved to re-commit the subject to the Committee on the Judiciary; which was disagreed to—yeas 127, nays 130 (not voting 33).

Mr. REAGAN's substitute was then disagreed to—yeas 72, nays 184 (not voting 33), as follow:

YEAS—Messrs. *Ashe*, *Atkins*, *J. H. Bagley, jr.*, J. H. Baker, BANKS, Bradley, *Bright*, *W. P. Caldwell*, *Candler*, Cannon, *Chapin*, *Clymer*, *Cochrane*, *Cook*, *Cowan*, *Douglas*, *Ellis*, *Ely*, *Faulkner*, *Felton*, *Forney*, *R. Hamilton*, *Hardenbergh*, *H. R. Harris*, *C. H. Harrison*, *Hatcher*, *A. S. Hewitt*, *G. W. Hewitt*, *Hill*, *Hopkins*, *House*, *Lane*, *B. B. Lewis*, *Luttrell*, E. W. M. Mackey, *L. A. Mackey*, *Maish*, *Milliken*, *Mills*, *Morgan*, *Payne*, *J. Phelps*, W. A. Phillips, *Piper*, A. POTTER, *Powell*, *Randall*, *Reagan*, *J. Reilly*, *J. B. Reilly*, *Riddle*, *J. Robbins*, *W. M. Robbins*, *C. B. Roberts*, *Scales*, *Schleicher*, *Sheakley*, *Singleton*, *Sparks*, *Teese*, *Throckmorton*, *Turney*, *R. B. Vance*, *Waddell*, *Walling*, *Ward*, *Warren*, *Whitehouse*, *A. S. Williams*, *J. D. Williams*, *Willis*, *C. Young*—72.

NAYS—Messrs. C. H. Adams, *Ainsworth*, ANDERSON, *Bagby*, G. A. Bagley, W. H. Baker, Ballou, *Banning*, *Barnum*, Bass, *Beebe*, *S. N. Bell*, *Blackburn*, Blaine, Blair, *Bland*, *Boone*, *Brad-*

ford, *J. Y. Brown*, W. R. Brown, *Buckner*, H. C. Burchard, *S. D. Burchard*, *Cabell*, *J. H. Caldwell*, CAMPBELL, *Cate*, *Caulfield*, Chittenden, *J. B. Clarke*, *J. B. Clark*, *jr.*, *Collins*, Conger, Crapo, Crounse, *Culberson*, *Cutler*, *Joseph J. Davis*, Davy, *DeBolt*, Denison, *Dibrell*, Dunnell, *Durand*, *Durham*, Eames, *Eden*, *Egbert*, Farwell, Fort, Foster, *Franklin*, C. Freeman, Frost, Frye, *Fuller*, Garfield, *Gause*, *Glover*, *A. H. Hamilton*, *Hancock*, Haralson, B. W. Harris, *J. T. Harris*, *Hartzell*, Hathorn, *Haymond*, Hendee, Henderson, *Henkle*, *Hereford*, *Holman*, *Hooker*, Hoskins, Hubbell, Hunter, *Hunton*, *Hurd*, Hurlbut, Hyman, *T. L. Jones*, Joyce, Kasson, *Kehr*, Ketchum, Kimball, King, *Knott*, *F. Landers*, *G. M. Landers*, Lapham, W. Lawrence, Leavenworth, *Levy*, *Lord*, Lynch, *Lynde*, Magoon, MacDougall, McCrary, J. W. McDill, *McMahon*, *Meade*, Miller, Monroe, *Morrison*, *Mutchler*, Nash, *Neal*, *New*, Norton, *O'Brien*, *Odell*, Oliver, O'Neill, Packer, Page, *E. Y. Parsons*, *J. F. Philips*, Pierce, Plaisted, T. C. Platt, *Poppleton*, Pratt, Rainey, *D. Rea*, *A. V. Rice*, M. S. Robinson, *M. Ross*, S. Ross, Rusk, Sampson, *Savage*, *M. Sayler*, *J. G. Schumaker*, Seelye, Sinnickson, *Slemons*, R. Smalls, A. H. Smith, *W. E. Smith*, *Southard*, *Springer*, Strait, *Stenger*, *Stevenson*, *Stone*, Stowell, *Swann*, *Tarbox*, *Terry*, *C. P. Thompson*, *P. F. Thomas*, Thornburgh, M. I. Townsend, W. Townsend, *Tucker*, Tufts, Van Vorhes, *J. L. Vance*, Waldron, *C. C. B. Walker*, *G. C. Walker*, A. S. Wallace, Walls, *Walsh*, *E. Wells*, G. W. Wells, Wheeler, J. D. White, *Whiting*, *Wigginton*, *Wike*, G. Willard, C. G. Williams, *J. N. Williams*, W. B. Williams, *Wilshire*, *B. Wilson*, J. Wilson, *F. Wood*, Woodburn, Woodworth, *Yeates*—184.

The joint resolution, reported from the Committee, was then disagreed to, (two-thirds not having voted in the affirmative)—yeas 145, nays 108 (not voting 36) as follow:

YEAS—Messrs. *Ainsworth*, *Ashe*, *Atkins*, *Bagby*, *J. H. Bagley*, *jr.*, BANKS, *Banning*, *Barnum*, *Beebe*, *S.N.Bell*, *Blackburn*, *Bland*, *Boone*, *Bradford*, *Bright*, *J. Y. Brown*, *Buckner*, *S. D. Burchard*, *Cabell*, *J. H. Caldwell*, *Candler*, *Cate*, *Caulfield*, *Chapin*, *J. B. Clarke*, *J. B. Clark*, *jr.*, *Clymer*, *Cochrane*, *Collins*, *Cook*, *Cowan*, Crounse, *Culberson*, *Cutler*, *Joseph J. Davis*, *DeBolt*, *Dibrell*, *Douglas*, Dunnell, *Durand*, *Durham*, *Eden*, *Egbert*, *Faulkner*, *Felton*, *Forney*, *Franklin*, Frost, *Fuller*, *Gause*, *Gibson*, *Glover*, *Goodin*, *A. H. Hamilton*, *Hancock*, *H. R. Harris*, *J. T. Harris*, *C. H. Harrison*, *Hartzell*, *Hatcher*, *Hereford*, *A. S. Hewitt*, *G. W. Hewitt*, *Hill*, *Holman*, *Hopkins*, *House*, *Hunton*, *Hurd*, *T. L. Jones*, *Knott*, *F. Landers*, *G. M. Landers*, *Lane*, *Levy*, *B. B. Lewis*, *Lord*, *Luttrell*, *Lynde*, *L. A. Mackey*, *Maish*, *McFarland*, *McMahon*, *Meade*, *Metcalfe*, *Milliken*, *Mills*, *Morgan*, *Morrison*, *Mutchler*, *Odell*, *E. Y. Parsons*, *Payne*, *J. Phelps*, *J. F. Philips*, W. A. Phillips, *Piper*, *Poppleton*, *Powell*, *Reagan*, *J. Reilly*, *A. V. Rice*, *Riddle*, *J. Robbins*, *W. M. Robbins*, *C. B. Roberts*, *M. Ross*, *Savage*, *M. Sayler*, *Scales*, *Schleicher*, *Sheakley*, *Singleton*, *Slemons*, *W. E. Smith*, *Southard*, *Sparks*, *Springer*, *Stenger*, *Stevenson*, *Stone*, *Tarbox*, *Terry*, *C. P. Thompson*, *Throckmorton*, *Tucker*, *Turney*, *J. L. Vance*, *R. B. Vance*, *Waddell*, *C. C. B. Walker*, *G. C. Walker*, *Walling*, *Ward*, *Warren*, *E. Wells*, *Whitehouse*, *Wigginton*, *A. S. Williams*, *J. D. Williams*, *J. N. Williams*, *Willis*, *Wilshire*, *B. Wilson*, *Yeates*—145.

NAYS—Messrs. C. H. Adams, ANDERSON, G. A. Bagley, J. H. Baker, W. H. Baker, Ballou, Blaine, Blair, Bradley, W. R. Brown, H. C. Burchard, Burleigh, CAMPBELL, Cannon, Chittenden, Conger, Crapo, Davy, Denison, Eames, Farwell, Fort, Foster, C. Freeman, Frye, Garfield, E. Hale, *R. Hamilton*, Haralson, *Hardenbergh*, B. W. Harris, Hathorn, *Haymond*, Hendee, Henderson, *Hooker*, Hoskins, Hubbell, Hunter, Hurlbut, Hyman, Joyce, Kasson, *Kehr*, Ketchum, Kimball, King, Lapham, W. Lawrence, Leavenworth, Lynch, E. W. M. Mackey, Magoon, MacDougall, McCrary, J. W. McDill, Miller, Monroe, Nash, *Neal*, *New*, Norton, Oliver, O'Neill, Packer, Page, Pierce, Plaisted, T. C. Platt, A. POTTER, Pratt, Purman, Rainey, *Randall*, M. S. Robinson, S. Ross, Rusk, Sampson, Seelye, Sinnickson, R. Smalls, A. H. Smith, Strait, Stowell, *Swann*, *Teese*, *P. F. Thomas*, Thornburgh, M. I. Townsend, W. Townsend, Tufts, Van Vorhes, Waldron, A. S. Wallace, Walls, *Walsh*, G. W. Wells, Wheeler, J. D. White, *Whiting*, *Wike*, G. Willard, C. G. Williams, W. B. Williams, J. Wilson, *F. Wood*, Woodburn, Woodworth—108.

XII.

THE AMNESTY BILL—FORTY-FOURTH CONGRESS.

IN HOUSE.

1875, December 15—Mr. RANDALL offered a bill (H. R. 214), to remove the disabilities imposed by the third section of the fourteenth article of the Amendments of the Constitution of the United States; which, after a brief discussion as to time, was made a special order for December 21.

The bill is as follows:

Be it enacted by the Senate and House of Representatives of the United States of America in Congress assembled (*two-thirds of each House concurring therein*), That all disabilities imposed and remaining upon any person by virtue of the third section of the fourteenth article of the amendments of the Constitution of the United States be, and the same are hereby, removed, and each and every person is hereby forever relieved therefrom.

SEC. 2. Whenever any persons from whom disabilities are removed by this act shall be elected or appointed to any post or office of honor or trust under the Government of the United States he shall take the oath prescribed by section 1757 of title 19 of the Revised Statutes of the United States or such other official oath as may be hereafter prescribed in such cases by any future act of Congress.

1875, December 21—The House was not in session.

1876, January 6—Mr. BLAINE obtained consent to have printed the following amendment, and he gave notice that he would offer it as an amendment to the bill, on Monday next:

Be it enacted, etc., That all persons now under the disabilities imposed by the fourteenth amendment to the Constitution of the United States, with the exception of Jefferson Davis, late president of the so-called Confederate States, shall be relieved of such disabilities upon their appearing before any judge of a United States Court and taking and subscribing in open Court the following oath, to be duly attested and recorded, namely: I, A. B., do solemnly swear, or affirm, that I will support and defend the Constitution of the United States against all enemies, foreign and domestic; that I will bear true faith and allegiance to the same; that I take this obligation freely, without any mental reservation or purpose of evasion; and that, to the best of my knowledge and ability, I will well and faithfully discharge the duties of a citizen of the United States.

January 10—Mr. RANDALL moved a suspension of the rules, so as to proceed to the consideration of the Amnesty bill, which was agreed to.

Mr. BLAINE desired to offer his amendment, in the nature of a substitute.

Mr. RANDALL, having the floor, demanded the previous question, stating that he desired to have it sustained, and that he then proposed to give to the gentleman on the other side of the House one-half of the time which may be allowed for discussion.

The previous question was decided on a count by tellers—ayes 159, noes 95. On ordering the main question, the yeas were 164, nays 100, (not voting 26), as follows:

YEAS—Messrs. *Ainsworth*, ANDERSON, *Ashe, Atkins, Bagby, J. H Bagley, jr., Barnum, Beebe, Blackburn, Bland, Blount, Boone, Bradford, Bright, J. Y. Brown, Buckner, S. D. Burchard, Cabell, J. H. Caldwell, W. P. Caldwell*, CAMPBELL, *Candler, Caulfield, Chapin, J. B. Clarke, J. B. Clark, jr., Clymer, Cochrane, Cook, Cowan, Cox, Culberson, Cutler*, Darrall, *Joseph J. Davis, DeBolt, Dibrell, Douglas, Durand, Durham, Eden, Egbert, Ely, Faulkner, Felton, Forney, Franklin, Fuller, Gause, Gibson, Glover, Goode, Goodin, Gunter, A. H. Hamilton, R. Hamilton, Hancock, Hardenbergh, H. R. Harris, J. T. Harris, C. H. Harrison, Hartridge, Hartzell, Hatcher, Haymond, Henkle, Hereford, G. W. Hewitt, Hill, Holman, Hooker, Hopkins, House, Hunton, Jenks, F. Jones, T. L. Jones, Knott, F. Landers, G. M. Landers, Lane, Levy, B. B. Lewis, Lord, Luttrell, Lynde, Maish, McFarland, McMahon, Meade, Metcalfe, Milliken, Mills, Money, Morey, Morgan, Morrison, Mutchler*, Nash, *Neal, New, O'Brien, E. Y. Parsons, J. Phelps, J. F. Philips, Piper, Poppleton, Powell, Randall, D. Rea, Reagan, J. Reilly, J. B. Reilly, A. V. Rice, Riddle, J. Robbins, W. M. Robbins, C. B. Roberts, M. Ross, Savage, M. Sayler, Scales, Schleicher, J. G. Schumaker, Sheakley, Singleton, Slemons, W. E. Smith, Southard, Sparks, Springer, Stenger, Stevenson, Stone, Tarbox, Teese, Terry, C. P. Thompson, P. F. Thomas, Throckmorton, Tucker, Turney, J. L. Vance, R. B. Vance, Waddell, C. C. B. Walker, G. C. Walker, Walling, Walsh, Ward, Warren, E. Wells, Whitthorne, Wike, A. S. Williams, J. Williams, J. D. Williams, J. N. Williams, Willis, Wilshire, B. Wilson, F. Wood, Yeates, C. Young*—164.

NAYS—Messrs. C. H. Adams, G. A. Bagley, J. H. Baker, W. H. Baker, Ballou, BANKS, Blaine, Blair, Bradley, W. R. Brown, H. C. Burchard, Burleigh, Cannon, Cason, Caswell, Cate, Chittenden, Conger, Crapo, Crounse, Danford, Davy, Denison, Dunnell, Eames, Evans, Fort, Foster, C. Freeman, Frost, Frye, Garfield, E. Hale, Haralson, B. W. Harris, Hathorn, Hendee, Henderson, G. F. Hoar, Hoskins, Hubbell, Hunter, Hurlbut, Hyman, Joyce, Kasson, *Kehr*, Ketchum, Kimball, King, Lapham, W. Lawrence, Leavenworth, Lynch, E. W. M. Mackey, Magoon, MacDougall, McCrary, J. W. McDill, Miller, Monroe, Norton, Oliver, O'Neill, Packer, Page, W. A. Phillips, Pierce, Plaisted, T. C. Platt, A. POTTER, Pratt, M. S. Robinson, S. Ross, Rusk, Sampson, Seelye, Sinnickson, R. Smalls, A. H. Smith, Starkweather, Strait, Stowell, Thornburgh, M. I. Townsend, W. Townsend, Tufts, Van Vorhes, Waldron, A. S. Wallace, J. W. Wallace, Wheeler, J. D. White, Whiting, G. Willard, C. G. Williams, W. B. Williams, J. Wilson, A. Wood, jr., Woodworth —100.

On the passage of the bill the yeas were 175, nays 97, (not voting 18,) two-thirds being required, as follow:

NAYS—Messrs. *Ainsworth*, ANDERSON, *Ashe, Atkins, Bagby, J. H. Bagley, jr.*, BANKS, *Barnum, Beebe, S.N.Bell, Blackburn, Bland, Blount, Boone, Bradford, Bright, J. Y. Brown, Buckner, S. D. Burchard, Cabell, J. H. Caldwell, W. P. Caldwell*, CAMPBELL, *Candler, Cate, Caulfield, Chapin, J. B. Clarke, J. B. Clark, jr., Clymer, Cochrane, Cook, Cowan, Cox, Culberson, Cutler, Joseph J. Davis, DeBolt, Dibrell, Douglas, Durand, Durham, Eden, Egbert, Ely, Faulkner, Felton, Forney, Franklin, Fuller, Gause, Gibson, Glover, Goode, Goodin, Gunter, A. H. Hamilton, R. Hamilton, Hancock, Hardenbergh, H. R. Harris, J. T. Harris, C. H. Harrison, Hartridge, Hartzell, Hatcher, Haymond, Henkle, Hereford, G. W. Hewitt, Hill, Holman, Hooker, Hopkins, House, Hunton, Hurd, Jenks, F. Jones, T. L. Jones, Kehr*, Kelley, *Knott, F. Landers, G. M. Landers, Lane, Levy, B. B. Lewis, Lord, Luttrell*, Lynch, *Lynde*, E. W. M. Mackey, *Maish, McFarland, McMahon, Meade, Metcalfe, Milliken, Mills, Money*, Morey, *Morgan, Morrison, Mutchler, Neal, New, O'Brien, E. Y. Parsons, Payne, J. Phelps, J. F. Philips*, Pierce, *Piper, Poppleton*, A. POTTER, *Powell, Randall, D. Rea, Reagan, J. Reilly, J. B. Reilly, A. V. Rice,*

Riddle, *J. Robbins*, *W. M. Robbins*, *C. B. Roberts*, *M. Ross*, *Savage*, *M. Sayler*, *Scales*, *Schleicher*, *J. G. Schumaker*, *Sheakley*, *Singleton*, *Slemons*, *W. E. Smith*, *Southard*, *Sparks*, *Springer*, *Stenger*, *Stevenson*, *Stone*, *Swann*, *Tarbox*, *Teese*, *Terry*, *C. P. Thompson*, *P. F. Thomas*, *Throckmorton*, *Tucker*, *Turney*, *J. L. Vance*, *R. B. Vance*, *Waddell*, *C. C. B. Walker*, *G. C. Walker*, *Walling*, *Walsh*, *Ward*, *Warren*, *E. Wells*, G. W. Wells, *Whitthorne*, *Wike*, *A. S. Williams*, *J. Williams*, *J. D. Williams*, *J. N. Williams*, *Willis*, *Wilshire*, *B. Wilson*, *F. Wood*, *Yeates*, *C. Young*—175.

NAYS—Messrs. C. H. Adams, G. A. Bagley, J. H. Baker, W. H. Baker, Ballou, Blaine, Blair, Bradley, W. R. Brown, H. C. Burchard, Burleigh, Cannon, Cason, Caswell, Chittenden, Conger, Crapo, Crounse, Danford, Davy, Denison, Dobbins, Dunnell, Eames, Evans, Foster, C. Freeman, Frost, Frye, Garfield, E. Hale, Haralson, B. W. Harris, Hathorn, Hendee, Henderson, G. F. Hoar, Hoskins, Hubbell, Hunter, Hurlbut, Hyman, Joyce, Kasson, Ketchum, Kimball, King, Lapham, W. Lawrence, Leavenworth, Magoon, MacDougall, McCrary, J. W. McDill, Miller, Monroe, Nash, Norton, Oliver, O'Neill, Packer, Page, W. A. Phillips, Plaisted, T. C. Platt, Pratt, Purman, Rainey, M. S. Robinson, S. Ross, Rusk, Sampson, Seelye, Sinnickson, R. Smalls, A. H. Smith, Starkweather, Strait, Stowell, Thornburgh, M. I. Townsend, W. Townsend, Tufts, Van Vorhes, Waldron, A. S. Wallace, J. W. Wallace, Walls, Wheeler, J. D. White, Whiting, G. Willard, C. G. Williams, W. B. Williams, J. Wilson, A. Wood, jr., Woodworth—97.

Mr. BLAINE moved to re-consider the vote by which the bill was rejected.

Which, after several days' debate, was agreed to without a division.

The question recurring on the passage of the bill,

January 13—Mr. BANKS offered the following words as a substitute for what follows the seventh line of the first section of the bill as printed on the files:

And shall be forever relieved therefrom, upon their appearing before a Judge of any Court of the United States or any Court of Record of the State in which they are resident, and taking and subscribing the following oath, to be duly attested and recorded, to wit: "I, A. B, do solemnly swear (or affirm) that I will support and defend the Constitution of the United States against all enemies, foreign and domestic; that I will bear true faith and allegiance to the same, and obey all laws made in pursuance thereof; and that I take this obligation freely, and without any mental reservation or purpose of evasion whatever."

Mr. EUGENE HALE objected to the amendment, unless the amendment of his colleague (Mr. BLAINE) was admitted.

The SPEAKER *pro tempore* (Mr. HOSKINS) said that the amendment had merely been read for the information of the House, and is not now in order.

Mr. RANDALL asked unanimous consent that the gentleman from Massachusetts have the opportunity of offering that amendment.

Mr. BLAINE objected.

After further debate,

Mr. RANDALL moved to commit the bill to the Committee on the Judiciary, with instructions to report it back with the amendment of the gentleman from Massachusetts (Mr. BANKS).

Which was agreed to.

January 14—Mr. KNOTT, from the Judiciary Committee, reported the same according to instructions, to read as follows:

Be it enacted, &c., That all the disabilities imposed and remaining upon any person, by virtue of the third section of the fourteenth article of the amendments of the Constitution of the United States, be, and the same are hereby, removed; and each and every person is and shall be forever relieved therefrom upon his appearing before a judge of any court of the United States or any court of record of the State in which he is resident, and taking and subscribing the following oath, to be duly attested and recorded, to wit: "I, A B, do solemnly swear (or affirm) that I will support and defend the Constitution of the United States against all enemies, foreign and domestic; that I will bear true faith and allegiance to the same, and obey all laws made in pursuance thereof, and that I take this obligation freely and without any mental reservation or purpose of evasion whatever."

Mr. KNOTT demanded the previous question upon the bill.

The main question was ordered, yeas 183, nays 92 (not voting 15), as follow:

YEAS—Messrs. *Ainsworth*, ANDERSON, *Ashe*, *Atkins*, *Bagby*, *J. H. Bagley, jr.*, BANKS, *Barnum*, *Beebe*, *S. N. Bell*, *Blackburn*, *Bland*, *Bliss*, *Blount*, *Boone*, *Bradford*, *Bright*, *J. Y. Brown*, *Buckner*, *S. D. Burchard*, *Cabell*, *J. H. Caldwell*, *W. P. Caldwell*, CAMPBELL, *Candler*, *Cate*, *Caulfield*, *Chapin*, *J. B. Clarke*, *J. B. Clark, jr.*, *Clymer*, *Cochrane*, *Collins*, *Cook*, *Cowan*, *Cox*, *Culberson*, *Cutler*, *Joseph J. Davis*, *DeBolt*, *Dibrell*, *Douglas*, *Durand*, *Durham*, *Eden*, *Egbert*, *Ellis*, *Ely*, *Faulkner*, *Felton*, *Forney*, *Franklin*, *Fuller*, *Gause*, *Gibson*, *Glover*, *Goodin*, *Gunter*, *A. H. Hamilton*, *R. Hamilton*, *Hancock*, Haralson, *Hardenbergh*, *H. R. Harris*, *J. T. Harris*, *C. H. Harrison*, *Hartridge*, *Hartzell*, *Hatcher*, *Henkle*, *Hereford*, *A. S. Hewitt*, *G. W. Hewitt*, *Hill*, *Holman*, *Hooker*, *Hopkins*, *House*, *Hunton*, *Hurd*, *Jenks*, *F. Jones*, *T. L. Jones*, *Kehr*, *Knott*, *Lamar*, *F. Landers*, *G. M. Landers*, *Lane*, *Levy*, *B. B. Lewis*, *Lord*, *Luttrell*, E. W. M. Mackey, *L. A. Mackey*, *Maish*, *McFarland*, *McMahon*, *Meade*, *Metcalfe*, *Milliken*, *Mills*, *Money*, *Morey*, *Morgan*, *Morrison*, *Mutchler*, *Neal*, *New*, *O'Brien*, *Odell*, *E. Y. Parsons*, *Payne*, *J. Phelps*, *J. F. Philips*, Pierce, *Piper*, *Poppleton*, A. POTTER, *Powell*, Rainey, *Randall*, *D. Rea*, *Reagan*, *J. Reilly*, *J. B. Reilly*, *A. V. Rice*, *Riddle*, *J. Robbins*, *W. M. Robbins*, *C. B. Roberts*, *M. Ross*, *Savage*, *M. Sayler*, *Scales*, *Schleicher*, *J. G. Schumaker*, Seelye, *Sheakley*, *Singleton*, *Slemons*, *W. E. Smith*, *Southard*, *Sparks*, *Springer*, *Stenger*, *Stevenson*, *Stone*, *Swann*, *Tarbox*, *Teese*, *Terry*, *C. P. Thompson*, *P. F. Thomas*, *Throckmorton* *Tucker*, *Turney*, *J. L. Vance*, *R. B. Vance*, *Waddell*, *C. C. B. Walker*, *G. C. Walker*, A. S. Wallace, *Walling*, *Walsh*, *Ward*, *Warren*, *E. Wells*, *Whitehouse*, *Whitthorne*, *Wigginton*, *Wike*, *A. S. Williams*, *J*

Williams, *J. D. Williams*, *J. N. Williams*, *Willis*, *Wilshire*, *B. Wilson*, *F. Wood*, Woodburn, *Yeates*, *C. Young*—183.

NAYS—Messrs. G. A. Bagley, J. H. Baker, W. H. Baker, Ballou, Blaine, Blair, Bradley, W. R. Brown, H. C. Burchard, Burleigh, Cannon, Cason, Caswell, Conger, Crapo, Crounse, Danford, Darrall, Davy, Denison, Dobbins, Dunnell, Eames, Evans, Fort, Foster, C. Freeman, Frost, Frye, Garfield, E. Hale, B. W. Harris, Hathorn, *Haymond*, Hendee, Henderson, G. F. Hoar, Hoskins, Hunter, Hurlbut, Hyman, Joyce, Kasson, Ketchum, King, Lapham, W. Lawrence, Leavenworth, Lynch, Magoon, MacDougall, McCrary, J. W. McDill, Miller, Monroe, Nash, Norton, Oliver, O'Neill, Packer, Page, W. A. Phillips, Plaisted, T. C. Platt, Pratt, M. S. Robinson, S. Ross, Rusk, Sampson, Sinnickson, R. Smalls, A. H. Smith, Starkweather, Stowell, Thornburgh, M. I. Townsend, W. Townsend, Tufts, Van Vorhes, Waldron, J. W. Wallace, Walls, G. W. Wells, Wheeler, J. D. White, Whiting, G. Willard, C. G. Williams, W. B. Williams, J. Wilson, A. Wood, jr., Woodworth—92.

On the final passage of the bill as reported from the Committee on the Judiciary, the yeas were 184, nays 97 (not voting 9), as follow:

YEAS—Messrs. *Ainsworth*, ANDERSON, *Ashe*, *Atkins*, *Bagby*, *J. H. Bagley, jr.*, BANKS, *Barnum*, *Beebe*, *S. N. Bell*, *Blackburn*, *Bland*, *Bliss*, *Blount*, *Boone*, *Bradford*, *Bright*, *J. Y. Brown*, *Buckner*, *S. D. Burchard*, *Cabell*, *J. H. Caldwell*, *W. P. Caldwell*, CAMPBELL, *Candler*, *Cate*, *Caulfield*, *Chapin*, *J. B. Clarke*, *J. B. Clark, jr.*, *Clymer*, *Cochrane*, *Collins*, *Cook*, *Cowan*, *Cox*, *Culberson*, *Cutler*, *Joseph J. Davis*, *De-Bolt*, *Dibrell*, *Douglas*, *Durand*, *Durham*, *Eden*, *Egbert*, *Ellis*, *Ely*, Farwell, *Faulkner*, *Felton*, *Forney*, *Franklin*, *Fuller*, *Gause*, *Gibson*, *Glover*, *Goode*, *Goodin*, *Gunter*, *A. H. Hamilton*, *R. Hamilton*, *Hancock*, Haralson, *Hardenbergh*, *H. R. Harris*, *J. T. Harris*, *C. H. Harrison*, *Hartridge*, *Hartzell*, *Hatcher*, *Henkle*, *Hereford*, *A. S. Hewitt*, *G. W. Hewitt*, *Hill*, *Holman*, *Hooker*, *Hopkins*, *House*, *Hunton*, *Hurd*, *Jenks*, *F. Jones*, *T. L. Jones*, *Kehr*, Kelley, *Knott*, *Lamar*, *F. Landers*, *G. M. Landers*, *Lane*, *Levy*, *B. B. Lewis*, *Lord*, *Luttrell*, E. W. M. Mackey, *L. A. Mackey*, *Maish*, *McFarland*, *McMahon*, *Meade*, *Metcalfe*, *Milliken*, *Mills*, *Money*, *Morey*, *Morgan*, *Morrison*, *Mutchler*, *Neal*, *New*, *O'Brien*, *Odell*, *E. Y. Parsons*, *Payne*, *J. Phelps*, *J. F. Philips*, Pierce, *Piper*, *Poppleton*, A. POTTER, *Powell*, *Randall*, *D. Rea*, *Reagan*, *J. Reilly*, *J. B. Reilly*, *A. V. Rice*, *Riddle*, *J. Robbins*, *W. M. Robbins*, *C. B. Roberts*, *M. Ross*, *Savage*, *M. Sayler*, *Scales*, *Schleicher*, *J. G. Schumaker*, Seelye, *Sheakley*, *Singleton*, *Slemons*, *W. E. Smith*, *Southard*, *Sparks*, *Springer*, *Stenger*, *Stevenson*, *Stone*, *Swann*, *Tarbox*, *Teese*, *Terry*, *C. P. Thompson*, *P. F. Thomas*, *Throckmorton*, *Tucker*, *Turney*, *J. L. Vance*, *R. B. Vance*, *Waddell*, *C. C. B. Walker*, *G. C. Walker*, *Walling*, *Walsh*, *Ward*, *Warren*, *E. Wells*, *Whitehouse*, *Whitthorne*, *Wigginton*, *Wike*, *A. S. Williams*, *J. Williams*, *J. D. Williams*, *J. N. Williams*, *Willis*, *Wilshire*, *Wilson*, *F. Wood*, Woodburn, *Yeates*, *C. Young*—184.

NAYS—Messrs. G. A. Bagley, J. H. Baker, W. H. Baker, Ballou, Blaine, Blair, Bradley, W. R. Brown, H. C. Burchard, Burleigh, Cannon, Cason, Caswell, Conger, Crapo, Crounse, Danford, Darrall, Davy, Denison, Dobbins, Dunnell, Eames, Evans, Fort, Foster, C. Freeman, Frost, Frye, Garfield, E. Hale, B. W. Harris, Hathorn, *Haymond*, Hendee, Henderson, G. F. Hoar, Hoge, Hoskins, Hubbell, Hunter, Hurlbut, Hyman, Joyce, Kasson, Ketchum, King, Lapham, W. Lawrence, Leavenworth, Lynch, Magoon, MacDougall, McCrary, J. W. McDill, Miller, Monroe, Nash, Norton, Oliver, O'Neill, Packer, Page, W. A. Phillips, Plaisted, T. C. Platt, Pratt, Purman, M. S. Robinson, S. Ross, Rusk, Sampson, Sinnickson, R. Smalls, A. H. Smith, Starkweather, Strait, Stowell, Thornburgh, M. I. Townsend, W. Townsend, Tufts, Van Vorhes, Waldron, A. S. Wallace, J. W. Wallace, Walls, G. W. Wells, Wheeler, J. D. White, Whiting, G. Willard, C. G. Williams, W. B. Williams, J. Wilson, A. Wood, jr., Woodworth—97.

NOT VOTING—Messrs. C. H. Adams, *Banning*, Bass, Chittenden, Hays, Kimball, *Lynde*, Rainey, A. Williams—9.

Mr. BLAINE moved that the vote last taken be reconsidered.

During the debate,

Mr. BLAINE asked unanimous consent to offer his amendment, offering to yield the floor at the same time to any gentleman who desires to move to strike out the exclusion of Jefferson Davis.

Mr. RANDALL objected.

Subsequently, on a renewal of the proposition,

Mr. WILLIAM M. ROBBINS objected.

Mr. BLAINE then withdrew the motion to reconsider, and the bill fell.

1876, January 17—Mr. JOHN D. WHITE moved that the rules be suspended so as to enable him to submit, and the House to agree to the following resolution:

Resolved, That the rules be suspended so as to enable the House to proceed forthwith to vote on the passage of the following bill:

A bill to remove the disabilities imposed by the Fourteenth Amendment to the Constitution of the United States.

Be it enacted, &c., That all persons now under the disabilities imposed by the fourteenth amendment to the Constitution of the United States, with the exception of Jefferson Davis, late president of the so-called Confederate States, shall be relieved of such disabilities upon their appearing before any judge of a United States court, and taking and subscribing, in open court, the following oath, to be duly attested and recorded, namely:

I, A.B., do solemnly swear (or affirm) that I will support and defend the Constitution of the United States against all enemies, foreign and domestic; that I will bear true faith and allegiance to the same; that I take this obligation freely, without any mental reservation or purpose of evasion; and that, to the best of my knowledge and ability, I will well and faithfully discharge the duties of a citizen of the United States.

The House first, however, voting on the following amendment thereto:

Strike out the following words: "with the exception of Jefferson Davis, late president of the so-called Confederate States."

Which motion was disagreed to—yeas 164, nays 111 (not voting 15), as follow:

YEAS—Messrs. C. H. Adams, *Ainsworth*, ANDERSON, *Bagby*, G. A. Bagley, J. H. Baker, W. H. Baker, Ballou, BANKS, Bass, *Beebe*, *S. N. Bell*, Blaine, Blair, *Bland*, *Bliss*, Bradley, W. R. Brown, H. C. Burchard, *S. D. Burchard*, Burleigh, *W. P. Caldwell*, CAMPBELL, Cannon, Cason, Caswell, *Cate*, Chittenden, *Cochrane*, Conger, *Cox*, Crapo, Crounse, Danford, Darrall, Davy, *DeBolt*, Denison, Dobbins, Dunnell, *Durand*, Eames, *Egbert*, *Ely*, Evans, Farwell, *Faulkner*, Fort, Foster, C. Freeman, Frost, Frye, *Fuller*, Garfield, *Goodin*, E. Hale, Haralson, *Hardenbergh*, B. W. Harris, *C. H. Harrison*, *Hartzell*, Hathorn, *Haymond*, Hendee, Henderson, *A. S. Hewitt*, *G. W. Hewitt*, G. F. Hoar, Hoge, *Holman*, Hoskins, Hubbell, Hunter, *Hurd*, Hurlbut, Hyman, *Jenks*, *F. Jones*, *T. L. Jones*, Joyce, Kasson, Kelley, Ketchum, Kimball, King, Lapham, W. Lawrence, Leavenworth, *Levy*, Lynch, Magoon, MacDougall, McCrary, J. W. McDill, *Meade*, Miller, Monroe, Morey, *Morgan*, *Mutchler*, Nash, *Neal*, *New*, Norton, *Odell*, Oliver, O'Neill, Packer, Page, *Payne*, *J. Phelps*, W. A. Phillips, Pierce, *Piper*, Plaisted, T. C. Platt, A. POTTER, *Powell*, Pratt, Purman, Rainey, *J. Reilly*, M. S. Robinson, S. Ross, Rusk, Sampson, *Savage*, Seelye, Sinnickson, R. Smalls, A. H. Smith, *Springer*, Starkweather, Strait, *Stevenson*, Stowell, *Tarbox*, *C. P. Thompson*, Thornburgh, *Throckmorton*, M. Townsend, W. Townsend, Tufts, Van Vorhes, *R. B. Vance*, Waldron, *C. C. B. Walker*, A. S. Wallace, J. W. Wallace, Walls, *Warren*, G. W. Wells, Wheeler, J. D. White, Whiting, G. Willard, C. G. Williams, *J. D. Williams*, W. B. Williams, *B. Wilson*, J. Wilson, A. Wood, jr., Woodburn, Woodworth—164.

NAYS—Messrs. *Ashe*, *Atkins*, *J. H. Bagley, jr.*, *Blackburn*, *Blount*, *Boone*, *Bradford*, *Bright*, *J. Y. Brown*, *Buckner*, *Cabell*, *J. H. Caldwell*, *Candler*, *Caulfield*, *Chapin*, *J. B. Clarke*, *J. B. Clark, jr.*, *Clymer*, *Collins*, *Cook*, *Cowan*, *Cutler*, *Joseph J. Davis*, *Dibrell*, *Douglas*, *Durham*, *Eden*, *Ellis*, *Felton*, *Forney*, *Franklin*, *Gause*, *Gibson*, *Glover*, *Goode*, *Gunter*, *A. H. Hamilton*, *R. Hamilton*, *Hancock*, *H. R. Harris*, *Hartridge*, *Hatcher*, *Henkle*, *Hereford*, *Hill*, *Hooker*, *Hopkins*, *House*, *Hunton*, *Kehr*, *Lamar*, *F. Landers*, *G. M. Landers*, *Lane*, *B. B. Lewis*, *Luttrell*, *L. A. Mackey*, *Maish*, *McFarland*, *McMahon*, *Metcalfe*, *Milliken*, *Mills*, *Money*, *Morrison*, *O'Brien*, *E. Y. Parsons*, *J. F. Philips*, *Poppleton*, *Randall*, *D. Rea*, *Reagan*, *A. V. Rice*, *Riddle*, *J. Robbins*, *W. M. Robbins*, *C. B. Roberts*, *M. Ross*, *M. Sayler*, *Scales*, *Schleicher*, *Sheakley*, *Singleton*, *Slemons*, *W. E. Smith*, *Southard*, *Sparks*, *Stenger*, *Stone*, *Swann*, *Terry*, *P. F. Thomas*, *Tucker*, *Turney*, *J. L. Vance*, *Waddell*, *G. C. Walker*, *Walling*, *Walsh*, *Ward*, *E. Wells*, *Whitehouse*, *Whitthorne*, *Wigginton*, *Wike*, *A. S. Williams*, *J. N. Williams*, *Wilshire*, *F. Wood*, *Yeates*, *C. Young*—111.

[For previous votes, see McPherson's Hand-Book of Politics for 1872, pp. 72, 73, 75–83; and Hand-Book for 1874, p. 214.]

XIII.

PRESIDENT GRANT'S CABINET, AND MEMBERS OF THE FORTY-FOURTH CONGRESS.

The Cabinet.

Secretary of State—HAMILTON FISH, of New York.

Secretary of the Treasury—LOT M. MORRILL, of Maine, July 7, 1876, *vice* BENJAMIN H. BRISTOW, of Kentucky, resigned June 20, 1876.

Secretary of War—J. DONALD CAMERON, of Pennsylvania, June 1, 1876, *vice* ALPHONSO TAFT, of Ohio, appointed March 11, 1876, in place of WILLIAM W. BELKNAP, of Iowa, resigned March 2, 1876.

Secretary of the Navy—GEORGE M. ROBESON, of New Jersey.

Secretary of the Interior—ZACHARIAH CHANDLER, of Michigan, October 19, 1875, *vice* COLUMBUS DELANO, of Ohio, resigned October 1, 1875.

Postmaster General—JAMES N. TYNER, of Indiana, July 12, 1876, *vice* MARSHALL JEWELL, of Connecticut, resigned July 10, 1876.

Attorney General—ALPHONSO TAFT, of Ohio, June 1, 1876, *vice* EDWARDS PIERREPONT, of New York, resigned that date, who was appointed May 15, 1875, in place of GEORGE H. WILLIAMS, of Oregon, resigned to take effect that day.

Members of Forty-Fourth Congress.

FIRST SESSION, DECEMBER 6, 1875—AUG. 15, 1876.

The Senate.

THOMAS W. FERRY, of Michigan, *President of the Senate pro tempore.*
George C. Gorham, of California, *Secretary.*

State	Senator	Term	Senator	Term
Alabama	George E. Spencer	(1879)	George Goldthwaite	(1877).
Arkansas	Stephen W. Dorsey	(1879)	Powell Clayton	(1877).
California	Newton Booth	(1881)	Aaron A. Sargent	(1879).
Connecticut	William W. Eaton	(1881)	William H. Barnum,*	(1879).
Delaware	Thomas F. Bayard	(1881)	Eli Saulsbury	(1877).
Florida	Charles W. Jones	(1881)	Simon B. Conover	(1879).
Georgia	John B. Gordon	(1879)	Thomas M. Norwood	(1877).
Illinois	Richard J. Oglesby	(1879)	John A. Logan	(1877).
Indiana	Joseph E. McDonald	(1881)	Oliver P. Morton	(1879).
Iowa	William B. Allison	(1879)	George G. Wright	(1877).
Kansas	John J. Ingalls	(1879)	James M. Harvey	(1877).
Kentucky	Thomas C. McCreery	(1879)	John W. Stevenson	(1877).
Louisiana	(Vacancy)	(1879)	J. Rodman West	(1877).
Maine	Hannibal Hamlin	(1881)	James G. Blaine†	(1877).
Maryland	William P. Whyte	(1881)	George R. Dennis	(1879).
Massachusetts	Henry L. Dawes	(1881)	George S. Boutwell	(1877).
Michigan	Isaac P. Christiancy	(1881)	Thomas W. Ferry	(1877).
Minnesota	S. J. R. McMillan	(1881)	William Windom	(1877).
Mississippi	Branch K. Bruce	(1881)	James L. Alcorn	(1877).
Missouri	Francis M. Cockrell	(1881)	Lewis V. Bogy	(1879).
Nebraska	Algernon S. Paddock	(1881)	Phineas W. Hitchcock	(1877).
Nevada	William Sharon‡	(1881)	John P. Jones	(1877).
New Hampshire	Bainbridge Wadleigh	(1879)	Aaron A. Cragin	(1877).
New Jersey	Theodore F. Randolph	(1881)	Fred'k. T. Frelinghuysen	(1877).
New York	Francis Kernan	(1881)	Roscoe Conkling	(1879).
North Carolina	Augustus S. Merrimon	(1879)	Matthew W. Ransom	(1877).
Ohio	Allen G. Thurman	(1881)	John Sherman	(1879).
Oregon	John H. Mitchell	(1879)	James K. Kelly	(1877).
Pennsylvania	William A. Wallace	(1881)	Simon Cameron	(1879).
Rhode Island	Ambrose E. Burnside	(1881)	Henry B. Anthony	(1877).
South Carolina	John J. Patterson	(1879)	Thomas J. Robertson	(1877).
Tennessee	Daniel M. Key§	(1881)	Henry Cooper	(1877).
Texas	Samuel B. Maxey	(1881)	Morgan C. Hamilton	(1877).
Vermont	George F. Edmunds	(1881)	Justin S. Morrill	(1879).
Virginia	Robert E. Withers	(1881)	John W. Johnston	(1877).
West Virginia	(Vacancy)¶	(1881)	Henry G. Davis	(1877).
Wisconsin	Angus Cameron	(1881)	Timothy O. Howe	(1879).

*Qualified May 22, 1876, under election by the Legislature, to fill the vacancy caused by the death of Orris S. Ferry, November 21, 1875—James E. English having qualified December 7, 1875, under Executive appointment, and served till the election of his successor.

†Mr. Blaine's credentials were presented July 12, 1876, to fill the vacancy caused by the resignation, July 7, 1876, of Lot M. Morrill, appointed Secretary of the Treasury. Mr. Blaine was absent from the Capital by reason of sickness, and did not qualify.

‡Qualified February 28, 1876.

§Qualified December 6, 1875, in place of Andrew Johnson, died July 31, 1875, who qualified March 4, 1875.

¶By the death of Allen T. Caperton, July 26, 1876.

NOTE.—At the close of the previous session of the Senate, THOMAS W. Ferry, of Michigan, was elected President of the Senate *pro tempore.* HENRY WILSON, *Vice-President* of the United States, died November 22d, 1875. At the opening of the first regular session of the Forty-fourth Congress, December 6th, 1875, Mr. FERRY resumed the chair. The questions which arose were settled by the Senate thus: January 10, 1876, the Senate adopted these resolutions reported by the Committee on Privileges and Elections:

Resolved, That the tenure of a President *pro tempore* of the Senate, elected at one session, does not expire at the meeting of Congress after the first recess, the Vice-President not having appeared to take the chair.

Resolved, That the death of the Vice-President does not have the effect to vacate the office of President *pro tempore* of the Senate.

Resolved, That the office of President *pro tempore* of the Senate is held at the pleasure of the Senate.

The first resolution was agreed to—yeas 59, nays none.

The second—yeas 62, nays none.

The third, January 12—yeas 34, nays 15.

THE LOUISIANA VACANCY.

NOTE.—The seat was claimed during the Forty-Third Congress by Pinckney B. S. Pinchback and W. L. M'Millan, but the right of either to it was not determined by the Senate, though frequently considered and long debated. In the Executive Session of the Senate, Forty-Fourth Congress, March 4th, 1875, it was revived, but not determined. In the first regular session it was again considered. December 9, 1875, Senator WEST presented the letter of W. L. M'Millan, asking permission to withdraw from the files of the Senate his credentials as Senator elect from the State of Louisiana, which was granted December 15—yeas 30, nays 28. Senator BAYARD, December 20, presented "a paper signed by John M'Enery, as Governor of Louisiana, and purporting to be the credentials of Robert H. Marr, appointed a Senator to fill the vacancy occasioned by the resignation of William L. M'Millan." Senator THURMAN, January 18, 1876, presented "papers purporting to be the credentials of J. B. Eustis, as a Senator from the State of Louisiana for the term ending March 3, 1879;" which, January 24, were referred to the Committee on Privileges and Elections. That Committee, January 28th, reported that "there is no vacancy in the office of Senator from the State of Louisiana, P. B. S. Pinchback having been elected in January, 1873, to the term beginning on the 4th of March, 1873." The question of seating Mr. Pinchback was considered and debated at different times from February 8 to March 8, 1876, when it was decided. The question being on the adoption of the resolution of the Committee on Privileges and Elections that Mr. Pinchback be admitted to the seat,

MR. EDMUNDS moved to insert the word "not" before the word "admitted;" which was agreed to—yeas 32, nays 29, as follow:

YEAS—Messrs. *Bayard*, *Caperton*, Christiancy, *Cockrell*, *Cooper*, *Davis*, *Dennis*, *Eaton*, Edmunds, *English*, *Cordon*, *Johnson*, *Jones* of Florida, *Kelly*, *Kernan*, *Key*, *McCreery*, *McDonald*, *Maxey*, *Merrimon*, Morrill of Maine, Morrill of Vermont, *Norwood*, Paddock, *Randolph*, *Ransom*, *Saulsbury*, *Stevenson*, *Thurman*, *Wallace*, *Whyte*, *Withers*—32.

NAYS—Messrs. Allison, Anthony, Boutwell, Bruce, Cameron of Pennsylvania, Conkling, Conover, Cragin, Dorsey, Ferry, Frelinghuysen, Hamilton, Hamlin, Harvey, Hitchcock, Howe, Ingalls, Jones of Nevada, Logan, McMillan, Mitchell, Morton, Patterson, Sargent, Sharon, Sherman, Spencer, West, Windom—29.

The resolution, as amended, was then agreed to, by the same vote.

The House of Representatives.

MICHAEL C. KERR, of Indiana, *Speaker*.

George M. Adams, of Kentucky, *Clerk*.

Alabama—Jere Haralson, Jeremiah N. Williams, Taul Bradford, Charles Hays, John H. Caldwell, Goldsmith W. Hewitt, Burwell B. Lewis, William H. Forney—8.

Arkansas—Lucien C. Gause, William F. Slemons, William W. Wilshire, Thomas M. Gunter—4.

California—William A. Piper, Horace F. Page, John K. Luttrell, Peter D. Wigginton—4.

Connecticut—George M. Landers, James Phelps, John T. Wait,* William H. Barnum,† —4.

Delaware—James Williams—1.

Florida—Jesse J. Finley,‡ William J. Purman —2.

Georgia—Julian Hartridge, William E. Smith, Philip Cook, Henry R. Harris, Milton A. Candler, James H. Blount, William H. Felton, Alexander H. Stephens, Benjamin H. Hill—9.

Illinois—Bernard G. Caulfield, Carter H. Harrison, J. V. LeMoyne,‖ Stephen A. Hurlbut, Horatio C. Burchard, Thomas J. Henderson, Alexander Campbell, Greenbury L. Fort, Richard H. Whiting, John C. Bagby, Scott Wike, William M. Springer, Adlai E. Stevenson, Joseph G. Cannon, John R. Eden, Wm. A. J. Sparks, William R. Morrison, William Hartzell, William B. Anderson—19.

Indiana—Benoni S. Fuller, James D. Williams, Michael C. Kerr, Jeptha D. New, William S. Holman, Milton S. Robinson, Franklin Landers, Morton C. Hunter, Thomas J. Cason, William S. Haymond, James L. Evans, Andrew H. Hamilton, John H. Baker—13.

Iowa—George W. McCrary, John Q. Tufts, Lucien L. Ainsworth, Henry O. Pratt, James Wilson, Ezekiel S. Sampson, John A. Kasson, James W. McDill, Addison Oliver—9.

Kansas—William A. Phillips, John R. Goodin, William R. Brown—3.

Kentucky—Andrew R. Boone, John Young Brown, Charles W. Milliken, J. Proctor Knott, Edward Y. Parsons,§ Thomas L. Jones, Joseph C. S. Blackburn, Milton J. Durham, John D. White, John B. Clarke—10.

Louisiana—Randall L. Gibson, E. John Ellis, Chester B. Darrall, William M. Levy, William B. Spencer,¶ Charles E. Nash—6.

Maine—John H. Burleigh, William P. Frye, James G. Blaine,** Harris M. Plaisted, Eugene Hale—5.

Maryland—Philip F. Thomas, Charles B. Roberts, William J. O'Brien, Thomas Swann, Eli J. Henkle, William Walsh—6.

Massachusetts—William W. Crapo,†† Benjamin W. Harris, Henry L. Pierce, Rufus S. Frost,‡‡ Nathaniel P. Banks, Charles P. Thompson, John K. Tarbox, William Wirt Warren, George F. Hoar, Julius H. Seelye, Chester W. Chapin—11.

Michigan—Alpheus S. Williams, Henry Waldron, George Willard, Allen Potter, William B.

* Qualified April 12, 1876, *vice* Henry H. Starkweather, died January 28, 1876.

† Mr. Barnum resigned, May 18, 1876, to take his seat in the Senate.

‡ Qualified April 19, 1876, *vice* Josiah T. Walls, unseated by a vote of 135 to 84.

‖ Qualified May 5, 1876, *vice* Charles B. Farwell, unseated May 3, by a vote of 129 to 89.

§ Died July 8, 1876.

¶ Qualified June 8, 1876, in place of Frank Morey, unseated May 31, 1876. The minority resolution that Mr. Spencer was not elected was disagreed to, yeas 74, nays 99, and the resolution that he was elected was then agreed to without a division. A substitute by Mr. McCrary, for additional time, &c., was lost—76 to 101.

** Resigned July 10, 1876, to accept appointment of Senator from Maine.

†† Elected November 2, 1875, to fill vacancy caused by the death of James Buffinton, March 7, 1875.

‡‡ July 14, 1876, Mr. Frost unseated—102 to 79—and Josiah G. Abbott declared entitled to the seat.

Williams, George H. Durand, Omar D. Conger, Nathan B. Bradley, Jay A. Hubbell—9.

Minnesota—Mark H. Dunnell, Horace B. Strait, William S. King—3.

Mississippi—Lucius Q. C. Lamar, G. Wiley Wells, Hernando D. Money, Otho R. Singleton, Charles E. Hooker, John R. Lynch—6.

Missouri—Edward C. Kehr, Erastus Wells, William H. Stone, Robert A. Hatcher, Richard P. Bland, Charles H. Morgan, John F. Philips, Benjamin J. Franklin, David Rea, Rezin A. DeBolt, John B. Clark, jr., John M. Glover, Aylett H. Buckner—13.

Nebraska—Lorenzo Crounse—1.

Nevada—William Woodburn—1.

New Hampshire—Frank Jones, Samuel N. Bell, Henry W. Blair—3.

New Jersey—Clement H. Sinnickson, Samuel A. Dobbins, Miles Ross, Robert Hamilton, Augustus W. Cutler, Frederick H. Teese, Augustus A. Hardenbergh—7.

New York—Henry B. Metçalfe, John G. Schumaker, Simeon B. Chittenden, Archibald M. Bliss, Edwin R. Meade, Samuel S. Cox, Smith Ely, jr., Elijah Ward, Fernando Wood, Abram S. Hewitt, Benjamin A. Willis, N. Holmes Odell, John O. Whitehouse, George M. Beebe, John H. Bagley, jr., Charles H. Adams, Martin I. Townsend, Andrew Williams, William A. Wheeler, Henry H. Hathorn, Samuel F. Miller, George A. Bagley, Scott Lord, William H. Baker, Elias W. Leavenworth, Clinton D. MacDougall, Elbridge G. Lapham, Thomas C. Platt, Charles C. B. Walker, John M. Davy, George G. Hoskins, Lyman K. Bass, Nelson I. Norton—33.

North Carolina—Jesse J. Yeates, John A. Hyman, Alfred M. Waddell, Joseph J. Davis, Alfred M. Scales, Thomas S. Ashe, William M. Robbins, Robert B. Vance—8.

Ohio—Milton Sayler, Henry B. Banning, John S. Savage, John A. McMahon, Americus V. Rice, Frank H. Hurd, Lawrence T. Neal, William Lawrence, Earley F. Poppleton, Charles Foster, John L. Vance, Ansel T. Walling, Milton I. Southard, Jacob P. Cowan, Nelson H. Van Vorhes, Lorenzo Danford, Laurin D. Woodworth, James Monroe, James A. Garfield, Henry B. Payne—20.

Pennsylvania—Chapman Freeman, Charles O'Neill, Samuel J. Randall, William D. Kelley, John Robbins, Washington Townsend, Alan Wood, jr., Hiester Clymer, A. Herr Smith, William Mutchler, Francis D. Collins, Winthrop W. Ketchum, James B. Reilly, John B. Packer, Joseph Powell, Sobieski Ross, John Reilly, William S. Stenger, Levi Maish Levi A. Mackey, Jacob Turney, James H. Hopkins, Alexander G. Cochrane, John W. Wallace, George A. Jenks, James Sheakley, Albert G. Egbert—27.

Rhode Island—Benjamin T. Eames, Latimer W. Ballou—2.

South Carolina—Joseph H. Rainey, Edmund W. M. Mackey,* Solomon L. Hoge, Alexander S. Wallace, Robert Smalls—5.

Tennessee—William McFarland, Jacob M. Thornburgh, George G. Dibrell, Haywood Y. Riddle,† John M. Bright, John F. House, Washington C. Whitthorne, John D. C. Atkins, William P. Caldwell, Casey Young—10.

Texas—John H. Reagan, David B. Culberson, James W. Throckmorton, Roger Q. Mills, John Hancock, Gustave Schleicher—6.

Vermont—Charles H. Joyce, Dudley C. Denison, George W. Hendee—3.

Virginia—Beverly B. Douglas, John Goode, jr.,‡ Gilbert C. Walker, William H. H. Stowell, George C. Cabell, John R. Tucker, John T. Harris, Eppa Hunton, William Terry—9.

West Virginia—Benjamin Wilson, Charles J. Faulkner, Frank Hereford—3.

Wisconsin—Charles G. Williams, Lucien B. Caswell, Henry S. Magoon, William P. Lynde, Samuel D. Burchard, Alanson M. Kimball, Jeremiah M. Rusk, George W. Cate—8.

THE DELEGATES FROM TERRITORIES.

Arizona—Hiram S. Stevens.
Colorado—Thomas M. Patterson.
Dakota—Jefferson P. Kidder.
Idaho—Stephen S. Fenn.§
Montana—Martin McGinnis.
New Mexico—Stephen B. Elkins.
Utah—George Q. Cannon.
Washington—Orange Jacobs.
Wyoming—William R. Steele.

* Committee on Elections reported, July 13, 1876, neither C. W. Butts nor Mr. Mackey lawfully elected.

† Qualified January 5, 1876, to fill the vacancy caused by the death of Hon. Samuel M. Fite, who died in the fall of 1875.

‡ A majority of Committee on Elections reported, July 17, 1876, that James H. Platt, jr., was legally elected.

§ Qualified June 23, 1876, in place of T. W. Bennett unseated that day.

XIV.

DECLARATORY RESOLUTIONS IN SENATE AND HOUSE.

The Theory of Government.

IN SENATE.

1875, December 15—Mr. MORTON submitted the following:

Resolved by the Senate, (the House of Representatives concurring,) That the people of the United States constitute a nation, and are one people in the sense of national unity.

Resolved, That the Government of the United States is not a compact between the States, in their municipal and corporate characters, but was formed by the people of the United States in their primary capacity; that the rights of the States are defined and guaranteed by the Constitution, and not by any outside theory of State sovereignty; and that the rights of the States cannot be enlarged or diminished except by an amendment to the Constitution.

Resolved, That the rights of the States have the same sanction and security in the Constitution as the rights and powers of the National Government, and that local domestic government by the States, within the limits of the Constitution, is an essential part of our free republican system.

Resolved, That the doctrine that a State has the right to secede from the Union is inconsistent with the idea of nationality, is in conflict with the spirit and structure of the Constitution, and should be regarded as having been forever extinguished by the suppression of the rebellion.

No vote was reached.

IN SENATE.

1876, January 10—Mr. WHYTE submitted the following:

Resolved by the Senate, (the House of Representatives concurring,) That the people of the several States, acting in their highest sovereign capacity as free and independent States, adopted the Federal Constitution and established a form of government in the nature of a confederated republic, and for the purpose of carrying into effect the objects for which it was formed, delegated to that Government certain rights enumerated in said Constitution, but reserved to the States respectively or to the people thereof all the residuary powers not delegated to the United States by the Constitution nor prohibited by it to the States.

No vote was reached.

Appointments to Office.

IN HOUSE.

1875, December 14th—Mr. FORT offered the following:

Resolved, That in all subordinate appointments, under any of the officers of this House, it is the judgment of this House that wounded Union soldiers, who are not disabled from performance of duty, should be preferred.

And he demanded the previous question, but the House refused to second it.

Mr. COX submitted the following amendment in the nature of a substitute:

Resolved, That inasmuch as the Union of the States has been restored, all the citizens thereof are entitled to consideration in all appointments to offices under this Government.

And he moved the reference to the Committee on Accounts, which was agreed to—yeas 168, nays 102 (not voting 19), as follow:

YEAS—Messrs. *Ainsworth, Anderson, Ashe, Atkins, Bagby, J. H. Bagley, jr., Banning, Barnum, Beebe, S. N. Bell, Blackburn, Bland, Bliss, Blount, Boone, Bradford, Bright, J. Y. Brown, Buckner, S. D. Burchard, Cabell, J. H. Caldwell, W. P. Caldwell, Candler, Cate, Caulfield, Chapin,* Chittenden, *J. B. Clarke, J. B. Clark, jr., Clymer, Cochrane, Cook, Cowan, Cox, Culberson, Cutler, Joseph J. Davis, DeBolt, Dibrell, Douglas, Durand, Eden, Egbert, Ellis, Ely, Faulkner, Felton, Forney, Franklin, Fuller, Gause, Gibson, Glover, Goode, Gunter, A. H. Hamilton, R. Hamilton, Hancock, Hardenbergh, H. R. Harris, J. T. Harris, C. H. Harrison, Hartridge, Hartzell, Hatcher, Haymond, Hereford, A. S. Hewitt, G. W. Hewitt, Hill, Holman, Hooker, Hopkins, House, Hunton, Hurd, Jenks, F. Jones, T. L. Jones, Kehr, Knott, Lamar, F. Landers, G. M. Landers, Lane, Levy, B. B. Lewis, Lord, Luttrell, Lynde, Maish, McFarland, McMahon, Meade, Metcalfe, Milliken, Mills, Money, Morgan, Morrison, Mutchler, Neal, New, O'Brien, Odell, E. Y. Parsons, Payne, J. Phelps, J. F. Philips, Piper, Poppleton, Randall, D. Rea, Reagan, J. Reilly, J. B. Reilly, A. V. Rice, J. Robbins, W. M. Robbins, M. Ross, Savage, M. Sayler, Scales, Schleicher, J. G. Schumaker,* Seelye, *Sheakley, Singleton, Slemons, W. E. Smith, Southard, Sparks, Springer, Stenger, Stone, Swann, Tarbox, Teese, Terry, C. P. Thompson, P. F. Thomas, Throckmorton, Tucker, Turney, J. L. Vance, R. B. Vance, Waddell, C. C. B. Walker, G. C. Walker, Walling, Ward, Warren, E. Wells, Whitehouse, Whitthorne, Wigginton, Wike, A. S. Williams, J. Williams, J. D. Williams, J. N. Williams, Willis, Wilshire, B. Wilson, F. Wood, Yeates, C. Young*—168.

NAYS—Messrs. C. H. Adams, G. A. Bagley, J. H. Baker, W. H. Baker, Ballou, Blaine, Blair, Bradley, W. R. Brown, H. C. Burchard, Burleigh, Cannon, Cason, Caswell, Conger, Crapo, Crounse, Danford, Darrall, Davy, Denison, Dobbins, Dunnell, Eames, Evans, Farwell, Fort, Foster, C. Freeman, Frost, Frye, Garfield, *Goodin*, E. Hale, Haralson, B. W. Harris, Henderson, G. F. Hoar, Hoge, Hoskins, Hubbell, Hunter, Hurlbut, Hyman, Joyce, Kasson, Kelley, Ketchum, Kimball, King, Lapham, W. Lawrence, Lynch, Magoon, MacDougall, McCrary, J. W. McDill, Miller, Monroe, Nash, Norton, Oliver, O'Neill, Packer, Page, W. A. Phillips, Pierce, Plaisted, Pratt, Purman, Rainey, M. S. Robinson, S. Ross, Rusk, Sampson, Sinnickson, R. Smalls, A. H. Smith, Starkweather, *Stevenson*, Stowell, Strait, Thornburgh, M. I. Townsend, W. Townsend, Tufts, Van Vorhes, Waldron, A. S. Wallace, J. W. Wallace, Walls, G. W. Wells, Wheeler, J. D. White, Whiting, G. Willard, C. G. Williams, W. B. Williams, J. Wilson, A. Wood, jr., Woodburn, Woodworth—102.

1876, January 5—Mr. CASON offered the following:

Whereas the people of these United States have lately passed through an internecine war, in which one section of the country has been arrayed against the other, brother against brother, and father against son; and whereas we owe the preservation of the Union, the establishment of peace, and the enforcement of law and order, to the bravery and patriotic devotion of the loyal soldiers to the Union and its cause: Therefore,

Be it resolved by the House of Representatives, That we recognize the brave and gallant services rendered by the loyal soldier to his country in the time of its greatest need and peril, and that we do earnestly recommend to the people of our common country the utmost care and watchfulness over the rights and interests of these brave men, securing to each one in need employment, and to such and their families the necessaries and common comforts of life; and in all cases of public employment and in the bestowment of the emoluments of office, that, all other things being equal, the soldier should have the preference over the civilian; and, as one branch of the legislative department of this Government, we are in favor of laws being enacted by Congress giving liberal pensions to the diseased and crippled soldiers, and to the widows and children and dependent fathers and mothers of those who have died of wounds or diseases contracted while in the service of the Union Army, and to each living soldier, and to the widows and heirs of those dead, such bounties and homesteads as a generous Government can afford to those who have won and preserved to the nation its unity and Constitution.

On which he demanded the previous question, and it was seconded, yeas 142, nays 9; and the resolution was agreed to.

Same day Mr. FORT offered the following:

Resolved, That the doctrine just announced by the House in the resolution of the gentleman from Indiana (Mr. CASON) is so wise and just that in the judgment of this House it should be followed by officers of the House in filling subordinate places under their authority; and that in all such cases they are hereby instructed to give to well-qualified Union soldiers preference over soldiers of the late confederate army.

On which he demanded the previous question, but it was not seconded, yeas 78, nays 103.

Mr. F. WOOD moved its reference to the Committee on the Centennial Celebration; which was agreed to—yeas 122, nays 93 (not voting 75), as follow:

YEAS—Messrs. *Ashe, Atkins, Bagby, J. H. Bagley, jr., Bland, Blount, Boone, Bradford, Bright, J. Y. Brown, Buckner, S. D. Burchard, Cabell, J. H. Caldwell, W. P. Caldwell, Candler, Chapin, J. B. Clark, jr., Clymer, Cochrane, Cook, Cowan, Cox, Culberson, Cutler, Joseph J. Davis, DeBolt, Dibrell, Douglas, Durham, Eden, Egbert, Faulkner, Felton, Forney, Franklin, Fuller, Gause, Glover, Goode, A. H. Hamilton, R. Hamilton, Hancock, H. R. Harris, J. T. Harris, C. H. Harrison, Hatcher, Hereford, A. S. Hewitt, Hill, Hooker, Hopkins, House, Hunton, Jenks, G. M. Landers, Lane, Levy, Lord, Lynde, L. A. Mackey, Maish, McFarland, McMahon, Metcalfe, Milliken, Mills, Money, Morrison, Mutchler, New, O'Brien, E. Y. Parsons, J. Phelps, J. F. Philips, Piper, Poppleton, Powell, Randall, D. Rea, Reagan, J. Reilly, J. B. Reilly, Riddle, J. Robbins, W. M. Robbins, C. B. Roberts, M. Ross, M. Sayler, Schleicher, Sheakley, Singleton, Slemons, W. E. Smith, Southard, Springer, Stenger, Stone, Tarbox, Terry, C. P. Thompson, Throckmorton, Tucker, Turney, J. L. Vance, Waddell, Walling, Walsh, Ward, Warren, E. Wells, Whitthorne, Wike, J. Williams, J. D. Williams, J. N. Williams, Willis, Wilshire, B. Wilson, F. Wood, Yeates, C. Young*—122.

NAYS—Messrs *Ainsworth*, ANDERSON, J. H. Baker, W. H. Baker, Ballou, BANKS, Blaine, Blair, W. R. Brown, H. C. Burchard, Burleigh, Cannon, Cason, *Caulfield*, Chittenden, Conger, Crapo, Crounse, Danford, Davy, Denison, Dobbins, Dunnell, Eames, Farwell, Fort, C. Freeman, Frost, Frye, Garfield, *Goodin*, E. Hale, Haralson, B. W. Harris, *Hartzell*, Hendee, Henderson, *Holman*, Hoskins, Hubbell, Hurlbut, Hyman, Joyce, Kasson, Kelley, Kimball, Lapham, W. Lawrence, Leavenworth, Lynch, McCrary, J. W. McDill, Monroe, Morey, *Neal*, Norton, Oliver, O'Neill, Page, W. A. Phillips, Pierce, Plaisted, Purman, Rainey, M. S. Robinson, S. Ross, Rusk, Sampson, *Savage*, Seelye, Sinnickson, R. Smalls, A. H. Smith, Starkweather, *Stevenson*, Thornburgh, M. I. Townsend, W. Townsend, Tufts, Van Vorhes, Waldron, Wheeler, J. D. White, Whiting, G. Willard, A. Williams, *A. S. Williams*, C. G. Williams, W. R. Williams, J. Wilson, A. Wood, jr. Woodburn, Woodworth—93.

Same day—Mr. CARTER H. HARRISON offered the following:

Resolved, That in the distribution of the patronage under the House of Representatives and in the Government generally, those duly elected, and who by law have the appointment of subordinates, should regard the Jeffersonian test—is he honest? is he faithful? is he capable?—and that recent events in Federal administration give peculiar emphasis to this democratic sentiment.

On which the previous question was demanded and seconded, and the resolution passed.

January 6—Mr. NEW offered the following:

Resolved, That the fraternal feeling and good-will now existing in all sections of the Union, and the manifest disposition and purpose of the men who battled against each other in the late civil war to join hands as one people in the future is a most auspicious ushering in of the centennial year; and while the people are thus making an honest effort to live together in peace and uphold the same flag for an undivided country, their representatives in Congress should do no act which will unnecessarily disturb the patriotic concord now existing and increasing, or wantonly revive the bitter memories of the past.

Which was unanimously agreed to—yeas 250, nays 0 (not voting 40).

Resumption of Specie Payments.

December 15—Mr. EUGENE HALE offered the following preamble and resolutions:

Whereas the country is suffering under the evils of an irredeemable currency, which causes uncertainty in business and stimulates speculation, to the prejudice of legitimate business and labor; and whereas both political parties in the United States stand committed against repudiation and in favor of a speedy return to specie payment; and whereas Congress established a like policy in the act of March 16, 1869, which was followed by the act of January 14, 1875, providing for the resumption of specie payments on the 1st day of January, 1879; therefore

Resolved, That, in the judgment of this House, prompt legislative measures should be taken to render said act of January 14, 1875, effective, by placing in the hands of the Secretary of the Treasury whatever power may be necessary to that end.

And he demanded the previous question upon it; but the House refused to second the same on a count—ayes 75, noes 143. And it was referred to the Committee on Banking and Currency.

Subsidies to Railroads.

December 15—Mr. HOLMAN offered the following:

Resolved, That in the judgment of this House, in the present condition of the financial affairs of the Government, no subsidies in money, bonds, public lands, indorsements, or by pledge of the public credit, should be granted by Congress to associations or corporations engaged or proposing to engage in public or private enterprises; and that all appropriations from the public treasury ought to be limited at this time to such amounts only as shall be imperatively demanded by the public service.

Which was agreed to—yeas 223, nays 33, (not voting 33,) as follow:

YEAS—Messrs. C. H. Adams, *Ainsworth*, ANDERSON, *Ashe*, *Bagby*, G. A. Bagley, *J. H. Bagley, jr.*, J. H. Baker, W. H. Baker, Ballou, *Banning*, *Beebe*, *S. N. Bell*, *Blackburn*, Blaine, Blair, *Bland*, *Bliss*, *Blount*, *Boone*, *Bradford*, Bradley, *J. Y. Brown*, W. R. Brown, H. C. Burchard, *S. D. Burchard*, Burleigh, *J. H. Caldwell*, *W. P. Caldwell*, CAMPBELL, *Candler*, Cannon, Cason, Caswell, *Cate*, *Caulfield*, *Chapin*, Chittenden, *J. B. Clarke*, *J. B. Clark, jr.*, *Clymer*, *Cochrane*, *Collins*, Conger, *Cook*, *Cowan*, *Cox*, Crapo, Crounse, *Culberson*, *Cutler*, Danford, *Joseph J. Davis*, Davy, *DeBolt*, Denison, *Dibrell*, Dobbins, *Durand*, Eames, *Eden*, *Egbert*, *Ellis*, *Ely*, Evans, *Faulkner*, *Felton*, *Forney*, Fort, Foster, *Franklin*, C. Freeman, Frost, Frye, *Fuller*, Garfield, *Gause*, *Gibson*, *Glover*, *Goodin*, *Gunter*, E. Hale, *A. H. Hamilton*, *R. Hamilton*, Haralson, *Hardenbergh*, B. W. Harris, *H. R. Harris*, *C. H. Harrison*, *Hartridge*, *Hartzell*, *Hatcher*, *Haymond*, Henderson, *Henkle*, *Hereford*, *A. S. Hewitt*, *G. W. Hewitt*, *Hill*, G. F. Hoar, *Holman*, *Hooker*, *Hopkins*, Hoskins, Hubbell, Hunter, *Hurd*, *Jenks*, *F. Jones*, Joyce, Kasson, Ketchum, Kimball, King, *Knott*, *F. Landers*, *G. M. Landers*, Lapham, W. Lawrence, Leavenworth, *Levy*, *B. B. Lewis*, *Lord*, *Luttrell*, Lynch, *Lynde*, *L. A. Mackey*, Magoon, *Maish*, MacDougall, McCrary, J. W. McDill, *McFarland*, *McMahon*, *Metcalfe*, Miller, *Milliken*, *Money*, Monroe, *Morgan*, *Morrison*, *Mutchler*, Nash, *Neal*, *New*, Norton, *O'Brien*, *Odell*, Oliver, Packer, Page, *Payne*, *J. F. Philips*, W. A. Phillips, Pierce, *Piper*, Plaisted, *Poppleton*, A. POTTER, Rainey, *Randall*, *D. Rea*, *J. B. Reilly*, *A. V. Rice*, *J. Robbins*, *W. M. Robbins*, *C. B. Roberts*, M. S. Robinson, *M. Ross*, Rusk, Sampson, *Savage*, *M. Sayler*, *Scales*, *Schumaker*, Seelye, *Sheakley*, *Singleton*, Sinnickson, A. H. Smith, *W. E. Smith*, *Southard*, *Sparks*, *Springer*, Starkweather, *Stenger*, *Stevenson*, Stowell, *Tarbox*, *Teese*, *C. P. Thompson*, *P. F. Thomas*, Thornburgh, M. I. Townsend, Tufts, *Turney*, Van Vorhes, *J. L. Vance*, *Waddell*, Waldron, *C. C. B. Walker*, A. S. Wallace, *Walling*, *Ward*, *Warren*, Wheeler, Whiting, *Whitthorne*, *Wigginton*, *Wike*, G. Willard, *A. S. Williams*, C. G. Williams, *J. Williams*, *J. D. Williams*, *J. N. Williams*, W. B. Williams, *Willis*, *B. Wilson*, J. Wilson, A. Wood, jr., *F. Wood*, Woodworth—223.

NAYS—Messrs. *Cabell*, Darrall, *Douglas*, Dunnell, *Goode*, *Hancock*, *J. T. Harris*, *House*, *Hunton*, Hyman, *T. L. Jones*, Kelley, *Lamar*, *Mills*, Morey, O'Neill, *E. Y. Parsons*, *Reagan*, *J. Reilly*, *Slemons*, R. Smalls, Strait, *Stone*, *Terry*, *Throckmorton*, *Tucker*, *R. B. Vance*, J. W. Wallace, *E. Wells*, G. W. Wells, J. D. White, *Yeates*, *C. Young*—33.

On "Third Term."

December 15—Mr. SPRINGER offered the following:

Resolved, That, in the opinion of this House, the precedent established by Washington and other Presidents of the United States, in retiring from the presidential office after their second term, has become, by universal concurrence, a part of our republican system of government, and that any departure from this time-honored custom would be unwise, unpatriotic, and fraught with peril to our free institutions.

Which was agreed to—yeas 234, nays 18 (not voting 37), as follow:

YEAS—Messrs. C. H. Adams, *Ainsworth*, ANDERSON, *Ashe*, *Atkins*, G. A. Bagley, *J. H. Bagley, jr.*, J. H. Baker, W. H. Baker, Ballou, *Banning*, *Beebe*, *S. N. Bell*, *Blackburn*, Blair, *Bland*, *Blount*, *Boone*, *Bradford*, *Bright*, *J. Y. Brown*, W. R. Brown, *Buckner*, H. C. Burchard, *S. D. Burchard*, Burleigh, *Cabell*, *J. H. Caldwell*, *W. P. Caldwell*, CAMPBELL, *Candler*, Cason, *Cate*, *Caulfield*, *Chapin*, Chittenden, *J. B. Clarke*, *J. B. Clark, jr.*, *Clymer*, *Cochrane*, *Collins*, Conger, *Cook*, *Cowan*, *Cox*, Crapo, Crounse, *Culberson*, *Cutler*, Danford, Darrall, *Joseph J. Davis*, Davy, *DeBolt*, *Dibrell*, *Douglas*, Dunnell, *Durand*, Eames, *Eden*, *Egbert*, *Ellis*, *Ely*, Evans, *Faulkner*, *Felton*, *Forney*, Fort, Foster, *Franklin*, C. Freeman, Frost, Frye, *Fuller*, Garfield, *Gause*, *Gibson*, *Glover*, *Goode*, *Goodin*, *Gunter*, E. Hale, *A. H. Hamilton*, *R. Hamilton*, *Hancock*, *Hardenbergh*, B. W. Harris, *H. R. Harris*, *J. T. Harris*, *C. H. Harrison*, *Hartridge*, *Hartzell*, *Hatcher*, Hathorn, *Haymond*, Henderson, *Henkle*, *Hereford*, *A. S. Hewitt*, *G. W. Hewitt*, *Hill*, G. F. Hoar, *Holman*, *Hooker*, *Hopkins*, Hoskins, *House*, Hunter, *Hunton*, *Jenks*, *F. Jones*, *T. L. Jones*, Joyce, Kasson, Kelley, Ketchum, *Knott*, *F. Landers*, *G. M. Landers*, *Lane*, Lapham, W. Lawrence, Leavenworth, *Levy*, *B. B. Lewis*, *Lord*, *Luttrell*, *Lynde*, *L. A. Mackey*, *Maish*, McCrary, J. W. McDill, *McMahon*, *Metcalfe*, Miller, *Milliken*, *Mills*, *Money*, Monroe, *Morgan*, *Morrison*, *Mutchler*, *Neal*, *New*, Norton, *O'Brien*, *Odell*, Oliver, O'Neill, Packer, *E. Y. Parsons*, *Payne*, *J. F. Philips*, W. A. Phillips, Pierce, *Piper*, *Poppleton*, A. POTTER, *Powell*, *Randall*, *D. Rea*, *Reagan*, *J. Reilly*, *J. B. Reilly*, *A. V. Rice*, *J. Robbins*, *W. M. Robbins*, *C. B. Roberts*, M. S. Robinson, *M. Ross*, S. Ross, Sampson, *Savage*, *M. Sayler*, *Scales*, *Schumaker*, Seelye, *Sheakley*, *Singleton*, Sinnickson, A. H. Smith, *W. E. Smith*, *Southard*, *Sparks*, *Springer*, Starkweather, *Stenger*, *Stevenson*, *Stone*, *Swann*, *Tarbox*, *Teese*, *Terry*, *C. P. Thompson*, *P. F. Thomas*, *Throckmorton*, M. I. Townsend, W. Townsend, *Tucker*, Tufts, *Turney*, Van Vorhes, *J. L. Vance*, *R. B. Vance*, *Waddell*, Waldron, *C. C. B. Walker*, *G. C. Walker*, J. W. Wallace, *Walling*, *Walsh*, *Ward*, *Warren*, *E. Wells*, Wheeler, *Whitehouse*, *Whitthorne*, *Wigginton*, *Wike*, G. Willard, *A. S. Williams*, C. G. Williams, *J. Williams*, *J. D. Williams*, *J. N. Williams*, W. B. Williams, *Willis*, *B. Wilson*, J. Wilson, A. Wood, jr., *F. Wood*, Woodworth, *Yeates*, *C. Young*—234.

NAYS—Messrs. Bradley, Denison, Haralson, Hoge, Hubbell, Hyman, Lynch, MacDougall, Nash, Page, Plaisted, Pratt, R. Smalls, A. S. Wallace, Walls, G. W. Wells, J. D. White, Whiting—18.

December 17—Mr. PAGE offered the following:

Whereas the Constitution of the United States, as framed by the fathers of the republic, imposes no limit upon the eligibility of any citizen to the office of President further than that he shall be native-born and of a certain age and time of residence: Therefore be it

Resolved, That in the judgment of this House the right of selecting candidates for the office of President can only be lawfully exercised by the people under existing constitutional restrictions, and has never been delegated by the people to the House of Representatives or to any members of the same, and that any attempt by the House of Representatives to limit or forestall the public will on a question of such importance is an invasion of powers reserved to the people at large, to be freely exercised by them without any interference from any legislative body whatever.

And he demanded the previous question upon it, but the House refused—yeas 30, nays 89.

May 22—The resolution coming up,

Mr. C. H. HARRISON and Mr. BLOUNT moved to lay it on the table; which was agreed to—yeas 147, nays 82 (not voting 60), as follow:

YEAS—Messrs. *Ashe, Atkins, Bagby, J. H. Bagley, jr., Beebe, S. N. Bell, Blackburn, Bland, Bliss, Blount, Boone, Bradford, Bright, J. Y. Brown, Buckner, S. D. Burchard, Cabell, J. H. Caldwell, W. P. Caldwell, Candler, Cate, J. B. Clarke, J. B. Clark, jr., Clymer, Collins, Cook, Cowan, Culberson, Cutler, Joseph J. Davis, De-Bolt, Dibrell, Durand, Durham, Eden, Egbert, Ellis, Ely, Faulkner, Felton, Finley, Forney, Franklin, Fuller, Gause, Gibson, Glover, Goode, Gunter, A. H Hamilton, R. Hamilton, Hancock, Hardenbergh, H. R. Harris, J. T. Harris, C. H. Harrison, Hartridge, Hartzell, Hatcher, Haymond, Henkle, Hereford, A. S. Hewitt, G. W. Hewitt, Hill, Hooker, Hopkins, House, Hunton, Hurd, Jenks, F. Jones, T. L. Jones, Kehr, Knott, Lamar, F. Landers, G. M. Landers, Le Moyne, Levy, B. B. Lewis, Lord, Luttrell, McFarland, Metcalfe, Milliken, Mills, Money, Morgan, Mutchler, Neal, New,* Oliver, *E. Y. Parsons, Payne, J. F. Philips,* Pierce, *Piper, Poppleton, Powell, Randall, D. Rea, Reagan, J. Reilly, J. B. Reilly, A. V. Rice, Riddle, J. Robbins, W. M. Robbins, C. B. Roberts, M. Ross, Savage, M. Sayler, Scales, Schleicher,* Seelye, *Singleton, Slemons, W. E. Smith, Southard, Sparks, Springer, Stenger, Stone, Tarbox, Teese, Terry, C. P. Thompson, Throckmorton, Tucker, Turney, R. B. Vance, Waddell, C. C. B. Walker, G. C. Walker, Walling, Walsh, Warren, Whitthorne, Wike, J. Williams, J. D. Williams, J. N. Williams, Willis, F. Wood, Yeates, C. Young*—147.

NAYS—Messrs. C. H. Adams, *Ainsworth*, ANDERSON, J. H. Baker, W. H. Baker, Ballou, BANKS, Bass, Bradley, W. R. Brown, H. C. Burchard, Burleigh, CAMPBELL, Caswell, Conger, Crapo, Danford, Davy, Denison, Dunnell, Eames, Fort, Foster, C. Freeman, Frost, Frye, *Goodin*, E. Hale, Haralson, B. W. Harris, Hathorn, Hendee, Hoge, Hoskins, Hunter, Hyman, Kasson, Kelley, Ketchum, W. Lawrence, Leavenworth, Lynch, *Lynde*, E. W. M. Mackey, Magoon, McDougall, McCrary, J. W. McDill, Monroe, Morey, Nash, Norton, O'Neill, Packer, Page, W. A. Phillips, Plaisted, T. C. Platt, A. POTTER, Pratt, Rainey, S. Ross, Rusk, Sampson, Sinnickson, R. Smalls, Thornburgh, M. I. Townsend, W. Townsend, Tufts, Wait, Waldron, A. S. Wallace, J. W. Wallace, G. W. Wells, J. D. White, G. Willard, C. G. Williams, W. B. Williams, J. Wilson, A. Wood, jr., Woodburn—82.

"The People a Nation."

1876, March 13—Mr. JOHN H. BAKER moved to suspend the rules so as to enable him to submit and the House to agree to, the following resolution:

Resolved, That the people of the United States constitute one nation and not a mere confederacy of States or nations; that the Constitution was formed by the people acting in their primary and individual capacity through their delegates thereto duly constituted; that the Government under the Constitution is one of the people, by the people, and for the people; that in its appropriate sphere the Government of this nation is sovereign and supreme; that in its nature it is permanent and indissoluble except by the act and consent of the whole people; that no State has the right or authority to judge of the constitutionality of the laws enacted by it, and to nullify or resist the execution of the same; and that all overt acts by any State or the people thereof of secession therefrom, or of rebellion against the same, constitute treason; and that the late war of the rebellion for the dismemberment of the Union was causeless and indefensible on any theory of right or constitutional law.

Which was disagreed to—yeas 97, nays 75, not voting 117, as follow:

YEAS—Messrs. *Ainsworth*, ANDERSON, J. H. Baker, Ballou, Bass, Blaine, Bradley, W. R. Brown, H. C. Burchard, CAMPBELL, Cannon, Cason, Caswell, Chittenden, Conger, Danford, Davy, Denison, Dobbins, Dunnell, Durand, Eames, Evans, Farwell, Fort, Foster, Frost, *Goodin, A. H. Hamilton, Hardenbergh*, B. W. Harris, Hathorn, *Haymond*, Hendee, Henderson, G. F. Hoar, Hoskins, Hubbell, Hunter, Hyman, *Jenks*, Joyce, Kasson, *Kehr*, Kelley, Lapham, W. Lawrence, Leavenworth, Lynch, Magoon, MacDougall, McCrary, J. W. McDill, Miller, Monroe, Nash, *New*, Norton, Oliver, O'Neill, Packer, Page, *J. Phelps*, W. A. Phillips, Pierce, Plaisted, T. C. Platt, A. POTTER, *Powell, J. B. Reilly*, M. S. Robinson, Rusk, Sampson, Seelye, Sinnickson, R. Smalls, A. H. Smith, Strait, *Stevenson, Teese*, Thornburgh, W. Townsend, Tufts, Van Vorhes, *J. L. Vance*, A. S. Wallace, J. W. Wallace, J. D. White, G. Willard, A. Williams, *A. S. Williams*, C. G. Williams, W. B. Williams, J. Wilson, A. Wood, jr., Woodburn, Woodworth—97.

NAYS—Messrs. *Ashe, Atkins, Beebe, Blackburn, Bland, Blount, Boone, Bright, J. Y. Brown, Cabell, J. H. Caldwell, W. P. Caldwell, Candler, Cate, J. B. Clarke, Cook, Cowan,*

Culberson, DeBolt, Dibrell, Douglas, Ellis, Faulkner, Felton, Forney, Franklin, Glover, Goode, Gunter, Hancock, H. R. Harris, Hartridge, G. W. Hewitt, Hill, Hooker, House, Hunton, Hurd, T. L. Jones, Knott, Levy, B. B. Lewis, Lord, Meade, Milliken, Mutchler, Odell, E. Y. Parsons, Payne, J. F. Philips, Piper, D. Rea, Reagan, A. V. Rice, Riddle, J. Robbins, W. M. Robbins, M. Ross, Scales, Sheakley, Singleton, W. E. Smith, Stone, Terry, Throckmorton, Tucker, R. B. Vance, Waddell, C. C. B. Walker, Ward, J. D. Williams, J. N. Williams, Willis, Yeates, C. Young—75.

NOT VOTING—Messrs. C. H. Adams, *Bagby*, G. A. Bagley, *J. H. Bagley, jr.*, W. H. Baker, BANKS, *Banning, Barnum, S. N. Bell*, Blair, *Bliss, Bradford, Buckner, S. D. Burchard*, Burleigh, *Caulfield, Chapin, J. B. Clark, jr., Clymer, Cochrane, Collins, Cox*, Crapo, Crounse, *Cutler*, Darrall, *Joseph J. Davis, Durham, Eden, Egbert, Ely*, C. Freeman, Frye, *Fuller*, Garfield, *Gause, Gibson*, E. Hale, *R. Hamilton*, Haralson, *J. T. Harris, C. H. Harrison, Hartzell, Hatcher*, Hays, *Henkle, Hereford, A. S. Hewitt*, Hoge, *Holman, Hopkins*, Hurlbut, *F. Jones*, Ketchum, Kimball, King, *Lamar, F. Landers, G. M. Landers, Lane, Luttrell, Lynde*, E. W. M. Mackey, *L. A. Mackey, Maish, McFarland, McMahon, Metcalfe, Mills, Money*, Morey, *Morgan, Morrison, Neal, O'Brien, Poppleton*, Pratt, Purman, Rainey, *Randall, J. Reilly, C. B. Roberts*, S. Ross, *Savage, M. Sayler, Schleicher, J. G. Schumaker, Slemons, Southard, Sparks, Springer, Stenger*, Stowell, *Swann, Tarbox, C. P. Thompson, P. F. Thomas*, M. I. Townsend, *Turney*, Waldron, *G. C. Walker, Walling*, Walls, *Walsh, Warren, E. Wells*, G. W. Wells, Wheeler, *Whitehouse*, Whiting, *Whitthorne, Wigginton, Wike, J. Williams, Wilshire, B. Wilson, F. Wood*—117.

March 13—Mr. Cox moved that the rules be suspended so as to enable him to submit, and the House to agree to, the following resolutions:

Resolved, That the people of the United States constitute a nation in the sense, to the extent, and for the purposes defined in the Federal Constitution.

Resolved, That the Government of the United States is a Federal Union, and was formed by the people of the several States in their sovereign capacity; That the rights and powers of the United States Government are defined and limited by the Federal Constitution, and these rights and powers cannot be enlarged nor diminished except by an amendment to the Constitution.

Resolved, That the rights of the States have the same sanction and security in the Constitution as the rights and powers of the Federal Government, and that local domestic government by the several States within the limits of the Constitution is absolutely necessary for the preservation of the liberties of the citizen and the continuance of our republican system of government.

Resolved, That the doctrine that a State has a right to secede from the Union is in conflict with the idea of a "perpetual union," as contemplated by the Constitution, and should be regarded as being forever extinguished by the results of the recent civil conflict.

Which was agreed to—Yeas 151, nays 42, not voting 96, as follow:

YEAS—Messrs. *Ainsworth*, ANDERSON, *Ashe, Atkins, J. H. Bagley, jr., Banning*, Bass, *Beebe, Blackburn, Bland Blount, Boone, Bright, J. Y. Brown, Buckner, Cabell, J. H. Caldwell, W. P. Caldwell*, CAMPBELL, Cannon, Cason, *Cate, Caulfield, J. B. Clarke, J. B. Clark, jr., Clymer, Cochrane, Cook, Cowan, Cox, Cutler*, Davy, *De-Bolt, Dibrell, Douglas, Durand, Eden, Ellis, Faulkner, Felton, Forney*, Fort, *Franklin, Fuller, Glover, Goode, Goodin, A. H. Hamilton, R. Hamilton, Hancock, Hardenbergh*, B. W. Harris, *H. R. Harris, Hartridge, Hartzell*, Hendee, *Henkle, G. W. Hewitt, Hill, Holman, Hooker, Hopkins, House, Hunton, Hurd, Jenks, T. L. Jones, Kehr*, Kelley, *Knott, F. Landers, G. M. Landers*, Leavenworth, *Levy, B. B. Lewis, Lord, Luttrell, Lynde, L. A. Mackey, Maish*, J. W. McDill, *McFarland, Meade, Milliken, Morgan, Morrison, Neal, New, O'Brien, Odell, E. Y. Parsons, Payne, J. Phelps, J. F. Philips*, W. A. Phillips, Pierce, *Piper, Poppleton*, A. POTTER, *Randall, D. Rea, Reagan, J. Reilly, J. B. Reilly, A. V. Rice, Riddle, J. Robbins, W. M. Robbins, C. B. Roberts, M. Ross*, Sampson, *Savage, M. Sayler, Scales, Schleicher, Sheakley, Singleton, W. E. Smith, Southard, Sparks*, Strait, *Stenger, Stevenson, Stone, Teese, Terry, C. P. Thompson, Throckmorton*, W. Townsend, *Tucker*, Tufts, *Turney, J. L. Vance, R. B. Vance, Waddell, C. C. B. Walker, Walling, Walsh, Ward, Warren, Wike*, G. Willard, *A. S. Williams, J. D. Williams, J. N. Williams*, W. B. Williams, *Willis*, J. Wilson, *Woodburn, Yeates, C. Young*—151.

NAYS—Messrs. J. H. Baker, Blaine, Bradley, H. C. Burchard, Conger, Denison, Dunnell, Eames, Evans, Farwell, Foster, G. F. Hoar, Hubbell, Hyman, Lapham, W. Lawrence, Lynch, Magoon, MacDougall, McCrary, Monroe, Nash, Norton, Oliver, Packer, Page, Plaisted, T. C. Platt, Purman, M. S. Robinson, Rusk, Seelye, Sinnickson, R. Smalls, Thornburgh, Van Vorhes, A. S. Wallace, J. W. Wallace, J. D. White, A. Williams, A. Wood, jr., Woodworth—42.

NOT VOTING—Messrs. C. H. Adams, *Bagby*, G. A. Bagley, W. H. Baker, Ballou, BANKS, *Barnum, S. N. Bell*, Blair, *Bliss, Bradford*, W. R. Brown, *S. D. Burchard*, Burleigh, *Candler*, Caswell, *Chapin*, Chittenden, *Collins*, Crapo, Crounse, *Culberson*, Danford, Darrall, *Joseph J. Davis*, Dobbins, *Durham, Egbert, Ely*, C. Freeman, Frost, Frye, Garfield, *Gause, Gibson, Gunter*, E. Hale, Haralson, *J. T. Harris, C. H. Harrison, Hatcher*, Hathorn, *Haymond*, Hays, Henderson, *Hereford, A. S. Hewitt*, Hoge, Hoskins, Hunter, Hurlbut, *F. Jones*, Joyce, Kasson, Ketchum, Kimball, King, *Lamar, Lane*, E. W. M. Mackey, *McMahon, Metcalfe*, Miller, *Mills, Money*, Morey, *Mutchler*, O'Neill, *Powell*, Pratt, Rainey, S. Ross, *J. G. Schumaker, Slemons*, A. H. Smith, *Springer*, Stowell, *Swann, Tarbox, P. F. Thomas*, M. I. Townsend, Waldron, *G. C. Walker*, Walls, *E. Wells*, G. W. Wells, Wheeler, *Whitehouse*, Whiting, *Whitthorne, Wigginton*, C. G. Williams, *J. Williams, Wilshire, B. Wilson, F. Wood*—96.

Tariff Legislation.

1876, May 29—Mr. CHARLES H. ADAMS offered the following resolution, and demanded the previous question; which was seconded, and the main question ordered:

Whereas the fact is apparent that all branches of manufacturing, mechanical and mining pursuits are at this time greatly depressed, and that all legislation which tends to embarrassment by the unsettling of values or the rendering of manufacturing, mechanical, or mining operations uncertain is unwise and injudicious: Therefore

Resolved, That in the judgment of this House legislation affecting the tariff is at this time inexpedient.

Mr. MORRISON moved to reconsider the vote ordering the main question; which was agreed to—yeas 120, nays 94 (not voting 75), as follow:

YEAS—Messrs. *Ainsworth*, ANDERSON, *Ashe*, *Atkins*, *Bagby*, *J. H. Bagley, jr.*, *Banning*, *Bland*, *Blount*, *Boone*, *Bradford*, *Bright*, *J. Y. Brown*, *Buckner*, H. C. Burchard, *S. D. Burchard*, *Cabell*, *J. H. Caldwell*, *W. P. Caldwell*, CAMPBELL, *Candler*, Cannon, *Cate*, *Chapin*, Chittenden, *J. B. Clarke*, *J. B. Clark, jr.*, *Cook*, *Cowan*, *Culberson*, *De Bolt*, *Dibrell*, *Douglas*, Dunnell, *Durham*, *Eden*, *Ellis*, *Faulkner*, *Felton*, *Finley*, *Forney*, Fort, *Franklin*, *Fuller*, *Gause*, *Glover*, *Goode*, *Goodin*, *Gunter*, *A. H. Hamilton*, *Hancock*, *J. T. Harris*, *C. H. Harrison*, *Hartridge*, *Hartzell*, *Hatcher*, *Haymond*, *Henkle*, *Hereford*, *G. W. Hewitt*, *Holman*, *Hooker*, *House*, *Hunton*, *Hurd*, *F. Jones*, *T. L. Jones*, *Knott*, *Le Moyne*, *B. B. Lewis*, *Lord*, *Lynde*, *McFarland*, *Metcalfe*, *Milliken*, *Mills*, *Money*, *Morey*, *Morgan*, *Morrison*, *Neal*, *O'Brien*, *E. Y. Parsons*, *Payne*, *J. F. Philips*, *Piper*, *Poppleton*, *D. Rea*, *Reagan*, *A. V. Rice*, *Riddle*, *Savage*, *M. Sayler*, *Scales*, *Schleicher*, *J. G. Schumaker*, Seelye, *Singleton*, *W. E. Smith*, *Sparks*, *Springer*, *Tarbox*, *Terry*, *P. F. Thomas*, *Throckmorton*, *R. B. Vance*, *G. C. Walker*, *Walling*, *Warren*, *E. Wells*, Whiting, *Whitthorne*, *Wigginton*, *J. Williams*, *J. D. Williams*, *J. N. Williams*, *Willis*, *F. Wood*, *Yeates*, *C. Young*—120.

NAYS—Messrs. C. H. Adams, G. A. Bagley, J. H. Baker, W. H. Baker, Ballou, BANKS, Bass, Blaine, Blair, Bradley, W. R. Brown, Caswell, *Clymer*, Crapo, Crounse, Cutler, Danford, Davy, Denison, Dobbins, Eames, *Egbert*, Frost, Frye, Garfield, Haralson, *Hardenbergh*, B. W. Harris, Hathorn, Hendee, Henderson, Hoge, *Hopkins*, Hoskins, Hubbell, Hunter, Hurlbut, Hyman, *Jenks*, Kasson, Kelley, Ketchum, Kimball, W. Lawrence, Leavenworth, Lynch, E. W. M. Mackey, Magoon, MacDougall, McCrary, Miller, Monroe, *Mutchler*, Nash, Norton, Oliver, O'Neill, Packer, Page, W. A. Phillips, Pierce, Plaisted, T. C. Platt, A. POTTER, *Powell*, *Randall*, *J. Reilly*, *J. Robbins*, Sampson, *Sheakley*, Sinnickson, *Slemons*, R. Smalls, *Stenger*, *Stone*, Stowell, *Teese*, *C. P. Thompson*, Thornburgh, M. I. Townsend, W. Townsend, Tufts, *Turney*, Van Vorhes, Wait, A. S. Wallace, J. W. Wallace, G. W. Wells, White, G. Willard, A. Williams, C. G. Williams, J. Wilson, Woodworth—94.

Debate arising upon it, the resolution went over.

June 5—It was referred to the Committee on Ways and Means—yeas 116, nays 99.

"Retrenchment and Reform."

1876, June 26—Mr. WILLIAM P. CALDWELL, offered the following resolution:

Resolved, That in the opinion of this House retrenchment and reform are now matters of imperative necessity. It is not the mere cry of demagogues, but a problem demanding the attention and worthy the highest ability of the Representatives of the people. No party is fit to govern this country that cannot solve it. It is vain to look to executive officers for reform; their power and influence depend upon executive patronage, and while we grant they will squander. The Senate is neither by the theory of our system nor by its composition fitted for the task. This House alone has the constitutional power to perfect a radical reform. The Constitution provides that no money shall be drawn from the Treasury but in consequence of appropriations made by law, and that all bills for raising revenue shall originate in the House of Representatives. These provisions were designed to invest in this House the entire control over the public purse, the power of supply. This is invested in the House of Commons, and has been zealously guarded by it; it is a pearl beyond price, without which constitutional liberty in England would long since have fallen under the despotism of the Crown.

On suspending the rules and passing the resolution, the yeas were 94, nays 35, as follow:

YEAS—Messrs. *Ainsworth*, ANDERSON, *Ashe*, *Atkins*, *Blackburn*, *Bland*, *Blount*, *Buckner*, *S. D. Burchard*, *Cabell*, *W. P. Caldwell*, *Candler*, *Caulfield*, *J. B. Clarke*, *J. B. Clark, jr.*, *Cook*, *Cowan*, *Culberson*, *Cutler*, *Joseph J. Davis*, *De Bolt*, *Dibrell*, *Durham*, *Ellis*, *Faulkner*, *Felton*, *Finley*, *Forney*, *Franklin*, *Fuller*, *Gibson*, *Goodin*, *A. H. Hamilton*, *R. Hamilton*, *Hardenbergh*, *H. R. Harris*, *J. T. Harris*, *Hartridge*, *Hartzell*, *Hatcher*, *Haymond*, *G. W. Hewitt*, *Holman*, *Hopkins*, *House*, *Jenks*, *T. L. Jones*, *Knott*, *F. Landers*, *B. B. Lewis*, *Lord*, *Maish*, *McFarland*, *McMahon*, *Metcalfe*, *Milliken*, *Mills*, *Morgan*, *Neal*, *New*, *Odell*, *Payne*, *J. Phelps*, *J. F. Philips*, *Powell*, *Randall*, *D. Rea*, *Reagan*, *J. B. Reilly*, *A. V. Rice*, *Riddle*, *J. Robbins*, *W. M. Robbins*, *C. B. Roberts*, *Savage*, *Scales*, *Sheakley*, *W. E. Smith*, *Southard*, *Sparks*, *Spencer*, *Springer*, *Stevenson*, *Tarbox*, *Terry*, *P. F. Thomas*, *Turney*, *R. B. Vance*, *Walsh*, *Wigginton*, *Wike*, *A. S. Williams*, *J. N. Williams*, *Yeates*—94.

NAYS—Messrs. J. H. Baker, W. H. Baker, BANKS, Bradley, Denison, Dobbins, Dunnell, Evans, Hendee, Hunter, Hyman, Kimball, Leavenworth, J. W. McDill, Page, Pierce, Piper, A. POTTER, Rainey, M. S. Robinson, Sampson, Seelye, Sinnickson, R. Smalls, Strait, *C. P. Thompson*, Tufts, Waldron, A. S. Wallace, J. D. White, G. Willard, W. B. Williams, J. Wilson, Woodburn, Woodworth—35.

No quorum voting, the House adjourned.

XV.

PRESIDENT GRANT'S SPECIAL MESSAGES, AND LETTERS.

Approving the Bill for the Resumption of Specie Payments, January 14, 1875.

To the Senate of the United States:

Senate bill No. 1044, "to provide for the resumption of specie payments," is before me, and this day receives my signature of approval.

I venture upon this unusual method of conveying the notice of approval to the "house in which the measure originated," because of its great importance to the country at large, and in order to suggest further legislation which seems to me essential to make this law effective.

It is a subject of congratulation that a measure has become law which fixes a date when specie resumption shall commence, and implies an obligation on the part of Congress—if in its power—to give such legislation as may prove necessary to redeem this promise.

To this end I respectfully call your attention to a few suggestions:

First. The necessity of an increased revenue to carry out the obligation of adding to the sinking-fund annually one per cent. of the public debt, amounting now to about thirty-four millions of dollars per annum, and to carry out the promises of this measure to redeem, under certain contingencies, eighty millions of the present legal tenders, and, without contingency, the fractional currency now in circulation.

How to increase the surplus revenue is for Congress to devise, but I will venture to suggest the duty on tea and coffee might be restored without permanently enhancing the cost to the consumers, and that the ten per cent. horizontal reduction of the tariff on articles specified in the law of June 6, 1872, be repealed. The supply of tea and coffee already on hand in the United States would in all probability be advanced in adopting this measure. But it is known that the adoption of free entry to those articles of necessity did not cheapen them, but merely added to the profits of the countries producing them, or of the middle-men in those countries, who have the exclusive trade in them.

Second. The first section of the bill now under consideration provides that the fractional currency shall be redeemed in silver coin as rapidly as practicable. There is no provision preventing the fluctuation in the value of the paper currency. With gold at a premium of anything over 10 per cent. above the currency in use, it is probable, almost certain, that silver would be bought up for exportation as fast as it was put out, or until change would become so scarce as to make the premium on it equal to the premium on gold, or sufficiently high to make it no longer profitable to buy for export, thereby causing a direct loss to the community at large and great embarrassment to trade.

As the present law commands final resumption on the first day of January, 1879, and as the gold receipts by the Treasury are larger than the gold payments and the currency receipts are smaller than the currency payments, thereby making monthly sales of gold necessary to meet currency expenses, it occurs to me that these difficulties might be remedied by authorizing the Secretary of the Treasury to redeem legal-tender notes whenever presented in sums not less than one hundred dollars and multiples thereof, at a premium for gold of ten per cent., less interest at the rate of two and one-half per cent. per annum from the 1st day of January, 1875, to the date of putting this law into operation, and diminishing this premium at the same rate until final resumption, changing the rate of premium demanded from time to time as the interest amounts to one-quarter of one per cent. I suggest this rate of interest because it would bring currency at par with gold at the date fixed by law for final resumption. I suggest ten per cent. as the demand premium at the beginning, because I believe this rate would insure the retention of silver in the country for change.

The provisions of the third section of the act will prevent combinations being made to exhaust the Treasury of coin.

With such a law it is presumable that no gold would be called for not required for legitimate business purposes. When large amounts of coin should be drawn from the Treasury, corresponding large amounts of currency would be withdrawn from circulation, thus causing a sufficient stringency in currency to stop the outward flow of coin.

The advantages of a currency of a fixed known value would also be reached. In my opinion, by the enactment of such a law, business and industries would revive, and the beginning of prosperity on a firm basis would be reached.

Other means of increasing revenue than those suggested should probably be devised, and also other legislation.

In fact, to carry out the first section of the act, another mint becomes necessary. With the present facilities for coinage, it would take a period probably beyond that fixed by law for final specie resumption to coin the silver necessary to transact the business of the country.

There are now smelting-furnaces for extracting the silver and gold from the ores brought from the mountain Territories, in Chicago, Saint Louis, and Omaha—three in the former city—and as much of the change required will be wanted in the Mississippi Valley States, and as the metals to be coined come from west of those States, and, as I understand, the charges for transportation of bullion from either of the cities named to the Mint in Philadelphia, or to New York City, amount to four dollars for each one thousand dollars' worth, with an equal expense for transportation back, it would seem a fair argument in favor of adopting one or more of those cities as the place or places for the establishment of new coining facilities.

I have ventured upon this subject with great diffidence, because it is so unusual to approve a measure—as I most heartily do this, even if no further legislation is attainable at this time—and to announce the fact by message. But I do so because I feel that it is a subject of such vital importance to the whole country that it should receive the attention of, and be discussed by, Congress and the people through the press, and in every way, to the end that the best and most satisfactory course may be reached of executing what I deem most beneficial legislation on a most vital question to the interests and prosperity of the nation. U. S. GRANT.

Executive Mansion, January 14, 1875.

Centennial Celebration, January 20, 1875.

To the House of Representatives:

I have the honor to transmit herewith a report from a board composed of one person named by the head of each executive department and of the Department of Agriculture and Smithsonian Institution, for the purpose of securing a complete and harmonious arrangement of the articles and materials designed to be exhibited from the Executive Departments of the Government at the international exhibition to be held in the city of Philadelphia in the year 1876 for the purpose of celebrating the one hundredth anniversary of the Independence of the United States. The report gives a statement of what is proposed to be exhibited by each Department, together with an estimate of the expense which will have to be incurred. Submitting to Congress the estimate made by the board, I recommend that Congress make a suitable appropriation to enable the different Departments to make a complete and creditable showing of the articles and materials designed to be exhibited by the Government, and which will undoubtedly form one of the most interesting features of the exhibition.

U. S. GRANT.

Executive Mansion, January 20, 1875.

Armament for Sea-Coast Defenses, January 20, 1875.

To the Senate and House of Representatives:

In my annual message of December 1, 1873, while inviting general attention to all the recommendations made by the Secretary of War, your special consideration was invited to "the importance of preparing for war in time of peace by providing proper armament for our sea-coast defenses. Proper armanent is of vastly more importance than fortifications. The latter can be supplied very speedily for temporary purposes when needed; the former cannot."

These views gain increased strength and pertinence as the years roll by, and I have now again the honor to call special attention to the condition of the "armament of our fortifications," and the absolute necessity for immediate provision by Congress for the procurement of heavy cannon. The large expenditures required to supply the number of guns for our forts is the strongest argument that can be adduced for a liberal annual appropriation for their gradual accumulation. In time of war such preparations cannot be made; cannon cannot be purchased in open market, nor manufactured at short notice; they must be the product of years of experience and labor.

I herewith inclose copies of a report of the Chief of Ordnance and of a board of ordnance officers on the trial of an eight-inch rifle converted from a ten-inch smooth-bore, which shows very conclusively an economical means of utilizing these useless smooth-bores and making them into eight-inch rifles capable of piercing seven inches of iron. The twelve hundred and ninety-four ten-inch Rodman guns should, in my opinion, be so utilized, and the appropriation requested by the Chief of Ordnance of $250,000 to commence these conversions is urgently recommended.

While convinced of the economy and necessity of these conversions, the determination of the best and most economical method of providing guns of still larger caliber should no longer be delayed. The experience of other nations, based on the new conditions of defense brought prominently forward by the introduction of iron-clads into every navy afloat, demands heavier metal and rifle-guns of not less than twelve inches in caliber. These enormous masses, hurling a shot of seven hundred pounds, can alone meet many of the requirements of the national defenses. They must be provided, and experiments on a large scale can alone give the data necessary for the determination of the question. A suitable proving-ground, with all the facilities and conveniences referred to by the Chief of Ordnance, with a liberal annual appropriation, is an undoubted necessity. The guns now ready for trial cannot be experimented with without funds, and the estimate of $250,000 for the purpose is deemed reasonable and is strongly recommended.

The constant appeals for legislation on the "armament of fortifications" ought no longer to be disregarded, if Congress desires in peace to prepare the important material without which future wars must inevitably lead to disaster.

This subject is submitted with the hope that the consideration it deserves may be given it at the present session. U. S. GRANT.

Executive Mansion, January 20, 1875.

Message Vetoing the Act to Reduce the Salary of the Executive, April 18, 1876.

To the Senate of the United States:

Herewith I return Senate bill No. 172, entitled "An act fixing the salary of the President of the United States," without my approval.

I am constrained to this course from a sense of duty to my successors in office, to myself, and to what is due to the dignity of the position of Chief Magistrate of a nation of more than forty millions of people.

When the salary of the President of the United States pursuant to the Constitution was fixed at $25,000 per annum, we were a nation of but three millions of people, poor from a long and exhaustive war, without commerce or manufactures, with but few wants and those cheaply supplied. The salary must then have been deemed small for the responsibilities and dignity of the position, but justifiably so from the impoverished condition of the Treasury and the simplicity it was desired to cultivate in the republic.

The salary of Congressmen under the Constitution was first fixed at $6 per day for the time actually in session—an average of about one hundred and twenty days to each session—or $720 per year, or less than one-thirtieth of the salary of the President.

Congress have legislated upon their own salaries from time to time since, until finally it reached $5,000 per annum, or one-fifth that of the President before the salary of the latter was increased.

No one having a knowledge of the cost of living at the national capital will contend that the present salary of Congressmen is too high, unless it is the intention to make the office one entirely of honor, when the salary should be abolished—a proposition repugnant to our republican ideas and institutions.

I do not believe the citizens of this republic desire their public servants to serve them without a fair compensation for their services. Twenty-five thousand dollars does not defray the expenses of the Executive for one year, or has not in my experience. It is not now one-fifth in value of what it was at the time of the adoption of the Constitution in supplying demands and wants.

Having no personal interest in this matter, I have felt myself free to return this bill to the House in which it originated with my objections, believing that in doing so I meet the wishes and judgment of the great majority of those who indirectly pay all the salaries and other expenses of Government. U. S. GRANT.

Executive Mansion, April 18, 1876.

President Grant's Message Respecting His Absence from the Seat of Government, May 4, 1876.

April 3—The House, on motion of Mr. BLACKBURN, passed this resolution:

Resolved, That the President of the United States be requested to inform this House, if, in his opinion, it is not incompatible with the public interest, whether since the 4th day of March, 1869, any executive offices, acts, or duties, and, if any, what, have been performed at a distance from the seat of Government established by law, and for how long a period at any one time, and in what part of the United States; also, whether any public necessity existed for such performance, and, if so, of what character, and how far the performance of such executive offices, acts, or duties at such distance from the seat of Government established by law, was in compliance with the act of Congress of the 16th day of July, 1790.

May 4—The PRESIDENT made this reply:

To the House of Representatives:

I have given very attentive consideration to a resolution of the House of Representatives passed on the 3d day of April, requesting the President of the United States to inform the House whether any executive offices, acts, or duties, and, if any, what, have within a specified period been performed at a distance from the seat of government established by law, etc.

I have never hesitated and shall not hesitate to communicate to Congress, and to either branch thereof, all the information which the Constitution makes it the duty of the President to give, or which my judgment may suggest to me or a request from either House may indicate to me will be useful in the discharge of the appropriate duties confided to them. I fail, however, to find in the Constitution of the United States the authority given to the House of Representatives (one branch of the Congress in which is vested the legislative power of the Government) to require of the Executive, an independent branch of the Government—co-ordinate with the Senate and House of Representatives—an account of his discharge of his appropriate and purely executive offices, acts, and duties, either as to when, where, or how performed.

What the House of Representatives may require as a right in its demand upon the Executive for information, is limited to what is necessary for the proper discharge of its powers of legislation or of impeachment.

The inquiry in the resolution of the House as to where executive acts have within the last seven years been performed, and at what distance from any particular spot or for how long a period at any one time, etc., does not necessarily belong to the province of legislation. It does not profess to be asked for that object.

If this information be sought through an inquiry of the President as to his executive acts in view or in aid of the power of impeachment vested in the House, it is asked in derogation of an inherent natural right, recognized in this country by a constitutional guarantee which protects every citizen, the President as well as the humblest in the land, from being made a witness against himself.

During the time that I have had the honor to occupy the position of President of this Government, it has been, and while I continue to occupy that position it will continue to be, my earnest endeavor to recognize and to respect the several trusts and duties and powers of the co-ordinate branches of the Government, not encroaching upon them nor allowing encroachments upon the proper powers of the office which the people of the United States have confided to me, but aiming to preserve in their proper relations the several powers and functions of each of the co-ordinate branches of the Government agreeably to the Constitution, and in accordance with the solemn oath which I have taken to "preserve, protect, and defend" that instrument.

In maintenance of the rights secured by the Constitution to the executive branch of the Government, I am compelled to decline any specific or detailed answer to the request of the House for information as to "any executive offices, acts, or duties, and, if any, what, have been performed at a distance from the seat of Government established by law, and for how long a period at any one time and in what part of the United States."

If, however, the House of Representatives desires to know whether during the period of upward of seven years during which I have held the office of President of the United States, I have been absent from the seat of government, and whether during that period I have performed or have neglected to perform the duties of my office, I freely inform the House that from the time of my entrance upon my office I have been in the habit, as were all of my predecessors, (with the exception of one who lived only one month after assuming the duties of his office, and one whose continued presence in Washington was necessary from the existence at the time of a powerful rebellion,) of absenting myself at times from the seat of government; and that during such absences I did not neglect or forego the obligations or the duties of my office, but continued to discharge all of the executive offices, acts, and duties which were required of me as the President of the United States. I am not aware that a failure occurred in any one instance of my exercising the functions and powers of my office in every case requiring their discharge, or of my exercising all necessary executive acts in whatever part of the United States I may at the time have been. Fortunately, the rapidity of travel and of mail communication, and the facility of almost instantaneous correspondence with the offices at the seat of government which the telegraph affords to the President, in whatever section of the Union he may be, enable him in these days to maintain as constant and almost as quick intercourse with the Departments at Washington as may be maintained while he remains in the capital.

The necessity of the performance of executive acts by the President of the United States exists and is devolved upon him, wherever he may be within the United States during his term of office, by the Constitution of the United States.

His civil powers are no more limited or capable of limitation as to the place where they shall be exercised than are those which he might be required to discharge in his capacity of Commander-in-chief of the Army and Navy, which latter powers, it is evident, he might be called upon to exercise possibly even without the limits of the United States. Had the efforts of those recently in rebellion against the Government been successful in driving a late President of the United States from Washington, it is manifest that he must have discharged his functions, both civil and military, elsewhere than in the place named by law as the seat of government.

No act of Congress can limit, suspend, or confine this constitutional duty. I am not aware of the existence of any act of Congress which assumes thus to limit or restrict the exercise of the functions of the Executive. Were there such acts, I should nevertheless recognize the superior authority of the Constitution, and should exercise the powers required thereby of the President.

The act to which reference is made in the resolution of the House relates to the establishing of the seat of government and the providing of suitable buildings and removal thereto of the offices attached to the Government, &c. It was not understood at its date and by General Washington to confine the President in the discharge of his duties and powers to actual presence at the seat of government. On the 30th of March, 1791, shortly after the passage of the act referred to, General Washington issued an executive proclamation having reference to the subject of this very act from Georgetown, a place remote from Philadelphia, which then was the seat of government, where the act referred to directed that "all offices attached to the seat of government" should for the time remain.

That none of his successors have entertained the idea that their executive offices could be performed only at the seat of government is evidenced by the hundreds upon hundreds of such acts performed by my predecessors, in unbroken line from Washington to Lincoln, a memorandum of the general nature and character of some of which acts is submitted herewith; and no question has ever been raised as to the validity of these acts, or as to the right and propriety of the Executive to exercise the powers of his office in any part of the United States. U. S. GRANT.

Washington, May 4, 1876.

Memorandum of absences of the Presidents of the United States from the national capital during each of the several administrations, and of public and executive acts performed during the time of such absences.

PRESIDENT WASHINGTON

was frequently absent from the Capital; he appears to have been thus absent at least one hundred and eighty-one days during his term.

During his several absences he discharged official and executive duties, among them:

In March, 1791, he issued a proclamation, dated at Georgetown, in reference to running the boundary for the territory of the permanent seat of the Government.

From Mount Vernon he signed an official letter to the Emperor of Morocco, and from the same place the commission of Oliver Walcott as Comptroller of the Treasury, and the proclamation respecting the whisky insurrection in Pennsylvania; also, various sea letters, the proclamation of the treaty of 1795 between the United States and Spain, the executive order of August 4, 1792, relative to the duties on distilled spirits, &c.

When at Germantown he signed the commission of John Brackenridge as attorney of the United States for Kentucky, and that of engineer of the United States Mint.

He proposed to have Mr. Trujo officially presented, as envoy extraordinary and minister plenipotentiary from Spain, to him at Mount Vernon; but, although Mr. Trujo went there for the purpose, the ceremony of presentation was prevented by Mr. Trujo's having accidentally left his credentials.

PRESIDENT JOHN ADAMS.

President John Adams was absent from the capital during his term of four years, on various occasions, three hundred and eighty-five days.

He discharged official duties and performed the most solemn public acts at Quincy, in the same manner as when at the seat of Government.

In 1797 (August 25) he forwarded to the Secretary of State a number of passports which he had signed at Quincy.

He issued at Quincy commissions to numerous officers of various grades, civil and military.

On the 28th of September, 1797, he forwarded to the Secretary of State a commission for a Justice of the Supreme Court, signed in blank at Quincy, instructing the Secretary to fill it with the name of John Marshall if he would accept, and if not, Bushrod Washington. He issued a proclamation opening trade with certain ports of Saint Domingo, and signed warrants for the execution of two soldiers, and for a pardon.

PRESIDENT JEFFERSON

was absent from the seat of Government, during his two terms of office, seven hundred and ninety-six days, more than one-fourth of the whole official period.

During his absence he signed and issued from Monticello seventy-five commissions, one letter to the Emperor of Russia, and nine letters of credence to diplomatic agents of the United States, accredited to other governments.

PRESIDENT MADISON

was absent from the seat of Government during his two presidential terms six hundred and thirty-seven days.

He signed and issued from Montpelier, during his absence from the capital, seventy-one commissions, one proclamation, and nine letters of credence to ministers, accrediting them to foreign governments; and, as it appears, transacted generally all the necesary routine business incident to the executive office.

PRESIDENT MONROE

was absent from the capital, during his presidential service of eight years, seven hundred and eight days, independent of the year 1824, and two months of 1825 for which period no data are found.

He transacted public business wherever he happened to be; sometimes at his farm in Virginia, again at his summer resort on the Chesapeake, and sometimes while traveling. He signed and issued from these several places, away from the capital, numerous commissions to civil officers of the Government, exequaturs to foreign consuls, letters of credence, two letters to sovereigns, and thirty-seven pardons.

PRESIDENT JOHN Q. ADAMS

was absent from the capital, during his presidential term of four years, two hundred and twenty-two days.

During such absence he performed official and public acts, signing and issuing commissions, exequaturs, pardons, proclamations, etc.

Referring to his absence in August and September, 1827, Mr. Adams, in his memoirs, volume 8, page 75, says: "I left with him (the chief clerk) some blank signatures to be used when necessary for proclamations, remission of penalties, and commissions of consuls, taking of him a receipt for the number and kind of blanks left with him, with directions to return me, when I came back, all the signed blanks remaining unused, and to keep and give me an account of all those that shall have been disposed of. This has been my constant practice with the respect to signed blanks of this description. I do the same with regard to patents and land grants."

PRESIDENT JACKSON

was absent from the capital during his presidential service of eight years five hundred and two days.

He also performed executive duties and public acts while absent.

He appears to have signed and issued while absent from the capital very many public papers, embracing commissions, letters of credence, exequaturs, pardons, and among them four executive proclamations.

On the 26th of June, 1833, he addressed a letter from Boston to Mr. Duane, Secretary of the Treasury, giving his views at large on the removal of the "deposits" from the United States Bank and placing them in the State banks, directing that the change with all its arrangements should be if possible completed by the 15th September following, and recommending that Amos Kendall should be appointed an agent of the Treasury Department to make the necessary arrangements with the State banks. Soon after, September 23, a paper signed by the President and purporting to have been read to the Cabinet was published in the newspapers of the day. Early in the next session of Congress a resolution passed the Senate inquiring of the President whether the paper was genuine or not, and if it was published by his authority, and requesting that a copy be laid before that body.

The President replied, avowing the genuineness of the paper and that it was published by his authority, but declined to furnish a copy to the Senate on the ground that it was purely executive business, and that the request of the Senate was an undue interference with the independence of the Executive, a co-ordinate branch of the Government.

In January 1837, (26th,) he refused the privilege to a committee under a resolution of the House of Representatives to make a general investigation of the Executive Departments without specific charges, on the ground, among others, that the use of the books, papers, etc., of the Departments for such purpose would interfere with the discharge of the public duties devolving upon the heads of the different Departments, and necessarily disarrange and retard the public business.

PRESIDENT VAN BUREN

was absent from the capital during his presidential term one hundred and thirty-one days.

He discharged executive duties and performed official and public acts during these absences.

Among the papers signed by President Van Buren during his absence from the seat of Government are commissions, one of these being for a United States judge of a district court, pardons, etc.

PRESIDENT TYLER

was absent from the capital during his presidential term one hundred and sixty-three days, and performed public acts and duties during such absences, signing public papers and documents to the number of twenty-eight, in which were included commissions, exequaturs, letters of credence, pardons, and one proclamation making public the treaty of 1842 between the United States and Ecuador.

PRESIDENT POLK

was absent from the capital during his presidential term thirty-seven days, and appears to have signed but two official public papers during such absence.

PRESIDENT TAYLOR

was absent from the capital during the time he served as President thirty-one days, and while absent signed two commissions, three "full powers," two exequaturs, and the proclamation of August 11, 1849, relative to a threatened invasion of Cuba or some of the provinces of Mexico.

PRESIDENT FILLMORE

was absent from the capital, during the time he served as President, sixty days. During such absence he signed pardons, commissions, exequaturs, etc.

PRESIDENT PIERCE

was absent from the capital in all during his presidential term fifty-seven days. The several periods of absence which make up this aggregate were each brief, and it does not appear that during these absences the President signed any public official documents except one pardon.

PRESIDENT BUCHANAN

was absent from the capital during his presidential term fifty-seven days, and the official papers which he is shown to have signed during such absence are three exequaturs and one letter of credence.

In addition to the public documents and papers executed by the several Presidents during their absences from the seat of Government, constant official correspondence was maintained by each with the heads of the different Executive Departments.

Message of the President Relating to the Extradition Treaty with Great Britain, June 20, 1876.

To the Senate and House of Representatives:

By the tenth article of the treaty between the United States and Great Britain, signed in Washington on the 9th day of August, 1842, it was agreed that the two governments should, upon mutual requisitions respectively made, deliver up to justice all persons who, being charged with certain crimes therein enumerated, committed within the jurisdiction of either, should seek an asylum or be found within the territories of the other.

The only condition or limitation contained in the treaty to the reciprocal obligation thus to deliver up the fugitive was that it should be done only upon such evidence of criminality as, according to the laws of the place where the fugitive or person so charged should be found, would justify his apprehension and commitment for trial if the crime or offense had there been committed.

In the month of February last a requisition was duly made, in pursuance of the provisions of the treaty, by this Government upon that of Great Britain for the surrender of one Ezra D. Winslow, charged with extensive forgeries and the utterance of forged paper, committed within the jurisdiction of the United States, who had sought an asylum, and was found within, the territories of Her Britannic Majesty, and was apprehended in London. The evidence of the criminality of the fugitive was furnished and heard, and, being found sufficient to justify his apprehension and commitment for trial, if the crimes had been committed in Great Britain, he was held and committed for extradition.

Her Majesty's government, however, did not deliver up the fugitive in accordance with the terms of the treaty, notwithstanding every requirement thereof had been met on the part of the United States; but, instead of surrendering the fugitive, demanded certain assurances or stipulations not mentioned in the treaty, but foreign to its provisions, as a condition of the performance by Great Britain of her obligations under the treaty.

In a recent communication to the House of Representatives and in answer to a call from that body for information on this case, I submitted the correspondence which has passed between the two governments with reference thereto. It will be found in Executive Document No. 173 of the House of Representatives of the present session, and I respectfully refer thereto for more detailed information bearing on the question.

It appears from the correspondence that the British government bases its refusal to surrender the fugitive and its demand for stipulations or assurances from this Government on the requirements of a purely domestic enactment of the British Parliament, passed in the year 1870.

This act was brought to the notice of this Government shortly after its enactment, and Her Majesty's government was advised that the United States understood it as giving continued effect to the existing engagements under the treaty of 1842 for the extradition of criminals; and, with this knowledge on its part and without dissent from the declared views of the United States as to the unchanged nature of the reciprocal rights and obligations of the two powers under the treaty, Great Britain has continued to make requisitions and to grant surrenders in numerous instances, without suggestion that it was contemplated to depart from the practice under the treaty which has obtained for more than thirty years until now, for the first time, in this case of Winslow, it is assumed that under this act of Parliament Her Majesty may require a stipulation or agreement not provided for in the treaty, as a condition to the observance by her government of its treaty obligations toward this country.

This I have felt it my duty emphatically to repel.

In addition to the case of Winslow, requisition was also made by this Government on that of Great Britain for the surrender of Charles J. Brent, also charged with forgery committed in the United States and found in Great Britain. The evidence of criminality was duly heard and the fugitive committed for extradition.

A similar stipulation to that demanded in Winslow's case was also asked in Brent's, and was likewise refused.

It is with extreme regret that I am now called upon to announce to you that Her Majesty's government has finally released both of these fugitives, Winslow and Brent, and set them at liberty, thus omitting to comply with the provisions and requirements of the treaty under which the extradition of fugitive criminals is made between the two governments.

The position thus taken by the British government, if adhered to, cannot but be regarded as the abrogation and annulment of the article of the treaty on extradition.

Under these circumstances it will not, in my judgment, comport with the dignity or self-respect of this Government to make demands upon that government for the surrender of fugitive criminals, nor to entertain any requisition of that character from that government under the treaty.

It will be a cause of deep regret if a treaty which has been thus far beneficial in its practical operation, which has worked so well and so efficiently, and which, notwithstanding the exciting and at times violent political disturbances of which both countries have been the scene during its existence, has given rise to no complaints on the part of either government against either its spirit or its provisions, should be abruptly terminated.

It has tended to the protection of society and to the general interests of both countries. Its violation or annulment would be a retrograde step in international intercourse.

I have been anxious and have made the effort to enlarge its scope, and to make a new treaty which would be a still more efficient agent for the punishment and prevention of crime. At the same time I have felt it my duty to decline to entertain a proposition made by Great Britain, pending its refusal to execute the existing treaty, to amend it by practically conceding by treaty the identical conditions which that government demands under its act of Parliament. In addition to the impossibility of the United States entering upon negotiations under the menace of an intended violation or a refusal to execute the terms of an existing treaty, I deemed it inadvisable to treat of only the one amendment proposed by Great Britain, while the United States desires an enlargement of the list of crimes for which extradition may be asked, and other improvements which experience has shown might be embodied in a new treaty.

It is for the wisdom of Congrèss to determine whether the article of the treaty relating to extradition is to be any longer regarded as obligatory on the Government of the United States or as forming part of the supreme law of the land. Should the attitude of the British government remain unchanged, I shall not, without an expression of the wish of Congress that I should do so, take any action either in making or granting requisitions for the surrender of fugitive criminals under the treaty of 1842.

Respectfully submitted. U. S. GRANT.

Washington, June 20, 1876.

Message from the President, touching the Condition of the Appropriation Bills, June 17, 1876.

To the Senate and House of Representatives:

The near approach of a new fiscal year, and the failure of Congress up to this time to provide the necessary means to continue all the functions of government, makes it my duty to call your attention to the embarrassments that must ensue if the fiscal year is allowed to close without remedial action on your part.

Article 1, Section 9, of the Constitution declares:

"No money shall be drawn from the Treasury but in consequence of appropriations made by law."

To insure economy of expenditures and security of the public treasure, Congress has from time to time enacted laws to restrain the use of public moneys except for the specific purpose for which appropriated and within the time for which appropriated, and to prevent contracting debts in anticipation of appropriate appropriations.

Revised Statutes, Section 3679, provides:

"No Department of the Government shall expend, in any one fiscal year, any sum in excess of appropriations made by Congress for that fiscal year, or involve the Government in any contract for the future payment of money in excess of such appropriations."

Section 3732 provides:

"No contract or purchase on behalf of the United States shall be made, unless the same is authorized by law or is under an appropriation adequate to its fulfillment, except in the War and Navy Departments, for clothing, subsistence, forage, fuel, quarters, or transportation, which, however, shall not exceed the necessities of the current year."

Section 3678, as follows:

"All sums appropriated for the various branches of expenditure in the public service shall be applied solely to the objects for which they are respectively made, and for no others."

Section 3690, that—

"All balances of appropriations contained in the annual appropriation bills, and made specifically for the service of any fiscal year, and remaining unexpended at the expiration of such fiscal year, shall only be applied to the payment of expenses properly incurred during that year, or to the fulfillment of contracts properly made within that year; and balances not needed for such purposes shall be carried to the surplus fund. This section, however, shall not apply to appropriations known as permanent or indefinite appropriations."

The effect of the laws quoted, taken in connection with the constitutional provision referred to, is, as above stated, to prohibit any outlay of public money toward defraying even the current and necessary expenses of Government after the expiration of the year for which appropriated, excepting when those expenses are provided for by some permanent appropriation, and excepting in the War and Navy Departments, under section 3732.

The number of permanent appropriations are very limited, and cover but few of the necessary expenditures of the Government. They are nearly all, if not quite all, embraced in sections 3687, 3688, and 3689 of the Revised Statutes. That contained in section 3687 *is applicable to expenses of collecting the revenue from customs*, that in section 3688 to the payment of interest on the *public debt*, and that in section 3689 to various objects too numerous to detail here.

It will be observed that while section 3679, quoted above, provides that *no* Department shall in any one fiscal year involve the Government in any contract for the future payment of money in excess of the appropriation for that year, section 3732, also quoted above, confers, by clear implication, upon the heads of the War and Navy Departments full authority, even in the absence of any appropriation, to purchase or contract for clothing, subsistence, forage, fuel, quarters, or transportation, not exceeding the necessities of the current year. The latter provision is special and exceptional in its character, and is to be regarded as excluded from the operation of the former more general one. But if any of the appropriation bills above enumerated should fail to be matured before the expiration of the current fiscal year, the Government would be greatly embarrassed for want of the necessary funds to carry on the service. Precluded from expending money not appropriated, the Departments would have to suspend the service, so far as the appropriations for it should have failed to be made.

A careful examination of this subject will demonstrate the embarrassed condition all branches of the Government will be in—and especially the executive—if there should be a failure to pass the necessary appropriation bills before the 1st of July, or otherwise provide.

I commend this subject most earnestly to your consideration, and urge that some measure be speedily adopted to avert the evils which would result from non-action by Congress. I will venture the suggestion, by way of remedy, that a joint resolution, properly guarded, might be passed through the two Houses of Congress, extending the provisions of all appropriations for the present fiscal year to the next in all cases where there is a failure on the 1st of July to supply such appropriation; each appropriation so extended to hold good until Congress shall have passed a corresponding appropriation applicable to the new fiscal year, when all moneys expended under laws enacted for this fiscal year shall be deducted from the corresponding appropriation for the next.

To make my ideas on this subject more clear, I have caused to be drawn up a "joint resolution" embodying them more fully.

U. S. GRANT.

Executive Mansion, June 17, 1876.

Joint resolution to provide for defraying temporarily the ordinary and necessary expenses of the public service.

Whereas the ordinary and necessary expenses of the public service in its various branches, comprising among others the expenses which especially pertain to the legislative, executive, and judicial departments of the Government, to the consular and diplomatic service, to the postal service, to the support of the Army and to the maintenance of the Navy, are generally met by annual appropriations which expire at the end of the current fiscal year; and whereas no public funds will be available to defray these expenses as the same shall accrue after that period, unless appropriations shall have been previously made therefor by law; and whereas to avoid the great embarrassment to the public service that might otherwise ensue, it is expedient to make provision for defraying temporarily such of these expenses as would be unprovided for in case some one of the usual annual appropriation bills designed to provide therefor should fail to be matured by the end of the fiscal year now current: Therefore,

Be it resolved by the Senate and House of Representatives of the United States of America in Congress assembled, That in case any of the following appropriation bills for the fiscal year ending June 30, 1877, shall not have passed by the commencement of such year, so that the funds to be appropriated thereby may then be available for expenditure, that is to say, the bill providing for the legislative, executive, and judicial expenses; the bill providing for the consular and diplomatic expenses; the bill providing for the service of the Post-office department; the bill providing for the support of the Army; and the bill providing for the naval service, the appropriation act for the current fiscal year corresponding in its general description and object to such appropriation bill shall extend to the fiscal year next ensuing until such appropriation bill is enacted and takes effect, to the end that the provisions of such appropriation act which apply to the ordinary and necessary expenses of the public service for the current fiscal year shall in like manner be applicable to similar expenses which may accrue during the period intervening between the end of the current fiscal year and the time when such appropriation bill for the next ensuing fiscal year shall be enacted and take effect.

President Grant's Letter on a "Third Term," May 29, 1875.

EXECUTIVE MANSION,
WASHINGTON, D. C., *May* 29, 1875.

DEAR SIR: A short time subsequent to the Presidential election of 1872, the press, a portion of it hostile to the Republican party, and particularly so to the Administration, started the cry of "Cæsarism" and "the Third Term," calling lustily for me to define my position on the latter subject. I believed it to be beneath the dignity of the office which I have been twice called upon to fill to answer such a question before the subject should be presented by competent authority to make a nomination, or by a body of such dignity and authority as not to make a reply a fair subject of ridicule. In fact, I have been surprised that so many sensible persons in the Republican party should permit their enemy to force upon them and their party an issue which cannot add strength to the party, no matter how met. But a body of the dignity and party authority of a convention to make nominations for the State officers of the second State in the Union having considered this question, I deem it not improper that I should speak.

In the first place, I never sought the office for a second, nor even for a first nomination. To the first I was called from a life position, one created by Congress expressly for me, for supposed services rendered to the Republic. The position vacated I liked. It would have been most agreeable to me to have retained it until such time as Congress might have consented to my retirement, with the rank and a portion of the emoluments which I so much needed, to a home where the balance of my days might be spent in peace and in the enjoyment of domestic quiet, relieved from the cares which have oppressed me so constantly now for fourteen years. But I was made to believe that the public good called me to make the sacrifice. Without seeking the office for the second term, the nomination was tendered to me by a unanimous vote of the delegates of all the States and Territories, selected by the Republicans of each to represent their whole number for the purpose of making their nomination. I cannot say that I was not pleased at this, and at the overwhelming indorsement which their action received at the election following. But it must be remembered that all the sacrifices except that of comfort had been made in accepting the first term. Then, too, such a fire of personal abuse and slander had been kept up for four years, notwithstanding the conscientious performance of my duties to the best of my understanding—though I admit, in the light of subsequent events, many times subject to fair criticism—that an indorsement from the people, who alone govern republics, was a gratification that it is only human to have appreciated and enjoyed.

Now, for the Third Term. I do not want it any more than I did the first. I would not write or utter a word to change the will of the people in expressing and having their choice. The question of the number of terms allowed to any one Executive can only come up fairly in the shape of a proposition to amend the Constitution, a shape in which all political parties can participate, fixing the length of time or the number of terms for which any one person shall be eligible for the office of President. Until such an amendment is adopted, the people cannot be restricted in their choice by resolution further than they are now restricted as to age, nativity, etc. It may happen in the future history of the country that to change an Executive because he has been eight years in office will prove unfortunate, if not disastrous. The idea that any man could elect himself President, or even renominate himself, is preposterous. It is a reflection upon the intelligence and patriotism of the people to suppose such a thing possible. Any man can destroy his chances for the office, but no one can force an election, or even a nomination.

To recapitulate: I am not, nor have I ever been, a candidate for a renomination. I would not accept a nomination if it were tendered, unless it should come under such circumstances as to make it an imperative duty—circumstances not likely to arise.

I congratulate the Convention over which you presided for the harmony which prevailed, and for the excellent ticket put in the field and which I hope may be triumphantly elected. With great respect, Your obedient servant,

U. S. GRANT.

To Gen. HARRY WHITE, President Pennsylvania Republican State Convention.

[The resolution which called for this reply was adopted May 26th, and was as follows: "That we declare a firm, unqualified adherence to the unwritten law of the Republic, which wisely and under the sanction of the most venerable examples limits the Presidential service of any citizen to two terms; and we, the Republicans of Pennsylvania, in recognition of this law, are unalterably opposed to the election to the Presidency of any person for a third term."]

President Grant's Speech at Des Moines, Iowa, September 29, 1875.

These remarks were made at the annual re-union of the Army of the Tennessee:

"Comrades: It always affords me much gratification to meet my old comrades in arms of ten and fourteen years ago, and to live over again in memory the trials and hardships of those days—hardships imposed for the preservation and perpetuation of our free institutions. We believed then, and believe now, that we had a good Government, worth fighting for, and, if need be, dying for. How many of our comrades of those days paid the latter price for our preserved Union! Let their heroism and sacrifices be ever green in our memory. Let not the results of their sacrifices be destroyed. The Union and the free institutions, for which they fell, should be held more dear for their sacrifices. We will not deny to any of those who fought against us any privileges under the Government which we claim for ourselves; on the contrary, we welcome all such who come forward in good faith to help build up the waste places and to perpetuate our institutions against all enemies, as brothers in full interest with us in a common heritage; but we are not prepared to apologize for the part we took in the war. It is to be hoped that like trials will never again befall our country. In this sentiment no class of people can more heartily join than the soldier who submitted to the dangers, trials and hardships of the camp and the battle-field. On whichever side they may have fought, no class of people are more interested in guarding against a recurrence of those days.

"Let us, then, begin by guarding against every enemy threatening the perpetuity of free Republican institutions. I do not bring into this assemblage politics, certainly not partisan politics; but it is a fair subject for soldiers in their deliberations to consider what may be necessary to secure the prize for which they battled in a Republic like ours. Where the citizen is the sovereign and the official the servant, where no power is exercised except by the will of the people, it is important that the sovereign—the people—should possess intelligence.

"The free school is the promoter of that intelligence which is to preserve us as a free nation. If we are to have another contest in the near future of our national existence, I predict that the dividing line will not be Mason's and Dixon's, but between patriotism and intelligence on the one side, and superstition, ambition and ignorance on the other. Now, in this Centennial year of our national existence, I believe it a good time to begin the work of strengthening the foundation of the house commenced by our patriotic forefathers, one hundred years ago, at Concord and Lexington. Let us all labor to add all needful guarantees for the more perfect security of free thought, free speech and free press, pure morals, unfettered religious sentiments, and of equal rights and privileges to all men, irrespective of nationality, color or religion. Encourage free schools, and resolve that not one dollar of money appropriated to their support, no matter how raised, shall be appropriated to the support of any sectarian school. Resolve that neither the State nor Nation, or both combined, shall support institutions of learning other than those sufficient to afford to every child, growing up in the land, the opportunity of a good common school education, unmixed with sectarian, pagan or atheistical tenets. Leave the matter of religion to the family altar, the Church and the private school, supported entirely by private contributions. Keep the Church and State forever separate. With these safeguards, I believe the battles which created the Army of the Tennessee will not have been fought in vain."

President Grant's Letter Interpreting It.

EXECUTIVE MANSION,
WASHINGTON, *November* 17, 1875.

Professor L. F. BARKER, *Iowa City, Iowa:*

DEAR SIR—Your letter of the 4th inst. was received about the time I was starting for New York city, one week ago yesterday. I expected to answer immediately on my return, but permitted the matter to escape my mind until this time.

What I said at Des Moines was hastily noted down in pencil, and may have expressed my views imperfectly. I have not the manuscript before me, as I gave it to the Secretary of the society. My idea of what I said is this: "Resolve that the State or Nation, or both combined, shall furnish to every child growing up in the land, the means of acquiring a good common school education."

Such is my idea, and such I intended to have said.

I feel no hostility to free education going as high as the State or National Government feels able to provide—protecting, however, every child in the privilege of a common school education before public means are appropriated to a higher education for the few.

Yours truly, U. S. GRANT.

President Grant's Letter on Privileged Communications, July 12, 1876.

EXECUTIVE MANSION,
WASHINGTON, *July* 12, 1876.

Hon. B. H. BRISTOW:

DEAR SIR—Through the press I learn that the committee of Congress investigating *whiskey frauds* have summoned you as a witness, and that you—with great propriety, as I think—have declined to testify, claiming that what occurs in Cabinet, or between a member of the Cabinet and the Executive officially, is privileged, and that a committee of Congress have no right to demand answer. I appreciate the position you have assumed on this question, but beg to relieve you from all obligation of secrecy on this subject, and desire not only that you may answer all questions asked relating to it, but wish that all members of my Cabinet, and ex-members of my Cabinet since I have been President, may also be called upon to testify in regard to the same matter.

With great respect, your obedient servant,

U. S. GRANT.

XVI.

IMPEACHMENT OF WILLIAM W. BELKNAP, LATE SECRETARY OF WAR.

IN HOUSE.

1876, March 2—Mr. CLYMER, by unanimous consent, from the Committee on Expenditures in the War Department, submitted a report in writing, relative to evidence of the malfeasance in office by William W. Belknap, late Secretary of War, accompanied by the following resolutions, viz:

Resolved, That William W. Belknap, late Secretary of War, be impeached of high crimes and misdemeanors while in office.

Resolved, That the testimony in the case of William W. Belknap, late Secretary of War, be referred to the Committee on the Judiciary, with instructions to prepare and report without unnecessary delay suitable articles of impeachment of said William W. Belknap, late Secretary of War.

Resolved, That a committee of five members of this House be appointed and instructed to proceed immediately to the bar of the Senate, and there impeach William W. Belknap, late Secretary of War, in the name of the House of Representatives and of all the people of the United States of America, of high crimes and misdemeanors while in office, and to inform that body that formal articles of impeachment will in due time be presented, and to request the Senate to take such order in the premises as they deem appropriate.

Which were agreed to.

The SPEAKER announced that he had appointed as the committee under the second resolution:

Mr. CLYMER, Mr. WILLIAM M. ROBBINS, Mr. BLACKBURN, Mr. BASS, and Mr. DANFORD.

IN SENATE.

1876, March 3—Mr. CLYMER, Mr. W. M. ROBBINS, Mr. BLACKBURN, Mr. BASS, and Mr. DANFORD appeared at the bar of the Senate and delivered the following message:

Mr. President: In obedience to the order of the House of Representatives we appear before you, and, in the name of the House of Representatives and of all the people of the United States of America, we do impeach William W. Belknap, late Secretary of War of the United

States, of high crimes and misdemeanors in office; and we further inform the Senate that the House of Representatives will in due time exhibit articles of impeachment against him and make good the same; and, in their name, we demand that the Senate shall take order for the appearance of said William W. Belknap to answer said impeachment.

The President *pro tempore* replied that the Senate would take order in the premises; and the committee withdrew.

On motion by Mr. EDMUNDS,

Ordered, That the message of the House of Representatives relating to the impeachment of William W. Belknap be referred to a select committee to consist of five Senators, to be appointed by the President *pro tempore;* and

The President *pro tempore* appointed Mr. EDMUNDS, Mr. CONKLING, Mr. FRELINGHUYSEN, Mr. THURMAN, and Mr. STEVENSON.

March 6—Mr. EDMUNDS, from the select committee to whom was referred the message of the House of Representatives in relation to the impeachment of William W. Belknap, reported the following resolution; which was considered, by unanimous consent, and agreed to:

Whereas the House of Representatives on the 3d day of March, 1876, by five of its members, Messrs. Clymer, Robbins, Blackburn, Bass, and Danford, at the bar of the Senate, impeached William W. Belknap, late Secretary of War, of high crimes and misdemeanors, and informed the Senate that the House of Representatives will in due time exhibit particular articles of impeachment against him and make good the same; and likewise demanded that the Senate take order for the appearance of the said William W. Belknap to answer the said impeachment: Therefore,

Ordered, That the Senate will, according to its standing rules and orders in such cases provided, take proper order thereon, (upon the presentation of articles of impeachment,) of which due notice shall be given to the House of Representatives.

April 3—The SENATE, having been informed that the House had appointed Managers to conduct the impeachment and had directed them to carry to the Senate the Articles agreed upon by the House,

Ordered, That the Secretary inform the House of Representatives that the Senate is ready to receive the Managers for the purpose of exhibiting articles of impeachment agreeably to such notice.

April 4—The Managers, Messrs. SCOTT LORD, J. PROCTOR KNOTT, WILLIAM P. LYNDE, JOHN A. MCMAHON, GEORGE A. JENKS, ELBRIDGE G. LAPHAM, and GEORGE F. HOAR—were received, and Mr. LORD, their chairman, read the following articles of impeachment:

Articles exhibited by the House of Representatives of the United States of America, in the names of themselves and of all the people of the United States of America, against William W. Belknap, late Secretary of War, in maintenance and support of their impeachment against him for high crimes and misdemeanors while in said office.

ARTICLE I.

That William W. Belknap, while he was in office as Secretary of War of the United States of America, to wit, on the eighth day of October, eighteen hundred and seventy, had the power and authority, under the laws of the United States, as Secretary of War as aforesaid, to appoint a person to maintain a trading-establishment at Fort Sill, a military post of the United States; that said Belknap, as Secretary of War as aforesaid, on the day and year aforesaid, promised to appoint one Caleb P. Marsh to maintain said trading-establishment at said military post; that thereafter, to wit, on the day and year aforesaid, the said Caleb P. Marsh and one John S. Evans entered into an agreement in writing substantially as follows, to wit:

Articles of agreement made and entered into this eighth day of October, in the year of our Lord eighteen hundred and seventy, by and between John S. Evans, of Fort Sill, Indian Territory, United States of America, of the first part, and Caleb P. Marsh, of No. 51 West Thirty-fifth street, of the city, county, and State of New York, of the second part, witnesseth, namely:

Whereas the said Caleb P. Marsh has received from General William W. Belknap, Secretary of War of the United States, the appointment of post-trader at Fort Sill aforesaid; and whereas the name of said John S. Evans is to be filled into the commission of appointment of said post-trader at Fort Sill aforesaid, by permission and at the instance and request of said Caleb P. Marsh, and for the purpose of carrying out the terms of this agreement; and whereas said John S. Evans is to hold said position of post-trader as aforesaid solely as the appointee of said Caleb P. Marsh, and for the purpose hereinafter stated:

Now, therefore, said John S. Evans, in consideration of said appointment and the sum of one dollar to him in hand paid by said Caleb P. Marsh, the receipt of which is hereby acknowledged, hereby covenants and agrees to pay to said Caleb P. Marsh the sum of twelve thousand dollars annually, payable quarterly in advance, in the city of New York aforesaid; said sum to be so payable during the first year of this agreement absolutely and under all circumstances, anything hereinafter contained to the contrary notwithstanding; and thereafter said sum shall be so payable, unless increased or reduced in amount, in accordance with the subsequent provisions of this agreement.

In consideration of the premises, it is mutually agreed between the parties aforesaid as follows, namely:

First. This agreement is made on the basis of seven cavalry companies of the United States Army, which are now stationed at Fort Sill aforesaid.

Second. If at the end of the first year of this agreement the forces of the United States Army stationed at Fort Sill aforesaid shall be increased or diminished not to exceed one hundred (100) men, then this agreement shall remain in full force and unchanged for the next year. If, however, the said forces shall be increased or diminished beyond the number of one hundred (100) men, then the amount to be paid under this agreement by said John S. Evans to said Caleb P. Marsh shall be increased or reduced in accordance therewith and in proper proportion thereto. The above rule laid down for the continuation of this agreement at the close of the first year thereof shall be applied at the close of each succeeding year, so long as this agreement shall remain in force and effect.

Third. This agreement shall remain in force and effect so long as said Caleb P. Marsh shall hold or control, directly or indirectly, the appointment and position of post-trader at Fort Sill aforesaid.

Fourth. This agreement shall take effect from the date and day the Secretary of War aforesaid shall sign the commission of post-trader at Fort Sill aforesaid, said commission to be issued to said John S. Evans at the instance and request of said Caleb P. Marsh, and solely for the purpose of carrying out the provisions of this agreement.

Fifth. Exception is hereby made in regard to the first quarterly payment under this agreement, it being agreed and understood that the same may be paid at any time within the next thirty days after the said Secretary of War shall sign the aforesaid commission of post-trader at Fort Sill.

Sixth. Said Caleb P. Marsh is at all times, at the request of said John S. Evans, to use any proper influence he may have with said Secretary of War for the protection of said John S. Evans while in the discharge of his legitimate duties in the conduct of the business as post-trader at Fort Sill aforesaid.

Seventh. Said John S. Evans is to conduct the said business of post-trader at Fort Sill aforesaid solely on his own responsibility and in his own name; it being expressly agreed and understood that said Caleb P. Marsh shall assume no liability in the premises whatever.

Eighth. And it is expressly understood and agreed that the stipulations and covenants aforesaid are to apply to and bind the heirs, executors, and administrators of the respective parties.

In witness whereof, the parties to these presents have hereunto set their hands and seals the day and year first above written.

John S. Evans. [Seal.]
C. P. Marsh. [Seal.]

Signed, sealed, and delivered in presence of
E. T. Bartlett.

That thereafter, to wit, on the tenth day of October, eighteen hundred and seventy, said Belknap, as Secretary of War aforesaid, did, at the instance and request of said Marsh, at the city of Washington, in the District of Columbia, appoint said John S. Evans to maintain said trading-establishment at Fort Sill, the military post aforesaid; and in consideration of said appointment of said Evans so made by him as Secretary of War as aforesaid, the said Belknap did, on or about the second day of November, eighteen hundred and seventy, unlawfully and corruptly receive from said Caleb P. Marsh the sum of one thousand five hundred dollars; and that at divers times thereafter, to wit, on or about the seventeenth day of January, eighteen hundred and seventy-one, and at or about the end of each three months during the term of one whole year, the said William W. Belknap, while still in office as Secretary of War as aforesaid, did unlawfully receive from said Caleb P. Marsh like sums of one thousand five hundred dollars, in consideration of the appointment of the said John S. Evans by him, the said Belknap, as Secretary of War as aforesaid, and in consideration of his permitting said Evans to continue to maintain the said trading-establishment at said military post during that time. Whereby the said William W. Belknap, who was then Secretary of War as aforesaid, was guilty of high crimes and misdemeanors in office.

Article II.

That said William W. Belknap, while he was in office as Secretary of War of the United States of America, did, at the city of Washington, in the District of Columbia, on the fourth day of November, one thousand eight hundred and seventy-three, willfully, corruptly, and unlawfully take and receive from one Caleb P. Marsh the sum of fifteen hundred dollars, in consideration that he would continue to permit one John S. Evans to maintain a trading-establishment at Fort Sill, a military post of the United States, which said establishment said Belknap, as Secretary of War as aforesaid, was authorized by law to permit to be maintained at said military post, and which the said Evans had been before that time appointed by said Belknap to maintain; and that said Belknap, as Secretary of War as aforesaid, for said consideration, did corruptly permit the said Evans to continue to maintain the said trading-establishment at said military post. And so the said Belknap was thereby guilty, while he was Secretary of War, of a high misdemeanor in his said office.

Article III.

That said William W. Belknap was Secretary of War of the United States of America before and during the month of October, eighteen hundred and seventy, and continued in office as such Secretary of War until the second day of March, eighteen hundred and seventy-six; that as Secretary of War as aforesaid said Belknap had authority, under the laws of the United States, to appoint a person to maintain a trading-establishment at Fort Sill, a military post of the United States, not in the vicinity of any city or town; that on the tenth day of October, eighteen hundred and seventy, said Belknap, as Secretary of War as aforesaid, did, at the city of Washington, in the District of Columbia, appoint one John S. Evans to maintain said trading-establishment at said military post, and that said John S. Evans, by virtue of said appointment, has since, till the second day of March, eighteen hundred and seventy-six, maintained a trading-establishment at said military post; and said Evans, on the eighth day of October, eighteen hundred and seventy, before he was so appointed to maintain said trading-establishment as aforesaid, and in order to procure said appointment and to be continued therein, agreed with one Caleb P. Marsh that, in consideration that said Belknap would appoint him, the said Evans, to maintain said trading-establishment at said military post, at the instance and request of said Marsh, he, the said Evans, would pay to him a large sum of money, quarterly, in advance, from the date of his said appointment by said Belknap, to wit, twelve thousand dollars during the year immediately following the tenth day of October, eighteen hundred and seventy, and other large sums of money, quarterly, during each year that he, the said Evans, should be permitted by said Belknap to maintain said trading-establishment at said post; that said Evans did pay to said Marsh said sum of money quarterly during each year after his said appointment, until the month of December, eighteen hundred and seventy-five, when the last of said payments was made; that said Marsh, upon the receipt of each of said payments, paid one-half thereof to him, the said Belknap. Yet the said Belknap, well knowing these facts, and having the power to remove said Evans from said position at any time, and to appoint some other person to maintain said trading-establishment, but criminally disregarding his duty as Secretary of War, and basely prostituting his high office to his lust for private gain, did unlawfully and corruptly continue said Evans in said position, and permit him to maintain said establishment at said military post during all of said time, to the great injury and damage of the officers and soldiers of the Army of the United States stationed at said post, as well as of emigrants, freighters and other citizens of the United States, against public policy and to the great disgrace and detriment of the public service. Whereby the said William W. Belknap was, as Secretary of War as aforesaid, guilty of high crimes and misdemeanors in office.

ARTICLE IV.

That said William W. Belknap, while he was in office and acting as Secretary of War of the United States of America, did, on the tenth day of October, eighteen hundred and seventy, in the exercise of the power and authority vested in him as Secretary of War as aforesaid by law, appoint one John S. Evans to maintain a trading-establishment at Fort Sill, a military post of the United States; and he, the said Belknap, did receive from one Caleb P. Marsh large sums of money for and in consideration of his having so appointed said John S. Evans to maintain said trading-establishment at said military post, and for continuing him therein, whereby he has been guilty of high crimes and misdemeanors in his said office.

Specification I.

On or about the second day of November, eighteen hundred and seventy, said William W. Belknap, while Secretary of War as aforesaid, did receive from Caleb P. Marsh fifteen hundred dollars, in consideration of his having appointed said John S. Evans to maintain a trading-establishment at Fort Sill aforesaid, and for continuing him therein.

Specification II.

On or about the seventeenth day of January, eighteen hundred and seventy-one, the said William W. Belknap, while Secretary of War as aforesaid, did receive from said Caleb P. Marsh fifteen hundred dollars, in consideration of his having appointed said John S. Evans to maintain a trading-establishment at Fort Sill aforesaid, and for continuing him therein.

Specification III.

On or about the eighteenth day of April, eighteen hundred and seventy-one, the said William W. Belknap, while Secretary of War as aforesaid, did receive from said Caleb P. Marsh fifteen hundred dollars, in consideration of his having appointed said John S. Evans to maintain a trading-establishment at Fort Sill aforesaid, and continuing him therein.

Specification IV.

On or about the twenty-fifth day of July, eighteen hundred and seventy-one, the said William W. Belknap, while Secretary of War as aforesaid, did receive from said Caleb P. Marsh fifteen hundred dollars, in consideration of his having appointed said John S. Evans to maintain a trading-establishment at Fort Sill aforesaid, and continuing him therein.

Specification V.

On or about the tenth day of November, eighteen hundred and seventy-one, the said William W. Belknap, while Secretary of War as aforesaid, did receive from said Caleb P. Marsh fifteen hundred dollars, in consideration of his having appointed said John S. Evans to maintain a trading-establishment at Fort Sill aforesaid, and continuing him therein.

Specification VI.

On or about the fifteenth day of January, eighteen hundred and seventy-two, the said William W. Belknap, while Secretary of War as aforesaid, did receive from said Caleb P. Marsh fifteen hundred dollars, in consideration of his having appointed said John S. Evans to maintain a trading-establishment at Fort Sill aforesaid, and continuing him therein.

Specification VII.

On or about the thirteenth day of June, eighteen hundred and seventy-two, the said William W. Belknap, while Secretary of War as aforesaid, did receive from said Caleb P. Marsh fifteen hundred dollars, in consideration of his having appointed said John S. Evans to maintain a trading-establishment at Fort Sill aforesaid, and continuing him therein.

Specification VIII.

On or about the twenty-second day of November, eighteen hundred and seventy-two, the said William W. Belknap, while Secretary of War as aforesaid, did receive from said Caleb P. Marsh fifteen hundred dollars, in consideration of his having appointed said John S. Evans to maintain a trading-establishment at Fort Sill aforesaid, and continuing him therein.

Specification IX.

On or about the twenty-eighth day of April, eighteen hundred and seventy-three, the said William W. Belknap, while Secretary of War as aforesaid, did receive from said Caleb P. Marsh one thousand dollars, in consideration of his having appointed said John S. Evans to maintain a trading-establishment at Fort Sill aforesaid, and continuing him therein.

Specification X.

On or about the sixteenth day of June, eighteen hundred and seventy-three, the said William W. Belknap, while Secretary of War as aforesaid, did receive from said Caleb P. Marsh seventeen hundred dollars, in consideration of his having appointed said John S. Evans to maintain a trading-establishment at Fort Sill aforesaid, and continuing him therein.

Specification XI.

On or about the fourth day of November, eighteen hundred and seventy-three, the said William W. Belknap, while Secretary of War as aforesaid, did receive from said Caleb P. Marsh fifteen hundred dollars, in consideration of his having appointed said John S. Evans to maintain a trading-establishment at Fort Sill aforesaid, and continuing him therein.

Specification XII.

On or about the twenty-second day of January, eighteen hundred and seventy-four, the said William W. Belknap, while Secretary of War as aforesaid, did receive from said Caleb P. Marsh fifteen hundred dollars, in consideration of his having appointed said John S. Evans to maintain a trading-establishment at Fort Sill, and continuing him therein.

Specification XIII.

On or about the tenth day of April, eighteen hundred and seventy-four, the said William W. Belknap, while Secretary of War as aforesaid, did receive from said Caleb P. Marsh fifteen hundred dollars, in consideration of his having appointed said John S. Evans to maintain a trading-establishment at Fort Sill aforesaid, and continuing him therein.

Specification XIV.

On or about the ninth day of October, eighteen hundred and seventy-four, the said William W. Belknap, while Secretary of War as aforesaid, did receive from said Caleb P. Marsh fifteen hundred dollars, in consideration of his having appointed said John S. Evans to maintain a trading-establishment at Fort Sill aforesaid, and continuing him therein.

Specification XV.

On or about the twenty-fourth day of May, eighteen hundred and seventy-five, the said William W. Belknap, while Secretary of War as aforesaid, did receive from said Caleb P. Marsh fifteen hundred dollars, in consideration of his having appointed said John S. Evans to maintain a trading-establishment at Fort Sill aforesaid, and continuing him therein.

Specification XVI.

On or about the seventeenth day of November, eighteen hundred and seventy-five, the said William W. Belknap, while Secretary of War as aforesaid, did receive from said Caleb P. Marsh fifteen hundred dollars, in consideration of his having appointed said John S. Evans to maintain a trading-establishment at Fort Sill aforesaid, and continuing him therein.

Specification XVII.

On or about the fifteenth day of January, eighteen hundred and seventy-six, the said William W. Belknap, while Secretary of War as aforesaid, did receive from said Caleb P. Marsh seven hundred and fifty dollars, in consideration of his having appointed said John S. Evans to maintain a trading-establishment at Fort Sill aforesaid, and continuing him therein.

ARTICLE V.

That one John S. Evans was on the tenth day of October, in the year eighteen hundred and seventy, appointed by the said Belknap to maintain a trading-establishment at Fort Sill, a military post on the frontier, not in the vicinity of any city or town, and said Belknap did, from that day continuously to the second day of March, eighteen hundred and seventy-six, permit said Evans to maintain the same; and said Belknap was induced to make said appointment by the influence and request of one Caleb P. Marsh; and said Evans paid to said Marsh, in consideration of such influence and request, and in consideration that he should thereby induce said Belknap to make said appointment, divers large sums of money, at various times, amounting to about twelve thousand dollars a year from the date of said appointment to the twenty-fifth day of March, eighteen hundred and seventy-two, and to about six thousand dollars a year thereafter until the second day of March, eighteen hundred and seventy-six, all which said Belknap well knew; yet said Belknap did, in consideration that he would permit said Evans to continue to maintain said trading-establishment, and in order that said payments might continue and be made by said Evans to said Marsh as aforesaid, corruptly receive from said Marsh, either to his, the said Belknap's, own use, or to be paid over to the wife of said Belknap, divers large sums of money at various times, viz: the sum of fifteen hundred dollars on or about the second day of November, eighteen hundred and seventy; the sum of fifteen hundred dollars on or about the seventeenth day of January, eighteen hundred and seventy-one; the sum of fifteen hundred dollars on or about the eighteenth day of April, eighteen hundred and seventy-one; the sum of fifteen hundred dollars on or about the twenty-fifth day of July, eighteen hundred and seventy-one; the sum of fifteen hundred dollars on or about the tenth day of November, eighteen hundred and seventy-one; the sum of fifteen hundred dollars on or about the fifteenth day of January, eighteen hundred and seventy-two; the sum of fifteen hundred dollars on or about the thirteenth day of June, eighteen hundred and seventy-two; the sum of fifteen hundred dollars on or about the twenty-second day of November, eighteen hundred and seventy-two; the sum of one thousand dollars on or about the twenty-eighth day of April, eighteen hundred and seventy-three; the sum of seventeen hundred dollars on or about the sixteenth day of June, eighteen hundred and seventy-three; the sum of fifteen hundred dollars on or about the fourth day of November, eighteen hundred and seventy-three; the sum of fifteen hundred dollars on or about the twenty-second day of January, eighteen hundred and seventy-four; the sum of fifteen hundred dollars on or about the tenth day of April, eighteen hundred and seventy-four; the sum of fifteen hundred dollars on or about the ninth day of October, eighteen hundred and seventy-four; the sum of fifteen hundred dollars on or about the twenty-fourth day of May, eighteen hundred and seventy-five; the sum of fifteen hundred dollars on or about the seventeenth day of November, eighteen hundred and seventy-five; the sum of seven hundred and fifty dollars on or about the fifteenth day of January, eighteen hundred and seventy-six: all of which acts and doings were while the said Belknap was Secretary of War of the United States, as aforesaid, and were a high misdemeanor in said office.

And the House of Representatives, by protestation, saving to themselves the liberty of exhibiting at any time hereafter any further articles or accusation or impeachment against the said William W. Belknap, late Secretary of War of the United States, and also of replying to his answers which he shall make unto the articles herein preferred against him, and of offering proof to the same and every part thereof, and to all and every other article, accusation, or impeachment which shall be exhibited by them, as the case shall require, do demand that the said William W. Belknap may be put to answer the high crimes and misdemeanors in office herein charged against him, and that such proceedings, examinations, trials and judgments may be thereupon had and given as may be agreeable to law and justice. MICHAEL C. KERR,

Speaker of the House of Representatives.

Attest:

GEORGE M. ADAMS,

Clerk of the House of Representatives.

April 5—Mr. EDMUNDS submitted the following resolution; which was considered, by unanimous consent, and agreed to:

Resolved, That a committee of two Senators be appointed by the Chair, to wait upon the Chief-Justice of the United States and invite him to attend in the Senate chamber at one o'clock after noon this day, and in case of his inability to attend, then to invite any one of the associate justices, to administer to Senators the oath required by the Constitution, in the matter of the impeachment of William W. Belknap, late Secretary of War; and

The President *pro tempore* appointed Mr. EDMUNDS and Mr. THURMAN as such committee.

After some time the Chief Justice, Hon. MORRISON R. WAITE, entered the chamber and administered the requisite oath to the Senators. Thereafter, on being notified, the Managers appeared and asked for process in the case, when the Senate adopted this order:

Ordered, That a summons be issued, as required by the rules of procedure and practice in the Senate when sitting for the trial of impeachments, to William W. Belknap, returnable on Monday, the 17th day of the present month, at one o'clock in the afternoon.

April 17—The defendant interposed the following plea:

In the Senate of the United States sitting as a Court of Impeachment.

THE UNITED STATES OF AMERICA *vs.* WILLIAM W. BELKNAP.	Upon articles of impeachment of the House of Representatives of the United States of America, of high crimes and misdemeanors.

And the said William W. Belknap, named in the said articles of impeachment, comes here before the honorable the Senate of the United States sitting as a court of impeachment, in his own proper person, and says that this honorable court ought not to have or take further cognizance of the said articles of impeachment exhibited and presented against him by the House of Representatives of the United States, because, he says, that before and at the time when the said House of Representatives ordered and directed that he, the said Belknap, should be impeached at the bar of the Senate, and at the time when the said articles of impeachment were exhibited and presented against him, the said Belknap, by the said House of Representatives, he, the said Belknap, was not, nor hath he since been, nor is he now, an officer of the United States; but at the said times was, ever since hath been, and now is, a private citizen of the United States and of the State of Iowa; and this he, the said Belknap, is ready to verify; wherefore he prays judgment whether this court can or will take further cognizance of the said articles of impeachment.

WM. W. BELKNAP.

The Managers were allowed till the 19th inst. to consider their replication.

April 19—The HOUSE adopted the following replication:

In the Senate of the United States, sitting as a Court of Impeachment.

THE UNITED STATES OF AMERICA *vs.* WILLIAM W. BELKNAP.	The replication of the House of Representatives of the United States in their own behalf, and also in the name of the people of the United States, to the plea of William W. Belknap to the articles of impeachment exhibited by them to the Senate against the said William W. Belknap.

The House of Representatives of the United States, prosecuting, on behalf of themselves and the people of the United States, the articles of impeachment exhibited by them to the Senate of the United States against said William W. Belknap, reply to the plea of said William W. Belknap, and say that the matters alleged in the said plea are not sufficient to exempt the said William W. Belknap from answering the said articles of impeachment, because they say that at the time all the acts charged in said articles of impeachment were done and committed, and thence continuously done, to the 2d day of March, A. D. 1876, the said William W. Belknap was Secretary of War of the United States, as in said articles of impeachment averred, and therefore, that by the Constitution of the United States the House of Representatives had power to prefer the articles of impeachment, and the Senate have full and the sole power to try the same. Wherefore, they demand that the plea aforesaid of the said William W. Belknap be not allowed, but that the said William W. Belknap be required to answer the said articles of impeachment.

II.

The House of Representatives of the United

States, so prosecuting in behalf of themselves and the people of the United States the said articles of impeachment exhibited by them to the Senate of the United States against the said William W. Belknap, for a second and further replication to the plea of the said William W. Belknap, say that the matters alleged in the said plea are not sufficient to exempt the said William W. Belknap from answering the said articles of impeachment, because they say that at the time of the commission by the said William W. Belknap of the acts and matters set forth in the said articles of impeachment he, said William W. Belknap, was an officer of the United States, as alleged in the said articles of impeachment; and they say that the said William W. Belknap, after the commission of each one of the acts alleged in the said articles, was and continued to be such officer, as alleged in said articles, until and including the 2d day of March, A. D. 1876, and until the House of Representatives, by its proper committee, had completed its investigation of his official conduct as such officer in regard to the matters and things set forth as official misconduct in the said articles, and the said committee was considering the report it should make to the House of Representatives upon the same, the said Belknap being at the time aware of such investigation, and of the evidence taken, and of such proposed report.

And the House of Representatives further say that, while its said committee was considering and preparing its said report to the House of Representatives recommending the impeachment of the said William W. Belknap for the matters and things set forth in the said articles, the said William W. Belknap, with full knowledge thereof, resigned his position as such officer on the said 2d day of March, A. D. 1876, with intent to evade the proceedings of impeachment against him. And the House of Representatives resolved to impeach the said William W. Belknap for said matters as in said articles set forth on said 2d day of March, A. D. 1876. And the House of Representatives say that by the Constitution of the United States the House of Representatives had power to prefer said articles of impeachment against the said William W. Belknap, and that the Senate sitting as a court of impeachment has full power to try the same.

Wherefore the House of Representatives demand that the plea aforesaid be not allowed, but that the said William W. Belknap be compelled to answer the said articles of impeachment.

The SENATE sitting as a court, made the following order:

Ordered, That the respondent file his rejoinder with the Secretary on or before the 24th day of April instant, who shall deliver a copy thereof to the Clerk of the House of Representatives, and that the House of Representatives file their sur-rejoinder, if any, on or before the 25th day of April, instant, a copy of which shall be delivered by the Secretary to the counsel for the respondent.

Ordered, That the trial proceed on the 27th day of April, instant, at twelve o'clock and thirty minutes afternoon.

April 24—The defendant submitted the following rejoinder:

In the Senate of the United States, sitting as a Court of Impeachment.

THE UNITED STATES OF AMERICA *vs.* WILLIAM W. BELKNAP.	Upon articles of impeachment of the House of Representatives of the United States of America, of high crimes and misdemeanors.

And the said William W. Belknap saith that the replication of the House of Representatives first above pleaded to the said plea of him the said Belknap, and the matters therein contained in manner and form as the same are above pleaded and set forth, are not sufficient in law for the said House of Representatives to have or maintain impeachment thereof against him, the said Belknap, and that he, the said Belknap, is not bound by law to answer the same.

And this the said defendant is ready to verify. Wherefore, by reason of the insufficiency of the said replication in this behalf, he, the said Belknap, prays judgment if the said House of Representatives ought to have or maintain this impeachment against him, etc.

WM. W. BELKNAP.

In the Senate of the United States sitting as a Court of Impeachment.

THE UNITED STATES OF AMERICA *vs.* WILLIAM W. BELKNAP.	Upon articles of impeachment of the House of Representatives of the United States of America, of high crimes and misdemeanors.

And the said William W. Belknap, as to the second replication of the House of Representatives of the United States, secondly above pleaded, saith that the said House of Representatives ought not, by reason of anything in that replication alleged, to have or maintain the said impeachment against him, the said Belknap, because he says that it is not true, as in that replication alleged, that he, the said Belknap, was Secretary of War of the United States from any time until and including the 2d day of March, A. D. 1876, and of this he, the said Belknap, demands trial according to law.

II.

And the said Belknap further saith, as to the said second replication of the House of Representatives of the United States, secondly above pleaded, that the said House of Representatives ought not, by reason of anything in that replication alleged, to have or maintain the said impeachment against him, the said Belknap, because he saith that it is not true, as in that replication alleged, that he, the said Belknap, was Secretary of War until the said House of Representatives, by any committee of the said House raised or instructed for that purpose, or having any authority from the House of Representatives in that behalf, had investigated the official conduct of him, the said Belknap, as Secretary of War, in regard to the matters and things set forth as official misconduct in the said articles of impeachment; and of this he, the said Belknap, demands trial according to law.

III.

And the said Belknap, as to the said second replication of the said House of Representatives of the United States, secondly above pleaded, further saith that the said House of Representatives ought not, by reason of anything in that replication alleged, to have or maintain the said impeachment against him, the said Belknap, because he says that at the city of Washington, in the District of Columbia, on the 2d day of March, A. D. 1876, at ten o'clock and twenty minutes in the forenoon of that day, he, the said Belknap, resigned the office of Secretary of War, by written resignation under his hand, addressed and delivered to the President of the United States, and the President of the United States then and there accepted the said resignation, by acceptance in writing under his hand, then and there indorsed upon the said written resignation; so that the said Belknap then and there ceased to be Secretary of War of the United States, and since that time he, the said Belknap, has not been an officer of the United States, but has been a private citizen of the United States and of the State of Iowa, as stated by said Belknap in his said plea; and that at the time he, the said Belknap, resigned as aforesaid, and the said resignation was accepted as aforesaid, the said House of Representatives had not taken any proceeding for the investigation or examination of any of the charges set forth in the said articles of impeachment as official misconduct of him, the said Belknap, as Secretary of War; nor had the said House of Representatives raised any committee of the said House, nor directed, nor instructed any committee of the said House to make inquiry or investigation in that behalf.

And this the said Belknap is ready to verify. Wherefor he prays judgment if the said House of Representatives ought to have or maintain the said impeachment against him the said Belknap.

IV.

And the said Belknap, as to the said second replication of the House of Representatives of the United States, secondly above pleaded, further saith that the said House of Representatives of the United States, by reason of anything in that replication alleged, ought not to have or maintain the said impeachment against him the said Belknap, because he says that, when the said House of Representatives took the first proceeding in relation to the impeachment of him, the said Belknap, and when the matter was first mentioned in the said House—that is, in the afternoon of the 2d day of March, A. D. 1876—the said House of Representatives was fully advised and well knew that he, the said Belknap, had before then resigned the said office of Secretary of War, by resignation in writing, under his hand addressed and delivered to the President of the United States, and that the President of the United States had also before that time, as President as aforesaid, accepted the said written resignation, by acceptance in writing, signed by him and indorsed on the said written resignation, and that he, the said Belknap, was not then an officer of the United States, as the facts were.

And this he, the said Belknap, is ready to verify. Wherefore he prays judgment if the said House of Representatives ought to have or maintain the said impeachment against him, the said Belknap.

V.

And the said Belknap, as to the said second replication of the House of Representatives of the United States, secondly above pleaded, further saith that the said House of Representatives of the United States, by reason of anything in that replication alleged, ought not to have or maintain the said impeachment against him, the said Belknap, because he says that, although true it is that a certain committee of the said House, called the Committee on the Expenditures of the War Department, had been pretending to make some inquiry into or investigation of the matters and things set forth in said articles of impeachment as official misconduct of him, the said Belknap, but without any authority from or direction by the House of Representatives in that behalf, yet he, the said Belknap, says that said committee had not completed its said pretended investigation, but was engaged in the examination of witnesses, when said committee was informed that the said Belknap had resigned as Secretary of War, by resignation in writing, under his hand, addressed and delivered to the President of the United States, and that the President of the United States had accepted the said resignation by acceptance in writing, under his hand, indorsed upon the said written resignation; that said committee received the said information during and before the completion of the said pretended investigation into the alleged facts in that behalf, to wit, at eleven o'clock in the forenoon of the second day of March, A. D. 1876, and that thereupon the said committee declared that they, the said committee, had no further duty to perform in the premises.

And this the said Belknap is ready to verify. Wherefore he prays judgment if the said House of Representatives ought to have or maintain the said impeachment against him, the said Belknap.

VI.

And said Belknap, as to said second replication of the House of Representatives of the United States, secondly above pleaded, further saith that the said House of Representatives ought not, by anything in that replication alleged, to have or maintain said impeachment against him, said Belknap, because he says that, although true it is that he did resign his position as Secretary of War on the 2d day of March, A. D., 1876, at ten o'clock and twenty minutes in the forenoon of that day, at the city of Washington in the District of Columbia, by a resignation in writing under his hand, addressed to and then and there delivered to the President of the United States, and the President of the United States did then and there accept said resignation, by acceptance in writing, under his hand, then and there by him indorsed upon said written resignation, nevertheless, it is not true, as alleged in that replication, that he, said Belknap, resigned his said position with intent to "*evade*" any proceedings of said House of Representatives to impeach him, said Belknap; but on the contrary thereof, he avers the fact to be that a standing committee of said House, known as the Committee on the Expenditures of the War Department, without any authority from or direction of said House of Representatives to examine, inquire, or investigate in regard to the matters and things set forth in said articles as official misconduct of him, said Belknap, had examined one Marsh, and he had made a statement to said committee, which said statement, if true, would not support articles of impeachment against him, said Belknap, but which said statement was of such a character in respect to other persons, some of whom had been and one of whom was so nearly connected with him, said Belknap, by domestic ties as greatly to afflict him, said Belknap, and make him willing to secure the suppression of so much of said statement as affected such other persons at any cost to himself, therefore he, said Belknap, proposed to said committee that, if said committee would suppress that part of said statement which related to said other persons, he, said Belknap, though contrary to the truth, would admit the receipt by him, said Belknap, of all the moneys stated by said Marsh to have been received by him from one Evans mentioned in said statement and paid over by said Marsh to any other person or persons, but said committee declined to accede to said proposition, and Hon. HIESTER CLYMER, chairman of said committee, then declared to said Belknap that he, said CLYMER, should move in the said House of Representatives, upon the statement of said Marsh, for the impeachment of him, said Belknap, unless the said Belknap should resign his position as Secretary of War before noon of the next day, to wit, March the 2d, A. D. 1876; and, said Belknap regarding this statement of said CLYMER, chairman as aforesaid, as an intimation that he, said Belknap, could by thus resigning avoid the affliction inseparable from a protracted trial in a forum which would attract the greatest degree of public attention, and the humiliation of availing himself of the defense disclosed in said statement itself which would cast blame upon said other persons, he yielded to the suggestion made by said CLYMER, chairman as aforesaid, believing that the same was made in good faith by the said CLYMER, chairman as aforesaid, and that he, said Belknap, would, by resigning his position as Secretary of War, secure the speedy dismissal of said statement from the public mind, which said statement, though it involved no criminality on his part, was deeply painful to his feelings; and did resign his said position as Secretary of War, as hereinbefore stated, at ten o'clock and twenty minutes in the forenoon of the 2d day of March, A. D. 1876; and at eleven o'clock in the forenoon of the day and year last aforesaid he, said Belknap, caused said committee to be notified of his said resignation and of the acceptance thereof by the President of the United States as aforesaid; all of which was in pursuance and in consequence of the said suggestion so made by said CLYMER; and thereupon said committee declared that they, the said committee, had no further duty to perform in the premises. And he, said Belknap, submits that, while said House of Representatives claims that said CLYMER was acting on its behalf in said pretended examination of said Marsh, said House ought, in honor and in law, to be estopped to deny that said CLYMER was also acting on behalf of said House in suggesting the resignation of him, said Belknap, as aforesaid, and ought not to be heard to complain of a resignation thus induced.

And this he, the said Belknap, is ready to verify. Wherefore he prays judgment if the said House of Representatives ought to have or maintain the impeachment against him, the said Belknap.

WM. W. BELKNAP.

April 25—The House adopted this joinder in demurrer and surrejoinder:

In the Senate of the United States, sitting as a Court of Impeachment.

THE UNITED STATES OF AMERICA *vs.* WILLIAM W. BELKNAP. } By the House of Representatives of the United States, April 25, 1876.

The House of Representatives of the United States, in the name of themselves and of all the people of the United States, say that the said first replication to the plea of the said William W. Belknap to the articles of impeachment exhibited against him as aforesaid, and the matters therein contained, in manner and form as the same are above set forth and stated, are sufficient in law for the said House of Representatives to have and maintain the said articles of impeachment against the said William W. Belknap, and that the Senate sitting as a court of impeachment has jurisdiction to hear, try, and determine the same; and the House of Representatives are ready to verify and prove the same, as the Senate sitting as a court of impeachment shall direct and award. Wherefore, inasmuch as the said William W. Belknap hath not answered the said articles of impeachment or in any manner denied the same, the said House of Representatives, in the name of themselves and of all the people of the United States, pray judgment thereon according to law, that the said William W. Belknap be adjudged guilty of the high crimes and misdemeanors aforesaid, and that the Senate sitting as a court of impeachment do adjudge accordingly.

And the said House of Representatives, as to the first and second subdivisions of the rejoinder to the second replication of the House of Representatives to the plea of the defendant to the articles of impeachment, wherein the said defendant demands trial according to law, the said House of Representatives, in behalf of themselves and all the people of the United States, do the like; and as to the third, fourth, fifth, and sixth subdivisions of the rejoinder of the said defendant to the said second replication, they say that the said House of Representatives by reason of anything by the said defendant in said last-named subdivisions of said rejoinder above alleged, ought not to be barred from having and maintaining the said articles of impeachment against the said defendant, because they say that, reserving to themselves all advantage of exception to the sufficiency of the said subdivisions of said rejoinder to said second replication, they deny each and every averment in said several rejoinders to said second replication contained, or either of them, which denies or traverses the acts and intents charged against said defendant in said second replication, and they re-affirm the truth of the matter stated therein. And this the said House of Representatives pray may be inquired of by the Senate sitting as a court of impeachment.

Wherefore the said House of Representatives, in the name of themselves and of the people of the United States, pray judgment thereon according to law, that the said William W. Belknap be adjudged guilty of the high crimes and misdemeanors aforesaid, and that the Senate sitting as a court of impeachment do adjudge and determine accordingly.

April 27—The defendant filed the following *similiter:*

In the Senate of the United States, sitting as a Court of Impeachment.

THE UNITED STATES OF AMERICA *vs.* WILLIAM W. BELKNAP.	Upon articles of impeachment of the House of Representatives of the United States of America of high crimes and misdemeanors.

And the said Belknap, as to the surrejoinder of said House of Representatives to the third, fourth, fifth, and sixth rejoinders of the said Belhnap to the second replication of said House of Representatives above pleaded, whereof said House of Representatives have demanded trial, the said Belknap doth the like.

WM. W. BELKNAP.

Same day, April 27—The defendant's counsel having moved a postponement of the trial until the first Monday in December next,

Mr. EDMUNDS moved, in private session, that it be denied.

After debate, and voting down two amendments,

Mr. EDMUNDS' motion was adopted—yeas 59, nays 0, not voting 12.

April 28—The SENATE adopted these orders:

Ordered, That the Senate proceed first to hear and determine the question whether W. W. Belknap, the respondent, is amenable to trial by impeachment for acts done as Secretary of War, notwithstanding his resignation of said office; and that the managers and counsel in such argument discuss the question whether the issues of fact are material and whether the matters in support of the jurisdiction alleged by the House of Representatives in the pleadings subsequent to the articles of impeachment can be thus alleged if the same are not averred in said articles.

Ordered, That the hearing proceed on the 4th of May, 1876, at twelve o'clock and thirty minute: p. m.; that the opening and close of the argument be given to the respondent; that three counsel and three managers may be heard in such order as may be agreed on between themselves; and that such time be allowed for argument as the managers and counsel may desire.

May 5—The argument of counsel began and was continued for several days, and then the SENATE in secret session debated the subject.

May 29—Debate having been concluded under the order of 28th ult.,

The PRESIDENT *pro tempore* announced that the proposition before the Senate now pending for determination was the inquiry submitted by Mr. MORTON on the 16th instant.

Mr. MORTON having modified his inquiry to read as follows—

Resolved, That the power of impeachment created by the Constitution does not extend to a person who is charged with the commission of a high crime while he was a civil officer of the United States and acting in his official character, but who had ceased to be such officer before the finding of articles of impeachment by the House of Representatives—

Mr. MORRILL, of Vermont, moved to amend the resolution by striking out all after the word "resolved" in the first line and in lieu thereof inserting:

That the demurrer of the respondent to the replication of the House of Representatives to the plea of the respondent be, and the same is hereby, overruled; and that the plea of the respondent to the jurisdiction of the Senate be, and the same is hereby, overruled; and that the articles of impeachment are sufficient to show that the Senate has jurisdiction of the case, and that the respondent answer to the merits of the accusation contained in the articles of impeachment.

Mr. CHRISTIANCY moved to amend the amendment of Mr. MORRILL, of Vermont, by striking out all after the words "resolved, that," and in lieu thereof inserting:

W. W. Belknap, the respondent, is not amenable to trial by impeachment for acts done as Secretary of War, he having resigned said office before the impeachment.

Mr. WRIGHT moved to lay the resolution of Mr. MORTON on the table.

Which was agreed to—yeas 36, nays 30, as follow:

YEAS—Messrs. *Bayard, Bogy,* Burnside, *Caperton, Cockrell, Cooper, Davis,* Dawes, *Dennis,* Edmunds, *Goldthwaite, Gordon,* Hamilton of Texas, Hitchcock, *Kelly, Kernan, Key, McCreery, McDonald, Maxey,* Mitchell, Morrill of Vermont, *Norwood, Randolph, Ransom,* Robertson, Sargent, *Saulsbury,* Sherman, *Stevenson, Thurman,* Wadleigh, *Wallace, Whyte, Withers,* Wright—36.

NAYS—Messrs. Allison, BOOTH, Boutwell, Bruce, Cameron of Pennsylvania, Cameron of Wisconsin, Christiancy, Clayton, Conkling, Cragin, Dorsey, *Eaton,* Ferry of Michigan, Frelinghuysen, Hamlin, Harvey, Howe, Ingalls, *Jones* of Florida, Jones of Nevada, Logan, McMillan, Morrill of Maine, Morton, Oglesby, Paddock, Patterson, Spencer, West, Windom—30.

Mr. THURMAN offered the following:

1. *Resolved,* That in the opinion of the Senate William W. Belknap, the respondent, is amenable to trial by impeachment for acts done as Secretary of War, notwithstanding his resignation of said office.

2. *Resolved,* That the House of Representatives and the respondent be notified that on the — day of ——, at twelve o'clock meridian, the Senate will deliver its judgment in open Senate on the question of jurisdiction raised by the pleadings, at which time the managers on the part of the House and the respondent are notified to attend.

3. *Resolved,* That at the time specified in the foregoing resolution the President of the Senate shall pronounce the judgment of the Senate as

follows: "It is ordered by the Senate sitting for the trial of the articles of impeachment preferred by the House of Representatives against William W. Belknap, late Secretary of War, that the demurrer of said William W. Belknap to the replication to the House of Representatives to the plea to the jurisdiction filed by said Belknap be, and the same hereby is, overruled; and going back to the first defect, and it being the opinion of the Senate that said plea is insufficient in law, and that said articles of impeachment are sufficient in law, it is therefore further ordered and adjudged that said plea be, and the same hereby is, overruled and held for naught, and said William W. Belknap is ordered to plead or answer to the merits within —— days; which judgment thus pronounced shall be entered upon the journal of the Senate sitting as aforesaid."

Mr. CONKLING moved to amend the first resolution by inserting at the end thereof "before he was impeached."

The amendment was agreed to.

Mr. CONKLING having demanded a division of the question embraced in the resolutions of Mr. THURMAN and a separate vote upon the first resolution,

On the question to agree thereto as amended,

Mr. PADDOCK moved to amend the said resolution, as amended, by striking out after the word "resolved" and in lieu thereof inserting:

That William W. Belknap, having ceased to be a civil officer of the United States by reason of his resignation before proceedings in impeachment were commenced against him by the House of Representatives, the Senate cannot take jurisdiction in this case.

Which was disagreed to—yeas 29, nays 37:

YEAS—Messrs. Allison, BOOTH, Boutwell, Bruce, Cameron of Wisconsin, Christiancy, Clayton, Conkling, Cragin, Dorsey, *Eaton*, Ferry of Michigan, Frelinghuysen, Hamlin, Harvey, Howe, Ingalls, *Jones* of Florida, Jones of Nevada, Logan, McMillan, Morrill of Maine, Morton, Oglesby, Paddock, Patterson, Spencer, West, Windom—29.

NAYS—Messrs. *Bayard*, *Bogy*, Burnside, Cameron of Pennsylvania, *Caperton*, *Cockrell*, *Cooper*, *Davis*, Dawes, *Dennis*, Edmunds, *Goldthwaite*, *Gordon*, Hamilton of Texas, Hitchcock, *Kelly*, *Kernan*, *Key*, *McCreery*, *McDonald*, *Maxey*, Mitchell, Morrill of Vermont, *Norwood*, *Randolph*, *Ransom*, Robertson, Sargent, *Saulsbury*, Sherman, *Stevenson*, *Thurman*, Wadleigh, *Wallace*, *Whyte*, *Withers*, Wright—37.

The first resolution of Mr. THURMAN, amended to read as follows:

Resolved, That in the opinion of the Senate William W. Belknap, the respondent, is amenable to trial by impeachment for acts done as Secretary of War, notwithstanding his resignation of said office before he was impeached—

Was then agreed to—yeas 37, nays 29:

YEAS—Messrs. *Bayard*, *Bogy*, Burnside, Cameron of Pennsylvania, *Caperton*, *Cockrell*, *Cooper*, *Davis*, Dawes, *Dennis*, Edmunds, *Goldthwaite*, *Gordon*, Hamilton of Texas, Hitchcock, *Kelly*, *Kernan*, *Key*, *McCreery*, *McDonald*, *Maxey*, Mitchell, Morrill of Vermont, *Norwood*, *Randolph*, *Ransom*, Robertson, Sargent, *Saulsbury*, Sherman, *Stevenson*, *Thurman*, Wadleigh, *Wallace*, *Whyte*, *Withers*, Wright—37.

NAYS—Messrs. Allison, BOOTH, Boutwell, Bruce, Cameron of Wisconsin, Christiancy, Clayton, Conkling, Cragin, Dorsey, *Eaton*, Ferry of Michigan, Frelinghuysen, Hamlin, Harvey, Howe, Ingalls, *Jones* of Florida, Jones of Nevada, Logan, McMillan, Morrill of Maine, Morton, Oglesby, Paddock, Patterson, Spencer, West, Windom—29.

The second resolution, as amended, as follows:

Resolved, That the House of Representatives and the respondent be notified that on Thursday, the 1st day of June, 1876, at one o'clock p. m., the Senate will deliver its judgment, in open Senate, on the question of jurisdiction raised by the pleadings, at which time the managers on the part of the House and the respondent are notified to attend—

Was then agreed to—yeas 45, nays, 4:

YEAS—Messrs. *Bayard*, *Bogy*, BOOTH, Boutwell, Burnside, *Caperton*, Christiancy, Clayton, *Cockrell*, *Cooper*, *Davis*, Dawes, *Dennis*, Edmunds, Ferry of Michigan, *Goldthwaite*, *Gordon*, Hamilton of Texas, Harvey, Hitchcock, *Kelly*, *Kernan*, *Key*, *McCreery*, *McDonald*, *Maxey*, Morrill of Vermont, *Norwood*, Oglesby, Paddock, *Randolph*, *Ransom*, Robertson, Sargent, *Saulsbury*, Sherman, *Stevenson*, *Thurman*, Wadleigh, *Wallace*, West, *Whyte*, Windom, *Withers*, Wright—45.

NAYS—Messrs. *Eaton*, Hamlin, McMillan, Morrill of Maine—4.

The third resolution, amended to read as follows:

Resolved, That at the time specified in the foregoing resolution the President of the Senate shall pronounce the judgment of the Senate as follows: "It is ordered by the Senate sitting for the trial of the articles of impeachment preferred by the House of Representatives against William W. Belknap, late Secretary of War, that the demurrer of said William W. Belknap to the replication of the House of Representatives to the plea to the jurisdiction filed by said Belknap be, and the same hereby is, overruled; and, it being the opinion of the Senate that said plea is insufficient in law and that said articles of impeachment are sufficient in law, it is therefore further ordered and adjudged that said plea be, and the same hereby is, overruled and held for naught;" which judgment thus pronounced shall be entered upon the journal of the Senate sitting as aforesaid—

Was then agreed to—yeas 35, nays 22:

YEAS—Messrs. *Bayard*, *Bogy*, Burnside, Cameron of Pennsylvania, *Caperton*, *Cockrell*, *Cooper*, *Davis*, Dawes, *Dennis*, Edmunds, *Goldthwaite*, *Gordon*, Hamilton of Texas, *Kelly*, *Kernan* *Key*, *McCreery*, *McDonald*, *Maxey*, Morrill of Vermont, *Norwood*, *Randolph*, *Ransom*, Robertson, Sargent, *Saulsbury*, Sherman, *Stevenson*, *Thurman*, Wadleigh, *Wallace*, *Whyte*, *Withers*, Wright—35.

NAYS—Messrs. Allison, BOOTH, Boutwell, Cameron of Wisconsin, Christiancy, Conkling, Cragin, *Eaton*, Ferry of Michigan, Frelinghuysen, Hamlin, Harvey, Howe, Jones of Nevada, Logan, McMillan, Morrill of Maine, Oglesby, Paddock, Spencer, West, Windom—22.

June 1—The PRESIDENT *pro tempore* of the Senate announced the judgment of the body, as follows:

On the question of jurisdiction raised by the pleadings in this trial, it is ordered by the Senate sitting for the trial of the articles of impeachment preferred by the House of Representatives against William W. Belknap, late Secretary of War, that the demurrer of said William W. Belknap to the replication of the House of Representatives to the plea to the jurisdiction filed by said Belknap be, and the same hereby is, overruled; and, it being the opinion of the Senate that said plea is insufficient in law and that said articles of impeachment are sufficient in law, it is therefore further ordered and adjudged that said plea be, and the same hereby is, overruled and held for naught. The Secretary will make the proper entry upon the journal.

Mr. WHYTE offered the following:

Ordered, That W. W. Belknap is hereby ordered to plead further or answer the articles of impeachment within ten days from this date.

After debate, the Court adjourned till Tuesday next, at one o'clock.

June 6—The question being on Mr. WHYTE'S motion,

Mr. SHERMAN moved to amend by striking out the words "is hereby ordered" and inserting the words "have leave;" which was agreed to.

The question being on the motion as amended,

Mr. THURMAN moved to add the following at the end of the order:

And that in default of an answer to the merits within ten days by respondent to the articles of impeachment, the trial shall proceed as upon a plea of not guilty.

Mr. BLACK, of counsel for the respondent, submitted the following motion:

In the Senate of the United States sitting as a Court of Impeachment.

THE UNITED STATES OF AMERICA
vs.
WILLIAM W. BELKNAP.

Here in Court comes the said William W. Belknap, and moves the Court now here, to vacate the order entered of record in the cause setting aside and holding as naught the plea of him, said Belknap, by him first above in this cause pleaded, for the reason that said order was not passed with the concurrence of two-thirds of the Senators present and voting upon the question of adopting and passing said order, as appears by the record in this cause.

WILLIAM W. BELKNAP.
J. S. BLACK,
MONTGOMERY BLAIR,
MATT. H. CARPENTER,
Of Counsel.

A motion by Mr. WHYTE, that the court adjourn till to-morrow at one o'clock to hear argument upon the above motion, was lost—yeas 18, nays 23.

Mr. THURMAN'S amendment was then agreed to, yeas 35, nays 7.

The question recurring on Mr. WHYTE'S motion as amended,

Mr. WHYTE moved to strike out the words "plead further or;" which was agreed to.

The order as amended was then agreed to—yeas 33, nays 4, reading as follows:

Ordered, That W. W. Belknap has leave to answer the articles of impeachment within ten days from this date; and that in default of an answer to the merits within ten days by respondent to the articles of impeachment, the trial shall proceed as upon a plea of not guilty.

Mr. Manager LORD offered the following:

Resolved, That on the 6th day of July, 1876, the Senate sitting as a court of impeachment will proceed to hear the evidence on the merits in the trial of this case.

Mr. SARGENT moved the same proposition except the date fixed was "19th day of June."

Mr. ANTHONY moved to substitute "11th of July."

Mr. CAMERON, of Penna., moved to substitute "6th of July;" which was agreed to.

The amendment, as amended, was then rejected.

After debate,

Mr. SARGENT modified his motion so as to read as follows:

Resolved, That further proceedings in this case, after the filing of his answer by the defendant, be postponed until the 6th day of December next.

Mr. EDMUNDS moved to amend by striking out "6th day of December next" and inserting "6th day of July."

Mr. COCKRELL moved to amend the amendment by striking out the words proposed to be inserted, and inserting "19th day of June instant."

The amendment to the amendment was then rejected—yeas 19, nays 27:

YEAS—Messrs. Allison, *Bayard*, *Bogy*, *Caperton*, *Cockrell*, *Dennis*, *Gordon*, Hamilton, *Johnston*, *Maxey*, Morrill of Vermont, *Norwood*, Sargent, *Saulsbury*, Sherman, *Stevenson*, *Thurman*, *Whyte*, *Withers*—19.

NAYS—Messrs. Anthony, BOOTH, Burnside, Clayton, Conkling, *Cooper*, Cragin, Dorsey, *Eaton*, Edmunds, Ferry of Michigan, *Goldthwaite*, Hamlin, Howe, *Kelly*, *Key*, Logan, *McCreery*, Mitchell, Morrill of Maine, Morton, Paddock, *Ransom*, Robertson, Wadleigh, Windom, Wright—27.

The amendment of Mr. EDMUNDS was then agreed to—yeas 36, nays 9:

YEAS—Messrs. Anthony, *Bayard*, *Bogy*, BOOTH, *Caperton*, *Cockrell*, Conkling, *Cooper*, Cragin, *Dennis*, *Eaton*, Edmunds, Ferry of Michigan, *Goldthwaite*, *Gordon*, Hamilton, Hamlin, Howe, *Johnston*, *Kelly*, *Key*, *McCreery*, *Maxey*, Mitchell, Morrill of Maine, Morrill of Vermont, *Norwood*, *Ransom*, Robertson, *Saulsbury*, *Stevenson*, *Thurman*, Wadleigh, *Whyte*, *Withers*, Wright—36.

NAYS—Messrs. Allison, Burnside, Clayton, Jones of Nevada, Morton, Paddock, Sargent, Sherman, Windom—9.

The resolution of Mr. SARGENT having been further amended, on the motion of Mr. EDMUNDS, was agreed to as follows;

Ordered, That on the 6th of July, 1876, at one o'clock p. m., the Senate sitting as a court of impeachment will proceed to hear the evidence on the merits of the trial in this case.

Mr. BLAIR, of counsel for respondent, offered the following motion:

In the Senate of the United States sitting as a Court of Impeachment.

THE UNITED STATES
vs.
WILLIAM W. BELKNAP.

William W. Belknap, by his counsel, moves the court that an order be made upon the managers on the part of the House of Representatives to furnish within twenty-four hours to the accused or his counsel a list of the witnesses whom they intend to call, together with the particulars of the facts which they expect to prove by them.

Which was rejected.

The SENATE then adopted the following order:

Ordered, That the managers furnish to the defendant, or his counsel, within four days, a list of witnesses, as far as at present known to them, that they intend to call in this case; and that, within four days thereafter, the respondent furnish to the managers a list of witnesses, as far as known, that he intends to summon.

Adjourned till June 16th, at 12 o'clock.

June 16—Mr. BLACK, of counsel, offered the following paper:

In the Senate of the United States sitting as a Court of Impeachment.

THE UNITED STATES OF AMERICA
vs.
WILLIAM W. BELKNAP.

And now, to wit, this 16th day of June, 1876, the said William W. Belknap comes into court, and being called upon to plead further to the said articles of impeachment, doth most humbly and with profound respect represent and show to this honorable court, that on the 17th day of April last he did plead to the said articles of impeachment, and in his said plea did allege that at the time when the House of Representatives of the United States ordered the said impeachment, and at the time when the said articles of impeachment were exhibited at the bar of the Senate against him, the said Belknap, he, the said Belknap, was and ever thereafter had been not a public officer of the United States, but a private citizen of the United States and of the State of Iowa; and that the plea aforesaid and all the matters and things therein contained were by him, said Belknap, fully verified by proofs, namely, by admissions of the said House of Representatives before said court; and the said Belknap further represents and shows to the court here, that the truth and sufficiency of the plea pleaded by him as aforesaid were thereupon debated by the managers of the said House of Representatives and the counsel of this respondent, and thereupon submitted to this court for its determination and judgment thereon; and that such proceedings were thereupon had in this court on that behalf in this cause; that afterward, to wit, on the 29th day of May last past, the members of this court, to wit, the Senators of the United States sitting as a court of impeachment as aforesaid, did severally deliver their several judgments, opinions, and votes on the truth and sufficiency in law of the said plea, when and whereby it was made duly to appear that only thirty-seven Senators concurred in pronouncing said plea insufficient or untrue; whereas twenty-nine Senators sitting in said court, by their opinions and votes, affirmed and declared their opinion to be that said plea was sufficient in law and true in point of fact; so that the said Belknap in fact saith that, on the day and year last aforesaid, twenty-nine Senators sitting in said court declared therein that the said Belknap, having ceased to be a public officer of the United States by reason of his resignation of the office of Secretary of War of the United States before proceedings in impeachment were commenced against him by the House of Representatives of the United States, the Senate cannot take jurisdiction of this cause; and that seven Senators did not vote upon said question, and only thirty-seven Senators, by their votes, declared their opinion to be that the Senate could take jurisdiction of said cause. And afterward thirty-seven Senators sitting in said court, and no more, concurred in a resolution declaring that "in the opinion of the Senate William W. Belknap is amenable to trial on impeachment for acts done as Secretary of War, notwithstanding his resignation of said office," and that twenty-nine of said Senators sitting in said court, by their votes, affirmed and declared their opinion to be to the contrary thereof. And afterward, on the day and year last aforesaid, it was proposed in said court that the President *pro tempore* of the said Senate should declare the judgment of the said Senate, sitting as aforesaid, to be that said plea of said respondent should be held for naught, and a vote was taken upon said proposition; and, as said vote showed, two-thirds of the said Senators present did not concur therein; but, on the contrary thereof, only thirty-six Senators did concur therein, and twenty-seven Senators then and there present, and voting on said proposition, did by their votes dissent from and vote against said proposition. All of which appears more fully and at large upon the record of this court in this cause, to which record he, said Belknap, prays leave to refer.

Therefore the said Belknap, referring to the Constitution of the United States, article 1, section 3, clause 6, which provides that "no person shall be convicted without the concurrence of two-thirds of the members present," (meaning on trial on impeachment,) avers that his said plea has not been overruled or held for naught by the Senate sitting as aforesaid, no such judgment having been concurred in by two-thirds of the Senators sitting in said court and voting thereon; but, on the contrary thereof, as the vote aforesaid fully shows, the said plea of the said respondent was sustained, and its truth in fact and sufficiency in law duly affirmed by the said Senate sitting as aforesaid, more than one-third of the Senators of said Senate, sitting as aforesaid, having by their votes so declared, to wit, twenty-seven Senators as aforesaid, and said twenty-seven Senators having by their votes declared and affirmed their opinion to be, that said plea of said respondent was true in fact, and was sufficient in law to prevent the Senate sitting as aforesaid from taking further cognizance of said articles of impeachment.

Wherefore the respondent avers that he has already been substantially acquitted by the Senate sitting as aforesaid; and that he, the said respondent, is not bound further to answer said articles of impeachment; the said order requiring this respondent to answer over not having been made with the concurrence of two-thirds of the said Senators sitting as aforesaid and voting upon the question of the passage of said order; and said order having been passed with the concurrence only of less than two-thirds of the said Senators sitting as aforesaid, and voting on the question of making and passing said order, the said order ought not to have been entered of record as an order of said court of impeachment in this cause; and said order appearing upon the whole record of said cause to be null and void, as an order of said court.

And the said respondent prays the court now here, as he has before formally moved said court, to vacate said order, and the said respondent hereby prays said court that he may be hence dismissed.

WILLIAM W. BELKNAP,
MATT. H. CARPENTER,
J. S. BLACK,
MONTGOMERY BLAIR,
Of Counsel for said Respondent.

Mr. Manager LORD offered the following order:

Ordered, That W. W. Belknap having made default to plead or answer to the merits within the time fixed in the order of the Senate, the trial proceed as upon a plea of not guilty, in pursuance of the former order.

Adjourned, for want of a quorum, till to-morrow.

June 17—Mr. BLACK, of counsel, offered the following order:

Ordered, That this cause be continued until some convenient day in the month of November.

Pending which, the Managers expressing a wish to consult the House, the Senate adjourned till June 19th.

IN HOUSE.

June 17—Mr. Manager LORD submitted the following:

Whereas in the impeachment of William W. Belknap the defendant has moved for a continuance, now on account of the lateness of the season, with the difficulty which will probably attend the retaining of a full organization of the court, and the urgency of other business:

Resolved, That the managers be authorized to consent to a continuance until the —— day of November next.

On which no definite action was taken; and June 20, by unanimous consent, it was withdrawn by the Managers.

June 20—Pending the motion of counsel for postponement,

Mr. THURMAN moved that it be overruled; which was agreed to.

The question being on filing the paper offered by Mr. BLACK on the 16th inst.,

Mr. SHERMAN moved it be filed, and the defendant having failed to answer the merits within ten days allowed by the order of the Senate of the 6th inst., the trial shall proceed on the 6th of July as upon a plea of not guilty.

Mr. THURMAN moved to insert the word "not" before filed; which was disagreed to—yeas 24, nays 24.

The first clause of Mr. SHERMAN'S motion (for filing the paper) was agreed to—yeas 26, nays 24.

On the second clause of Mr. SHERMAN'S motion,

Mr. ALLISON moved to amend by striking out the "6th of July" and inserting "19th of November;" which was disagreed to—yeas 9, nays 37:

YEAS—Messrs. Allison, Christiancy, Clayton, Jones of Nevada, Logan, Morrill of Maine, Wadleigh, Windom, Wright—9.

NAYS—Messrs. Alcorn, *Bogy*, BOOTH, *Cockrell*, Conkling, Cragin, *Davis*, Dawes, *Eaton*, Edmunds, Ferry of Michigan, Frelinghuysen, *Goldthwaite*, Hamilton, Howe, Ingalls, *Johnston*, *Jones* of Florida, *Kelly*, *Kernan*, *Key*, *McCreery*, *Maxey*, Morrill of Vermont, Morton, *Norwood*, Oglesby, Paddock, Patterson, *Ransom*, Robertson, Sargent, *Saulsbury*, Sherman, *Stevenson*, *Wallace*, *Withers*—37.

Mr. MORTON moved to amend the clause by inserting at the end thereof the following words:

Provided, That the impeachment can only proceed in the presence of the House of Representatives.

Mr. FRELINGHUYSEN moved to amend the amendment by striking out "in the presence of the House of Representatives" and in lieu thereof inserting "while Congress is in session."

The amendment to the amendment was agreed to.

The question recurring on the amendment of Mr. MORTON as amended,

Mr. MORTON asked, and obtained, leave to withdraw the amendment.

The question again recurring on the second clause of the order proposed by Mr. SHERMAN,

Mr. CONKLING moved to amend the clause by inserting at the end thereof the words:

Provided, That the impeachment can only proceed while Congress is in session.

Which was agreed to—yeas 21, nays 19, as follow:

YEAS—Messrs. Alcorn, Allison, Clayton, Conkling, Dawes, Ferry of Michigan, Frelinghuysen, Hamlin, Ingalls, Logan, *Maxey*, Morrill of Vermont, Oglesby, Paddock, Patterson, *Randolph*, Sargent, Sherman, Spencer, Wadleigh, *Wallace*—21.

NAYS—Messrs. *Bogy*, BOOTH, Christiancy, *Cockrell*, Cragin, *Davis*, *Eaton*, Edmunds, *Goldthwaite*, Hamilton, *Kelly*, *Kernan*, *Key*, *McCreery*, *Ransom*, *Saulsbury*, *Thurman*, *Withers*, Wright—19.

Mr. MORTON moved further to amend the last clause of the order proposed by Mr. Sherman, by inserting at the end thereof the words:

And in the presence of the House of Representatives.

Mr. SAULSBURY moved to amend the amendment by inserting at the end thereof, "or its managers."

Mr. THURMAN moved to lay the second clause of the order of Mr. SHERMAN on the table.

Which was disagreed to—yeas 21, nays 26, as follow:

YEAS—Messrs. *Bogy*, *Caperton*, *Cockrell*, *Davis*, Dawes, *Eaton*, Hamilton, *Johnston*, *Jones* of Florida, *Kelly*, *Kernan*, *Key*, *McCreery*, *Norwood*, *Randolph*, *Ransom*, *Saulsbury*, *Stevenson*, *Thurman*, *Wallace*, *Withers*—21.

NAYS—Messrs. Allison, BOOTH, Christiancy, Clayton, Conkling, Cragin, Edmunds, Ferry of Michigan, Frelinghuysen, Hamlin, Howe, Ingalls, Logan, *Maxey*, Morrill of Maine, Morrill of Vermont, Morton, Paddock, Patterson, Sargent, Sherman, Spencer, Wadleigh, West, Windom, Wright—26.

Mr. SAULSBURY'S amendment was rejected.

Mr. MORTON'S amendment was then rejected —yeas 9 (Messrs. Allison, Conkling, Ferry of Michigan, Morrill of Vermont, Morton, Sargent, Spencer, West, Windom), nays 28.

Mr. SHERMAN'S second clause as amended as follows:

And the defendant having failed to answer to the merits within ten days allowed by the order of the Senate of the 6th instant, the trial shall proceed on the 6th of July next as upon a plea of not guilty: *Provided*, The impeachment can only proceed while Congress is in session—

Was agreed to—yeas 21, nays 16:

YEAS—Messrs. Allison, BOOTH, Clayton, Conkling, Cragin, Dawes, Frelinghuysen, *Johnston*, *Kelly*, *Key*, *Maxey*, Morrill of Maine, Morrill of Vermont, Oglesby, Paddock, Patterson, Sargent, Sherman, Spencer, Wadleigh, West—21.

NAYS—Messrs. *Bogy*, *Caperton*, Christiancy, *Cockrell*, *Davis*, Edmunds, Ferry of Michigan, Howe, *Kernan*, *McCreery*, *Norwood*, *Randolph*, *Ransom*, *Stevenson*, *Thurman*, Windom—16.

On motion of Mr. EDMUNDS, the following order was adopted:

Ordered, That the Secretary issue subpœnas that may be applied for by the respondent for such witnesses to be summoned at the expense of the United States as shall be allowed by a committee to consist of Senators FRELINGHUYSEN, THURMAN, and CHRISTIANCY; and that subpœnas for all other witnesses for the respondent shall contain the statement that the witnesses therein named are to attend upon the tender on behalf of the respondent of their lawful fees.

Adjourned till July 6.

July 6—The examination of witnesses was begun, and continued on various days, till July 26, when the case was closed.

August 1—The SENATE voted. On the first article, thirty-five voted guilty, and twenty-five not guilty. On the second, third and fourth, Mr. MAXEY made the thirty-sixth who voted guilty. On the fifth, Mr. MORTON made the thirty-seventh who voted guilty. The vote on first was:

VOTING GUILTY—Messrs. *Bayard*, BOOTH, Cameron of Pennsylvania, *Cockrell*, *Cooper*, *Davis*, Dawes, *Dennis*, Edmunds, *Gordon*, Hamilton, Harvey, Hitchcock, *Kelly*, *Kernan*, *Key*, *McCreery*, *McDonald*, *Merrimon*, Mitchell, Morrill of Vermont, *Norwood*, Oglesby, *Randolph*, *Ransom*, Robertson, Sargent, *Saulsbury*, Sherman, *Stevenson*, *Thurman*, Wadleigh, *Wallace*, *Whyte*, *Withers*—35.

VOTING NOT GUILTY—Messrs. Allison, Anthony, Boutwell, Bruce, Cameron of Wisconsin, Christiancy, Conkling, Conover, Cragin, Dorsey, *Eaton*, Ferry of Michigan, Frelinghuysen, Hamlin, Howe, Ingalls, Jones of Nevada, Logan, McMillan, Paddock, Patterson, Spencer, West, Windom, Wright—25.

Mr. BOGY was absent because of the death of his daughter.

Mr. JONES of Florida declined to vote. Those "voting not guilty" generally denied jurisdiction, and so voted accordingly.

XVII.

FINANCIAL VOTES IN FORTY-FOURTH CONGRESS.

Act to Redeem Fractional Currency.

IN HOUSE.

1876, March 27—Pending the following bill (H. R. 2450), reported from the Committee on Appropriations:

A bill to provide for a deficiency in the Printing and Engraving Bureau in the Treasury Department, and for the issue of silver coin of the United States in place of fractional currency.

Be it enacted, &c., That there be and hereby is, appropriated, out of any money in the Treasury not otherwise appropriated, the sum of one hundred and sixty-three thousand dollars, to provide for engraving, printing, and other expenses of making and issuing United States notes.

SEC. 2. That the Secretary of the Treasury is hereby directed to issue silver coins of the United States of the denomination of ten, twenty, twenty-five, and fifty cents, of standard value, in redemption of an equal amount of fractional currency, whether the same be now in the Treasury awaiting redemption, or wherever it may be presented for redemption; and the Secretary of the Treasury may, under regulations of the Treasury Department, provide for such redemption and issue by substitution at the regular sub-treasuries and public depositories of the United States, until the whole amount of fractional currency outstanding shall be redeemed.

Amendments offered by Messrs. PAGE, H. C. BURCHARD, ANDREW WILLIAMS, A. S. HEWITT, F. LANDERS, W. A. PHILLIPS, W. TOWNSEND, DUNNELL, REAGAN and OLIVER, were voted down, on a division.

Mr. HOLMAN moved the following new section:

SEC. 3. The Secretary of the Treasury is hereby prohibited from making any further increase in the interest-bearing debt of the United States by the issue and sale of bonds for the purchase of silver bullion for coinage. But silver bullion shall, under regulations to be prescribed by the Secretary of the Treasury, be received by the several mints for fabrication into subsidiary coins, and paid for in such coins at a rate or price per ounce to be fixed from time to time, according to the market rate, by the Director of the Mint, with the approval of the Secretary of the Treasury, on the basis of the difference between the par value of such coin and the value of such bullion, and an addition not exceeding one per cent., in the discretion of the Secretary of the Treasury, shall be made to the purchasing price as an allowance for the transportation of the coin. And the excess of the par value of such coin over the value of the bullion so deposited, less the amount that shall be allowed for transportation, as aforesaid, determined as above provided, shall be from time to time covered into the Treasury, as the Secretary of the Treasury shall direct: *Provided, however*, That such silver coins of the denominations aforesaid, and the silver bullion now owned by the United States, shall not exceed in par value, the par value of the fractional currency now authorized by law.

Mr. E. WELLS moved the following proviso to the proposed new section:

Provided, That if silver bullion is not presented for coinage in sufficient quantity for the redemption of fractional currency, the Secretary of the Treasury may, under the provisions of the act entitled "An act to provide for the resumption of specie payments," approved January 14, 1875, purchase silver bullion for the purposes of coinage as provided in said act.

Which was agreed to—yeas 118, nays 106 (not voting 65), as follow:

YEAS—Messrs. C. H. Adams, *Bagby*, G. A. Bagley, *J. H. Bagley, jr.*, W. H. Baker, Ballou, *S. N. Bell*, Blair, *Blount*, Bradley, H. C. Burchard, Burleigh, Cannon, Caswell, Chittenden, Conger, Crapo, Crounse, *Cutler*, Danford, Denison, *Durand*, Eames, Farwell, Fort, Foster, Frost, Frye, Garfield, E. Hale, *R. Hamilton*, *Hancock*, Haralson, *Hardenbergh*, B. W. Harris, Hathorn, Hendee, Henderson, *Henkle*, *G. W. Hewitt*, Hoge, Hoskins, Hubbell, *Jenks*, Joyce, Kasson, *Kehr*, Kimball, Lapham, Leavenworth, *B. B. Lewis*, *Luttrell*, Lynch, Magoon, McCrary, *Meade*, *Metcalfe*, Miller, Monroe, *Mutchler*, Norton, *O'Brien*, *Odell*, O'Neill, Page, *Payne*, *J. Phelps*, Pierce, *Piper*, Plaisted, T. C. Platt, A. POTTER, *Powell*, *Randall*, *Reagan*, *M. Ross*, Rusk, Sampson, *J. G. Schumaker*, Seelye, *Singleton*, Sinnickson, R. Smalls, A. H. Smith, Strait, *Stenger*, Stowell, *Tarbox*, *Teese*, *Terry*, *P. F. Thomas*, *C. P. Thompson*, Thornburgh, *Throckmorton*, M. I. Townsend, W. Townsend, Van Vorhes, Waldron, A. S. Wallace, J. W. Wallace, Walls, *Ward*, *Warren*, *E. Wells*, G. W. Wells, Wheeler, J. D. White, *Whitehouse*, Whiting, *Wike*, G. Willard, A. Williams, *A. S. Williams*, C. G. Williams, *J. Williams*, W. B. Williams, J. Wilson, A. Wood, jr.—118.

NAYS—Messrs. ANDERSON, *Ashe*, *Atkins*, J. H. Baker, *Banning*, *Blackburn*, *Boone*, *Bradford*, *Bright*, *J. Y. Brown*, W. R. Brown, *Cabell*, *J. H. Caldwell*, *W. P. Caldwell*, CAMPBELL, Cason, *Cate*, *Caulfield*, *J. B. Clarke*, *J. B. Clark, jr.*, *Cochrane*, *Collins*, *Cook*, *Culberson*, *Joseph J. Davis*, *DeBolt*, *Dibrell*, Dobbins, *Douglas*, Dunnell, *Durham*, *Eden*, *Egbert*, *Ellis*, *Ely*, Evans, *Felton*, *Forney*, *Franklin*, *Fuller*, *Gibson*, *Glover*, *Goode*, *Goodin*, *Gunter*, *A. H. Hamilton*, *H. R. Harris*, *J. T. Harris*, *Hartzell*, *Haymond*, Hays, *Hereford*, *A. S. Hewitt*, *Hill*, *Holman*, *Hooker*, *Hopkins*, *House*, Hunter, *Hunton*, Hyman, *T. L. Jones*, Kelley, *F. Landers*, *Lynde*, *McFarland*, *Milliken*, *Money*, *Morgan*, *Neal*, *New*, Oliver, Packer, *E. Y. Parsons*, *J. F. Philips*, W. A. Phillips, *Poppleton*, *D. Rea*, *J. Reilly*, *J. B. Reilly*, *A. V. Rice*, *Riddle*, *W. M. Robbins*, M. S. Robinson, *Savage*, *Scales*, *Sheakley*, *Southard*, *Sparks*, *Springer*, *Stevenson*, *Stone*, *Swann*, *Tucker*, Tufts, *Turney*, *J. L. Vance*, *R. B. Vance*, *Waddell*, *G. C. Walker*, *Walling*, *Walsh*, *J. D. Williams*, *J. N. Williams*, Woodworth, *Yeates*—106.

Mr. REAGAN offered the following amendment:

Insert as section 4 the following:

That the silver coins of the United States of the denomination of one dollar shall be a legal tender at their nominal value for any amount not exceeding fifty dollars in any one payment. And silver coins of the United States of denominations of less than one dollar shall be a legal tender at their nominal value for any amount not exceeding twenty-five dollars in any one payment.

Which was agreed to—yeas 124, nays 94 (not voting 71), as follow:

YEAS—Messrs. ANDERSON, *Ashe*, *Atkins*, *Bagby*, J. H. Baker, W. H. Baker, BANKS, *Banning*, *S. N. Bell*, *Blackburn*, Blair, *Boone*, *Bradford*, Bradley, *Bright*, *J. Y. Brown*, W. R. Brown, H. C. Burchard, *J. H. Caldwell*, *W. P. Caldwell*, CAMPBELL, Cason, Caswell, *Cate*, *Caulfield*, *J B. Clark, jr.*, *Clymer*, *Cochrane*, *Collins*, Conger, *Culberson*, *Joseph J. Davis*, *DeBolt*, *Dibrell*, *Douglas*, *Durham*, *Eden*, *Egbert*, *Ellis*, Evans, *Felton*, *Forney*, *Fuller*, *Gibson*, *Glover*, *Goode*, *Goodin*, *Gunter*, *A. H. Hamilton*, *R. Hamilton*, *H. R. Harris*, *J. T. Harris*, *C. H. Harrison*, *Hartzell*, *Haymond*, *Henkle*, *G. W. Hewitt*, *Holman*, *Hooker*, *Hopkins*, *House*, Hunter, Hyman, *Jenks*, *T. L. Jones*, Leavenworth, *Levy*, *B. B. Lewis*, *Maish*, *McFarland*, *McMahon*, *Meade*, *Metcalfe*, *Money*, *Morgan*, *Mutchler*, *Neal*, *New*, *Odell*, *E. Y. Parsons*, *J. Phelps*, *J. F. Philips*, *Poppleton*, *Powell*, *D. Rea*, *Reagan*, *J. Reilly*, *J. B. Reilly*, *A. V. Rice*, *Riddle*, *W. M. Robbins*, M. S. Robinson, *M. Ross*, *Savage*, *M. Sayler*, *Scales*, *Sheakley*, *Singleton*, *Sparks*, *Springer*, *Stenger*, *Stevenson*, *Stone*, *Teese*, *Throckmorton*, Tufts, *Turney*, Van Vorhes, *J. L. Vance*, *R. B. Vance*, *Waddell*, Waldron, *Walling*, *Walsh*, G. W. Wells, J. D. White, Whiting, *Wike*, *A. S. Williams*, *J. D. Williams*, *J. N. Williams*, W. B. Williams, Woodworth, *Yeates*—124.

NAYS—Messrs. C. H. Adams, G. A. Bagley, Ballou, *Blount*, Burleigh, *Cabell*, Cannon, Chittenden, *J. B. Clarke*, *Cook*, Crapo, Crounse, *Cutler*, Danford, Denison, Dobbins, Dunnell, Eames, *Ely*, Farwell, Fort, Foster, *Franklin*, Frye, Garfield, E. Hale, *Hardenbergh*, B. W. Harris, Hathorn, Hendee, Henderson, *A. S. Hewitt*, *Hill*, Hoge, Hoskins, Hubbell, *Hunton*, Joyce, Kasson, *Kehr*, Kelley, Kimball, Lapham, *Luttrell*, Lynch, Magoon, McCrary, Miller, *Milliken*, Monroe, Morey, *Morrison*, Nash, Norton, Oliver, O'Neill, Packer, Page, *Payne*, W. A. Phillips, Pierce, *Piper*, Plaisted, T. C. Platt, A. POTTER, Pratt, *Randall*, Sampson, Seelye, Sinnickson, *Slemons*, R. Smalls, A. H. Smith, Strait, Stowell, *Tarbox*, *Terry*, *C. P. Thompson*, Thornburgh, W. Townsend, *Tucker*, A. S. Wallace, J. W. Wallace, *Ward*, *Warren*, *E. Wells*, Wheeler, *Whitehouse*, G. Willard, A. Williams, C. G. Williams, *J. Williams*, J. Wilson, A. Wood, jr. —94.

March 31—The amendment offered by Mr. HOLMAN, as amended on motion of Mr. E. WELLS, was then disagreed to—yeas 68, nays 77.

The bill—being the bill as reported by the Committee of Appropriations, amended by the addition of the last amendment offered by Mr. REAGAN—reading as follows:

That there be, and hereby is, appropriated, out of any money in the Treasury not otherwise appropriated, the sum of one hundred and sixty-three thousand dollars, to provide for engraving, printing, and other expenses of making and issuing United States notes.

SEC. 2. That the Secretary of the Treasury is hereby directed to issue silver coins of the United States, of the denomination of ten, twenty, twenty-five, and fifty cents, of standard value, in redemption of an equal amount of fractional currency, whether the same be now in the Treasury awaiting redemption, or whether it may be presented for redemption; and the Secretary of the Treasury may, under regulations of the Treasury Department, provide for such redemption and issue, by substitution, at the regular sub-treasuries and public depositories of the United States, until the whole amount of fractional currency outstanding shall be redeemed.

SEC. 3. That the silver coins of the United States of the denomination of one dollar shall be a legal tender at their nominal value for any amount not exceeding fifty dollars in any one payment. And silver coins of the United States of denominations of less than one dollar shall be a legal tender at their nominal value for any amount not exceeding twenty-five dollars in any one payment.

Was then passed—yeas 122, nays 100, (not voting 67,) as follow:

YEAS—Messrs. C. H. Adams, *Bagby*, G. A. Bagley, *J. H. Bagley, jr.*, W. H. Baker, Ballou, BANKS, Blair, *Blount*, Bradley, H. C. Burchard, Burleigh, Cannon, *Caulfield*, *Chapin*, Chittenden, *Clymer*, *Cochrane*, Conger, Crounse, *Culberson*, *Cutler*, Danford, Denison, *B. B. Douglas*, *Durand*, Eames, Farwell, Fort, Foster, Frost, Frye, Garfield, *Gibson*, *Goode*, *Gunter*, E. Hale, *Hancock*, Haralson, *Hardenbergh*, *C. H. Harrison*, Hathorn, Hendee, Henderson, *G. W. Hewitt*, Hoge, Hoskins, Hubbell, Hyman, *Jenks*, Joyce, Kasson, *Kehr*, Kimball, Lapham, Leavenworth, *Levy*, *Luttrell*, Lynch, *Lynde*, Magoon, MacDougall, McCrary, *Meade*, Miller, *Mills*, Monroe, Morey, *Morrison*, *Mutchler*, Norton, *O'Brien*, *Odell*, O'Neill, *Page*, *J. Phelps*, *Piper*, Plaisted, T. C. Platt, A. POTTER, *Powell*, Pratt, *Randall*, *Reagan*, *J. Robbins*, *M. Ross*, Rusk, Sampson, *Schleicher*, *J. G. Schumaker*, *Singleton*, Sinnickson, R. Smalls, Strait, *Teese*, *Terry*, Thornburgh, *Throckmorton*, M. I. Townsend, W. Townsend, Tufts, *Turney*, Waldron, A. S. Wallace, J. W. Wallace, Walls, *E. Wells*, G. W. Wells, Wheeler, J. D. White, Whiting, *Wigginton*, *Wike*, G. Willard, A. Williams, *A. S. Williams*, W. B. Williams, *Wilshire*, J. Wilson, A. Wood, jr., Woodburn, *Yeates*—122.

NAYS—Messrs. ANDERSON, *Ashe*, *Atkins*, J. H. Baker, *Banning*, *S. N. Bell*, *Blackburn*, *Boone*, *Bradford*, *Bright*, *J. Y. Brown*, W. R. Brown, *Cabell*, *J. H. Caldwell*, *W. P. Caldwell*, CAMPBELL, Cason, *Cate*, *J. B. Clarke*, *J. B. Clark, jr.*, *Cook*, Crapo, *Joseph J. Davis*, *DeBolt*, *Dibrell*, Dunnell, *Durham*, *Eden*, *Egbert*, Evans, *Felton*, *Forney*, *Franklin*, Fuller, *Glover*, *Goodin*, *A. H. Hamilton*, B. W. Harris, *H. R. Harris*, *J. T. Harris*, *Hartzell*, *Hatcher*, *Haymond*, *Hereford*, *A. S. Hewitt*, *Hopkins*, *House*, Hunter, *Hunton*, *T. L. Jones*, *F. Landers*, *Lord*, *McFarland*, *McMahon*, *Milliken*, *Money*, *Morgan*, *Neal*, *New*, Oliver, Packer, *J. F. Philips*, W. A. Phillips, Pierce, *Poppleton*, *D. Rea*, *J. Reilly*, *J. B. Reilly*, *A. V. Rice*, *Riddle*, *W. M. Robbins*, M. S. Robinson, *Savage*, *M. Sayler*, *Scales*, Seelye, *Sheakley*, *Slemons*, *Sparks*, *Springer*, *Stevenson*, *Stone*, *Tarbox*, *C. P. Thompson*, *Tucker*, Van Vorhes, *J. L. Vance*, *R. B. Vance*, *Waddell*, *G. C. Walker*, *Walling*, *Walsh*, *Ward*, *Warren*, *Whitehouse*, *J. D. Williams*, J. N. Williams, *Willis*, Woodworth, *C. Young*—100.

IN SENATE.

April 10—Mr. SHERMAN reported the bill from the Committee on Finance with these amendments:

The first amendment was in section 2, line 6, to strike out the word "whether" and insert "whenever;" which was agreed to.

The next amendment was to amend section 3, so as to make it read as follows:

SEC. 3. That there shall be coined at the mints of the United States a silver dollar of the weight of four hundred and twelve and eight-tenths grains troy, of standard silver, the emblems, devices and inscriptions of which shall conform to those prescribed by law for the gold and silver coins of the United States, with such modifications thereof as may be necessary to render the said dollar readily distinguishable from the trade-dollar; and in the coinage and delivery thereof, the same deviations from standard weight and fineness shall be allowed as are prescribed by law for the trade-dollar; and the said dollar herein authorized shall be a legal tender at its nominal value for any amount not exceeding $20 in any one payment, except for customs-duties and interest on the public debt; and the trade-dollar shall not hereafter be a legal tender.

The next amendment was to add a new section:

SEC. 4. That the Secretary of the Treasury is hereby authorized to exchange the silver dollars herein authorized for an equal amount of United States notes, which shall be retired and canceled, and not be again replaced by other notes. And he is authorized to exchange such silver coin at its nominal value for silver bullion at its market value, to be ascertained and announced from time to time by the Director of the Mint, with the approval of the Secretary of the Treasury. And the United States notes and fractional currency redeemed under this act shall be held to be a part of the sinking-fund provided for by existing law.

After debate,

Mr. SHERMAN moved to strike out all after the second section of the bill; which was agreed to.

Mr. MORRILL of Maine moved an amendment appropriating $48,000 for engraving and printing national bank-notes; which was agreed to.

Mr. SHERMAN moved to add to the second section these words:

And all fractional currency redeemed under this act shall be held to be part of the sinking-fund provided for by existing law, the interest to be computed thereon as in the case of bonds redeemed under the acts relating to the sinking-fund; which was agreed to.

And the bill passed finally, without division.

IN HOUSE.

April 11 and 12—The House concurred in the amendments of the Senate. The vote on concurring in the amendment striking out the third section (Mr. REAGAN'S amendment), was—ayes 96, noes 55.

[In SENATE, it was stated that the object in striking out was to disembarrass this bill of the provision, leaving it to the future to consider the question as an independent one. The statement was repeated in the HOUSE.]

Bill for the Issue of Silver Coin.

IN HOUSE.

1876, June 10—Mr. COX, from the Committee on Banking and Currency, reported this joint resolution:

That the Secretary of the Treasury, under such limits and regulations as will best secure a just and fair distribution of the same through the country, may issue the silver coin now in the Treasury to an amount not exceeding ten million dollars, in exchange for an equal amount of legal-tender notes; and the notes so received in exchange shall be kept as a special fund, separate and apart from all other money in the Treasury, and be re-issued only upon the retirement and destruction of a like sum of fractional currency received at the Treasury in payment of dues to the United States; and said fractional currency, when so substituted, shall be destroyed and held as part of the sinking-fund, as provided in the act approved April seventeen, 1876.

Mr. COX demanded the previous question, which was seconded, ayes 85, noes 54, and the main question ordered—yeas 106, nays 86 (not voting 98), as follow:

YEAS—Messrs. C. H. Adams, *Bagby*, G. A. Bagley, *J. H. Bagley, jr.*, W. H. Baker, Ballou, BANKS, *Beebe*, *S. N. Bell*, Blaine, Blair, Bradley, W. R. Brown, H. C. Burchard, *S. D. Burchard*, *Candler*, Cannon, Caswell, *Caulfield*, *Chapin*, *Cochrane*, *Cox*, Crapo, Crounse, *Cutler*, Danford, Denison, Dunnell, *Durand*, *Durham*, Eames, Foster, Frost, Garfield, *Gause*, *Goode*, *R. Hamilton*, *Hancock*, Haralson, *Hardenbergh*, B. W. Harris, *Hartridge*, *Haymond*, Hendee, Henderson, *Hurd*, Hurlbut, *Jenks*, Joyce, Kasson, *Kehr*, Kimball, *G. M. Landers*, *Lane*, Lapham, Leavenworth, *Le Moyne*, *Levy*, *Lord*, *Luttrell*, Lynch, *Lynde*, Magoon, *Maish*, McCrary, J. W. McDill, *Meade*, Miller, Monroe, *Morrison*, Norton, O'Neill, Packer, Page, *Piper*, A. POTTER, Rainey, *Randall*, *J. Robbins*, Sampson, *Schleicher*, Sinnickson, A. H. Smith, Strait, *Stenger*, *Tarbox*, *C. P. Thompson*, *Throckmorton*, M. I. Townsend, W. Townsend, Tufts, Van Vorhes, J. W. Wallace, *Ward*, *E. Wells*, G. W. Wells, *Whitehouse*, *Wigginton*, *Wike*, G. Willard, C. G. Williams, *J. Williams*, *J. N. Williams*, *Willis*, J. Wilson, Woodworth—106.

NAYS—Messrs. *Ainsworth*, ANDERSON, *Ashe*, J. H. Baker, *Banning*, *Blackburn*, *Bland*, *Blount*, *Boone*, *Bradford*, *Bright*, *J. Y. Brown*, *Buckner*, *Cabell*, *J. H. Caldwell*, *W. P. Caldwell*, CAMPBELL, Cason, *Cate*, *J. B. Clarke*, *J. B. Clark, jr.*, *Clymer*, *Collins*, *Cook*, *Culberson*, *Joseph J. Davis*, *De Bolt*, *Dibrell*, *Eden*, *Ellis*, Evans, *Felton*, *Finley*, *Forney*, *Franklin*, *Glover*, *A. H. Hamilton*, *J. T. Harris*, *Hartzell*, *Hatcher*, *Hereford*, *G. W. Hewitt*, *Hill*, *Holman*, *Hooker*, Hunter, *Hunton*, *T. L. Jones*, *F. Landers*, W. Lawrence, *B. B. Lewis*, *McFarland*, *McMahon*, *Milliken*, *Mills*, *Morgan*, Nash, *Neal*, Oliver, *J. F. Philips*, W. A. Phillips, *Poppleton*, *D. Rea*, *Reagan*, *J. Reilly*, *A. V. Rice*, *Riddle*, M. S. Robinson, *Savage*, *M. Sayler*, *Scales*, *W. E. Smith*, *Southard*, *Sparks*, *Spencer*, *Springer*, *Terry*, *Tucker*, *Turney*, *R. B. Vance*, *Walsh*, *Whitthorne*, *F. Wood*, *Yeates*, *C. Young*—86.

The joint resolution was then passed, without a division, the yeas and nays being refused, ayes 28, noes 93.

IN SENATE.

1876, June 21—The joint resolution was considered, amended by striking out the word "now" after the word "coin" and by adding the second section, and passed without division. It reads as follows:

Be it enacted, &c., That the Secretary of the Treasury, under such limits and regulations as will best secure a just and fair distribution of the same through the country, may issue the silver coin in the Treasury to an amount not exceeding $10,000,000, in exchange for an equal amount of legal-tender notes; and the notes so received in exchange shall be kept as a special fund, separate and apart from all other money in the Treasury, and be re-issued only upon the retirement and destruction of a like sum of fractional currency received at the Treasury in payment of dues to the United States; and said fractional currency, when so substituted, shall be destroyed and held as part of the sinking fund, as provided in the act approved April 17, 1876.

SEC. 2. That the trade-dollar shall not hereafter be a legal tender, and the Secretary of the Treasury is hereby authorized to limit from time to time the coinage thereof to such an amount as he may deem sufficient to meet the export demand for the same.

IN HOUSE.

June 28—Mr. PAYNE, from the Committee on Banking and Currency, reported back the amendments, recommending concurrence.

On concurring in the first amendment, which was to strike out the word "now" after the word "coin" where it first occurs, and before the phrase "in the Treasury"—the yeas were 82, nays 97, (not voting 110,) as follow:

YEAS—Messrs. C. H. Adams, G. A. Bagley, W. H. Baker, BANKS, Bradley, W. R. Brown, H. C. Burchard, *Candler*, Cannon, Caswell, Conger, Crounse, *Cutler*, Danford, Davy, Denison, Dunnell, *Durand*, Eames, Foster, Frost, Frye, E. Hale, *R. Hamilton*, *Hancock*, *Hardenbergh*, B. W. Harris, *Haymond*, Hendee, Henderson, Hoge, Hubbell, Hurlbut, Joyce, Kasson, Kimball, Leavenworth, Lynch, Magoon, MacDougall, McCrary, J. W. McDill, Miller, Norton, Oliver, Packer, Page, *Payne*, Pierce, *Piper*, T. C. Platt, A. POTTER, *Powell*, Rainey, *J. Robbins*, Rusk,

Sampson, *Schleicher*, Seelye, Sinnickson, A. H. Smith, Strait, *Tarbox*, *Teese*, *C. P. Thompson*, Thornburgh, M. I. Townsend, Tufts, Wait, Waldron, A. S. Wallace, J. W. Wallace, *Warren*, *E. Wells*, J. D. White, *Wike*, G. Willard, A. Williams, *A. S. Williams*, W. B. Williams, J. Wilson, Woodworth—82.

NAYS—Messrs. *Ainsworth*, ANDERSON, *Ashe*, *Atkins*, J. H. Baker, *Blackburn*, *Blount*, *Boone*, *Bright*, *Buckner*, *Cabell*, *J. H. Caldwell*, *W. P. Caldwell*, CAMPBELL, *Cate*, *J. B. Clarke*, *J. B. Clark, jr.*, *Cook*, *Cowan*, *Culberson*, *Joseph J. Davis*, *DeBolt*, *Dibrell*, Dobbins, *Douglas*, *Durham*, *Ellis*, Evans, *Faulkner*, *Felton*, *Finley*, *Forney*, Fort, *Franklin*, *Gause*, *Goodin*, *Gunter*, *A. H. Hamilton*, *J. T. Harris*, *Hartridge*, *Hatcher*, *Hereford*, *G. W. Hewitt*, *Holman*, *Hooker*, *House*, Hunter, *Hunton*, *Jenks*, *F. Jones*, *T. L. Jones*, *F. Landers*, *Lane*, *B. B. Lewis*, *Lord*, *Lynde*, *L. A. Mackey*, *Maish*, *McFarland*, *McMahon*, *Metcalfe*, *Milliken*, *Mills*, *Morgan*, *Neal*, *New*, *Odell*, *J. Phelps*, *J. F. Philips*, W. A. Phillips, *Randall*, *D. Rea*, *Reagan*, *J. B. Reilly*, *A. V. Rice*, *Riddle*, *W. M. Robbins*, M. S. Robinson, *Savage*, *Scales*, *Sheakley*, *Singleton*, *W. E. Smith*, *Southard*, *Sparks*, *Spencer*, *Springer*, *Stevenson*, *Terry*, *P. F. Thomas*, *Turney*, *Waddell*, *C. C. B. Walker*, *Walsh*, *Wigginton*, *J. N. Williams*, *Yeates*, *C. Young*—97.

On concurring in the second amendment of the Senate, which was to add the second section, the yeas were 59, nays 108 (not voting 122).

But, on motion of Mr. RANDALL, the vote on concurring was reconsidered.

Mr. RANDALL then moved to concur in the second amendment of the Senate, with an amendment to add the following sections:

That, in addition to the amount of subsidiary coin authorized by law to be issued in redemption of the fractional currency, it shall be lawful to manufacture at the several mints, and issue through the Treasury and its several offices, such coin to the amount of $20,000,000.

That the silver bullion required for this purpose shall be purchased, from time to time, at market rate, by the Secretary of the Treasury, with any money in the Treasury not otherwise appropriated; and the resulting coin may be issued in the ordinary disbursement of the Treasury; but no purchase of bullion shall be made under this act when the market rate for the same shall be such as will not admit of the coinage and issue as herein provided without loss to the Treasury; and any gain or seigniorage arising from this coinage shall be accounted for and paid into the Treasury, as provided under existing laws relative to the subsidiary coinage: *Provided*, That the amount of money at any one time invested in such silver bullion, exclusive of such resulting coin, shall not exceed $1,000,000.

Mr. F. LANDERS moved to amend further by adding the following:

And be it further provided, That the Secretary of the Treasury is directed to authorize the coinage of the standard silver dollar of the same weight and fineness in use January 1, 1861; and said dollar shall be a legal tender in payment of all debts, public and private.

The amendment offered by Mr. F. LANDERS was then agreed to—yeas 110, nays 55 (not voting 124), as follow:

YEAS—Messrs. *Ainsworth*, ANDERSON, *Ashe*, *Atkins*, J. H. Baker, W. H. Baker, *Blackburn*, *Bland*, *Boone*, Bradley, *Bright*, W. R. Brown, *Buckner*, H. C. Burchard, *Cabell*, *J. H. Caldwell*, *W. P. Caldwell*, CAMPBELL, Cannon, *J. B. Clarke*, *J. B. Clark, jr.*, Conger, *Cowan*, Crounse, *Culberson*, *Cutler*, *Joseph J. Davis*, *DeBolt*, *Dibrell*, Dobbins, *Douglas*, Dunnell, *Durham*, *Ellis*, Evans, *Faulkner*, *Felton*, *Finley*, *Forney*, Fort, *Franklin*, *Gause*, *Goodin*, *Gunter*, *A. H. Hamilton*, *R. Hamilton*, *Hardenbergh*, *H. R. Harris*, *J. T. Harris*, *Hartridge*, *Hatcher*, *Haymond*, *Hereford*, *G. W. Hewitt*, *Hill*, *Holman*, *House*, Hubbell, Hunter, *Hunton*, *T. L. Jones*, *F. Landers*, *Lane*, *B. B. Lewis*, *Luttrell*, *Lynde*, *L. A. Mackey*, Magoon, J. W. McDill, *McFarland*, *Milliken*, *Morgan*, *Neal*, *Odell*, *J. Phelps*, *J. F. Philips*, *Randall*, *D. Rea*, *Reagan*, *J. B. Reilly*, *A. V. Rice*, *Riddle*, *J. Robbins*, *W. M. Robbins*, M. S. Robinson, *Savage*, *Scales*, *Sheakley*, Sinnickson, *W. E. Smith*, *Southard*, *Sparks*, *Spencer*, *Springer*, *Stevenson*, *Teese*, *Terry*, *P. F. Thomas*, Tufts, *Turney*, *Waddell*, Whiting, *Wigginton*, G. Willard, *J. N. Williams*, W. B. Williams, J. Wilson, Woodworth, *Yeates*, *C. Young*—110.

NAYS—Messrs. C. H. Adams, G. A. Bagley, BANKS, *Candler*, *Cook*, Davy, Denison, *Durand*, Eames, Foster, Frost, Frye, *Hancock*, B. W. Harris, Hendee, Joyce, Kasson, Kimball, Leavenworth, Lynch, *Maish*, MacDougall, *Meade*, *Metcalfe*, Miller, Norton, Oliver, Packer, *Payne*, W. A. Phillips, Pierce, *Piper*, T. C. Platt, A. POTTER, *Powell*, Rainey, Sampson, *Schleicher*, Seelye, R. Smalls, A. H. Smith, Strait, *Tarbox*, *C. P. Thompson*, Thornburgh, Wait, Waldron, A. S. Wallace, J. W. Wallace, *Warren*, *E. Wells*, J. D. White, *Wike*, A. Williams, *A. S. Williams*, —55.

The amendment offered by Mr. RANDALL, as amended, was then agreed to—yeas 110, nays 45 (not voting 134), as follow:

YEAS—Messrs. ANDERSON, *Ashe*, *Atkins*, J. H. Baker, BANKS, *Bland*, *Blount*, *Boone*, Bradley, *Bright*, W. R. Brown, *Buckner*, H. C. Burchard, *Cabell*, *J. H. Caldwell*, *W. P. Caldwell*, CAMPBELL, Cannon, *J. B. Clarke*, *J. B. Clark, jr.*, Conger, *Cowan*, Crounse, *Culberson*, *Cutler*, *Joseph J. Davis*, *De Bolt*, Denison, *Dibrell*, *Douglas*, Dunnell, *Durham*, *Ellis*, Evans, *Faulkner*, *Felton*, *Forney*, *Franklin*, *Goodin*, *Gunter*, *A. H. Hamilton*, *R. Hamilton*, *H. R. Harris*, *J. T. Harris*, *Hatcher*, *Haymond*, Henderson, *Hereford*, *G. W. Hewitt*, *Holman*, *Hooker*, *House*, Hunter, *Hunton*, *Jenks*, *T. L. Jones*, Kimball, *Knott*, *Lamar*, *F. Landers*, Leavenworth, *B. B. Lewis*, *Lord*, *Luttrell*, *Lynde*, *L. A. Mackey*, Magoon, *Maish*, J. W. McDill, *McFarland*, *McMahon*, *Metcalfe*, *Milliken*, *Mills*, *Neal*, *Odell*, *Randall*, *D. Rea*, *Reagan*, *J. B. Reilly*, *A. V. Rice*, *Riddle*, *W. M. Robbins*, M. S. Robinson, Sampson, *Savage*, *Scales*, *Sheakley*, *W. E. Smith*, *Southard*, *Sparks*, *Spencer*, *Springer*, *Stevenson*, *Teese*, *Terry*, Tufts, *Waddell*, *Walsh*, *E. Wells*, Whiting, *Wigginton*, G. Willard, *A. S. Williams*, *J. N. Williams*, W. B. Williams, J. Wilson, Woodworth, *Yeates*, *C. Young*—110.

NAYS—Messrs. C. H. Adams, *Ainsworth*, W. H. Baker, *Blackburn*, *Candler*, Caswell, Davy, Eames, Foster, Frost, Frye, *Hancock*, *Hardenbergh*, B. W. Harris, Hendee, Hubbell, *F. Jones*, Joyce, Lynch, *Morgan*, Norton, Oliver, Packer, *Payne*, W. A. Phillips, Pierce, *Piper*, T. C. Platt, A. POTTER, Rainey, *J. Robbins*, *Schleicher*, Seelye, R. Smalls, A. H. Smith, Strait, *Tarbox*, *C. P. Thompson*, Waldron, A. S. Wallace, J. W. Wallace, *Warren*, J. D. White, A. Williams, *Wilshire*—45.

IN SENATE.

June 29—The bill, with amendments, was referred to the Committee on Finance.

July 1—The Committee reported the amendments, with a recommendation that they be non-concurred in, and a Committee of Conference appointed; which was agreed to, without a division. Messrs. SHERMAN, BOUTWELL and BOGY were appointed conferees.

July 6—The HOUSE agreed to the conference, and Messrs. PAYNE, RANDALL and F. LANDERS were appointed conferees.

Report of the Conference.

IN HOUSE.

July 13—The Committee of Conference made this report, unanimous except as to Mr. F. Landers:

The committee of conference on the disagreeing votes of the two Houses on the amendments to the joint resolution (H. R. No. 109) for the issue of silver coin, having met, after full and free conference, have agreed to recommend, and do recommend to their respective Houses, as follows:

That the House recede from its disagreement to the first amendment of the Senate to said joint resolution, and agree thereto, amended as follows:

In line 4 strike out the word "now" and insert "at any time."

And the Senate agree to the same.

That the Senate recede from its disagreement to the amendment of the House to the second amendment of the Senate to said joint resolution, and agree to a substitute for said House amendment, as follows:

Add to the second amendment of the Senate the following:

SEC. 3. That in addition to the amount of subsidiary silver coin authorized by law to be issued in redemption of the fractional currency, it shall be lawful to manufacture at the several mints and issue through the Treasury and its several offices such coin to an amount that, including the amount of subsidiary silver coin and of fractional currency outstanding, shall in the aggregate not exceed at any time fifty millions of dollars.

SEC. 4. That the silver bullion required for the purposes of this act shall be purchased from time to time, at market rate, by the Secretary of the Treasury, with any money in the Treasury not otherwise appropriated; but no purchase of bullion shall be made under this act when the market rate for the same shall be such as will not admit of the coinage and issue, as herein provided, without loss to the Treasury; and any gain or seigniorage arising from this coinage shall be accounted for and paid into the Treasury, as provided under existing laws relative to the subsidiary coinage: *Provided*, That the amount of money at any one time invested in such silver bullion, exclusive of such resulting coin, shall not exceed two hundred thousand dollars.

And the House agree to the same.

Which was agreed to—yeas 129, nays 76 (not voting 82), as follow:

YEAS—Messrs. C. H. Adams, *Bagby*, G. A. Bagley, *J. H. Bagley, jr.*, Ballou, BANKS, *Banning*, *Beebe*, *S. N. Bell*, Blair, *Bliss*, Bradley, W. R. Brown, *Buckner*, H. C. Burchard, *S. D. Burchard*, Burleigh, *Candler*, Cannon, Caswell, *Caulfield*, *Cochrane*, *Collins*, Conger, *Cook*, *Cox*, Crapo, Crounse, *Cutler*, Danford, Darrall, Davy, *Durand*, Eames, *Ellis*, *Ely*, C. Freeman, Frye, Garfield, *Gause*, *Gibson*, *Hancock*, *Hardenbergh*, B. W. Harris, *C. H. Harrison*, *Hartridge*, *Haymond*, Hays, *Henkle*, *A. S. Hewitt*, *Hill*, G. F. Hoar, Hoskins, Hubbell, *Hurd*, Hurlbut, *Jenks*, *F. Jones*, Kasson, *Kehr*, Kimball, *Lamar*, *G. M. Landers*, Lapham, W. Lawrence, Leavenworth, *Le Moyne*, *Lynde*, Magoon, *Maish*, MacDougall, J. W. McDill, *Meade*, *Milliken*, *Mills*, Monroe, *Mutchler*, Nash, Norton, Oliver, O'Neill, Packer, Page, *Payne*, *J. Phelps*, Pierce, *Piper*, Plaisted, A. POTTER, *Powell*, Pratt, Rainey, *Randall*, *J. Reilly*, *J. Robbins*, *M. Ross*, Rusk, Sampson, *Schleicher*, *Singleton*, Sinnickson, R. Smalls, A. H. Smith, Strait, *Tarbox*, *Teese*, *P. F. Thomas*, *C. P. Thompson*, Thornburgh, M. I. Townsend, W. Townsend, *Tucker*, Tufts, *Turney*, *Waddell*, Wait, Waldron, *C. C. B. Walker*, A. S. Wallace, J. W. Wallace, *E. Wells*, *Whitehouse*, Whiting, *Wike*, A. Williams, *A. S. Williams*, *J. Williams*, *J. N. Williams*, *Willis*—129.

NAYS—Messrs. *Ainsworth*, ANDERSON, *Ashe*, *Atkins*, J. H. Baker, *Blackburn*, *Bland*, *Boone*, *Bradford*, *Bright*, *J. Y. Brown*, *Cabell*, *J. H. Caldwell*, *W. P. Caldwell*, CAMPBELL, Cason, *Cate*, *J. B. Clark, jr.*, *Clymer*, *Cowan*, *Culberson*, *Joseph J. Davis*, *De Bolt*, *Dibrell*, Dobbins, *Douglas*, Dunnell, *Eden*, *Egbert*, Evans, *Finley*, *Forney*, Fort, *Glover*, *Goodin*, *Gunter*, *J. T. Harris*, *Hartzell*, *Hatcher*, Henderson, *Holman*, *Hopkins*, *House*, Hunter, Kelley, *F. Landers*, *Lane*, E. W. M. Mackey, *L. A. Mackey*, *McFarland*, *Morgan*, *New*, W. A. Phillips, *Poppleton*, *D. Rea*, *Reagan*, *J. B. Reilly*, *H. Y. Riddle*, M. S. Robinson, *Savage*, *Slemons*, *Sparks*, *Spencer*, *Springer*, *Stevenson*, *Stone*, *Terry*, *Throckmorton*, Van Vorhes, *J. L. Vance*, *R. B. Vance*, *G. C. Walker*, G. Willard, *J. D. Williams*, *B. Wilson*, Woodburn—76.

IN SENATE.

July 14—The report was adopted without division.

Bill for the issue of Subsidiary Coin.

IN HOUSE.

1876, June 10—Mr. COX, from the Committee on Banking and Currency, reported the following (H. R. 3398):

That, in addition to the amount of subsidiary coin authorized by law to be issued in redemption of the fractional currency, it shall be lawful to manufacture at the several mints, and issue through the Treasury and its several offices, such coin to the amount of twenty millions of dollars.

SEC. 2. That the silver bullion required for this purpose shall be purchased from time to time, at market rate, by the Secretary of the Treasury, with any money in the Treasury not otherwise appropriated; and the resulting coin may be issued in the ordinary disbursements of the Treasury or in exchange for legal-tender notes at par; but no purchase of bullion shall be made under this act when the market rate for the same shall be such as will not admit of the coinage and issue or exchange as herein provided without loss to the Treasury, and any gain or seigniorage arising from this coinage shall be accounted for and paid into the Treasury as provided under existing laws relative to the subsidiary coinage: *Provided*, That the amount of money at any one time invested in such silver bullion, exclusive of such resulting coin, shall not exceed one million dollars.

SEC. 3. That the trade-dollar shall not hereafter be a legal-tender; and the Secretary of the Treasury is hereby authorized to limit, from time to time, the coinage thereof to such an amount as he may deem sufficient to meet the export demand for the same.

Mr. WASHINGTON TOWNSEND moved to substitute $10,000,000 for $20,000,000.

Mr. REAGAN moved to strike out, in line four of Sec. 2, of printed bill, the words "or in exchange for legal-tender notes at par," and after the words "coinage and issue," the words "or exchange."

The amendment of Mr. TOWNSEND was not agreed to.

The amendment of Mr. REAGAN was then agreed to—ayes 64, noes not counted.

The bill was then passed, without a division.

IN SENATE.

1876, June 27—This bill came up in order, the question being on the amendment reported by the Committee on Finance, to strike out the whole of the House bill, after the enacting clause, and insert as follows:

That there shall be coined at the mints of the United States a silver dollar of the weight of 412.8 grains troy of standard silver, the emblems, devices, and inscriptions of which shall conform to those prescribed by law for the gold and silver coins of the United States, with such modifications thereof as may be necessary to render the said dollar readily distinguishable from the trade-dollar; and in the coinage and delivery thereof the same deviations from standard weight and fineness shall be allowed as are prescribed by law for the trade-dollar; and the said dollar herein authorized shall be a legal tender at its nominal value for any amount not exceeding $20 in any one payment, except for customs, duties and interest on the public debt, and shall be receivable in payment of all dues to the United States except duties on imports.

SEC. 2. That the Secretary of the Treasury is hereby authorized to exchange the silver dollars herein authorized, and also the subsidiary coins of the United States, for an equal amount of United States notes, which shall be retired and canceled and not be again replaced by other notes. And all United States notes redeemed under this act shall be held to be a part of the sinking fund provided for by existing law, the interest to be computed thereon as in the case of bonds redeemed under the acts relating to the sinking fund.

SEC. 3. That the silver bullion required for this purpose shall be purchased from time to time at market rate by the Secretary of the Treasury with any money in the Treasury not otherwise appropriated; but no purchase of bullion shall be made under this act when the market rate for the same shall be such as will not admit of the coinage and issue as herein provided without loss to the Treasury; and any gain or seigniorage arising from this coinage shall be accounted for and paid into the Treasury, as provided under existing laws relative to the subsidiary coinage: *Provided*, That the amount of money at any one time invested in such silver bullion, exclusive of such resulting coin, shall not exceed $1,000,000.

SEC. 4. That the trade-dollar shall not hereafter be a legal tender, and the Secretary of the Treasury is hereby authorized to limit, from time to time, the coinage thereof to such an amount as he may deem sufficient to meet the export demand for the same.

June 28—Mr. BOGY moved to amend by striking out in the first section the words "not exceeding $20;" on which the vote was—yeas 18, nays 14, as follow:

YEAS—Messrs. *Bogy*, *Caperton*, Clayton, *Cockrell*, Conover, Ferry of Michigan, Hitchcock, Ingalls, Jones of Nevada, *Key*, *McCreery*, *Norwood*, Paddock, Patterson, Spencer, *Whyte*, Windom, *Withers*—18.

NAYS—Messrs. BOOTH, Christiancy, Cragin, *Eaton*, *Goldthwaite*, Hamilton of Texas, Hamlin, Howe, Logan, *Maxey*, Mitchell, Morrill of Vermont, Oglesby, Sherman—14.

There being no quorum, the Senate adjourned, and June 29 the bill, with the amendment, was recommitted to the Committee on Finance, and was not reported back.

Resolution for Issue of Silver Coin.

IN HOUSE.

MAY 15—Mr. PAYNE moved to suspend the rules and pass the following joint resolution:

Resolved by the Senate and House of Representatives, &c., That the Secretary of the Treasury, under such limitations and regulations as will best secure a just and fair distribution of the same through the country, may issue the silver coin now in the Treasury to an amount not exceeding $10,000,000 in exchange for an equal amount of legal tender notes; and the notes so received in exchange shall be kept as a special fund, separate and apart from all other money in the Treasury, and be re-issued only upon the retirement and destruction of a like sum of fractional currency received at the Treasury in payment of dues to the United States; and said fractional currency, when so substituted, shall be destroyed and held as part of the sinking fund, as provided in the act approved April 17, 1876,

Which was disagreed to—yeas 135, nays 73 (not voting 82), as follow:

YEAS—Messrs. C. H. Adams, *Bagby*, *J. H.*

Bagley, jr., Ballou, BANKS, *Banning*, *Beebe*, *S. N. Bell*, Blair, Bradley, W. R. Brown, *Buckner*, H. C. Burchard, *S. D. Burchard*, Burleigh, *Candler*, Cannon, Caswell, *Caulfield*, *Clymer*, *Cochrane*, Conger, *Cowan*, Crapo, *Cutler*, Danford, Davy, Denison, *Durand*, *Ellis*, *Felton*, Foster, C. Freeman, Frost, Garfield, *Gause*, *Goode*, E. Hale, *R. Hamilton*, *Hancock*, *Hardenbergh*, B. W. Harris, *Hartridge*, *Haymond*, Hendee, *Henkle*, *A. S. Hewitt*, *G. W. Hewitt*, *Hill*, G. F. Hoar, Hoskins, *Jenks*, Joyce, *Kehr*, Ketchum, *G. M. Landers*, Lapham, Leavenworth, *Le Moyne*, *Levy*, *B. B. Lewis*, *Lord*, Lynch, *Lynde*, E. W. M. Mackey, *L. A. Mackey*, *Maish*, MacDougall, McCrary, J. W. McDill, *Metcalfe*, Miller, *Mills*, *Money*, Monroe, Morey, *Morrison*, *Mutchler*, Norton, *O'Brien*, *Odell*, O'Neill, Page, *E. Y. Parsons*, *Payne*, *J. F. Philips*, *Piper*, Plaisted, A. POTTER, *Powell*, Pratt, Rainey, *Randall*, *Reagan*, *J. Reilly*, *J. Robbins*, *M. Ross*, Rusk, Sampson, *Scales*, *Schleicher*, *J. G. Schumaker*, R. Smalls, A. H. Smith, Strait, Stowell, *Tarbox*, *Teese*, *C. P. Thompson*, *Throckmorton*, W. Townsend, Tufts, Van Vorhes, *Waddell*, Wait, *C. C. B. Walker*, A. S. Wallace, J. W. Wallace, *Ward*, *Warren*, *E. Wells*, G. W. Wells, Wheeler, J. D. White, *Wigginton*, G. Willard, *A. S. Williams*, C. G. Williams, *J. N. Williams*, W. B. Williams, *Willis*, J. Wilson, A. Wood, jr., Woodburn, *C. Young*—135.

NAYS—Messrs. *Ainsworth*, ANDERSON, *Atkins*, J. H. Baker, *Bland*, *Blount*, *Boone*, *Bright*, *J. Y. Brown*, *Cabell*, *J. H. Caldwell*, *W. P. Caldwell*, CAMPBELL, Cason, *Cate*, *Cook*, *Culberson*, *Joseph J. Davis*, *De Bolt*, *Dibrell*, Dobbins, *Douglas*, Dunnell, *Durham*, *Eden*, *Egbert*, Evans, *Faulkner*, *Finley*, *Franklin*, *Fuller*, *Glover*, *Gunter*, *A. H. Hamilton*, *H. R. Harris*, *J. T. Harris*, *Hartzell*, *Hatcher*, *Holman*, *Hooker*, *Hopkins*, *House*, *Hunter*, Hyman, *T. L. Jones*, *F. Landers*, *McMahon*, *Milliken*, *Morgan*, W. A. Phillips, *Poppleton*, *D. Rea*, *A. V. Rice*, *Riddle*, *W. M. Robbins*, *Sheakley*, *W. E. Smith*, *Southard*, *Sparks*, *Springer*, *Stone*, *Terry*, *Tucker*, *Turney*, *J. L. Vance*, *R. B. Vance*, *G. C. Walker*, *Walsh*, *Whitthorne*, *J. D. Williams*, *Wilshire*, *F. Wood*, *Yeates*—73.

Votes on the Repeal of the Resumption Act of 1875.

IN HOUSE.

1876, January 17—Mr. HOLMAN moved a suspension of the rules to enable him to submit the following resolution:

Resolved, That it is unwise and inexpedient at this time that a specific and arbitrary period should be prescribed by law at which legal-tender notes of the United States should be paid by the Secretary of the Treasury in coin; and therefore the act entitled "An act to provide for the resumption of specie payment," approved January 14, 1875, ought to be repealed; and the Committee on Banking and Currency is instructed at as early a period as may be practicable to report to the House a bill for that purpose.

The motion was disagreed to—yeas 112, nays 158 (not voting 20), two-thirds being required, as follow:

YEAS—Messrs. *Ainsworth*, ANDERSON, *Ashe*, *Atkins*, *J. H. Bagley, jr.*, *Blackburn*, *Bland*, *Blount*, *Boone*, *Bradford*, *Bright*, *J. Y. Brown*, *Buckner*, *Cabell*, *J. H. Caldwell*, *W. P. Caldwell*, CAMPBELL, Cason, *Cate*, *J. B. Clarke*, *J. B. Clark, jr.*, *Clymer*, *Cochrane*, *Collins*, *Cook*, *Cowan*, *Joseph J. Davis*, *DeBolt*, *Dibrell*, Dobbins, *Douglas*, *Durham*, *Eden*, *Egbert*, Evans, *Faulkner*, *Felton*, *Forney*, *Franklin*, *Fuller*, *Gause*, *Glover*, *Goode*, *Goodin*, *Gunter*, *A. H. Hamilton*, *H. R. Harris*, *J. T. Harris*, *C. H. Harrison*, *Hartridge*, *Hartzell*, *Hatcher*, *Haymond*, *Hereford*, *G. W. Hewitt*, *Hill*, *Holman*, *Hopkins*, *House*, *Hunton*, *Jenks*, *T. L. Jones*, Kelley, *Knott*, *F. Landers*, *B. B. Lewis*, *L. A. Mackey*, *McFarland*, *McMahon*, *Milliken*, *Morgan*, *Neal*, *New*, Oliver, *J. Phelps*, *J. F. Philips*, W. A. Phillips, *Piper*, *Poppleton*, *D. Rea*, *J. Reilly*, *A. V. Rice*, *Riddle*, *W. M. Robbins*, *C. B. Roberts*, M. S. Robinson, *Savage*, *M. Sayler*, *Scales*, *Sheakley*, *Slemons*, *W. E. Smith*, *Southard*, *Sparks*, *Springer*, *Stenger*, *Stevenson*, *Stone*, *Terry*, *Tucker*, *Turney*, *J. L. Vance*, *R. B. Vance*, *Waddell*, *G. C. Walker*, *Walling*, *Whitthorne*, *J. D. Williams*, *J. N. Williams*, *Yeates*, *C. Young*—112.

NAYS—Messrs. C. H. Adams, *Bagby*, G. A. Bagley, J. H. Baker, W. H. Baker, Ballou, BANKS, Bass, *Beebe*, *S. N. Bell*, Blaine, Blair, *Bliss*, Bradley, W. R. Brown, H. C. Burchard, *S. D. Burchard*, Burleigh, *Candler*, Cannon, Caswell, *Caulfield*, *Chapin*, Chittenden, Conger, *Cox*, Crapo, Crounse, *Cutler*, Danford, Darrall, Davy, Denison, Dunnell, *Durand*, Eames, *Ellis*, *Ely*, Farwell, Fort, Foster, C. Freeman, Frost, Frye, Garfield, *Gibson*, E. Hale, *R. Hamilton*, *Hancock*, Haralson, *Hardenbergh*, B. W. Harris, Hathorn, Hendee, Henderson, *Henkle*, *A. S. Hewitt*, G. F. Hoar, Hoge, *Hooker*, Hoskins, Hubbell, Hunter, *Hurd*, Hyman, *F. Jones*, Joyce, Kasson, *Kehr*, Ketchum, King, *Lamar*, *G. M. Landers*, *Lane*, Lapham, W. Lawrence, Leavenworth, *Levy*, *Luttrell*, Lynch, Magoon, *Maish*, MacDougall, McCrary, J. W. McDill, *Meade*, *Metcalfe*, Miller, *Mills*, *Money*, Monroe, *Morrison*, *Mutchler*, Norton, *O'Brien*, *Odell*, O'Neill, Packer, Page, *E. Y. Parsons*, *Payne*, Pierce, Plaisted, T. C. Platt, A. POTTER, *Powell*, Pratt, Rainey, *Randall*, *Reagan*, *J. Robbins*, *M. Ross*, S. Ross, Rusk, Sampson, *Schleicher*, Seelye, *Singleton*, Sinnickson, R. Smalls, A. H. Smith, Starkweather, Strait, Stowell, *Tarbox*, *C. P. Thompson*, *P. F. Thomas*, Thornburgh, *Throckmorton*, M. I. Townsend, W. Townsend, Tufts, Van Vorhes, Waldron, *C. C. B. Walker*, A. S. Wallace, J. W. Wallace, Walls, *Walsh*, *Ward*, *Warren*, *E. Wells*, G. W. Wells, Wheeler, J. D. White, *Whitehouse*, Whiting, *Wigginton*, *Wike*, G. Willard, *A. S. Williams*, C. G. Williams, *J. Williams*, W. B. Williams, J. Wilson, A. Wood, jr., *F. Wood*, Woodburn—158.

1876, February 7—Mr. KASSON moved to suspend the rules so as to allow the House to vote upon and agree to the following resolutions separately:

Resolved, That the constitutional authority of Congress to "coin money, regulate the value thereof and of foreign coin" does not include the authority to issue the paper of the Government as money; and in the judgment of this House the Constitution nowhere confers upon Congress the power to issue in time of peace the promises or obligations of the Government as a legal tender in payment of debts.

Resolved, That any legislation touching the legal-tender currency of the Government should keep steadily in view the resumption of specie payments, and should tend to enhance the value of that currency for the resumption of which the faith of the United States has been pledged to its citizens.

Which was disagreed to—yeas 97, nays 146 (not voting 46), as follow:

YEAS—Messrs. C. H. Adams, *Bagby*, G. A. Bagley, J. H. Baker, W. H. Baker, Ballou, *S. N. Bell*, Blaine, Blair, Bradley, H. C. Burchard, Burleigh, Cannon, Chittenden, Conger, Crapo, Darrall, Davy, Denison, Dunnell, *Durand*, Eames, Farwell, Fort, Foster, Frost, Frye, Garfield, E. Hale, *R. Hamilton*, Haralson, *Hardenbergh*, B. W. Harris, Hathorn, Hendee, Henderson, G. F. Hoar, Hoge, Hoskins, Hubbell, Hurlbut, Joyce, Kasson, *Kehr*, Ketchum, Kimball, Lapham, W. Lawrence, Leavenworth, *Luttrell*, Lynch, Magoon, MacDougall, McCrary, J. W. McDill, Miller, Monroe, Nash, Norton, Oliver, O'Neill, Packer, Page, Pierce, Plaisted, T. C. Platt, A. POTTER, *Powell*, Pratt, Rainey, S. Ross, Rusk, Sampson, Seelye, Sinnickson, A. H. Smith, Strait, Stowell, *Teese*, Thornburgh, M. I. Townsend, W. Townsend, Tufts, Van Vorhes, Waldron, A. S. Wallace, J. W. Wallace, Walls, Wheeler, J. D. White, Whiting, G. Willard, C. G. Williams, *Willis*, J. Wilson, A. Wood, jr., Woodburn—97.

NAYS—Messrs. *Ainsworth*, ANDERSON, *Ashe, Atkins, Banning, Barnum, Beebe, Blackburn, Bland, Blount, Boone, Bradford, Bright, J. Y. Brown, Buckner, S. D. Burchard, J. H. Caldwell, W. P. Caldwell*, CAMPBELL, *Candler*, Cason, *Cate, Caulfield, J. B. Clarke, J. B. Clark, jr., Clymer, Cochrane, Collins, Cowan, Cox*, Crounse, *Culberson, Cutler, DeBolt, Dibrell, Douglas, Durham, Eden*, Evans, *Faulkner, Felton, Forney, Franklin, Fuller, Gause, Glover, Goode, Goodin, Gunter, A. H. Hamilton, Hancock, H. R. Harris, C. H. Harrison, Hartzell, Hatcher, Haymond, Hereford, A. S. Hewitt, G. W. Hewitt, Hill, Holman, Hooker, Hopkins, House*, Hunter, *Hunton*, Hyman, *T. L. Jones*, Kelley, *Knott, F. Landers, Levy, B. B. Lewis, Lord, Lynde, L. A. Mackey, Maish, McFarland, McMahon, Metcalfe, Milliken, Mills, Money, Morgan, Morrison, Mutchler, Neal, New, O'Brien, E. Y. Parsons, Payne, J. Phelps, J. F. Philips*, W. A. Phillips, *Piper, Poppleton, Randall, D. Rea, Reagan, J. Reilly, A. V. Rice, Riddle, J. Robbins, W. M. Robbins*, M. S. Robinson, *M. Ross, Savage, M. Sayler, Scales, Sheakley, Singleton, Slemons, W. E. Smith, Southard, Sparks, Springer, Stenger, Stevenson, Swann, Tarbox, Terry, C. P. Thompson, P. F. Thomas, Throckmorton, Tucker, Turney, J. L. Vance, R. B. Vance, Waddell, C. C. B. Walker, Walling, Warren, E. Wells, Whitehouse, Wike*, A. Williams, *A. S. Williams, J. D. Williams, J. N. Williams, Wilshire, B. Wilson, F. Wood*, Woodworth, *Yeates, C. Young*—146.

February 14—Mr. EUGENE HALE moved that the rules be suspended, and the House agree to the following preamble and resolutions:

Whereas the currency now in use among the people of the United States consists of the national bank notes and the greenbacks, the latter being a debt of the Government widely distributed among the people, and the former being redeemable in the greenback and subject to like fluctuation with it; and whereas the United States Treasury has thus far failed to meet its obligations and to redeem its notes, thereby depreciating the value of the people's money and keeping it at a large discount, which depreciation varies from day to day, causing risk and uncertainty in business affairs, to the great prejudice of all legitimate industry and enterprise; and whereas Congress by its enactments, and both the political parties by resolutions adopted in their several national conventions, stand committed to the early resumption of specie payments; Therefore,

Be it resolved by the House of Representatives in Congress assembled, That prompt measures should be taken by such legislation as is needed to render effective the policy to a resumption of specie payments, by placing in the hands of the Secretary of the Treasury all necessary powers to carry out said objects, to the end that a sound and stable currency may be provided for the people.

Which was disagreed to—yeas 85, nays 139 (not voting 65), as follows:

YEAS—Messrs. C. H. Adams, *Bagby*, G. A. Bagley, W. H. Baker, Ballou, Bass, *S. N. Bell*, Blaine, Blair, *Bliss*, Bradley, H. C. Burchard, Burleigh, Chittenden, Conger, Crapo, Crounse, Darrall, Davy, Denison, Dunnell, *Durand*, Eames, Farwell, C. Freeman, Frost, Frye, Garfield, E. Hale, Haralson, B. W. Harris, Hendee, Hoskins, Hubbell, Joyce, Kasson, *Kehr*, Ketchum, Kimball, Lapham, W. Lawrence, Leavenworth, Lynch, McDougall, McCrary, J. W. McDill, Miller, Monroe, Nash, Norton, Packer, Page, Pierce, T. C. Platt, A. POTTER, *Powell*, Pratt, Rainey, Rusk, Sampson, Seelye, Sinnickson, R. Smalls, Strait, Stowell, *Tarbox*, Thornburgh, M. I. Townsend, W. Townsend, Tufts, Van Vorhes, Waldron, A. S. Wallace, Wheeler, J. D. White, Whiting, G. Willard, A. Williams, *A. S. Williams*, C. G. Williams, W. B. Williams, *Willis*, J. Wilson, A. Wood, jr., Woodburn—85.

NAYS—Messrs. *Ainsworth, Ashe*, J. H. Baker, *Barnum, Beebe, Blackburn, Bland, Blount, Boone, Bradford, Bright, J. Y. Brown, Buckner, S. D. Burchard, Cabell, J. H. Caldwell, W. P. Caldwell*, CAMPBELL, *Candler*, Cason, *Cate, Caulfield, J. B. Clarke, J. B. Clark, jr., Collins, Cook, Cowan, Cox, Culberson, Cutler, Joseph J. Davis, DeBolt, Dibrell, Douglas, Durham, Eden, Egbert, Ellis*, Evans, *Felton, Forney*, Fort, *Franklin, Fuller, Gause, Glover, Goode, Goodin, Gunter, Hancock, Hardenbergh, H. R. Harris, J. T. Harris, C. H. Harrison, Hartridge, Hartzell, Haymond, Henkle, Hereford, A. S. Hewitt, G. W. Hewitt, Hill, Holman, Hooker, Hopkins, House*, Hunter, *Hunton, Hurd*, Hyman, *F. Jones, T. L. Jones*, Kelley, *Knott, Lamar, F. Landers, G. M. Landers, Lynde, L. A. Mackey, McFarland, McMahon, Meade, Metcalfe, Milliken, Money, Morgan, Morrison, Mutchler, Neal, New, O'Brien*, Oliver, *E. Y. Parsons, Payne, J. Phelps, J. F. Philips*, W. A. Phillips, *Piper, Poppleton, Randall, D. Rea,*

Reagan, *J. Reilly*, *J. B. Reilly*, *A. V. Rice*, *Riddle*, *J. Robbins*, *W. M. Robbins*, M. S. Robinson, *M. Ross*, *Savage*, *M. Sayler*, *Scales*, *Schleicher*, *Slemons*, *W. E. Smith*, *Southard*, *Sparks*, *Springer*, *Stenger*, *Stone*, *Terry*, *C. P. Thompson*, *Throckmorton*, *Tucker*, *J. L. Vance*, *R. B. Vance*, *Waddell*, *G. C. Walker*, J. W. Wallace, *Walsh*, *Warren*, *Wike*, *J. D. Williams*, *J. N. Williams*, *Wilshire*, *B. Wilson*, Woodworth, *Yeates*—139.

1876, March 20—Mr. ATKINS offered the following bill:

Be it enacted, etc., That all of the provisions of the act entitled "An act to provide for the resumption of specie payment," approved January 14, 1875, which authorize the Secretary of the Treasury to redeem or cancel United States notes and to sell United States bonds for the accomplishment of that purpose be, and the same are hereby, repealed.

And moved that the rules be suspended and the bill passed.

Which was disagreed to—yeas 110, nays 108 (not voting 71), as follow:

YEAS—Messrs. *Ainsworth*, ANDERSON, *Ashe*, *Atkins*, J. H. Baker, *Banning*, *Blackburn*, *Bland*, *Blount*, *Boone*, *Bradford*, *Bright*, *J. Y. Brown*, *S. D. Burchard*, *Cabell*, *J. H. Caldwell*, *W. P. Caldwell*, CAMPBELL, Cannon, *Cate*, *Caulfield*, *J. B. Clarke*, *J. B. Clark, jr.*, *Clymer*, *Cochrane*, *Cook*, *Cowan*, *DeBolt*, *Dibrell*, *Douglas*, *Durham*, *Eden*, *Egbert*, *Ellis*, Evans, *Faulkner*, *Forney*, Fort, *Franklin*, *Fuller*, *Goode*, *Goodin*, *Gunter*, *A. H. Hamilton*, *H. R. Harris*, *J. T. Harris*, *C. H. Harrison*, *Hartridge*, *Hartzell*, *Haymond*, Hays, *Hereford*, *G. W. Hewitt*, *Holman*, *Hopkins*, *House*, Hunter, *Hunton*, *Hurd*, Hyman, *Jenks*, *T. L. Jones*, Kelley, *Knott*, *F. Landers*, *B. B. Lewis*, *Lynde*, *McFarland*, *McMahon*, *Milliken*, *Morgan*, *Neal*, *New*, Oliver, *J. Phelps*, *J. F. Philips*, W. A. Phillips, *Poppleton*, *D. Rea*, *J. Reilly*, *J. B. Reilly*, *A. V. Rice*, *Riddle*, *W. M. Robbins*, M. S. Robinson, *Savage*, *M. Sayler*, *Scales*, *Sheakley*, *W. E. Smith*, *Southard*, *Sparks*, *Springer*, *Stevenson*, *Stone*, *Terry*, *Tucker*, Van Vorhes, *J. L. Vance*, *R. B. Vance*, *Waddell*, *G. C. Walker*, J. W. Wallace, *E. Wells*, *Whitthorne*, *J. D. Williams*, *J. N. Williams*, Woodworth, *Yeates*, *C. Young*—110.

NAYS—Messrs. *Bagby*, G. A. Bagley, *J. H. Bagley, jr.*, W. H. Baker, Ballou, BANKS, *Barnum*, Bass, *Beebe*, Blaine, Blair, *Bliss*, Bradley, W. R. Brown, H. C. Burchard, Caswell, Chittenden, Conger, *Cox*, Crapo, *Cutler*, Denison, Dunnell, *Durand*, Eames, *Ely*, Farwell, Foster, C. Freeman, Frost, Frye, Garfield, E. Hale, *R. Hamilton*, *Hancock*, *Hardenbergh*, Hathorn, Hendee, *Henkle*, *A. S. Hewitt*, G. F. Hoar, Hoge, *Hooker*, Hubbell, Hurlbut, Joyce, *Kehr*, Kimball, *G. M. Landers*, Lapham, Leavenworth, *Luttrell*, Lynch, *Maish*, McCrary, J. W. McDill, *Metcalfe*, Miller, *Money*, Monroe, *Morrison*, Nash, Norton, *O'Brien*, Page, *Payne*, Pierce, *Piper*, Plaisted, A. POTTER, *Powell*, Pratt, *Randall*, *Reagan*, *J. Robbins*, Sampson, *Schleicher*, *J. G. Schumaker*, Seelye, *Singleton*, R. Smalls, A. H. Smith, Strait, *Stenger*, Stowell, *Tarbox*, *C. P. Thompson*, Thornburgh, *Throckmorton*, W. Townsend, Tufts, *C. C. B. Walker*, A. S. Wallace, *Ward*, *Warren*, Wheeler, *Whitehouse*, Whiting, *Wike*, G. Willard, A. Williams, *A. S. Williams*, C. G. Williams, *J. Williams*, W. B. Williams, *Willis*, J. Wilson, A. Wood, jr.—108.

Democratic Caucus Bill on the Money Question.

March 27—Mr. PAYNE moved that the rules be suspended so to allow him to introduce, and the House to pass, the following bill to provide for the gradual resumption of specie payments:

A BILL to provide for the gradual resumption of specie payments.

Be it enacted, etc., That it shall be the duty of the Secretary of the Treasury, during each and every year from and after July 1, 1876, and until the legal tender notes of the United States shall have appreciated to par value with gold and shall be convertible into coin, to cause to be set aside and retained in coin an amount equal to three per centum of such legal tender notes outstanding; and from the date of such convertibility as aforesaid, the amount of coin set aside and retained, as aforesaid, shall be held as a resumption fund in respect to said legal tender notes, and shall at no time be less than thirty per centum of such outstanding legal tender notes: *Provided, however*, that the coin so set aside and retained as above provided shall be counted as a part of the sinking fund for the purchase or payment of the public debt, as required by section 3,694 of the revised statutes.

SEC. 2. That it shall be the duty of each national banking association during each and every year from and after July 1, 1876, and until the full and complete resumption of the payment in specie of its circulating notes, to set aside and retain from the coin receivable as interest on the bonds deposited with the Treasurer of United States as security for its circulation an amount equal to three per centum of its circulating notes issued to such association and not surrendered; and from the date of its resumption of specie payments as aforesaid, the amount of coin to be held and maintained as a resumption fund shall at no time be less than thirty per centum of its outstanding circulation; *Provided, however*, That the coin by this section directed to be set aside and retained shall be counted as a part of the lawful money reserve which said associations are by existing laws required to maintain.

SEC. 3. That so much of section three of an act entitled "an act to provide for the resumption of specie payments" approved January 14, 1875, as requires the Secretary of the Treasury to redeem legal tender notes to the amount of eighty per centum of the sum of national bank notes issued to any banking association increasing its capital or circulation, or to any association newly organized as provided in said section, and also so much of said section three as relates to or provides for the redemption in coin of the United States legal-tender notes on and after January 1, 1879, and all other provisions of law inconsistent with this act, are hereby repealed.

Mr. HOLMAN asked if it was in order to divide the several propositions embraced in the bill, so as to have a separate vote on the last section.

The SPEAKER said: It is not.

Others made the same request. But Mr. PAYNE refused to yield for any purpose.

The vote was then taken on the motion; and it was disagreed to, (two-thirds being required) —yeas 81, nays 157 (not voting 51), as follow:

YEAS—Messrs. *Ashe, Bagby, J. H. Bagley, jr., Barnum, S. N. Bell, Blount, Bradford, J. Y. Brown, Cabell, J. H. Caldwell, Caulfield, Chapin, Clymer, Cochrane, Collins, Cook, Cox, Culberson, Cutler, DeBolt, Douglas, Durham, Felton, Forney, Gibson, Goode, Gunter, Hancock, Hardenbergh, H. R. Harris, C. H. Harrison, Hartridge, Henkle, G. W. Hewitt, Hooker, Hopkins, Hunton, Hurd, Knott, G. M. Landers, Lane, Levy, Luttrell, Lynde, Maish, Meade, Metcalfe, Milliken, Money, Morrison, Mutchler, E. Y. Parsons, Payne, J. Phelps, Piper, Powell, Randall, Reagan, W. M. Robbins, C. B. Roberts, M. Ross, Schleicher, Singleton, Slemons, W. E. Smith, Stenger, Swann, Terry, P. F. Thomas, Throckmorton, Tucker, Turney, R. B. Vance, Walsh, Wigginton, Wike, A. S. Williams, J. Williams, J. N. Williams, Yeates, C. Young*—81.

NAYS—Messrs. C. H. Adams, ANDERSON, *Atkins*, G. A. Bagley, J. H. Baker, W. H. Baker, Ballou, BANKS, *Beebe, Blackburn*, Blair, *Boone*, Bradley, *Bright*, W. R. Brown, H. C. Burchard, Burleigh, *W. P. Caldwell*, CAMPBELL, Cannon, Cason, Caswell, *Cate*, Chittenden, *J. B. Clarke, J. B. Clark, jr.*, Conger, Crapo, Crounse, Danford, *Joseph J. Davis*, Denison, *Dibrell*, Dobbins, Dunnell, *Durand*, Eames, *Eden, Egbert, Ely*, Evans, Farwell, *Faulkner*, Fort, Foster, *Franklin, Fuller*, Garfield, *Glover, Goodin*, E. Hale, *A. H. Hamilton, R. Hamilton, Hartzell*, Hathorn, *Haymond*, Hendee, Henderson, *Hereford, A. S. Hewitt*, G. F. Hoar, *Holman*, Hoskins, Hubbell, Hunter, Hurlbut, Hyman, *T. L. Jones*, Joyce, Kasson, *Kehr*, Kelley, Kimball, King, *F. Landers*, Lapham, Leavenworth, Lynch, Magoon, McCrary, *McFarland, McMahon*, Miller, Monroe, Morey, *Morgan*, Nash, *Neal, New*, Norton, *O'Brien*, Oliver, O'Neill, Packer, Page, *J. F. Philips*, W. A. Phillips, Pierce, Plaisted, T. C. Platt, *Poppleton*, A. POTTER, *J. Reilly, A. V. Rice, Riddle, J. Robbins*, M. S. Robinson, S. Ross, Rusk, Sampson, *Savage, M. Sayler, Scales*, Seelye, *Sheakley*, Sinnickson, R. Smalls, A. H. Smith, *Southard, Sparks, Springer*, Strait, *Stevenson, Stone*, Stowell, *Tarbox, Teese, C. P. Thompson*, Thornburgh, M. I. Townsend, W. Townsend, Tufts, Van Vorhes, *J. L. Vance, Waddell*, Waldron, A. S. Wallace, J. W. Wallace, *Walling*, Walls, *Ward, Warren*, G. W. Wells, Wheeler, J. D. White, Whiting, *Whitthorne*, G. Willard, A. Williams, C. G. Williams, *J. D. Williams*, W. B. Williams, *Willis*, J. Wilson, A. Wood, jr., Woodburn, Woodworth—157.

[This bill is understood to have been adopted, in a caucus of Democratic Representatives, March 15, 1876, by a vote of 69 to 46, and ordered presented to the House, "as the best practicable compromise of differing opinions on the financial question."]

May 1—Mr. HOLMAN moved that the rules be suspended so as to enable him to introduce, and the House to pass, a bill to repeal so much of the act entitled "An act to provide for the resumption of specie payments," approved January 14, 1875, as authorizes the Secretary of th Treasury to redeem and cancel United State notes and to issue and sell United States bond for the accomplishment of that purpose.

Which was disagreed to, (two-thirds not havin voted in the affirmative,) yeas 115, nays 111 (nc voting 64), as follow:

YEAS—Messrs. *Ainsworth*, ANDERSON, *At kins*, J. H. Baker, *Banning, Blackburn, Blana Blount, Bradford, J. Y. Brown, Buckner, S D. Burchard, Cabell, J. H. Caldwell, W. F Caldwell*, Cannon, Cason, *Cate, Caulfield, J. B Clark, jr., Clymer, Cochrane, Collins, Cook Cowan, Culberson, Joseph J. Davis, De Bolt Dibrell, Douglas, Durham, Eden, Ellis*, Evans *Faulkner, Felton, Finley, Forney*, Fort, *Frank lin, Fuller, Glover, Goode, Goodin, A. H. Ham ilton, H. R. Harris, J. T. Harris, C. H. Har rison, Hartridge, Hartzell, Hatcher, Haymond Hereford, Hill, Holman, Hopkins, House*, Hun ter, *Hunton*, Kelley, *F. Landers*, W. Lawrence *McFarland, McMahon, Milliken, Morgan, Neal New*, Packer, *E. Y. Parsons, Payne, Phelps, J F. Philips*, W. A. Phillips, *Poppleton, Randall, D Rea, Reagan, J. Reilly, J. B. Reilly, A. V. Rice Riddle, J. Robbins, W. M. Robbins, C. B. Rob erts*, M. S. Robinson, *Savage, M. Sayler, Scales Sheakley, Slemons, W. E. Smith, Southard Sparks, Springer, Stenger, Stevenson, Stone Terry, Tucker, Turney, J. L. Vance, R. B Vance, G. C. Walker*, J. W. Wallace, *Walling Walsh, E. Wells, Whitthorne, J. D. Williams J. N. Williams, Wilshire*, Woodworth, *Yeates C. Young*—115.

NAYS—Messrs. C. H. Adams, G. A. Bagley *J. H. Bagley, jr.*, BANKS, *Barnum, Beebe, S. N. Bell*, Blaine, Blair, Bradley, H. C. Burchard Burleigh, *Candler, Chapin*, Chittenden, Conger, Crapo, Crounse, *Cutler*, Danford, Davy, Denison, Dunnell, Eames, *Ely*, Farwell, Foster, Frost, Frye, Garfield, *Gibson*, E. Hale, *R. Hamilton*, Haralson, *Hardenbergh*, Hendee, Henderson, *Henkle, G. W. Hewitt*, Hoge, Hoskins, Hubbell, Joyce, *Kehr*, Ketchum, Kimball, *Lamar, G. M. Landers*, Lane, Leavenworth, *Levy, Luttrell*, Lynch, *Maish*, MacDougall, McCrary, J. W. McDill, *Metcalfe*, Miller, Monroe, *Morrison, Mutchler*, Norton, *O Brien*, O'Neill, Page, Pierce, *Piper*, Plaisted, T. C. Platt, A. POTTER, *Powell*, Pratt, Rainey, Rusk, Sampson, *Schleicher, J. G. Schumaker*, Seelye, *Singleton*, Sinnickson, R. Smalls, A. H. Smith, Stowell, *Tarbox, C. P. Thompson*, Thornburgh, *Throckmorton*, M. I. Townsend, W. Townsend, Tufts, Wait, Waldron, A. S. Wallace, *Warren*, Wells, Wheeler, J. D. White, *Whitehouse*, Whiting, *Wigginton*, G. Willard, A. Williams, *A. S. Williams*, C. G. Williams, *J. Williams*, W. B. Williams, J. Wilson, A. Wood, jr., *F. Wood*, Woodburn—110.

Change of Rule to facilitate a report from the Committee on Banking and Currency.

1876, June 6—Mr. RANDALL, from the Committee on Rules, reported the following as an addition to rule 74, relating to reports from the Committee on Banking and Currency:

And on any question referred to them by the House in relation to the currency, the said committee may during the present session report at any time.

Which was agreed to—yeas 115, nays 97:

YEAS—Messrs. *Ainsworth*, ANDERSON, *Ashe*, *Atkins*, *Banning*, *Blackburn*, *Bland*, *Blount*, *Boone*, *Bradford*, *Bright*, *J. Y. Brown*, *Buckner*, *Cabell*, *J. H. Caldwell*, *W. P. Caldwell*, CAMPBELL, *Cate*, *Caulfield*, Chittenden, *J. B. Clarke*, *J. B. Clark*, *jr.*, *Clymer*, *Cochrane*, *Collins*, *Cook*, *Cutler*, *Joseph J. Davis*, *DeBolt*, *Dibrell*, *Douglas*, *Durham*, *Eden*, *Egbert*, *Felton*, *Finley*, *Forney*, *Franklin*, *Fuller*, *Glover*, *Goodin*, *Gunter*, *A. H. Hamilton*, *R. Hamilton*, *J. T. Harris*, *C. H. Harrison*, *Hartridge*, *Hartzell*, *Haymond*, *Henkle*, *Hereford*, *A. S. Hewitt*, *G. W. Hewitt*, *Hill*, *Hopkins*, *House*, *Hunton*, *Hurd*, *Jenks*, *T. L. Jones*, *Knott*, *F. Landers*, *G. M. Landers*, *Le Moyne*, *Levy*, *B. B. Lewis*, *Maish*, *McFarland*, *Meade*, *Metcalfe*, *Milliken*, *Mills*, *Money*, *Morgan*, *Mutchler*, *Neal*, *Odell*, *E. Y. Parsons*, *J. F. Philips*, *Piper*, *Poppleton*, *Randall*, *D. Rea*, *Reagan*, *J. Reilly*, *A. V. Rice*, *Riddle*, *J. Robbins*, *C. B. Roberts*, *M. Ross*, *Savage*, *Scales*, *Sheakley*, *Singleton*, *W. E. Smith*, *Southard*, *Sparks*, *Springer*, *Stenger*, *Stone*, *Swann*, *Teese*, *P. F. Thomas*, *Throckmorton*, *R. B. Vance*, *G. C. Walker*, *Walling*, *Walsh*, *E. Wells*, *Whitthorne*, *Wigginton*, *J. D. Williams*, *J. N. Williams*, *F. Wood*, *Yeates*—115.

NAYS—Messrs. C. H. Adams, *Bagby*, G. A. Bagley, *J. H. Bagley*, *jr.*, J. H. Baker, W. H. Baker, Ballou, *Beebe*, *S. N. Bell*, Blaine, Blair, Bradley, W. R. Brown, H. C. Burchard, Burleigh, *Candler*, Cason, Caswell, *Chapin*, Crapo, Crounse, Danford, Davy, Denison, Dunnell, *Durand*, Eames, Frye, Garfield, E. Hale, *Hardenbergh*, B. W. Harris, Hendee, Henderson, Hoge, Hoskins, Hunter, Hurlbut, Joyce, Kasson, *Kehr*, Kelley, Ketchum, Kimball, King, W. Lawrence, Leavenworth, Lynch, E. W. M. Mackey, Magoon, MacDougall, McCrary, J. W. McDill, Miller, Monroe, Nash, Norton, *O'Brien*, Oliver, O'Neill, Packer, Page, W. A. Phillips, Pierce, Platt, A. POTTER, *Powell*, Pratt, Rainey, M. S. Robinson, Sampson, *Schleicher*, Seelye, Sinnickson, R. Smalls, A. H. Smith, Strait, *Tarbox*, Thornburgh, M. I. Townsend, W. Townsend, Tufts, Van Vorhes, Waldron, *C. C. B. Walker*, A. S. Wallace, *Ward*, *Warren*, Whiting, G. Willard, A. Williams, C. G. Williams, W. B. Williams, *Willis*, J. Wilson, A. Wood, jr., Woodworth—97.

June 26—Mr. NEAL offered this bill:

A bill to repeal the act entitled "An act to provide for the resumption of specie payments," approved January 14, 1875.

Be it enacted, etc., That the act entitled "An act to provide for the resumption of specie payments," approved January 14, 1875, be, and the same is hereby, repealed.

And demanded the previous question on its passage, which was not seconded—ayes 77, noes 100.

Mr. KASSON rose to debate it, and it went over, under the rule.

July 10—Mr. HOLMAN moved to suspend the rules, and pass this resolution:

Resolved, That the Committee on Banking and Currency be, and they are hereby, instructed to report to the House the following bill, and that the same be made the special order for Thursday next after the morning hour, and be open for consideration and amendment, to wit:

A bill relating to the currency.

Be it enacted, etc., That so much of the act entitled "An act to provide for the resumption of specie payments," approved January 14, 1875, as authorized the Secretary of the Treasury to redeem in coin United States notes be, and the same is hereby, repealed.

Which was disagreed to—yeas 105, nays 96 (not voting 86), two-thirds being necessary, as follow:

YEAS—Messrs. *Ainsworth*, ANDERSON, *Ashe*, *Atkins*, J. H. Baker, *Banning*, *Bland*, *Blount*, *Boone*, *Bradford*, *Bright*, *J. Y. Brown*, *Buckner*, *S. D. Burchard*, *Cabell*, *J. H. Caldwell*, *W. P. Caldwell*, CAMPBELL, Cannon, Cason, *Cate*, *Caulfield*, *J. B. Clark*, *jr.*, *Clymer*, *Cochrane*, *Cook*, *Cowan*, *Culberson*, *Joseph J. Davis*, *Dibrell*, Dobbins, *Douglas*, *Eden*, *Ellis*, Evans, *Faulkner*, *Felton*, *Finley*, *Fuller*, *Gause*, *Goodin*, *Gunter*, *J. T. Harris*, *C. H. Harrison*, *Hartridge*, *Hartzell*, *Hatcher*, *Haymond*, Hays, *Henkle*, *Hereford*, *Hill*, *Holman*, *House*, Hubbell, Hunter, *Hunton*, *Jenks*, Kelley, *Knott*, *F. Landers*, *Lane*, *B. B. Lewis*, *Lynde*, *L. A. Mackey*, *McFarland*, *Milliken*, *Morgan*, *New*, *J. Phelps*, *J. F. Philips*, *Poppleton*, *Randall*, *D. Rea*, *J. Reilly*, *J. B. Reilly*, *A. V. Rice*, *Riddle*, *C. B. Roberts*, M. S. Robinson, *Savage*, *Scales*, *Singleton*, *Slemons*, *W. E. Smith*, *Southard*, *Sparks*, *Spencer*, *Springer*, *Stevenson*, *Stone*, *Terry*, *Turney*, *J. L. Vance*, *R. B. Vance*, J. W. Wallace, *Walling*, *Walsh*, *E. Wells*, *Wigginton*, *J. D. Williams*, *J. N. Williams*, *B. Wilson*, *Yeates*, *C. Young*—105.

NAYS—Messrs. C. H. Adams, *Bagby*, G. A. Bagley, *J. H. Bagley*, *jr.*, W. H. Baker, Ballou, BANKS, *S. N. Bell*, Blair, Bradley, W. R. Brown, H. C. Burchard, Burleigh, *Candler*, Caswell, Conger, Crapo, Crounse, *Cutler*, Davy, Dunnell, *Durand*, Eames, *Ely*, Foster, C. Freeman, Frost, Garfield, E. Hale, *R. Hamilton*, *Hancock*, *Hardenbergh*, B. W. Harris, Henderson, *A. S. Hewitt*, G. F. Hoar, Hoskins, *Hurd*, Hurlbut, Kasson, *Kehr*, Ketchum, Kimball, *G. M. Landers*, Lapham, *Le Moyne*, *Levy*, *Luttrell*, E. W. M. Mackey, Magoon, *Maish*, MacDougall, J. W. McDill, *Meade*, Miller, Monroe, *Morrison*, *Mutchler*, Norton, *O'Brien*, O'Neill, Page, Pierce, *Piper*, T. C. Platt, A. POTTER, *Powell*, *J. Robbins*, *M. Ross*, Rusk, Sampson, *Schleicher*, Seelye, Sinnickson, R. Smalls, A. H. Smith, Strait, Stowell, *Tarbox*, *C. P. Thompson*, Thornburgh, M. I. Townsend, W. Townsend, Tufts, Wait, Waldron, A. S. Wallace, *Ward*, G. W. Wells, Whiting, *Wike*, G. Willard, *J. Williams*, W. B. Williams, *Willis*, Woodburn—96.

July 17—Mr. SPRINGER moved to suspend the rules and pass a resolution instructing the Committee on Banking and Currency to report tomorrow a bill to repeal the act for the resumption of specie payments, to be open for amendment; which was disagreed to—yeas 102, nays 92 (not voting 92), two-thirds being necessary.

IN HOUSE.

1876, July 17—Mr. JOHN L. VANCE moved to suspend the rules, and pass this resolution:

Resolved, That the Committee on Banking and Currency be, and they are hereby instructed to report to the House immediately after the reading of the journal to-morrow a bill to repeal the resumption day clause of the act entitled "An act to provide for the resumption of specie payment," approved January 14, 1875.

Pending which, a motion to adjourn was agreed to—yeas 100, nays 90 (not voting 96).

Coinage of Silver Dollars.

IN HOUSE.

1876, July 24—Mr. KELLEY moved to suspend the rules and pass this bill:

A Bill to provide for the coining of the standard silver dollar of the United States, and for restoring its legal tender character.

Whereas by the omission to name the legal tender silver dollar in the enumeration of the silver coins of the United States in the act of February 12, 1873, the authority to coin said dollar was withheld: Therefore,

Be it enacted, etc., That there shall be, from time to time, struck and coined, at the several mints of the United States, silver dollars of the weight of 412½ grains, as provided for in the act of January 18, 1837, upon which shall be the devices and legends provided by said act; and that the said dollar shall be a legal tender of payment for any sums whatever.

Which was disagreed to—yeas 119, nays 66 (not voting 99)—two-thirds being required—as follow:

YEAS—Messrs. *Ainsworth*, ANDERSON, *Atkins*, J. H. Baker, *Bland*, *Boone*, *Bradford*, Bradley, *Bright*, *J. Y. Brown*, W. R. Brown, *Buckner*, H. C. Burchard, *S. D. Burchard*, *Cabell*, *J. H. Caldwell*, *W. P. Caldwell*, CAMPBELL, *Candler*, Cannon, Cason, *Cate*, *Caulfield*, *J. B. Clarke*, *J. B. Clark, jr.*, *Clymer*, *Cochrane*, Conger, *Cook*, *Joseph J. Davis*, *De Bolt*, *Dibrell*, Dobbins, *Douglas*, Dunnell, *Durham*, *Eden*, *Egbert*, Evans, *Felton*, *Finley*, *Forney*, Fort, *Franklin*, *Goode*, *Goodin*, *Gunter*, *A. H. Hamilton*, *Hartzell*, Hays, *Hereford*, *Hill*, *Holman*, *Hopkins*, *House*, Hunter, Hurlbut, *T. L. Jones*, Kelley, *Knott*, *F. Landers*, *Lane*, *Levy*, *Luttrell*, *Lynde*, *L. A. Mackey*, J. W. McDill, *McFarland*, *McMahon*, *Milliken*, *Mills*, *Neal*, *New*, Page, *J. Phelps*, W. A. Phillips, *Piper*, Purman, *Randall*, *D. Rea*, *Reagan*, *J. Reilly*, *J. B. Reilly*, *A. V. Rice*, *Riddle*, *W. M. Robbins*, M. S. Robinson, Rusk, Sampson, *Savage*, *Scales*, *Sheakley*, *Singleton*, *Slemons*, *W. E. Smith*, *Springer*, *Stevenson*, *Stone*, *Terry*, Thornburgh, Tufts, *Turney*, Van Vorhes, *J. L. Vance*, *R. B. Vance*, *Waddell*, *E. Wells*, J. D. White, Whiting, *Whitthorne*, *Wigginton*, G. Willard, C. G. Williams, *J. D. Williams*, *J. N. Williams*, W. B. Williams, J. Wilson, Woodburn, Woodworth—119.

NAYS—Messrs. C. H. Adams, G. A. Bagley, W. H. Baker, Ballou, *S. N. Bell*, Burleigh, Caswell, Chittenden, Crapo, *Cutler*, Danford, Darrall, Davy, *Durand*, Eames, *Ely*, Frye, Garfield, *Gibson*, E. Hale, *Hancock*, *Hardenbergh*, B. W. Harris, Hendee, Hoskins, Habbell, *F. Jones*, *Kehr*, Kimball, *Lamar*, Leavenworth, Lynch, Magoon, MacDougall, *Meade*, *Metcalfe*, Miller, Monroe, *Mutchler*, Norton, O'Neill, Packer, *Payne*, Pierce, Plaisted, A. POTTER, Rainey, *J. Robbins*, *Schleicher*, Seelye, Sinnickson, R. Smalls, Stowell, *Tarbox*, *Teese*, *C. P. Thompson*, M. I. Townsend, W. Townsend, *Tucker*, Wait, *C. C. B. Walker*, *Ward*, *Warren*, G. W. Wells, *Wike*, *A. S. Williams*, *J. Williams*, *Willis*—68.

Amendment of Funding Act.

[For text of the Funding Act of July 14, 1870, and the votes on its passage, and in intermediate stages, see McPherson's History of Reconstruction, pp.597–604.]

IN SENATE.

1876, February 25—Mr. SHERMAN moved to proceed to consider the bill (S. 478) amendatory of the Funding Acts of July 14, 1870, and January 20, 1871, as follows:

Be it enacted, etc., That the acts to authorize the refunding of the national debt, approved July fourteenth, eighteen hundred and seventy, and January twentieth, eighteen hundred and seventy-one, be so amended that the amount of bonds bearing four and one-half per centum interest, authorized to be issued, be increased to five hundred millions of dollars; and that they be payable at the pleasure of the United States after thirty years from the date of their issue, instead of after fifteen years.

SEC. 2. That this act shall not be construed to authorize any increase of the total amount of bonds provided for by the acts to which this act is an amendment, nor to authorize any increase whatever of the bonded debt of the United States; and all provisions of the acts to which this act is amendatory not inconsistent with the provisions of this act are hereby continued in force and effect.

[The changes proposed are to make the 4½ per cent. bonds provided for in 1870 payable in thirty years, instead of fifteen, and to increase the amount of them from three hundred million dollars to five hundred million dollars.]

IN SENATE.

1876, February 25—Mr. McDONALD moved to amend by striking out, in line six, section one, of printed bill, the words "that the amount of bonds bearing four and one-half per centum interest, authorized to be issued, be increased to five hundred millions of dollars; and that they be payable at the pleasure of the United States after thirty years from the date of their issue, instead of after fifteen years."

And inserting in lieu thereof the following:

That the bonds now authorized to be issued, bearing four and one-half per cent. interest, be made payable at the pleasure of the United States after thirty years from date of their issue instead of after fifteen years.

Which was disagreed to—yeas 14, nays 43, as follow:

YEAS—Messrs. BOOTH, *Cockrell*, *Davis*, *Gordon*, *McCreery*, *McDonald*, *Maxey*, *Merrimon*, *Norwood*, *Randolph*, Robertson, *Saulsbury*, *Thurman*, *Wallace*—14.

NAYS—Messrs. Allison, Anthony, Boutwell, Bruce, Cameron of Pennsylvania, Cameron of Wisconsin, *Caperton*, Christiancy, Clayton, Conkling, Dawes, Dorsey, *Eaton*, Edmunds, *English*,

Ferry, Frelinghuysen, Hamilton, Hamlin, Harvey, Howe, Ingalls, *Johnston*, *Jones* of Florida, *Kelly*, *Kernan*, *Key*, Logan, McMillan, Mitchell, Morrill of Maine, Morrill of Vermont, Morton, Oglesby, Sargent, Sherman, Spencer, Wadleigh, West, *Whyte*, Windom, *Withers*, Wright—43.

The bill then passed—yeas 51, nays 5 (Messrs. *Cockrell*, *Eaton*, *McCreery*, *McDonald*, Robertson).

IN HOUSE.

Referred, February 29, to Ways and Means, and not reported by that Committee.

Silver Coinage Bill.

IN HOUSE.

1876, July 19—Mr. BLAND reported from the Committee on Mines and Mining, the following bill (H. R. 3635):

A bill to utilize the product of gold and silver mines, and for other purposes.

Be it enacted, &c., That coin notes of the denomination of $50, and multiples thereof up to $10,000, may, in the mode hereinafter provided, be paid by the several mints and assay offices at San Francisco, Carson City, Philadelphia, and New York, for the net value of gold and silver bullion deposited thereat; and of the bullion thus received not less than 75 per cent. in coin or fine bars shall at all times be kept on hand for redemption of the coin notes, gold for gold, and silver for silver. The gold deposited shall be computed at its coining value, and silver at the rate of 412.8 grains standard silver to the dollar, less the lawful mint charges, and such charge for transportation from the several assay offices to the mints for coinage, and from the latter to the assistant treasuries respectively at which the coin notes shall be payable; and there shall be coined at the mints of the United States the silver dollar hereinbefore mentioned.

SEC. 2. That for bullion deposited at the mints of San Francisco and Carson, the coin notes issued shall be redeemable on demand at the assistant treasury at San Francisco; and for bullion deposited at the Philadelphia mint and assay office at New York, the notes shall be redeemed at the assistant treasury.

SEC. 3. That the Secretary of the Treasury shall, from time to time, cause coin and fine mint-bars (stamped) to be transferred from the mint to the assistant treasuries at San Francisco and New York in such amounts as may be necessary for the redemption of the coin notes.

SEC. 4. That the coin notes issued under the provisions of this act shall be receivable without limit for all dues to the United States; and the coin mentioned in this act shall be a legal tender for all debts, public and private, not specified to be paid in gold coin.

SEC. 5. That the gold coin notes issued under this act shall be redeemed, on presentation, in gold coin or fine bars, and silver in silver dollars or fine bars.

SEC. 6. That the coin notes authorized by this act to be issued shall be prepared under the direction of the Secretary of the Treasury, and shall be transferred to the mints and assay offices named in this act as a part of the bullion fund, and from which fund deposits shall be paid for in coin or coin notes at the option of the depositor.

SEC. 7. That the fine gold and silver bars by this act authorized to be issued shall bear the mint stamp of fineness, weight, and value, and the value of the gold bars shall be computed according to their coining rate, and the silver bars at their coining value in dollars.

SEC. 8. That the Secretary of the Treasury shall prescribe the necessary regulations for carrying into effect the provisions of this act.

A direct vote upon it has not been reached up to the time this page was stereotyped.

XVIII.

GENERAL POLITICAL VOTES, FORTY-FOURTH CONGRESS.

Supplement to the Present Statutes in Aid and Defense of the Constitutional Rights of Citizens.

IN SENATE.

1876, June 23—The following bill (S. 686) was considered the entire day, and finally passed as follows:

A Bill supplementary to the present statutes in aid and defense of the constitutional rights of citizens.

Be it enacted, &c., That if, by or under the authority of the constitution or laws of the United States, or of any State, or the laws of any Territory, any act is or shall be required to be done as a prerequisite or qualification for voting, and by such constitution or laws any persons or officers shall be charged with the performance of duties in furnishing to citizens an opportunity to perform such prerequisite, or to become qualified to vote, it shall be the duty of every such person and officer to give, and every such person and officer respectively shall give, to all citizens of the United States the same and equal opportunity to perform such prerequisite and to become qualified to vote, without distinction of race, color, or previous condition of servitude; and if any such person or officer shall refuse or knowingly omit to execute and give full effect to the foregoing provisions of this section, on account of the race, color, or previous condition of servitude of the applicant or person seeking to perform such prerequisite or qualification for voting, he shall, for every such offense, forfeit and pay the sum of five hundred dollars to the person aggrieved thereby, to be recovered by an action on the case, with full cost, and such allowance for counsel-fees as the court shall deem just; and shall, also, for every such offense, be deemed guilty of a misdemeanor, and shall, on conviction thereof, be fined not less than five hundred dol.

lars or be imprisoned not less than one month and not more than one year, or both, at the discretion of the court.

SEC. 2. That if any person or officer of the United States, or officer of any State, or any person exercising power or authority under the United States or any State, shall deny or abridge to any citizen of the United States, entitled by the laws of such State, or by the Constitution or laws of the United States, to vote at any election, the right and opportunity so to vote at such election by reason of his race, color, or previous condition of servitude, or shall for said cause fail to allow and furnish such citizen, so entitled to vote as aforesaid, a full, fair, impartial and equal opportunity, under the laws, with all other citizens entitled to vote at any such election, to exercise his right of voting, every person and officer so offending shall be deemed guilty of a misdemeanor, and shall, on conviction thereof, be punished by a fine not exceeding one thousand dollars, and be imprisoned not exceeding two years.

SEC. 3. That whenever by or under the authority of the constitution or laws of any State, or the laws of any Territory, or the laws of the United States, any act is or shall be required to be done by any citizen as a pre-requisite to qualify or entitle him to vote, the offer of any such citizen to perform the act required to be done as aforesaid shall, if it fail to be carried into execution by reason of the wrongful act or omission of the person or officer charged with the duty of receiving or permitting such performance or offer to perform or acting thereon, proceeding from the race, color, or previous condition of servitude of such citizen, be deemed and held as a performance in law of such act, and of the due performance by such person or officer of his duty in the premises; and the person so offering and failing as aforesaid, and being otherwise qualified, shall be entitled to vote in the same manner and to the same extent as if he had in fact performed such act, and as if such person or officer had done his duty in the premises; and any judge, inspector, or other officer of election, whose duty it is, or shall be, to receive, count, certify, register, report, or give effect to the lawful vote of any citizen, who shall wrongfully refuse or omit to receive, count, certify, register, report, or give effect to the lawful vote of any citizen, who shall wrongfully refuse or omit to receive, count, certify, register, report, or give effect to the vote of such citizen, so having offered and failed to perform as aforesaid, upon the presentation by him of his affidavit stating that he had a right to qualify as a voter, and such offer, and the time and place thereof, and the name of the officer or person whose duty it was to act thereon, and that he was wrongfully prevented by such officer or person from performing such act by reason of his race, color, or previous condition of servitude, shall, for every such offense, forfeit and pay the sum of five hundred dollars to the person aggrieved thereby, to be recovered by an action on the case, with full costs, and such allowance for counsel-fees as the court shall deem just; and shall also, for every such offense, be deemed guilty of a misdemeanor, and shall, on conviction thereof, be fined not less than five hundred dollars, or be imprisoned not less than one month and not more than one year, or both, in the discretion of the court. And if any person so making and presenting such affidavit shall willfully and contrary to his oath in that behalf state or subscribe any material matter which he does not believe to be true, he shall be deemed guilty of perjury and shall on conviction be liable to the penalty provided in section 5392 of the statutes of the United States.

SEC. 4. That if any person, by force, bribery, threats, or intimidation, or other unlawful means, shall hinder, delay, prevent, or obstruct, or shall combine and confederate with others to hinder, delay, prevent, or obstruct, any citizen from doing any act required by law to be done to qualify him to vote, or from voting at any election as aforesaid, on account of the race, color, or previous condition of servitude of such citizen, such person shall, for every such offense, forfeit and pay the sum of five hundred dollars to the person aggrieved thereby, to be recovered by an action on the case, with full cost, and such allowance for counsel-fees as the court shall deem just; and shall also, for every such offense, be guilty of a misdemeanor, and shall, on conviction thereof, be fined not less than five hundred dollars, or be imprisoned not less than one month and not more than one year, or both, at the discretion of the court.

SEC. 5. That if any person shall prevent, hinder, control, or intimidate, or shall attempt to prevent, hinder, control, or intimidate, any person having the right of suffrage from exercising, or in exercising, the right of suffrage, on account of the race, color, or previous condition of servitude of such person, by means of bribery, force, or intimidation, or by threats of depriving any such person of employment or occupation, or of ejecting such person from any house, lands, or other property, or by threats of refusing to renew leases or contracts for labor, or by threats of violence to himself or family, every such person so offending shall be deemed guilty of a misdemeanor, and shall, on conviction thereof, be fined not less than five hundred dollars, or be imprisoned not less than one month and not more than one year, or both, at the discretion of the court.

Pending its consideration,

Mr. THURMAN moved to strike from the second section, in the first line, the words "person or."

Which was disagreed to—yeas 14, nays 25:

YEAS—Messrs. *Caperton*, *Cockrell*, *Eaton*, *Goldthwaite*, *Johnston*, *Kelly*, *McCreery*, *Maxey*, *Merrimon*, *Norwood*, *Ransom*, *Thurman*, *Whyte*, *Withers*—14.

NAYS—Messrs. Alcorn, Allison, Anthony, BOOTH, Conkling, Dawes, Dorsey, Edmunds, Ferry of Michigan, Frelinghuysen, Hamilton, Hamlin, Harvey, Howe, Ingalls, Logan, Mitchell, Morrill of Maine, Morrill of Vermont, Oglesby, Paddock, Robertson, Sargent, Sherman, Wadleigh—25.

Mr. WHYTE moved to strike out the word "fail" in the ninth line of printed bill, and insert in lieu thereof the word "refuse," which was disagreed to—yeas 15, nays 26. The affirmative was the same as on last vote, with Mr. KEY additional. The negative was the same also, except that Messrs. BRUCE, CRAGIN and HITCH-

COCK were additional, and Messrs. PADDOCK and WADLEIGH did not vote.

Mr. CHRISTIANCY moved to amend by striking out all after the word "any" in the first line of the second section down to the end of the third line, as follows:

"Person or officer of the United States, or officer of any State, or any person exercising power or authority under the United States or any State."

And in lieu of them to insert:

"Officer of the United States, or officer of any State, or any person exercising power or authority under the United States or any State, or pretending to be such officer, or assuming to exercise such authority."

Which was disagreed to—yeas 16, nays 26:

YEAS—Messrs. *Caperton*, Christiancy, *Cockrell*, *Eaton*, *Goldthwaite*, *Johnston*, *Kelly*, *Key*, *McCreery*, *Maxey*, *Merrimon*, Paddock, *Ransom*, *Thurman*, *Whyte*, *Withers*—16.

NAYS—Messrs. Alcorn, Allison, Anthony, BOOTH, Bruce, Conkling, Cragin, Dawes, Dorsey, Edmunds, Ferry of Michigan, Frelinghuysen, Hamilton, Hamlin, Harvey, Hitchcock, Howe, Ingalls, Logan, Mitchell, Morrill of Maine, Morrill of Vermont, Oglesby, Robertson, Sargent, Sherman—26.

On agreeing to the third section of the bill, the yeas and nays were called, and were—yeas 21, nays 16:

YEAS—Messrs. Alcorn, Anthony, Bruce, Clayton, Conkling, Conover, Cragin, Dawes, Edmunds, Ferry of Michigan, Frelinghuysen, Hamilton, Hitchcock, Howe, Ingalls, Morrill of Vermont, Oglesby, Paddock, Robertson, Sargent, Wadleigh—21.

NAYS—Messrs. *Bogy*, BOOTH, *Caperton*, *Cockrell*, *Eaton*, *Goldthwaite*, *Johnston*, *Key*, *McCreery*, *Maxey*, *Merrimon*, *Norwood*, *Ransom*, *Thurman*, *Whyte*, *Withers*—16.

The bill was then passed—yeas 25, nays 13:

YEAS—Messrs. Alcorn, Allison, Anthony, BOOTH, Bruce, Clayton, Conkling, Conover, Cragin, Dawes, Edmunds, Ferry of Michigan, Frelinghuysen, Hamilton, Hitchcock, Howe, Ingalls, Logan, Morrill of Maine, Morrill of Vermont, Oglesby, Paddock, Robertson, Sargent, Wadleigh—25.

NAYS—Messrs. *Caperton*, *Cockrell*, *Eaton*, *Goldthwaite*, *Johnston*, *Key*, *McCreery*, *Maxey*, *Merrimon*, *Ransom*, *Thurman*, *Whyte*, *Withers*—13.

IN HOUSE.

No vote was reached.

Proposed Repeal of Act for Registration of Voters and Appointment of Supervisors of Election.

IN HOUSE.

1876, June 23—Pending the Sundry Civil Appropriation bill, a separate vote was had on the following provision in the bill, as reported by the Committee on Appropriations:

Provided, That all of the provisions of title 26 of the Revised Statutes of the United States in relation to the registration of voters and the appointment of supervisors of elections, and deputy and special deputy marshals, and touching the supervision of elections, are hereby repealed.

Mr. KASSON moved to strike it from the bill, which was disagreed to—yeas 57, nays 93 (not voting 140):

YEAS—Messrs. C. H. Adams, J. H. Baker, Ballou, BANKS, Blair, W. R. Brown, Cannon, Caswell, Conger, Crounse, Davy, Denison, Dobbins, Dunnell, Eames, Fort, Foster, Frost, *Goodin*, Hendee, Henderson, Hunter, Hurlbut, Hyman, Kasson, *Kehr*, Kimball, Leavenworth, Lynch, McCrary, McDill, Miller, Norton, Oliver, O'Neill, Packer, Page, Pierce, Plaisted, A. POTTER, Rainey, M. S. Robinson, Rusk, Sampson, Seelye, R. Smalls, Strait, Thornburgh, W. Townsend, Tufts, J. D. White, Whiting, Willard, A. Williams, W. B. Williams, J. Wilson, Woodburn —57.

NAYS—Messrs. *Ainsworth*, ANDERSON, *Atkins*, *Banning*, *Blackburn*, *Bland*, *Blount*, *Boone*, *Bradford*, *Bright*, *Buckner*, *Cabell*, *J. H. Caldwell*, *W. P. Caldwell*, *Candler*, *Caulfield*, *J. B. Clarke*, *J. B. Clark, jr.*, *Cook*, *Cowan*, *Culberson*, *Cutler*, *Joseph J. Davis*, *De Bolt*, *Dibrell*, *Durham*, *Ellis*, *Forney*, *Franklin*, *Fuller*, *Goode*, *Gunter*, *A. H. Hamilton*, *R. Hamilton*, *Hancock*, *C. H. Harrison*, *Hartridge*, *Hartzell*, *G. W. Hewitt*, *Holman*, *Hooker*, *Hopkins*, *House*, *Hunton*, *Jenks*, *F. Jones*, *T. L. Jones*, *B. B. Lewis*, *Lord*, *Luttrell*, *Lynde*, *Maish*, *McFarland*, *Meade*, *Metcalfe*, *Milliken*, *Mills*, *Neal*, *Payne*, *J. F. Philips*, *Randall*, *D. Rea*, *Reagan*, *J. Reilly*, *A. V. Rice*, *Riddle*, *W. M. Robbins*, *Savage*, *Sayler*, *Scales*, *Schleicher*, *J. G. Schumaker*, *Sheakley*, *Singleton*, *W. E. Smith*, *Sparks*, *Springer*, *Stevenson*, *Tarbox*, *Terry*, *P. F. Thomas*, *C. P. Thompson*, *Throckmorton*, *Turney*, *R. B. Vance*, *C. C. B. Walker*, *Walling*, *Walsh*, *E. Wells*, *Wike*, *A. Williams*, *J. N. Williams*, *Wilshire*—93.

IN SENATE.

1876, June 30—The motion to strike the above from the bill was agreed to—yeas 26, nays 11, as follow:

YEAS—Messrs. Allison, BOOTH, Boutwell, Bruce, Cameron of Pennsylvania, Clayton, Conkling, Conover, Cragin, Dorsey, Edmunds, Ferry of Michigan, Frelinghuysen, Hamlin, Harvey, Hitchcock, Howe, Ingalls, Logan, McMillan, Morrill of Vermont, Paddock, Sargent, Sherman, Wadleigh, West—26.

NAYS—Messrs. *Bayard*, *Bogy*, *Caperton*, *Cockrell*, *Goldthwaite*, *Gordon*, *Key*, *McCreery*, *Maxey*, *Randolph*, *Withers*—11.

In Committee of Conference, the House conferees, under instructions from a Democratic caucus, receded from the amendment, and the proviso was stricken out.

Contributions to Election Funds.

1876, March 21—Mr. CAULFIELD, from the Committee on the Judiciary, reported back, with an amendment, the bill (H. R. 876):

Be it enacted, etc., That from and after the passage of this act it shall not be lawful for any person or persons in the employment of the United States to demand from any other person so employed any money or other valuables to be used as an election-fund or to defray the expenses of an election in any State, county, or national election in the United States.

SEC. 2. That it shall not be lawful for any person or persons employed in the service of the United States, in any manner whatever, to contribute any money or other valuable thing to be used as an election-fund or to aid in the expenses of any election or canvass for an election in any State, county, or district in the United States.

SEC. 3. That any person violating the provisions of either of the preceding sections shall, upon conviction, be deemed guilty of a misdemeanor, and shall be fined not exceeding $1,000 and imprisoned not exceeding one year, at the discretion of the judge trying the cause.

SEC. 4. That the judges of the district and circuit courts shall give this act in charge to grand juries.

[The amendment reported by the committee was as follows: In section 1, line 5, after the word "demand," insert the words "or solicit;" so that it will read "it shall not be lawful for any person or persons in the employment of the United States to demand or solicit from any other person so employed," &c.]

Mr. J. Y. BROWN, from the Committee on Reform in the Civil Service, moved an amendment in the nature of a substitute, as follows:

That no officer or employé of the Government shall require or request, give to or receive from, any other officer or employé of the same or other person, directly or indirectly, any money, property, or other thing of value, for political purposes; and any such officer or employé who shall offend against the provisions of the act shall at once be dismissed from the service of the United States, and also be deemed guilty of a high misdemeanor, and on conviction thereof fined not less than five hundred nor more than three thousand dollars, and imprisoned not more than one year, at the discretion of the judge trying the case.

SEC. 2. That the district courts of the United States shall have jurisdiction of the offenses created by this act.

SEC. 3. That the judges of the district and circuit courts shall give this act in charge to the grand juries.

Mr. G. F. HOAR moved to add the following words, at the end of the second section of the bill:

Provided, Nothing herein shall be construed to prevent voluntary contributions for the purpose of circulating documents or procuring public addresses for the purpose of giving information on questions of public interest.

Mr. GOODE offered the following amendment:

After section 3 in the bill, and after section 1 in the substitute, add the following:

SEC. 2. That if any person, with a view to the election to or obtaining votes for the office of President, Vice-President, or the post of Senator, Representative, or Delegate in the Congress of the United States, or to the appointment to any office or post of honor or emolument under the Government of the United States, of himself or any other person, shall use force or duress, by menace or violence to life, limb, property, or liberty, or shall commit bribery, or use money, property, or other thing of value to influence any elector, voter, officer, or other person in or in respect to any election or appointment to any such office or post, he shall, upon conviction thereof, be fined not less than $500 nor more than $3,000, and be imprisoned not more than one year, at the discretion of the judge trying the case.

Notice of other amendments was given, as follow:

By Mr. REAGAN—

Amend section 1 of the substitute by striking out of the first line of said section the words "of the Government," and by inserting in lieu thereof the following:

Or other person, intending thereby to corruptly influence the election of any Senator or Representative in Congress or the election or appointment of any other officer of the United States.

By Mr. G. W. HEWITT—

SECTION 1. That it shall be unlawful for any person to solicit of any officer or employé of the Government of the United States any contribution of money or other thing of value with intent to aid in securing the election of any person to any State or Federal office whatever.

SEC. 2. That from and after the passage of this act it shall be unlawful for any officer of the United States, postmaster, clerk, or employé of the same to give, directly or indirectly, any money or thing of value to any political organization or person with intent to assist or forward the interest of any political party or the election of any particular person or persons to any office, State or Federal.

SEC. 3. That any person violating the provisions of the foregoing sections of this act shall be guilty of a misdemeanor, and, upon conviction before a court of competent jurisdiction, shall be fined not less than $1,000 and imprisoned for a period not less than six months, and shall be removed from office upon such conviction being certified by the clerk of the court before which such conviction was had to the appointing power.

March 22—Mr. BLAINE moved the following amendment to the text of the original bill, and a similar amendment to the text of the substitute:

Amend section 2, line 2, by inserting after the words "United States" the following words:

Or any Senator, Representative, or Delegate in Congress.

And at the close of section add:

And the contribution of money or other valuable thing as herein prohibited by any Senator or Representative or Delegate in Congress, while he was a candidate for such position, shall subject the offender to the penalties herein prescribed.

Mr. WASHINGTON TOWNSEND moved to add this proviso to the first section of the bill, and the substitute:

From and after the passage of this act it shall not be lawful for any person or persons in the employment of the United States to demand from any other person so employed any money or other valuables to be used as an election-fund or to defray the expenses of an election in any State, county, or national election in the United States.

Mr. REAGAN gave notice of an amendment to insert the following in lieu of section 1 of the substitute offered by the gentleman from Kentucky [Mr. BROWN]:

That from and after the passage of this act it shall be unlawful for any officer of the United

States, postmaster, clerk, employé, Senator or Representative in Congress, or other person, to give, directly or indirectly, any money or any thing of value to any person or persons, or political party, or other organization or association, for the purpose or with the intent to assist or forward the interests of any person or persons, or political organization or party, in any election for any officer of the United States. And it shall be unlawful for any officer of the United States, postmaster, clerk, or employé, Senator or Representative in Congress, or other person or persons, to solicit, ask, receive, or accept any gift or donation of any money or other valuable thing for the purpose or with the intent that the same shall be used to assist in or influence the election of any officer of the United States. And such officer, postmaster, clerk, Senator or Representative in Congress, or other person shall, on conviction of a violation of this act, by any court of the United States having jurisdiction of such offense, be fined in any sum not exceeding $500, and shall be imprisoned for any time not exceeding six months. And any such officer of the United States, postmaster, clerk, employé, or Senator or Representative in Congress, shall, on conviction of a violation of the provisions of this act, be dismissed from such office or position of postmaster, clerk, employé, or Senator or Representative in Congress.

The amendment to the bill, reported by the Committee on the Judiciary, was then agreed to.

The amendment offered by Mr. W. TOWNSEND was not agreed to.

The amendment offered by Mr. BLAINE was agreed to—yeas 129, nays 87, (not voting 72,) as follow:

YEAS—Messrs. ANDERSON, G. A. Bagley, *J. H. Bagley, jr.*, J. H. Baker, W. H. Baker, Ballou, BANKS, *Barnum*, Bass, *Beebe*, Blaine, Blair, Bradley, H. C. Burchard, Caswell, Chittenden, *Clymer*, Conger, *Cox*, Crapo, Crounse, *Cutler*, Denison, Dunnell, *Durham*, Eames, *Ellis*, *Ely*, Evans, Farwell, *Faulkner*, Fort, Foster, Frost, Frye, *Fuller*, Garfield, *Goodin*, E. Hale, *A. H. Hamilton*, *R. Hamilton*, *Hardenbergh*, *Hartzell*, Hathorn, *Haymond*, Hendee, Henderson, G. F. Hoar, *Holman*, *Hopkins*, Hubbell, Hunter, Hurlbut, Hyman, Joyce, *Kehr*, Kelley, Kimball, *G. M. Landers*, Leavenworth, Lynch, Magoon, McCrary, J. W. McDill, Monroe, Morey, *Morgan*, Nash, *Neal*, *New*, Norton, *O'Brien*, Oliver, O'Neill, Packer, Page, *Payne*, *J. Phelps*, W. A. Phillips, Pierce, *Piper*, Plaisted, A. POTTER, Pratt, *D. Rea*, *J. Reilly*, *J. B. Reilly*, *Riddle*, M. S. Robinson, S. Ross, Rusk, Sampson, *Savage*, Seelye, Sinnickson, R. Smalls, A. H. Smith, *Springer*, Strait, *Stevenson*, *Stone*, Stowell, *Tarbox*, *Teese*, *Thornburgh*, M. I. Townsend, W. Townsend, Tufts, *Turney*, Van Vorhes, *C. C. B. Walker*, A. S. Wallace, J. W. Wallace, *Walsh*, G. W. Wells, Wheeler, J. D. White, Whiting, G. Willard, A. Williams, *A. S. Williams*, C. G. Williams, *J. D. Williams*, W. B. Williams, *Wilshire*, J. Wilson, A. Wood, jr., Woodburn, Woodworth—129.

NAYS—Messrs. *Ainsworth*, *Ashe*, *Atkins*, *Bagby*, *Blackburn*, *Bliss*, *Blount*, *Boone*, *Bradford*, *Bright*, *J. Y. Brown*, *Cabell*, *J. H. Caldwell*, *W. P. Caldwell*, *Cate*, *Caulfield*, *J. B. Clarke*, *J. B. Clark, jr.*, *Cook*, *Cowan*, *Culberson*, *Joseph J. Davis*, *De Bolt*, *Dibrell*, *Douglas*, *Eden*, *Felton*, *Forney*, *Franklin*, *Glover*, *Goode*, *Hunter*, *Hancock*, *H. R. Harris*, *J. T. Harris*, *C. H. Harrison*, *Hartridge*, *Hereford*, *A. S. Hewitt*, *G. W. Hewitt*, *Hill*, *Hooker*, *House*, *Hunton*, *Hurd*, *Jenks*, *T. L. Jones*, *B. B. Lewis*, *Luttrell*, *Lynde*, *McFarland*, *Metcalfe*, *Milliken*, *Morrison*, *Mutchler*, *E. Y. Parsons*, *J. F. Philips*, *Poppleton*, *Reagan*, *A. V. Rice*, *J. Robbins*, *W. M. Robbins*, *C. B. Roberts*, *M. Ross*, *M. Sayler*, *Scales*, *Singleton*, *Slemons*, *W. E. Smith*, *Southard*, *Sparks*, *Terry*, *C. P. Thompson*, *Throckmorton*, *Tucker*, *J. L. Vance*, *R. B. Vance*, *Waddell*, *G. C. Walker*, *Warren*, *E. Wells*, *Whitehouse*, *Whitthorne*, *Wike*, *J. Williams*, *J. N. Williams*, *Yeates*—87.

The amendment offered by Mr. G. F. HOAR was disagreed to—yeas 93, nays 119 (not voting 77), as follow:

YEAS—Messrs. G. A. Bagley, J. H. Baker, W. H. Baker, Ballou, Bass, *Blackburn*, Blaine, Blair, Bradley, H. C. Burchard, *W. P. Caldwell*, Cannon, Caswell, Conger, Crapo, Crounse, Denison, Dunnell, Eames, Evans, Farwell, Fort, Foster, Frost, Frye, *Goodin*, E. Hale, Hathorn, *Haymond*, Hays, Hendee, Henderson, G. F. Hoar, Hubbell, Hunter, *Hurd*, Hurlbut, Hyman, Joyce, *Kehr*, Kelley, Kimball, Leavenworth, Lynch, Magoon, McCrary, J. W. McDill, Monroe, Morey, Nash, *New*, Norton, Oliver, O'Neill, Packer, Page, *J. Phelps*, *J. F. Philips*, W. A. Phillips, Pierce, Plaisted, Pratt, *J. B. Reilly*, M. S. Robinson, S. Ross, Rusk, Sampson, Seelye, Sinnickson, R. Smalls, A. H. Smith, *W. E. Smith*, Strait, Stowell, Thornburgh, M. I. Townsend, W. Townsend, Tufts, Van Vorhes, A. S. Wallace, J. W. Wallace, G. W. Wells, Wheeler, J. D. White, Whiting, A. Williams, C. G. Williams, *J. D. Williams*, W. B. Williams, J. Wilson, A. Wood, jr., Woodburn, Woodworth—93.

NAYS—Messrs. *Ainsworth*, ANDERSON, *Ashe*, *Atkins*, *Bagby*, BANKS, *Barnum*, *Beebe*, *Blount*, *Boone*, *Bradford*, *Bright*, *J. Y. Brown*, *Cabell*, CAMPBELL, *Cate*, Chittenden, *J. B. Clarke*, *J. B. Clark, jr.*, *Clymer*, *Cook*, *Cowan*, *Culberson*, *Cutler*, *Joseph J. Davis*, *DeBolt*, *Dibrell*, *Douglas*, *Durand*, *Durham*, *Eden*, *Ellis*, *Ely*, *Faulkner*, *Felton*, *Forney*, *Franklin*, *Fuller*, *Glover*, *Goode*, *Gunter*, *A. H. Hamilton*, *R. Hamilton*, *Hancock*, *Hardenbergh*, *H. R. Harris*, *J. T. Harris*, *C. H. Harrison*, *Hartridge*, *Hartzell*, *A. S. Hewitt*, *G. W. Hewitt*, *Hill*, *Holman*, *Hooker*, *Hopkins*, *House*, *Hunton*, *Jenks*, *T. L. Jones*, *F. Landers*, *G. M. Landers*, *B. B. Lewis*, *Luttrell*, *McMahon*, *Metcalfe*, *Milliken*, *Money*, *Morgan*, *Morrison*, *Mutchler*, *Neal*, *O'Brien*, *E. Y. Parsons*, *Payne*, *Piper*, *Poppleton*, A. POTTER, *D. Rea*, *Reagan*, *J. Reilly*, *A. V. Rice*, *Riddle*, *J. Robbins*, *W. M. Robbins*, *C. B. Roberts*, *M. Ross*, *Savage*, *M. Sayler*, *Scales*, *Slemons*, *Southard*, *Sparks*, *Springer*, *Stone*, *Tarbox*, *Teese*, *Terry*, *C. P. Thompson*, *P. F. Thomas*, *Throckmorton*, *Tucker*, *Turney*, *J. L. Vance*, *R. B. Vance*, *Waddell*, *G. C. Walker*, *Walsh*, *Warren*, *E. Wells*, *Whitehouse*, *Wike*, G. Willard, *A. S. Williams*, *J. Williams*, *J. N. Williams*, *Willis*, *Yeates*—119.

The amendment to the bill offered by Mr. GOODE was then agreed to.

Mr. W. TOWNSEND's amendment to section one of the substitute was then disagreed to.

The amendment to the substitute offered by Mr. BLAINE:

Add to the first section the following:

And the contribution of any money or valuable thing, as herein prohibited, by any Senator, Representative, or Delegate in Congress, while he was a candidate for such position, shall be deemed a misdemeanor, and the offender on conviction shall be fined not less than $500 nor more than $3,000, and imprisoned not more than one year, at the discretion of the judge trying the same.

Was then disagreed to—yeas 102, nays 108 (not voting 79), as follow:

YEAS—Messrs. G. A. Bagley, J. H. Baker, W. H. Baker, Ballou, BANKS, Bass, Blaine, Blair, Bradley, H. C. Burchard, Cannon, Caswell, Chittenden, *Clymer*, Conger, Crapo, Denison, Dunnell, *Durham*, Eames, Evans, Farwell, Fort, Foster, Frost, Frye, Garfield, E. Hale, *A. H. Hamilton*, *R. Hamilton*, Hathorn, *Haymond*, Hays, Hendee, Henderson, G. F. Hoar, *Holman*, Hubbell, Hunter, Hurlbut, Hyman, Joyce, *Kehr*, Kelley, Kimball, Leavenworth, Lynch, Magoon, McCrary, J. W. McDill, Monroe, Morey, *Morgan*, Nash, *Neal*, *New*, Norton, *O'Brien*, Oliver, O'Neill, Packer, Page, *J. Phelps*, W. A. Phillips, Pierce, Plaisted, A. POTTER, Pratt, *Riddle*, M. S. Robinson, S. Ross, Rusk, Sampson, *Savage*, Seelye, Sinnickson, R. Smalls, A. H. Smith, Strait, *Stevenson*, *Stone*, Stowell, *Teese*, Thornburgh, M. I. Townsend, W. Townsend, Tufts, Van Vorhes, A. S. Wallace, J. W. Wallace, G. W. Wells, Wheeler, J. D. White, Whiting, G. Willard, A. Williams, C. G. Williams, *J. D. Williams*, W. B. Williams, J. Wilson, A. Wood, jr., Woodworth—102.

NAYS—Messrs. *Ainsworth*, ANDERSON, *Ashe*, *Atkins*, *Bagby*, *J. H. Bagley, jr.*, *Banning*, *Barnum*, *Beebe*, *Blackburn*, *Bliss*, *Blount*, *Boone*, *Bradford*, *Bright*, *J. Y. Brown*, *Cabell*, *J. H. Caldwell*, *W. P. Caldwell*, *Cate*, *Caulfield*, *J. B. Clarke*, *J. B. Clark, jr.*, *Cook*, *Cox*, *Culberson*, *Cutler*, *Joseph J. Davis*, *DeBolt*, *Dibrell*, *Douglas*, *Durand*, *Eden*, *Ellis*, *Ely*, *Felton*, *Forney*, *Franklin*, *Glover*, *Goode*, *Goodin*, *Gunter*, *Hancock*, *H. R. Harris*, *J. T. Harris*, *C. H. Harrison*, *Hartridge*, *Hartzell*, *Henkle*, *Hereford*, *A. S. Hewitt*, *G. W. Hewitt*, *Hill*, *Hooker*, *House*, *Hunton*, *Hurd*, *Jenks*, *T. L. Jones*, *G. M. Landers*, *Luttrell*, *Lynde*, *McMahon*, *Metcalfe*, *Milliken*, *Money*, *Morrison*, *Mutchler*, *E. Y. Parsons*, *Payne*, *J. F. Philips*, *Poppleton*, *D. Rea*, *Reagan*, *J. Reilly*, *J. B. Reilly*, *A. V. Rice*, *J. Robbins*, *W. M. Robbins*, *C. B. Roberts*, *M. Ross*, *M. Sayler*, *Scales*, *Schleicher*, *Singleton*, *Slemons*, *W. E. Smith*, *Southard*, *Sparks*, *Springer*, *Tarbox*, *Terry*, *C. P. Thompson*, *P. F. Thomas*, *Throckmorton*, *Tucker*, *Turney*, *J. L. Vance*, *R. B. Vance*, *Waddell*, *G. C. Walker*, *E. Wells*, *Whitehouse*, *Wike*, *J. Williams*, *J. N. Williams*, *Willis*, *Yeates*—108.

The amendment offered by Mr. G. F. HOAR to the substitute was then disagreed to.

The motion of Mr. GOODE to amend the substitute offered by Mr. J. Y. BROWN, by inserting as section two of the substitute, the following:

That if any person, with a view to the election to or obtaining votes for the office of President, Vice-President, or the post of Senator, Representative, or Delegate in the Congress of the United States, or to the appointment to any office or post of honor or emolument under the Government of the United States of himself or any other person, shall use force or duress, by menace or violence to life, limb, property, or liberty, or shall commit bribery, or use money, property, or other thing of value to influence any elector, voter, officer, or other person, in or in respect to any election or appointment to any such office or post, he shall, upon conviction thereof, be fined not less than $500, nor more than $3,000, and be imprisoned not more than one year, at the discretion of the judge trying the case.

Was then agreed to—yeas 211, nays 3 (Messrs. *Bradford*, *Lynde* and *Walsh*), not voting 75.

Mr. AINSWORTH moved to table the bill; which was disagreed to.

Mr. REAGAN's motion to amend was then disagreed to—on a count, ayes 35, noes not counted.

The substitute offered by Mr. J. Y. BROWN, as amended by the adoption of the amendment offered by Mr. GOODE, was then agreed to, and the bill passed—yeas 175, nays 8: Messrs. *Ainsworth*, *W. P. Caldwell*, *Hancock*, Hyman, McCrary, *C. B. Roberts*, *Slemons*, *Wigginton*.

The title was amended so as to read as follows: "A bill to prevent the solicitation, contribution, or acceptance by any officer or employé of the Government, of money, property, or other thing of value for political purposes, and for other purposes."

IN SENATE.

No action was taken.

Repealing Homestead Law as to Certain States.

IN SENATE.

1876, February 15—This bill (S. 2) passed:

A Bill to repeal section two thousand three hundred and three of the Revised Statutes of the United States, making restrictions in the disposition of the public lands in the States of Alabama, Mississippi, Louisiana, Arkansas and Florida, and for other purposes.

Be it enacted, etc., That section 2303 of the Revised Statutes of the United States, confining the disposal of the public lands in the States of Alabama, Mississippi, Louisiana, Arkansas and Florida to the provisions of the homestead law, be, and the same is hereby, repealed: *Provided*, That the repeal of said section shall not have the effect to impair the right, complete or inchoate, of any homestead settler, and no land occupied by such settler at the time this act shall take effect shall be subject to entry, pre-emption or sale: *And provided*, That the public lands affected by this act shall be offered at public sale, as soon as practicable, from time to time, and according to the provisions of existing law, and shall not be subject to private entry until they are so offered.

Yeas 41, nays 17, as follow:

YEAS—Messrs. Alcorn, *Bayard*, *Bogy*, BOOTH, *Caperton*, Clayton, *Cockrell*, *Cooper*, *Davis*, *Dennis*, Dorsey, *English*, Ferry, *Goldthwaite*, Harvey, Hitchcock, Howe, *Johnston*, *Jones* of

Florida, *Kelly*, *Kernan*, *Key*, *McCreery*, *McDonald*, McMillan, *Maxey*, *Merrimon*, Morton, *Norwood*, Paddock, *Ransom*, Robertson, *Saulsbury*, Sherman, Spencer, *Stevenson*, Wadleigh, *Wallace*, West, *Whyte*, Windom—41.

NAYS—Messrs. Allison, Anthony, Boutwell, Cameron of Pennsylvania, Cameron of Wisconsin, Christiancy, Dawes, Frelinghuysen, Hamilton, Hamlin, Ingalls, Jones of Nevada, Morrill of Maine, Morrill of Vermont, Oglesby, Sargent, Wright—17.

IN HOUSE.

1876, June 7—It was passed finally—yeas 108, nays 97 (not voting 83), as follow:

YEAS—Messrs. *Atkins*, *Bagby*, *J. H. Bagley, jr.*, *Beebe*, *S. N. Bell*, *Blackburn*, *Bland*, *Boone*, *Bradford*, *J. Y. Brown*, *Buckner*, *S. D. Burchard*, *Cabell*, *J. H. Caldwell*, *W. P. Caldwell*, *Candler*, *Cate*, *J. B. Clarke*, *J. B. Clark, jr.*, *Cochrane*, *Cook*, *Cox*, *Culberson*, *Joseph J. Davis*, *De Bolt*, *Dibrell*, *Douglas*, *Eden*, *Egbert*, *Felton*, *Finley*, *Forney*, *Franklin*, *Gause*, *Goode*, *Gunter*, *A. H. Hamilton*, *R. Hamilton*, *Hardenbergh*, *C. H. Harrison*, *Hartridge*, *A. S. Hewitt*, *G. W. Hewitt*, *Hill*, Hoge, *Hooker*, *Hopkins*, *House*, *Hurd*, *Jenks*, *T. L. Jones*, *Lamar*, *G. M. Landers*, *Levy*, *B. B. Lewis*, *Lord*, *McFarland*, *Meade*, *Metcalfe*, *Milliken*, *Mills*, *Money*, *Morgan*, *O'Brien*, *Odell*, *E. Y. Parsons*, *J. Phelps*, *J. F. Philips*, *D. Rea*, *Reagan*, *J. Reilly*, *Riddle*, *J. Robbins*, *C. B. Roberts*, *M. Ross*, *Scales*, *Schleicher*, *J. G. Schumaker*, *Sheakley*, *Singleton*, *Slemons*, *W. E. Smith*, *Southard*, *Sparks*, *Springer*, *Stenger*, *Stone*, *Swann*, *Teese*, *Terry*, *P. F. Thomas*, *C. P. Thompson*, *Throckmorton*, *Tucker*, *R. B. Vance*, *C. C. B. Walker*, *G. C. Walker*, *Walling*, *Walsh*, *E. Wells*, *Whitthorne*, *Wike*, *J. Williams*, *J. D. Williams*, *J. N. Williams*, *Willis*, *F. Wood*, *Yeates*—108.

NAYS—Messrs. C. H. Adams, *Ainsworth*, ANDERSON, G. A. Bagley, W. H. Baker, Ballou, Blair, Bradley, W. R. Brown, H. C. Burchard, Burleigh, CAMPBELL, Cannon, Cason, Caswell, Chittenden, *Clymer*, *Collins*, Crapo, Crounse, Cutler, Danford, Davy, Denison, Dobbins, Dunnell, *Durand*, Eames, Evans, Foster, Garfield, *Goodin*, E. Hale, B. W. Harris, Hartzell, Hathorn, *Haymond*, Hendee, Henderson, G. F. Hoar, *Holman*, Hunter, Hurlbut, Joyce, Kasson, Kelley, Ketchum, Kimball, *F. Landers*, Lapham, Leavenworth, *Le Moyne*, Lynch, E. W. M. Mackey, *L. A. Mackey*, McCrary, J. W. McDill, Miller, Monroe, Nash, *Neal*, Norton, Oliver, O'Neill, Packer, Page, Pierce, *Piper*, T. C. Platt, A. POTTER, Pratt, Rainey, *Randall*, M. S. Robinson, Sampson, *Savage*, Seelye, Sinnickson, R. Smalls, A. H. Smith, Strait, *Tarbox*, Thornburgh, W. Townsend, Van Vorhes, Waldron, A. S. Wallace, J. W. Wallace, G. W. Wells, *Whitehouse*, Whiting, G. Willard, A. Williams, C. G. Williams, J. Wilson, A. Wood, *C. Young*—97.

Bill Fixing the Salary of the President of the United States.

IN SENATE.

1876, February 28—Mr. WRIGHT, from the Committee on Civil Service and Retrenchment, reported the bill as follows:

Be it enacted, etc., That from and after the fourth day of March, eighteen hundred and seventy-seven, the salary of the President of the United States shall be twenty-five thousand dollars per annum; and that all acts and parts of acts inconsistent herewith be, and the same are hereby, repealed.

March 15—The SENATE passed the bill—yeas 26, nays 20, as follow:

YEAS—Messrs. Allison, *Bogy*, Christiancy, Clayton, *Cockrell*, Conkling, Dawes, Ferry, *Goldthwaite*, Hamilton, Harvey, Hitchcock, *Kernan*, *Key*, Logan, *McCreery*, *McDonald*, *Maxey*, Morrill of Vermont, Morton, Patterson, *Stevenson*, *Thurman*, *Wallace*, *Whyte*, Wright—26.

NAYS—Messrs. *Bayard*, Boutwell, *Cooper*, *Davis*, Dorsey, Frelinghuysen, Hamlin, Howe, Ingalls, *Jones* of Florida, Jones of Nevada, McMillan, Mitchell, Paddock, Robertson, Sargent, Sharon, Spencer, Windom, *Withers*—20.

1876, April 3—The motion to reconsider the vote passing the bill, was disagreed to—yeas 24, nays 31:

YEAS—Messrs. Anthony, *Bayard*, BOOTH, Boutwell, Cameron of Pennsylvania, Christiancy, *Cooper*, Cragin, Dorsey, Edmunds, Frelinghuysen, Hamlin, Ingalls, *Jones* of Florida, Jones of Nevada, McMillan, Mitchell, Morrill of Maine, Paddock, Sargent, Sharon, Spencer, Wadleigh, Windom—24.

NAYS—Messrs. *Bogy*, Bruce, *Caperton*, Clayton, *Cockrell*, *Davis*, Dawes, Ferry, *Goldthwaite*, *Gordon*, Hamilton, Harvey, *Kelly*, *Kernan*, *Key*, Logan, *McCreery*, *McDonald*, *Maxey*, *Merrimon*, Morrill of Vermont, Morton, *Norwood*, Oglesby, Sherman, *Stevenson*, *Thurman*, *Wallace*, *Whyte*, *Withers*, Wright—31.

IN HOUSE.

April 6—Mr. HOLMAN reported the bill from the Committee on Appropriations; and it passed without a division.

[For President's GRANT's objections to the bill, see page 148.]

May 25—Mr. WRIGHT, from the Committee, reported back the bill, and recommended its passage, notwithstanding the objections of the PRESIDENT. But no vote was reached.

IN SENATE.

June 3—Pending the Legislative Appropriation bill (the HOUSE having appropriated for the salary of the PRESIDENT at the rate of $50,000 up to March 4, 1877, and $25,000 after that date, and provided that after March 4, 1877, "the salary of the President of the United States shall be $25,000 per annum")—

The Committee on Appropriation of the SENATE reported an amendment striking out the above and inserting the words "in compensation of the President of the United States, $50,000."

On agreeing to the amendment, the yeas were 31, and the nays 11, as follow:

YEAS—Messrs. Allison, Anthony, *Bayard*, BOOTH, Boutwell, Christiancy, Clayton, *Cooper*, Cragin, *Davis*, Edmunds, Frelinghuysen, Hamlin, Howe, *Johnston*, Logan, McMillan, Mitchell, Morrill of Maine, Morrill of Vermont, Morton, *Norwood*, Paddock, Patterson, *Ransom*,

Robertson, Sargent, Sherman, Spencer, Windom, *Withers*—31.

NAYS—Messrs. *Bogy*, *Cockrell*, *Eaton*, *Goldthwaite*, Hitchcock, *Kelly*, *Key*, *McCreery*, *Maxey*, *Stevenson*, *Thurman*—11.

Civil Service Appointments.

IN SENATE.

1876, June 5—Pending the Legislative Appropriation bill,

Mr. CLAYTON offered, from the Committee on Civil Service, the following amendment, to be added to section 3:

That the appointments in all the Executive Departments of the Government shall be so arranged as to be equally distributed between the several States of the United States, Territories, and the District of Columbia, according to population; and the principle of equal distribution of appointments as above provided for shall apply in making reductions of force in said Departments.

Mr. EDMUNDS moved to amend the amendment by adding to it the words:

And all such appointments shall be made upon a careful and impartial examination of the candidate therefor by a board composed of not less than five persons, to be appointed by the President, by and with the advice and consent of the Senate; and the most capable and worthy of the competitors so examined shall be selected for such appointments.

Mr. MORRILL of Maine moved to lay on the table the amendment offered by Mr. CLAYTON; which was disagreed to—yeas 13, nays 22.

June 7—The amendment of Mr. EDMUNDS was rejected—yeas 11, nays 28:

YEAS—Messrs. Allison, Anthony, Christiancy, Conkling, Cragin, Edmunds, Ferry of Michigan, Hamlin, *Kelly*, Morrill of Vermont, Wadleigh—11.

NAYS—Messrs. *Barnum*, *Bogy*, Bruce, *Caperton*, Clayton, *Cooper*, *Dennis*, *Eaton*, Hamilton, Howe, *Johnston*, *Jones* of Florida, Jones of Nevada, *Key*, *McCreery*, *Maxey*, *Merrimon*, Mitchell, Morrill of Maine, *Norwood*, Paddock, Robertson, *Saulsbury*, Sherman, *Stevenson*, *Whyte*, Windom, Wright—28.

Mr. CHRISTIANCY moved to amend the amendment of Mr. CLAYTON, by adding to it these words:

Provided, That the District of Columbia shall be entitled to three times the number of appointments to which it would be entitled on the basis of population.

Which was rejected.

Mr. EDMUNDS moved to add the following proviso to the amendment:

Provided, That the foregoing provision shall be subject to the provisions of section 1754 of the Revised Statutes of the United States.

[That section is as follows: Persons honorably discharged from the military or naval service by reason of disability resulting from wounds or sickness incurred in the line of duty shall be preferred for appointments to civil offices, provided they are found to possess the business capacity necessary for the proper discharge of the duties of such offices.]

Which was agreed to—yeas 37, nays 3:

YEAS—Messrs. Allison, Anthony, *Barnum*, *Bogy*, Bruce, Burnside, *Caperton*, Christiancy, Clayton, *Cockrell*, Conkling, *Cooper*, Cragin, Edmunds, Ferry of Michigan, Hamilton, Hamlin, Hitchcock, Howe, Ingalls, *Jones* of Florida, Jones of Nevada, *Kelly*, *Key*, *Maxey*, Mitchell, Morrill of Maine, Morrill of Vermont, Paddock, Robertson, Sherman, *Stevenson*, Wadleigh, *Whyte*, Windom, *Withers*, Wright—37.

NAYS—Messrs. *McCreery*, *Merrimon*, *Saulsbury*—3.

The amendment offered by Mr. CLAYTON, as amended, was then rejected—yeas 22, nays 23:

YEAS—Messrs. Allison, *Barnum*, *Bogy*, Bruce, *Caperton*, Clayton, *Cockrell*, Dorsey, Ferry of Michigan, *Gordon*, Hitchcock, Ingalls, Jones of Nevada, *Kelly*, *Key*, *McCreery*, *Maxey* Mitchell, Paddock, Robertson, *Stevenson*, Wright—22.

NAYS—Messrs. Anthony, BOOTH, Cameron of Pennsylvania, Christiancy, Conkling, *Cooper*, *Dennis*, *Eaton*, Edmunds, *Goldthwaite*, Hamilton, Hamlin, Howe, *Johnston*, *Merrimon*, Morrill of Maine, Morrill of Vermont, *Norwood*, Sargent, *Saulsbury*, Sherman, Windom, *Withers*—23.

Mr. CLAYTON then moved the following, to come in at the end of the third section:

Provided, That, in making any reduction of force in any of the Executive Departments, the head of such Department shall retain those persons who may be qualified who have been honorably discharged from the military or naval service of the United States, and the widows and orphans of deceased soldiers and sailors.

Which was agreed to—yeas 43, nays 0:

YEAS—Messrs. Allison, Anthony, *Barnum*, *Bogy*, BOOTH, Bruce, Cameron of Pennsylvania, *Caperton*, Christiancy, Clayton, *Cockrell*, Conkling, *Cooper*, *Dennis*, Dorsey, Edmunds, Ferry of Michigan, *Goldthwaite*, Hamilton, Hamlin, Hitchcock, Howe, Ingalls, Jones of Nevada, *Kelly*, *Key*, *McCreery*, *Maxey*, *Merrimon*, Mitchell, Morrill of Vermont, Morton, *Norwood*, Paddock, *Ransom*, Robertson, Sargent, Sherman, *Stevenson*, *Whyte*, Windom, *Withers*, Wright—43.

NAYS—0.

At a later stage in the progress of the bill, Mr. CLAYTON renewed his amendment first offered, and

Mr. EDMUNDS renewed his amendment.

On motion of Mr. MORRILL of Maine, the amendment was laid on the table—yeas 21, nays 18:

YEAS—Messrs. Anthony, BOOTH, Christiancy, Cragin, *Eaton*, Edmunds, *Gordon*, Hamilton, Hamlin, *Johnston*, Jones of Nevada, Morrill of Maine, Morrill of Vermont, *Norwood*, Sargent, *Saulsbury*, Sherman, *Stevenson*, *Whyte*, Windom, *Withers*—21.

NAYS—Messrs. Allison, Cameron of Pennsylvania, Clayton, *Cockrell*, *Cooper*, Dorsey, Ferry of Michigan, *Goldthwaite*, Hitchcock, Ingalls, *Kelly*, *McCreery*, *Maxey*, *Merrimon*, Paddock, West, Wright—18.

[For previous action on Civil Service, see McPherson's Hand Book of Politics for 1874, pp. 113, 119, 126, 128, 129, 143, and 221; and Hand-Book of Politics for 1872, pp. 21, 27, 40, 42, 64, 65—69.]

On admitting New Mexico as a State.

IN SENATE.

1876, March 10—The bill passed finally—yeas 35, nays 15:

YEAS—Messrs. *Bogy*, BOOTH, Bruce, Cameron of Wisconsin, Christiancy, Conover, *Cooper*, *Davis*, *Dennis*, Dorsey, Ferry, *Goldthwaite*, Hamilton, Hamlin, Harvey, Hitchcock, Howe, Ingalls, Jones of Nevada, *Kelley*, *Kernan*, Logan, McMillan, *Maxey*, Mitchell, Paddock, *Ransom*, Robertson, Sargent, Sharon, Sherman, West, Windom, *Withers*, Wright—35.

NAYS—Messrs. Allison, *Bayard*, *Eaton*, Edmunds, Frelinghuysen, *Key*, *McCreery*, *McDonald*, Morrill of Vermont, *Norwood*, *Randolph*, *Saulsbury*, *Stevenson*, *Wallace*—15.

IN HOUSE.

No vote was reached.

[For votes on this subject, in Forty-third Con gress, see McPherson's Hand-Book of Politics for 1874, p. 220.]

Relative to the Pacific Railroad Companies.

IN HOUSE.

1876, July 7—The bill (H. R. 3672), reported from the Committee on the Judiciary, by Hon. W. LAWRENCE, was brought to a vote, and was passed—yeas 159, nays 9 (not voting 121), as follow:

YEAS—Messrs. *Ainsworth*, ANDERSON, *Ashe*, *Atkins*, *J. H. Bagley, jr.*, J. H. Baker, *Banning*, *S. N. Bell*, *Blackburn*, *Blount*, *Boone*, *Bradford*, Bradley, *Bright*, *Buckner*, H. C. Burchard, *S. D. Burchard*, Burleigh, *Cabell*, *J. H. Caldwell*, *W. P. Caldwell*, CAMPBELL, *Candler*, Cannon, *Caulfield*, *J. B. Clarke*, *J. B. Clark, jr.*, *Clymer*, *Cochrane*, Conger, *Cook*, *Cox*, Crounse, *Culberson*, *Cutler*, *Joseph J. Davis*, Davy, *Dibrell*, Dobbins, *Douglas*, Dunnell, *Durand*, Eames, *Egbert*, *Ellis*, Evans, *Felton*, *Finley*, *Forney*, Fort, *Goode*, *Goodin*, *Hancock*, *Hardenbergh*, *H. R. Harris*, *J. T. Harris*, *C. H. Harrison*, *Hartzell*, *Hatcher*, *Haymond*, Hendee, *Hereford*, *Holman*, *Hooker*, *Hopkins*, *House*, Hunter, *Hunton*, *T. L. Jones*, Kelley, Ketchum, *F. Landers*, W. Lawrence, Leavenworth, *Levy*, *B. B. Lewis*, *Luttrell*, *L. A. Mackey*, Magoon, *Maish*, J. W. McDill, *McFarland*, Miller, *Milliken*, *Mills*, Monroe, *Morgan*, *Morrison*, *Mutchler*, *New*, Norton, Oliver, O'Neill, Packer, Page, *Payne*, *J. F. Philips*, *Piper*, Plaisted, *Poppleton*, A. POTTER, *Powell*, *Randall*, *D. Rea*, *Reagan*, *J. Reilly*, *J. B. Reilly*, *A. V. Rice*, *Riddle*, *J. Robbins*, *W. M. Robbins*, M. S. Robinson, *M. Ross*, S. Ross, Rusk, Sampson, *Scales*, *Schleicher*, *Singleton*, Sinnickson, *Slemons*, R. Smalls, A. H. Smith, *Southard*, *Sparks*, *Spencer*, *Springer*, Strait, *Stevenson*, *Stone*, *Tarbox*, *Terry*, *C. P. Thompson*, Thornburgh, M. I. Townsend, W. Townsend, *Tucker*, Tufts, *Turney*, Van Vorhes, *J. L. Vance*, *R. B. Vance*, *G. C. Walker*, A. S. Wallace, *Walling*, *Walsh*, *Warren*, *E. Wells*, J. D. White, Whiting, *Wike*, G. Willard, *J. Williams*, *J. D. Williams*, *J. N. Williams*, W. B. Williams, *B. Wilson*, J. Wilson, *Yeates*—159.

NAYS—Messrs. *Bagby*, B. W. Harris, *Hurd*, *Lamar*, *Le Moyne*, MacDougall, *Meade*, Pierce, G. W. Wells—9.

The principal section of the bill is the fourth, which is as follows:

SEC. 4. That it shall be the duty of the several railroad companies to which bonds were issued under any of the several acts of which this act is amendatory, to provide a sinking fund for the payment, according to law, of the interest and principal of such bonds, and for re-imbursing the United States for such sums as have been, and may from time to time be, advanced and paid by the United States upon such bonds and interest, and which may not be re-imbursed from compensation for services as now provided by law, and from 5 per cent. of net earnings. And for the purpose of providing such sinking fund said companies shall severally be required to pay into the Treasury of the United States, in addition to the said compensation for services and 5 per cent. of net earnings, the following annual installments, to wit: The Union Pacific Railroad Company shall, during the period of ten years from and after the 1st day of July, 1876, pay annually into the Treasury of the United States the sum of $750,000, to be paid one-half on July 1 and the other half on January 1 in each of said years. And during each and every year, commencing with the expiration of said period of ten years, the said Union Pacific Railroad Company shall pay into the Treasury of the United States $1,000,000, until the whole amount of bonds issued to said company, together with interest, shall have been fully paid, one-half of each annual installment to be paid on the 1st of July, and the other half on the 1st of January. And the said Central Pacific Railroad Company, on its own account and on account of the Western Pacific Railroad Company, shall, during the period of ten years from and after the 1st day of July, 1876, pay annually into the Treasury of the United States the sum of $568,210, to be paid one-half on July 1 and the other half on January 1 in each of said years. And during each and every year, commencing with the expiration of said period of ten years, the said Central Pacific Railroad Company shall pay into the Treasury of the United States the sum of $760,330, until the whole amount of bonds issued to said company, together with interest, shall have been paid, one-half of each annual installment to be paid on the 1st day of July and the other half on the 1st day of January: *Provided*, That the sums paid into the sinking fund under this act shall apply first to the extinguishment of interest, and the balance to the principal of the aforesaid bonds. And there shall be paid into the Treasury on account of said sinking fund, annually, one-half on the 1st day of July and the other half on the 1st day of January in each year, by the Kansas Pacific Railway Company, $87,327; by the Central Branch Union Pacific Railroad Company, $22,296; and by the Sioux City and Pacific Railroad Company, $20,723, until the bonds issued to said companies respectively, and the interest thereon, shall be fully paid. And said several companies shall owe and be indebted to the United States in the several sums required to be by them respectively paid as aforesaid. And any company may pay any sum herein required to be paid in bonds, Treasury notes, or other evidences of debt against the United States, to be allowed at par.

The total sum required to be paid by any company in any one year by virtue of this act, and including said 5 per cent. of net earnings, and said compensation for services as now required by law, shall not exceed the several sums following, to wit: By the Central Pacific Railroad Company, on its own account, $4,869,484, and on account of the Western Pacific Railroad Company, $133,588; the Union Pacific Railroad Company, $1,989,462; the Kansas Pacific Railway Company, $489,034; the Central Branch Union Pacific Railroad Company, $124,856; and the Sioux City and Pacific Railroad Company, $116,050.

IN SENATE.

No action was taken to date of closing this page.

On Repealing the Bankruptcy Act.

1876, February 8—Mr. LYNDE, from the Committee on the Judiciary, reported a bill (H. R. 390), to repeal the act entitled "An act to establish a uniform system of bankruptcy throughout the United States," approved March 21, 1867, and all laws and parts of laws amendatory thereof.

It provides that the act entitled "An act to establish a uniform system of bankruptcy throughout the United States," approved March 2, 1867, and all other laws and parts of laws amendatory of said act and supplemental thereunto, and all amendments thereto, be, and the same hereby are, repealed.

The second section provides that all suits and proceedings now pending in the courts of the United States wherein an adjudication in bankruptcy has been made shall be proceeded with and governed by the provisions of existing laws, which are hereby continued in force only for the purpose of closing up suits and proceedings now pending.

The third section provides that this act shall take effect from and after the 1st day of January, 1877.

Which was passed—yeas 187, nays 59 (not voting 44), as follow:

YEAS—Messrs. C. H. Adams, *Ainsworth*, ANDERSON, *Ashe*, *Atkins*, *Bagby*, G. A. Bagley, *J. H. Bagley, jr.*, J. H. Baker, W. H. Baker, *Banning*, Bass, *Beebe*, *S. N. Bell*, *Blackburn*, *Bland*, *Boone*, *Bradford*, Bradley, *Bright*, *J. Y. Brown*, W. R. Brown, *Buckner*, H. C. Burchard, *S. D. Burchard*, Burleigh, *J. H. Caldwell*, *W. P. Caldwell*, CAMPBELL, *Candler*, Cannon, Cason, Caswell, *Cate*, *Caulfield*, Chittenden, *J. B. Clarke*, *J. B. Clark, jr.*, *Clymer*, *Collins*, Conger, *Cowan*, *Cox*, Crapo, Crounse, *Culberson*, *Cutler*, Darrall, Davy, *DeBolt*, Denison, *Dibrell*, *Douglas*, *Durand*, *Durham*, *Eden*, *Egbert*, *Ellis*, Evans, Farwell, *Faulkner*, *Forney*, Fort, Foster, *Franklin*, Frost, *Fuller*, *Glover*, *Goodin*, *A. H. Hamilton*, *Hancock*, Haralson, *Hardenbergh*, B. W. Harris, *J. T. Harris*, *C. H. Harrison*, *Hartridge*, *Hartzell*, *Hatcher*, *Haymond*, *Henkle*, *Hereford*, G. F. Hoar, *Holman*, *Hooker*, *Hopkins*, Hoskins, *House*, Hunter, Hyman, *T. L. Jones*, Joyce, *Kehr*, Kimball, *Knott*, *F. Landers*, Lapham, W. Lawrence, *B. B. Lewis*, *Luttrell*, Lynch, *Lynde*, *L. A. Mackey*, Magoon, *Maish*, McCrary, J. W. McDill, *McFarland*, *McMahon*, *Meade*, *Metcalfe*, Miller, *Milliken*, *Mills*, *Money*, Monroe, *Morgan*, *Morrison*, *Neal*, *New*, Norton, Packer, Page, *E. Y. Parsons*, *Payne*, *J. Phelps*, *J. F. Philips*, W. A. Phillips, *Piper*, *Poppleton*, A. POTTER, *Powell*, Rainey, *Randall*, *D. Rea*, *Reagan*, *J. Reilly*, *J. B. Reilly*, *A. V. Rice*, *Riddle*, M. S. Robinson, Sampson, *Savage*, *Scales*, *Schleicher*, *J. G. Schumaker*, Seelye, *Sheakley*, *Singleton*, Sinnickson, R. Smalls, A. H. Smith, *Southard*, *Sparks*, *Springer*, Strait, *Stenger*, *Stevenson*, *Tarbox*, *Terry*, *C. P. Thompson*, *P. F. Thomas*, Thornburgh, *Throckmorton*, M. I. Townsend, *Tucker*, Tufts, *Turney*, *Waddell*, Waldron, A. S. Wallace, *Walsh*, *E. Wells*, Wheeler, J. D. White, *Wike*, G. Willard, *A. S. Williams*, C. G. Williams, *J. D. Williams*, *J. N. Williams*, *Willis*, *B. Wilson*, J. Wilson, A. Wood, jr., Woodburn, *C. Young*—187.

NAYS—Messrs. Ballou, BANKS, Blaine, Blair, *Blount*, *Cook*, Dunnell, Eames, *Felton*, C. Freeman, Frye, Garfield, *Gause*, *Gunter*, *R. Hamilton*, *H. R. Harris*, Hathorn, Hendee, Henderson, *A. S. Hewitt*, *G. W. Hewitt*, Hubbell, *Hunton*, *Hurd*, Hurlbut, Kasson, Kelley, Ketchum, King, *Lamar*, Leavenworth, MacDougall, Oliver, O'Neill, Pierce, Plaisted, T. C. Platt, Purman, *J. Robbins*, *W. M. Robbins*, *Slemons*, *W. E. Smith*, Stowell, *Teese*, W. Townsend, Van Vorhes, *J. L. Vance*, *R. B. Vance*, J. W. Wallace, *Walling*, *E. Ward*, *Warren*, *Whitehouse*, Whiting, A. Williams, W. B. Williams, *F. Wood*, *Yeates*—59.

IN SENATE.

June 20—Reported from Committee on Judiciary, and recommended to be postponed till next session.

The Centennial Appropriation.

IN HOUSE.

1876, January 6—Mr. HOPKINS, from the Committee on the Centennial Celebration, reported the following bill:

Whereas by the act of Congress entitled "An act to provide for the celebrating of the one-hundredth anniversary of American independence by holding an international exhibition of arts, manufacture, and products of the soil and mine, in the city of Philadelphia, and State of Pennsylvania, in the year 1876," approved March 3, 1875, provision was made for the celebration of the centennial anniversary of the Declaration of American Independence by "an exhibition of American and foreign arts, products, and manufactures," to be "held under the auspices of the Government of the United States, in the city of Philadelphia, in the year 1876; and

Whereas by the act of Congress entitled "An act relative to the Centennial International Exhibition to be held in the city of Philadelphia, State of Pennsylvania, in the year 1876," approved June 1, 1872, the Centennial Board of Finance was incorporated, with authority to raise the capital necessary to carry into effect the provisions of the said act of March 3, 1871; and

Whereas the President of the United States, in compliance with a joint resolution of Congress approved June 5, 1874, did "extend, in the name of the United States, a respectful and cordial invitation to the governments of other nations to be represented and take part in the international exposition to be held at Philadelphia, under the auspices of the Government of the United States," and as the governments so invited, to the number of thirty-eight, have so accepted such invitation, and many of them are making extensive preparations to embrace the courtesy so extended to them, thereby rendering proper arrangements for the coming ceremonies on the part of the Government of the United States a matter of honor and good faith; and

Whereas the preparations designed by the United States Centennial Commission, and in part executed by the Centennial Board of Finance, are in accordance with the spirit of the acts of Congress relating thereto, and are on a scale creditable to the Government and people of the United States; Therefore,

Be it enacted, etc., That the sum of one million five hundred thousand dollars, to complete the Centennial buildings and other preparations, be, and the same is hereby, appropriated out of any moneys in the United States Treasury not otherwise appropriated, which shall be paid on the drafts of the president and treasurer of the Centennial Board of Finance, one-third immediately after the passage of this act, and the remainder in four equal monthly payments: *Provided*, That in the distribution of any moneys that may remain in the treasury of the Centennial Board of Finance after the payment of its debts, as provided for by the tenth section of the act of Congress, approved June 1, 1872, incorporating said Centennial Board of Finance, the appropriation hereinbefore made shall share equally with the holders of the said Centennial stock, and a like percentage thereon be paid into the United States Treasury as may be paid to the holders of the said stock: *Provided, also*, That the Government of the United States shall not, under any circumstances, be liable for any debt or obligation of the United States Centennial Commission or the Centennial Board of Finance, or any payment in addition to the foregoing sum.

January 25—Mr. SPRINGER moved to amend by striking from the bill the words, in the first proviso, beginning with "share equally with," etc., and ending with the word "stock" at the end of the proviso, and inserting these words in their place: "be paid in full into the Treasury of the United States before any dividend or percentage of the profits shall be paid to the holders of said stock."

Which was agreed to.

Mr. KASSON moved to add this, as a second section:

SEC. 2. That the money by this act appropriated shall be paid to the treasurer of the Centennial Board of Finance only after he and the President of the Board shall execute a bond in the sum of five hundred thousand dollars, to the United States, with sufficient security, to be approved by the Secretary of the Treasury, for the safe-keeping and faithful disbursement of the sum hereby appropriated.

Which was agreed to.

The bill as amended was then passed finally—yeas 145, nays 130 (not voting 15), as follow:

YEAS—Messrs. C. H. Adams, G. A. Bagley, W. H. Baker, Ballou, BANKS, *Banning*, *Barnum*, Bass, Blaine, Blair, *Bliss*, Bradley, W. R. Brown, Burleigh, Cason, Caswell, *Chapin*, Chittenden, *Clymer*, Crapo, Crounse, *Cutler*, Danford, Darrall, Davy, Denison, Dobbins, Dunnell, Eames, *Egbert*, *Ellis*, Farwell, *Forney*, Foster, C. Freeman, Frost, Frye, Garfield, *Gause*, *Gibson*, E. Hale, *Hancock*, Haralson, *Hardenbergh*, B. W. Harris, *C. H. Harrison*, Hathorn, *A. S. Hewitt*, *Hill*, G. F. Hoar, *Hopkins*, Hubbell, Hunter, Hurlbut, Hyman, *Jenks*, *T. L. Jones*, Kasson, Kelley, Ketchum, King, *Lamar*, *G. M. Landers*, *Lane*, Lapham, Leavenworth, *Levy*, *Luttrell*, E. W. M. Mackey, *L. A. Mackey*, Magoon, *Maish*, MacDougall, McCrary, J. W. McDill, *Meade*, Miller, *Money*, Monroe, Morey, *Morgan*, *Mutchler*, Nash, Norton, *O'Brien*, Oliver, O'Neill, Page, W. A. Phillips, Pierce, *Piper*, Plaisted, T. C. Platt, *Powell*, Pratt, Purman, Rainey, *Randall*, *Reagan*, *J. Reilly*, *J. Robbins*, *W. M. Robbins*, *C. B. Roberts*, *M. Ross*, S. Ross, Sampson, *Schleicher*, *J. G. Schumaker*, Seelye, Sinnickson, *Slemons*, R. Smalls, A. H. Smith, Strait, Stowell, *Swann*, *Tarbox*, *Teese*, *C. P. Thompson*, *Throckmorton*, M. I. Townsend, W. Townsend, Van Vorhes, *Waddell*, A. S. Wallace, J. W. Wallace, Walls, *E. Ward*, *Warren*, *E. Wells*, G. W. Wells, Wheeler, *Whitehouse*, Whiting, *Wigginton*, A. Williams, *A. S. Williams*, C. G. Williams, *Wilshire*, A. Wood, jr., *F. Wood*, Woodburn, Woodworth, *C. Young*—145.

NAYS—Messrs. *Ainsworth*, ANDERSON, *Ashe*, *Atkins*, *Bagby*, *J. H. Bagley, jr.*, J. H. Baker, *Beebe*, *S. N. Bell*, *Blackburn*, *Bland*, *Blount*, *Boone*, *Bradford*, *Bright*, *J. Y. Brown*, *Buckner*, H. C. Burchard, *S. D. Burchard*, *Cabell*, *J. H. Caldwell*, *W. P. Caldwell*, CAMPBELL, *Candler*, Cannon, *Cate*, *Caulfield*, *J. B. Clarke*, *J. B. Clark, jr.*, *Cochrane*, *Collins*, Conger, *Cook*, *Cowan*, *Cox*, *Culberson*, *Joseph J. Davis*, *De Bolt*, *Dibrell*, *Douglas*, *Durham*, *Eden*, Evans, *Faulkner*, *Felton*, Fort, *Franklin*, *Fuller*, *Glover*, *Goode*, *Goodin*, *Gunter*, *A. H. Hamilton*, *H. R. Harris*, *J. T. Harris*, *Hartridge*, *Hartzell*, *Hatcher*, *Haymond*, Hendee, Henderson, *Henkle*, *Hereford*, *G. W. Hewitt*, *Holman*, *Hooker*, Hoskins, *House*, *Hunton*, *Hurd*, *F. Jones*, Joyce, *Kehr*, Kimball, *Knott*, *F. Landers*, *B. B. Lewis*, *Lord*, *Lynde*, *McFarland*, *McMahon*, *Metcalfe*, *Milliken*, *Mills*, *Morrison*, *Neal*, *New*, *J. Phelps*, *J. F. Philips*, *Poppleton*, A. POTTER, *D. Rea*, *A. V. Rice*, *Riddle*, M. S. Robinson, Rusk, *Savage*, *M. Sayler*, *Scales*, *Sheakley*, *Singleton*, *W. E. Smith*, *Southard*, *Sparks*, *Springer*, *Stenger*, *Stevenson*, *Stone*, *Terry*, *P. F. Thomas*, Thornburgh, *Tucker*, Tufts, *Turney*, *J. L. Vance*, *R. B. Vance*, Waldron, *G. C. Walker*, *Walling*, *Walsh*, *Whitthorne*, *Wike*, G. Willard, *J. Williams*, *J. D. Williams*, W. B. Williams, *Willis*, *B. Wilson*, J. Wilson, *Yeates*—130.

IN SENATE.

February 9—Mr. MCCREERY moved to amend by striking out the preamble, and all after the enacting clause, and inserting the following:

That it be recommended to the people of the United States to assemble on the 4th of July next, in such numbers and manner as may be convenient, in their respective cities, towns, villages, neighborhoods, or wherever they may be, publicly to testify their joy at the one hundredth return of that auspicious day by suitable eulogies, orations, and discourses, or by public prayers and such religious exercises and ceremonies as may be appropriate to the occasion and sanctioned by their own consciences:

Which was disagreed to—yeas 12, nays 45, as follow:

YEAS—Messrs. Alcorn, *Cooper*, *Eaton*, *Goldthwaite*, *Kernan*, *Key*, *McCreery*, *Stevenson*, *Thurman*, Wadleigh, *Whyte*, *Withers*—12.

NAYS—Messrs. Allison, Anthony, *Bayard*, BOOTH, Boutwell, Bruce, Cameron of Pennsylvania, Cameron of Wisconsin, *Caperton*, Clayton, Conkling, Conover, Cragin, Dawes, *Dennis*, Dorsey, Edmunds, *English*, Ferry of Michigan, Frelinghuysen, Hamlin, Harvey, Hitchcock, Ingalls, *Jones* of Florida, Jones of Nevada, *McDonald*, McMillan, *Maxey*, Mitchell, Morrill of Maine, Morrill of Vermont, Morton, Oglesby, Paddock, Patterson, *Randolph*, *Ransom*, Robertson, Sargent, Spencer, *Wallace*, West, Windom, Wright—45.

February 11—The bill passed finally—yeas 41, nays, 15, as follow:

YEAS—Messrs. Allison, Anthony, *Bayard*, Boutwell, Cameron of Pennsylvania, *Caperton*, Clayton, Conkling, Conover, Cragin, Dawes, *Dennis*, Dorsey, Edmunds, Ferry of Michigan, Frelinghuysen, Hamlin, Harvey, Hitchcock, Ingalls, *Jones* of Florida, Jones of Nevada, *Kelly*, Logan, *McDonald*, McMillan, *Maxey*, Mitchell, Morrill of Maine, Morrill of Vermont, Morton, Oglesby, Paddock, Patterson, *Randolph*, *Ransom*, Robertson, Sargent, Spencer, *Wallace*, Windom—41.

NAYS—Messrs. Alcorn, *Cooper*, *Eaton*, *Goldthwaite*, Hamilton, Howe, *Kernan*, *Key*, *McCreery*, *Merrimon*, *Stevenson*, *Thurman*, Wadleigh, *Whyte*, *Withers*—15.

The preamble was agreed to—yeas 37, nays 16.

[The bill was approved by President Grant, February 16, 1876.]

Commission on the Alcoholic-liquor Traffic.

IN SENATE.

1876, January 25—The bill (S. 124) to provide a commission on the subject of the alcoholic-liquor traffic, as follows:

Be it enacted, etc., That for the purpose of obtaining information which may serve as a guide to the system of legislation best fitted for the District of Columbia, the several Territories of the United States, and other places subject to the legislation of Congress in reference to the question of revenue from the manufacture and sale of alcoholic and fermented liquors, and the effect of the use of such liquors upon the morals and welfare of the people of such District, Territories, and places, there shall be appointed by the President, by and with the advice and consent of the Senate, a commission of five persons, neither of whom shall be the holder of any office of profit or trust in the General or a State Government, and all of whom shall not be advocates of prohibitory legislation or total abstinence in relation to alcoholic or fermented liquors. The said commissioners shall be selected solely with reference to personal fitness and capacity for an honest, impartial, and thorough investigation, and shall hold office until their duties shall be accomplished, but not to exceed one year. It shall be their duty to investigate the alcoholic and fermented liquor traffic and manufacture, having special reference to revenue and taxation, distinguishing as far as possible, in the conclusions they arrive at, between the effects produced by the use of distilled or spirituous liquors, and the use of fermented or malt liquors, in their economic, criminal, moral, and scientific aspects, in connection with pauperism, crime, social vice, the public health, and general welfare of the people; and also inquire and take testimony as to the practical results of license and restrictive legislation for the prevention of intemperance in the several States, and the effect produced by such legislation upon the consumption of distilled or spirituous liquors and fermented or malt liquors; also to ascertain whether the evils of drunkenness have been increased or decreased, and whether public morals have been improved thereby. It shall also be the duty of said commissioners to gather information and take testimony as to whether the evil of drunkenness exists to the same extent, or more so, in other civilized countries, and whether those foreign nations that are considered the most temperate in the use of stimulants are so through prohibitory laws; and also to what degree prohibitory legislation has affected the consumption and manufacture of malt and spirituous liquors in this country.

SEC. 2. That the said commissioners shall serve without salary, shall be authorized to employ a secretary at a reasonable compensation, not to exceed $2,000 per annum, which, with the necessary expenses incidental to said investigation, in all not exceeding $10,000, of both the secretary and commissioners, shall be paid out of any money in the Treasury not otherwise appropriated, upon vouchers to be approved by the Fifth Auditor of the Treasury. It shall be the further duty of said commissioners to report the result of their investigation and the expenses attending the same to the President, to be by him transmitted to Congress.

Was agreed to—yeas 37, nays 20:

YEAS—Messrs. Allison, BOOTH, Boutwell, Bruce, Cameron of Pennsylvania, Cameron of Wisconsin, Christiancy, Clayton, Conkling, Conover, Cragin, Dawes, Dorsey, Ferry, Frelinghuysen, Hamilton, Hamlin, Harvey, Howe, Ingalls, Jones of Nevada, Logan, McMillan, Mitchell, Morrill of Maine, Morrill of Vermont, Morton, Oglesby, Paddock, Patterson, Sargent, Sherman, Spencer, West, Windom, *Withers*, Wright—37.

NAYS—Messrs. *Bayard*, *Bogy*, *Caperton*, *Cooper*, *Davis*, *Dennis*, *Eaton*, *English*, *Goldthwaite*, *Gordon*, *Johnston*, *Jones* of Florida, *Key*, *McCreery*, *McDonald*, *Maxey*, *Norwood*, *Ransom*, *Stevenson*, *Wallace*—20.

IN HOUSE.

No action was taken.

Counting of the Electoral Vote.

Forty-third Congress—Second Session.

1875, February 6—Mr. MORTON, from the Committee on Privileges and Elections, reported the following bill (S. 1251), which was passed to a second reading:

IN SENATE.

Be it enacted etc., That the two Houses of Congress shall assemble in the hall of the House of Representatives, at the hour of one o'clock, on the last day of January next succeeding the meeting of the electors of President and Vice-President of the United States, and the President of the Senate shall be their presiding officer; one teller shall be appointed on the part of the Senate, and two on the part of the House of Representatives, to whom shall be handed, as they are opened by the President of the Senate, the certificates of the electoral votes; and said tellers, having read the same in the presence and hearing of the two Houses then assembled, shall make a list of the votes as they shall appear from the said certificates; and the votes having been counted, the result of the same shall be delivered to the President of the Senate, who shall thereupon announce the state of the vote, and the names of the persons, if any, elected, which announcement shall be deemed a sufficient declaration of the persons elected President and Vice-President of the United States, and, together with a list of the votes, be entered on the journals of the two Houses. If, upon the reading of any such certificate by the tellers, any question shall arise in regard to counting the votes therein certified, the same having been stated by the presiding officer, the Senate shall thereupon withdraw, and said question shall be submitted to the body for its decision; and the Speaker of the House of Representatives, shall, in like manner, submit said question to the House of Representatives for its decision; and no electoral vote or votes from any State, to the counting of which objections have been made, shall be rejected except by the affirmative vote of the two Houses. When the two Houses have voted, they shall immediately re-assemble, and the presiding officer shall then announce the decision of the question submitted. And any other question pertinent to the object for which the two Houses are assembled may be submitted and determined in like manner.

SEC. 2. That if more than one return shall be received by the President of the Senate from a State, purporting to be the certificates of electoral votes given at the last preceding election for President and Vice-President in such State, all such returns shall be opened by him in the presence of the Houses when assembled to count the votes; and that return from such State shall be counted which the two Houses acting separately shall decide to be the true and valid return.

SEC. 3. That when the two Houses separate to decide upon an objection that may have been made to the counting of any electoral vote or votes from any State, or for the decision of any other question pertinent thereto, each Senator and Representative may speak to such objection or question ten minutes, and not oftener than once: *Provided*, That after such debate has lasted two hours, it shall be in the power of a majority of each House to direct that the main question shall be put without further debate.

SEC. 4. At such joint meeting of the two Houses, seats shall be provided as follows: For the President of the Senate, the Speaker's chair; for the Speaker, immediately upon his left; the Senators in the body of the hall upon the right of the presiding officer; for the Representatives, in the body of the hall not provided for the Senators; for the tellers, Secretary of the Senate, and Clerk of the House of Representatives, at the Clerk's desk; for the other officers of the two Houses, in front of the Clerk's desk and upon each side of the Speaker's platform. Such joint meeting shall not be dissolved until the electoral votes are all counted and the result declared; and no recess shall be taken unless a question shall have arisen in regard to counting any such votes, in which case it shall be competent for either House, acting separately, in the manner hereinbefore provided, to direct a recess not beyond the next day at the hour of ten o'clock in the forenoon.

Feb. 25—Mr. THURMAN moved to strike out "one teller," and insert "two tellers," in section 1; which was agreed to. And also to insert after the clause "electoral votes" in the first section, the following:

Which certificates shall be opened, presented, and acted upon in the alphabetical order of the names of the States, beginning with the letter A.

Which was agreed to.

Also to strike out the last sentence of section one; which was agreed to.

Also to strike out the words "or for the decision of any other question pertinent thereto," in section three; which was agreed to.

Mr. MERRIMON moved to strike out of section one, the words, "the two Houses of Congress," and insert, "the Senate and House of Representatives;" which was agreed to. Also to amend in section one, by inserting after the words "one o'clock," the letters, "p. m.;" which was agreed to.

Mr. WRIGHT moved to amend the bill in section two, after the word "return," where it first occurs, in the last clause, by inserting the word "only," and after the word "shall" inserting "each;" so as to read: "And that return only from such State shall be counted which the two Houses, acting separately, shall each decide to be the true and valid return;" which was agreed to.

Mr. EDMUNDS moved to amend by striking out all after the enacting clause and inserting the following:

That within not more than ten and not less than three days next prior to the last Monday in January next following any election for President or Vice-President, the Senate shall appoint four Senators and the House of Representatives shall appoint four Members, and such eight persons shall constitute a Committee upon Elections of President and Vice-President. A majority of said committee shall be a quorum thereof, and the concurrence of such majority shall be necessary in any action thereof. Each member of such committee shall, before he enters upon the duties by this act imposed on such committee, take and subscribe the following oath:

"I, ——— ———, do solemnly swear that I

will faithfully and impartially perform all the duties imposed upon me by the act entitled 'An act to provide for and regulate the counting of votes for President and Vice-President;' so help me God."

And such oaths of Senators shall be filed in the archives of the Senate, and of Members of the House of Representatives in the archives of the House.

SEC. 2. That Congress shall be in session on the last Monday in January next after any election for President and Vice-President shall have occurred; and the Senate and House of Representatives shall meet in the Hall of the House of Representatives, at one o'clock afternoon of that day, and from day to day, (Sundays excepted,) at the same hour, until the duties required by this act shall have been performed; the President of the Senate shall preside, and whenever the Senate shall withdraw, from time to time, the Speaker of the House shall resume his chair; having so met, the President of the Senate shall, in the presence of the Senate and House of Representatives, open all the certificates and papers, purporting to be certificates of votes given at the last preceding election for President and for Vice-President, respectively, and which shall have come to his possession; and the votes shall then be counted in the manner and with effect hereinafter provided.

SEC. 3. That when the certificates of votes for President of the United States shall be opened by the President of the Senate, in the presence of the Senate and House of Representatives, as provided in the Constitution and by this act, the same shall, with the votes therein contained or stated, be then and there delivered to the committee provided for in section 1 of this act; which committee shall forthwith proceed to examine the same, and shall count the votes which shall appear to have been legally given and duly certified and returned. And said committee shall report in writing as soon as may be to said meeting their proceedings, the state of the votes, and what persons, if any, have been pursuant to law elected President and Vice-President respectively; and if, on such report, any question shall be made by any Senator or Member of the House of Representatives touching the legal validity of any vote or votes so delivered to said committee, or touching any action of said committee, the Senate shall withdraw, and each House shall proceed to consider the question; and if the two Houses concur in the decision thereof, their judgment shall stand, and the report of such committee shall be modified accordingly; but if they do not so concur, the report of such committee shall stand; and if such committee shall be equally divided in opinion, the vote in question shall be counted unless both Houses concur in rejecting the same. And the persons so declared elected shall respectively be deemed entitled to exercise the functions of their offices.

SEC. 4. That section 142 of the Revised Statutes of the United States, and all provisions inconsistent with this act are hereby repealed.

Which was disagreed to.

Mr. EATON moved the indefinite postponement of the bill, which was disagreed to—yeas 14, nays 31 (not voting 28), as follow:

YEAS—Messrs. *Bayard*, Carpenter, Conkling, *Cooper*, *Davis*, *Dennis*, *Eaton*, *Goldthwaite*, *Hager*, *Kelly*, *McCreery*, *Merrimon*, *Ransom*, *Stockton*—14.

NAYS—Messrs. Boreman, Boutwell, Chandler, Clayton, Conover, Cragin, Dorsey, Edmunds, Ferry of Michigan, Flanagan, Frelinghuysen, Hamlin, Harvey, Hitchcock, Ingalls, Jones of Nevada, Logan, Mitchell, Morrill of Vermont, Morton, Oglesby, Patterson, Pease, Sargent, Scott, Spencer, Sprague, Stewart, Washburn, West, Windom—31.

The bill was then ordered to be engrossed and read a third time, and passed—yeas 28, nays 20 (not voting 25), as follow:

YEAS—Messrs. Allison, Boreman, Boutwell, Chandler, Clayton, Conover, Cragin, Dorsey, Ferry of Michigan, Flanagan, Frelinghuysen, Hamilton of Texas, Harvey, Hitchcock, Logan, Mitchell, Morrill of Vermont, Morton, Oglesby, Patterson, Pease, Ramsey, Sargent, Sherman, Spencer, Washburn, West, Wright—28.

NAYS—Messrs. *Bayard*, *Bogy*, Carpenter, Conkling, *Cooper*, *Davis*, *Dennis*, *Eaton*, Edmunds, *Goldthwaite*, *Hager*, Jones of Nevada, *Kelly*, *Merrimon*, *Ransom*, *Saulsbury*, Sprague, Stewart, *Stockton*, *Windom*—20.

IN HOUSE.

No action was taken.

Forty-Fourth Congress—First Session.

IN SENATE.

1875, December 8—Mr. MORTON offered the same bill precisely, as is printed above; which was referred to the Committee on Privileges and Elections.

1876, March 3—It was reported without amendment.

March 21—The Senate being as in committee of the whole, Mr. COOPER moved to add to the second section these words:

And if the two Houses do not agree as to which return shall be counted, then that vote shall be counted which the House of Representatives, voting by States in the manner provided by the Constitution when the election devolves upon the House, shall decide to be the true and valid return.

Mr. FRELINGHUYSEN moved to strike out all after the word "agree" in the first line, and substitute the following:

The difference shall be immediately referred to the Chief Justice of the Supreme Court, the presiding officer of the Senate, and the Speaker of the House, whose decision shall be final. If the Chief Justice is absent or unable to attend, the senior associate justice of the Supreme Court present in the Capitol or other place of meeting shall act in his place.

Which was disagreed to—yeas 20, nays 29, as follow:

YEAS—Messrs. Allison, Anthony, Bruce, Burnside, Cameron of Pennsylvania, Conkling, Dawes, Ferry of Michigan, Frelinghuysen, Hamlin, Howe, Logan, McMillan, Morrill of Vermont, Morton, Paddock, Robertson, Sharon, West, Windom—20.

NAYS—Messrs. *Bayard*, *Bogy*, BOOTH, Boutwell, Christiancy, *Cooper*, *Davis*, *Eaton*, *Gold-*

thwaite, *Gordon*, Ingalls, *Johnston*, *Jones* of Florida, *Kelly*, *Kernan*, *Key*, *McCreery*, *McDonald*, *Maxey*, *Merrimon*, Mitchell, *Norwood*, *Randolph*, *Ransom*, *Saulsbury*, *Stevenson*, *Thurman*, *Whyte*, *Withers*—29.

Mr. JOHNSTON moved to strike out all after the word "and" in the first line, and substitute the following:

If the Senate should vote for counting one certificate and the House of Representatives another, the joint meeting of the two Houses shall finally determine which shall be counted by States, the representation from each State, including the Senators therefrom, having one vote, but if the representation of any State shall be equally divided, its vote shall not be counted.

Which was disagreed to—yeas 11, nays 39, as follow:

YEAS—Messrs. Allison, *Bogy*, *Davis*, *Johnston*, *Kelly*, *McCreery*, *Ransom*, Sargent, *Saulsbury*, *Thurman*, *Withers*—11.

NAYS—Messrs. BOOTH, Boutwell, Burnside, Cameron of Pennsylvania, Cameron of Wisconsin, Christiancy, *Cockrell*, Conkling, *Cooper*, Dawes, *Dennis*, *Eaton*, Edmunds, Ferry of Michigan, Frelinghuysen, *Gordon*, Hamilton, Hitchcock, Howe, Ingalls, *Jones* of Florida, *Key*, Logan, *McDonald*, McMillan, *Maxey*, *Merrimon*, Mitchell, Morton, *Norwood*, Oglesby, Paddock, *Randolph*, Robertson, Sharon, West, *Whyte*, Windom, Wright—39.

The amendment of Mr. COOPER was then disagreed to—yeas 13, nays 35, as follow:

YEAS—Messrs. *Bogy*, *Caperton*, *Cooper*, *Davis*, *Gordon*, *Johnston*, *Kelly*, *McCreery*, *McDonald*, *Ransom*, *Saulsbury*, *Thurman*, *Withers*—13.

NAYS—Messrs. Allison, BOOTH, Boutwell, Burnside, Cameron of Pennsylvania, Cameron of Wisconsin, Christiancy, *Cockrell*, Conkling, Dawes, *Dennis*, *Eaton*, Edmunds, Ferry of Michigan, Frelinghuysen, Hamilton, Hitchcock, Howe, Ingalls, *Jones* of Florida, *Key*, Logan, McMillan, *Maxey*, *Merrimon*, Mitchell, Morton, Oglesby, Paddock, Robertson, Sargent, West, *Whyte*, Windom, Wright—35.

Mr. MAXEY moved to amend the bill by adding to section two the words:

But if the two Houses fail to agree as to which of the returns shall be counted, then the President of the Senate shall decide which is the true and valid return, and the same shall then be counted.

Which was disagreed to—yeas 7, nays 38, as follow:

YEAS—Messrs. *Bogy*, Cameron of Pennsylvania, Hamlin, *Maxey*, Robertson, Sargent, *Withers*—7.

NAYS—Messrs. Allison, Anthony, *Bayard*, BOOTH, Boutwell, Burnside, Cameron of Wisconsin, *Caperton*, Christiancy, Conkling, Dawes, *Dennis*, *Eaton*, Edmunds, *English*, Ferry of Michigan, Frelinghuysen, *Goldthwaite*, *Gordon*, Hamilton, Howe, Ingalls, *Johnston*, *Jones* of Florida, Jones of Nevada, Kelly, *Key*, *McCreery*, *McDonald*, *Merrimon*, Mitchell, Morrill of Maine, Morton, *Norwood*, Oglesby, Sharon, *Whyte*, Wright—38.

March 23—Mr. RANDOLPH moved to add these new sections:

SEC. —. To insure each State the count of the electoral vote, except it shall be rejected as provided for in section one of this act, it is declared the duty of each house of Congress to record its vote by ayes and noes upon all questions as to which are the true and valid returns of a State; and it shall be the duty of the presiding officer of each house to immediately forward to the other a true and detailed return of such vote.

SEC. —. Should it then appear that the two houses have failed to agree as to which are the true and valid returns, they shall immediately reassemble, and the President of the Senate shall announce those returns as valid which shall have received a majority of all the votes cast in both houses of Congress, considered as if in joint meeting assembled.

SEC. —. Should it occur that the aggregate vote of both houses be equally divided upon the question, then, and in that event only, the President of the Senate shall give the casting vote.

Which was disagreed to—yeas 12, nays 37, as follow:

YEAS— Messrs. *Bayard*, *Caperton*, *Cooper*, *Davis*, *Gordon*, *Johnston*, *McCreery*, *Randolph*, *Ransom*, *Saulsbury*, *Thurman*, *Withers*—12.

NAYS— Messrs. *Bogy*, Boutwell, Burnside, Cameron of Wisconsin, Christiancy, Conkling, Cragin, Dawes, *Dennis*, Dorsey, *Eaton*, Edmunds, Ferry of Michigan, Frelinghuysen, *Goldthwaite*, Hamlin, Howe, *Jones* of Florida, *Kelly*, *Key*, Logan, *McDonald*, McMillan, *Merrimon*, Mitchell, Morrill of Maine, Morton, Oglesby, Paddock, Patterson, Sargent, Spencer, Wadleigh, West, *Whyte*, Windom, Wright—37.

March 24—Mr. BAYARD moved to add to section two these words:

And if the two houses do not agree as to which return shall be counted, then that vote shall be counted which the House of Representatives, voting by States in the manner provided by the Constitution when the election devolves upon the House, shall decide to be the true and valid return.

Which was disagreed to—yeas 18, nays 34, as follow:

YEAS—Messrs. *Bayard*, *Bogy*, *Caperton*, *Cooper*, *Davis*, *Goldthwaite*, *Johnston*, *Kelly*, *Key*, *McCreery*, *McDonald*, *Maxey*, *Randolph*, *Ransom*, *Saulsbury*, *Thurman*, *Wallace*, *Withers*—18.

NAYS—Messrs. Allison, Anthony, BOOTH, Burnside, Cameron of Pennsylvania, Cameron of Wisconsin, Christiancy, Conkling, Dawes, *Dennis*, Dorsey, *Eaton*, Edmunds, *English*, Ferry of Michigan, Frelinghuysen, Hamilton, Hamlin, Howe, Jones of Nevada, Logan, McMillan, *Merrimon*, Mitchell, Morrill of Maine, Morton, Oglesby, Paddock, Patterson, Sargent, Sherman, *Whyte*, Windom, Wright—34.

Mr. WRIGHT moved to add, in section two, after the word "return," where it first occurs in the last clause of the section, the words "and that only;" which was agreed to.

Other amendments by Mr. BURNSIDE and Mr. WHYTE were offered, and rejected, without a record of yeas and nays, and they are not inserted.

The bill, as amended on motion of Mr. WRIGHT, was than passed—yeas 32, nays 26, as follow:

YEAS—Messrs. Allison, Anthony, BOOTH,

Burnside, Cameron of Pennsylvania, Cameron of Wisconsin, Christiancy, Dawes, Dorsey, Ferry, Frelinghuysen, Hamilton, Hamlin, Hitchcock, Ingalls, Jones of Nevada, *Key*, Logan, McMillan, *Merrimon*, Mitchell, Morrill of Maine, Morton, Oglesby, Paddock, Patterson, Sargent, Sherman, Spencer, *Thurman*, Windom, Wright—32.

NAYS—Messrs. *Bayard*, *Bogy*, *Caperton*, *Cockrell*, Conkling, *Cooper*, *Davis*, *Dennis*, *Eaton*, Edmunds, *English*, *Goldthwaite*, Howe, *Johnston*, *Jones* of Florida, *Kelly*, *McCreery*, *McDonald*, *Maxey*, *Randolph*, *Ransom*, *Saulsbury*, *Stevenson*, *Wallace*, *Whyte*, *Withers*—26.

MR. THURMAN moved to reconsider this vote; which was postponed.

April 19—The motion to reconsider was agreed to—yeas 31, nays 23, as follow:

YEAS—Messrs. *Bayard*, *Bogy*, *Caperton*, *Cockrell*, Conkling, *Cooper*, *Davis*, Dawes, *Dennis*, *Eaton*, Edmunds, *English*, *Goldthwaite*, *Gordon*, Hamilton, Howe, *Kelly*, *Kernan*, *Key*, *McCreery*, *Maxey*, *Merrimon*, *Norwood*, Paddock, *Randolph*, *Ransom*, *Saulsbury*, *Stevenson*, *Thurman*, *Wallace*, *Withers*—31.

NAYS—Messrs. Anthony, BOOTH, Boutwell, Burnside, Cameron of Pennsylvania, Cameron of Wisconsin, Clayton, Cragin, Ferry, Frelinghuysen, Hamlin, Harvey, Ingalls, Jones of Nevada, Logan, McMillan, Morrill of Maine, Morrill of Vermont, Morton, Oglesby, Robertson, Sargent, Windom—23.

Nothing further was done to the date of closing this page.

The Joint Rules.

IN SENATE.

1876, January 20—This resolution was adopted:

Resolved by the Senate (*the House of Representatives concurring*), That the joint rules of the Senate and House of Representatives in force at the close of the last session of Congress, excepting the twenty-second joint rule, be, and the same are hereby, adopted as the joint rules of the two houses for the present session.

[The twenty-second rule provides the mode for counting and declaring the electoral vote for PRESIDENT and VICE-PRESIDENT.]

The Geneva Award.

1876, July 5—The House came to a vote on the bill (H. R. 2685) "for the distribution of the unappropriated moneys of the Geneva award."

The important sections are these:

Section one directs the Commissioners to receive and examine claims mentioned below, and to enter judgment for the amounts allowed therefor in two classes.

Section two provides that the first class shall be for claims directly resulting from damage done on the high seas by Confederate cruisers during the late rebellion, including vessels and cargoes attacked or taken on the high seas or pursued therefrom, although destroyed within four miles of the shore, except as provided for in section eleven of said chapter four hundred and fifty-nine. The second class shall be for claims for the payment of premiums for war-risks, whether paid to corporations, agents, or individuals, after the sailing of any Confederate cruiser.

SEC. 3. That in examining claims in the second class, it shall be the duty of the court to deduct any sum in any way received by or repaid to the claimant, diminishing the amount paid for any such premium, so that the actual loss of the claimant only shall be allowed.

SEC. 5. That judgments entered in the first class shall be paid before judgments of the second class are paid. If the sum of money so unappropriated shall be insufficient to pay the judgments of the first class, they shall be paid according to the proportions which they severally bear to the whole amount of such unappropriated sum. If such sum shall be sufficient to pay the judgments of the first class, and not sufficient to pay the judgments of the second class, the latter judgments shall be paid according to the proportions which they severally bear to the residue of such unappropriated sum.

Mr. KNOTT moved this substitute for the bill:

Be it enacted, &c., That so much of the twelfth section of the said act as provides that "no claim shall be admissable or allowed by the court by or in behalf of any insurance company or insurer, either in its or his own right, or as assignee or otherwise in the right of a person or party insured, unless such claimant shall show to the satisfaction of said court that during the late rebellion the sum of its or his losses in respect to its or his war risks exceeded the sum of its or his premiums or other gains upon or in respect to such war risks; and in case of any such allowance, the same shall not be greater than such excess of loss," be, and the same is hereby repealed.

SEC 2. That any claimant excluded by the provision hereby repealed shall have the like period of time within which to present, file, and prove its or his claim after the passage of this amendment as he could have had after the passage of the said act if not so excluded. And the time of the duration of the court created by the said act, and its powers, are hereby extended for a period sufficient to enable it to hear and dispose of such additional claims and the claims already referred to it; which period shall not exceed one year from the expiration of the time for filing claims under this section.

Mr. WILLIAM LAWRENCE moved this substitute for the above:

That all bonds of the United States in which the money awarded to the United States by the tribunal of arbitration at Geneva has been invested, after paying all charges thereon and judgments as determined by the court of commissioners of Alabama claims under existing law, shall be canceled by the Secretary of State, and the Secretary of the Treasury; and all money, if any, arising from said award or from bonds in which it has been invested, shall be covered into the Treasury.

Which was disagreed to—yeas 59, nays 109 (not voting 121). The YEAS were Messrs. C. H. Adams, *Ainsworth*, ANDERSON, *Atkins*, *Bagby*, G. A. Bagley, *S. N. Bell*, *Blackburn*, *Bland*, *Buckner*, H. C. Burchard, *S. D. Burchard*, *Cabell*, *J. H. Caldwell*, *W. P. Caldwell*, Cannon, Cason, *J. B. Clark, jr.*, *Cowan*, *Culberson*, *Dibrell*, *Felton*, *Goodin*, *Gunter*, *H. R. Harris*, *C. H. Harrison*, *Hartzell*, *Hatcher*, *Haymond*, *Holman*, *F.*

Landers, *Lane*, W. Lawrence, *B. B. Lewis*, Magoon, *McFarland*, *Mills*, *Money*, *Morrison*, *New*, *J. Phelps*, *J. F. Philips*, *Poppleton*, *Reagan*, S. Ross, A. H. Smith, *Southard*, *Sparks*, *Springer*, *Stevenson*, *Stone*, *Tarbox*, *Terry*, Thornburgh, Van Vorhes, *Walling*, *E. Wells*, *Wigginton*, G. Willard.

The proposed substitute of Mr. KNOTT was then disagreed to—yeas 35, nays 151 (not voting 103).

The YEAS were Messrs. *Ashe*, *Atkins*, *Blackburn*, *Blount*, *Boone*, *Buckner*, *J. B. Clarke*, *Clymer*, *Cox*, *Joseph J. Davis*, *Douglas*, Garfield, *Hancock*, *Hardenbergh*, Hathorn, Hubbell, *T. L. Jones*, *Kehr*, *Knott*, *Lamar*, Leavenworth, *Milliken*, *Mills*, *Money*, Pierce, T. C. Platt, *Reagan*, *W. M. Robbins*, *Scales*, *Slemons*, *Spencer*, *R. B. Vance*, Waldron, J. W. Wallace, *Willis*—35.

On a motion to table the bill, the yeas were 96, nays 113 (not voting 80).

The bill then passed—yeas 107, nays 96 (not voting 86), as follow:

YEAS—Messrs. *Bagby*, *J. H. Bagley, jr.*, J. H. Baker, *Banning*, *S. N. Bell*, Bradley, W. R. Brown, H. C. Burchard, *S. D. Burchard*, Burleigh, CAMPBELL, Cason, Caswell, *Caulfield*, Conger, *Cowan*, Crapo, Crounse, Dobbins, Dunnell, Eames, *Ellis*, Evans, *Finley*, Fort, C. Foster, E. Hale, Haralson, B. W. Harris, *C. H. Harrison*, *Haymond*, Hendee, *Hereford*, *A. S. Hewitt*, *Hopkins*, Hunter, *Hunton*, *Jenks*, *F. Jones*, Joyce, Kasson, Kelley, Ketchum, Kimball, Lapham, *Levy*, *Lord*, *Luttrell*, *Maish*, MacDougall, McCrary, J. W. McDill, *Meade*, Miller, *Morgan*, Norton, *O'Brien*, Oliver, O'Neill, *Payne*, *J. Phelps*, W. A. Phillips, *Piper*, Plaisted, *Poppleton*, A. POTTER, *Powell*, Pratt, *Randall*, *D. Rea*, *J. Reilly*, *J. B. Reilly*, *A. V. Rice*, *Riddle*, *J. Robbins*, M. S. Robinson, S. Ross, Rusk, Sampson, *Schleicher*, Seelye, Sinnickson, R. Smalls, Strait, *Stenger*, *Stevenson*, Stowell, *C. P. Thompson*, M. I. Townsend, W. Townsend, Tufts, Van Vorhes, Wait, *G. C. Walker*, A. S. Wallace, J. W. Wallace, *Warren*, G. W. Wells, J. D. White, Whiting, *Wigginton*, *Wike*, *A. S. Williams*, *J. Williams*, W. B. Williams, J. Wilson, *Yeates*—107.

NAYS—Messrs. C. H. Adams, *Ainsworth*, ANDERSON, *Ashe*, *Atkins*, G. A. Bagley, W. H. Baker, *Blackburn*, *Bland*, *Blount*, *Boone*, *Bradford*, *Buckner*, *Cabell*, *J. H. Caldwell*, *W. P. Caldwell*, *Candler*, Cannon, *J. B. Clarke*, *J. B. Clark, jr.*, *Clymer*, *Cochrane*, *Cook*, *Culberson*, Cutler, Davy, *Dibrell*, *Douglas*, *Durand*, *Faulkner*, *Felton*, *Forney*, *Fuller*, Garfield, *Gause*, *Gibson*, *Goodin*, *Gunter*, *Hancock*, *Hardenbergh*, *H. R. Harris*, *Hartridge*, *Hartzell*, *Hatcher*, Hathorn, Henderson, *Hill*, *Holman*, *Hooker*, Hubbell, *T. L. Jones*, *Kehr*, *Knott*, *Lamar*, *F. Landers*, W. Lawrence, Leavenworth, *B. B. Lewis*, *L. A. Mackey*, *McFarland*, *Milliken*, *Mills*, *Money*, *Morrison*, *New*, Packer, *J. F. Philips*, Pierce, T. C. Platt, *Reagan*, *W. M. Robbins*, *M. Ross*, *Scales*, *Singleton*, *Slemons*, A. H. Smith, *W. E. Smith*, *Southard*, *Sparks*, *Spencer*, *Springer*, *Stone*, *Tarbox*, *Terry*, Thornburgh, *J. L. Vance*, *R. B. Vance*, *Waddell*, Waldron, *Walling*, *E. Wells*, G. Willard, *J. N. Williams*, *Willis*, *B. Wilson*, *C. Young*—96.

IN SENATE.

No action was taken, up to date of closing this page.

[For previous act on this subject, see McPherson's Hand-Book of Politics for 1874, page 214.]

The Bill to promote the Efficiency of the Army, Provide for its Gradual Reduction, &c.

IN HOUSE.

1876, June 1—The House was brought to final action on the bill.

[It reduces the cavalry regiments from ten to eight, infantry from 25 to 20, abolishes the regimental organization of the artillery, consolidates into one the Quartermaster's and Subsistence Departments, reorganizes the Medical Department, limits second lieutenant appointments to graduates of West Point, and contains many provisions of minor importance. It also repeals sections eleven hundred and four and eleven hundred and eight of the Revised Statutes, providing that the enlisted men of two regiments of cavalry, and of two regiments of infantry, shall be colored men. It also repeals sections eleven hundred and thirteen and twelve hundred and eighteen of the Revised Statutes. The former refers to Military Academy cadets; the latter is as follows:

No person who has served in any capacity in the military, naval, or civil service of the so-called Confederate States, or of either of the States in insurrection during the late rebellion, shall be appointed to any position in the Army of the United States.]

Pending the bill,

Mr. R. SMALLS asked to have this amendment considered pending:

Insert at line 19, section 1, after the word "service," the following:

Provided further, That hereafter in the enlistment of men in the Army, or the merging of enlisted men into other organizations, no distinction whatever shall be made on account of race or color.

Objection was made.

Mr. HURLBUT, with the consent of the Military Committee, offered this substitute for the bill:

Be it enacted &c., That the President of the United States be requested and directed to appoint a commission of seven officers of the Army of distinguished service and knowledge, who shall report through the President, as soon as practicable, their opinions upon the best method of reorganizing the Army of the United States, and especially upon the best method of organizing the staff departments with a view to economy and efficiency.

Which was disagreed to—yeas 88, nays 113 (not voting 87).

The bill then passed—yeas 123, nays 82 (not voting 83), as follow:

YEAS—Messrs. *Ainsworth*, ANDERSON, *Ashe*, *Atkins*, *J. H. Bagley, jr.*, *Banning*, *Beebe*, *Bland*, *Blount*, *Boone*, *Bradford*, *Bright*, *J. Y. Brown*, *Buckner*, *Cabell*, *J. H. Caldwell*, *W. P. Caldwell*, *Candler*, *Cate*, *Caulfield*, *Chapin*, *J. B. Clarke*, *J. B. Clark, jr.*, *Clymer*, *Cochrane*,

Collins, Cutler, DeBolt, Dibrell, Douglas, Durand, Durham, Eden, Ellis, Ely, Felton, Finley, Forney, Franklin, Fuller, Gause, Glover, Goode, Gunter, A. H. Hamilton, R. Hamilton, Hardenbergh, C. H. Harrison, Hartridge, Hartzell, Hatcher, Haymond, Henkle, Hereford, G. W. Hewitt, Hill, Holman, House, Hunton, Hurd, Jenks, F. Jones, T. L. Jones, Lamar, F. Landers, Le Moyne, B. B. Lewis, Lord, Lynde, McFarland, McMahon, Metcalfe, Milliken, Money, Morrison, Mutchler, Neal, O'Brien, Odell, E. Y. Parsons, Payne, J. F. Philips, Piper, Poppleton, A. POTTER, *Powell, Randall, D. Rea, J. Reilly, A. V. Rice, Riddle, J. Robbins, M. Ross, Savage, M. Sayler, Scales, Sheakley, Singleton, Slemons, W. E. Smith, Southard, Springer, Stenger, Tarbox, Teese, Terry, P. F. Thomas, C. P. Thompson, Turney, R. B. Vance, Walling, Ward, E. Wells, Whitthorne, Wigginton, Wike, J. Williams, J. D. Williams, J. N. Williams, Willis, F. Wood, Yeates, C. Young*—123.

NAYS—Messrs. C. H. Adams, G. A. Bagley, J. H. Baker, W. H. Baker, Ballou, BANKS, Blaine, Blair, Bradley, W. R. Brown, H. C. Burchard, Caswell, Crapo, Crounse, *Culberson*, Danford, Davy, Denison, Dobbins, Dunnell, Eames, Frye, Garfield, Haralson, B. W. Harris, Hathorn, Hays, Hendee, Henderson, Hunter, Hurlbut, Joyce, Kasson, *Kehr*, Kelley, Ketchum, Kimball, King, W. Lawrence, Leavenworth, *Levy*, Lynch, E. W. M. Mackey, Magoon, McDougall, McCrary, J. W. McDill, Miller, *Mills*, Monroe, *Morgan*, Nash, Norton, O'Neill, Packer, Page, W. A. Phillips, Pierce, Plaisted, T. C. Platt, Pratt, M. S. Robinson, Rusk, Sampson, *Schleicher*, Seelye, Sinnickson, R. Smalls, *Spencer, Throckmorton*, M. I. Townsend, W. Townsend, Tufts, Waldron, A. S. Wallace, G. W. Wells, J. D. White, Whiting, G. Willard, A. Williams, C. G. Williams, W. B. Williams, Woodworth—82.

The bill was not acted upon in the SENATE.

Troops in the States.

IN HOUSE.

1876, July 19—Pending the joint resolution (H. R. 96) to provide for the protection of the Texas frontier, and the question being on concurring in the following proviso inserted in Committee of the Whole:

Provided, That no part of the troops provided for by this resolution shall be taken from any State or service where troops may now or hereafter be stationed, if, in the judgment of the President, the public service requires the continuation of troops in such localities.

The yeas were 80, nays 98 (not voting 108), as follow:

YEAS—Messrs. *Ainsworth*, ANDERSON, J. H. Baker, W. H. Baker, Ballou, BANKS, *S. N. Bell*, Blair, Bradley, W. R. Brown, H. C. Burchard, Burleigh, Cannon, Conger, Darrall, Davy, Dobbins, Dunnell, *Durand*, Eames, Evans, Foster, Garfield, E. Hale, *Hancock, Hardenbergh*, Hendee, Hoge, *Holman*, Hoskins, Hunter, Kasson, Kelley, Kimball, W. Lawrence, Leavenworth, *Le Moyne*, Magoon, MacDougall, J. W. McDill, Miller, Monroe, *Morgan*, Nash, Norton, Oliver, O'Neill, Packer, Page, *Payne*, W. A. Phillips, Plaisted, T. C. Platt, A. POTTER, Pratt, Rainey, *J. Reilly, J. B. Reilly*, Rusk, Sampson, *Savage*, Sinnickson, R. Smalls, A. H. Smith, *Stevenson, Tarbox*, Thornburgh, M. I. Townsend, W. Townsend, Tufts, Van Vorhes, Wait, *C. C. B. Walker*, A. S. Wallace, Willard, *A. S. Williams*, C. G. Williams, *J. D. Williams*, W. B. Williams, *Willis*—80.

NAYS—Messrs. *Ashe, Atkins, Bagby, J. H. Bagley, jr., Banning, Blackburn, Bland, Boone, Bradford, Bright, J. Y. Brown, Buckner, S. D. Burchard, Cabell, J. H. Caldwell, W. P. Caldwell, Candler, Cate, Caulfield, J. B. Clarke, Clymer, Cochrane, Collins, Cook, Cox, Culberson, Cutler, Joseph J. Davis, DeBolt, Dibrell, Douglas, Eden, Felton, Finley, Forney*, Fort, *Gibson, Glover, Goode, Gunter, A. H. Hamilton, J. T. Harris, Hartridge, Hartzell, Hatcher, Henkle, Hereford, A. S. Hewitt, Hill, House, T. L. Jones, Kehr, Lamar, F. Landers, Lane, Levy, B. B. Lewis, Luttrell, L. A. Mackey, Maish, McFarland, Metcalfe, Milliken, Mills, Mutchler, New, J. Phelps, Piper, Randall, Reagan, A. V. Rice, Riddle, W. M. Robbins, M. Ross, Scales, Schleicher, Singleton, W. E. Smith, Southard, Spencer, Springer, Stone, Terry, C. P. Thompson, P. F. Thomas, Throckmorton, Tucker, Turney, J. L. Vance. R. B. Vance, Waddell, Warren, E. Wells, Whitehouse, Wigginton, J. Williams, J. N. Williams, C. Young*—98.

XIX.

MISCELLANEOUS.

The text of the "Wheeler Adjustment" of Affairs in Louisiana.*

NEW ORLEANS, *March*, 1875.

Whereas, It is desirable to adjust the difficulties growing out of the general election in this State, in 1872, the action of the Returning Board in declaring and promulgating the results of the general election, in the month of November last, and the organization of the House of Representatives, on the 4th day of January last, such adjustment being deemed necessary to the re-establishment of peace and order in this State.

Now, therefore, the undersigned members of the Conservative party, claiming to have been elected members of the House of Representatives, and that their certificates of election have been illegally withheld by the Returning Board, hereby severally agree to submit their claims to seats in the House of Representatives to the award and arbitrament of George F. Hoar, Wil-

* Referred to on page 40.

liam A. Wheeler, William P. Frye, Charles Foster, William Walter Phelps, Clarkson N. Potter, and Samuel S Marshall, who are hereby authorized to examine and determine the same upon the equities of the several cases; and when such awards shall be made, we hereby severally agree to abide by the same:

And such of us as may become members of the House of Representatives, under this arrangement, hereby severally agree to sustain by our influence and votes the joint resolution hereinafter set forth.

[Here follow the signatures of the Democrats who claimed that their certificates of election as members of the House of Representatives had been illegally withheld by the Returning Board.]

And the undersigned claiming to have been elected Senators from the Eighth and Twenty-Second Senatorial Districts, hereby agree to submit their claims to the foregoing award and arbitrament, and in all respects to abide the results of the same.

[Here follow the signatures of the Democrats, who made a like claim as to seats in the Senate.]

And the undersigned, holding certificates of election from the Returning Board, hereby severally agree that upon the coming in of the award of the foregoing arbitrators they will, when the same shall have been ratified by the report of the Committee on Elections and Qualifications of the body in session at the State House claiming to be the House of Representatives, attend the sitting of the said House for the purpose of adopting said report, and if said report shall be adopted, and the members embraced in the foregoing report shall be seated, then the undersigned severally agree that immediately upon the adoption of said report they will vote for the following joint resolution:

[Here follow the signatures of the Democratic members of the House of Representatives in relation to whose seats there was no controversy.]

JOINT RESOLUTION.

Resolved, by the General Assembly of the State of Louisiana, That said Assembly, without approving the same, will not disturb the present State Government claiming to have been elected in 1872, known as the Kellogg Government, or seek to impeach the Governor for any past official acts, and that henceforth it will accord to said Governor all necessary and legitimate support in maintaining the laws and advancing the peace and prosperity of the people of this State; and that the House of Representatives, as to its members, as constituted under the award of George F. Hoar, W. A. Wheeler, W. P. Frye, Charles Foster, Samuel S. Marshall, Clarkson N. Potter and William Walter Phelps, shall remain without change except by resignation or death of members until a new general election, and that the Senate, as now organized, shall also remain unchanged except so far as that body shall make changes on contests.

TEXT OF THE AWARD.

NEW YORK, *March* 13, 1875.

The undersigned having been requested to examine the claims of the persons hereinafter named to seats in the Senate and House of Representatives of the State of Louisiana, and having examined the returns and the evidence relating to such claims, are of opinion, and do hereby find, award and determine, that F. S. Goode is entitled to a seat in the Senate from the Twenty-second Senatorial District; and that J. B. Elam is not entitled to a seat in the Senate from the Eighth Senatorial District; and that the following named persons are entitled to seats in the House of Representatives from the following named parishes respectively: From the Parish of Assumption, R. R. Beasely, E. F. X. Dugas; from the Parish of Bienville, James Brice; from the Parish of De Soto, J. S. Scales, Charles Schuler; from the Parish of Jackson, E. Kidd; from the Parish of Rapides, James Jeffries, R. C. Luckett, G. W. Stafford; from the Parish of Terrebone, Edward McCollum, W. H. Keyes; from the Parish of Winn, George A. Kelley. And that the following named persons are not entitled to seats which they claim from the following named parishes respectively, but that the persons now holding seats from said parishes are entitled to retain the seats now held by them; from the Parish of Avoyelles, J. O. Quinn; from the Parish of Iberie, W. F. Schwing; from the Parish of Caddo, A. D. Land, T. R. Vaughan, J. J. Horan. We are of opinion that no person is entitled to a seat from the Parish of Grant.

In regard to most of the cases, the undersigned are unanimous; as to the others the decision is that of a majority.

GEORGE F. HOAR,
W. A. WHEELER,
W. P. FRYE,
CHARLES FOSTER,
CLARKSON N. POTTER,
WILLIAM WALTER PHELPS,
SAMUEL S. MARSHALL.

Illinois.

In McPherson's Hand-Book of Politics for 1874, pp. 200–202, the Railroad Act of May 2, 1873, is given in full. It remains unchanged, except that section 8 thereof has been stricken out, and this substituted for it, by act of March 26, 1874, in force July 1, 1874:

SECTION 8.

Schedules.—The Railroad and Warehouse Commissioners are hereby directed to make, for each of the railroad corporations doing business in this State, as soon as practicable, a schedule of reasonable maximum rates of charges for the transportation of passengers and freights and cars on each of said railroads; and said schedule shall, in all suits brought against any such railroad corporations, wherein is in any way involved the charges of any such railroad corporation for the transportation of any passenger or freight or cars, or unjust discrimination in relation thereto, be deemed and taken in all courts of this State as *prima facie* evidence that the rates therein fixed are reasonable maximum rates of charges for the transportation of passengers and freights and cars upon the railroads for which said schedules may have been respectively prepared.

Said commissioners shall from time to time, and as often as circumstances may require, change and revise said schedules.

When any schedule shall have been made or revised, as aforesaid, it shall be the duty of said commissioners to cause publication thereof to be made for three successive weeks, in some public newspaper published in the city of Springfield, in this State.

All such schedules, heretofore or hereafter made, purporting to be printed and published as aforesaid, shall be received and held in all such suits as *prima facie*. The schedules of said commissioners, without further proof than the production of the schedule desired to be used as evidence, with a certificate of the railroad and warehouse commissioners that the same is a true copy of a schedule prepared by them for the railroad company or corporation therein named, and that the same has been published as required by law, stating the name of the paper in which the same was published, together with the date of such publication.

Wisconsin.

On pages 202–205, of McPherson's Hand-Book of Politics for 1874, will be found in full a copy of the Railroad Law of 1874, popularly known as the "Potter Law."

At the late session of the Legislature a new act was passed, popularly known as the "Vance Law," which repealed ten of the nineteen sections of the "Potter Act," and substituted others in their stead. A comparison of the two acts will show the points of difference. The new act passed the SENATE—yeas 20, nays 7; the HOUSE—yeas 56, nays 30; and was approved by Governor LUDDINGTON, February 24, 1876.

Below is a digest of the various Railroad Laws (of 1874, 1875 and 1876), now in force in that State, as prepared and printed by the Railroad Commissioner:

SECTION 1. Within ten days after the passage and publication of this act, the governor, by and with the consent of the senate, shall appoint a railroad commissioner, who shall hold his office for the term of two years from the fifteenth day of February, and until his successor is appointed and qualified. Every two years thereafter, the governor, by and with the advice and consent of the senate, shall appoint a railroad commissioner, who shall hold his office for the term of two years, and until his successor shall be appointed and qualified. And the nomination of railroad commissioner shall hereafter be sent to the senate by the governor during the month of January, immediately preceding the beginning of such commissioner's term of office. The governor shall have power to remove such commissioner, and appoint another to fill the vacancy, at any time in his discretion. No person owning any bonds, stock or property in any railroad company, or who is in the employment of, or in any way or manner pecuniarily interested in any railroad corporation, shall be so appointed.

SEC. 2. The railroad commissioner shall inquire into any neglect or violation of the laws of this State by any railroad corporation doing business therein, or by the officers, agents, or employees thereof, and shall also, from time to time, carefully examine and inspect the condition of each railroad in the State, and of its equipment, and the manner of its conduct and management with relation to the public safety and convenience. He shall also examine and ascertain the pecuniary condition and the manner of financial management of each and every railroad corporation doing business in this State.

SEC. 3. To enable said commissioner to make the report and return required by section twelve (12), of the act of which this is amendatory, the president or managing officer of each railroad corporation in the State, shall annually make to the railroad commissioner, in the month of October, such returns and in the form he may prescribe, as will afford the information required for his said official report. Such returns shall be verified by the oath of the officer making them, and any railroad corporation whose return shall not be made, as herein prescribed, within the month of October, shall be liable to a penalty of one hundred dollars ($100) for each and every day after the thirty-first day of October that such return shall be wilfully delayed or refused.

SEC. 4. Said railroad commissioner shall, during the month of January in each year, ascertain and make return to the State Treasurer, as hereinafter provided. 1st. The actual cost of each railroad in this State up to and including the 31st day of the next preceding December, and if such railroad shall be partly in and partly out of this State, then the actual cost of so much thereof as is in this State. 2d. The total gross receipts resulting from the operation of every such railroad during the next preceding year ending on the 31st day of December, or that part of the same which is in this State. 3d. The total net earnings resulting from the operation of any such railroad during the next preceding year, ending on the 31st day of December, or that part of the same which is in this State. 4th. The total interest-bearing indebtedness of the company owning or operating such railroad, and the amount of interest paid by such company during the next preceding year ending on the 31st day of December, and if any part of such indebtedness has been incurred in consequence of the construction, maintenance, repair, removal, or operation of any part of such railroad which is not in this State, or for equipment for such part, such railroad commissioner shall ascertain and determine in such manner as he shall think just and equitable how much of its indebtedness is justly chargeable to that part of said railroad that is in this State, and how much interest shall have been paid by such company during such year ending on the 31st day of the next preceding December, or [on] that part of such indebtedness which is justly chargeable to that part of said railroad that is in this State. The commissioner shall prescribe the form and manner in which all reports required from railroad companies under the provisions of this act shall be made, aud suitable blanks for that purpose, as by said commissioner directed, shall be provided by the Secretary of State. The record of said commissioner shall at all times be open to inspection by the Governor, Secretary of State, Attorney-General, and Legislature.

SEC. 5. Said railroad commissioner shall have power to administer oaths or affirmations, to send for persons or papers under such regulations as he may prescribe, and shall at any and all times have access to any and all books and papers in any railroad office, kept for and used in any railroad office, by any railroad company in this State.

SEC. 6. Said railroad commissioner, in making any examination as contemplated in this act, for the purpose of obtaining information pursuant to this act, shall have power to issue subpœnas for the attendance of witnesses by such rules as he may prescribe. In case any person shall willfully fail or refuse to obey such subpœna, it shall be the duty of the Circuit Court of any county, upon the application of the said commissioner, to issue an attachment for such witness and compel such witness to attend before the commissioner and give his testimony upon such matters as shall be lawfully required by such commissioner, and said court shall have power to punish for contempt as in other cases of refusal to obey the process and order of such Court.

SEC. 7. Any person who shall willfully neglect or refuse to obey the process of subpœna issued by said commissioner, and appear and testify as therein required, shall be deemed guilty of a misdemeanor, and shall be liable to arraignment and trial in any Court of competent jurisdiction, and on conviction thereof shall be punished for such offense by fine not less than fifty dollars nor more than five hundred dollars, or by imprisonment of not more than thirty days, or both, in the discretion of the Court before which such conviction shall be had.

SEC. 8. No railroad corporation shall charge, demand, or receive from any person, company, or corporation for the transportation of persons or property, a greater sum than it shall at the same time charge, demand, or receive from any other person or corporation for a like service from the same place; and no railroad corporation shall charge or receive a larger sum per car-load, from one person, than any other, shipping from the same place; but this last provision shall not apply to shipments from connecting points.

SEC. 9. No railroad corporation shall charge, demand, or receive from any person, company, or corporation, an unreasonable price for the transportation of persons or property, or for the handling or storing of any freight, or for the use of its cars, or for any privilege or service afforded by it in the transaction of its business as a railroad corporation.

SEC. 10. It shall be the duty of any railroad corporation, when within their power so to do, and upon reasonable notice, to furnish suitable cars to any and all persons who may apply therefor, for the transportation of any and all usual kinds of freight, and to receive and transport such freight with all reasonable dispatch, and to provide and keep suitable facilities for the receiving and handling the same at any depot on the line of its road.

SEC. 11. Any railroad corporation who shall violate any of the provisions of this act as to extortion or unjust discrimination, or the provisions hereof establishing rates, shall forfeit for each and every offense to the company, person, or corporation aggrieved thereby, three times the actual damage sustained, together with the costs of suit, to be recovered in a civil action therefor, and all prosecutions shall be made at the expense of the State; and it shall be the duty of said railroad commissioner, on receiving complaint in writing from any citizen of this State, stating that any railroad corporation has violated any of the provisions of this act, and specifying the acts complained of, to investigate such alleged violation, and if on such examination he shall find such complaint well founded, he may, in his discretion, report the facts to the attorney-general, and thereupon it shall be the duty of the attorney-general to prosecute said complaint at the expense of the State for the benefit of the party aggrieved.

SEC. 12. No railroad corporation shall consolidate the stock, property, or franchise of such corporation with, or lease or purchase the works or franchises of, or in any way control any other railroad corporation owing or having under its control a parallel or competing line; nor shall any officer of such railroad corporation act as the officer of any other railroad corporation, owning or having the control of parallel or competing lines, and the question whether such railroads are parallel or competing lines shall, when demanded by the complainant, be decided by a jury as in other civil issues; *provided*, that the provisions of this section shall not apply to any contracts now existing, where one corporation has become responsible for the liabilities of another, either by advances heretofore made or by the guarantee of bonds previous to the passage of this act; nor shall it apply to any railroad corporation which, prior to the passage of this act, shall have been authorized to purchase or hold stock in any other railroad corporation.

SEC. 13. No president, director, officer, agent or employee of any railroad or transportation company, shall be interested directly or indirectly in the furnishing of material or supplies to such company, or in the business of transportation as a common carrier of freights or passengers, over the lines owned, leased, controlled, or operated by such company.

SEC. 14. In the construction of this act, the phrase railroad shall be construed to include all railroads and railways operated by steam, and whether operated by the corporation owning them, or by other corporations, or otherwise. The phrase railroad corporation shall be construed to mean the corporation which constructs, maintains, or operates a railroad operated by steam power.

SEC. 15. The Chicago, Milwaukee and St. Paul Railway Company shall file with the railroad commissioner, before the day when this act shall take effect, the regular published schedule of their tariff rates for the transportation of persons and property, which was in force on their railroads on the 15th day of June, A. D. 1872, duly verified by the oath of the general freight agent of said company thereto attached, and that company and the Western Union Railroad Company, and the Chicago and Northwestern Railway Company, shall not demand, collect, or receive a greater compensation for the transportation of persons and property than is fixed in such schedule for corresponding distances. This provision shall also apply to such lines of railroads as have been built and put into operation by either of said companies and operated under lease or otherwise, since the date above mentioned; *provided*, that the Chicago, Milwaukee and St. Paul Railway Company, and the Western Union Railroad Company, and the Chicago and Northwestern Railway Company, shall sell at all ticket stations, on their respective lines, within this State, tickets for five hundred miles, which shall be transferable; also round-trip tickets, good for first-class passengers to and from any station within this State, on their respective lines of road, at a uniform rate of three cents per mile; *and provided further*, that no railroad corporation shall be compelled to accept less than five cents for the transportation of any passenger between any points.

SEC. 16. All the powers, duties and privileges conferred on the board of railroad commissioners by the acts to which this act is amendatory, and not herein repealed, are hereby conferred on the railroad commissioner to be appointed under the provisions of this act.

SEC. 17. The commissioner shall have the right of passing, in the performance of his duties concerning railroads, on all railways and railway trains in this State, free of charge.

SEC. 18. Nothing contained in this act shall be taken as in any manner abridging or controlling the rates for freight charged by any railroad company in this State for carrying freight which comes from beyond the boundaries of the State, and to be carried across or through the State, but said railroad company shall possess the same power and right to charge such rates for carrying such freight as they possessed before the passage of this act.

SEC. 19. All those railroad companies whose lines of road are now incomplete or are in process of construction, and to aid in the building of which the general government has donated grants of land, and which are not exempted from taxation on said lands for the next five years, are hereby exempted from the payment of the license fees required by law for said five years.

SEC. 20. Before entering upon the duties of his office, said commissioner shall make and subscribe and file with the secretary of state an affidavit in the following form: "I do solemnly swear (or affirm) that I will support the constitution of the United States and the constitution of the State of Wisconsin, and that I will faithfully discharge the duties of railway commissioner according to the best of my ability; that I am not a stockholder, officer, or employee of any railroad or freight company, or in any way interested therein;" and shall enter into bonds, with security to be approved by the governor, in the sum of twenty thousand dollars, conditioned for the faithful performance of his duty as such commissioner.

SEC. 21. The commissioner appointed under the provisions of this act shall receive for his services the sum of three thousand dollars per annum, payable monthly, at the end of each month, and three dollars per day for traveling expenses, for each and every day actually traveled in the performance of the duties hereby required. He shall be furnished with all office-furniture and stationery, and necessary books and maps, at the expense of the State; and the said commissioner is hereby authorized and empowered to employ a clerk at an annual salary of twelve hundred dollars, payable at the end of each month. The office of said commissioner shall be kept at Madison, and all sums of money authorized to be paid by this act, out of the state treasury, shall be paid only on the order of the governor; *provided*, that the total sums of money to be expended by said commissioner for office-rent, furniture, and stationery, shall in no case exceed the total sum of eight hundred dollars per annum.

SEC. 22. Sections one, two, three, four, five, six, seven, eight, thirteen, and fourteen, of chapter 273, of the laws of 1874, of which this is amendatory; chapter 341, of the laws of 1874, entitled, "An act in relation to railroads;" chapter 334, of the laws of 1875, entitled, "An act to amend chapter 273, of the laws of 1874, entitled, 'an act relating to railroad, express, and telegraph companies in the State of Wisconsin,'" and the first section of chapter 113, of the laws of 1875, are hereby repealed; *provided*, that nothing herein contained shall in any manner affect any litigation now pending in any of the courts of this State, or any court or courts of the United States.

Female Attorneys.

IN HOUSE.

1876, June 20—A bill (H. R. 2622) providing that every person shall be entitled to be admitted in every court of the United States to practice as an attorney and counselor at law and solicitor in chancery, who may be properly qualified according to law, without regard to sex, was reported back from the Judiciary Committee, with an adverse report. And the bill was accordingly laid on the table.

Woman Suffrage.

1876, February 23—In the Massachusetts Senate, the Committee on Woman Suffrage reported this bill:

An Act to secure to Women the right to Vote on Municipal Affairs in Cities and Towns, and to hold Municipal Offices.

Be it enacted by the Senate and House of Representatives, in General Court assembled, and by the authority of the same, as follows:

SEC. 1. Every woman who is a citizen of this Commonwealth, of twenty-one years of age and upwards, and has the educational qualifications required by the twentieth article of the amendments to the constitution (excepting paupers and persons under guardianship), who shall have resided within this Commonwealth one year, and within the city or town in which she seeks a right to vote, six months preceding any meeting of citizens, either in wards or in general meeting for municipal purposes, and who shall have paid by herself, or her parents, or guardian, a state or county, city or town tax, which within two years next preceding such meeting has been assessed upon her in any city or town, shall have a right to vote at such town and city meetings for town and city officers, and upon all questions concerning municipal affairs, and to hold any city or town office to which she may be elected or appointed.

SEC. 2. This act shall take effect upon its passage.

March 3—The bill was defeated—yeas 11, nays 19.

1876, June 20—The Connecticut House of Representatives, by a vote of one hundred and six yeas to seventy nays, passed a bill providing that women who pay taxes on property worth five hundred dollars, and which they own, shall have a right to vote at local elections at any time within one year after they have paid their taxes.

1876, January 25—In Senate of the U. S., Mr. SARGENT presented a petition of women, citizens of the United States, praying the establishment of a government in the District of Columbia which shall secure to women the right to vote; which was referred to the Committee on the District of Columbia, and ordered to be printed.

Constitutional Amendments in Connecticut.

In addition to the record given (pp. 98, 99), the legislature which recently adjourned passed five proposed amendments to the Constitution of the State, which go over to the next legislature, and will require therein a two-thirds majority, before being submitted to the people. Their titles are as follow:

Amendment prohibiting special legislation on corporations, county seats, voting places, railroads, etc.

Amendment prohibiting extra pay to public officers.

Amendment limiting each town to one representative.

Amendment increasing the senatorial districts to 27 or 31.

Amendment prohibiting use of money in elections.

Rescinding a Resolution of Censure. Forty-Third Congress, Second Session.

1875, March 2—Mr. SCOFIELD submitted this resolution, which was agreed to:

Whereas the House of Representatives, on the 30th day of April, 1862, adopted a resolution censuring Simon Cameron for certain irregular proceedings as Secretary of War in the matter of purchasing military supplies at the outbreak of the rebellion; and whereas on the 26th day of the ensuing month the then President of the United States, Abraham Lincoln, in a special message to Congress, assumed for the Executive Department of the Government the full responsibility of the proceedings complained of, declaring in said message that he should be wanting equally in candor and in justice if he should leave the censure to rest exclusively or chiefly on Mr. Cameron, and added that it was due to Mr. Cameron to say that, although he fully approved the proceedings, they were not moved nor suggested by him, and that not only the President but all the other heads of Departments were at least equally responsible with him for whatever error, wrong, or fault was committed in the premises; therefore

Resolved, That this House, as an act of personal justice to Mr. Cameron and as a correction of its own records, hereby directs that said resolution be rescinded, and that "rescission" be entered on the margin of the Journal where said resolution is recorded.

[For copy of President LINCOLN'S Message, referred to, and resolution, see McPherson's Rebellion, p. 333.]

The Law Governing Election of Representatives in Congress.

All the Representatives in Congress are now elected on the first Tuesday after the first Monday in November, except in the States of INDIANA, MAINE, and OHIO, and for the alternate Congresses in IOWA.

The law of the United States on the subject is as follows:

February 2, 1872, a law was passed establishing the Tuesday next after the first Monday in November, 1876, as the day for the election of Representatives and Delegates in the Forty-fifth Congress; and the Tuesday next after the first Monday in November, in every second year thereafter, for the election of succeeding Congresses.

March 3, 1875, a law was passed modifying the above "so as not to apply to any State that has not yet changed its day of election, and whose Constitution must be amended in order to effect a change in the day of the election of State officers in said State."

The proposed new Constitution of OHIO—in which the day of election was changed to November—having been voted down August 18, 1874, this section relieved that difficulty. INDIANA and MAINE were the only other States to which its terms applied. CONNECTICUT has since March 3, 1875, by Constitutional Amendment fixed its election for State officers on the same day in November, and NEW HAMPSHIRE did at the late session of the Legislature. The Constitution of IOWA is peculiar, in providing that in Presidential years, members of Congress and State officers shall be elected on the day of the Presidential election, and on the alternate years, on the second Tuesday of October. Thus members of the Forty-fifth Congress will be chosen in that State in November, 1876; of Forty-sixth, in October, 1878.

By act of 28th February, 1871, all votes for Representatives in Congress must be by written or printed ballot; and all votes allowed or received contrary to this section shall be of no effect.

Rhode Island.

The proposed amendments printed on page 115 were ratified by the late General Assembly, June 14, 1876, the first-named in the Senate by a vote of 28 to 0, and in the House 46 to 21. The second-named was ratified in the Senate 27 to 1, and in the House 51 to 16. The last-named was ratified in the Senate, yeas 28, nays 0, and in the House, yeas 66, nays 0. These amendments are to be voted on, November 7, 1876, and if approved by three-fifths of the electors voting, will become a part of the Constitution.

Changes in List of Congressmen.

Since pages 138–140 have been stereotyped, the following changes have taken place:

In HOUSE—Winthrop W. Ketchum, of Pennsylvania, resigned July 19, 1876, to accept the Judgeship of the United States for the Western District of that State.

Edmund W. M. Mackey was unseated, July 19, 1876, by a vote of the House—the seat being declared vacant.

John Goode, July 28, 1876, was voted—yeas 105, nays 99—entitled to hold a seat as a Representative from Virginia, the majority of the committee on elections having reported that Hon. James H. Platt, jr., was duly elected.

Josiah G. Abbott, of Massachusetts, qualified July 28, 1876, in place of Mr. Frost, unseated July 14, by a vote of 102 to 79.

President Grant's Message Respecting the Provisions of the Sundry Civil Appropriation Act, July 31, 1876.

To the House of Representatives:

The act making appropriations for sundry civil expenses of the Government for the fiscal year ending June 30, 1877, is so defective in what it omits to provide for that I cannot announce its approval without at the same time pointing out what seem to be its defects. It makes but inadequate provision for the service at best, and in some instances fails to make any provision whatever.

Notably among the first class is the reduction in the ordinary annual appropriations for the revenue-cutter service, to the prejudice of the customs revenue.

The same may be said of the Signal Service, as also the failure to provide for the increased expenses devolved upon the mints and assay offices by recent legislation, and thus tending to defeat the objects of that legislation.

Of this class, also, are public buildings, for the protection, preservation, and completion of which there is no adequate appropriation, while the sum of $100,000 only is appropriated for the repairs of the different navy-yards and stations and the preservation of the same, the ordinary and customary appropriations for which are not less than $1,000,000.

A similar reduction is made in the expenses for armories and arsenals.

The provision for the ordinary judicial expenses is much less than the estimated amount for that important service, the actual expenditures of the last fiscal year, and the certain demands of the current year.

The provision for the expenses of the surveys of public lands is less than one-half of the usual appropriation for that service and what are understood to be its actual demands.

Reduction in the expenditures for light-houses, beacons, and fog-stations is also made in similar proportion.

Of the class for which no appropriation is made, among the most noticeable, perhaps, is that portion of the general expenses of the District of Columbia, on behalf of the United States, as appropriated in former years, and the judgments of the Court of Claims. The failure to make a reasonable contribution to the expenses of the nation's capital is an apparent dereliction on the part of the United States, and rank injustice to the people here who bear the burdens; while to refuse or neglect to provide for the payment of solemn judgments of its own courts is, apparently, to repudiate. Of a different character, but as prejudicial to the Treasury, is the omission to make provision to enable the Secretary of the Treasury to have the rebel archives and records of captured and abandoned property examined and information furnished therefrom for the use of the Government.

Finally, without further specification of detail, it may be said that the act which in its title purports to make provision for a diverse and greatly extended civil service, unhappily appropriates an amount not more than 65 per cent. of its ordinary demands.

The legislative department establishes and defines the service, and devolves upon the Executive Departments the obligation of submitting annually the needful estimates of expenses of such service. Congress properly exacts implicit obedience to the requirements of the law in the administration of the public service, and rigid accountability in the expenditures therefor. It is submitted that a corresponding responsibility and obligation rests upon it to make the adequate appropriations to render possible such administration, and tolerable such exaction. Anything short of an ample provision for a specified service is necessarily fraught with disaster to the public interests, and is a positive injustice to those charged with its execution.

To appropriate and to execute are corresponding obligations and duties, and the adequacy of the former is the necessary measure of the efficiency of the execution.

In this eighth month of the present session of Congress—nearly one month of the fiscal year to which this appropriation applies having passed—I do not feel warranted in vetoing an absolutely necessary appropriation bill; but in signing it I deem it a duty to show where the responsibility belongs for whatever embarrassments may arise in the execution of the trust confided to me.

U. S. GRANT.

EXECUTIVE MANSION, *July* 31, 1876.

President Grant's Message relating to the Slaughter of American Citizens at Hamburg, South Carolina, August 1, 1876.

To the Senate of the United States:

In response to the resolution of the Senate of July 20, 1876, calling upon the President to communicate to the Senate, if in his opinion not incompatible with the public interest, any information in regard to the slaughter of American citizens at Hamburg, South Carolina, I have the honor to submit the following inclosures, to wit:

No. 1. Letter of the 22d of July, 1876, from Governor D. H. Chamberlain, of South Carolina, to me.

No. 2. My reply thereto.

No. 3. Report of Hon. William Stone, attorney-general of South Carolina.

No. 4. Report of General H. W. Purvis, adjutant and inspector-general of South Carolina.

No. 5. Copy of evidence taken before a coroner's jury investigating facts relating to the Hamburg massacre.

No. 6. Printed copy of statement of M. C. Butler, of South Carolina.

No. 7. Printed letter from the same to the editors of the *Journal of Commerce.*

No. 8. Copy of letter from Governor Chamberlain to Hon. T. J. Robertson.

No. 9. An address to the American people by the colored citizens of Charleston, South Carolina.

No. 10. An address by a committee appointed at a convention of leading representatives of Columbia, South Carolina.

No. 11. Copy of letter of July 15, 1876, from the district attorney of Mississippi to the Attorney-General of the United States.

No. 12. Letter from same to same.

No. 13. Copy of report of a grand jury lately in session in Oxford, Mississippi.

These inclosures embrace all the information in my possession touching the late disgraceful and brutal slaughter of unoffending men at the town of Hamburg, South Carolina. My letter to Governor Chamberlain contains all the comments I wish to make on the subject. As allusion is made in that letter to the condition of other States, and particularly to Louisiana and Mississippi, I have added to the inclosures letters and testimony in regard to the lawless condition of a portion of the people of the latter State.

In regard to Louisiana affairs, murders and massacres of innocent men for opinion's sake, or on account of color, have been of too recent date and of too frequent occurrence to require recapitulation or testimony here. All are familiar with their horrible details, the only wonder being that so many justify them or apologize for them.

But recently a committee of the Senate of the United States visited the State of Mississippi to take testimony on the subject of frauds and violence in elections. Their report has not yet been made public; but I await its forthcoming with a feeling of confidence that it will fully sustain all that I have stated relating to fraud and violence in the State of Mississippi.

U. S. GRANT.

EXECUTIVE MANSION, *July* 31, 1876.

The following is the President's letter to Gov. CHAMBERLAIN, referred to above:

EXECUTIVE MANSION,
WASHINGTON, *July* 26, 1876.

DEAR SIR: I am in receipt of your letter of the 22d of July, and all the enclosures enumerated therein, giving an account of the late barbarous massacre of innocent men at the town of Hamburg, S. C. The views which you express as to the duty you owe to your oath of office and the citizens to secure to all their civil rights, including their right to vote according to the dictates of their own consciences, and the further duty of the Executive of the nation to give all needful aid, when properly called on to do so, to enable you to insure this inalienable right, I fully concur in.

The scene at Hamburg, as cruel, bloodthirsty, wanton, unprovoked, and as uncalled for as it was, is only a repetition of the course that has been pursued in other States within the last few years, notably in Mississippi and Louisiana. Mississippi is governed to-day by officials chosen through fraud and violence, such as would scarcely be accredited to savages, much less to a civilized and Christian people. How long these things are to continue, or what is to be the final remedy, the great Ruler of the Universe only knows. But I have an abiding faith that the remedy will come, and come speedily, and I earnestly hope that it will come peacefully. There has never been a desire on the part of the North to humiliate the South; nothing is claimed for one State that is not freely accorded to all others, unless it may be the right to kill negroes and Republicans without fear of punishment and without loss of caste or reputation. This has seemed to be a privilege claimed by a few States.

I repeat again, that I fully agree with you as to the measure of your duties in the present emergency, and as to my duties. Go on, and let every Governor, where the same dangers threaten the peace of his State, go on in the conscientious discharge of his duties to the humblest as well as the proudest citizen, and I will give every aid for which I can find law or constitutional power. A government that cannot give protection to the life, property, and all guaranteed civil rights (in this country the greatest is an untrammeled ballot) to the citizen is, in so far, a failure, and every energy of the oppressed should be exerted (always within the law and by constitutional means) to regain lost privileges or protection.

Too long denial of guaranteed rights is sure to lead to revolution, bloody revolution, where suffering must fall upon the innocent as well as the guilty. Expressing the hope that the better judgment and co-operation of the citizens of the State over which you have presided so ably may enable you to secure a fair trial, and punishment of all offenders without distinction of race, color, or previous condition of servitude, and without aid from the Federal Government, but with the promise of such aid on the conditions named in the foregoing, I subscribe myself very respectfully your obedient servant,

U. S. GRANT.

To the Hon. D. H. CHAMBERLAIN, Governor of South Carolina.

[From the newspapers.]

CHINESE IMMIGRATION.—Official returns made to the Bureau of Statistics show that during the fiscal year ended June 30, 1876, there arrived in the United States 22,572 Chinese immigrants, of whom only 259 were females. Of this number 21,262 arrived in San Francisco, 915 in Oregon and 395 in Puget Sound. During the corresponding period of 1875 the total immigration to the United States from China was 16,437, of whom 382 were females. This shows an increase in 1876 over 1875 of 6,135.

THE STATE OF COLORADO.—The President, in accordance with the provisions of the act of Congress, approved March 3, 1875, issued a proclamation, August 1, 1876, declaring and proclaiming the fact that the fundamental conditions imposed by Congress on the State of Colorado to entitle that State to admission to the Union, have been ratified and accepted, and that the admission of said State into the Union is now complete.

Public Debt Statement, July 31, 1876.

This statement is taken from the newspapers:

Debt bearing interest in coin.	
Bonds at 6 per cent	$ 984,999,650 00
Bonds at 5 per cent	711,685,800 00
	$1,696,685,450 00
Debt bearing interest in lawful money.	
Navy pension fund at 3 per cent	14,000,000 00
Debt on which interest has ceased since maturity	$ 3,297,706 26
Debt bearing no interest.	
Old demand and legal-tender notes	$ 369,686,020 50
Certificates of deposit	32,815,000 00
Fractional currency	32,902,880 39
Coin certificates	29,313,000 00
	$ 464,717,900 89
Total debt	$2,178,700,111 15
Interest	$ 24,850,234 16
Total debt, principal and interest	$2,230,550,345 31
Cash in the Treasury.	
Coin	$ 59,843,684 73
Currency	12,590,349 52
Special deposit held for redemption of certificates of deposit as provided by law	32,815,000 00
	$ 105,249,034 25
Debt, less cash in the Treasury, Aug. 1, 1876	$2,098,301,311 06
Debt, less cash in the Treasury, July 1, 1876	$2,099,439,344 99
Decrease of debt during the month	$ 1,138,033 93
Decrease of debt since June 30, 1876	$ 1,138,033 93

Bonds issued to the Pacific Railway Companies, interest payable in lawful money—Principal outstanding, $64,623,512.00; interest accrued and not yet paid, $323,117.56; interest paid by the United States, $32,080,218.42; interest repaid by transportation of mails, etc., $6,909,-204.91; balance of interest paid by the United States, $25,171,013.51.

CURRENCY FIGURES TO AUGUST 1.—The Comptroller of the Currency has made a statement showing the issue and retirement of national bank notes and legal tender notes under the acts of June 20, 1874, and January 14, 1875, to August 1, 1876. The amount of national bank circulation retired and surrendered from January 14, 1875, to August 1, 1876, is $39,697,990. The amount issued between the same dates is $15,475,965, showing a decrease of national bank circulation of $24,222,025. The amount of legal tender notes deposited from June 20, 1874 (including $3,813,675 on deposit at that date), to August 1, 1876, for the purpose of retiring national bank circulation, was $61,590,141, of which amount $25,310,349 remained on deposit August 1, 1875. The additional circulation issued since January 14, 1875, is $15,475,-965, of which amount 80 per cent. in legal tender notes, or $12,380,722 has been retired, leaving the amount of legal tender notes outstanding August 1, 1876, $369,619,228.

The following is a statement of the United States currency outstanding at that date:

Old demand notes	$66,792 50
Legal tender notes, new issue	27,435,078 00
Legal tender notes, series of 1869	223,635,488 00
Legal tender notes, series of 1874	61,892 554 00
Legal tender notes, series of 1875	56,656,108 00
One-year notes of 1863	61,045 00
Two-year notes of 1863	18,850 00
Two-year coupon notes of 1863	24,800 00
Compound interest notes	328,620 00
Fractional currency, 1st issue	4,294,854 92
Fractional currency, 2d issue	3,117,076 28
Fractional currency, 3d issue	3,066,479 83
Fractional currency, 4th issue, 1st series	4,221,856 08
Fractional currency, 4th issue, 2d series	1,061,226 55
Fractional currency, 4th issue, 3d series	1,903 006,65
Fractional currency, 5th issue	15,238,380,08
Total	$403,022,215 89

Gold Coin in the Treasury.

The following letter was presented to the House July 31, 1876:

TREASURY DEPARTMENT, *July* 29, 1876.

SIR: I am in receipt of the resolution of the House of Representatives, dated the 24th instant, requesting me to report to the House within one week from the passage of the resolution the amount of gold coin and gold bullion, respectively, in the Treasury and actually owned by the Government, with a full detailed statement of the amount of gold certificates outstanding, gold interest due and unpaid, called bonds, and all other obligations payable in gold on demand on that date, and in reply I have the honor to state that the available coin balance at the close of business on the 24th instant was $61,158,223 45

Made up as follows:

Gold coin	$41,627,450 56	
Gold bullion	11,030,095 87	
Silver coin and bullion	8,500,677 02	
		61,158,223 45
Against which there were matured obligations, payable on demand, as follows:		
Coin interest	10,456,386 29	
Bonds called or matured and interest thereon	3,026,627 51	
Coin certificates	30,230,100 00	
Old demand notes	66,907 50	
		43,780,021 30
Leaving a balance in excess of all such obligations of		17,378,202 15

Very respectfully,

LOT M. MORRILL, *Secretary.*

Hon. MILTON SAYLER,
Speaker pro tempore, House of Representatives.

Constitutional Amendment.

The following was omitted from its proper place, on page 131:

HOUSE OF REPRESENTATIVES.

1876, April 26.—Mr. LAPHAM proposed the following: Whenever any appropriation bill shall have passed the House of Representatives and the Senate, and shall be presented to the President for his approval, he may withhold his approval to any clause or clauses, or provision or provisions, in such bill, and approve the remainder; and in such case he shall state his objections to the portions disapproved in the same manner as is provided in article first, section seven of the Constitution; and all provisions of said section as to bills not approved shall apply to the item or items so disapproved.

XX.

REPUBLICAN NATIONAL CONVENTION, 1876.

This body met in Cincinnati, Ohio, on the 14th of June, in pursuance of the following call:

The next Union Republican National Convention for the nomination of candidates for President and Vice-President of the United States will be held in the city of Cincinnati, on Wednesday, the fourteenth day of June, 1876, at 12 o'clock noon, and will consist of delegates from each State equal to twice the number of its Senators and Representatives in Congress, and of two delegates from each organized Territory and the District of Columbia.

In calling the conventions for the election of delegates, the committees of the several States are recommended to invite all Republican electors, and all other voters, without regard to past political differences or previous party affiliations, who are opposed to reviving sectional issues, and desire to promote friendly feeling and permanent harmony throughout the country by maintaining and enforcing all the constitutional rights of every citizen, including the full and free exercise of the right of suffrage without intimidation and without fraud; who are in favor of the continued prosecution and punishment of all official dishonesty, and of an economical administration of the Government by honest, faithful, and capable officers; who are in favor of making such reforms in government as experience may from time to time suggest; who are opposed to impairing the credit of the nation by depreciating any of its obligations, and in favor of sustaining in every way the national faith and financial honor; who hold that the common-school system is the nursery of American liberty, and should be maintained absolutely free from sectarian control; who believe that, for the promotion of these ends, the direction of the Government should continue to be confided to those who adhere to the principles of 1776, and support them as incorporated in the Constitution and the laws; and who are in favor of recognizing and strengthening the fundamental principle of National Unity in this Centennial Anniversary of the birth of the Republic.

E. D. MORGAN, *Chairman*,
WM. E. CHANDLER, *Secretary*,
Republican National Committee.

WASHINGTON, *January* 13, 1876.

At 12 o'clock it was called to order by EDWIN D. MORGAN, of New York, on whose motion, after some remarks, THEODORE M. POMEROY, of New York, was elected temporary President.

On motion, committees were appointed, consisting of one from each State and Territory, elected by the delegations respectively, on Permanent Organization; on Rules and Order of Business; on Credentials; and on Resolutions.

After some time, during which speeches were made by JOHN A. LOGAN, JOSEPH R. HAWLEY, EDWARD F. NOYES, HENRY HIGHLAND GARNET, WILLIAM A. HOWARD, and FREDERICK DOUGLASS, the Committee on Permanent Organization, through GEO. B. LORING, of Massachusetts, reported a list of officers, who were elected—EDWARD MCPHERSON, of Pennsylvania, being the permanent President.

June 15—After some preliminary business, JOHN CESSNA, of Pennsylvania, from the Committee on Rules and Order of Business, reported the following rules for the government of the Convention:

RULES AND ORDER OF BUSINESS.

RULE 1. Upon all subjects before the Convention the States shall be called in alphabetical order, and next the Territories and the District of Columbia.

RULE 2. Each State shall be entitled to double the number of its Senators and Representatives in Congress, according to the late apportionment, and each Territory and the District of Columbia shall be entitled to two votes. The votes of each delegation shall be reported by its chairman.

RULE 3. The report of the Committee on Credentials shall be disposed of before the report of the Committee on Platform and Resolutions is acted upon, and the report of the Committee of Platform and Resolutions shall be disposed of before the Convention proceeds to the nomination of candidates for President and Vice-President.

RULE 4. In making the nominations for President and Vice-President, in no case shall the calling of the roll be dispensed with. When it shall appear that any candidate has received the majority of the votes cast, the President of the Convention shall announce the question to be: "Shall the nomination of the candidate be made unanimous?" but if no candidate shall have received a majority of the votes, the Chair shall direct the vote to be again taken, which shall be repeated until some candidate shall have received a majority of the votes cast; and when any State has announced its vote it shall so stand until the ballot is announced, unless in case of numerical error.

RULE 5. When a majority of the delegates of any two States shall demand that a vote be recorded, the same shall be taken by States, Territories and the District of Columbia; the Secretary calling the roll of the States and Territories in the order heretofore stated, and the District of Columbia.

RULE 6. In the record of the vote by States the vote of each State, Territory and the District of Columbia, shall be announced by the Chairman, and in case the votes of any State, Territory or the District of Columbia shall be divided, the Chairman shall announce the number of votes cast for any candidate or for or against any proposition.

RULE 7. When the previous question shall be demanded by the majority of the delegates from any State, and the demand seconded by two or more States, and the call sustained by a majority of the Convention, the question will then be proceeded with and disposed of according to the rules of the House of Representatives in similar cases.

RULE 8. No member shall speak more than once upon the same question, nor longer than five minutes, unless by leave of the Convention; except that delegates presenting the name of a candidate shall be allowed ten minutes in presenting the name of such candidate.

RULE 9. The rules of the House of Representatives shall be the rules of this Convention, so far as they are applicable, and not inconsistent with the foregoing rules.

RULE 10. A Republican National Committee shall be appointed, to consist of one member from each State, Territory and District represented in this Convention. The roll shall be called, and the delegation from each State, Territory and District shall name, through their chairman, a person to act as a member of such committee.

Which were adopted.

The Committee on Credentials then made report. The majority of the committee reported through JOHN T. ENSOR, of Maryland, in favor of admitting the Haralson delegation from Alabama; the minority, through CHARLES N. HARRIS, of Nevada, in favor of the Spencer delegation. The minority report was rejected—yeas 354, nays 375, and the majority report then adopted. The Bowen delegation from the District of Columbia were seated, and the Conover delegation from Florida.

Resolutions.

JOSEPH R. HAWLEY, Chairman of the Committee,* reported the following:

When, in the economy of Providence, this land was to be purged of human slavery, and when the strength of government of the people, by the people, and for the people, was to be demonstrated, the Republican party came into power. Its deeds have passed into history, and we look back to them with pride. Incited by their memories to high aims for the good of our country and mankind, and looking to the future with unfaltering courage, hope and purpose, we, the representatives of the party in National Convention assembled, make the following declarations of principles:

1. The United States of America is a Nation, not a league. By the combined workings of the National and State Governments, under their respective constitutions, the rights of every citizen are secured, at home and abroad, and the common welfare promoted.

2. The Republican party has preserved these Governments to the hundredth anniversary of the Nation's birth, and they are now embodiments of the great truths spoken at its cradle—"that all men are created equal; that they are endowed by their Creator with certain inalienable rights, among which are life, liberty and the pursuit of happiness; that for the attainment of these ends Governments have been instituted among men, deriving their just powers from the consent of the governed." Until these truths are cheerfully obeyed, or, if need be, vigorously enforced, the work of the Republican party is unfinished.

3. The permanent pacification of the Southern section of the Union and the complete protection of all its citizens in the free enjoyment of all their rights, is a duty to which the Republican party stands sacredly pledged. The power to provide for the enforcement of the principles embodied in the recent constitutional amendments, is vested by those amendments in the Congress of the United States, and we declare it to be the solemn obligation of the legislative and executive departments of the Government to put into immediate and vigorous exercise all their constitutional powers for removing any just causes of discontent on the part of any class, and for securing to every American citizen complete liberty and exact equality in the exercise of all civil, political and public rights. To this end we imperatively demand a Congress and a Chief Executive whose courage and fidelity to these duties shall not falter until these results are placed beyond dispute or recall.

4. In the first act of Congress signed by President Grant, the National Government assumed to remove any doubts of its purpose to discharge all just obligations to the public creditors, and "solemnly pledged its faith to make provision at the earliest practicable period for the redemption of the United States notes in coin." Commercial prosperity, public morals and National credit demand that this promise be fulfilled by a continuous and steady progress to specie payment.

5. Under the Constitution the President and heads of departments are to make nominations for office; the Senate is to advise and consent to appointments, and the House of Representatives is to accuse and prosecute faithless officers. The best interest of the public service demands that these distinctions be respected; that Senators and Representatives who may be judges and accusers should not dictate appointments to office. The invariable rule in appointments should have reference to the honesty, fidelity and capacity of the appointees, giving to the party in power those places where harmony and vigor of adminstration require its policy to be represented, but permitting all others to be filled by persons selected with sole reference to the efficiency of the public service, and the right of all citizens to share in the honor of rendering faithful service to the country.

6. We rejoice in the quickened conscience of the people concerning political affairs, and will

---

* The committee consisted of the following persons: *Arkansas*—C. C. Waters; *Arizona*—R. C. McCormick; *California*—Chas. F. Reed; *Connecticut*—Jos. R. Hawley; *Colorado*—James B. Belford; *Dakota*—Andrew McHench; *Delaware*—Eli R. Sharp: *Georgia*—Henry M. Turner; *Illinois*—C. B. Farwell; *Indiana*—R. W. Thompson; *Iowa*—Hiram Price; *Idaho*—Austin Savage; *Kansas*—J. D. Thatcher; *Kentucky*—James Speed; *Louisiana*—Henry Demoss; *Maine*—Nelson Dingley, jr.; *Maryland*—L. H. Steiner; *Massachusetts*—Edward L. Pierce; *Michigan*—H. P. Baldwin; *Minnesota*—J. E. Wakefield; *Mississippi*—C. W. Clarke; *Missouri*—R. T. Van Horn; *Montana*—W. F. Sanders; *New Mexico*—S. B. Axtell; *Nebraska*—A. R. Pinnéy; *Nevada*—J. P. Jones; *New Hampshire*—Chas. Burns; *New Jersey*—Frederick A. Potts; *New York*—Chas. E. Smith; *North Carolina*—P. C. Badger; *Ohio*—Edward Cowles; *Oregon*—H. K. Hines; *Pennsylvania*—H. W. Oliver; *Rhode Island*—Chas. Nourse; *South Carolina*—D. H. Chamberlain; *Texas*—E. J. Davis; *Tennessee*—A. A. Freeman; *Utah*—J. B. McKean; *Vermont*—G. H. Bigelow; *Virginia*—Wm. Miller; *West Virginia*—J. W. Davis; *Wisconsin*—Gen. Jas. H. Howe; *Washington*—Elwood Evans; *Wyoming*—Wm. Hinton.

hold all public officers to a rigid responsibility, and engage that the prosecution and punishment of all who betray official trusts shall be swift, thorough and unsparing.

7. The public school system of the several States is the bulwark of the American Republic, and with a view to its security and permanence we recommend an amendment to the Constitution of the United States forbidding the application of any public funds or property for the benefit of any schools or institutions under sectarian control.

8. The revenue necessary for current expenditures and the obligations of the public debt must be largely derived from duties upon importations, which, so far as possible, should be adjusted to promote the interests of American labor and advance the prosperity of the whole country.

9. We reaffirm our opposition to further grants of the public lands to corporations and monopolies, and demand that the National domain be devoted to free homes for the people.

10. It is the imperative duty of the Government so to modify existing treaties with European Governments, that the same protection shall be afforded to the adopted American citizen that is given to the native born; and that all necessary laws should be passed to protect emigrants in the absence of power in the States for that purpose.

11. It is the immediate duty of Congress to fully investigate the effect of the immigration and importation of Mongolians upon the moral and material interests of the country.

12. The Republican party recognizes with approval the substantial advances recently made towards the establishment of equal rights for women by the many important amendments effected by Republican Legislatures in the laws which concern the personal and property relations of wives, mothers, and widows, and by the appointment and election of women to the superintendence of education, charities and other public trusts. The honest demands of this class of citizens for additional rights, privileges and immunities should be treated with respectful consideration.

13. The Constitution confers upon Congress sovereign power over the Territories of the United States for their government, and in the exercise of this power it is the right and duty of Congress to prohibit and extirpate, in the Territories, that relic of barbarism—polygamy; and we demand such legislation as shall secure this end and the supremacy of American institutions in all the Territories.

14. The pledges which the Nation has given to her soldiers and sailors must be fulfilled, and a grateful people will always hold those who imperiled their lives for the country's preservation, in the kindest remembrance.

15. We sincerely deprecate all sectional feeling and tendencies. We therefore note with deep solicitude that the Democratic party counts, as its chief hope of success, upon the electoral vote of a united South, secured through the efforts of those who were recently arrayed against the Nation; and we invoke the earnest attention of the country to the grave truth that a success thus achieved would reopen sectional strife and imperil National honor and human rights.

16. We charge the Democratic party with being the same in character and spirit as when it sympathized with treason; with making its control of the House of Representatives the triumph and opportunity of the Nation's recent foes; with reasserting and applauding in the National Capitol the sentiments of unrepentant rebellion; with sending Union soldiers to the rear, and promoting Confederate soldiers to the front; with deliberately proposing to repudiate the plighted faith of the Government; with being equally false and imbecile upon the overshadowing financial questions; with thwarting the ends of justice by its partisan mismanagements and obstruction of investigation; with proving itself, through the period of its ascendency in the Lower House of Congress, utterly incompetent to administer the Government; and we warn the country against trusting a party thus alike unworthy, recreant and incapable.

17. The National Administration merits commendation for its honorable work in the management of domestic and foreign affairs, and President Grant deserves the continued hearty gratitude of the American people for his patriotism and his eminent services, in war and in peace.

18. We present as our candidates for President and Vice-President of the United States two distinguished statesmen, of eminent ability and character, and conspicuously fitted for those high offices, and we confidently appeal to the American people to intrust the administration of their public affairs to Rutherford B. Hayes and William A. Wheeler.

[The last resolution was adopted after the nominations were made, on motion of Mr. SMITH, of New York.]

Upon the reading of the resolutions,

EDWARD L. PIERCE, of Massachusetts, moved to strike out the eleventh resolution; which, after debate, was disagreed to—yeas 215, nays 532.

EDMUND J. DAVIS, of Texas, moved to strike out the fourth resolution and substitute for it the following:

Resolved, That it is the duty of Congress to provide for carrying out the act known as the Resumption Act of Congress, to the end that the resumption of specie payments may not be longer delayed.

Which, after a brief debate, was disagreed to on a *viva voce* vote.

The resolutions were then adopted without a division.

NOMINATION OF CANDIDATES.

Nominations were then made for President of the United States:

By CONNECTICUT—MARSHALL JEWELL.
By INDIANA—OLIVER P. MORTON.
By KENTUCKY—BENJAMIN H. BRISTOW.
By MAINE—JAMES G. BLAINE.
By NEW YORK—ROSCOE CONKLING.
By OHIO—RUTHERFORD B. HAYES.
By PENNSYLVANIA—JOHN F. HARTRANFT.

After the speeches in favor of these nominees, the Convention adjourned till to-morrow at 10 o'clock.

June 16—Seven ballots were then taken with the following result:

	1st	2d	3d	4th	5th	6th	7th
HAYES	61	64	67	68	104	113	384
BLAINE	285	296	293	292	286	308	351
MORTON	125	120	113	108	95	85	
BRISTOW	113	114	121	126	114	111	21
CONKLING	99	93	90	84	82	81	...
HARTRANFT	58	63	68	71	69	50	...
JEWELL	11	(withdrawn.)					
WM. A. WHEELER	3	3	2	2	2	2	...
ELLIHU B. WASHBURNE	...	1	1	3	3	5	...
Whole No. of votes	754	754	755	754	755	755	756
Necessary to a choice	378	378	378	378	378	378	379

On motion of Mr. FRYE of Maine, Governor HAYES was unanimously declared the nominee of the Convention.

Messrs. WILLIAM A. WHEELER of New York, STEWART L. WOODFORD of New York, MARSHALL JEWELL of Connecticut, FREDERICK T. FRELINGHUYSEN of New Jersey, and JOSEPH R. HAWLEY of Connecticut, were nominated for Vice-President; but before the roll-call was completed, it being apparent that WILLIAM A. WHEELER had received a majority of the votes cast, other candidates were by consent withdrawn, and he was unanimously declared the nominee of the Convention.

After the transaction of some unimportant business, the Convention adjourned *sine die.*

NOTE—On the second ballot for a candidate for President, four delegates from Pennsylvania rose to a question of privilege, and demanded that under the rules of the Convention they had the right to record their votes independently of a majority of the delegation. The CHAIR held, that under the Sixth Rule of the Convention, which was the paramount law on the subject, they had this right. The ruling was appealed from, and after discussion, sustained, on a vote by States—yeas 395, nays 354.

Gov. Hayes's Letter of Acceptance.

COLUMBUS, O., *July* 8, 1876.

To the Hons. EDWARD MCPHERSON, WM. A. HOWARD, JOS. H. RAINEY, *and others, Committee of the National Republican Convention.*

GENTLEMEN: In reply to your official communication of June 17, by which I am informed of my nomination for the office of President of the United States by the Republican National Convention at Cincinnati, I accept the nomination with gratitude, hoping that, under Providence, I shall be able, if elected, to execute the duties of the high office as a trust for the benefit of all the people. I do not deem it necessary to enter upon any extended examination of the declaration of principles made by the Convention. The resolutions are in accord with my views, and I heartily concur in the principles they announce. In several of the resolutions, however, questions are considered which are of such importance that I deem it proper to briefly express my convictions in regard to them. The fifth resolution adopted by the Convention is of paramount interest. More than forty years ago a system of making appointments to office grew up, based upon the maxim "to the victors belong the spoils." The old rule, the true rule, that honesty, capacity and fidelity constitute the only real qualification for office, and that there is no other claim, gave place to the idea that party services were to be chiefly considered. All parties in practice have adopted this system. It has been essentially modified since its first introduction. It has not, however, been improved. At first the President, either directly or through the heads of department, made all the appointments, but gradually the appointing power, in many cases, passed into the control of members of Congress. The offices in these cases have become not merely rewards for party services, but rewards for services to party leaders. This system destroys the independence of the separate departments of the Government. "It tends directly to extravagance and official incapacity." It is a temptation to dishonesty; it hinders and impairs that careful supervision and strict accountability by which alone faithful and efficient public service can be secured; it obstructs the prompt removal and sure punishment of the unworthy; in every way it degrades the civil service and the character of the Government. It is felt, I am confident, by a large majority of the members of Congress, to be an intolerable burden and an unwarrantable hindrance to the proper discharge of their legitimate duties. It ought to be abolished. The reform should be thorough, radical, and complete. We should return to the principles and practice of the founders of the Government—supplying by legislation, when needed, that which was formerly the established custom. They neither expected nor desired from the public officers any partisan service. They meant that public officers should give their whole service to the Government and to the people. They meant that the officer should be secure in his tenure as long as his personal character remained untarnished and the performance of his duties satisfactory. If elected, I shall conduct the administration of the Government upon these principles, and all constitutional powers vested in the Executive will be employed to establish this reform. The declaration of principles by the Cincinnati Convention makes no announcement in favor of a single Presidential term. I do not assume to add to that declaration, but believing that the restoration of the civil service to the system established by Washington and followed by the early Presidents can be best accomplished by an Executive who is under no temptation to use the patronage of his office to promote his own reelection, I desire to perform what I regard as a duty in stating now my inflexible purpose, if elected, not to be a candidate for election to a second term.

On the currency question I have frequently expressed my views in public, and I stand by my record on this subject. I regard all the laws of the United States relating to the payment of the public indebtedness, the legal tender notes included, as constituting a pledge and moral obligation of the Government, which must in good faith be kept. It is my conviction that the feeling of uncertainty inseparable from an irredeemable paper currency, with its fluctuations of value, is one of the great obstacles to a revival of confidence and business, and to a return of prosperity. That uncertainty can be ended in but one way—the resumption of specie payments. But the longer the instability of our money system is permitted to continue, the greater will be the injury inflicted upon our economical interests and all classes of society. If elected, I shall approve every appropriate measure to accomplish the desired end; and shall oppose any step backward. The resolution with respect to the public school system is one which should receive the hearty support of the American people. Agitation upon this subject is to be apprehended, until, by constitutional amendment the schools are placed beyond all danger of sectarian control or interference. The Republican party is pledged to secure such an amendment.

The resolution of the Convention on the subject of the permanent pacification of the country, and the complete protection of all its citizens in the free enjoyment of all their constitutional rights, is timely and of great importance. The condition of the Southern States attracts the attention and commands the sympathy of the people of the whole Union. In their progressive recovery from the effects of the war, their first necessity is an intelligent and honest administration of government which will protect all classes of citizens in their political and private rights. What the South most needs is "peace," and peace depends upon the supremacy of the law. There can be no enduring peace if the constitutional rights of any portion of the people are habitually disregarded. A division of political parties resting merely upon sectional lines is always unfortunate and may be disastrous. The welfare of the South, alike with that of every other part of this country, depends upon the attractions it can offer to labor and immigration, and to capital. But laborers will not go, and capital will not be ventured where the Constitution and the laws are set at defiance, and distraction, apprehension, and alarm take the place of peace-loving, and law-abiding social life. All parts of the Constitution are sacred and must be sacredly observed—the parts that are new no less than the parts that are old. The moral and national prosperity of the Southern States can be most effectually advanced by a hearty and generous recognition of the rights of all, by all—a recognition without reserve or exception. With such a recognition fully accorded it will be practicable to promote, by the influence of all legitimate agencies of the General Government, the efforts of the people of those States to obtain for themselves the blessings of honest and capable local government. If elected, I shall consider it not only my duty, but it will be my ardent desire to labor for the attainment of this end.

Let me assure my countrymen of the Southern States that if I shall be charged with the duty of organizing an administration, it will be one which will regard and cherish their truest interests—the interests of the white and of the colored people both, and equally; and which will put forth its best efforts in behalf of a civil policy which will wipe out forever the distinction between North and South in our common country. With a civil service organized upon a system which will secure purity, experience, efficiency, and economy, a strict regard for the public welfare solely in appointments, and the speedy, thorough, and unsparing prosecution and punishment of all public officers who betray official trusts; with a sound currency; with education unsectarian and free to all; with simplicity and frugality in public and private affairs, and with a fraternal spirit of harmony pervading the people of all sections and classes, we may reasonably hope that the second century of our existence as a nation will, by the blessing of God, be preëminent as an era of good feeling and a period of progress, prosperity, and happiness. Very respectfully, your fellow-citizen, R. B. HAYES.

Mr. Wheeler's Acceptance.

MALONE, July 15, 1876.

Hon. Edward McPherson, and others, of the Committee of the Republican National Convention:

GENTLEMEN:—I received, on the 6th inst., your communication advising me that I had been unanimously nominated by the National Convention of the Republican party, held at Cincinnati on the 14th ult., for the office of Vice-President of the United States; and requesting my acceptance of the same, and asking my attention to the summary of Republican doctrines contained in the platform adopted by the Convention.

A nomination made with such unanimity implies a confidence on the part of the Convention which inspires my profound gratitude. It is accepted with a sense of the responsibility which may follow. If elected, I shall endeavor to perform the duties of the office in the fear of the Supreme Ruler, and in the interest of the whole country.

To the summary of doctrines enunciated by the Convention I give my cordial assent. The Republican party has intrenched in the organic law of our land the doctrine that liberty is the supreme, unchangeable law for every foot of American soil. It is the mission of that party to give full effect to this principle by "securing to every American citizen complete liberty and exact equality in the exercise of all civil, political and public rights." This will be accomplished only when the American citizen, without regard to color, shall wear this panoply of citizenship as fully and as securely in the canebrakes of Louisiana as on the banks of the St. Lawrence.

Upon the question of our Southern relations, my views were recently expressed as a member of the Committee of the United States House of Representatives upon Southern Affairs. Those views remain unchanged, and were thus expressed:

"We of the North delude ourselves in expecting that the masses of the South, so far behind in many of the attributes of enlightened improvement and civilization, are, in the brief period of ten or fifteen years, to be transformed into our model Northern communities. That can only come through a long course of patient waiting, to which no one can now set certain bounds. There will be a good deal of unavoidable friction, which will call for forbearance, and which will have to be relieved by the temperate, fostering care of the government. One of the most potent, if not indispensable agencies in this direction, will be the devising of some system to aid in the education of the masses. The fact that there are whole counties in Louisiana in which there is not a solitary school-house, is full of suggestion. We compelled these people to remain in the Union, and now duty and interest demand that we leave no just means untried to make them good, loyal citizens. How to diminish the friction, how to stimulate the elevation of this portion of our country, are problems addressing themselves to our best and wisest statesmanship. The foundation for these efforts must be laid in satisfying the Southern people that they are to have equal, exact justice accorded to them. Give them, to the fullest extent, every blessing which the government confers upon the most favored—give them no just cause for complaint, and then hold them, by every necessary means, to an exact, rigid observance of all their duties and obligations under the Constitution and its amendments to secure to *all* within their borders manhood and citizenship, with every right thereto belonging."

The just obligations to public creditors, created when the government was in the throes of threatened dissolution, and as an indispensable condition of its salvation—guaranteed by the lives and blood of thousands of its brave defenders—are to be kept with religious faith, as are all the pledges subsidiary thereto and confirmatory thereof.

In my judgment the pledge of Congress of January 14, 1875, for the redemption of the notes of the United States in coin is the plighted faith of the nation, and national honor, simple honesty, and justice to the people whose permanent welfare and prosperity are dependent upon true money, as the basis of their pecuniary transactions, all demand the scrupulous observance of this pledge, and it is the duty of Congress to supplement it with such legislation as shall be necessary for its strict fulfillment.

In our system of government intelligence must give safety and value to the ballot. Hence the common schools of the land should be preserved in all their vigor; while, in accordance with the spirit of the Constitution, they and all their endowments should be secured by every possible and proper guaranty against every form of sectarian influence or control.

There should be the strictest economy in the expenditures of the government consistent with its effective administration, and all unnecessary offices should be abolished. Offices should be conferred only upon the basis of high character and particular fitness, and should be administered only as public trusts, and not for private advantage.

The foregoing are chief among the cardinal principles of the Republican party, and to carry them into full, practical effect is the work it now has in hand. To the completion of its great mission we address ourselves in hope and confidence, cheered and stimulated by the recollection of its past achievements; remembering that, under God, it is to that party we are indebted in this centennial year of our existence for a preserved, unbroken Union; for the fact that there is no master or slave throughout our broad domains, and that emancipated millions look upon the ensign of the Republic as the symbol of the fulfilled declaration that all men are created free and equal, and the guaranty of their own equality, under the law, with the most highly favored citizen of the land.

To the intelligence and conscience of all who desire good government, good will, good money and universal prosperity, the Republican party, not unmindful of the imperfection and short-comings of human organizations, yet with the honest purpose of its masses promptly to retrieve all errors and to summarily punish all offenders against the laws of the country, confidently submits its claims for the continued support of the American people.

Respectfully,

WILLIAM A. WHEELER.

XXI.

DEMOCRATIC NATIONAL CONVENTION.

Call for the Convention.

The National Democratic Committee, to whom is delegated the power of fixing the time and place of holding the National Democratic Convention of 1876, have appointed Tuesday, the 27th day of June next, noon, as the time, and selected St. Louis as the place, of holding such Convention. Each State will be entitled to a representation equal to double the number of its Senators and Representatives in the Congress of the United States, and the Territory of Colorado, whose admission in July as a State will give it a vote in the next electoral college, is also invited to send delegates to the Convention. Democratic, Conservative and other citizens of the United States, irrespective of past political associations, desiring to coöperate with the Democratic party in its present efforts and objects, are cordially invited to join in sending delegates to the National Convention. Coöperation is desired from all persons who would change an administration that has suffered the public credit to become and remain inferior to other and less-favored nations; has permitted commerce to be taken away by foreign powers; has stifled trade by unjust, unequal and pernicious legislation; has imposed unusual taxation and rendered it most troublesome; has changed growing prosperity to widespread suffering and want; has squandered the public moneys recklessly and defiantly, and shamefully used the power that should have been swift to punish crime, to protect it.

For these and other reasons the National Democratic party deem the public danger imminent, and earnestly desirous of securing to our country the blessing of an economical, pure and free government, cordially invite the coöperation of their fellow-citizens in the effort to attain this object.

AUGUSTUS SCHELL, *Chairman.*

The Convention met as per the call, and Mr. SCHELL, after making some remarks, nominated HENRY WATTERSON, of Kentucky, as temporary chairman, who was elected.

The rules of the last National Democratic Convention were adopted. Committees on Credentials, Permanent Organization and on Resolutions were appointed.

Adjourned till 5 o'clock, p. m.

The Territories and the District of Columbia were given the right of representation as States, but not the right to vote.

The Committee on Permanent Organization, through Mr. HANNA, reported a list of officers, with Gen. JOHN A. McCLERNAND, of Illinois, as the permanent President.

Adjourned till to-morrow at 11 o'clock.

June 28—The convention met, listened to speeches from Col. WM. P. BRECKINRIDGE, of Kentucky, Hon. B. GRATZ BROWN, of Missouri, Hon. WM. A. WALLACE, of Pennsylvania, Hon. JAMES R. DOOLITTLE, of Wisconsin, and others. At 2½ o'clock the convention re-assembled, and the Committee on Resolutions made the following report through Mr. DORSHEIMER, of New York:

We, the delegates of the Democratic party of the United States in National Convention assembled, do hereby declare the administration of the Federal Government to be in urgent need of immediate reform; do hereby enjoin upon the nominees of this Convention, and of the Democratic party in each State, a zealous effort and coöperation to this end; and do hereby appeal to our fellow-citizens of every former political connection to undertake with us this first and most pressing patriotic duty.

For the Democracy of the whole country, we do here re-affirm our faith in the permanence of the Federal Union, our devotion to the Constitution of the United States, with its amendments universally accepted as a final settlement of the controversies that engendered civil war, and do here record our steadfast confidence in the perpetuity of republican self-government.

In absolute acquiescence in the will of the majority—the vital principle of republics; in the supremacy of the civil over the military authority; in the total separation of Church and State, for the sake alike of civil and religious freedom; in the equality of all citizens before just laws of their own enactment; in the liberty of individual conduct, unvexed by sumptuary laws; in the faithful education of the rising generation, that they may preserve, enjoy, and transmit these best conditions of human happiness and hope, we behold the noblest products of a hundred years of changeful history; but while upholding the bond of our Union and great charter of these our rights, it behooves a free people to practice also that eternal vigilance which is the price of liberty.

Reform is necessary to rebuild and establish in the hearts of the whole people, the Union, eleven years ago happily rescued from the danger of a secession of States; but now to be saved from a corrupt centralism which, after inflicting upon ten States the rapacity of carpet-bag tyrannies, has honeycombed the offices of the Federal Government itself with incapacity, waste, and fraud; infected States and municipalities with the contagion of misrule, and locked fast the prosperity of an industrious people in the paralysis of "hard times."

Reform is necessary to establish a sound currency, restore the public credit, and maintain the national honor.

We denounce the failure, for all these eleven years of peace, to make good the promise of the legal-tender notes, which are a changing standard of value in the hands of the people, and the non-payment of which is a disregard of the plighted faith of the nation.

We denounce the improvidence which, in eleven years of peace, has taken from the people in Federal taxes thirteen times the whole amount of the legal-tender notes, and squandered four times their sum in useless expense without accumulating any reserve for their redemption.

We denounce the financial imbecility and immorality of that party, which, during eleven years of peace, has made no advance toward resumption, no preparation for resumption, but instead has obstructed resumption, by wasting our resources and exhausting all our surplus income; and, while annually professing to intend a speedy return to specie payments, has annually enacted fresh hindrances thereto. As such hindrance we denounce the resumption clause of the act of 1875 and we here demand its repeal.

We demand a judicious system of preparation by public economies, by official retrenchments, and by wise finance, which shall enable the nation soon to assure the whole world of its perfect ability and its perfect readiness to meet any of its promises at the call of the creditor entitled to payment.

We believe such a system, well devised, and, above all, intrusted to competent hands for execution, creating at no time an artificial scarcity of currency, and at no time alarming the public mind into a withdrawal of that vaster machinery of credit by which ninety-five per cent. of all business transactions are performed—a system open, public, and inspiring general confidence, would from the day of its adoption bring healing on its wings to all our harassed industries, set in motion the wheels of commerce, manufactures, and the mechanic arts, restore employment to labor, and renew in all its natural sources the prosperity of the people.

Reform is necessary in the sum and modes of Federal taxation, to the end that capital may be set free from distrust, and labor lightly burdened.

We denounce the present Tariff, levied upon nearly 4,000 articles, as a master-piece of injustice, inequality and false pretence. It yields a dwindling, not a yearly rising revenue. It has impoverished many industries to subsidize a few. It prohibits imports that might purchase the products of American labor. It has degraded American commerce from the first to an inferior rank on the high seas. It has cut down the sales of

American manufactures at home and abroad and depleted the returns of American agriculture—an industry followed by half our people. It costs the people five times more than it produces to the Treasury, obstructs the processes of production, and wastes the fruits of labor. It promotes fraud, fosters smuggling, enriches dishonest officials, and bankrupts honest merchants. We demand that all Custom House taxation shall be only for revenue.

Reform is necessary in the scale of public expense—Federal, State, and Municipal. Our Federal taxation has swollen from sixty millions gold, in 1860, to four hundred and fifty millions currency, in 1870; our aggregate taxation from one hundred and fifty-four millions gold, in 1860, to seven hundred and thirty millions currency, in 1870; or in one decade from less than five dollars per head to more than eighteen dollars per head. Since the peace, the people have paid to their tax gatherers more than thrice the sum of the national debt, and more than twice that sum for the Federal Government alone. We demand a rigorous frugality in every department, and from every officer of the government.

Reform is necessary to put a stop to the profligate waste of public lands, and their diversion from actual settlers by the party in power, which has squandered 200,000,000 of acres upon railroads alone, and out of more than thrice that aggregate has disposed of less than a sixth directly to tillers of the soil.

Reform is necessary to correct the omissions of a Republican Congress, and the errors of our treaties and our diplomacy which have stripped our fellow citizens of foreign birth and kindred race recrossing the Atlantic, of the shield of American citizenship, and have exposed our brethren of the Pacific coast to the incursions of a race not sprung from the same great parent stock, and in fact now by law denied citizenship through naturalization as being neither accustomed to the traditions of a progressive civilization nor exercised in liberty under equal laws. We denounce the policy which thus discards the liberty-loving German and tolerates a revival of the coolie trade in Mongolian women imported for immoral purposes and Mongolian men held to perform servile labor contracts, and demand such modification of the treaty with the Chinese Empire or such legislation within constitutional limitations as shall prevent further importation or immigration of the Mongolian race.

Reform is necessary and can never be effected but by making it the controlling issue of the elections, and lifting it above the two false issues with which the office-holding class and the party in power seek to smother it:

1. The false issue with which they would enkindle sectarian strife in respect to the public schools, of which the establishment and support belong exclusively to the several States, and which the Democratic party has cherished from their foundation, and is resolved to maintain without prejudice or preference for any class, sect or creed, and without largesses from the treasury to any.

2. The false issue by which they seek to light anew the dying embers of sectional hate between kindred peoples once estranged, but now reunited in one indivisible republic and a common destiny.

Reform is necessary in the Civil Service. Experience proves that efficient, economical conduct of the governmental business is not possible if its civil service be subject to change at every election, be a prize fought for at the ballot-box, be a brief reward of party zeal, instead of posts of honor assigned for proved competency and held for fidelity in the public employ; that the dispensing of patronage should neither be a tax upon the time of all our public men, nor the instrument of their ambition. Here again promises falsified in the performance, attest that the party in power can work out no practical or salutary reform.

Reform is necessary even more in the higher grades of the public service. President, Vice-President, Judges, Senators, Representatives, Cabinet officers, these and all others in authority are the people's servants. Their offices are not a private perquisite; they are a public trust.

When the annals of this Republic show the disgrace and censure of a Vice-President; a late Speaker of the House of Representatives marketing his rulings as a presiding officer; three Senators profiting secretly by their votes as law-makers; five chairmen of the leading committees of the late House of Representatives exposed in jobbery; a late Secretary of the Treasury forcing balances in the public accounts; a late Attorney-General misappropriating public funds; a Secretary of the Navy enriched or enriching friends by percentages levied off the profits of contractors with his department; an Ambassador to England censured in a dishonorable speculation; the President's private secretary barely escaping conviction upon trial for guilty complicity in frauds upon the revenue; a Secretary of War impeached for high crimes and misdemeanors—the demonstration is complete, that the first step in reform must be the people's choice of honest men from another party, lest the disease of one political organization infect the body politic, and lest by making no change of men or parties we get no change of measures and no real reform.

All these abuses, wrongs, and crimes, the product of sixteen years' ascendency of the Republican party, create a necessity for reform confessed by Republicans themselves; but their reformers are voted down in convention and displaced from the Cabinet. The party's mass of honest voters is powerless to resist the 80,000 office-holders, its leaders and guides.

Reform can only be had by a peaceful civic revolution. We demand a change of system, a change of Administration, a change of parties, that we may have a change of measures and of men.

Resolved, That this Convention, representing the Democratic party of the United States, do cordially indorse the action of the present House of Representatives in reducing and curtailing the expenses of the Federal Government, in cutting down salaries, extravagant appropriations, and in abolishing useless offices and places not required by the public necessities, and we shall trust to the firmness of the Democratic members of the House that no committee of conference and no misinterpretation of the rules will be allowed to defeat these wholesome measures of economy demanded by the country.

Resolved, That the soldiers and sailors of the Republic and the widows and orphans of those who have fallen in battle have a just claim upon the care, protection, and gratitude of their fellow-citizens.

[The Committee consisted of the following persons: *Alabama*, Leroy P. Walker; *Arkansas*, L. V. Maguire; *California*, John S. Hager; *Colorado*, F. J. Marshall; *Connecticut*, R. D. Hubbard; *Delaware*, George Gray; *Florida*, John Westcott; *Georgia*, C. F. Howell; *Illinois*, John A. McClernand; *Indiana*, D. W. Voorhees; *Iowa*, H. H. Trimble; *Kansas*, Thomas L. Davis; *Kentucky*, Alvin Duval; *Louisiana*, R. H. Mann; *Maine*, D. R. Hastings; *Maryland*, George Freaner; *Massachusetts*, Edward Avery; *Michigan*, William L. Bancroft; *Minnesota*, Daniel Bucks; *Mississippi*, A. M. Clayton; *Missouri*, C. H. Hardin; *Nebraska*, George L. Emlen; *Nevada*, A. C. Ellis; *New Hampshire*, E. C. Barley; *New Jersey*, Joseph Gates; *New York*, William Dorsheimer; *North Carolina*, Thomas L. Clingman; *Ohio*, Thomas Ewing; *Oregon*, M. V. Brown; *Pennsylvania*, Malcolm Hay; *Rhode Island*, W. B. Beach; *South Carolina*, Sam. McGowan; *Tennessee*, John C. Brown; *Texas*, Ashbel Smith; *Vermont*, James H. Williams; *Virginia*, John A. Meredith; *West Virginia*, John J. Davis; *Wisconsin*, Alex. Mitchell.

The above is believed to be a correct copy of the Platform as adopted. For a time, some confusion existed on this question, caused by the publication in the N. Y. *Sun*, of July 7, 1876, (and probably other papers,) of a copy, purporting to be "official," but which was noticeably inaccurate and incomplete.—EDITOR.]

Pending the report,

Mr. THOMAS EWING, of Ohio, presented the following minority report:

The undersigned members of the Committee recommend that the following clause in the resolutions reported by the Committee be stricken out: "As such hindrance we denounce the resumption clause of the act of 1875, and we here demand its repeal." And they recommend that there be substituted for that clause the following: "The law for the resumption of specie payments on the 1st of January, 1879, having been enacted by the Republican party without deliberation in Congress or discussion before the people, and being both ineffective to secure its objects and highly injurious to the business of the country, ought to be forthwith repealed."

T. EWING, Ohio.
D. W. VOORHEES, Indiana.
J. C. BROWN, Tennessee.
MALCOLM HAY, Penn.
H. H. TRIMBLE, Iowa.
J. J. DAVIS, West Virginia.
T. L. DAVIS, Kansas.
E. H. HARDIN, Missouri.

After debate, the Convention rejected the minority report—yeas 219, nays 550.

The Platform, as reported, was then adopted—yeas 651, nays 83.

NOMINATION OF CANDIDATES.

By DELAWARE—THOMAS F. BAYARD.
By INDIANA—THOMAS A. HENDRICKS.
By NEW JERSEY—JOEL PARKER.
By NEW YORK—SAMUEL J. TILDEN.
By OHIO—WILLIAM ALLEN.
By PENNSYLVANIA—WINFIELD S. HANCOCK.

After speech making and seconding these nominations, the Convention balloted, and with this result:

	1st.	*2d.*
Samuel J. Tilden	417	535
Thomas A. Hendricks	140	60
Winfield S. Hancock	75	59
William Allen	56	54
Thomas F. Bayard	33	11
Joel Parker	18	18
Allen G. Thurman	00	7
	739	744

Mr. TILDEN'S nomination was made unanimous, and the Convention adjourned till to-morrow.

June 29—Hon. THOMAS A. HENDRICKS, of Indiana, was nominated by acclamation.

Mr. WEBBER, of Michigan, offered this resolution:

Resolved, That it be recommended to future National Democratic Conventions, as the sense of the Democracy here in Convention assembled, that the so-called two-thirds rule be abolished as unwise and unnecessary; and that the States be requested to instruct their delegates to the Democratic National Convention which is to be held in 1880 whether it is desirable to continue the two-thirds rule longer in force in the National Conventions, and that the National Committee insert such request in their call for the Convention.

A division of the question was called, to end with the word "unnecessary."

The first division was disagreed to, and the second agreed to.

After transacting some routine business the Convention adjourned *sine die*.

Gov. Tilden's Letter of Acceptance.

ALBANY, July 31, 1876.

GENTLEMEN: When I had the honor to receive a personal delivery of your letter on behalf of the Democratic National Convention, held on the 28th of June at St. Louis, advising me of my nomination as the candidate of the constituency represented by that body for the office of President of the United States, I answered that, at my earliest convenience, and in conformity with usage, I would prepare and transmit to you a formal acceptance. I now avail myself of the first interval in unavoidable occupations to fulfill that engagement. The convention, before making its nominations, adopted a declaration of principles, which, as a whole, seems to me a wise exposition of the necessities of our country, and of the reforms needed to bring back the Government to its true functions, to restore purity of administration, and to renew the prosperity of the people. But some of these reforms are so urgent that they claim more than a passing approval.

The necessity of a reform "in the scale of

public expense—Federal, State, and Municipal," —and "in the modes of Federal taxation," justifies all the prominence given to it in the declaration of the St. Louis Convention. The present depression in all the business and industries of the people, which is depriving labor of its employment, and carrying want into so many homes, has its principal cause in excessive Governmental consumption. Under the illusions of a specious prosperity engendered by the false policies of the Federal Government a waste of capital has been going on ever since the peace of 1865, which could only end in universal disaster. The Federal taxes of the last eleven years reach the gigantic sum of four thousand five hundred millions. Local taxation has amounted to two-thirds as much more. The vast aggregate is not less than seven thousand five hundred millions. This enormous taxation followed a civil conflict that had greatly impaired our aggregate wealth, and had made a prompt reduction of expenses indispensable. It was aggravated by most unscientific and ill-adjusted methods of taxation that increased the sacrifices of the people far beyond the receipts of the Treasury. It was aggravated, moreover, by a financial policy which tended to diminish the energy, skill and economy of production, and the frugality of private consumption, and induced miscalculation in business and an unremunerative use of capital and labor. Even in prosperous times, the daily wants of industrious communities press closely upon their daily earnings. The margin of possible national savings is at best a small percentage of national earnings. Yet now for these eleven years, governmental consumption has been a larger portion of the national earnings than the whole people can possibly save even in prosperous times for all new investments. The consequences of these errors are now a present public calamity. But they were never doubtful, never invisible. They were necessary and inevitable, and were foreseen and depicted when the waves of that fictitious prosperity ran highest. In a speech made by me on the 24th of September, 1868, it was said of these taxes:

"They bear heavily upon every man's income, upon every industry and every business in the country, and year by year they are destined to press still more heavily, unless we arrest the system that gives rise to them. It was comparatively easy when values were doubling under repeated issues of legal tender paper money, to pay out of the froth of our growing and apparent wealth these taxes, but when values recede and sink toward their natural scale, the tax-gatherer takes from us not only our income, not only our profits, but also a portion of our capital. * * * I do not wish to exaggerate or alarm; I simply say that we cannot afford the costly and ruinous policy of the Radical majority of Congress. We cannot afford that policy toward the South. We cannot afford the magnificent and oppressive centralism into which our Government is being converted. We cannot afford the present magnificent scale of taxation."

To the Secretary of the Treasury I said, early in 1865:

"There is no royal road for a government more than for an individual or a corporation. What you want to do now is to cut down your expenses and live within your income. I would give all the legerdemain of finance and financiering—I would give the whole of it for the old, homely maxim, 'Live within your income.'"

This reform will be resisted at every step, but it must be pressed persistently. We see to-day the immediate representatives of the people in one branch of Congress, while struggling to reduce expenditures, compelled to confront the menace of the Senate and the Executive that unless the objectionable appropriations be consented to, the operations of the Government thereunder shall suffer detriment or cease. In my judgment an amendment of the Constitution ought to be devised separating into distinct bills the appropriations for the various departments of the public service, and excluding from each bill all appropriations for other objects and all independent legislation. In that way alone can the revisory power of each of the two houses and of the Executive be preserved and exempted from the moral duress which often compels assent to objectionable appropriations rather than stop the wheels of Government.

An accessory cause enhancing the distress in business is to be found in the systematic and insupportable misgovernment imposed upon the States of the South. Besides the ordinary effects of ignorant and dishonest administration, it has inflicted upon them enormous issues of fraudulent bonds, the scanty avails of which were wasted or stolen, and the existence of which is a public discredit, tending to bankruptcy or repudiation. Taxes, generally oppressive, in some instances have confiscated the entire income of property and totally destroyed its marketable value. It is impossible that these evils should not re-act upon the prosperity of the whole country. The nobler motives of humanity concur with the material interests of all in requiring that every obstacle be removed, to a complete and durable reconciliation between kindred populations once unnaturally estranged, on the basis recognized by the St. Louis platform, of the "Constitution of the United States, with its amendments universally accepted as a final settlement of the controversies which engendered civil war." But, in aid of a result so beneficent, the moral influence of every good citizen, as well as every governmental authority, ought to be exerted, not alone to maintain their just equality before the law, but likewise to establish a cordial fraternity and good will among citizens, whatever their race or color, who are now united in the one destiny of a common self-government. If the duty shall be assigned to me, I should not fail to exercise the powers with which the laws and the Constitution of our country clothe its Chief Magistrate, to protect all its citizens, whatever their former condition, in every political and personal right.

"Reform is necessary," declares the St. Louis Convention, "to establish a sound currency, restore the public credit and maintain the national honor; and it goes on to "demand a judicious system of preparation by public economies, by official retrenchments, and by wise finance, which shall enable the nation soon to assure the whole world of its perfect ability and its perfect readiness to meet any of its promises at the call of the creditor entitled to payment." The object demanded by the Convention is a resumption of specie payments on the legal-tender notes of the United States. That would not only "restore the public credit" and "maintain the national honor," but it would "establish a sound currency" for the people. The methods by which this object is to be pursued, and the means by which it is to be attained, are disclosed by what the Convention demanded for the future, and by what it denounced in the past.

Resumption of specie payments by the Government of the United States on its legal-tender notes would establish specie payments by all the banks on all their notes. The official statement, made on the 12th of May, shows that the amount of the bank notes was three hundred millions, less twenty millions held by themselves. Against these two hundred and eighty millions of notes the banks held one hundred and forty-one millions of legal-tender notes, or a little more than fifty per cent. of their amount But they also held on deposit in the Federal Treasury, as security for these notes, bonds of the United States worth in gold about three hundred and sixty millions, available and current in all the foreign money markets. In resuming, the banks, even if it were possible for all their notes to be presented for payment, would have five hundred millions of specie funds to pay two hundred and eighty millions of notes, without contracting their loans to their customers, or calling on any private debtor for payment. Suspended banks undertaking to resume have usually been obliged to collect from needy borrowers the means to redeem excessive issues and to provide reserves. A vague idea of distress is, therefore, often associated with the process of resumption. But the conditions which caused distress in those former instances do not now exist. The Government has only to make good its own promises, and the banks can take care of themselves without distressing anybody. The Government is, therefore, the sole delinquent.

The amount of the legal-tender notes of the United States now outstanding is less than three hundred and seventy millions of dollars, besides thirty-four millions of dollars of fractional currency. How shall the Government make these notes at all times as good as specie? It has to provide, in reference to the mass which would be kept in use by the wants of business, a central reservoir of coin, adequate to the adjustment of the temporary fluctuations of international balances, and as a guaranty against transient drains artificially created by panic or by speculation. It has also to provide for the payment in coin of such fractional currency as may be presented for redemption, and such inconsiderable portions of the legal tenders as individuals may from time to time desire to convert for special use, or in order to lay by in coin their little stores of money.

To make the coin now in the Treasury available for the objects of this reserve, to gradually strengthen and enlarge that reserve, and to provide for such other exceptional demands for coin as may arise, does not seem to me a work of difficulty. If wisely planned and discreetly pursued, it ought not to cost any sacrifice to the business of the country. It should tend, on the contrary, to a revival of hope and confidence. The coin in the Treasury on the 30th of June, including what is held against coin certificates, amounted to nearly seventy-four millions. The current of precious metals which has flowed out of our country for the eleven years from July 1, 1865, to June 30, 1876, averaging nearly seventy-six millions a year, was eight hundred and thirty-two millions in the whole period, of which six hundred and seventeen millions were the product of our own mines. To amass the requisite quantity, by intercepting from the current flowing out of the country, and by acquiring from the stocks which exist abroad without disturbing the equilibrium of foreign money markets, is a result to be easily worked out by practical knowledge and judgment. With respect to whatever surplus of legal-tenders the wants of business may fail to keep in use, and which, in order to save interest, will be returned for redemption, they can either be paid or they can be funded. Whether they continue as currency, or be absorbed into the vast mass of securities held as investments, is merely a question of the rate of interest they draw. Even if they were to remain in their present form, and the Government were to agree to pay on them a rate of interest making them desirable as investments, they would cease to circulate and take their place with Government, State, Municipal, and other corporate and private bonds, of which thousands of millions exist among us. In the perfect ease with which they can be changed from currency into investments lies the only danger to be guarded against in the adoption of general measures intended to remove a clearly ascertained surplus; that is, the withdrawal of any which are not a permanent excess beyond the wants of business. Even more mischievous would be any measure which affects the public imagination with the fear of an apprehended scarcity. In a community where credit is so much used, fluctuations of values and vicissitudes in business are largely caused by the temporary beliefs of men even before those beliefs can conform to ascertained realities.

The amount of the necessary currency at a given time cannot be determined arbitrarily, and should not be assumed on conjecture. That amount is subject to both permanent and temporary changes. An enlargement of it, which seemed to be durable, happened at the beginning of the civil war by a substituted use of currency in place of individual credits. It varies with certain states of business. It fluctuates, with considerable regularity, at different seasons of the year. In the autumn, for instance, when buyers of grain and other agricultural products begin their operations, they usually need to borrow capital or circulating credits by which to make their purchases, and want these funds in currency capable of being distributed in small sums among numerous sellers. The additional need of currency at such times is five or more per cent, of the whole volume, and, if a surplus beyond what is required for ordinary use does not happen to have been on hand at the money centres, a scarcity of currency ensues, and also a stringency in the loan market. It was in reference to such experiences that, in a discussion of this subject in my annual Message to the New-York Legislature of January 5, 1875, the suggestion was made that:

"The Federal Government is bound to redeem every portion of its issues which the public do not wish to use. Having assumed to monopolize the supply of currency and enacted exclusions against everybody else, it is bound to furnish all which the wants of business require." * * * "The system should passively allow the volume of circulating credits to ebb and flow, according to the ever-changing wants of business. It should imitate, as closely as possible, the natural laws of trade, which it has superseded by artificial contrivances." And in a similar discussion in my Message of January 4, 1876, it was said that resumption should be effected "by such measures as would keep the aggregate amount of the currency self-adjusting during all the process, without creating, at any time, an artificial scarcity, and without exciting the public imagination with alarms which impair confidence, contract the whole large machinery of credit, and disturb the natural operations of business."

"Public economies, official retrenchments, and wise finance" are the means which the St. Louis Convention indicates as provision for reserves and redemptions. The best resource is a reduction of the expenses of the Government below its income; for that imposes no new charge on the people. If, however, the improvidence and waste which have conducted us to a period of falling revenues, oblige us to supplement the results of economies and retrenchments by some resort to loans, we should not hesitate. The Government ought not to speculate on its own dishonor, in order to save interest on its broken promises, which it still compels private dealers to accept at a fictitious par. The highest national honor is not only right, but would prove profitable. Of the public debt nine hundred and eighty-five millions bear interest at six per cent. in gold, and seven hundred and twelve millions at five per cent. in gold. The average interest is 5.58 per cent. A financial policy which should secure the highest credit, wisely availed of, ought gradually to obtain a reduction of one per cent. in the interest on most of the loans. A saving of one per cent. on the average would be seventeen millions a year in gold. That saving regularly invested at four and a half per cent. would, in less than thirty-eight years, extinguish the principal. The whole seventeen hundred millions of funded debt might be paid by this saving alone, without cost to the people.

The proper time for resumption is the time when wise preparations shall have ripened into a perfect ability to accomplish the object with a certainty and ease that will inspire confidence and encourage the reviving of business. The earliest time in which such a result can be brought about is the best. Even when the preparations shall have been matured, the exact date would have to be chosen with reference to the then existing state of trade and credit operations in our own country, the course of foreign commerce, and the condition of the exchanges with other nations. The specific measures and the actual date are matters of detail having reference to ever-changing conditions. They belong to the domain of practical administrative statesmanship. The captain of a steamer about starting from New York to Liverpool does not assemble a council over his ocean chart and fix an angle by which to lash the rudder for the whole voyage. A human intelligence must be at the helm to discern the shifting forces of the waters and the winds. A human hand must be on the helm to feel the elements day by day, and guide to a mastery over them.

Such preparations are everything. Without them, a legislative command fixing a day, an official promise fixing a day, are shams. They are worse—they are a snare and a delusion to all who trust them. They destroy all confidence among thoughtful men whose judgment will at last sway public opinion. An attempt to act on such a command or such a promise, without preparation, would end in a new suspension. It would be a fresh calamity, prolific of confusion, distrust, and distress.

The act of Congress of the 14th of January, 1875, enacted that, on and after the 1st of January, 1879, the Secretary of the Treasury shall redeem in coin the legal-tender notes of the United States on presentation at the office of the Assistant Treasurer in the City of New-York. It authorized the Secretary "to prepare and provide for" such resumption of specie payments by the use of any surplus revenues not otherwise appropriated; and by issuing, in his discretion, certain classes of bonds. More than one and a half of the four years have passed. Congress and the President have continued ever since to unite in acts which have legislated out of existence every possible surplus applicable to this purpose. The coin in the Treasury claimed to belong to the Government had, on the 30th of June, fallen to less than forty-five millions of dollars, as against fifty-nine millions on the 1st of January, 1875, and the availability of a part of that sum is said to be questionable. The revenues are falling faster than appropriations and expenditures are reduced, leaving the Treasury with diminishing resources. The Secretary has done nothing under his power to issue bonds. The legislative command, the official promise fixing a day for resumption, have thus far been barren. No practical preparations toward resumption have been made. There has been no progress. There have been steps backward. There is no necromancy in the operations of government. The homely maxims of every-day life are the best standards of its conduct. A debtor who should promise to pay a loan out of surplus income, yet be seen every day spending all he could lay his hands on in riotous living would lose all character for honesty and veracity. His offer of a new promise or his profession as to the value of the old promise would alike provoke derision.

The St. Louis platform denounces the failure for eleven years to make good the promise of the legal tender notes. It denounces the omission to accumulate "any reserve for their redemption." It denounces the conduct "which, during eleven years of peace, has made no advances toward resumption, no preparation for resumption, but instead has obstructed resumption by wasting our resources and exhausting all our surplus income; and, while professing to intend a speedy return to specie payments, has annually enacted fresh hindrances thereto." And having first denounced the barrenness of the promise of a day of resumption, it next denounces that barren promise as "a hindrance" to resumption. It then demands its repeal and also demands the establishment of "a judicious system of preparation," for resumption. It cannot be doubted that the substitution of "a system of preparation" without the promise of a day for the worthless promise of a day without "a system of preparation" would be the gain of the substance of resumption in exchange for its shadow. Nor is the denunciation unmerited of that improvidence which, in the eleven years since the peace, has consumed four thousand five hundred millions of dollars, and yet could not afford to give the people a sound and stable currency. Two and a half per cent. on the expenditures of these eleven years, or even less, would have provided all the additional coin needful to resumption.

The distress now felt by the people in all their business and industries, though it has its principal cause in the enormous waste of capital occasioned by the false policies of our Government, has been greatly aggravated by the mismanagement of the currency. Uncertainty is the prolific parent of mischiefs in all business. Never were its evils more felt than now. Men do nothing because they are unable to make any calculations on which they can safely rely. They undertake nothing because they fear a loss in everything they would attempt. They stop and wait. The merchant dares not buy for the future consumption of his customers. The manufacturer dares not make fabrics which may not refund his outlay. He shuts his factory and discharges his workmen. Capitalists cannot lend on security they consider safe, and their funds lie almost without interest. Men of enterprise who have credit, or securities to pledge, will not borrow. Consumption has fallen below the natural limits of a reasonable economy. Prices of many things are under their range in frugal, specie-paying times before the civil war. Vast masses of currency lie in the banks unused. A year and a half ago the legal tenders were at their largest volume, and the twelve millions since retired have been replaced by fresh issues of fifteen millions of bank notes. In the meantime the banks have been surrendering about four millions a month, because they cannot find a profitable use for so many of their notes. The public mind will no longer accept shams. It has suffered enough from illusions. An insecure policy increases distrust. An unstable policy increases uncertainty. The people need to know that the Government is moving in the direction of ultimate safety and prosperity, and that it is doing so through prudent, safe, and conservative methods, which will be sure to inflict no new sacrifice on the business of the country. Then the inspiration of new hope and well-founded confidence will hasten the restoring processes of nature, and prosperity will begin to return. The St. Louis Convention concludes its expression in regard to the currency by a declaration of its convictions as to the practical results of the system of preparations it demands. It says: "We believe such a system, well devised, and above all, intrusted to competent hands for execution, creating at no time an artificial scarcity of currency, and at no time alarming the public mind into a withdrawal of that vaster machinery of credit by which ninety-five per cent. of all business transactions are performed—a system open, public, and inspiring general confidence would, from the day of its adoption, bring healing on its wings to all our harassed industries, set in motion the wheels of commerce, manufactures, and the mechanic arts, restore employment to labor, and renew in all its natural sources the prosperity of the people." The Government of the United States, in my opinion, can advance to a resumption of specie payments on its legal tender notes by gradual and safe processes tending to relieve the present business distress. If charged by the people with the administration of the Executive office, I should deem it a duty so to exercise the powers with which it has been or may be invested by Congress as best and soonest to conduct the country to that beneficent result.

The Convention justly affirms that reform is necessary in the civil service, necessary to its purification, necessary to its economy and its efficiency, necessary in order that the ordinary employment of the public business may not be "a prize fought for at the ballot-box, a brief reward of party zeal instead of posts of honor assigned for proved competency, and held for fidelity in the public employ." The Convention wisely added that "Reform is necessary even more in the highest grades of the public service. President, Vice-President, Judges, Senators, Representatives, Cabinet officers, these and all others in authority are the people's servants. Their offices are nor a private perquisite, they are a public trust." Two evils infest the official service of the Federal Government. One is the prevalent and demoralizing notion that the public service exists not for the business and benefit of the whole people, but for the interest of the office holders, who are in truth but the servants of the people. Under the influence of this pernicious error public employments have been multiplied; the numbers of those gathered into the ranks of office-holders have been steadily increased beyond any possible requirement of the public business, while inefficiency, peculation, fraud, and malversation of the public funds, from the high places of power to the lowest, have overspread the whole service like a leprosy. The other evil is the organization of the official class into a body of political mercenaries, governing the caucuses and dictating the nominations of their own party, and attempting to carry the elections of the people by undue influence and by immense corruption funds systematically collected from the salaries or fees of office-holders. The official class in other countries, sometimes by its own weight, and sometimes in alliance with the army, has been able to rule the unorganized masses even under universal suffrage. Here, it has already grown into a gigantic power, capable of stifling the inspirations of a sound public opinion, and of resisting an easy change of administration, until misgovernment becomes intolerable and public spirit has been stung to the pitch of a civic revolution. The first step in reform is the elevation of the standard by which the appointing power selects agents to execute official trusts. Next in importance is a conscientious fidelity in the exercise of the authority to hold to account and displace untrustworthy or incapable subordinates. The public interest in an honest, skillful performance of official trust must not be sacrificed to the usufruct of the incumbents. After these immediate steps, which will insure the exhibition of better examples, we may wisely go on to the abolition of unnecessary offices, and finally to the patient, careful organization of a better civil-service system, under the tests, wherever practicable, of proved competency and fidelity. While much may be accomplished by these methods, it might encourage delusive expectations if I withheld here the expression of my conviction that no reform of the civil service in this country will be complete and permanent until its Chief Magistrate is constitutionally disqualified for re-election, experience having repeatedly exposed the futility of self-imposed restrictions by candidates or incumbents. Through this solemnity only can he be effectually delivered from his greatest temptation to misuse the power and patronage with which the Executive is necessarily charged.

Educated in the belief that it is the first duty of a citizen of the Republic to take his fair allotment of care and trouble in public affairs, I have, for forty years, as a private citizen, fulfilled that duty. Though occupied in an unusual degree during all that period with the concerns of Government, I have never acquired the habit of official life. When, a year and a half ago, I entered upon my present trust, it was in order to consummate reforms to which I had already devoted several of the best years of my life. Knowing as I do, therefore, from fresh experience, how great the difference is between gliding through an official routine and working out a reform of systems and policies, it is impossible for me to contemplate what needs to be done in the Federal Administration without an anxious sense of the difficulties of the undertaking. If summoned by the suffrages of my countrymen to attempt this work, I shall endeavor, with God's help, to be the efficient instrument of their will.

SAMUEL J. TILDEN.

To Gen. John A. McClernand, Chairman; Gen. W. B. Franklin, Hon. J. G. Abbott, Hon. H. J. Spannhorst, Hon. H. J. Redfield, Hon. F. S. Lyon, and others, Committee, &c.

Gov. Hendricks' Letter of Acceptance.

INDIANAPOLIS, July 24, 1876.

GENTLEMEN: I have the honor to acknowledge the receipt of your communication, in which you have formally notified me of my nomination by the National Democratic Convention, at St. Louis, as their candidate for the office of Vice-President of the United States. It is a nomination which I had neither expected nor desired; and yet I recognize and appreciate the high honor done me by the Convention. The choice of such a body, pronounced with such unusual unanimity, and accompanied with so generous an expression of esteem and confidence ought to outweigh all merely personal desires and preferences of my own. It is with this feeling, and I trust also from a deep sense of public duty, that I now accept the nomination, and shall abide the judgment of my countrymen.

It would have been impossible for me to accept the nomination if I could not heartily indorse the platform of the Convention. I am gratified, therefore, to be able unequivocally to declare that I agree in the principles, approve the policies, and sympathize with the purposes enunciated in that platform.

The institutions of our country have been sorely tried by the exigencies of civil war, and, since the peace, by a selfish and corrupt management of public affairs, which has shamed us before civilized mankind. By unwise and partial legislation every industry and interest of the people have been made to suffer, and in the executive departments of the Government dishonesty, rapacity and venality have debauched the public service. Men known to be unworthy have been promoted, while others have been degraded for fidelity to official duty. Public office has been made the means of private profit, and the country has been offended to see a class of men who boast the friendship of the sworn protectors of the State amassing fortunes by defrauding the public treasury and by corrupting the servants of the people. In such a crisis of the history of the country I rejoice that the Convention at St. Louis has so nobly raised the standard of reform. Nothing can be well with us or with our affairs until the public conscience, shocked by the enormous evils and abuses which prevail, shall have demanded and compelled an unsparing reformation of our National Administration, "in its head and in its members." In such a reformation the removal of a single officer, even the President, is comparatively a trifling matter, if the system which he represents, and which has fostered him as he has fostered it, is suffered to remain. The President alone must not be made the scapegoat for the enormities of the system which infects the public service, and threatens the destruction of our institutions. In some respects I hold that the present Executive has been the victim rather than the author of that vicious system. Congressional and party leaders have been stronger than the President. No one man could have created it, and the removal of no one man can amend it. It is thoroughly corrupt, and must be swept remorselessly away by the selection of a Government composed of elements entirely new, and pledged to radical reform.

The first work of reform must evidently be the restoration of the normal operation of the Constitution of the United States, with all its amendments. The necessities of war cannot be pleaded in time of peace; the right of local self-government as guaranteed by the Constitution of the Union must be everywhere restored, and the centralized (almost personal) imperialism which has been practiced must be done away or the first principles of the Republic will be lost.

Our financial system of expedients must be reformed. Gold and silver are the real standard of values, and our national currency will not be a perfect medium of exchange until it shall be convertible at the pleasure of the holder. As I have heretofore said, no one desires a return to specie payments more earnestly than I do; but I do not believe that it will or can be reached in harmony with the interests of the people by artificial measures for the contraction of the currency, any more than I believe that wealth or permanent prosperity can be created by an inflation of the currency. The laws of finance can not be disregarded with impunity. The financial policy of the Government, if indeed, it deserves the name of policy at all, has been in disregard of those laws, and therefore has disturbed commercial and business confidence, as well as hindered a return to specie payments. One feature of that policy was the resumption clause of the act of 1875, which has embarrassed the country by the anticipation of a compulsory resumption for which no preparation has been made, and without any assurance that it would be practicable. The repeal of that clause is necessary that the natural operation of financial laws may be restored, that the business of the country may be relieved from its disturbing and depressing influence, and that a return to specie payments may be facilitated by the substitution of wiser and more prudent legislation which shall mainly rely on a judicious system of public economies and official retrenchments, and above all on the promotion of prosperity in all the industries of the people.

I do not understand the repeal of the resumption clause of the act of 1875 to be a backward step in our return to specie payments, but the recovery of a false step; and, although the repeal may, for a time, be prevented, yet the determination of the Democratic party on this subject has now been distinctly declared. There should be no hindrances put in the way of the return to specie payments. "As such a hindrance," says the platform of the St. Louis Convention, "we denounce the resumption clause of the act of 1875, and demand its repeal."

I thoroughly believe that by public economy, by official retrenchments, and by wise finance enabling us to accumulate the precious metals, resumption, at an early period, is possible without producing an "artificial scarcity of currency," or disturbing public or commercial credit; and that these reforms, together with the restoration of pure government, will restore general confidence, encourage the useful investment of capital, furnish employment to labor, and relieve the country from the "paralysis of hard times."

With the industries of the people there have been frequent interferences. Our platform truly says that many industries have been impoverished to subsidize a few. Our commerce has been degraded to an inferior position on the high seas; manufactures have been diminished; agriculture has been embarrassed, and the distress of the industrial classes demands that these things shall be reformed.

The burdens of the people must also be lightened by a great change in our system of public expenses. The profligate expenditures which increased taxation from $5 per capita in 1860, to $18 in 1870, tells its own story of our need of fiscal reform.

Our treaties with foreign powers should also be revised and amended, in so far as they leave citizens of foreign birth in any particular less secure in any country on earth than they would be if they had been born upon our own soil; and the iniquitous coolie system which, through the agency of wealthy companies, imports Chinese bondmen, and establishes a species of slavery, and interferes with the just rewards of labor on our Pacific coast should be utterly abolished.

In the reform of our civil service I most heartily indorse that section of the platform which declares that the civil service ought not to be "subject to change at every election," and that it ought not to be made "the brief reward of party zeal, but ought to be awarded for proved competency and held for fidelity in the public employ." I hope never again to see the cruel and remorseless proscription for political opinions which has disgraced the Administration of the last eight years. Bad as the civil service now is, as all know, it has some men of tried integrity and proved ability. Such men, and such men only, should be retained in office; but no man should be retained, on any consideration, who has prostituted his office to the purposes of partisan intimidation or compulsion, or who has furnished money to corrupt the elections. This is done, and has been done in almost every county of the land. It is a blight upon the morals of the country, and ought to be reformed.

Of sectional contentions, and in respect to our common schools, I have only this to say: That in my judgment, the man or party that would involve our schools in political or sectarian controversy is an enemy to the schools. The common schools are safer under the protecting care of all the people than under the control of any party or sect. They must be neither sectarian nor partisan, and there must be neither division nor misappropriation of the funds for their support. Likewise I regard the man who would arouse or foster sectional animosities and antagonisms among his countrymen as a dangerous enemy to his country. All the people must be made to feel and know that once more there is established a purpose and policy under which all citizens of every condition, race, and color, will be secure in the enjoyment of whatever rights the Constitution and laws declare or recognize; and that in controversies that may arise the Government is not a partisan, but within its constitutional authority the just and powerful guardian of the rights and safety of all. The strife between the sections and between races will cease as soon as the power for evil is taken away from a party that makes political gain out of scenes of violence and bloodshed, and the constitutional authority is placed in the hands of men whose political welfare requires that peace and good order shall be preserved everywhere.

It will be seen, gentlemen, that I am in entire accord with the platform of the Convention by which I have been nominated as a candidate for the office of Vice-President of the United States. Permit me, in conclusion, to express my satisfaction at being associated with a candidate for the Presidency who is first among his equals as a representative of the spirit and of the achievements of reform. In his official career as the Executive of the great State of New York, he has, in a comparatively short period, reformed the public service and reduced the public burdens, so as to have earned at once the gratitude of his State and the admiration of the country. The people know him to be thoroughly in earnest;

he has shown himself to be possessed of powers and qualities which fit him, in an eminent degree, for the great work of reformation which this country now needs; and if he shall be chosen by the people to the high office of President of the United States, I believe that the day of his inauguration will be the beginning of a new era of peace, purity, and prosperity in all departments of our Government. I am, gentlemen, your obedient servant,

THOMAS A. HENDRICKS,

To Hon. John A. McClernand, Chairman, and others of the Committee of the National Democratic Convention.

XXII.

"GREENBACK" AND PROHIBITION CONVENTIONS.

"Greenback" National Platform.

The Independent ("Greenback") National Convention met at Indianapolis, Indiana, on the 18th day of May, and nominated Mr. PETER COOPER, of New York city, for President, and Hon. NEWTON BOOTH, of California, for Vice-President.

The Platform adopted is as follows:

The Independent party is called into existence by the necessities of the people, whose industries are prostrated, whose labor is deprived of its just reward by a ruinous policy which the Republican and Democratic parties refuse to change, and in view of the failure of these parties to furnish relief to the depressed industries of the country, thereby disappointing the just hopes and expectations of the suffering people, we declare our principles and invite all independent and patriotic men to join our ranks in this movement for financial reform and industrial emancipation:

First. We demand the immediate and unconditional repeal of the specie resumption act of January 14, 1875, and the rescue of our industries from ruin and disaster resulting from its enforcement; and we call upon all patriotic men to organize in every Congressional District of the country with a view of electing representatives to Congress who will carry out the wishes of the people in this regard and stop the present suicidal and destructive policy of contraction.

Second. We believe that a United States note issued directly by the Government and convertible on demand into United States obligations, bearing a rate of interest not exceeding one cent a day on each one hundred dollars, and exchangeable for United States notes at par, will afford the best circulating medium ever devised. Such United States notes should be full legal-tenders for all purposes except for the payment of such obligations as are by existing contracts especially made payable in coin, and we hold that it is the duty of the Government to provide such circulating medium, and insist, in the language of Thomas Jefferson, that "bank paper must be suppressed and the circulation restored to the nation, to whom it belongs."

Third. It is the paramount duty of the Government, in all its legislation to keep in view the full development of all legitimate business, agricultural, mining, manufacturing and commercial.

Fourth. We most earnestly protest against any further issue of gold bonds for sale in foreign markets, by which we would be made for a long period "hewers of wood and drawers of water" to foreigners, especially as the American people would gladly and promptly take at par all bonds the Government may need to sell, provided they are made payable at the option of the holder and bearing interest at 3 65 per cent. per annum, or even a lower rate.

Fifth. We further protest against the sale of Government bonds for the purpose of purchasing silver to be used as a substitute for our more convenient and less fluctuating fractional currency, which, although well calculated to enrich owners of silver mines, yet in operation it will still further oppress in taxation an already over-burdened people.

A subsequent resolution against railroad subsidies was adopted.

Peter Cooper's Acceptance.

The Hon. MOSES W. FIELD, *Chairman, and the Hon.* THOMAS J. DURANT, *Secretary, National Executive Committee, Independent party.*

GENTLEMEN: Your formal official notification of the unanimous nomination tendered by the National Convention of the Independent party at Indianapolis on the 17th inst., to me for the high office of President of the United States, and to the Hon. Newton Booth, of California, for Vice-President, is before me, together with an authenticated copy of the admirable platform which the Convention adopted. While I most heartily thank the Convention through you for the great honor they have thus conferred upon me, kindly permit me to say that there is a bare possibility—if wise counsels prevail—that the sorely needed relief from the blighting effects of past unwise legislation relative to finance which the people so earnestly seek, may yet be had through either the Republican or Democratic party, both of them meeting in National Convention at an early date. It is unnecessary for me to assure you that while I have no aspiration for the position of Chief Magistrate of this great Republic, I will most cheerfully do what I can to forward the best interests of my country. I therefore accept your nomination conditionally, expressing the earnest hope that the Independent party may yet attain its exalted aims, while permitting me to step aside and remain in that quiet which is most congenial to my nature and time of life. Most respectfully, your obedient servant,

PETER COOPER.

Mr. BOOTH declined the nomination for Vice-President, and Hon. SAMUEL F. CARY, of Ohio, has been substituted for him by the National Executive Council of that party.

Prohibition National Convention.

This body met at Cleveland, Ohio, on the 17th of May, and nominated Rev. GREEN CLAY SMITH, of Kentucky, for President, and G. T. STEWART, of Ohio, for Vice-President.

The Platform adopted is as follows:

The Prohibition Reform party of the United States, organized in the name of the people, to revive, enforce and perpetuate in the Government the doctrines of the Declaration of Independence, submit in this Centennial year of the Republic for the suffrages of all good citizens the following platform of national reforms and measures:

First—The legal prohibition in the District of Columbia, the Territories, and in every other place subject to the laws of Congress, of the importation, exportation, manufacture and traffic of all alcoholic beverages, as high crimes against society; an amendment of the national Constitution to render these prohibitory measures universal and permanent; and the adoption of treaty stipulations with foreign powers to prevent the importation and exportation of all alcoholic beverages.

Second—The abolition of class legislation and of special privileges in the Government, and the adoption of equal suffrage and eligibility to office without distinction of race, religious creed, property or sex.

Third—The appropriation of the public lands in limited quantities to actual settlers only; the reduction of the rates of inland and ocean postage; of telegraphic communication; of railroad and water transportation and travel to the lowest practical point by force of laws, wisely and justly framed, with reference not only to the interests of capital employed, but to the higher claims of the general good.

Fourth—The suppression, by laws, of lotteries and gambling in gold, stocks, produce and every form of money and property, and the penal inhibition of the use of the public mails for advertising schemes of gambling and lotteries.

Fifth—The abolition of those foul enormities, polygamy and the social evil, and the protection of purity, peace and happiness of homes by ample and efficient legislation.

Sixth—The national observance of the Christian Sabbath, established by laws prohibiting ordinary labor and business in all departments of public service and private employments, (works of necessity, charity and religion excepted,) on that day.

Seventh—The establishment by mandatory provisions in National and State constitutions, and by all necessary legislation, of a system of free public schools for the universal and forced education of all the youth of the land.

Eighth—The free use of the Bible, not as a ground of religious creeds, but as a text-book of purest morality, the best liberty and the noblest literature, in our public schools, that our children may grow up in its light and that its spirit and principles may pervade our nation.

Ninth—The separation of the Government in all its departments and institution, including the public schools and all funds for their maintenance, from the control of every religious sect or other association, and the protection alike of all sects by equal laws, with entire freedom of religious faith and worship.

Tenth—The introduction into all treaties hereafter negotiated with foreign governments, of a provision for the amicable settlement of international difficulties by arbitration.

Eleventh—The abolition of all barbarous modes and instruments of punishment. The recognition of the laws of God and the claims of humanity in the discipline of jails and prisons, and of that higher and wiser civilization worthy of our age and nation, which regards the reform of criminals as a means for the prevention of crime.

Twelfth—The abolition of executive and legislative patronage, and the election of President, Vice-President, United States Senators, and of all civil officers, so far as practicable, by the direct vote of the people.

Thirteenth—The practice of a friendly and liberal policy to immigrants from all nations, the guaranty to them of ample protection, and of equal rights and privileges.

Fourteenth—The separation of the money of Government from all banking institutions. The National Government only should exercise the high prerogative of issuing paper money, and that should be subject to prompt redemption on demand, in gold and silver, the only equal standards of value recognized by the civilized world.

Fifteenth—The reduction of the salaries of public officers in a just ratio with the decline of wages and market prices, the abolition of sinecures, unnecessary offices and official fees and perquisites; the practice of strict economy in government expenses, and a free and thorough investigation into any and all alleged abuses of public trusts.

XXIII.

STATE PLATFORMS, 1875 AND 1876.

1875.

NEW YORK.

Republican, Sept. 9, 1875.

"The Republicans of New York, faithful to justice and liberty, to the supremacy of the Constitution, to the national unity and the just rights of the States, make the following declaration of principles:

"1. The national government should remain in the hands of those who sustain the guaranties of the amended Constitution, and in pursuance of the past action of the Republican party and its good results, the welfare of the country requires a just, generous and forbearing national policy in the southern States, a firm refusal to use military power, except for purposes clearly defined in the Constitution, and the local enforcement of national authority by those only who are in sympathy with such a policy and will heartily support it.

"2. We demand honesty, economy, and efficiency in every branch of the State and National administrations, prompt investigation of all charges of wrong-doing, and summary exposure, prosecution and punishment of wrong-doers. We therefore heartily commend the action of all officers, whether of the State or National government, in their honest efforts for the correction of public abuses. We pledge to them our constant and faithful support, and we charge every nominee of this convention to co-operate in every honorable way to secure pure government and to bring offenders to justice.

"3. The people should nominate for the legislature only men who are pledged by their known character to provide and sustain measures calculated to rescue and preserve the State from every form of corruption and mal-administration.

"4. The guilty offenders in the management of the canals should be brought to speedy punishment, and the Executive, under the powers already conferred upon him, should suspend all officers who have violated the law.

"5. The Republican party has proved itself from the beginning the party of practical reform and sound economy. In the affairs of this State it has, within the last four years, provided for the payment of $20,000,000 of the public debt, and practically extinguished the general State indebtedness, and by this action has made it certain that the tax for the next year will be reduced about $5,000,000.

"6. Further inflation of the currency, under any pretence whatever, would be a public calamity. The interests of honest industry and the common welfare demands the speediest possible return to specie payments.

"7. The whole subject of taxation ought to be carefully and wisely reviewed, to the end that its burdens should bear equally upon all.

"8. Recognizing as conclusive the President's public declaration that he is not a candidate for renomination, and with the sincerest gratitude for his patriotic services, we declare our unalterable opposition to the election of any President for a third term.

"9. The free public school is the bulwark of the American republic; we therefore demand the unqualified maintenance of the public school system, and its support by equal taxation. We are opposed to all sectarian appropriations; and we denounce as a crime against liberty and republican institutions any project for a sectarian division or perversion of the school fund of the State.

"10. The national administration, by its steadfast fidelity to the principles of commercial honor, by its opposition to unsound financial projects, by its calm avoidance of collisions with foreign powers, by its reliance on justice and reason, rather than force, in the settlement of disputes, by its firm vindication of the national dignity and authority, by rigidly executing the laws, correcting abuses, punishing offenders and enforcing retrenchment without boastful, ostentatious pretension, deserves the gratitude of the American people, and adds lustre to the services in the war of the distinguished soldier and patriot who stands at its head."

Democratic, September 16, 1875.

The Democratic party of New York renew their pledge of fidelity to the principles adopted and affirmed unanimously by the delegates representing the Democrats of all the United States together assembled in their latest National Convention, and since reapproved and indorsed by Democratic majorities in fifteen States, comprising more than half the total population of the Union.

[*From the National Democratic Platform, Baltimore, July* 10, 1872.]

Seventh—The public credit must be sacredly maintained, and we denounce repudiation in every form and guise.

Eighth—A speedy return to specie payment is demanded alike by the highest considerations of commercial morality and honest government.

To these authentic declarations of Democratic principle and policy the time gives proof. The present depression of business is caused by the reaction from the unhealthy stimulus of an excessive, depreciated and irredeemable currency; by enormous and ill-adjusted municipal, state and federal taxation, and by extravagance, waste and peculation in the administration of public affairs. The remedy for this evil is not to be found in the renewal of any of the causes. In face of the fact that the existing volume of currency is greater than can be absorbed by business; in face of the fact that the recent fall of prices has followed repeated inflations, any attempt to increase the currency would be worse than ineffectual to revive prosperity, for it would interrupt the healing processes of industry; it would be worse than futile to restore confidence, for it would create distrust and new uncertainties in business, paralyze the beginnings of enterprise, rob labor of its too scanty employment, and while stifling the progress of legislative reforms, would inflict lasting dishonor upon the credit, the intelligence and the character of the country.

[*From the New York Democratic Platform, Syracuse, September* 16, 1874.]

First—Gold and silver the only legal tender: no currency inconvertible with coin.

Second—Steady steps toward Specie Payments: no step backward.

Third—Honest payment of the public debt in coin: sacred preservation of the public faith.

Fourth—Revenue reform: Federal taxation for revenue only: no government partnership with protected monopolies.

Fifth—Home Rule: to limit and localize most jealously the few powers intrusted to public servants—municipal, state and federal: no centralization.

Sixth—Equal and exact justice to all men: no partial legislation; no partial taxation.

Seventh—A free press: no gag laws.

Eighth—Free men: a uniform excise law: no sumptuary laws.

Ninth—Official accountability enforced by better civil and criminal remedies: no private use of public funds by public officers.

Tenth—Corporations chartered by the State always supervisable by the State in the interest of the people.

Eleventh—The party in power responsible for all legislation while in power.

Twelfth—The Presidency a public trust, not a private perquisite: no third term.

Thirteenth—Economy in the public expense, that labor may be lightly burdened.

The Democrats of New York, in convention assembled, pledge themselves, their nominees and their representatives in Senate and Assembly, to follow where an honest and fearless chief magistrate has dared to lead in reforming the administration of our great canals, so long despoiled in their construction, maintenance, repairs and revenues: to carry on with unwavering purpose and fidelity wise measures to increase the efficiency of all departments of the public works and service, and to persist in reducing our State tax, in which the burdens have already been lightened by the retrenchments and reforms of a single year to the amount of nearly $3,000,000! And upon this paramount, immediate and practical issue of administrative reform we cordially invite the co-operation of every true Democrat, every Liberal Republican, and all our fellow-citizens of whatever name who are willing in the coming State elections to unite with us in supporting reform candidates upon a reform platform.

OHIO.

Republican, June 2, 1875.

The Republicans of Ohio in Convention assembled, reaffirming the cardinal principles of their organization, which have become received maxims of policy, State and National, declare on specific points the series of sentiments following:

1. The States are one as a Nation, and all citizens are equal under the laws, and entitled to their fullest protection.

2. That a policy of finance should be steadily pursued which, without unnecessary shock to business or trade, will ultimately equalize the purchasing capacity of the coin and paper dollar.

3. We are in favor of a tariff for revenue, with incidental protection to American industry.

4. We stand by free education, our public school system, the taxation of all for its support, and no division of the school fund.

5. Under our Republican system of Government, there should be no connection direct or indirect, between Church and State, and we oppose all legislation in the interest of any particular sect. Upon this subject we should not fail to profit by the experience of foreign Governments, where the efforts of the Church to control the State constitute an evil of great magnitude, and endangers the power and prosperity of the people.

6. We demand such a revision of the patent laws as will relieve industry from the oppression of monopolies in administration.

7. A grateful people can never cease to remember the services of our soldiers and sailors, and it is due to them that liberality and generosity should obtain in the adjustment of pay and bounties.

8. That we demand that the public domain shall be scrupulously reserved for occupancy by actual settlers.

9. The determination of the Government to collect the revenue and prevent and punish frauds has our unqualified approval.

10. That the power of municipal corporations to create debts should be restricted, and local and other expenditures should be so reduced as to diminish taxation.

11. The observance of Washington's example in retiring at the close of a second Presidential term will be in the future, as it has been in the past, regarded as a fundamental rule in the unwritten law of the Republic.

12. The distinguished success of his administration, which to the fame of the patriot and soldier has added that of the capable and judicious statesman, entitles President Grant to the gratitude of his countrymen.

Democratic, June 17, 1875.

The Democratic party of Ohio, in State Convention assembled, proclaim the following propositions of political faith and action:

1. A sacred adherence to the principles of government declared and put in practical operation by the fathers of the Republic.

2. Opposition to aggressions by either department of the Government upon the functions of the other, and to the exercise by Federal authorities of any of the powers reserved by the Constitution to the States respectively, or to the people.

3. The protection of the Government to all citizens, without regard to race, color, or previous condition of servitude.

4. The President's services should be limited to one term, at a salary of $25,000 a year.

5. Retrenchment and reform in every depart-

ment of the Government—Federal, State and local.

6. No grants of land or money by the Government, or use of its credit to railroad, steamship or other companies.

7. The preservation of the remnant of the public lands for the benefit of the citizens of the United States and foreign emigrants who have declared their intention to become such, who will occupy and cultivate the same.

8. That the contraction of the currency heretofore made by the Republican party, and the further contraction proposed by it, with a view to the forced resumption to specie payment, has already brought disaster to the business of the country, and threatens general bankruptcy. We demand that this policy be abandoned and that the volume of currency be made and kept equal to the wants of trade, leaving the restoration of legal-tenders to par, gold, to be brought about by promoting the industries of the people and not by destroying them.

9. That the policy already initiated by the Republican party of abolishing legal-tenders and giving National banks the power to furnish all the currency will increase the power of an already dangerous monopoly and the enormous burdens now oppressing the people without any corresponding advantage, and that we oppose the policy, and demand that all the National bank circulation be promptly and permanently retired, and legal tenders be issued in their place.

10. That the public interest demands the Government should cease to discredit its own currency, and should make its legal tenders receivable for all public dues, except where respect for the obligations of contracts requires payment in coin; and that we favor the payment of at least one-half of the customs in legal tenders.

11. The extinction of the present National banks, and the establishment in their stead of a system of free banks of discount and deposit, under such regulations as the States may respectively prescribe; and no paper currency except such as may be issued directly by and upon the faith of the General Government.

12. A tariff for the sole purpose of revenue.

13. We favor the complete separation of Church and State; religious independence and absolute freedom of opinion; equal and exact justice to all religious societies, and purely secular education at the expense of taxpayers, without division among or control by any sect, directly or indirectly, of any portion of the Public School Fund. In view of the admirable provisions of our State Constitution upon these subjects, which are due to the energy and wisdom of the Democratic party, we denounce the Republican platform as an insult to the intelligence of the people of Ohio, and a base appeal to sectarian prejudices.

14. That we are opposed to the passage of what are called Sumptuary Laws, or any interference with social habits or customs not in themselves criminal; and we reprobate any espionage by one class of citizens upon another under any pretense whatever. With this declaration of principles and policy, we arraign the leaders of the Republican party for their extravagant expenditure and profligate waste of the people's money; for their oppressive, unjust, and defective system of finance and taxation; for their continued tyranny and cruelty to the Southern States of the Union; for squandering the public lands; for the continuance of incompetent and corrupt men in office at home and abroad; and for their general mismanagement of the Government; and we cordially invite all men, without regard to past party associations, to coöperate with us in expelling them from office, and in securing such an administration of public affairs as characterized the purer and better days of the Republic.

PENNSYLVANIA.

Republican, May 26, 1875.

The Republicans of Pennsylvania, affirming their continued adhesion to the party whose perpetuation is rendered necessary by the causes which called it into existence, make declaration of the fundamental principles of their political faith as follows:

1.—The equality of all men before the law, equal justice to all, and special favors to none.

2.—The harmony of the National and State governments; both are parts of one system, alike necessary for the common prosperity, peace and security.

3.—The unity of the nation; we are one people; the Constitution of the United States forms a government, not a league.

4.—A faithful execution of the laws, an economical administration of the government, integrity in office, honesty in all branches of the civil service, and a rigid accountability of public officers.

5.—Protection to home industry, and a home market for home products.

6.—The right of the laborer to protection and encouragement, and the promotion of harmony between labor and capital.

7.—Cheap transportation, and the advancement of closer intercourse between all parts of the country.

8.—Free banking, a safe and uniform national currency adjusted to the growing wants of the business interests of the country, and a steady reduction of the national debt.

9.—The public domain, being the heritage of the people, should be preserved for actual settlers exclusively.

10.—The equalization of the bounties of soldiers, and a speedy settlement of all just claims arising out of the late war.

11.—Honest men in office, men with brains enough to know dishonesty when they see it, and courage enough to fight it when they find it.

Resolved, That we declare a firm, unqualified adherence to the unwritten law of the republic, which wisely and under the sanction of the most venerable examples, limits the Presidential service of any citizen to two terms; and we, the Republicans of Pennsylvania, in recognition of this law, are unalterably opposed to the election to the Presidency of any person for a third term.*

---

* See President GRANT's reply to this resolution, page 154.

Democratic, September 8, 1875.

Resolved, 1. That we hereby declare our unfaltering devotion to the fundamental principles of democratic government as enunciated by Thomas Jefferson in his first inaugural address, to wit: Equal and exact justice to all men, of whatsoever state or persuasion, religious or political; the support of the State governments in all their rights as the most competent administration for our domestic concerns, and the surest bulwarks against anti-republican tendencies; the supremacy of the civil over military authority; economy in the public expense, that labor may be lightly burdened; the honest payment of our just debts and the sacred preservation of the public faith; freedom of religion, freedom of the press, freedom of person under the protection of the great writ of *habeas corpus*, and trial by juries impartially selected.

2. That the widespread depression and suffering which affect every business and employment that is capable of being touched by legislation show beyond a doubt the ignorance, insufficiency, and wickedness of the leaders of the party that has ruled the State and nation for a period of years, and calls for their immediate and permanent removal from the places which they have so long dishonored and disgraced.

3. That the contraction of the money currency and circulating medium heretofore made by the Republican party, and the further contraction proposed by it with a view to the forced resumption of specie payments, has already brought disaster to the business of the country and threatens general bankruptcy. We demand that this policy be abandoned, and that the volume of money be made and kept equal to the wants of trade, leaving the restoration of legal tenders to par in gold to be brought about by promoting the industries of the people, and not by destroying them.

4. That the policy already initiated by the Republican party of abolishing legal tenders and giving the national banks the power to furnish all the currency will increase the power of an already dangerous monopoly and the enormous burden now oppressing the people without compensating advantage, and that all the national bank circulation be promptly and permanently retired and full legal tenders be issued in their place.

5. That the public interest demands that the Government should cease to discredit its own money and should make its legal tenders receivable for all public dues, except where respect for the obligations of contracts requires payment in coin.

6. Demands the extinction of the present national banks, and the establishment in their stead of a system of free banks of discount and deposit, under such regulations as the States respectively may prescribe, and no paper money except such as may be issued directly and upon the faith of the Federal Government, affording practically a currency based on the gold and silver and other property of the whole people of the country.

7. That with this declaration of principles and policy, we arraign the leaders of the Republican party for their extravagant expenditures and profligate waste of the people's money; for their corruption; for their peculation; for their contempt of constitutional obligations; for their extortionate increase of the salaries of our public officers; for their oppressive, unjust and defective system of taxes, finance and currency; for their continuance of incompetent and corrupt men in office, and for their general mismanagement of both the State and Federal Governments, and we cordially invite the Liberal Republicans and other men, without regard to past party associations, to coöperate with us in expelling them from power, and establishing such an administration of our public affairs as characterized the purer and better days of the Republic.

INDIANA.

Republican, February 22, 1876.

The following is an abstract of the Platform:

First. After recounting the record of the Republican party it declares that they will remain faithful to it.

Second. Denying the right of any State to interfere in the execution of the national laws.

Third. Declaring that the United States is a nation, and not a mere confederation of States.

Fourth. Holding the National and State Governments to be entirely independent of each other within their own proper spheres.

Fifth. Expressing a willingness to restore entirely the amicable relations between the people of the North and South who engaged in the rebellion, and with that view are ready to forgive and grant amnesty to those who sincerely desire it, but not to those who are still unrepentant; and at the same time declaring that the war for the Union was right and rebellion wrong, and that thus it should forever stand in history.

Sixth. That while they have no wish to disfranchise any who fought for the Confederacy, it is a flagrant insult when faithful Union soldiers, who risked their lives for the nation and are honestly discharging the duties of their offices, are removed to make place for those who fought against the country, and it deserves the rebuke and condemnation of the whole country and every loyal soldier.

Seventh. In conducting the civil service, officers shold be selected because of their qualification, integrity and moral character, and the patronage of the government should be so disposed in the matter of faithfulness and economy that it shall not be brought in conflict with the freedom of elections.

Eighth. The equality of all is maintained, that equal justice should be done to all and especial privileges conferred on none.

Ninth. Perfect religious freedom and freedom of conscience is insisted upon: the union of Church and State is opposed, and it is declared incompatible with American citizenship to pay allegiance to any foreign power, civil or ecclesiastical.

Tenth. The duty of the government is to so regulate its revenue system as to give all needful encouragement to our agricultural, mechanical, mining and manufacturing enterprises, so that harmonious relations may be established between labor and capital and just remuneration secured to both.

Eleventh. Taxes should give the greatest possible exemption to necessities, and be placed more heavily upon the luxuries and wealth of the country.

Twelfth. The government's duty in furnishing currency is to so regulate it as to provide for its ultimate redemption in gold and silver; that any attempt to hasten this period more rapidly than brought about by laws of trade and commerce is inexpedient; therefore so much of the so-called resumption act as fixes the time for resuming specie payments should be repealed, and then the currency should remain undisturbed, neither contracted nor expanded, so that the financial troubles of the country will be cured by the natural laws of trade, and by persevering in that course of policy which Republicans have constantly maintained of steadily looking to the ultimate resumption of specie payments.

Thirteenth. The greenback currency was created by the Republican party as a war measure; the Democracy avowed the measure was unconstitutional, and that the notes would become worthless; therefore, if the Democracy were sincere, one of its objects in now seeking to obtain control of the government must be to destroy this currency along with that furnished the national banks, so that the country may be compelled to return to the system which existed under Buchanan.

Fourteenth. When the Republicans came into power in 1861, the expenditures of the country were greater than its receipts; commerce and trade were deranged by maladministration; the credit of the United States below par. Now, notwithstanding the financial embarrassments and the gigantic war, the credit of the nation is above par and its bonds sought after in all the great money markets of the world.

Fifteenth. Irrevocable opposition is declared to the payment of any part of the rebel debt, or for emancipated slaves, or for the property of rebels destroyed in the war.

Sixteenth. The strictest economy consistent with public safety in National and State affairs is demanded.

Seventeenth. Favoring and encouraging schools and the means of education necessary for extending the principles of civil and religious liberty; regarding all opponents of the common school system as assailing the fundamental principle of free government; demanding faithful administration of school laws, so that schools may become what they were designed to be, the schools of the people.

The *Eighteenth* and *Nineteenth* thank the soldiers and sailors of Indiana during the Rebellion, declaring that the honor of the nation is pledged to provide bounties and pensions for them, and take care of widows and orphans of those who lost their lives.

Twentieth. Praising Grant's administration, and commending his example of removing his own appointees when found unfaithful, and causing them to be so prosecuted that "none guilty may escape."

Democratic, April 19, 1876.

The following are the principal planks in the platform adopted:

We believe in our ancient doctrine that gold and silver are the true and the safe basis for the currency, and we are in favor of measures and policies that will produce uniformity in value in the coin and paper money of the country without destroying or embarrassing the business interests of the people.

We oppose the contraction of the volume of our paper currency, and declare in favor of the adoption of measures looking to the gradual retirement of the circulation of the national banks and the substitution therefor of circulating notes issued by authority of the Government.

We recognize with patriotic satisfaction the vast recuperative energies with which our country is endowed, and we observe that, in spite of the interference with the laws of commerce which has been practiced, our currency has improved in proportion as our wealth has increased, and the sense of national and local security has been confirmed. We are therefore of the opinion that a national return to specie payments will be promoted by the increase of national wealth and industries, by the assurance of harmony at home and peace abroad, and by strengthening our public credit under a wise and economical administration of our national affairs.

The legal tender notes constitute a safe currency, and one especially valuable to the debtor classes, because of its legal tender quality, and we demand the repeal of the legislation enacted by the Republican party, providing for its withdrawal from circulation, and the substitution therefor of national bank paper.

The act of Congress for the resumption of specie payments on the 1st of January, 1879, was a party measure devised in secret caucus for party ends, and forced through the House of Representatives without the allowance of amendment or debate, under party discipline. It paralyzes industry, creates distrust of the future, turns the laborer and producer out of employment, is a standing threat upon business men, and should at once be repealed, without any condition whatever.

NEW YORK.

Republican, March 22, 1876.

The Republicans of New York, in this centennial of the nation, reaffirm the sacred truths and principles of their fathers, and make the following declaration:

First. We are for the unity of the nation and the just rights of the States; for the full reconciliation and enduring harmony of all sections; for the inviolate preservation of the results of the war and the constitutional rights of every citizen; for grateful recognition of the brave soldiers of the Republic; for thorough retrenchment and reform; for the unsparing pursuit, exposure and punishment of public frauds and official dishonesty; for the elevation of the public service, and pure and efficient government; for maintaining untarnished the National credit and honor; for a sound currency of coin, or paper convertible into coin, and for common schools absolutely free from sectarian influence.

Second. We charge the Democratic party with being the same in character and spirit as when it sympathized with treason; with making its control of the House of Representatives the triumph and opportunity of the nation's recent foes; with reasserting and applauding, in the National Capital, the sentiments of unrepentant rebellion; with sending Union soldiers to the rear and promoting Confederate soldiers to the front; with deliberately proposing to repudiate the plighted faith of the Government; with being equally false and imbecile upon the overshadowing financial questions; with thwarting the ends of justice by its partisan mismanagement and obstruction of investigation through the four months of its ascendency in the lower House of Congress; with proving itself utterly incompetent to administer the Government; and we warn the country against trusting a party alike unworthy, recreant, and incapable.

Third. Without regard to past differences, we cordially invite all who believe that the direction of the Government should not pass into the hands that sought to destroy it, and who seek pure and economical government by honest and capable officers, to unite with us in fraternal and mutually considerate coöperation for the promotion of these ends.

Fourth. We emphatically condemn the dishonesty and treachery of every official who is faithless to his trust, and approve the injunction to let no guilty man, however high, escape. We believe the virtue of the people, which saved the nation through the storm of war, will preserve it from the dangers of corruption. We commend the good work of the National Administration in protecting the public treasury and punishing public offenders, and in laying down his trust at the close of the period for which he has been chosen, President Grant will carry with him the lasting gratitude of the American people for his patriotic services in war and peace.

Democratic, April 27, 1876.

The Democratic party of New York renew their fidelity to the principles set forth in their platform adopted in 1874 and 1875, thrice approved at the ballot boxes of the Empire State, well vindicated in the illustrious administration of Governor Samuel J. Tilden, and commended anew to their faith and adoption by the endorsement of an increasing majority of their fellow Democrats of sister States throughout the Union. The Democratic party of New York re-adopt also their resolution adopted in the State conventions of 1864, 1868 and 1872, to wit:

Resolved, That the delegates to the Democratic National Convention to be appointed are hereby instructed to enter that Convention as a unit, in accordance with the will of a majority of the members thereof, and in case any of its members shall be appointed a delegate thereof by another organization, and should not forthwith, in writing, decline such appointment, his seat shall be regarded as vacated, and the delegation shall proceed to fill the same, and they are hereby also empowered to supply all vacancies by death, absence, resignation or otherwise. The Democratic party of New York, while committing to their delegates the duty of joining with the delegates of their fellow Democrats of all the States in the momentous deliberations of the National Convention, declare their settled principles: The frugal expenditure and the administrative purity of the founders of the Republic as the first and most imperious necessity of the times, the commanding issue now before the people of the Union.

"Greenback," (Democratic,) June 1, 1876.

First. Unconditional repeal of the Republican forced Resumption act.

Second. The substitution of legal tenders for National bank notes.

Third. Legal tenders to be receivable for all debts, public and private, and all taxes and customs.

Fourth. No forced inflation, no forced contraction, but a circulation equal to the wants of trade and industry, to be regulated in volume and gradually equalized with gold by appropriate legislation.

Fifth. Legislation for the development of the resources and wealth of the country by the people to the exclusion of monopolies.

Sixth. A faithful compliance with the nation's just obligations.

Seventh. No centralization. Local self-government.

Eighth. We denounce the present corruption in the affairs of the Federal Government, and demand searching investigation and prompt punishment of the guilty, independent of party and irrespective of persons.

Ninth. We oppose the reëlection of every Congressman, Senator or Assemblyman who has opposed, directly or indirectly, the repeal of the iniquitous Resumption act.

OHIO.

Republican, March 29, 1876.

The Republicans of Ohio renew their allegiance to the Republican party and reaffirm its principles of free government as declared and defined by the grand men of 1776, and endeared to the people of our times by the sacrifices of war and the blessings of an assured union of the States, based upon universal liberty.

Second. The citizens of the several States of the Union are also citizens of the nation, and are equal in the Constitution and laws in all rights of citizenship, and are entitled to full and equal protection in their exercise.

Third. We favor an honest and economical administration of the Government, and favor retrenchment and reform in the public service. Personal integrity and fidelity should be required of all officials, and when found to be dishonored and corrupt they should be prosecuted and punished; and we cordially commend the vigorous prosecution of public offenders by the present National Administration.

Fourth. The national credit and honor must be sacredly maintained.

Fifth. We recognize gold as the true standard value, and the only steady and safe basis for a circulating medium, and declare that that policy of finance should be steadily pursued which, with out unnecessary injury to business or trade, will ultimately equalize the value of the coin and paper dollar.

Sixth. We favor a tariff of revenue, with incidental protection to American industry.

Seventh. We stand by our system of free common schools, supported by general taxation. There must be no division of the school fund and no sectarian interference with the schools.

Eighth. To the soldiers and sailors who fought for the Union the nation owes a debt of gratitude, and they and the widows and orphans of those who have fallen are justly entitled to liberal bounties and pensions.

Ninth. The thanks of the people are due to President Grant for his faithful adherence to Republican principles, and we assure him of the gratitude of the country for the distinguished service he has rendered as a soldier and civilian.

Democratic, May 17th, 1876.

Resolved, That recognizing the duty of the Democratic party as the time-honored champion of the rights of the many against the aggressions of the few, to express its purposes on the pending currency conflict without reserve or equivocation, we declare that we shall urge against all opposition, come from what quarter it may, measures to effect the following objects:

First. The immediate and unconditional repeal of the Republican Resumption law.

Second. The defeat of all schemes for resumption which involve either contraction of the currency, perpetuation of bank issues, or increase of the interest burden of the debt.

Third. The gradual but early substitution of legal tenders for national bank notes.

Fourth. The issue by the general Government alone of all the circulating medium whether paper or metallic.

Fifth. No forced inflation, no forced contraction, but sound currency, equal to the wants of trade and industry, to be regulated in volume, and gradually equalized with gold by means of appropriate legislation, such as making it receivable for customs and interconvertible at the pleasure of the holder with a bond bearing an interest not to exceed 3.65 per cent., payable in gold, so that the volume of currency shall not be determined by the pleasure or caprice of either Congress or the banks.

Sixth. A graduated income tax to meet at least the premium on gold needed to pay interest on the public debt.

Seventh. That public policy and sense of common justice require that silver issued by the Government should be a legal tender in payment of all debts, public or private, and that we demand the unconditional repeal of the so-called silver act, so far as the same limits the amount for which said silver coinage shall be a legal tender.

Eighth. That we are in favor of a tariff for revenue only, and we denounce the Republican scheme of resumption as intended, and operating through a large increase of bonded debt, a sudden and enormous contraction of the currency, to double the burdens of taxation, rob debtors of their property, paralyze productive and commercial industries, cast laborers out of employment and fill the land with want and misery for the wicked purpose of doubling the values of money securities and subjugating the mass of the people to the imperious sway of a money oligarchy.

These were adopted by a vote of 386 to 266, the minority of the Convention preferring the subjoined resolutions reported by the majority of the committee:

Resolved, That we favor a return to specie payments when the same can be done without seriously disturbing the business of the country, and to that end and in order that the debtor class may not be further embarrassed, we demand the repeal of the resumption act of 1875, and oppose any measure of legislation which shall arbitrarily fix a day for such resumption.

2. That the charters of the national banks ought not to be renewed, and each of the said banks should be wound up at the expiration of the time for which it is chartered, and in lieu of circulating notes, Treasury notes of the United States, convertible into coin on demand, and receivable for all debts or taxes due to the United States, should be issued to the extent required by the necessities of the Government.

3. That we favor a tariff for revenue only.

PENNSYLVANIA.

Republican, March 29, 1876.

Resolved, That we hereby reaffirm the platform adopted by the Republican State Convention at Lancaster in 1875, and in view of recent events at Washington, we emphatically endorse that part of it which demands honest men in office, men with brains enough to know dishonesty when they see it, and courage enough to fight it wherever they find it. The Republican party is committed by its origin, its traditions, its history and its duties, to an intrepid and honest administration of public affairs; and whenever, in National, State or municipal life, maladministration has existed or does exist, we demand that it be exposed, corrected, and the guilty punished, and to this end we pledge the full measure of our support as citizens and as voters.

Resolved, That the Republicans of Pennsylvania, having nothing in their past history which they wish to blot out, or to apologize for, or would have the nation forget, arraign the Democratic leaders in Congress and their abettors for the preference shown to the deadly principles, and for the subserviency shown to the defiant leaders, of the late Confederacy now dominating them; for their removal from office of Union soldiers and appointment of Confederate soldiers; for the repeated indication of their purpose, only controlled by fear, to open the Treasury of the nation to alarming and unjust pecuniary demands from the insurrectionary States; for their persistent effort to force amnesty upon men too proud or unrepentant to ask it, or too guilty to deserve it; and for the combined recklessness and cowardice of their course on financial questions—a recklessness which mischievously holds out a threat to overthrow existing laws, and a cowardice or incapacity to originate a substitute for them—all of which expose the Democratic party as without national instinct, or an unsectional impulse, or an affirmative policy, and as unfit to be trusted by the country which, when last under their control, they madly hurried into the vortex of civil war.

Resolved, That recent events in the late slave States clearly expose a purpose on the part of the Democratic party to seize them all and wield them as a unit in the next Presidential election, and to this end brutal and bloody conspiracies have been made to coerce voters, and base Legislative conspiracies are at this moment in operation in order that an unprincipled and fraudulent majority may deprive properly chosen officers of their rights, and as against these outrages we take an appeal to the people of the nation.

Resolved, That the common safety demands that our public schools shall not only be free to all, but shall be preserved from all special or partial control. All attempts to divide the school fund for any purpose whatever, or to divert any portion of it into a channel not under popular control, is to be frowned upon and resisted with unyielding firmness. The recent defeat in the Democratic Legislature of Maryland of a constitutional amendment to secure the common school fund of that State against division reveals at once a grave danger and its source, and, with other like facts, makes plain the duty of Congress to submit such an amendment to the Constitution of the United States as, when adopted, will effectually defend the common school system from all enemies, open or covert.

Resolved, That the attempt of the Democratic House of Representatives at Washington, in the face of the depressed condition of American industry, to inflict upon the nation a free-trade tariff, is an insult to the intelligence of the people and an evidence of the inability of the Democratic party to meet the present wants of the country. The remedy for our suffering is in a higher, not a lower tariff.

Democratic, March 22, 1876.

The Democracy of Pennsylvania reasserts its devotion to all of the provisions of the Federal Constitution and to a perpetual union of the States; pledges itself to rigid fidelity to the public trust; to a pure and economical administration of the Federal, State and municipal governments; to local self-government in every section; to the honest payment of the public debt, and to the sound preservation of the public faith. They see with humiliation and alarm the evidences of bribery, fraud, and peculation in high places, the distress that prevails, and the wide-spread financial ruin that impends over the people of the State, and they charge that these evils are the direct results of the personal government, unwise legislation, vicious financial policy, extravagance and corruption of the Republican party. They declare, first, that the Civil Service of the Government has become corrupt, and is made the object of personal gain, and infidelity to public trust has become the rule and not the exception. We believe that honesty, capacity and fidelity are the only tests of fitness for public station, and that the wholesome penalties of the law should be used with rigor to enforce official accountability.

Second. That the recent and repeated exposures of fraud and corruption in the administration of public affairs call for a searching and thorough investigation of the conduct and condition of every branch of the public service, to the end that all corrupt practices may be brought to light, and that all who have abused and betrayed their public trusts, whatever may be their station, may be exposed and punished: and we urge those in charge of this subject at Washington to a prompt, thorough and exhaustive examination of their respective fields of labor.

Third. That retrenchment and economy are indispensable in the Federal, State, and municipal administration as an essential means towards lessening the burdens of the people; and we commend the efforts of the majority in the House of Representatives for the reduction of the expenditures of the Federal Government to a just standard, and their determination to lessen the number of useless officials.

Fourth. That general amnesty of all persons implicated in the late rebellion against the Government of the United States who have not already been relieved from disabilities by the action of Congress and of the President, would be an allowable and proper exercise of Governmental power in the year of the Centennial celebration of American Independence, and that the recommendation of such measure by President Grant in a public message, and its endorsement and passage by a Republican House of Representatives at a former session, constitute full proof that such a measure is fit, judicious, and timely.

Fifth. That we approve of those provisions of the State Constitution which protect not only the school funds but other public moneys from appropriation to sectarian uses, and that they fitly illustrate the doctrine of the separation of Church and State, which always has been a cardinal one with the Democratic party.

Sixth. That the statute for the resumption of specie payments on the 1st day of January, 1879, is impossible to execute. It is a deliberate proclamation that at that date the United States will go into bankruptcy. It paralyzes industry, creates distrust of the future, turns the laborer and producer out of employment, is a standing threat upon the business men, and ought to be forthwith repealed.

Seventh. That gold and silver are the only true basis for the currency of the Republic, and that Congress should take such steps for the resumption of specie payments as will most surely and speedily reach that result, without destroying the business interests of the people.

Eighth. That the present depression of all our National industries, which checks the wholesome flow of capital through the channels of enterprise, and denies to honest labor a decent livelihood, is the direct, inevitable fruit of extravagance and of reckless and dishonest Republican tampering with the finances of the country; and we denounce the authors of that legislation as officials who have unsettled the foundations alike of the State and of the home. We call upon the people to aid us to halt them in this fatal career, and to set their faces in the direction of practical measures which shall eventually enable the Treasury of the United States to keep its plighted faith with rich and poor alike. We demand legislation through the power of the Federal Government which shall give us performances for promises, and restore solvency to the nation by restoring prosperity to the people.

XXIV.

ADDENDA.

Bill to Repeal the Resumption-day Clause of the Resumption Act.

IN HOUSE.

August 5—Mr. COX, from Committee on Banking and Currency, reported the following bill:

A Bill to repeal the resumption-day clause in the resumption act of 1875:

Be it enacted, etc., That the resumption-day clause in section 3 of an act entitled "An act to provide for the resumption of specie payments," approved January 14, 1875, which clause is in the words following, to wit:

"On and after the 1st day of January, 1879, the Secretary of the Treasury shall redeem in coin the United States legal-tender notes then outstanding on their presentation for redemption at the office of the assistant treasurer of the United States in the city of New York, in sums of not less than $50"—

Be and the same is hereby repealed.

Mr. A. S. HEWITT offered the following as a substitute for the above:

A Bill to provide for a commission to consider the resumption of specie payments.

Be it enacted, etc., That a commission is hereby authorized and constituted, to consist of three Senators, to be appointed by the Senate, three members of the House of Representatives, to be appointed by the Speaker, and three experts, to be selected by and associated with them, with authority to determine the time and place of meeting, and to take evidence; whose duty it shall be to consider what measures are necessary and practicable in order to bring about the resumption of specie payments at the earliest possible time, consistent with a due regard to the interests of the country, and to report a bill embodying the results of their investigations on or before the 15th day of December, A. D. 1876.

Which was disagreed to—yeas 92, nays 104 (not voting 89), as follow:

YEAS—Messrs. *Abbott*, C. H. Adams, *Bagby*, G. A. Bagley, *J. H. Bagley, jr.*, W. H. Baker, Ballou, *S. N. Bell*, Blair, W. R. Brown, H. C. Burchard, Caswell, Chittenden, Conger, Crounse, *Cutler*, Danford, Davy, *Durand*, Eames, *Ely*, C. Freeman, Frye, *Glover*, E. Hale, *Hancock*, *Hardenbergh*, B. W. Harris, Henderson, *A. S. Hewitt*, G. F. Hoar, Hoge, *Hooker*, *Hurd*, Hurlbut, Hyman, Joyce, Kasson, *Kehr*, Kimball, *Lamar*, Lapham, W. Lawrence, *Levy*, *Lord*, Lynch, MacDougall, McCrary, *Meade*, *Metcalfe*, Miller, Monroe, *Morrison*, Nash, Norton, *O'Brien*, *Odell*, O'Neill, Packer, Page, Pierce, *Piper*, T. C. Platt, A. POTTER, *Powell*, Pratt, Rainey, *M. Ross*, Rusk, Sampson, *Schleicher*, Sinnickson, R. Smalls, A. H. Smith, Strait, Stowell, *C. P. Thompson*, Thornburgh, W. Townsend, Tufts, Wait, *C. C. B. Walker*, *Ward*, *Warren*, G. W. Wells, J. D. White, Whiting, G. Willard, *A. S. Williams*, *Willis*, J. Wilson, Woodburn—92.

NAYS—Messrs. *Ainsworth*, ANDERSON, *Atkins*, BANKS, *Banning*, *Bland*, *Boone*, *Bradford*, *Bright*, *J. Y. Brown*, Cabell, *J. H. Caldwell*, *W. P. Caldwell*, CAMPBELL, Cannon, Cason, *Cate*, *Caulfield*, *J. B. Clarke*, *J. B. Clark, jr.*, *Clymer*, *Cochrane*, *Collins*, *Cook*, *Cox*, *Dibrell*, *Douglas*, *Durham*, *Eden*, Evans, *Faulkner*, *Felton*, *Finley*, *Forney*, Fort, *Franklin*, *Gause*, *Goode*, *Goodin*, *Gunter*, *C. H. Harrison*, *Hartzell*, *Haymond*, *Henkle*, *Hereford*, *Holman*, *Hopkins*, *House*, Hubbell, *Hunton*, *T. L. Jones*, *F. Landers*, *Lane*, *B. B. Lewis*, *Lynde*, *L. A. Mackey*, *Maish*, *McFarland*, *McMahon*, *Milliken*, *Mills*, *Morgan*, *Mutchler*, *Neal*, *New*, *Payne*, *J. Phelps*, *Poppleton*, *Randall*, *D. Rea*, *Reagan*, *J. Reilly*, *A. V. Rice*, *Riddle*, M. S. Robinson, *Savage*, *Sheakley*, *Singleton*, *Slemons*, *W. E. Smith*, *Southard*, *Springer*, *Stenger*, *Stevenson*, *Stone*, *Teese*, *P. F. Thomas*, *Throckmorton*, *Tucker*, *Turney*, Van Vorhes, *J. L. Vance*, *Waddell*, *G. C. Walker*, *Walsh*, *E. Wells*, *Whitthorne*, *J. D. Williams*, *J. N. Williams*, *Wilshire*, *B. Wilson*, *Yeates*, *C. Young*—104.

The bill reported by Mr. COX was then passed—yeas 106, nays 86 (not voting 93), as follow:

YEAS—Messrs. *Ainsworth*, ANDERSON, *Atkins*, *Banning*, *Bland*, *Boone*, *Bradford*, *Bright*, *J. Y. Brown*, W. R. Brown, *Cabell*, *J. H. Caldwell*, *W. P. Caldwell*, CAMPBELL, Cannon, Cason, *Cate*, *Caulfield*, *J. B. Clarke*, *J. B. Clark, jr.*, *Clymer*, *Cochrane*, *Collins*, *Cook*, *Cox*, *Dibrell*, *Douglas*, *Durham*, *Eden*, Evans, *Faulkner*, *Felton*, *Finley*, *Forney*, Fort, *Franklin*, *Gause*, *Goode*, *Goodin*, *Gunter*, *C. H. Harrison*, *Hartzell*, *Haymond*, *Henkle*, *Hereford*, *Holman*, *Hooker*, *Hopkins*, *House*, Hubbell, *Hunton*, *Hurd*, *T. L. Jones*, *F. Landers*, *Lane*, W. Lawrence, *B. B. Lewis*, *Lynde*, *L. A. Mackey*, *Maish*, *McFarland*, *McMahon*, *Milliken*, *Mills*, *Morgan*, *Mutchler*, *Neal*, *New*, *Payne*, *J. Phelps*, *Poppleton*, *Randall*, *D. Rea*, *Reagan*, *J. Reilly*, *A. V. Rice*, *Riddle*, M. S. Robinson, *Savage*, *Sheakley*, *Singleton*, *Slemons*, *W. E. Smith*, *Southard*, *Springer*, *Stenger*, *Stevenson*, *Stone*, *Teese*, *P. F. Thomas*, *Throckmorton*, *Tucker*, *Turney*, Van Vorhes, *J. L. Vance*, *Waddell*, *G. C. Walker*, *Walsh*, *E. Wells*, *Whitthorne*, *J. D. Williams*, *J. N. Williams*, *Wilshire*, *B. Wilson*, *Yeates*, *C. Young*—106.

NAYS—Messrs. *Abbott*, C. H. Adams, *Bagby*, G. A. Bagley, *J. H. Bagley, jr.*, W. H. Baker, Ballou, BANKS, *S. N. Bell*, Blair, H. C. Burchard, Caswell, Chittenden, Conger, Crounse, *Cutler*, Danford, Davy, *Durand*, Eames, *Ely*, C. Freeman, Frye, *Gibson*, E. Hale, *Hancock*, *Hardenbergh*, B. W. Harris, Henderson, *A. S. Hewitt*, G. F. Hoar, Hoge, Hyman, Joyce, Kasson, *Kehr*, Kimball, *Lamar*, Lapham, *Levy*, Lynch, MacDougall, McCrary, *Meade*, *Metcalfe*, Miller, Monroe, *Morrison*, Nash, Norton, *O'Brien*, *Odell*, O'Neill, Packer, Page, Pierce,

Piper, T. C. Platt, A. POTTER, *Powell*, Pratt, Rainey, *M. Ross*, Rusk, Sampson, *Schleicher*, Sinnickson, R. Smalls, A. H. Smith, Strait, Stowell, *C. P. Thompson*, Thornburgh, W. Townsend, Tufts, Wait, *C. C. B. Walker*, *Ward*, *Warren*, G. W. Wells, J. D. White, Whiting, *A. S. Williams*, *Willis*, J. Wilson, Woodburn—86

IN SENATE.

No action was taken up to the time of closing this page.

Same day—the House passed yeas 132, nays 31—a joint resolution, for the appointment of a commission of three Senators and three Representatives to investigate during the recess the whole subject, and report at the next session the results of it; which, slightly amended, was agreed to by the Senate, and became a law.

Affairs in Mississippi.

IN SENATE.

August 7—The special committee, to investigate how far the rights of the people of that State were violated at the election held in it in November, 1875, made report, by a majority, and a minority. Both reports are elaborate.

The majority, through Mr. BOUTWELL, find that the stipulation made by Gen. J. Z. George with Gov. Ames, was systematically disregarded by the Democrats in the larger portion of the State, while the stipulation by Gov. Ames was faithfully kept. The following is a summary of their conclusions as contained in the Associated Press dispatch:

1. The committee find that the young men of the State, especially those who reached manhood during the war, or who have arrived at that condition since the war, constitute the nucleus and the main force of the dangerous element. As far as the testimony taken by the committee throws any light upon the subject, it tends, however, to establish the fact that the Democratic organizations, both in the counties and in the State, encouraged the young men in their course, accepted the political advantages of their conduct, and are in a large degree responsible for the criminal results.

2. There was a general disposition on the part of white employers to compel the laborers to vote the Democratic ticket.

3. Democratic clubs were organized in all parts of the State, and the able-bodied members were also organized into military companies and furnished with the best arms that could be procured in the country. The fact of their existence was no secret, although persons not in sympathy with the movement were excluded from membership. Indeed their object was more fully attained by public declarations of their organization in connection with the intention, everywhere expressed, that it was their purpose to carry the election at all hazards. In many places these organizations possessed one or more pieces of artillery. These pieces of artillery were carried over the counties and discharged upon the roads in the neighborhood of Republican meetings, and at meetings held by the Democrats. For many weeks before the election members of this military organization traversed the various counties, menacing the voters and discharging their guns by night as well as by day.

4. It appears from the testimony that, for some time previous to the election, it was impossible, in a large number of the counties, to hold Republican meetings.

5. The riots at Vicksburg on the 5th of July, and at Clinton on the 4th of September, were the results of a special purpose on the part of the Democrats to break up the meetings of the Republicans, to destroy the leaders and to inaugurate an era of terror, not only in those counties, but throughout the State, which would deter Republicans, and particularly the negroes, from organizing or attending meetings, and especially deter them from the free exercise of the right to vote on the day of the election. The results sought for were in a large degree attained.

6. Following the riot at Clinton, the country for the next two days was scoured by detachments from these Democratic military organizations over a circuit of many miles, and a large number of unoffending persons was killed. The number has never been ascertained correctly, but it may be estimated fairly as between thirty and fifty.

7. The committee find, from the testimony of Captain Montgomery, supported by numerous facts stated by other witnesses, that the military organization extended to most of the counties in the State where the Republicans were in the majority; that it embraced a proportion not much less than one-half of all the white voters, and that in the respective counties the men could be summoned by signals given by firing cannons or anvils, and that probably in less than a week the entire force of the State could be brought out under arms.

9. The committee find that in several of the counties the Republican leaders were so overawed and intimidated, both white and black, that they were compelled to withdraw from the canvass those who had been nominated, and to substitute others who were named by the Democratic leaders, and that finally they were compelled to vote for the ticket so nominated, under threats that their lives would be taken if they did not do it.

10. The committee find that the candidates in some instances were compelled, by persecution or through fear of bodily harm, to withdraw their names from the ticket and even to unite themselves ostensibly with the Democratic party.

11. The committee find that on the day of the election, at several voting places armed men assembled, some times not organized and in other cases organized; that they controlled the elections, intimidated Republican voters, and, in fine, deprived them of the opportunity to vote the Republican ticket.

12. The gravity of these revolutionary proceedings is expressed in the single fact that the Chairman of the Republican State Committee, General Warner, owes the preservation of his life on the day of the election to the intervention of General George, chairman of the Democratic State Committee.

13. The committee find in several cases, where intimidation and force did not result in securing a Democratic victory, that fraud was resorted to

in conducting the election and in counting the votes.

14. The evidence shows that the civil authorities have been unable to prevent the outrages set forth in this report, or to punish the offenders. This is true not only of the Courts of the State, but also of the District Court of the United States, as appears from the report of the Grand Jury made at the term held in June last, when the evidence of the offences committed at the November election and during the canvass was laid before that body.

15. The committee find that outrages of the nature set forth in this report were perpetrated in the counties of Alcorn, Amite, Chickasaw, Claiborne, Clay, Copiah, De Soto, Grenada, Hinds, Holmes, Kemper, Lee, Lowndes, Madison, Marshall, Monroe, Noxubee, Rankin, Scott, Warren, Washington and Yazoo, and that the Democratic victory in the State was due to the outrages so perpetrated.

16. The committee find that if in the counties named there had been a free election, Republican candidates would have been chosen, and the character of the Legislature so changed that there would have been 66 Republicans to 50 Democrats in the House, and 26 Republicans to 11 Democrats in the Senate; and that consequently the present Legislature of Mississippi is not a legal body, and its acts are not entitled to recognition by the political department of the Government of the United States, although the President may, in his discretion, recognize it as a government *de facto* for the preservation of the public peace.

17. Your committee find that the resignation of Governor Ames was effected by a body of men calling themselves the Legislature of the State of Mississippi, by measures unauthorized by law, and that he is of right the Governor of that State.

18. The evidence shows further that the State of Mississippi is at present under the control of political organizations composed largely of armed men whose common purpose is to deprive the negroes of the free exercise of the right of suffrage and to establish and maintain the supremacy of the white-line Democracy, in violation alike of the constitution of their own State and of the Constitution of the United States.

THE REMEDY.

The power of the National Government will be invoked, and honor and duty will alike require its exercise. The nation cannot witness, with indifference, the dominion of lawlessness and anarchy in a State, with their incident evils and a knowledge of the inevitable consequences. It owes a duty to the citizens of the United States residing in Mississippi, and this duty it must perform. It has guaranteed to the State of Mississippi a republican form of government, and this guarantee must be made good.

The measures necessary and possible in an exigency are three:

1. Laws may be passed by Congress for the protection of the rights of citizens in the respective States.

2. States in anarchy, or wherein the affairs are controlled by bodies of armed men, should be denied representation in Congress.

3. The constitutional guarantee of a republican form of government to every State will require the United States, if these disorders increase or even continue and all milder measures shall prove ineffectual, to remand the State to a territorial condition, and through a system of public education and kindred means of improvement change the ideas of the inhabitants and reconstruct the government upon a republican basis.

The minority (Messrs. BAYARD and McDONALD), after criticising President Grant's references to Mississippi, in his Message on the Hamburg (S. C.) massacre proceed to argue that when Governor Ames took his seat on the 1st day of January, 1874—elected in the month of November previous—there was not an official in the State who was not a member of the Republican party. There was not a county official to be appointed by the Governor who was not in close affinity with him. In all the Republican counties—and all were Republican in which negroes were in a majority—every official was a member of the same party. Thus the entire control of the State was in the hands of Governor Ames and his party associates. In all these Republican strongholds, in which charges of turbulence and misgovernment are alleged to have existed, it is noted that the entire local power was in Republican hands. The minority then speak of the effects of the Republican system of misgovernment upon real estate property, and show at some length that Governor Ames prostituted his office and bargained with appointees, and speak of the State militia being organized preparatory to the campaign, and the officials being among the most notorious and unscrupulous partisans—black and white—of the State administration, many of them being unable to read. This created great alarm among the white population, and violence, bloodshed and force, as the only arbiters of the election, were first suggested in a time of a profound peace in the State of Mississippi, by Governor Ames and his political associates. The minority say to justify any legislation by Congress to enforce the Fifteenth Amendment, obstruction of the "right to vote," must be for the sole reason of race or color or previous condition, &c., and there is no power in Congress to interfere for any other cause whatever. There is not, from beginning to end of this testimony, a single case of obstruction of a voter because he was a colored man. A vast majority of the people of Mississippi have every element that constitutes a good American citizen, but they have been victims of a misrule which they sought in vain to avoid or remedy.

The reformation in the legislation and administration of Mississippi by the party in control since January, 1876, has been important and marked with great benefits to the entire community. The minority make a few remarks upon the condition of Mississippi in June last, saying no act of a turbulent or disorderly nature was witnessed by the committee, and no signs of enmity or incivility were exhibited, but on the contrary, courtesy and respect were on all hands extended to the committee. The poverty of the people was apparent in their garb, the appearance of their houses, and the marked absence of good and comfortable vehicles. The only exhibition of pleasure-seeking witnessed was by the colored people, whose processions passed the committee-room, and whose holiday excursions by railway started from the depot opposite. The only cannon sound was from their Republican ratification meeting, and theirs was the only music heard by us in Mississippi. The poverty of the colored people also was often painfully apparent in the groups of witnesses who clustered upon the long galleries, wretched in appearance and miserably clad, giving to the hotel the appearance of a county almshouse. Interference by Federal authority in State elections and internal affairs has, since the close of the war, frequently taken place—never without deplorable and disastrous results; and, on the other hand, applications of minorities, defeated by the popular vote, to be nevertheless installed in office, have never been denied by Federal authorities without such denial being followed by beneficent results. Such interference has always been followed (and very naturally) by local discontent and disorder, as in the case of Louisiana and Alabama, while Tennessee, Virginia, North Carolina, Georgia, Texas and Arkansas are living proofs, in their increased prosperity and tranquility, of the wisdom of non-interference.

Dates of Elections in 1876.

ALABAMA: Will elect State officers on Monday, Aug. 7; Congressmen on Tuesday, Nov. 7.

ARKANSAS: Will elect State officers on Monday, Sept. 4; Congressmen on Tuesday, Nov. 7.

CALIFORNIA: Will elect Congressmen on Tuesday, Nov. 7; State officers will next be chosen in September, 1879.

COLORADO: Will elect State officers and Congressman on Tuesday, Oct. 10.

CONNECTICUT: Will elect State officers and Congressmen on Tuesday, Nov. 7.

DELAWARE: Will elect Congressman on Tuesday, Nov. 7. State officers will next be elected in November, 1878.

FLORIDA: Will elect State officers and Congressmen on Tuesday, Nov. 7.

GEORGIA: Will elect Governor on Wednesday, Oct. 4; Congressmen on Tuesday, Nov. 7.

ILLINOIS: Will elect State officers and Congressmen on Tuesday, Nov. 7.

INDIANA: Will elect State officers and Congressmen on Tuesday, Oct. 10.

IOWA: Will elect State officers and Congressmen on Tuesday, Nov. 7.

KANSAS: Will elect State officers and Congressmen on Tuesday, Nov. 7.

KENTUCKY: Will elect county officials and Congressmen in the Fifth District, to fill vacancy, on Monday, Aug. 7; Congressmen on Tuesday, Nov. 7. State officers will next be chosen on the first Monday in August, 1879.

LOUISIANA: Will elect State officers and Congressmen on Monday, Nov. 6. Five proposed amendments to the Constitution of the State will be voted upon at the same time.

MAINE: Will elect Governor and Congressmen on Monday, Sept. 11.

MARYLAND: Will elect Congressmen on Tuesday, Nov. 7. State officers will next be chosen in November, 1879.

MASSACHUSETTS: Will elect State officers and Congressmen on Tuesday, Nov. 7.

MICHIGAN: Will elect State officers and Congressmen on Tuesday, Nov. 7. Three proposed amendments to the Constitution of the State will be voted upon on the same day.

MINNESOTA: Will elect Congressmen on Tuesday, Nov. 7. State officers will next be chosen in November, 1877.

MISSISSIPPI: Will elect Congressmen on Tuesday, Nov. 7. State officers will next be chosen in November, 1877.

MISSOURI: Will elect State officers and Congressmen on Tuesday, Nov. 7.

NEBRASKA: Will elect State officers and Congressmen on Tuesday, Nov. 7.

NEVADA: Will elect Congressmen on Tuesday, Nov. 7. State officers will next be chosen in November, 1878.

NEW HAMPSHIRE: Will elect Governor and Congressmen on Tuesday, March 13, 1877.

NEW JERSEY: Will elect Congressmen on Tuesday, Nov. 7. State officers will next be elected in November, 1877.

NEW YORK: Will elect State officers and Congressmen on Tuesday, Nov. 7. Two proposed amendments to the Constitution of the State will be voted upon on the same day.

NORTH CAROLINA: Will elect State officers and Congressmen on Tuesday, Nov. 7. Certain proposed amendments to the Constitution of the State will be voted upon on the same day.

OHIO: Will elect minor State officers and Congressmen on Tuesday, Oct. 10. The regular election for Governor will next occur in October, 1877.

OREGON: Will elect Congressmen on Tuesday, Nov. 7. The next election of Governor will occur in June, 1878.

PENNSYLVANIA: Will elect Congressmen on Tuesday, Nov. 7. State officers will next be chosen in November, 1878.

RHODE ISLAND: Will elect Congressmen on Tuesday Nov. 7. State officers on Wednesday, April 4, 1877.

SOUTH CAROLINA: Will elect State officers and Congressmen on Tuesday, Nov. 7.

TENNESSEE: Will elect Governor and Congressmen on Tuesday, Nov. 7.

TEXAS: Will elect Congressmen on Tuesday, Nov. 7. State officers will next be chosen in Nov. 1877.

VERMONT: Will elect State officers and Congressmen on Tuesday, Sept. 5.

VIRGINIA: Will elect Congressmen on Tuesday, Nov. 7. State officers will next be chosen in Nov. 1877.

WEST VIRGINIA: Will elect State officers on Tuesday, Oct. 10; Congressmen, November 7.

WISCONSIN: Will elect Congressmen on Tuesday, Nov. 7. State officers will next be chosen in Nov., 1877.—*N. Y. Times.*

Imports and Exports.

In the eleven months ending May 31, 1876, the total imports of merchandise, in value, were	$490,535,488
During the eleven months ending May 31, 1875, they were	426,551,860
Decrease of imports	$63,983,628

During the same period in 1876, the gold values of merchandise of domestic origin, exported, were....$480,839,000
During the same period in 1875, they were...... 463,376,514

Increase of exports.... $17,463,486

The following tables will present in a compact form the falling off in imports and the increase in our exports of a number of the leading articles of commerce:

IMPORTS.

COMMODITIES.	Eleven months ended May 31, 1875.	1876.
Fancy goods	$5,361,556	$4,336,020
Manufactures of flax (by yard)...	13,332,560	11,719,830
Hemp (raw)	2,962,892	2,072,653
Bar iron	1,628,129	1,468,380
Sheet iron	845,533	716,504
Old and scrap iron	771,919	381,030
Hardware	289,360	125,526
Anchors, cables and chains	326,326	214,602
Firearms	608,096	470,143
Steel ingots, bars, sheets and wire	2,336,186	1,667,438
Railroad bars or rails of steel	2,619,847	314,282
Cutlery	1,392,355	1,042,971
Files	330,378	209,125
Other manufactures of iron and steel not elsewhere specified	3,982,183	3,306,983
Lead and manufactures of	1,335,805	508,327
Leather of all kinds	5,615,670	3,669,773
Precious stones	3,231,092	2,344,400
Flaxseed or linseed	5,796,790	3,506,743
Straw and palmleaf, manufactures of	2,215,740	1,776,403
Brown sugar	60,043,093	48,571,098
Molasses	9,583,046	7,104,889
Tin and manufactures of	11,976,746	9,328,330
Watches and material for	2,155,978	1,382,537
Wines, spirits and cordials	7,028,622	5,993,598
Wool (unmanufactured)	10,140,706	7,782,548
Cloths and cassimeres	12,857,135	9,538,343
Shawls	2,112,806	1,436,136
Carpets	2,616,381	1,501,321
Dress goods	19,268,446	13,860,048

EXPORTS.

COMMODITIES.	Eleven months ended May 31, 1875.	1876.
Bark, for tanning	$157,524	$217,270
Indian corn	23,229,082	27,877,336
Wheat	53,115,185	60,615,742
Copper and manufactures of	1,637,601	3,078,481
Cotton (unmanufactured)	182,727,005	186,290,473
Leather and manufactures of	6,639,089	9,439,213
Lubricating oil	23,999,396	26,236,193
Shot and shell	3,290	510,747
Bacon and hams	27,015,359	36,368,390
Quicksilver	995,439	1,539,189
Refined sugar	1,769,093	5,107,949
Timber, sawed and hewed	2,030,347	3,214,914

Electoral College.

NEW ENGLAND AND MIDDLE.		WESTERN.	
Connecticut	6	Illinois	21
Maine	7	Indiana	15
Massachusetts	13	Iowa	11
New Hampshire	5	Kansas	5
New Jersey	9	Michigan	11
New York	35	Minnesota	5
Pennsylvania	29	Nebraska	3
Rhode Island	4	Ohio	22
Vermont	5	Wisconsin	10
	113		103

FORMER SLAVE.		PACIFIC.	
Alabama	10	California	6
Arkansas	6	Colorado	3
Delaware	3	Nevada	3
Florida	4	Oregon	3
Georgia	11		
Kentucky	12		15
Louisiana	8		
Maryland	8	Total	369
Mississippi	8	Majority	185
Missouri	15		
North Carolina	10		
South Carolina	7		
Tennessee	12		
Texas	8		
Virginia	11		
West Virginia	5		
	138		

Reduction of Debt.

United States debt, including accrued interest thereon, less cash in the Treasury:

1869, March 1	$2,525,463,260 01
1876, August 1	2,098,301,311 06
Reduction between those dates	$427,161,948 95

Monthly interest charge:

1869, March 1	$10,532,462 50
1876, August 1	7,925,355 75
Reduction between those dates	$2,607,106 75

Receipts and Expenditures for the Fiscal Year ending June 30, 1876.

RECEIPTS.

Customs	$148,071,984 61
Internal Revenue	116,700,732 03
Direct Tax	93,798 80
Public Lands	1,129,466 95
Miscellaneous	17,456,776 19
	$283,452,758 58

EXPENDITURES.

Civil and Miscellaneous	$66,958,373 78
War Department	38,070,888 64
Navy Department	18,963,309 82
Indians	5,966,558 17
Pensions	28,257,395 69
	$158,216,526 20

[The above statement could not be obtained from the Treasury Department in time to place it in its proper position in the tables following, and is accordingly inserted here.—EDITOR.]

President Grant's Message Asking for Troops against the Indians, August 11, 1876.

To the Senate and House of Representatives:

I transmit herewith a telegram of the 5th of August, inst., from Lieut-Gen. Sheridan to Gen. Sherman, a letter of the 11th of the present month from Gen. Sherman to the Secretary of War, and a letter from the latter of the same date to me, all setting forth the possible needs of the army in consequence of existing hostilities. I would strongly urge upon Congress the necessity for making some provision for a contingency which may arise during the vacation for more troops in the Indian country than it is now possible to send. It would seem to me to be much more economical and better to authorize an increase of the present cavalry force by 2,500 privates; but if this is not deemed advisable, then that the President be authorized to call out not exceeding five regiments, 1,000 strong each, of volunteers to serve for a period not exceeding six months. Should this latter authority be given, I would not order out any volunteers unless, in my opinion, based upon reports from the scene of war, I deemed it absolutely necessary, and then only the smallest number considered sufficient to meet the emergency. U. S. GRANT.

EXECUTIVE MANSION, *August* 11, 1876.

The following is Gen. Sheridan's letter to Gen. Sherman:

CHICAGO, Aug. 5, 1876.

To Gen. W. T. SHERMAN, *Washington, D. C.:*

I have not yet been able to reënforce the garrison at Red Cloud, at Spotted Tail, or at Standing Rock, to be strong enough to attempt to count the Indians, or to arrest and disarm those coming in. I beg of you to see the Military Committee of the House and urge on it the necessity of increasing the cavalry regiments to 100 to each company. Gen. Crook's total strength is 1,774; Terry's 1,873; and to give this force to them I have stripped every post from the line of Manitoba to Texas. We want more mounted men. We have not exceeded the law in enlisting Indian scouts; in fact have not as many as the law allows us. The whole number in this division is only 114. The Indians with Gen. Crook are not enlisted, or even paid. They are not worth paying. They are with him only to gratify their desire for a fight and their thirst for revenge on the Sioux.

P. H. SHERIDAN, Lieut.-General.

The letter of Gen. Sherman to the Secretary of War indorses the recommendations of Gen. Sheridan, and the letter of the Secretary of War recommends the same to the President.

Protection of Right of Suffrage.

IN HOUSE.

August 10—Mr. LORD asked unanimous consent to offer this preamble and resolution:

Whereas the right of suffrage prescribed by the constitutions of the several States is subject to the fifteenth amendment of the Constitution of the United States, which is as follows:

"ARTICLE XV.

"SECTION 1. The right of citizens of the United States to vote shall not be denied or abridged by the United States or by any State on account of race, color, or previous condition of servitude.

"SEC. 2. The Congress shall have power to enforce this article by appropriate legislation."

And whereas the exercise of the right of suffrage so prescribed and regulated should be faithfully maintained and observed by the United States and the several States and the citizens thereof; and whereas it is asserted that the exercise of the right of suffrage is in some of the States, notwithstanding the efforts of all good citizens to the contrary, resisted and controlled by fraud, intimidation, and violence, so that in such cases the object of the amendment is defeated; and whereas all citizens, without distinction of race, or class, or color, are entitled to the protection conferred by such article: Therefore,

Be it resolved by the House of Representatives, That all attempts by force, fraud, terror, intimidation, or otherwise, to prevent the free exercise of the right of suffrage in any State, should meet with certain, condign, and effectual punishment, and that in any case which has heretofore occurred or that may hereafter occur in which violence or murder has been or shall be committed by one race or class upon the other, the prompt prosecution and punishment of the criminal or criminals in any court having jurisdiction is imperatively demanded, whether the crime be one punishable by fine or imprisonment or one demanding the penalty of death.

Mr. CONGER objected to the resolution, but on its being again read, withdrew his objection.

Consent being given, the resolution was offered; and

Mr. LORD demanded the previous question.

Mr. CLYMER moved its reference to the Committee on the Judiciary.

The demand for the previous question taking precedence, there were 83 ayes, 53 noes—no quorum. By tellers, the vote was 79 ayes, 19 noes—no quorum. A call of the House was ordered—ayes 69, noes 46; and 173 members answered to their names, more than a quorum. Further proceedings were then suspended.

Tellers resumed their places on the question of seconding the demand for the previous question, when there were 90 ayes and 21 noes—not a quorum. Another call of the House was ordered—ayes 85, noes 30—when 178 members answered.

On another vote, by tellers, the demand for the previous question was seconded—ayes 133, noes 18.

Mr. CLYMER asked a division of the vote on the preamble and the resolution.

On adopting the resolution, the yeas were 174, nays 2 (not voting 109), as follow:

YEAS—Messrs. *Ainsworth*, ANDERSON, *Ashe*, *Atkins*, *Bagby*, *G. A. Bagley*, *J. H. Bagley, jr.*, J. H. Baker, W. H. Baker, Ballou, BANKS, *Banning*, *Beebe*, Blair, *Boone*, *Bradford*, Bradley, *Bright*, W. R. Brown, H. C. Burchard, Burleigh, *Cabell*, *J. H. Caldwell*, Cannon, Caswell, *Cate*, *J. B. Clarke*, *J. B. Clark, jr.*, *Clymer*, *Cochrane*, Conger, *Cook*, *Cox*, Crounse, *Cutler*, Danford, Darrall, *Joseph J. Davis*, Davy, *Dibrell*, *Durand*, *Durham*, Eames, *Eden*, *Egbert*, Evans, *Faulkner*, *Felton*, *Finley*, *Forney*, Fort, Foster, *Franklin*, C. Freeman, Frye, Garfield, *Gause*, *Goodin*, *Gunter*, E. Hale, *A. H. Hamilton*, *Hancock*, *Hardenbergh*, B. W. Harris, *J. T. Harris*, *Hartzell*, *Haymond*, Henderson, *Hereford*, *G. W. Hewitt*, G. F. Hoar, *Holman*, *Hooker*, *Hopkins*, *House*, *Hunton*, *Hurd*, Hurlbut, Hyman, *T. L. Jones*, Joyce, Kasson, *Kehr*, Kimball, King, *F. Landers*, *Lane*, Lapham, W. Lawrence, *Levy*, *B. B. Lewis*, *Lord*, *Luttrell*, Lynch, *Lynde*, Magoon, *Maish*, MacDougall, McCrary, J. W. McDill, *McFarland*, *McMahon*, *Metcalfe*, Miller, Monroe, *Morgan*, *Morrison*, *Mutchler*, Nash, *New*, Norton, *Odell*, Packer, *Payne*, Pierce, *Piper*, *Poppleton*, A. POTTER, Pratt, Rainey, *D. Rea*, *J. Reilly*, *J. B. Reilly*, *A. V. Rice*, *Riddle*, *J. Robbins*, *W. M. Robbins*,

C. B. Roberts, M. S. Robinson, *M. Ross*, Rusk, Sampson, *Savage*, *Scales*, *Schleicher*, *Sheakley*, *Singleton*, Sinnickson, *Slemons*, A. H. Smith, *W. E. Smith*, *Spencer*, *Springer*, Strait, *Stenger*, *Stevenson*, *Stone*, *Tarbox*, *Terry*, *P. F. Thomas*, *C. P. Thompson*, Thornburgh, W. Townsend, Tufts, *Turney*, Van Vorhes, *J. L. Vance*, *R. B. Vance*, *Waddell*, Wait, *E. Wells*, Whiting, *Whitthorne*, *Wigginton*, G. Willard, *A. S. Williams*, *J. Williams*, *J. D. Williams*, *J. N. Williams*, W. B. Williams, *Willis*, *Wilshire*, J. Wilson, *Yeates*—174.

NAYS—Messrs. *Bland*, *Reagan*—2.

The preamble was then agreed to—yeas 125, nays 31 (not voting 129), as follow:

YEAS—Messrs. *Ainsworth*, ANDERSON, *Ashe*, *Atkins*, *Bagby*, *J. H. Bagley*, *jr.*, W. H. Baker, Ballou, BANKS, *Banning*, Blair, *Boone*, Bradley, W. R. Brown, H. C. Burchard, Burleigh, Cannon, Caswell, *Cate*, Conger, Crounse, *Cutler*, Danford, *Joseph J. Davis*, Davy, *Durand*, Eames, *Eden*, *Egbert*, Evans, *Finley*, Fort, Foster, C. Freeman, Frye, Garfield, *Goodin*, *Gunter*, E. Hale, *A. H. Hamilton*, *Hancock*, *Hardenbergh*, B. W. Harris, *Hartzell*, *Haymond*, Henderson, G. F. Hoar, *Hooker*, *Hopkins*, *House*, Hurlbut, Hyman, *T. L. Jones*, Joyce, Kasson, *Kehr*, Kimball, King, *F. Landers*, *Lane*, Lapham, W. Lawrence, *Lord*, *Luttrell*, Lynch, *Lynde*, Magoon, *Maish*, MacDougall, McCrary, J. W. McDill, *McFarland*, *McMahon*, *Metcalfe*, Miller, Monroe, *Morgan*, Nash, *New*, Norton, Packer, *Payne*, Pierce, A. POTTER, Pratt, Rainey, *D. Rea*, *J. Reilly*, *J. B. Reilly*, *Riddle*, *J. Robbins*, M. S. Robinson, Rusk, Sampson, *Savage*, *Singleton*, Sinnickson, *Slemons*, A. H. Smith, *W. E. Smith*, *Spencer*, *Springer*, Strait, *Stenger*, *Stevenson*, *Stone*, *C. P. Thompson*, Thornburgh, W. Townsend, Tufts, *Turney*, Van Vorhes, *R. B. Vance*, Wait, J. D. White, Whiting, *Whitthorne*, *Wigginton*, G. Willard, *A. S. Williams*, *J. Williams*, W. B. Williams, *Willis*, J. Wilson, *Yeates*—125.

NAYS—Messrs. *Bland*, *Bradford*, *Bright*, *Cabell*, *J. H. Caldwell*, *J. B. Clarke*, *Clymer*, *Cook*, *Dibrell*, *Durham*, *Felton*, *Forney*, *Franklin*, *Hereford*, *G. W. Hewitt*, *Hunton*, *Hurd*, *B. B. Lewis*, *Mutchler*, *Piper*, *Poppleton*, *Reagan*, *A. V. Rice*, *W. M. Robbins*, *Tarbox*, *Terry*, *P. F. Thomas*, *Throckmorton*, *J. L. Vance*, *Waddell*, *J. N. Williams*—31.

Public School Amendment.*

IN HOUSE.

1876, August 4—Mr. LORD, from the Judiciary Committee, reported the Constitutional Amendment offered by Mr. BLAINE on the 14th of December, 1875, and referred to that committee [for which see page 129], in these words:

ARTICLE 16. No State shall make any law respecting an establishment of religion, or prohibiting the free exercise thereof; and no money raised by taxation in any State for the support of public schools, or derived from any public fund therefor, nor any public lands devoted thereto, shall ever be under the control of any religious sect or denomination; nor shall any money so raised, or lands so devoted be divided between religious sects or denominations. This article shall not vest, enlarge or diminish legislative power in Congress.

[The last sentence was added by the Committee, and the words "or denomination" where they first occur.]

After a brief debate, the resolution as reported was agreed to—yeas 180, nays 7, not voting 98, as follow:

YEAS—Messrs. *Abbott*, C. H. Adams, *Ainsworth*, *Atkins*, *Bagby*, *J. H. Bagley*, *jr.*, W. H. Baker, Ballou, BANKS, *Banning*, *S. N. Bell*, Blair, *Bland*, *Boone*, *Bright*, *J. Y. Brown*, W. R. Brown, H. C. Burchard, *S. D. Burchard*, *Cabell*, Cannon, Cason, Caswell, *W. P. Caldwell*, *Cate*, *Caulfield*, Chittenden, *J. B. Clark*, *jr.*, *Clymer*, *Cochrane*, Conger, *Cook*, *Cox*, Crounse, *Cutler*, Danford, Darrall, *Joseph J. Davis*, Davy, *Dibrell*, Dobbins, Dunnell, *Durand*, *Durham*, Eames, *Eden*, Evans, *Felton*, *Finley*, Fort, Foster *Franklin*, C. Freeman, Frye, Garfield, *Gause*, *Goode*, *Goodin*, *Gunter*, E. Hale, *A. H. Hamilton*, *Hancock*, *Hardenbergh*, B. W. Harris, *C. H. Harrison*, *Hartridge*, *Hartzell*, *Haymond*, Henderson, *Henkle*, *A. S. Hewitt*, G. F. Hoar, *Holman*, *Hopkins*, *Hunton*, *Hurd*, Hyman, *Jenks*, *T. L. Jones*, Joyce, Kasson, *Kehr*, *Lamar*, *F. Landers*, *Lane*, Lapham, W. Lawrence, Leavenworth, *Levy*, *B. B. Lewis*, *Lord*, Lynch, *Lynde*, *L. A. Mackey*, *Maish*, MacDougall, McCrary, J. W. McDill, *McFarland*, *McMahon*, *Metcalfe*, Miller, *Milliken*, *Mills*, Monroe, *Morgan*, *Morrison*, *Mutchler*, *Neal*, *New*, O'Neill, Packer, Page, *Payne*, W. A. Phillips, Pierce, *Piper*, Plaisted, T. C. Platt, *Poppleton*, A. POTTER, *Powell*, Pratt, Rainey, *Randall*, *D. Rea*, *Reagan*, *J. Reilly*, *A. V. Rice*, *Riddle*, *J. Robbins*, *W. M. Robbins*, *C. B. Roberts*, M. S. Robinson, *M. Ross*, Rusk, Sampson, *Savage*, *Scales*, *Singleton*, Sinnickson, *Slemons*, R. Smalls, A. H. Smith, *W. E. Smith*, *Southard*, *Springer*, *Stenger*, *Stevenson*, *Stone*, *Terry*, *P. F. Thomas*, *C. P. Thompson*, *Throckmorton*, W. Townsend, Tufts, *Turney*, Van Vorhes, *J. L. Vance*, *Waddell*, *C. C. B. Walker*, *G. C. Walker*, *Walsh*, *Ward*, *Warren*, *E. Wells*, J. D. White, *Whitthorne*, *Wigginton*, G. Willard, *A. S. Williams*, *J. Williams*, *J. D. Williams*, *J. N. Williams*, *Willis*, *B. Wilson*, *J. Wilson*, Woodburn, *Yeates*—180.

NAYS—Messrs. *Blackburn*, *Bradford*, *J. H. Caldwell*, *J. B. Clarke*, *Forney*, *Knott*, *O'Brien*—7.

NOT VOTING—Messrs. ANDERSON, *Ashe*, G. A. Bagley, J. H. Baker, Bass, *Beebe*, *Bliss*, *Blount*, Bradley, *Buckner*, Burleigh, *Candler*, *Chapin*, *Collins*, *Cowan*, Crapo, *Culberson*, Danford, *De Bolt*, Denison, *Douglas*, *Egbert*, *Ellis*, *Ely*, *Faulkner*, *Fuller*, Garfield, *Gibson*, *Glover*, *R. Hamilton*, Haralson, *H. R. Harris*, *J. T. Harris*, *Hatcher*, Hathorn, Hays, Hendee, *Hereford*, *G. W. Hewitt*, *Hill*, Hoge, *Hooker*, *Hos-*

*August 8—In HOUSE, Mr. W. LAWRENCE proposed this constitutional amendment, which was referred to the Committee on the Judiciary:

SECTION 1. No State shall make any law respecting an establishment of religion, or prohibiting the free exercise thereof.

SEC. 2. No public property or money raised by taxation or from any public fund or property in any State or place subject to the legislative power of Congress shall ever be given to or be under the control of any religious sect or denomination.

SEC. 3. Congress shall have power to enforce this article by appropriate legislation.

kins, *House*, Hubbell, Hunter, Hurlbut, *F. Jones*, Kelley, Kimball, King, *G. M. Landers*, *Le Moyne*, *Luttrell*, Magoon, *Meade*, *Money*, Monroe, Nash, Norton, *Odell*, Oliver, O'Neill, *J. Phelps*, *J. F. Philips*, Purman, *J. B. Reilly*, S. Ross, *M. Sayler*, *Schleicher*, *Schumaker*, Seelye, *Sheakley*, *Sparks*, *Spencer*, Strait, Stowell, *Swann*, *Tarbox*, Thornburgh, M. I. Townsend, *Tucker*, *R. B. Vance*, Wait, Waldron, A. S. Wallace, J. W. Wallace, *Walling*, G. W. Wells, Wheeler, *Whitehouse*, Whiting, *Wike*, A. Williams, C. G. Williams, W. B. Williams, *Wilshire*, A. Wood, jr., *F. Wood*, Woodworth, *C. Young*—113.

IN SENATE.

August 7—It was referred to the Committee on the Judiciary, and the following which were offered as substitutes for it:

By Mr. SARGENT—Article 16. There shall be maintained in each State and Territory a system of free common schools; but neither the United States nor any State, or Territory, county, or municipal corporation shall aid in the support of any school wherein the peculiar tenets of any religious denomination shall be taught.

SECTION 2. The Congress shall have power to enforce by appropriate legislation the provisions of this article.

By Mr. FRELINGHUYSEN—No State shall make any law respecting an establishment of religion or prohibiting the free exercise thereof; and no public property and no money raised by taxation in any State, Territory, or District, or derived from public lands, or other public source, shall be appropriated to any school, educational, or other institution that is under the control of any religious sect or denomination; and no such appropriation shall be made to any religious sect or denomination or to promote its interests; nor shall any public money, land, or property be divided between religious sects or denominations.

SECTION 2. The Congress shall have power to enforce by appropriate legislation the provisions of this article.

By Mr. CHRISTIANCY—No State shall make any law respecting the establishment of religion or prohibiting the free exercise thereof; nor shall Congress nor any State raise by taxation, donate, or appropriate any money or property for the support of any church or religious society, nor for the support or in aid of any theological school or seminary, or of any school or seminary teaching the peculiar religious doctrines, or subject in any respect to the control or direction of any church, religious society, sect, or denomination. And no special or denominational system of religion or religious belief shall in any State or Territory or in the District of Columbia constitute any part of the course of study or instruction in any school or institution of learning supported wholly or in part by taxation, or by the donation of any money or property by any State or by the United States.

August 9—Mr. EDMUNDS, from the Committee on the Judiciary, reported the joint resolution with an amendment in the nature of a substitute, as follows:

ARTICLE XVI.

No State shall make any law respecting an establishment of religion, or prohibiting the free exercise thereof; and no religious test shall ever be required as a qualification to any office or public trust under any State. No public property and no public revenue of, nor any loan of credit by or under the authority of the United States, or any State, Territory, District, or municipal corporation, shall be appropriated to or made or used for the support of any school, educational or other institution under the control of any religious or anti-religious sect, organization, or denomination, or wherein the particular creed or tenets of any religious or anti-religious sect, organization, or denomination shall be taught. And no such particular creed or tenets shall be read or taught in any school or institution supported in whole or in part by such revenue or loan of credit; and no such appropriation or loan of credit shall be made to any religious or anti-religious sect, organization, or denomination, or to promote its interests or tenets. This article shall not be construed to prohibit the reading of the Bible in any school or institution; and it shall not have the effect to impair rights of property already vested.

SEC. 2. Congress shall have power, by appropriate legislation, to provide for the prevention and punishment of violations of this article.

August 11—The subject was briefly debated, and the substitute of the committee was agreed to—yeas 27, nays 15, as follow:

YEAS—Messrs. Allison, Anthony, BOOTH, Boutwell, Burnside, Cameron of Wisconsin, Christiancy, Conkling, Cragin, Edmunds, Ferry of Michigan, Frelinghuysen, Harvey, Hitchcock, Howe, Ingalls, Logan, McMillan, Mitchell, Morrill of Vermont, Oglesby, Paddock, Patterson, Sargent, Spencer, Wadleigh, West—27.

NAYS—Messrs. *Bogy*, *Cockrell*, *Cooper*, *Davis*, *Eaton*, *Gordon*, *Kelly*, *Kernan*, *Key*, *McCreery*, *Maxey*, *Norwood*, *Randolph*, *Ransom*, *Stevenson*—15.

August 14—The SENATE voted on the passage of the joint resolution, as amended, when it was disagreed to—yeas 28, nays 16, as follow (two-thirds being necessary):

YEAS—Messrs. Allison, Anthony, BOOTH, Boutwell, Bruce, Burnside, Cameron of Wisconsin, Christiancy, Clayton, Conkling, Cragin, Edmunds, Ferry of Michigan, Frelinghuysen, Harvey, Jones of Nevada, Logan, McMillan, Mitchell, Morrill, Morton, Oglesby, Paddock, Patterson, Sargent, Spencer, Wadleigh, West—28.

NAYS—Messrs. *Bogy*, *Cockrell*, *Cooper*, *Davis*, *Eaton*, *Gordon*, *Jones* of Florida, *Kelly*, *Kernan*, *Key*, *McCreery*, *McDonald*, *Maxey*, *Norwood*, *Randolph*, *Stevenson*—16.

And the joint resolution failed.

Prohibiting Contributions for Political Purposes.

In the Committee of Conference on the legislative bill, the following section was inserted, as part of the conference report, which was agreed to, in each house, without a division:

"SEC. —. That all executive officers or employés of the United States not appointed by the President, with the advice and consent of the Senate, are prohibited from requesting, giving to, or receiving from any other officer or employé of the Government any money or property or other thing of value for political purposes; and any such officer or employé who shall offend against the provisions of this section shall be at once discharged from the service of the United States; and he shall also be deemed guilty of a misdemeanor, and, on conviction thereof, shall be fined in a sum not exceeding $500.

Previous Legislation on Gold and Silver Coin, from 1792 to 1873.

THE ACT OF APRIL 2, 1792, entitled "An Act establishing a Mint and regulating the coins of the United States," enacts

SEC. 9. That there shall be from time to time struck and coined at the said mint, coins of gold, silver, and copper, of the following denominations, values and descriptions, viz.: EAGLES—each to be of the value of ten dollars or units, and to contain two hundred and forty-seven grains and four-eighths of a grain of pure, or two hundred and seventy grains of standard gold. HALF EAGLES—each to be of the value of five dollars, and to contain one hundred and twenty-three grains and six-eighths of a grain of pure, or one hundred and thirty-five grains of standard gold. QUARTER EAGLES—each to be of the value of two dollars and a half dollar, and to contain sixty-one grains and seven-eighths of a grain of pure, or sixty-seven grains and four-eighths of a grain of standard gold. DOLLARS OR UNITS—each to be of the value of a Spanish milled dollar as the same is now current, and to contain three hundred and seventy-one grains and four sixteenth parts of a grain of pure, or four hundred and sixteen grains of standard silver. HALF DOLLARS—each to be of half the value of the dollar or unit, and to contain one hundred and eighty-five grains and ten sixteenth parts of a grain of pure, or two hundred and eight grains of standard silver. QUARTER DOLLARS—each to be of one-fourth the value of the dollar or unit, and to contain ninety-two grains and thirteen sixteenth parts of a grain of pure, or one hundred and four grains of standard silver. DISMES—each to be of the value of one-tenth of a dollar or unit, and to contain thirty-seven grains and two-sixteenth parts of a grain of pure, or forty-one grains and three-fifth parts of a grain of standard silver. HALF DISMES—each to be of the value of one-twentieth of a dollar and to contain eighteen grains and nine sixteenth parts of a grain of pure, or twenty grains and four fifth parts of a grain of standard silver.

SEC. 11. That the proportional value of gold to silver in all coins which shall by law be current as money within the United States, shall be as fifteen to one, according to quantity in weight, of pure gold or pure silver; that is to say, every fifteen pounds weight of pure silver shall be of equal value in all payments, with one pound weight of pure gold, and so in proportion as to any greater or less quantities of the respective metals.

SEC. 12. That the standard for all gold coins of the United States shall be eleven parts fine to one part alloy; and accordingly that eleven parts in twelve of the entire weight of each of the said coins shall consist of pure gold, and the remaining one-twelfth part of alloy; and the said alloy shall be composed of silver and copper, in such proportions, not exceeding one-half silver, as shall be found convenient.

SEC. 13. That the standard for all silver coins of the United States, shall be one thousand four hundred and eighty-five parts fine to one hundred and seventy-nine parts alloy; and accordingly that one thousand four hundred and eighty-five parts in one thousand six hundred and sixty-four parts of the entire weight of each of the said coins shall consist of pure silver, and the remaining one hundred and seventy-nine parts of alloy; which alloy shall be wholly of copper.

THE ACT OF FEBRUARY 9, 1793, entitled "An act regulating foreign coins, and for other purposes," enacts in its first section

That from and after the first day of July next, foreign gold and silver coins shall pass current as money within the United States, and be a legal tender for the payment of all debts and demands, at the several and respective rates following, and not otherwise, viz: * * *

* * * Spanish milled dollars, at the rate of one hundred cents for each dollar, the actual weight whereof shall not be less than seventeen pennyweights and seven grains; and in proportion for the parts of a dollar. * * *

But no foreign coin that may have, or shall be issued subsequent to the first day of January, 1792, shall be a tender, as aforesaid, until samples thereof shall have been found, by assay, at the mint of the United States, to be conformable to the respective standards required, and proclamation thereof shall have been made by the President of the United States.

THE ACT OF JUNE 28, 1834, entitled "An act concerning the gold coins of the United States, and for other purposes," enacts

That the gold coins of the United States shall contain the following quantities of metal, that is to say: each eagle shall contain two hundred and thirty-two grains of pure gold, and two hundred and fifty-eight grains of standard gold; each half eagle one hundred and sixteen grains of pure gold, and one hundred and twenty-nine grains of standard gold; each quarter eagle shall contain fifty-eight grains of pure gold, and sixty-four and a half grains of standard gold; every such eagle shall be of the value of ten dollars; every such half eagle shall be of the value of five dollars; and every such quarter eagle shall be of the value of two dollars and fifty cents; and the said gold coins shall be receivable in all payments, when of full weight, according to their respective values; and when of less than full weight, at less values, proportioned to their respective actual weights.

SEC. 3. That all gold coins of the United States, minted anterior to the thirty-first day of July next, shall be receivable in all payments at the rate of ninety-four and eight-tenths of a cent per pennyweight.

THE ACT OF JANUARY 18, 1837, entitled "An act supplementary to the act entitled 'An act establishing a mint, and regulating the coins of the United States,'" enacts

SEC. 8. That the standard for both gold and silver coins of the United States shall hereafter be such, that of one thousand parts by weight, nine hundred shall be of pure metal, and one hundred of alloy; and the alloy of the silver coins shall be of copper; and the alloy of the gold coins shall be of copper and silver, provided that the silver do not exceed one-half of the whole alloy.

SEC. 9. That of the silver coins, the dollar shall be of the weight of four hundred and twelve and one-half grains; the half dollar of the weight of two hundred and six and one-fourth grains; the quarter dollar of the weight of one hundred and three and one-eighth grains; the dime, or tenth part of a dollar, of the weight of forty-one and a quarter grains; and the half dime, or twentieth part of a dollar, of the weight of twenty grains and five-eighths of a grain. And that dollars, half dollars, and quarter dollars, dimes, and half dimes, shall be legal tenders of payment, according to their nominal value, for any sums whatever.

SEC. 10. That of the gold coins, the weight of the eagle shall be two hundred and fifty-eight grains; that of the half eagle one hundred and twenty-nine grains; and that of the quarter eagle sixty-four and one-half grains. And that for all sums whatever, the eagle shall be a legal tender of payment for ten dollars; the half eagle for five dollars; and the quarter eagle for two and a half dollars.

SEC. 11. That the silver coins heretofore issued at the mint of the United States, and the gold coins issued since the thirty-first day of July, 1834, shall continue to be legal tenders of payment for their nominal values, on the same terms as if they were of the coinage provided for by this act.

THE ACT OF MARCH 3, 1849, authorized a double eagle of gold, value of twenty dollars, or units, and a gold dollar, each to be for all sums whatever a legal tender to those amounts.

THE ACT OF MARCH 3, 1851, authorized the coinage of a three cent piece, to be a legal tender for all sums of thirty cents and under.

THE ACT OF FEBRUARY 21, 1853, entitled "An act amendatory of existing laws relative to the Half Dollar, Quarter Dollar, Dime, and Half Dime," enacts

That from and after the first day of June, 1853, the weight of the half dollar, or piece of fifty cents, shall be one hundred and ninety-two grains, and the quarter dollar, dime, and half dime, shall be, respectively, one-half, one-fifth, and one-tenth of the weight of said half dollar.

SEC. 3. That the silver coins issued in conformity with the above section, shall be legal tenders in payment of debts for all sums not exceeding five dollars.

THE ACT OF FEBRUARY 21, 1857, entitled "An act relating to Foreign Coins and to the Coinage of Cents at the Mint of the United States," enacts

That the pieces, commonly known as the quarter, eighth, and sixteenth of the Spanish pillar dollar, and of the Mexican dollar, shall be receivable at the Treasury of the United States and its several offices, and at the several post-offices and land-offices, at the rates of valuation following—that is to say, the fourth of a dollar, or piece of two reals, at twenty cents; the eighth of a dollar, or piece of one real, at ten cents; and the sixteenth of a dollar, or half real, at five cents.

Section second requires said coins to be recoined.

SEC. 3. That all former acts authorizing the currency of foreign gold or silver coins, and declaring the same a legal tender in payment for debts, are hereby repealed.

THE ACT OF MARCH 3, 1865, authorized the coinage of a three-cent piece, and to be a legal tender to the amount of sixty cents.

THE ACT OF MAY 16, 1866, authorized the coinage of a five-cent piece, and to be a legal tender to the amount of one dollar.

THE ACT OF FEBRUARY 12, 1873, entitled "An act revising and amending the laws relative to the Mints, Assay-offices and Coinage of the United States," enacts

SEC. 13. That the standard for both gold and silver coins of the United States shall be such that of one thousand parts by weight, nine hundred shall be of pure metal and one hundred of alloy; and the alloy of the silver coins shall be of copper, and the alloy of the gold coins shall be of copper, or of copper and silver; but the silver in no case shall exceed one-tenth of the whole alloy.

SEC. 14. That the gold coins of the United States shall be a one-dollar piece, which, at the standard weight of twenty-five and eight-tenths grains, shall be the unit of value; a quarter-eagle, or two-and-a-half dollar piece; a three-dollar piece; a half-eagle, or five-dollar piece; an eagle, or ten-dollar piece; and a double-eagle, or twenty-dollar piece. And the standard weight of the gold dollar shall be twenty-five and eight-tenths grains; of the quarter-eagle, or two-and-a-half dollar piece, sixty-four and a half grains; of the three-dollar piece, seventy-seven and four-tenths grains; of the half-eagle, or five-dollar piece, one hundred and twenty-nine grains; of the eagle, or ten-dollar piece, two hundred and fifty-eight grains; of the double-eagle, or twenty-dollar-piece, five hundred and sixteen grains; which coins shall be a legal tender in all payments at their nominal value when not below the standard weight and limit of tolerance provided in this act for the single piece, and, when reduced in weight, below said standard and tolerance, shall be a legal tender at valuation in proportion to their actual weight; and any gold coin of the United States, if reduced in weight by natural abrasion not more than one-half of one per centum below the standard weight prescribed by law, after a circulation of twenty years, as shown by its date of coinage, and at a ratable proportion for any period less than twenty years, shall be received at their nominal value by the United States Treasury and its offices, under such regulations as the Secretary of the Treasury may prescribe for the protection of the Government against fraudulent abrasion or other practices; and any gold coins in the Treasury of the United States reduced in weight below this limit of abrasion shall be recoined.

SEC. 15. That the silver coins of the United States shall be a trade-dollar, a half-dollar, or fifty-cent piece, a quarter-dollar, or twenty-five cent piece, a dime, or ten-cent piece; and the weight of the trade-dollar shall be four hundred and twenty grains troy; the weight of the half-dollar shall be twelve grammes and one-half of a gramme; * the quarter-dollar † and the dime ‡

* A gramme is 15.432 grains, and a half-dollar is equal to 192.9 grains.

† 96.45 grains. ‡ 38.58 grains.

shall be respectively one-half and one-fifth of the weight of said half-dollar; and said coins shall be a legal tender at their nominal value for any amount not exceeding five dollars in any one payment.

SEC. 16 makes a five-cent, a three-cent and a one-cent piece the minor coins, and a legal tender to the amount of twenty-five cents.

SEC. 17. That no coins, either of gold, silver or minor coinage, shall hereafter be issued from the mint other than those of the denominations, standards and weights herein set forth.

[In the Revised Statutes—sections 3511–3516, 3567, 3584–3587, the various provisions above, supposed to have the force of law at the time of their enactment (December 1, 1873), will be found re-enacted.]

From the Reports of the Director of the Mint it appears that from the organization of the Mint (1793), to June 30, 1873, the coinage was as follows:

GOLD.	
Double Eagles	$646,727,980.00
Eagles	55,514,000.00
Half-Eagles	68,259,745.00
Three Dollars	1,169,913.00
Quarter Eagles	26,218,517.50
Dollars	19,015,633.00
SILVER.	
Dollars	$8,045,838.00
Half-Dollars	99,845,235.50
Quarter-Dollars	22,001,218.50
Dimes	9,060,795.50
Half-Dimes	4,906,946.90
Three-Cents	1,281,850.20
MINOR COINAGE.	
Five-Cents	$5,276,140.00
Three-Cents	805,350.00
Two-Cents	912,020.00
Cents	4,886,452.44
Half-Cents	39,926.11

Value of Gold	$816,905,878.50
" Silver	145,141,884.60
" Minor Coinage	11,919,888.55
Total	$973,967,651.65

Of gold coinage, $15,680,158.50 were prior to 1835; and $221,011,348 from 1835 to 1852, inclusive; and $580,011,000 from 1853 to 1873, inclusive.

Of silver coinage (less minor), $39,690,079.90 were prior to 1835, $39,523,289 were from 1835 to 1852, inclusive, and $69,929,000 from 1853 to 1873, inclusive.

During the fiscal year ending June 30, 1874, the coinage was as follows, under act of 1873:

Gold	$56,838,216.30
Silver	5,983,601.30
Minor Coinage	411,925.00
Total	$63,233.742.66

During the fiscal year ending June 30, 1875, the coinage was as follows:

Gold	$33,553,965.00
Silver	10,070,368.00
Minor Coinage	230,375.00
Total	$43,854,708.00

Act of February 12th, 1873, Revising and Amending the Laws relative to the Mints and Assay Offices of the United States.

As general attention has recently been called to this law, I state the facts attending its passage.

IN HOUSE.

SECOND SESSION—FORTY SECOND CONGRESS.

1872, February 9—Mr. SAMUEL HOOPER, of Massachusetts, by unanimous consent, reported from the Committee on Coinage, Weights and Measures, a bill (H. R. 1427), with above title, which was read a first and second time, recommitted, and ordered printed.

February 13—Mr. HOOPER reported the bill from the committee. A question was raised by Mr. MCNEELY, whether the committee had authorized the reporting of the bill. After some discussion, the point appears to have been waived; and the second Tuesday of March was fixed for its consideration as a special order.

Same day—Mr. HOOPER moved that the bill reported by him be printed as it has been corrected; which was agreed to.

April 9—The bill came up as the regular order, the question being on ordering it to be engrossed and read a third time. In the course of his speech on it, Mr. HOOPER called attention to the 16th section "as reducing in weight the silver dollar from 412½ to 384 grains, thus making it a subsidiary coin in harmony with the silver coins of less denomination, to secure its concurrent circulation with them." He stated "that the silver dollar of 412½ grains, by reason of its bullion or intrinsic value, long since ceased to be a coin of circulation, and is melted by manufacturers of silverware;" and that it "does not circulate now in commercial transactions with any country," small stamped bars of the same standard supplying its place. The coinage of the half-dime is to be discontinued, its place being supplied by the copper-nickel five-cent piece. Section 17th is alluded to, and the effect of it stated to be "to discontinue the coinage of the one and two-cent bronze coins."

Mr. STOUGHTON, of Michigan, a member of the committee, alluded to one feature of the bill in these words: "The value of silver depends, in a great measure, upon the fluctuations of the market, and the supply and demand. Gold is, practically, the standard of value among all civilized nations, and the time has come in this country when the gold dollar should be distinctly declared to be the coin representative of the money unit."

Messrs. CLARKSON N. POTTER, WILLIAM D. KELLEY, THOMPSON W. MCNEELY, FERNANDO WOOD, AARON A. SARGENT, JAMES BROOKS, and others participated in the debate.

May 27—Mr. HOOPER called up the bill for the purpose of offering a substitute for it (H. R. 2934)—one which has been very carefully prepared—and "which I have submitted to the different gentlemen in this House, who have taken a special interest in the bill. I find that it meets with universal approbation in the form in which I offer it."

Mr. HOOPER moved to suspend the rules, dispense with the reading of the substitute, and pass it; which was not agreed to.

Mr. HOOPER then moved to suspend the rules, and pass it, on its being read.

The CLERK began the reading, when questions as to particular features of the substitute were asked by Messrs. WM. S. HOLMAN, JAMES A. GARFIELD, CLINTON L. MERRIAM, MICHAEL C. KERR, JAS. BROOKS, JAS. R. McCORMICK, and answered by Mr. HOOPER, when

Mr. HOLMAN asked for an explanation of the leading changes made in the existing laws, especially in reference to coinage, as it would seem that all the small coinage of the country is intended to be recoined.

Mr. HOOPER replied that this bill "makes no changes in the existing law in that regard. It does not require the recoinage of the small coins." He stated, in reply to Mr. MERRIAM, that the Secretary of the Treasury not only approved the bill, but strongly urged its passage, as deemed important to correct irregularities in the Mint now which cannot be controlled by existing laws.

After further remarks on comparatively unimportant points,

Mr. McNEELY said: "As a member of the Committee on Coinage, Weights and Measures, having carefully examined every section and line of this bill, and generally well understanding the subject before us, I am satisfied the bill ought to pass."

The motion of Mr. HOOPER was then agreed to—ayes 110, noes 13, and the bill passed.

IN SENATE.

SECOND SESSION, FORTY-SECOND CONGRESS.

May 28—The bill was received from the House, and May 29, was referred to the Committee on Finance. No further action was taken that session.

THIRD SESSION.

1872, December 16—Mr. SHERMAN reported the bill from the Committee on Finance, with amendments. He stated that this bill in substance had passed the Senate in the last session of the last Congress.

1873, January 17—It was taken up, and amendments reported, discussed, and passed without a division.

January 21—In HOUSE, the Senate amendments were ordered printed.

January 23—The HOUSE non-concurred in the Senate amendments, and asked a committee of conference.

January 27—The SENATE agreed to the conference, and appointed Messrs. JOHN SHERMAN, JOHN SCOTT, and THOMAS F. BAYARD its conferees. Messrs. SAMUEL HOOPER, WILLIAM L. STOUGHTON, and THOMPSON W. McNEELY were the House conferees.

February 6—The SENATE adopted the report of the Committee of Conference; and, February 7, the HOUSE adopted it; all its members signed it, except Mr. McNEELY.

The changes made in the section respecting silver coins (the 15th section of the law), were these:

In bill (H. R. 1427), being that introduced by Mr. HOOPER, February 9, 1872, that section read as follows, being the 16th:

That the silver coins of the United States shall be a dollar, a half-dollar, or fifty-cent piece, a quarter-dollar, or twenty-five cent piece, and a dime, or ten-cent piece; and the weight of the dollar shall be three hundred and eighty-four grains; the half-dollar, quarter-dollar, and the dime shall be, respectively, one-half, one-quarter, and one-tenth of the weight of said dollar; which coins shall be a legal tender, at their denominational value, for any amount not exceeding five dollars in any one payment.

In the bill, reported by Mr. HOOPER on the 13th of February, 1872, this section remained the same.

In the bill (H. R. 2934), which Mr. HOOPER, May 27, 1872, offered as a substitute, and which passed the House, the section remained the same.

One of the amendments proposed by the Committee on Finance of the Senate and reported December 16, 1872, was to strike out that section and insert these words as a substitute for it:

That the silver coins of the United States shall be a trade dollar, a half-dollar, or fifty-cent piece, a quarter-dollar, or twenty-five cent piece; and the weight of the trade dollar shall be four hundred and twenty grains troy; the weight of the half-dollar shall be twelve grains and one-half of a gram; the quarter-dollar and the dime shall be, respectively, one-half and one-fifth of the weight of said half-dollar; and said coins shall be a legal tender at their nominal value for any amount not exceeding five dollars in any one payment.

The bill was considered in the Senate, as in Committee of the Whole, January 17, 1873, and this amendment was agreed to without debate, or a division.* Sundry other amendments were agreed to, in which the House non-concurred in gross. The report of the Committee of Conference recommended, on this point, that the House should recede from its disagreement, with an amendment (verbal) to substitute the word "gram" for "grain" where it twice occurred. This report was adopted without division in either house. The fifteenth section of the original bill, relating to abraded gold coin, having been struck out, the silver section thus became the 15th of the law.

*The original records in the Senate show that this amendment was agreed to, though the report of proceedings in the *Congressional Globe*, 3d Sess., 43d Cong., part 1, 672, omits all mention of it.—EDITOR.

President Grant's Message on the River and Harbor Bill, August 14, 1876.

To the House of Representatives:

In affixing my signature to the river and harbor bill, No. 3822, I deem it my duty to announce to the House of Representatives my objections to some features of the bill, and the reason I sign it. If it was obligatory upon the Executive to expend all the money appropriated by Congress, I should return the river and harbor bill with my objections, notwithstanding the great inconvenience to the public interests resulting therefrom, and the loss of expenditures from previous Congresses upon incompleted works. Without enumerating, many appropriations are made for works of purely private or local interest, in no sense national. I cannot give my sanction to these, and will take care that during my term of office no public money shall be expended upon them.

There is very great necessity for economy of expenditures at this time, growing out of the loss of revenue likely to arise from a deficiency of appropriations to insure a thorough collection of the same. The reduction of revenue districts, diminution of special agents, and total abolition of supervisors, may result in great falling off of the revenue. It may be a question to consider whether any expenditure can be authorized under the river and harbor appropriation further than to protect works already done and paid for. Under no circumstances will I allow expenditures upon works not clearly national. U. S. GRANT.

EXECUTIVE MANSION, *August* 14, 1876.

President Grant's Message on the Consular and Diplomatic Bill, August 15, 1876.

To the House of Representatives:

In announcing, as I do, that I have attached my signature of official approval to the "Act making appropriations for the Consular and Diplomatic service of the government for the year ending June 30, 1877, and for other purposes," it is my duty to call attention to a provision in the act directing that notice be sent to certain of the Diplomatic and Consular officers of the government "to close their offices."

In the literal sense of this direction, it would be an invasion of the Constitutional prerogative and duty of the executive.

By the Constitution the President "shall have power by and with the advice and consent of the Senate, to make treaties, provided two-thirds of the Senators present consent, and he shall nominate, and by and with the advice and consent of the Senate, shall appoint Ambassadors, other public Ministers and Consuls," etc.

It is within the power of Congress to grant, or withhold, appropriation of money for the payment of salaries and expenses of the Foreign Representatives of the Government.

In the early days of the government, a sum in gross was appropriated, leaving it to the Executive to determine the grade of the officers, and the countries to which they should be sent.

Latterly, for many years, specific sums have been appropriated for designated missions or employments, and, as a rule, the omission by Congress to make an appropriation for any specific post, has heretofore been accepted as an indication of a wish on the part of Congress, which the Executive Branch of the Government respected and complied with.

In calling attention to the passage which I have indicated, I assume that the intention of the provision is only to exercise the Constitutional prerogative of Congress over the expenditures of the Government, and to fix a time at which the compensation of certain diplomatic and consular offices shall cease; and not to invade the Constitutional rights of the Executive, which I should be compelled to resist, and my present object is not to discuss or dispute the wisdom of failing to appropriate for several offices, but to guard against the construction that might possibly be placed on the language used, as implying a right in the legislative branch to direct the closing or discontinuing of any of the diplomatic or consular offices of the government.

U. S. GRANT.

EXECUTIVE MANSION,
WASHINGTON, *Aug* 14, 1876.

HENRY WATTERSON, of Kentucky, elected to fill the vacancy in the House of Representatives caused by the death of EDWARD Y. PARSONS, qualified August 14, 1876.

Congress adjourned on Tuesday, the 15th of August, at 7:30, P. M.

Statement

Showing the purchase of bonds on account of the Sinking Fund from its institution in May, 1869, to and including June 30, 1875:

		Principal Redeemed.
For the year ending June 30, 1869		$8,691,000 00
" " June 30, 1870		28,151,900 00
" " June 30, 1871		29,936,250 00
" " June 30, 1872		32,618,450 00
" " June 30, 1873		28,678,000 00
" " June 30, 1874		12,936,450 00
" " June 30, 1875		25,170,400 00
June 30, 1876—Six per cent. bonds purchased	$18,444,050	
Fractional currency redeemed	7,062,142 19	
		25,506,192 19
Legal tender notes redeemed under resumption act, but not applied, $5,990,296		
Total		$191,688,642 19

XXV.

STATISTICAL TABLES.

Statement

Of Appropriations made for fiscal year ending June 30, '76, at Second Session, Forty-third Congress:

Pensions		$30,000,000 00
Deficiencies for the year ending June 30, 1876, and prior years, as follows, viz.:		
Senate	$48,833 00	
House of Representatives	62,874 33	
District of Columbia	186,333 56	
Department of State	500 00	
Foreign Intercourse	13,287 30	
Territorial Governments	13,891 99	
Mints and Assay Offices	187,289 80	
Miscellaneous	253,897 04	
Public Buildings	284,548 34	

War Department	$662,170 40	
Navy Department	166,000 00	
Marine Corps	15,793 43	
Miscellaneous and Post Office Department	1,031,802 87	
State Department	1,596 77	
Treasury Department	220,000 00	
War Department	1,523,390 50	
Interior Department	10,590 66	
Department of Justice	20,900 79	$4,703,699 18
Indian Department		5,360,554 55
Legislative, Executive and Judicial Expenses		18,902,236 99
Sundry Civil Expenses as follows, viz.:		
Public Printing and Binding	$1,665,507 66	
Life Boat Stations	241,580 00	
Revenue Cutter Service	1,027,883 40	
National Currency	253,000 00	
National Loan	1,625,000 00	
Judiciary	3,105,200 00	
Miscellaneous	2,294,461 54	
Coast Survey	869,600 00	
Light House Establishment	1,899,000 00	
Light Houses, Fog Signals and Beacons	915,400 00	
Public Lands	958,790 00	
Expenses of the collection of revenue from sales of Public Lands	601,640 00	
Capitol Extension	263,500 00	
Botanic Gardens, Metropolitan Police, etc	670,994 23	
War Department, Armories and Arsenals, and Signal Office	1,055,165 00	
Miscellaneous Objects	1,722,998 27	
Buildings and Grounds in and around Washington	234,250 00	
Navy Yards and Stations	1,250,000 00	
Department of Agriculture	11,900 00	
Public Buildings under the Treasury Department	5,216,893 99	
Miscellaneous	256,496 00	
Centennial Expenses for Executive Department	505,000 00	26,644,350 09
Naval Service		17,001,006 40
Rivers and Harbors		6,643,517 50
Armory		27,933,830 00
Post-office Department (of which amount the sum of $6,852,705.00 is appropriated from the Treasury) the balance to be paid from the revenues of the Post-office Department		37,524,361 00
Consular		1,374,985 00
Military Academy		364,740 00
Fortifications		850,000 00
Payment of Claims reported by the Commissioner of Claims		729,653 62
Miscellaneous		1,133,275 57
Total Appropriations made for the fiscal year ending June 30, 1876		$179,166,209 90

Statement

Of Appropriations made for fiscal year ending June 30, '77, at First Session, Forty-fourth Congress:

By the act making appropriations for the payment of invalid and other pensions for the year ending June 30, 1877:			
Army Pensions		$28,400,000 00	
Fees for preparing vouchers, etc		250,000 00	
Fees of Examining Surgeons		100,000 00	
Compensation to Pension Agents, etc		200,000 00	
For artificial limbs		50,000 00	
Navy Pensions		525,000 00	
Miscellaneous		8,500 00	$29,533,500 00
By the act making appropriations for fortifications and for other works of defence for the year ending June 30, 1877:			
For the protection, etc., of fortifications		100,000 00	
For armament of sea-coast fortifications and guns		165,000 00	
For torpedoes		50,000 00	315,000 00
By the act making appropriations to supply deficiencies for the fiscal year ending June 30, 1876, and prior years:			
House of Representatives		$93,525 10	
Senate		32,920 19	
Department of State, being a transfer of accounts involving no expenditure of money, from the Treasury and not included in the aggregate, $47,117.38.			
Treasury Department and Treasury Miscellaneous		173,582 24	
War Department		309,444 55	
Interior Department		36,564 26	
Miscellaneous		119,461 40	
Judicial		71,000 00	
Unexpended balance of appropriations for the pay of the army for the year ending 1874, reappropriated		1,165,000 00	
Balance of appropriations carried to the surplus fund and reappropriated for the following purposes, viz.:			
Treasury Department	$30,000 00		
War Department	875,183 10		
Interior Department	1,496 25	906,679 35	2,908,177 09
By the act making appropriations for the naval service for the year ending June 30, 1877:			
For pay of the Navy		$5,750,000 00	
Bureau of Navigation		204,600 00	
Bureau of Ordnance		227,500 00	
Bureau of Equipments and Recruiting		1,045,000 00	
Bureau of Yards and Docks		512,973 00	
Bureau of Medicine and Surgery		80,000 00	
Bureau of Provisions and Clothing		990,000 00	
Bureau of Construction and Repair		1,750,000 00	

Bureau of Steam Engineering	942,500 00	
Naval Academy	197,582 40	
Marine Corps	875,000 00	
Miscellaneous	167,000 00	12,742,155 40
By the act making appropriations for the Post Office Department for the year ending June 30, 1877:		
For compensations to Postmasters	$7,000,000 00	
For compensation to P. O. Clerks	3,290,000 00	
For compensation to letter carriers	1,900,000 00	
For rent, light and fuel	390,000 00	
For transportation on star routes and steamboats	6,737,851 00	
For transportation by railroad	9,100,000 00	
For compensation to railway P. O. clerks	1,225,000 00	
For route agents	972,500 00	
For mail messengers	670,500 00	
For mail bags and catchers	175,000 00	
For manufacture of stamped envelopes and newspaper wrappers	535,878 00	
For manufacture of postal cards	216,760 00	
For transportation of foreign mails	220,000 00	
For official postage stamps	850,000 00	
For steamship service	250,000 00	
Miscellaneous	1,052,221 00	34,585,701 00
By the act making appropriations for the support of the army for the fiscal year ending June 30, 1877:		
For the pay of officers and privates	$9,918,574 50	
For travel, pay and commutation of subsistence to discharged soldiers	500,000 00	
For retained pay to discharged men	703,860 00	
For pay for clothing not drawn	360,000 00	
For additional pay to enlisted men	356,520 00	
For mileage of officers	230,000 00	
For subsistence	2,200,000 00	
For Quartermaster's Department	3,750,000 00	
For incidental expenses	850,000 00	
For purchase of horses	250,000 00	
For transportation	3,500,000 00	
For hire of quarters	1,150,000 00	
For purchase of clothing, etc	400,000 00	
Miscellaneous	1,818,213 40	25,987,167 90
By the act making appropriations for sundry civil expenses of the Government for the fiscal year ending June 30, 1877, and for other purposes:		
House of Representatives, Miscellaneous, Botanical Gardens, etc	111,644 96	
Public Printing and Binding	1,136,865 50	
District of Columbia	43,170 00	
Life boat stations and revenue cutter service	1,112,351 10	
Judiciary	2,588,500 00	
Government Hospital for the Insane, Columbia Institution for the Deaf and Dumb, Columbia Hospital, Smithsonian, Reform School, Metropolitan Police, and Miscellaneous	785,500 00	
Public Buildings under Treasury Department	2,791,500 00	
Light houses, etc	2,378,800 00	
Armories and arsenals	214,175 00	
Navy yards and stations	150,000 00	
Surveys	100,000 00	
Buildings and grounds in and around Washington	174,500 00	
Miscellaneous, including improvement of Capitol Grounds	211,200 00	
Under Department of Agriculture	6,450 00	
Bureau of Engraving and Printing	838,000 00	
Coast Survey	618,000 00	
Miscellaneous objects	889,467 40	
Under the War Department	345,000 00	
Miscellaneous objects	161,632 02	
National Home for disabled soldiers, etc	769,580 39	
Interior Department	141,380 00	
Survey of public lands and public tracts	783,158 21	16,350,874 58
By the act making appropriations for the support of the Military Academy for the fiscal year ending June 30, 1877		289,985 00
By the act making appropriations for the construction, repair, preservation and completion of certain public works, on rivers and harbors, and for other purposes, for the fiscal year, ending June 30, 1877		5,015,000 00
By the act making appropriations for the Legislative, Executive and Judicial expenses of the government for the fiscal year ending June 30, 1877, and for other purposes		15,373,960 00
By the act making appropriations for the Consular and Diplomatic expenses of the government for the fiscal year ending June 30, 1877		1,158,579 50
By the act making appropriations for the current and contingent expenses of the Indian Department, and for fulfilling treaty stipulations with various Indian tribes for the year ending June 30, 1877, and for other purposes		4,670,117 02
Miscellaneous, in which are included appropriation for P. O. St. Louis	$75,000 00	
Centennial	1,500,000 00	
Subsistence Sioux Indians	150,000 00	
Bureau of Engraving and Printing	211,000 00	
Supplies for Apache Indians	50,000 00	
Washington Monument	200,000 00	
Military Posts on Yellowstone	200,000 00	
Claims reported by accounting officers of Treasury Department	271,000 00	
Report of Court of Claims (about)	430,000 00	
For expenses of troops against the Indians	1,634 700 00	
Indefinite, and others estimated	413,000 00	5,134,700 00
Total appropriations, First Session Forty-fourth Congress		$154,064,917 49

This statement has been made on the same plan as the Statements in previous Hand-Books, and by the same person.

A.—Statement

Showing the Receipts and Disbursements of the Government from January 1, 1834, to June 30, 1875; exhibiting also the amount of defalcations and the ratio of losses per $1,000 to the aggregate received and disbursed, arranged in periods, as nearly as practicable, of four years each, and also in the periods prior and subsequent to June 30, 1861; prepared under the direction of the Secretary of the Treasury, to accompany his answer to a resolution of the United States Senate, dated February 9, 1876, calling for a detailed statement of balances due from public officers no longer in the public service, which have arisen since 1830.

Receipts, Losses, and Ratio of Loss per $1,000 to Aggregate of Receipts.

PERIOD.	CUSTOMS.			INTERNAL REVENUE.			MISCELLANEOUS.		
	Receipts.	Losses.	Loss on $1,000.	Receipts.	Losses.	Loss on $1,000.	Receipts.	Losses.	Loss on $1,000.
January 1, 1834, to December 31, 1837	$70,185,498 66	$1,211,566 25	$17 26	$20,519 41	....	....	$62,796,953 70	$172,259 16	$2 74
January 1, 1838, to December 31, 1841	67,283,444 08	264,502 94	3 93	9,964 20	....	....	26,832,178 67	127,825 40	4 76
January 1, 1842, to June 30, 1845	78,946,436 31	254,939 03	3 23	5,892 71	....	....	8,545,683 07	175,042 36	20 48
July 1, 1845, to June 30, 1849	110,564,342 31	7,719 11	06	3,647 26	....	....	12,019,158 04	10,390 87	86
July 1, 1849, to June 30, 1853	194,957,446 48	215,749 08	1 10	....	....	....	12,624,329 01	60,521 50	4 79
July 1, 1853, to June 30, 1857	245,148,753 03	131,277 05	53	....	....	....	37,024,174 86	81,724 73	2 20
July 1, 1857, to June 30, 1861	184,125,082 85	38,776 03	21	....	....	....	12,838,290 35	155,227 80	12 09
July 1, 1861, to June 30, 1865	305,360,453 61	31,261 99	10	356,846,137 30	$423,288 60	$1 18	67,251,745 08	53,943 01	80
July 1, 1865, to June 30, 1869	699,977,488 65	254,498 55	36	924,698,401 12	2,126,602 16	2 29	91,743,064 44	181,621 19	1 97
July 1, 1869, to June 30, 1873	805,268,591 96	20,935 15	02	572,369,401 98	826,265 67	1 44	79,624,848 56	107,497 86	1 35
July 1, 1873, to June 30, 1875	320,271,556 04	3,407 28	01	212,417,278 48	283,195 63	1 33	51,273,027 73	35,581 01	69
Total	3,082,089,093 98	2,434,632 46	78	2,066,371,242 46	3,659,352 06	1 77	462,573,453 51	1,161,634 89	2 51
January 1, 1834, to June 30, 1861	$951,211,003 72	$2,124,529 49	$2 23	$40,023 58	....	....	$172,680,767 70	$782,991 82	$4 53
July 1, 1861, to June 30, 1875	2,130,878,090 26	310,102 97	14	2,066,331,218 88	$3,659,352 06	$1 77	289,892,685 81	378,643 07	1 30

PERIOD.	NET TOTAL.			GROSS TOTAL.		
	Receipts.	Losses.	Loss on $1,000.	Receipts.*	Losses.	Loss on $1,000.
January 1, 1834, to December 31, 1837	$133,002,971 77	$1,383,825 41	$10 40	$135,995,960 92	$1,383,825 41	$10 17
January 1, 1838, to December 31, 1841	94,125,586 95	392,328 34	4 16	129,948,548 91	392,328 34	3 01
January 1, 1842, to June 30, 1845	87,498,012 09	429,981 39	4 91	116,736,004 87	429,981 39	3 68
July 1, 1845, to June 30, 1849	122,587,147 61	18,109 98	14	201,857,508 45	18,109 98	08
July 1, 1849, to June 30, 1853	207,581,775 49	276,270 58	1 33	211,908,612 91	276,270 58	1 30
July 1, 1853, to June 30, 1857	282,172,927 89	213,001 78	75	282,179,829 56	213,001 78	75
July 1, 1857, to June 30, 1861	196,963,373 20	194,003 83	98	312,359,679 56	194,003 83	62
July 1, 1861, to June 30, 1865	729,458,335 99	508,493 60	69	4,670,460,137 61	508,493 60	10
July 1, 1865, to June 30, 1869	1,716,418,954 21	2,562,721 90	1 49	4,042,316,438 46	2,562,721 90	63
July 1, 1869, to June 30, 1873	1,457,262,842 50	954,698 68	65	2,576,645,585 22	954,698 68	37
July 1, 1873, to June 30, 1875	583,961,862 25	322,183 92	55	1,420,222,898 62	322,183 92	22
Total	5,611,033,789 95	7,255,619 41	1 29	14,100,631,205 09	7,255,619 41	51
January 1, 1834, to June 30, 1861	$1,123,931,795 00	$2,907,521 31	$2 58	$1,390,986,145 18	$2,907,521 31	$2 09
July 1, 1861, to June 30, 1875	4,487,101,994 95	4,348,098 10	96	12,709,645,059 91	4,348,098 10	34

*Includes receipts for loans.

A.—Disbursements, Losses, and Ratio of Loss Per $1,000 to Aggregate Disbursements.

PERIOD.	WAR.			NAVY.			INDIANS.			PENSIONS.		
	Disbursements.	Losses.	Loss on $1000	Disbursements.	Losses.	Loss on $1000	Disbursements	Losses.	Loss on $1000	Disbursements	Losses.	Loss on $1000
Jan. 1, 1834, to Dec. 31, '37.	$36,885,422 32	$502,062 83	$13 60	$20,275,832 24	$213,405 94	$10 53	$12,095,456 75	$130,256 56	$10 76	$10,873,957 03	$17,906 63	$1 65
Jan. 1, 1838, to Dec. 31, '41.	37,711,097 43	206,873 89	5 48	24,428,848 64	101,256 23	4 14	12,879,740 60	4,215 61	32	10 290,804 48	101,951 64	9 90
Jan. 1, 1842, to June 30, '45.	20,483,584 91	48,359 58	2 35	24,920,331 48	54,291 93	2 17	4,573,354 42	10,585 29	2 31	6,650,769 55	11,553 38	1 74
July 1, 1845, to June 30, '49.	88,500,208 38	747,275 33	8 44	33,550,831 62	115,666 69	3 45	5,084,563 30	11,768 92	2 31	6,112,345 31	71,196 44	11 64
July 1, 1849, to June 30, '53.	40,280,994 37	373,158 05	9 26	36,771,937 67	141,493 87	3 85	11,417,463 40	69,497 61	6 08	8,318,428 22	1,257 41	15
July 1, 1853, to June 30, '57.	62,492,668 32	378,333 37	6 05	50,843,720 68	377,505 68	7 42	11,322,013 17	38,088 97	3 36	5,316,887 56	18,840 51	3 54
July 1, 1857, to June 30, '61.	88,307,575 55	287,516 48	3 25	52,645,998 89	183,510 52	3 49	14,325,403 42	982,417 05	68 58	4,577,393 06	4,649 51	1 01
July 1, 1861, to June 30, '65.	2,713,569,422 83	4,241,868 55	1 56	314,223,986 21	1,079,639 44	3 43	13,169,317 75	136,582 62	10 37	23,263,779 07	29,650 45	1 27
July 1, 1865 to June 30, '69.	583,749,510 99	542,547 69	92	120,173,925 90	98,422 02	81	19,135,153 08	73,973 97	3 86	88,810,848 02	94,540 67	1 06
July 1, 1869, to June 30, '73.	175,150,962 73	169,900 39	97	85,987,323 86	180,964 68	2 10	25,848,369 29	23,557 44	91	120,676,926 67	230,826 93	1 90
July 1, 1873, to June 30, '75.	83,434,573 20	23,742 80	28	52,430,213 69	26,670 77	50	15,077,118 91	2,676 38	17	58,494,630 88	....	....
Total........................	3,930,566,021 03	7,521,638 96	1 91	816,252,950 88	2,572,827 77	3 15	144,927,954 09	1,483,620 42	10 23	343,386,769 85	582,373 57	1 69
Jan. 1, 1834, to June 30, 61.	$374,661,551 28	$2,543,579 53	$6 79	$243,437,501 22	$1,187,130 86	$4 87	$71,697,995 06	$1,246,830 01	$17 39	$52,140,585 21	$227,355 52	$4 36
July 1, 1861, to June 30, 75.	3,555,904,469 75	4,978,059 43	1 39	572,815,449 66	1,385,696 91	2 41	73,229,959 03	236,790 41	3 23	291,246,184 64	355,018 05	1 21

PERIOD.	MISCELLANEOUS.			POST OFFICE.			NET TOTAL, EXCLUSIVE OF POST OFFICE.			GROSS TOTAL, EXCLUSIVE OF POST OFFICE.		
	Disbursements.	Losses.	Loss on $1000	Disbursements	Losses.	Loss on $1000.	Disbursements.	Losses.	Loss on $1000.	Disbursements.*	Losses.	Loss on $1000.
Jan. 1, '34, to Dec. 31, '37.	$23,921,077 47	$300,154 05	$12 54	$11,697,884 18	$13,696 51	$1 17	$104,051,745 81	$1,163,786 01	$11 18	$110,308,325 19	$1,163,786 01	$10 55
Jan. 1, '38, to Dec. 31, '41.	25,372,936 06	2,485,356 47	97 95	18,284,961 77	51,809 86	2 83	110,683,427 21	2,899,653 84	26 19	137,094,438 34	2,899,653 84	21 15
Jan. 1, '42, to June 30, '45.	21,535,282 45	1,008,452 22	46 82	18,666,750 20	2,679 46	14	78,163,322 81	1,133,242 40	14 49	109,187,401 24	1,133,242 40	10 37
July 1, '45, to June 30, '49.	32,133,077 73	766,262 44	23 84	16,861,478 41	2,571 24	15	165,381,026 34	1,712,169 82	10 35	205,194,700 57	1,712,169 82	8 34
July 1, '49, to June 30, '53.	68,899,995 00	899,785 74	13 05	26,582,570 74	52,946 20	1 99	165,688 818 66	1,485,192 68	8 96	194,370,493 14	1,485,192 68	7 64
July 1, '53, to June 30, '57.	111,122,107 75	862,084 11	7 75	40,439,110 70	280,128 05	6 92	241,097,397 48	1,674,852 64	6 94	285,638,875 65	1,674,852 64	5 86
July 1, '57, to June 30, '61.	101,502,826 81	834,731 96	8 22	56,957,922 74	172,278 46	3 02	261,359,197 73	2,292,825 52	8 77	328,183,268 39	2,292,825 52	6 98
July 1, '61, to June 30, '65.	115,145,844 93	1,111,281 85	9 65	48,779,085 45	93,467 63	1 91	3,179,372,350 79	6,599,022 91	2 07	4,667,457,921 22	6,599,022 91	1 41
July 1, '65, to June 30, '69.	201,926,036 61	1,080,156 82	5 34	81,016,286 91	167,236 74	2 06	1,013,795,474 60	1,889,641 17	1 86	3,891,576,259 10	1,889,641 17	48
July 1, '69, to June 30, '73.	248,032,245 27	440,953 04	1 77	104,132,079 69	117,797 60	1 13	655,695,827 82	1,046,202 48	1 59	2,601,158,569 90	1,046,202 48	40
July 1, '73, to June 30, '75.	156,212,296 59	317,248 86	2 03	65,737,724 03	34,970 63	53	365,648,833 27	370,338 81	1 01	1,406,699,819 31	370,338 81	26
Total.....................	1,105,803,726 67	10,106,467 56	9 13	489,155,854 82	989,582 38	2 02	6,340,937,422 52	22,266,928 28	3 51	13,936,870,072 05	22,266,928 28	1 59
Jan. 1, '34, to June 30, '61.	$384,487,303 27	$7,156,826 99	$18 61	$189,490,678 74	$576,109 78	$3 04	$1,126,424,936 04	$12,361,722 91	$10 97	$1,369,977,502 52	$12,361,722 91	$9 02
July 1, '61, to June 30, '75.	721,316,423 40	2,949,640 57	4 08	299,665,176 08	413,472 60	1 38	5,214,512,486 48	9,905,205 37	1 89	12,566,892,569 53	9,905,205 37	78

*Includes expenditures for public debt.

POSTAL MONEY ORDERS.—Amount involved to June 30, 1875, $389,718,785 38. Loss, $156,818 42. Loss per $1000, 40 cents.

NOTES.—1. In cases where the accounts of defaulting officers embraced more than one period, the losses, unless known to have occurred in other periods, have been charged to the periods in which the accounts were opened in this Department. In cases of defaulting banks, however, for want of other information, the losses have been charged to the periods in which they are reported on the books, though, doubtless, in several instances, they actually occurred in previous periods. No losses of the latter kind, however, have been included, unless known to have occurred within the period covered by this statement.

2. No deductions have been made for amounts which may be collected hereafter, though a large percentage of the recent losses will doubtless be yet recovered.

3. In preparing this statement, the receipts and disbursements since June 30, 1843, have been classified by fiscal years, as in the published official reports; the losses have in all cases been classified by calendar years, it not being practicable to separate the losses occurring in the fractional years of each period; but the periods compared being of the same length, the result is substantially correct.

Statement

Of the Comptroller of the Currency, showing by States the amount of National Bank circulation issued, and the amount of Legal-tender Notes deposited in the U. S. Treasury to retire National Bank circulation, from June 20, 1874, to July 1, 1876.

STATES AND TERRITORIES.	Additional National Bank Circulation Issued from June 20, 1874, to July 1, 1876.	LEGAL TENDER NOTES DEPOSITED IN THE U. S. TREASURY TO RETIRE NATIONAL BANK CIRCULATION, FROM JUNE 20, 1874, TO JULY 1, 1876.		
		Deposits for Redemption of Notes of Liquidating National Banks.	Deposits to Retire Circulation under Act of June 20, '74.	TOTAL DEPOSITS.
Maine	$741,440	$41,200	$480,000	$521,200
New Hampshire	362,760	27,400	....	27,400
Vermont	752,280	134,807	296,400	431,207
Massachusetts	5,001,045	96,400	4,184,295	4,280,695
Rhode Island	156,200	....	374,790	374,390
Connecticut	628,810	27,050	803,200	830,250
New York	1,539,810	614,000	12,861,341	13,475,341
New Jersey	457,335	23,060	502,640	525,700
Pennsylvania	2,771,820	426,407	3,492,200	3,918,607
Delaware	4,900	....	....	....
Maryland	105,510	166,600	1,033,100	1,199,700
District of Columbia	153,000	299,719	427,500	727,219
Virginia	207,100	706,864	592,415	1,299,279
West Virginia	35,370	731,060	204,300	935,360
North Carolina	305,060	....	413,400	413,400
South Carolina	6,700	....	908,380	908,380
Georgia	90,000	169,000	326,000	495,000
Florida	45,000	....	....	....
Alabama	90,000	....	....	....
Louisiana	32,130	592,062	1,844,250	2,436,312
Texas	62,100	....	184,340	184,340
Arkansas	....	....	90,000	90,000
Kentucky	1,919,640	315,000	786,000	1,101,000
Tennessee	234,000	191,501	408,859	600,360
Missouri	110,470	146,391	3,383,559	3,529,950
Ohio	796,520	786,331	1,262,990	2,049,321
Indiana	1,282,570	430,577	3,164,752	3,595 329
Illinois	785,475	677,300	5,435,460	6,112,760
Michigan	300,920	116,400	1,551,800	1,668,200
Wisconsin	50,900	292,800	687,400	980,200
Iowa	553,500	304,067	1,336,050	1,640,117
Minnesota	326,620	108,309	879,840	988,149
Kansas	30,600	400,571	121,500	522,071
Nebraska	....	45,000	40,480	85,480
Colorado	126,000	58,925	135,000	193,925
Utah	....	161,191	196,800	357,991
Montana	....	....	45,000	45,000
Total	$20,065,585	$8,089,992	$48,453,641	$56,543,633
Legal-tender notes which had been deposited prior to June 20, 1874, remaining at that date	....	....	....	$3,813,675
Total deposits	....	....	....	$60,357,308

Statement

Of the Comptroller of the Currency, showing the Issue and Retirement of National Bank Notes and Legal-tender Notes under the acts of June 20, 1874, and January 14, 1875, to July 1, 1876.

National Bank Notes outstanding when act of June 20, 1874, was passed		$349,894,182
" " " issued from June 20, 1874, to January 14, 1875	$4,734,500	
" " " redeemed and retired between same dates	2,767,232	
" " " increase from June 20, 1873, to January 14, 1875		1,967,268
" " " outstanding January 14, 1875		351,861,450
" " " redeemed and retired from January 14, 1875, to July 1, 1876	$30,675,911	
" " " surrendered between same dates	5,617,478	
Total redeemed and surrendered	36,293,389	
" " " issued between same dates	15,331,085	
Decrease from January 14, 1875, to July 1, 1876		20,962,304
Amount outstanding July 1, 1876		330,899,146
Greenbacks on deposit in the Treasury June 20, 1874, to retire notes of insolvent and liquidating Banks		$3,813,675
Greenbacks deposited from June 20, 1874, to July 1, 1876, to retire National Bank Notes		56,543,633
Total deposits		60,357,308
Circulation redeemed by Treasurer between same dates without reissue		33,447,976
Balance of deposits July 1, 1876		26,909,332
Greenbacks retired under act of January 14, 1875		$12,227,716
Greenbacks outstanding July 1, 1876		369,772,284

NOTE.—The amount of National Bank Notes received from the Engravers from June 30, 1874, to July 1, 1876, was $272,376,512. The amount of new currency issued during the same period was $218,050,814. The amount of new currency issued in the last fiscal year was $90,730,565. The total amount of mutilated currency received during the same year was $106,473,100. The amount of currency in the vaults on July 1, 1876, was $89,800,200.

Revenues of the Government.

For each Fiscal Year (ending June 30), from each Source since 1865.

	1866.	1867.	1868.	1869.	1870.	1871.	1872.	1873.	1874.	1875.
Customs	$179,046,651 58	$176,417,810 88	$164,464,579 56	$180,048,426 63	$194,538,374 44	$206,270,408 05	$216,370,286 77	$188,089,522 70	$163,103,833 69	$157,167,722 35
Internal Revenue	309,226,813 42	266,027,537 43	191,087,589 41	158,356,460 86	184,899,756 49	143,098,153 63	130,642,177 72	113,729,314 14	102,409,784 90	110,007,493 58
Direct Taxes	1,974,754 12	4,200,233 70	1,788,145 85	765,685 16	229,102 88	580,355 37	....	315,254 51	....	....
Public Lands	665,031 03	1,163,575 76	1,348,715 41	4,020,344 34	3,350,481 76	2,388,646 68	2,575,714 19	2,882,312 38	1,852,428 93	1,413,640 17
Miscellan's. Sources	29,036,314 23	15,037,522 15	17,745,403 59	13,997,338 65	12,942,118 30	22,093,541 21	15,106,051 23	17,161,270 05	32,575,043 32	15,431,915 31
Totals	$519,949,564 38	$462,846,679 92	$376,434,453 82	$357,188,255 64	$395,959,833 87	$374,431,104 94	$364,694,229 91	$322,177,673 78	$299,941,090 84	$284,020,771 41

Expenditures of the Government.

For each Fiscal Year (ending June 30) since 1865.

	1866.	1867.	1868.	1869.	1870.	1871.	1872.	1873.	1874.	1875.
Civil List	$12,287,828 55	$15,585,489 55	$11,950,156 58	$12,443,712 07	$19,031,283 56	$18,760,779 46	$16,187,059 20	$19,348,521 01	$17,627,115 09	$17,346,929 53
Foreign Intercourse	1,338,388 18	1,548,589 26	1,441,344 05	8,365,416 77	1,490,776 25	1,604,373 87	1,839,369 14	1,571,362 85	1,508,064 27	1,265,418 23
Navy Department	43,363,654 17	31,034,011 04	25,775,502 72	20,000,757 97	21,780,229 87	19,431,027 21	21,249,809 99	23,526,256 79	30,932,587 42	21,497 626 27
War Department	286,776,456 13	95,224,415 63	123,246,648 62	78,501,990 61	57,655,675 40	35,799,991 82	35,372,157 20	46,323,138 31	42,313,927 22	41,120,645 98
Pensions	15,615,287 75	20,936,551 71	23,782,386 78	28,476,621 78	28,340,202 17	34,443,894 88	28,533,402 76	29,359,426 86	29,038,414 66	29,456,216 22
Indians	3,349,015 93	4,642,531 77	4,100,682 32	7,042,923 06	3,407,938 15	7,426,997 44	7,061,728 82	7,951,704 88	6,692 462 09	8,384,656 82
Miscellaneous	27,705,666 96	33,976,144 91	39,618,367 04	35,664,932 69	32,715,401 75	40,116,762 90	42,958,329 08	52,408,226 20	50,506,414 25	*50,528,536 22
Totals	$390,436,297 67	$202,947,732 87	$229,915,088 11	$190,496,354 95	$164,421,507 15	$157,583,827 58	$153,201,856 19	$180,488,636 90	$178,618,985 00	$169,600,029 27
Int. on Public Debt.	$133,070,513 39	$143,781,591 91	$140,424,045 71	$130,694,242 80	$129,235,498 00	$125,576,565 93	$117,357,839 72	$104,750,688 44	$107,119,815 21	$103,093,544 57

*Exclusive of award of $1,929,819 to British claimants.

Statement of the Public Debt of the United States for the Month of June, 1876.

Debt bearing Interest in Coin.

Title of Loan.	Authorizing Act.	Rate of Interest.	When Redeemable.	When Payable.	Interest Payable.	Amount Outstanding.			Interest Due and Unpaid.	Accrued Interest to Date.
						Registered.	Coupon.	Total.		
Loan of 1858	June 14, 1858	5 per cent.	After Jan. 1, 1874	....	Jan. and July	$260,000 00	....	$260,000 00	....	$6,500 00
Loan of Feb., 1861, ('81's)	February 8, 1861	6 per cent.	....	Dec. 31, 1880*	Jan. and July	13,795,000 00	$4,620,000 00	18,415,000 00	$18,750 00	552,450 00
Oregon War Debt	March 2, 1861	6 per cent.	....	July 1, 1881.	Jan. and July	....	945,000 00	945,000 00	5,870 75	28,350 00
L'n of J'y & Aug. '61 ('81's)	July 17 and Aug. 5, 1861.	6 per cent.	After June 30, 1881.	....	Jan. and July	126,049,500 00	63,271,850 00	189,321,350 00	210,935 29	5,679,640 50
Loan of 1863, ('81's)	March 3, 1863	6 per cent.	After June 30, 1881.	....	Jan. and July	53,706,950 00	21,293,050 00	75,000,000 00	60,152 55	2,250,000 00
Ten-forties of 1864	March 3, 1864	5 per cent.	After Mar. 1, 1874	Mar. 1, 1904.	Mar. and Sept.	141,808,100 00	52,758,200 00	194,566,300 00	180,658 36	3,242,771 67
Five-twenties of 1865	March 3, 1865	6 per cent.	After Nov. 1, 1870.	Nov. 1, 1885.	May and Nov.	34,262,150 00	116,296,500 00	150,558,650 00	400,238 31	1,505,586 50
Consols of 1865	March 3, 1665	6 per cent.	After July 1, 1870	July 1, 1885.	Jan. and July	60,290,900 00	142,372,200 00	202,663,100 00	646,759 52	6,079,893 00
Consols of 1867	March 3, 1865	6 per cent.	After July 1, 1872	July 1, 1887.	Jan. and July	92,465,550 00	218,157,200 00	310,622,750 00	974,525 19	9,318,682 50
Consols of 1868	March 3, 1865	6 per cent.	After July 1, 1873	July 1, 1888.	Jan. and July	14,913,500 00	22,560,300 00	37,473,800 00	136,797 75	1,124,214 00
Funded Loan of 1881	J'y 14, '70 & Jan. 20, '71.	5 per cent.	After May 1, 1881.	....	Feb., May, Aug. and Nov.	219,342,550 00	297,516,950 00	516,859,500 00	1,338,649 00	4,307,162 50
Funded Loan of 1886	J'y 14, '70 & Jan. 20, '71.	4½ per ct.	After May 1, 1886.	....		....	....	....	....	....
Funded Loan of 1901	J'y 14, '70 & Jan. 20, '71.	4 per cent.	After May 1, 1901.	....		....	....	....	....	....
Aggregate of Debt bearing Interest in Coin						756,894,200 00	939,791,250 00	1,696,685,450 00	3,973,336 72	34,095,250 67

Debt bearing Interest in Lawful Money.

Navy Pension Fund	July 23, 1868	3 per cent.	Int. only applic'le to pay't of pen's	Jan. and July			$14,000,000 00		$210,000 00

Debt on which Interest has Ceased since Maturity.

Old Debt	Various prior to 1837	4 to 6 p. c.	Matured at various dates prior to Jan. 1, 1837				$57,665 00	$64,174 81	
Mexican Indemnity Stock	August 10, 1846	5 per cent.	Matured at various dates in 1851 and 1852				1,104 91	85 74	
Loan of 1847	January 28, 1847	6 per cent.	Matured December 31, 1867				1,250 00	22 00	
Bounty Land Scrip	February 11, 1847	6 per cent.	Matured July 1, 1849				3,400 00	216 55	
Texan Indemnity Stock	September 9, 1850	5 per cent.	Matured December 31, 1864				21,000 00	3,045 00	
Loan of 1858	June 14, 1858	5 per cent.	Matured after January 1, 1874				8,000 00		
Loan of 1860	June 22, 1860	5 per cent.	Matured January 1, 1871				10,000 00	600 00	
5-20's of 1862 (called)	February 25, 1862	6 per cent.	Matured Dec. 1, 1871, and at subsequent dates				1,011,550 00	8,644 11	
5-20's of Mar., 1864 (cal'd)	March 3, 1864	6 per cent.	Matured November 13, 1875				6,000 00	1,506 23	
5-20's of June, 1864 (cal'd)	June 30, 1864	6 per cent.	Matured Nov. 13, 1875, and at sbusequent dates				1,854,100 00	42,965 08	
5-20's of 1865 (called)	March 3, 1865	6 per cent.	Matured February 15, 1876				186,450 00	3,470 62	
Treas. Notes prior to 1846	Various, prior to 1846	1-10to6p.c.	Matured at various dates from 1838 to 1844				82,575 35	2,670 76	
Treasury Notes of 1846	July 22, 1846	1- to 6 p.c.	Matured at various dates in 1847 and 1848				6,000 00	206 00	
Treasury Notes of 1847	January 28, 1847	6 per cent.	Matured at various dates in 1848 and 1849				950 00	57 00	
Treasury Notes of 1857	December 23, 1857	3 to 6 p.c.	Matured at various dates in 1858 and 1859				1,900 00	105 00	
Treasury Notes of 1861	March 2, 1861	6 per cent.	Matured March 1, 1863				3,100 00	372 00	
Seven-thirties of 1861	July 17, 1861	7 3-10 p. c.	Matured August 19 and October 1, 1864				17,050 00	1,198 43	
One-year Notes of 1863	March 3, 1863	5 per cent.	Matured at various dates in 1865				61,055 00	3,064 85	
Two-year Notes of 1863	March 3, 1863	5 per cent.	Matured at various dates in 1866				43,650 00	2,648 12	
Compound-interest Notes	Mar. 3, '63; June 30, '64.	6 per cent.	Matured June 10, 1867, and May 15, 1868.				328,760 00	66,000 69	
Seven-thirties of '64 & '65.	June 30, '64; Mar. 3, '65.	7 3-10 p. c.	Matured Aug. 15, '67, and June 15 and J'y 15, '68.				183,800 00	12,955 47	
Certific's of Indebtedness.	Mar. 1, 17, '62; Mar. 3, '63.	6 per cent.	Matured at various dates in 1866				5,000 00	313 48	
Temporary Loan	June 30, 1864	4 to 6 p.c.	Matured October 15, 1866				3,060 00	256 06	
3 per cent. Certif's (called)	Mar. 2, '67; July 25, '68.	3 per cent.	Matured February 28, 1873				5,000 00	394 31	
Aggregate of Debt on which Interest has ceased since Maturity							3,902,420 26	214,972 31	

Debt bearing no Interest.

Old Demand Notes	July 17, 1861; February 12, 1862						$66,917 50		
Legal-tender Notes	February 25, 1862; July 11, 1862; March 3, 1863		Issues prior to 1869		$27,859,978 00		369,772,284 00		
			Series of 1869		226,398,115 00				
			Series of 1874		62,591,604 00				
			Series of 1875		52,922,587 00				
Certificates of Deposit	June 8, 1872						32,840,000 00		
Fractional Currency	July 17, 1862; March 3, 1863; June 30, 1864		First Issue		4,294,854 92		34,446,595 39		
			Second Issue		3,117,076 28				
			Third Issue		3,067,144 83				
			Fourth Issue		7,360,184 28				
			Fifth Issue		16,607,335 08				
Coin Certificates	March 3, 1863						28,681,400 00		
Unclaimed Interest								$20,444 84	
Aggregate of Debt bearing no Interest							465,807,196 89	20,444 84	

Recapitulation.

			Principal.	Interest.	Totals.
Debt bearing Interest in Coin	Bonds at 6 per cent	$984,999,650 00			
	Bonds at 5 per cent	711,685,800 00			
	Bonds at 4½ per cent				
	Bonds at 4 per cent				
			$1,696,685,450 00	$38,068,587 39	
Debt bearing Interest in Lawful Money	Navy Pension Fund at 3 per cent		14,000,000 00	210,000 00	
Debt on which Interest has Ceased since Maturity			3,902,420 26	214,972 31	
Debt bearing no Interest	Old Demand and Legal-tender Notes	369,839,201 50			
	Certificates of Deposit	32,840,000 00			
	Fractional Currency	34,446,595 39			
	Coin Certificates	28,681,400 00			
			465,807,196 89		
	Unclaimed interest			20,444 84	
Total Debt			2,180,395,067 15	38,514,004 54	$2,218,909,071 69
Cash in the Treasury—Coin				73,625,584 97	
Currency				13,004,141 73	
Special deposit held for redemption of certificates of deposit as provided by law				32,840,000 00	
					119,469,726 70
Debt, less Cash in the Treasury July 1, 1876					2,099,439,344 99
Debt, less Cash in the Treasury, June 1, 1876					2,103,320,742 55
Decrease of Debt during the month					3,881,397 56
Decrease of Debt since June 30, 1875					$29,249,381 33

Bonds issued to the Pacific Railway Companies, Interest payable in Lawful Money.

Name of Railway.	Authorizing Acts.	Rate of Interest.	When Payable.	Interest Payable.	Principal Outstanding.	Interest Accrued and not yet Paid.	Interest Paid by the United States.	Interest Re-paid by Transportation of Mails, etc.	Balance of Interest Paid by the United States.
Central Pacific	July 1, 1862, and July 2, 1864.	6 per cent.	30 years from date	Jan. and July.	$25,885,120 00	$776,553 60	$11,804,251 27	$1,231,213 76	$10,573,037 51
Kansas Pacific	July 1, 1862, and July 2, 1864.	6 per cent.	30 years from date	Jan. and July.	6,303,000 00	189,090 00	3,292,983 09	1,448,327 39	1,844,655 70
Union Pacific	July 1, 1862, and July 2, 1864.	6 per cent.	30 years from date	Jan. and July.	27,236,512 00	817,095 36	12,701,420 01	4,079,704 77	8,621,715 24
Central Branch Union Pacific.	July 1, 1862, and July 2, 1864.	6 per cent.	30 years from date	Jan. and July.	1,600,000 00	48,000 00	829,808 26	44,408 05	785,400 21
Western Pacific	July 1, 1862, and July 2, 1864.	6 per cent.	30 years from date	Jan. and July.	1,970,560 00	59,116 80	781,496 94	9,367 00	772,129 94
Sioux City and Pacific	July 1, 1862, and July 2, 1864.	6 per cent.	30 years from date	Jan. and July.	1,628,320 00	48,849 60	731,553 49	39,470 28	692,083 21
Totals					64,623,512 00	1,938,705 36	30,141,513 06	6,852,491 25	23,289,021 81

(New Series, No. 67.)

The foregoing is a correct statement of the Public Debt, as appears from the Books and Treasurer's Returns in the Department at the close of business, June 30, 1876.

CHAS. F. CONANT, *Assistant Secretary of the Treasury.*

Popular and Electoral Vote

In Presidential Election of 1872, and State Elections in 1874, 1875, and 1876.

STATES.	1872. Popular Vote.		Electoral College.	1872. Electoral Vote.		‖ State Elections.				
	Republican. Grant.	Liberal and Democratic. Greeley.		Republican. Grant.	Liberal and Democratic.*	1874. Republican.	1874. Democratic and Liberal.	1875. Republican.	1875. Democratic and Liberal.	1875. Independent.
Alabama	90,272	79,444	10	10	...	93,928	107,118	...	...	...
Arkansas	¶41,373	¶37,927	†6	...	...	22,808	42,671	...	...	...
California	54,020	40,718	6	6	...	...	...	31,322	61,509	30,097
Connecticut	50,638	45,880	6	6	...	39,973	46,755	44,272	53,752	2,959
Delaware	11,115	10,206	3	3	...	11,259	12,488	...	...	...
Florida	17,763	15,427	4	4	...	18,609	17,555	...	...	...
Georgia	62,550	76,356	†11	...	8	33,161	93,347	...	...	...
Illinois	241,944	184,938	21	21	...	163,024	128,169	...	...	...
Indiana	186,147	163,632	15	15	...	164,902	182,154	...	...	...
Iowa	131,566	71,196	11	11	...	107,243	79,060	125,069	93,324	...
Kansas	67,048	32,970	5	5	...	48,824	35,308	...	...	...
Kentucky	88,766	99,995	12	...	12	53,504	114,348	90,795	126,976	...
Louisiana	¶71,663	¶57,029	†8	...	...	69,544	68,586	...	...	...
Maine	61,422	29,087	7	7	...	53,131	41,734	57,852	53,077	...
Maryland	66,760	67,687	8	...	8	53,377	67,503	72,530	85,454	...
Massachusetts	133,472	59,260	13	13	...	89,344	96,376	83,639	78,333	11,213
Michigan	138,455	78,355	11	11	...	111,519	105,550	...	...	...
Minnesota	55,117	34,423	5	5	...	51,996	42,111	47,041	35,174	1,600
Mississippi	82,175	47,288	8	8	...	...	...	67,000	97,922	...
Missouri	119,196	151,434	15	...	15	112,104	149,566	...	...	...
Nebraska	18,329	7,812	3	3	...	20,874	8,471	31,226	15,091	...
Nevada	8,413	6,236	3	3	...	7,754	10,339	...	...	...
New Hampshire	37,168	34,424	5	5	...	34,138	35,598	39,293	39,121	792
New Jersey	91,656	76,456	9	9	...	84,050	97,283	...	...	...
New York	440,736	387,281	35	35	...	366,074	416,391	375,401	390,211	...
North Carolina	94,769	70,094	10	10	...	84,595	98,217	...	...	...
Ohio	281,852	244,321	22	22	...	221,204	238,406	297,813	292,264	2,591
Oregon	11,819	7,730	3	3	...	9,163	9,713	9,106	9,373	1,182
Pennsylvania	349,589	212,041	29	29	...	272,516	277,195	304,175	292,145	13,244
Rhode Island	13,665	5,329	4	4	...	12,335	1,589	8,368	5,166	8,728
South Carolina	72,290	22,703	7	7	...	80,403	68,814	...	...	...
Tennessee	85,655	94,391	12	...	12	55,842	103,061	...	...	...
Texas	47,468	66,546	8	...	8	52,353	99,984	...	...	...
Vermont	41,481	10,927	5	5	...	33,582	13,257	...	...	...
Virginia	93,468	91,654	11	11	...	84,139	93,895	...	...	...
West Virginia	32,315	29,451	5	5	...	28,874	37,823	...	...	...
Wisconsin	104,997	86,477	10	10	...	93,127	93,484	85,155	84,314	...
Total	3,597,132	2,834,125	§366	286	63					

Charles O'Conor, Straight Democrat, received 29,489 votes; and James Black, Temperance, 5,608.

* Owing to the death of Horace Greeley, the vote of no Electoral College was given for him. The Democratic Electoral vote was for B. Gratz Brown, 18; Thomas A. Hendricks, 42; Charles J. Jenkins, 2; David Davis, 1.

† Not counted, 17; of these, three votes cast in Georgia for Horace Greeley were excluded, he having died before the votes were so cast—the House voting to exclude, the Senate to receive. The vote of Arkansas was rejected—the House voting to receive, the Senate to reject. The vote of Louisiana was rejected, both Houses concurring.

§ Total counted, 349—necessary to a choice, 175.

¶ There were two counts in ARKANSAS and LOUISIANA. The other returns were: in ARKANSAS, Grant, 90,272; Greeley, 79,444; in LOUISIANA, Grant, 59,975; Greeley, 66,467.

‖ In 1874: In ARKANSAS, the vote given is on Congress. A. H. Garland received 76,871 votes for Governor; there was no opposition. In CONNECTICUT, Smith, Temperance, received 4,960 votes. In ILLINOIS, the vote given is for State Treasurer, besides which Gore, Independent Reform, received 75,580; and Simpson, Prohibitionist, 516 votes. For Superintendent of Public Instruction, Powell, Republican, received 166,984 votes, and Etter, Opposition, 197,490 votes. In KANSAS, Marshall, Independent, received 2,277 votes. In LOUISIANA, the vote given is that of the Returning Board; the Conservative count is, Moncure, Democratic, 74,670, Dubuclet, Republican, 69,719. In MASSACHUSETTS, the vote for Lieutenant Governor was: Knight, Republican, 99,151; Smith, Democratic, 87,138. In MICHIGAN, Carpenter, Prohibition, received 3,937 votes for Governor. In NEBRASKA, Gardner, Independent, received 3,987, and Church, Temperance, 1,257 votes for Governor. In NEW YORK, Clark, Prohibition, received 11,768 votes for Governor. In NEW HAMPSHIRE, Blackmer, Temperance, received 2,100 votes for Governor. In OHIO, Buchtel, Prohibition, received 7,815 votes. In PENNSYLVANIA, Bradford, Temperance, received 4,649 votes. In OREGON, Campbell, Independent, received 6,532 votes.

In 1875: Of 30,097 Independent votes in CALIFORNIA, Bidwell received 29,732. In CONNECTICUT, 2,932 of the Independent were Prohibition. In MASSACHUSETTS, of 11,213 Independent, 9,124 were Prohibition, 1,497 for Chas. F. Adams, Sr., 316 for Wendell Phillips, and 276 scattering. In MINNESOTA, the 1,600 were Prohibition; also the 2,591 in OHIO, the 13,244 in PENNSYLVANIA, and most of the 792 in NEW HAMPSHIRE. In OREGON, 345 were Prohibition, and 837 Independent. In RHODE ISLAND, 724 were for Prohibition and Independent Republican, and 4 scattering.

Elections of 1876.

Elections for State officers were held in the following States, with the annexed results, in March and April, 1876:

CONNECTICUT: *Governor*—Charles R. Ingersoll, Democrat, 51,138; Henry C. Robinson, Republican, 43,510; Charles Atwater, "Greenback," 1,970; Henry D. Smith, Prohibition, 1,983; scattering, 19. Ingersoll's majority over all, 3,656.

NEW HAMPSHIRE: *Governor*—Person C. Cheney, Republican, 41,756; Daniel Marcy, Democrat, 38,500; scattering, 439. Cheney's majority over all, 2,817.

RHODE ISLAND: *Governor*—Henry Lippitt, Regular Republican, 8,689; Albert C. Howard, Independent and Temperance, 6,732; William B. Beach, Democrat, 3,599; scattering, 16. There having been no choice by the people, the Legislature, May 30, 1876, chose Henry Lippitt Governor, by a vote of 74 to 23 for Albert C. Howard. A like vote selected the other State officers, except Secretary of State, to which Joshua M. Addeman, Republican, was chosen by the people, having received 15,395 votes to 3,684 for John B. Pierce.

Orders on Suffrage.

1876, August 15—The following letter has been addressed to General SHERMAN:

SIR: The House of Representatives of the United States, on the 10th inst., passed the following preamble and resolution, viz: [For text of resolution and vote on it, see p. 239.]

The PRESIDENT directs that in accordance with the spirit of the above, you are to hold all the available force under your command, not now engaged in subduing the savages on the Western frontier, in readiness to be used upon the call or requisition of the proper legal authorities for protecting all citizens, without distinction of race, color or political opinion, in the exercise of the right to vote, as guaranteed by the Fifteenth Amendment, and to assist in the enforcement of "certain, condign and effectual punishment" upon all persons who shall "attempt by force, fraud, terror, intimidation, or otherwise to prevent the free exercise of the right of suffrage," as provided by the law of the United States, and have such force so distributed and stationed as to be able to render prompt assistance in the enforcement of the law. Such additional orders as may be necessary to carry out the purpose of these instructions will be given to you from time to time, after consultation with the law officers of the Government.

Very respectfully, your obedient servant,

J. D. CAMERON,
Secretary of War.

Circular of the Attorney-General to U. S. Marshals, September 4, 1876.

SIR: The laws of the United States having made it my duty to exercise general direction over the marshals as to the manner of discharging their offices, I have prepared for their use this circular letter of instructions as to the coming elections, intending the same also as a reply, once for all, to numerous applications in like connection from private citizens in various States.

In the present condion of legislation the United States occupy a position toward voters and voting which varies according as the election is for State and other local officers only, or for members of Congress and Presidential Electors. In elections at which members of the House of Representatives are chosen, which by law include elections at which electors for President and Vice-President are appointed, the United States secure voters against whatever in general hinders or prevents them from a free exercise of the election franchise, extending that care alike to the registration lists, the act of voting, and the personal freedom and security of the voter, as well against violence on account of any vote he may intend to give, as against conspiracy because of any that he may already nave given.

The peace of the United States, therefore, which you are to preserve, and whose violation you are to suppress, protects, among others, the rights specified in the last paragraph, and any person who by force violates those rights breaks that peace and renders it your duty to arrest him, and to suppress any riots incident thereto, or that threaten the integrity of the registration or election, to the end that the will of the people in such election may be ascertained and take effect, and that offenders may be brought before the courts for punishment. Notorious events in several States, which recently and in an unusual manner have been publicly reprobated, render it a grave duty of all marshals who have cause to apprehend a violation of the peace of the United States, connected as above with the elections to be held upon the Tuesday after the first Monday in November next, to be prepared to preserve and restore such peace. As the chief executive officer of the United States in your district, you will be held responsible for all breaches of peace of the United States which diligence on your part might have prevented, and for the arrest and security of all persons who violate the peace in any of the points above enumerated.

Diligence in these matters requires, of course, that you be and continue present in person or by deputy, at all places of registration or election at which you have reason to suspect that the peace is threatened, and that, whenever an embodiment of the *posse comitatus* is required to enforce the laws, such embodiment be effected. You will observe that the "special" deputies mentioned in Section 2,021 of the Revised Statutes have peculiar duties assigned to them, duties which otherwise do not belong to deputy marshals. Such "special" deputies can be appointed only in cities of 20,000 inhabitants or upward. But the duties assigned to marshals and their deputies by Section 2,022, or other like statutes, belong to all duly appointed deputies, whether they be general or be "special" within the meaning of that and the preceding section. Deputies to discharge this latter class of duties may be appointed to any number whatever, according to the discretion of the marshal, in all States in which sheriffs have a similar power. Section 2,030 has no practical bearing upon this point in States where no limit is imposed upon the appointment of deputies by sheriffs, because in such States the laws of the United States "prior to the 10th of June, 1872," left marshals also unlimited as to the number of their deputies.

In discharging the duties above mentioned, you will doubtless receive the countenance and support of all good citizens of the United States in your respective districts. It is not necessary to say that it is upon such countenance and support that the United States mainly rely in their endeavor to enforce the right to vote which they have given or have secured. The present instructions are intended only to counteract that partial malice, wrongheadedness, or inconsideration which sometimes triumphs at critical moments over the conservative and in general prevailing forces of society, and to which the present and passing condition of the country gives more than ordinary strength, and therefore requires the Government to particularly observe and provide against. In this connection I advise that you and each of your deputies, general and "special," have a right to summon to your assistance, in preventing and quelling disorder, "every person in the district above fifteen years of age, whatever may be their occupation, whether civilians or not, and including the military of all denominations—militia, soldiers, marines—all of whom are alike bound to obey you. The fact that they are organized as military bodies, whether of State or of the United States, under the immediate command of their own officers, does not in any wise affect their legal character. They are still the *posse comitatus*." I prefer to quote the above statement of the laws upon this point from an opinion of my predecessor, ex-Attorney-General Cushing, because it thus appears to have been well settled for many years. (6 Opinions, 466, May 27, 1854.)

I need hardly add that there can be no State law or State official in this country who has jurisdiction to oppose you in discharging your official duties under laws of the United States. If such interference shall take place, a thing not anticipated, you are to disregard it entirely. The laws of the United States are supreme, and so, consequently, is the action of officials of the United States in enforcing them. There is, as virtually you have already been told, no officer of a State whom you may not by summons embody into your own *posse*, and any State *posse* already embodied by a sheriff will, with such sheriff, be obliged, upon your summons, to become part of the United States *posse*, and obey you or your deputy acting *virtute officio*. The responsibility which devolves upon an officer clothed with such powers and required to guard the highest rights of citizens corresponds in degree with those powers and rights, and exacts of such officer consideration, intelligence, and courage. It is proper to advise you that, in preparing this circular, I have considered recent important judgments given by the Supreme Court of the United States upon acts of Congress which regulate this general topic.

I have founded the above instructions upon such acts as are affected by such judgments. I need in this place add no more than that these judgments do not concern State elections. You will find appended, in full or by reference, such statutory provisions as it seems important that you and your deputies shall in this connection read and consider. In matters of doubt you are of course entitled to the advice of the United States Attorney for your district. These instructions have been submitted to the President, and have his approval.

Very respectfully, your obedient servant,

ALPHONSO TAFT, Attorney-General.

INDEX TO HAND-BOOK OF 1876.

www.ingramcontent.com/pod-product-compliance
Lightning Source LLC
LaVergne TN
LVHW010233110826
845151LV00004B/1284
* 9 7 8 1 4 2 5 5 2 4 6 3 0 *